Capital Controls and Capital Flows in Emerging Economies

A National Bureau
of Economic Research
Conference Report

Capital Controls and Capital Flows in Emerging Economies

Policies, Practices, and Consequences

Edited by **Sebastian Edwards**

The University of Chicago Press

Chicago and London

SEBASTIAN EDWARDS is the Henry Ford II Professor of International Business Economics at the Anderson Graduate School of Management at the University of California, Los Angeles, and a research associate of the National Bureau of Economic Research.

The University of Chicago Press, Chicago 60637
The University of Chicago Press, Ltd., London
© 2007 by The University of Chicago
All rights reserved. Published 2007
Printed in the United States of America

16 15 14 13 12 11 10 09 08 07   1 2 3 4 5
ISBN-13: 978-0-226-18497-5 (cloth)
ISBN-10: 0-226-18497-8 (cloth)

Library of Congress Cataloging-in-Publication Data

Capital controls and capital flows in emerging economies : policies,
        practices and consequences / edited by Sebastian Edwards.
            p. cm. — (NBER conference report)
        Includes bibliographical references and index.
        ISBN-13: 978-0-226-18497-5 (cloth : alk paper)
        ISBN-10: 0-226-18497-8 (cloth : alk paper)
            1. Capital movements—Developing countries—Congresses.
        I. Edwards, Sebastian, 1953–
        HG3891 .C356 2007
        332'.042409172—dc22

                                                                    2006045683

⊗ The paper used in this publication meets the minimum requirements of the American National Standard for Information Sciences— Permanence of Paper for Printed Library Materials, ANSI Z39.48-1992.

Relation of the Directors to the
Work and Publications of the
National Bureau of Economic Research

1. The object of the NBER is to ascertain and present to the economics profession, and to the public more generally, important economic facts and their interpretation in a scientific manner without policy recommendations. The Board of Directors is charged with the responsibility of ensuring that the work of the NBER is carried on in strict conformity with this object.

2. The President shall establish an internal review process to ensure that book manuscripts proposed for publication DO NOT contain policy recommendations. This shall apply both to the proceedings of conferences and to manuscripts by a single author or by one or more co-authors but shall not apply to authors of comments at NBER conferences who are not NBER affiliates.

3. No book manuscript reporting research shall be published by the NBER until the President has sent to each member of the Board a notice that a manuscript is recommended for publication and that in the President's opinion it is suitable for publication in accordance with the above principles of the NBER. Such notification will include a table of contents and an abstract or summary of the manuscript's content, a list of contributors if applicable, and a response form for use by Directors who desire a copy of the manuscript for review. Each manuscript shall contain a summary drawing attention to the nature and treatment of the problem studied and the main conclusions reached.

4. No volume shall be published until forty-five days have elapsed from the above notification of intention to publish it. During this period a copy shall be sent to any Director requesting it, and if any Director objects to publication on the grounds that the manuscript contains policy recommendations, the objection will be presented to the author(s) or editor(s). In case of dispute, all members of the Board shall be notified, and the President shall appoint an ad hoc committee of the Board to decide the matter; thirty days additional shall be granted for this purpose.

5. The President shall present annually to the Board a report describing the internal manuscript review process, any objections made by Directors before publication or by anyone after publication, any disputes about such matters, and how they were handled.

6. Publications of the NBER issued for informational purposes concerning the work of the Bureau, or issued to inform the public of the activities at the Bureau, including but not limited to the NBER Digest and Reporter, shall be consistent with the object stated in paragraph 1. They shall contain a specific disclaimer noting that they have not passed through the review procedures required in this resolution. The Executive Committee of the Board is charged with the review of all such publications from time to time.

7. NBER working papers and manuscripts distributed on the Bureau's web site are not deemed to be publications for the purpose of this resolution, but they shall be consistent with the object stated in paragraph 1. Working papers shall contain a specific disclaimer noting that they have not passed through the review procedures required in this resolution. The NBER's web site shall contain a similar disclaimer. The President shall establish an internal review process to ensure that the working papers and the web site do not contain policy recommendations, and shall report annually to the Board on this process and any concerns raised in connection with it.

8. Unless otherwise determined by the Board or exempted by the terms of paragraphs 6 and 7, a copy of this resolution shall be printed in each NBER publication as described in paragraph 2 above.

Contents

Acknowledgments

The editor wishes to thank Carl Beck and Rob Shannon from the National Bureau of Economics Research Conference Department for their help in organizing the conference. We are grateful to Helena Fitz-Patrick from the NBER Publications Department and Parker Smathers from the University of Chicago Press for their assistance in putting together this volume. Marty Feldstein supported the project throughout its different stages; without his help, it would not have been possible. Finally, I thank the Andrew W. Mellon Foundation and the Starr Foundation for their generous financial support.

Introduction

Sebastian Edwards

For a number of years economists have debated the optimal speed and sequencing of economic reform. These debates have been particularly heated regarding the lifting of capital controls and the opening of the capital account of the balance of payments. While for some authors the free movement of capital across borders is welfare enhancing, for others it represents a clear peril, especially for the emerging nations. According to the latter view, free capital mobility—and in particular the free mobility of fixed income securities—increases macroeconomic volatility and makes emerging countries vulnerable to the destabilizing effects of external shocks. Thus, the theory goes, restrictions on capital movements should be lifted gradually, toward the end of the reform process and only after other markets have been liberalized. The supporters of freer capital mobility, on the other hand, have argued that there are no reasons for postponing the opening of the capital account. These authors point out that restricting capital mobility results in serious economic costs in the form of capital market inefficiencies and resource misallocation. Discussions on the role of capital controls and capital flows—and, in particular, speculative capital flows—became particularly pointed in the aftermath of the East Asian currency crisis of 1997. According to Stiglitz (2002), for instance, the relaxation of capital controls was at the center of the crisis and of the East Asian nations' currency collapses.[1]

Questions related to the speed and sequencing of reform are not new in

Sebastian Edwards is the Henry Ford II Professor of International Business Economics at the Anderson Graduate School of Management at the University of California, Los Angeles (UCLA), and a research associate of the National Bureau of Economic Research (NBER).

1. In preparing this introduction I have drawn on some of my previous writings on capital controls, capital account liberalization, and economic reform.

policy discussions. In fact, since the beginning of the economics profession these issues have arisen over and over again. Adam Smith, for example, argued in *The Wealth of Nations* that determining the appropriate sequencing was a difficult issue that involved, primarily, political considerations (see Smith 1776/1937, book IV, chapter VII, part III, p. 121). Moreover, Smith supported gradualism on the grounds that cold-turkey liberalization would result in a significant increase in unemployment. Consider the following passage from *The Wealth of Nations:* "To open the colony trade all at once . . . might not only occasion some transitory inconvenience, but a great permanent loss. . . . [T]he sudden loss of employment . . . might alone be felt very sensibly" (vol. II, chap. VII, part III, p. 120).

Speed and sequencing also became central in analyses on how to design a reform strategy for the former Communist countries. In discussing the problems faced by Czechoslovakia during the early period of its transition, then finance minister Vaclav Klaus (1991) pointed out that one of the main problems was deciding on "sequencing as regards domestic institutional and price measures on the one hand, and liberalization of foreign trade and rate of exchange on the other" (p. 18).

In the 1980s the World Bank became particularly interested in exploring issues related to sequencing and speed of reform and, in particular, issues related to the role of capital controls during the reform process. As a result of the discussion surrounding this work, a consensus of sorts developed on sequencing and speed of reform. The most important elements of this consensus included the following: (a) trade liberalization should be gradual and buttressed with substantial foreign aid;[2] (b) an effort should be made to minimize the unemployment consequences of reform; (c) in countries with very high inflation, fiscal imbalances should be dealt with very early on in the reform process; (d) financial reform requires the creation of modern supervisory and regulatory agencies; and (e) the capital account should be liberalized at the very end of the process, and only once the economy has been able to expand successfully its export sector. Of course, not everyone agreed with all of these recommendations, but most economists involved with reform did. In particular, people at the International Monetary Fund (IMF) did not object, or at least did not object openly and strongly, these general principles. For example, Jacob Frenkel, who was to become the IMF's Economic Counsellor, had argued in the mid-1980s in an *IMF Staff Papers* article (Frenkel 1983) that the capital account should, indeed, be opened gradually and toward the end of the reform process.

Some time during the early 1990s this received wisdom on capital restrictions, capital account liberalization, sequencing, and speed began to be challenged, and some authors began to call for simultaneous and very fast

---

2. Although what exactly was meant by "gradual" was never specified. Indeed, the (implicit) definition of "gradualism" seemed to change through time.

reforms. To a large extent the argument was based on political economy considerations. If reforms are not implemented rapidly and simultaneously, the argument went, opponents would successfully block liberalization efforts. In the early 1990s the U.S. government also began to argue that the time had come for the East Asian nations to liberalize their capital account restrictions and to allow capital to move more freely. Policymakers and academics throughout East Asia became concerned about these recommendations. They had two main worries. On the one hand, they argued that lifting capital controls and liberalizing the capital account would result in massive real exchange rate appreciation, something that had indeed happened in a number of Latin American countries during the early 1980s. The problem, of course, was that an appreciating real exchange rate was in contradiction with East Asia's decades-old policies of maintaining a highly competitive real exchange rate as a way of encouraging exports. The main worry was based on the possibility of a sudden stop of capital inflows. More specifically, it was argued that if after entering the country capital flows suddenly declined or, worse yet, reversed, the country would be left permanently with a smaller export market. A second concern was that massive capital inflows were likely to feed a real estate boom and bubble that would make the economy particularly vulnerable to financial shocks.

In a paper delivered at a conference organized by Korea University, Robert Mundell argued that most concerns on the rapid and early lifting of capital controls were well founded. Consider the following quotation:

> Unfortunately . . . there are some negative externalities [of an early capital account liberalization]. One is that the borrowing goes into consumption rather than into investment, permitting the capital-importing country to live beyond its means . . . without any offset in future output with which to service the loans. Even if the liabilities are entirely in private hands, the government may feel compelled to transform the unrepayable debt into sovereign debt rather than allow execution of mortgages or other collateral. (Mundell 1995, p. 20)

At the same conference the late Manuel Guitián, then a senior official at the IMF, argued in favor of moving quickly toward capital account convertibility. Guitián's paper—suggestively titled "Capital Account Liberalization: Bringing Policy in Line with Reality"—was one of the first written pieces to document the IMF's change in views regarding sequencing and capital account convertibility. After discussing the evolution of the international financial markets and expressing reservations about the "capital-account-last" sequencing recommendation, Guitián summarized his views as follows: "There does not seem to be an a priori reason why the two accounts [current and capital] could not be opened up simultaneously. . . . [A] strong case can be made in support of rapid and decisive liberalization in capital transactions" (Guitián 1995, pp. 85–86).

During the second half of the 1990s the view that most emerging countries should lift capital controls and open up their capital account became dominant at the IMF and the U.S. Treasury. Starting in 1995 more and more emerging countries began to relax their controls on capital mobility. In doing this, however, they tended to follow different strategies and paths. While some countries relaxed bank lending only, other countries allowed only long-term capital movements, and yet others—such as Chile—used market-based mechanisms to slow down the rate at which capital was flowing into the country. Many countries, however—including some that later faced severe crisis—did not need any prodding by the IMF or the United States to open their capital account. Indonesia and Mexico, to mention just two important cases, had a long tradition of free capital mobility.

Malaysia's reliance on capital controls on outflows after the collapse of its currency in 1997 generated new debates in academic circles. It recovered fast after the 1997 crisis—although not as fast as South Korea—but it is not clear whether recovery was the result of the imposition of capital controls and of fixing of the exchange rate. In a paper presented at an NBER conference Kaplan and Rodrik (2002) provided a detailed discussion of Malaysia's unorthodox reaction to the currency upheaval of 1997–98. The authors note that the imposition of capital controls by Malaysia, in September 1998, was greeted with great skepticism by most analysts and observers. In particular, IMF officials and investment banks' analysts argued that these controls—and the accompanying decisions to peg the exchange rate and lower domestic interest rates—would result in a slower recovery and in a significant reduction in foreign direct investment (FDI) into Malaysia. This latter (potential) effect of the controls was considered to be particularly devastating, as Malaysia has traditionally relied heavily on FDI. Kaplan and Rodrik argue that this general perception is incorrect, and that once the appropriate econometric techniques are used there is evidence suggesting that Malaysia's unorthodox program yielded very positive results. The late Rudi Dornbusch (2002) took issue with this view, and argued that the relatively good performance of the Malaysian economy in the postcrisis period had little to do with the controls. In his opinion, a very friendly international environment—driven mostly by successive cuts in interest rates by the Federal Reserve—was the main force behind Malaysia's recovery of 1999–2000.

The papers and commentary presented in this volume were presented at a conference held in December 2004 in Santa Barbara, California. The main purpose of the conference was to analyze the mechanisms that different countries have used to slow down, or control, capital inflows, and in particular capital inflows associated with fixed income securities. We were interested in exploring country experiences and in evaluating whether the tools chosen by different countries were effective in reducing the flow of capital, altering the maturity of the resulting external debt, and reducing macroeconomic vulnerability. We were also interested in investigating the extent to which the different tools used to (partially) control capital inflows implied efficiency costs. One of the salient features of the country-specific papers collected in this volume is that they all provide detailed chronologies on the evolution of capital controls in each of the countries. These chronologies focus on the specific tools used to control flows, as well as on the liberalization efforts undertaken during the last few years. They also provide information on crises and other important events.

The volume is divided into two parts. Part one contains five chapters that deal with systemic issues related to capital mobility, with an emphasis on fixed income securities. These chapters discuss analytical and theoretical issues and provide cross-country evidence on the effectiveness, consequences, and costs of restricting capital mobility. Part two comprises nine policy and applied papers. There are eight country case studies, for Chile, Brazil, Argentina, South Korea, Malaysia, China, Singapore, and India, and a broad paper that evaluates, from a comparative perspective, the effects of capital controls on economic performance.

Capital Controls in the Emerging Countries:
Analytical Issues and Cross-Country Evidence

The first chapter is "Capital Flows in a Globalized World: The Role of Policies and Institutions," by Laura Alfaro, Sebnem Kalemli-Ozcan, and Vadym Volosovych. In this chapter the authors use data for 1970–2000 to analyze the patterns of international capital flows. They are particularly interested in analyzing what determines capital flow in certain directions, and what the main determinants of capital flow volatility are. In analyzing these issues Alfaro, Kalemli-Ozcan, and Volosovych pay particular attention to the role played by economic policy and by the quality of national institutions. The authors point out that in spite of their large increase during the last few years, capital flows to the emerging countries continue to be significantly lower than what is predicted by theory (this is the so-called Lucas paradox). Using data on flows extracted from balance-of-payments statistics, Alfaro, Kalemli-Ozcan, and Volosovych use regression analysis to determine whether institutional factors can explain (at least partially) the Lucas paradox. They conclude that the quality of institutions—measured by variables such as the origin of the country's legal system and the mortality rate of original colonial settlers—plays an important role in explaining the direction and magnitude of capital flows in the 1970–2000 period. But institutions are not the only determinant of capital inflows. The authors find that, for given institutional quality, economic policy plays an important role. This is particularly the case when policy is measured by inflation, the degree of financial development, and the extent of capital controls. The authors also provide evidence suggesting that the quality of institutions and economic policy have played an important role in the determination of the (relatively) high degree of volatility of capital flows to the emerging markets in the 1970–2000 period. A particularly interesting finding reported by Alfaro, Kalemli-Ozcan, and Volosovych is that local financial structure—measured as the share of bank credit in total credit—has been positively related to capital flows' volatility in the 1970–2000 period.

In "Capital Controls, Sudden Stops, and Current Account Reversals," I use a broad multicountry data set to analyze the relationship between restrictions to capital mobility and currency crises. My analysis focuses on two manifestations of external crises: (a) sudden stops of capital inflows, where capital flowing into a country experiences a major reduction (at least 4 percent of gross domestic product [GDP] in one year); and (b) current account reversals, where a country reduces its deficit by at least 3 percent of GDP in one year. I address two important policy-related issues. First, I analyze whether the extent of capital mobility affect countries' degree of vulnerability to external crises. In doing this I consider several manifestations of external crises. Second, I analyze whether the extent of capital mobility determines the depth of external crises—as measured by the decline in growth—once a crisis occurs. I use a new index of the degree of capital mobility, which has greater country coverage and allows for a broader spectrum of policies than previous indexes. I use both nonparametric statistical techniques and regression analyses. In particular, I rely on treatment models, where the probability of facing a crisis and the effects of the crisis on growth are estimated simultaneously. Overall, my results cast some doubts on the assertion that increased capital mobility has caused heightened macroeconomic vulnerability and has increased the probability of an external crisis. I find no systematic evidence suggesting that countries with higher capital mobility tend to have a higher incidence of crises, or tend to face a higher probability of having a crisis, than countries with lower mobility. My results do suggest, however, that once a crisis occurs, countries with higher capital mobility may face a higher cost in terms of growth decline. My results also indicate that a country's degree of trade openness is an important determinant of the growth costs of current account reversals. Countries that are more open to international trade tend to suffer smaller declines in GDP growth than countries that are less open to international trade.

In "Currency Mismatches, Debt Intolerance, and Original Sin: Why They Are Not the Same and Why It Matters," Barry Eichengreen, Ricardo Hausmann, and Ugo Panizza analyze the role of balance sheet effects in financial crises. Their work focuses on problems with the structure of global financial markets that result in the inability of economies to borrow abroad in their own currencies. In particular, they inquire whether the degree of capital mobility affects countries' ability to borrow internationally in their own currency. Eichengreen, Hausmann, and Panizza analyze the impact of balance sheet variables on the volatility of output, the volatility of capital flows, the management of exchange rates, and the creditworthiness of countries. They argue that when considering the behavior of such variables it is important to distinguish clearly three concepts: "original sin," "debt intolerance," and "currency mismatches." They argue that macroeconomic stability, strong institutions, and a record of low inflation are not enough for countries to be able to borrow in their own currency. Chile, they point out, is a case in point. Being unable to borrow in its own currency, Chile relied on controls on capital inflows as a way of reducing its vulnerability to external shocks. The authors show that countries that are unable to borrow in their own currency tend to hold larger stocks of international reserves and tend to have more rigid exchange rate regimes. The extent of currency mismatches, however, has no effect on exchange rate policy. It does affect, on the other hand, the level of international reserves held by the monetary authorities. Eichengreen and his coauthors also show that the degree of debt intolerance has no statistical effect on the volatility of GDP growth. It does appear to affect, however, the degree of volatility of capital flows. Eichengreen and his coauthors investigate why some countries are unable to borrow internationally in their own currency. Their results suggest that original sin is robustly related to country size and to countries' status as financial centers, advanced economies, or emerging markets, but that it is only weakly related to institutional variables like rule of law and measures of policy like inflation and fiscal history.

In "The Microeconomic Evidence on Capital Controls: No Free Lunch" Kristin J. Forbes discusses the microeconomic consequences of capital controls. She argues that although macroeconomic analyses of capital controls are useful, they have faced a number of imposing challenges and have yielded inconclusive results. In order to have a more complete sense of the effects of capital controls it is important to understand how this policy affects incentives and microeconomic decisions. In this paper Forbes surveys an emerging literature that evaluates various microeconomic effects of capital controls and capital account liberalization. Several key themes emerge. This literature has focused on several microeconomic effects of capital controls. First, controls on capital mobility—controls on both inflows and outflows—tend to reduce the supply of capital, raise the cost of financing, and increase financial constraints. This is particularly the case for smaller firms that don't have access to international capital markets or to preferential lending. Second, capital controls affect market discipline. There is indeed evidence suggesting that the existence of controls leads to a more inefficient allocation of capital and resources. Third, the existence of capital controls distorts decision making by firms and individuals. This is because economic agents will spend time and resources attempting to evade the controls or minimize their costs. Fourth, the effects of capital controls can vary across firms and countries, and may even magnify existing economic distortions. Finally, Forbes also argues that capital controls (on both inflows and outflows) can be difficult and costly to enforce, even in countries with sound institutions and low levels of corruption. A particularly useful contribution of Forbes's paper is that she summarizes the evidence on the microeconomic consequences of the well-known and often praised Chilean controls on capital inflows. She argues that this policy generated nontrivial microeconomic costs, through resource misallocation and by increasing the reliance on retained earnings as a source of firms' financing.

The next paper is by Linda S. Goldberg. In "The International Exposure of U.S. Banks: Europe and Latin America Compared" she documents the changing international exposures of U.S. bank balance sheets since the mid-1980s. Goldberg does this by using a new and unique data set on cross-border transactions by U.S. banks. The data set is a time series panel of individual U.S. exposure to foreign markets. Each bank reports a country-by-country distribution of foreign claims. In addition, the data set contains detailed information on the type of claims, valuation of derivatives positions, maturity composition, and categories of recipient of the claims. Goldberg finds that U.S. banks have foreign positions heavily concentrated in Europe. She also finds that in recent years some cross-border claims on Latin American countries have declined, while claims extended locally by the branches and subsidiaries of U.S. banks have grown. Goldberg investigates whether bank size matters for explaining foreign claims' volatility. She finds that the foreign exposures of larger U.S. banks have tended to be less volatile than claims of smaller banks, and locally issued claims have tended to be more stable than cross-border flows. Goldberg also analyzes the way in which the cycle affects foreign claims of U.S. banks. She finds that business cycle variables have mixed influence on U.S. bank cross-border and local claims. The cross-border claims of U.S. banks on European customers tend to be procyclical. This contrasts with the case of local claims and cross-border claims on Latin American customers of U.S. banks. Neither of these claims is significantly related to variables that capture either the U.S. or the international business cycle. U.S. banks do not appear to be an important channel for transmitting U.S. cycles to smaller economies (including emerging economies). Indeed, Goldberg's results suggest that U.S. banks may even play a positive role in helping reduce the amplitude of business cycles in smaller nations.

Country Studies

In "International Borrowing, Capital Controls, and the Exchange Rate: Lessons from Chile" Kevin Cowan and José De Gregorio discuss Chile's experience with capital account restrictions and exchange rate policy. During the late 1970s and early 1980s syndicated loans were the most important form of capital inflows into Chile. As a way of controlling capital inflows and avoiding (real) exchange rate appreciation, the authorities imposed severe restrictions on bank lending to Chile. Only longer-maturity loans (maturities in excess of sixty-six months) were allowed freely; any loan with a maturity shorter than twenty-four months was forbidden. In spite of these severe restrictions, in 1982 Chile experienced a deep and highly traumatic currency crisis. The authors argue that one of the reasons for the severity of this crisis was that in the 1980s the Chilean economy was characterized by significant currency mismatches. Many of the firms that had borrowed in foreign currency produced nontradable goods and had peso-denominated assets. In the main part of the paper Cowan and De Gregorio analyze the effectiveness of Chile's well-known and often-discussed policy of controlling capital inflows during the 1990s. They conclude that capital controls were only partially effective and that the main source of macroeconomic vulnerability during the 1990s was an overly rigid exchange rate policy. In their analysis the authors discuss three important characteristics of the Chilean experience during the 1990s. First, most international borrowing was done directly by firms and thus was not intermediated by the banking system. Second, the free trade agreement between Chile and the United States put some limits on Chile's ability to rely on capital controls in the future. And third, after examining Chile's experience after the Asian-Russian crisis, they conclude that Chile did not suffer a sudden stop but a current account reversal due to policy reactions and a "sudden start" in capital outflows.

Kathryn M. E. Dominguez and Linda L. Tesar deal with the case of Argentina. In "International Borrowing and Macroeconomic Performance in Argentina" Dominguez and Tesar analyze the evolution of capital flows and macroeconomic performance in Argentina from the adoption of the Convertibility Plan in 1991 until the collapse of the pegged exchange rate regime in early 2002. The authors place particular emphasis on the external shocks that affected the Argentine economy during this period. In the first part of their paper Dominguez and Tesar analyze the analytical and policy underpinning of the 1991 Convertibility Plan, which established a currency board type of monetary system. They also deal with the structural reforms aimed at opening the economy and privatizing state-owned enterprises. The authors argue that in spite of these reforms the Argentine economy was vulnerable to external shocks and, in particular, to sudden stops of capital inflows. In section 7.3 of their paper Dominguez and Tesar analyze in great detail how the major emerging countries' crises of the 1990s affected the Argentine economy. But external shocks are only part of the story. Argentina also made some serious policy mistakes. In section 7.4 of their chapter, Dominguez and Tesar argue that the inability to control fiscal finances was at the heart of Argentina's problems. This forced the country to borrow heavily; much of the borrowing took place overseas. Dominguez and Tesar provide a detailed discussion of the unraveling of the Argentine experience with a currency board and unrestricted capital mobility. They point out that after exchange and capital controls were imposed in late 2001—through the so-called *Corralito*—the stock market experienced a 50 percent gain. They attribute this to the fact that the purchase of Argentine stock had become the only way of transferring money abroad via American depository receipts.

The chapter by Ilan Goldfajn and André Minella deals with Brazil's experience with capital controls. In "Capital Flows and Controls in Brazil: What Have We Learned?" the authors deal with the 1974–2004 period, and discuss Brazil's experience with several currency crises. The authors provide useful stylized facts regarding the evolution of the balance of payments and its components, focusing on current account cycles, capital flow cycles and composition, and debt accumulation. The authors argue that during the last three decades—and in spite of the crises—there has been significant progress in macroeconomic management. Throughout the 1970s and 1980s Brazil had pervasive controls on capital. During the 1990s, however, a process of gradual capital account liberalization begun. By 1993, capital inflows had increased significantly, putting significant appreciating pressure on the currency. At that time the government adopted a mechanism for restricting capital inflows. The private sector rapidly discovered ways of circumventing the controls, and capital inflows continued. In 1997–98, however, conditions changed as a result of the East Asian and Russian currency crises, and controls on inflows were relaxed. In the year 2000, Brazil adopted a floating exchange rate regime and implemented inflation targeting. This allowed the country to liberalize the current account further. According to the authors, in spite of the significant progress in terms of capital account liberalization and currency convertibility attained since the early 1990s, current regulations continue to be cumbersome and complex.

The chapter by Eswar Prasad and Shang-Jin Wei, "The Chinese Approach to Capital Inflows: Patterns and Possible Explanations," deals with China's experience with capital flows and capital account restrictions. In order to provide a benchmark for comparison the authors adopt a cross-country perspective to examine the evolution of capital flows into China since the early 1980s. Their analysis focuses both on the volume of capital flows and on their composition. China's inflows have generally been dominated by FDI. According to Prasad and Wei this is a positive pattern in light of the recent literature on the experiences of developing countries with financial globalization, capital flow volatility, and macroeconomic vulnerability. The authors provide detailed data and analysis of the evolution of China's capital controls, and discuss the possible determinants of the pattern of capital inflows. The authors argue that, contrary to popular belief, capital flows into China come mainly from other advanced Asian countries that have net trade surpluses with China, rather than from the

United States and Europe, which constitute China's main export markets. They also show that China has maintained its external debt at low levels; non-FDI private capital inflows have typically been quite low, until very recently. In section 9.3 of their paper Prasad and Wei discuss the recent surge in international reserve accumulation in China. According to them a key finding is that the drastic surge in the pace of reserve accumulation since 2001 is mostly the consequence of an increase in non-FDI capital inflows; reserve accumulation has not been the result of an increased current account surplus. Prasad and Wei discuss the costs and benefits of holding a stock of reserves in the neighborhood of 40 percent of GDP. The authors analyze why capital flows into China have been concentrated so heavily on FDI flows. In order to do this they analyze in great detail the nature of China's capital account restrictions. They argue that "while controls on non-FDI inflows as well as tax and other incentives appear to be proximate factors for explaining the FDI-heavy composition of inflows, other factors may also have contributed to this outcome." They also argue that the evidence in existence does not support the view that the composition of capital flows into China is the result of a deliberate neomercantilist policy aimed at accumulating inordinate amounts of international reserves.

In "South Korea's Experience with International Capital Flows," Marcus Noland discusses the way in which South Korea has managed the capital account during the last twenty years. During the 1980s (and 1970s, for that matter) Korea had a highly regulated domestic capital market and maintained tight controls on capital mobility. Growth during this period was nothing short of spectacular. In the early 1990s Korea initiated a process of capital account liberalization. According to Noland this process was implemented for pragmatic reasons. Liberalization, however, was uneven and asymmetric and encouraged short-term bank borrowing. By 1997 the amount of short-term debt accumulated by Korean banks and large conglomerates was very high, increasing the country's vulnerability to external shocks. In late 1997, in the midst of a massive speculative attack, Korea succumbed to a major currency and financial crisis. Noland argues that until the late 1980s the control of capital mobility—and overall "financial repression," for that matter—was a key (and required) component of an export-led development strategy that was mostly managed by the state. According to Noland one of the fundamental objectives of capital controls was to ensure that the complex system of domestic controls, prohibitions, and subsidies would be operative and effective. This meant that until the late 1990s capital inflows—including FDI and remittances—were closely monitored and controlled. Until early 1980 Korea's exchange rate was pegged to the U.S. dollar. At that point a basket peg was adopted, an effort by the authorities to maintain an undervalued currency. In the late 1980s the U.S. Treasury labeled Korea an "exchange rate manipulator," and urged the country to adopt a more flexible regime that would reflect market forces. In 1990 Korea implemented a band system. During the late 1980s and early 1990s the U.S. pressured Korea to open its capital markets to international flows. During the mid-1990s Korea authorized the creation of merchant banks. These had a close relationship to local conglomerates (*chaebol*) and engaged in heavy related lending. Many of these loans were used to finance questionable projects, and by early 1997 the Korean financial system was overextended and highly vulnerable.

The next chapter, "Malaysian Capital Controls: Macroeconomics and Institutions," is by Simon Johnson, Kalpana Kochhar, Todd Mitton, and Natalia Tamirisa. The authors' goal is to evaluate Malaysia's experience with capital controls in 1998–99. They provide background information going back to the early 1990s, and discuss the authorities' objectives when imposing the controls. At least on paper, the objective of the controls, as explained by Mahathir's administration, was to help deinternationalize the ringgit. In September 1998 the administration required investors to repatriate ringgit held in offshore accounts, and prohibited trading the Malaysian currency in offshore markets. According to the authors the controls were imposed after Malaysia's crisis had already reached its peak, and it is not clear whether they were really needed. In addition, in their view it is not clear that the controls helped Malaysia to recover. In late 1998, shortly after Malaysia imposed the controls, all East Asian countries— Malaysia as well as those nations that did not impose controls—began to recover. Finally, the authors find no evidence suggesting that the imposition of the controls had negative macroeconomic effects. In the main part of the paper the authors look at firm-level data to determine which firms won and which ones lost as a result of the controls. They argue that in Malaysia this type of analysis is particularly pertinent, since large firms usually have close ties with senior politicians. Their analysis focuses on the connection between large firms and two politicians: the prime minister (Mohammad Mahathir) and the finance minister (Anwar Ibrahim). In 1998 there was a falling out between Mahathir and Ibrahim, and the latter was sent to jail. After analyzing in great detail a number of micro performance indicators, such as growth of sales, investment, indebtedness, profitability, and leverage, the authors conclude that the imposition of controls benefited firms associated with Prime Minister Mahathir. The authors also conclude that the data are inconclusive with regard to the macroeconomic benefits and costs of Malaysia's experience with controls.

In "Capital Flows and Exchange Rate Volatility: Singapore's Experience," Basant K. Kapur discusses the behavior of capital flows in Singapore, as well as Singapore's experience with capital account regulations. He argues that, in contrast with the rest of the East Asian nations, Singapore's experience with international capital flows over the past two decades has been a rather—although not completely—benign one. The reason for this has to do with Singapore's strong fundamentals and generally well-conceived macroeconomic policies, including its fiscal policy. In order to provide a point of comparison, Kapur begins his analysis with a discussion of the experience of Hong Kong during the 1998 crisis. Hong Kong is another city-state with a well-developed and sophisticated banking system and equities market. It also has a currency board (CB) system similar to that of Singapore, although with some differences. Using Hong Kong as a point of comparison, Kapur discusses Singapore's early experience and policy stance. In his analysis he emphasizes Singapore's exchange rate policy and its policy of noninternationalization of the Singapore dollar. He also analyzes the interaction and interplay between equity and currency markets. Kapur shows that Singapore emerged relatively unscathed from the 1997 Asian crisis. Finally, Kapur presents an extensive discussion on the evolution of Singapore's debt markets. He shows that, in order to promote it, debt market restrictions on capital account convertibility—and, more specifically, the noninternationalization policy—have been progressively relaxed, while at the same time some key safeguards have been maintained.

In "India's Experience with Capital Flows: The Elusive Quest for a Sustainable Current Account Deficit" Ajay Shah and Ila Patnaik discuss India's policies toward capital flows during the last two decades. The authors open their paper with an analysis of India's reforms. They point out that since the early 1990s India has implemented policies aimed at liberalizing trade and deregulating investment decisions. Throughout most of this period India has maintained strong controls on debt flows and has encouraged FDI and portfolio flows. At the same time the Indian authorities have adopted a pegged nominal exchange rate regime. According to Shah and Patnaik domestic institutional factors have resulted in relatively small FDI flows and relatively large portfolio flows. They also point out that one of India's most severe policy dilemmas during this period has been related to the tension between capital flows and the currency regime. As in a large number of emerging countries—both in Asia and elsewhere—large capital inflows have put significant appreciation pressure on the real exchange rate. This has affected the country's degree of international competitiveness, and has eroded the support to the liberalization policies. According to Shah and Patnaik, many tactical details of the intricate reforms to the capital controls derive from the interlocking relationships between monetary policy, the currency regime, and capital flows. The authors point out that recently the accumulation of international reserves has played an important role. An additional manifestation of the tension between exchange rate policy and capital flows has been the significant increase in the volatility of nominal rupee-dollar returns. The authors argue that in spite of the progress achieved since the reforms were adopted, the goal of the early 1990s—of finding a consistent way to augment investment using current account deficits—has remained elusive.

The volume closes with a broad and comprehensive evaluation of the functioning of capital controls and their effects on macroeconomic performance. In "Capital Controls: An Evaluation," Nicolas Magud and Carmen M. Reinhart analyze the literature on capital controls and economic performance. They argue that this literature is confusing and has been characterized by at least five major shortcomings. First, there is no unified theoretical framework to analyze the macroeconomic consequences of capital controls; this is the case both for controls on outflows and for controls on inflows. Second, most of the literature has not taken into account the fact that there is a significant heterogeneity across countries and time in the control measures implemented. Not all countries are similar; moreover, different episodes in the same country tend to have significant differences. Third, there are many (and very different) definitions of what constitutes a successful experience with capital controls. Many times authors don't specify what specific criterion they are using for defining success. Fourth, the existing empirical studies lack a common methodology. Finally, the empirical evidence on the effects and effectiveness of capital controls has been dominated by the experiences of only two countries: Chile and Malaysia. In this paper, Magud and Reinhart address some of these shortcomings in several ways. First, the authors are very explicit about what measures are construed as capital controls. Also, given that "success" is measured so differently across studies, Magud and Reinhart try to standardize the results of more than thirty empirical studies on capital controls and economic performance. This standardization process was done by constructing two indexes of capital controls. The first one is called the Capital Controls Effectiveness index (CCE index), and the second one is referred to as the Weighted Capital Control Effectiveness index (WCCE index). The difference between the two is that the WCCE controls for the differentiated degree of methodological rigor used in each of the papers. Also, the authors present evidence on episodes with capital controls that are not as well known as those of Chile and Malaysia.

References

Dornbusch, Rudiger. 2002. Malaysia: Was it different? In *Preventing currency crises in emerging markets,* ed. Sebastian Edwards and Jeffrey Frankel, 441–54. Chicago: University of Chicago Press.

Frenkel, Jacob A. 1983. Panel discussion on the Southern Cone. *International Monetary Fund Staff Papers* 30 (1): 164–73.

Guitián, Manuel. 1995. Capital account liberalization: Bringing policy in line with reality. In *Capital controls, exchange rates, and monetary policy in the world economy,* ed. Sebastian Edwards, 71–90. Cambridge: Cambridge University Press.

Kaplan, Ethan, and Dani Rodrik. 2002. Did the Malaysian capital controls work?

In *Preventing currency crises in emerging markets,* ed. Sebastian Edwards and Jeffrey Frankel, 393–431. Chicago: University of Chicago Press.

Klaus, Vaclav. 1991. A perspective on economic transition in Czechoslovakia and Eastern Europe. Paper presented at the World Bank Annual Conference on Development Economics. Washington, DC.

Mundell, Robert. 1995. Stabilization and liberalization policies in semi-open economies. In *Capital controls, exchange rates, and monetary policy in the world economy,* ed. Sebastian Edwards, 19–34. Cambridge: Cambridge University Press.

Smith, Adam. 1776/1937. *An inquiry into the nature and causes of the wealth of nations.* Repr. Ed. Edwin Cannan. New York: Random House.

Stiglitz, Joseph E. 2002. *Globalization and its discontents.* New York: Norton.

Capital Controls in the Emerging Countries
Analytical Issues and Cross-Country Evidence

1

Capital Flows in a Globalized World
The Role of Policies
and Institutions

Laura Alfaro, Sebnem Kalemli-Ozcan, and
Vadym Volosovych

1.1 Introduction

Controversy regarding the costs and benefits of globalization has taken center stage in policy and academic circles. While concerns over the benefits of capital mobility once voiced by John Maynard Keynes during the design of the Bretton Woods System were nearly forgotten in the 1970s and 1980s, the crises of the last decade have revived the debate over the merits of international financial integration.

The most powerful argument in favor of international capital mobility, voiced by, among others, Stanley Fischer, Maurice Obstfeld, Kenneth Rogoff, and Larry Summers, is that it facilitates an efficient global allocation of savings by channelling financial resources to their most productive uses, thereby increasing economic growth and welfare around the world. But some other prominent academics are among the skeptics of international financial integration. Paul Krugman (1998), for example, argues that countries that experience full-blown crises should use capital controls. Dani Rodrik (1998) claims that international financial liberalization creates a higher risk of crises for developing countries. Even Jagdish Bhagwati, a fierce proponent of free trade, wonders if the risks of international finan-

Laura Alfaro is an associate professor at Harvard Business School and a faculty associate at Harvard's Weatherhead Center for International Affairs. Sebnem Kalemli-Ozcan is an associate professor of economics at the University of Houston and a faculty research fellow of the National Bureau of Economic Research (NBER). Vadym Volosovych is an assistant professor of economics at Florida Atlantic University.

The authors thank Franklin Allen, Sebastian Edwards, Martin Feldstein, Jeff Frieden, Gerd Haeusler, Ayhan Kose, Gian Maria Milesi-Ferretti, Simon Johnson, David Papell, Eswar Prasad, Nouriel Roubini, Bent Sorensen, and participants at the NBER Conference on International Capital Flows and the Federal Reserve Bank of New York Conference on Financial Globalization for valuable comments and suggestions.

cial integration might outweigh its benefits (Bhagwati 1998). As a result, recent research has focused on how to minimize the instability associated with international capital markets. Without a comprehensive understanding of the determinants of capital flows and their volatility, however, it is difficult to evaluate the different proposals that have been put forth to mitigate the negative effects of international capital mobility.

The determinants of international capital flows and their consequences for economic growth have been one of the most important issues in the international macroeconomics literature.[1] However, there is no consensus. This is mainly due to the fact that different researchers focus on different samples of countries (Organization for Economic Cooperation and Development [OECD] countries versus emerging markets), different time periods (1970s versus 1980s versus 1990s), and different forms of capital flows (foreign direct investment/portfolio equity flows versus debt flows or public flows versus private flows). For example, Calvo, Leiderman, and Reinhart (1996) focus on the role of external (push) and internal (pull) factors as potential determinants of foreign investment using a cross section of developing countries. They find that low interest rates in the United States played an important role in accounting for the renewal of capital flows to these countries in the 1990s. Edwards (1991) shows that government size and openness are important determinants of inward foreign direct investment (FDI) from OECD to developing countries during the period 1971–81. Wei (2000) and Wei and Wu (2002) use data on bilateral FDI from eighteen industrialized source countries to fifty-nine host countries during 1994–96 and find that corruption reduces the volume of inward FDI and affects the composition of flows by increasing the loan-to-FDI ratio during this period.[2] Using data on bilateral portfolio equity flows from a set of fourteen industrialized countries during 1989–96, Portes and Rey (2005) find evidence that imperfections in the international credit markets can affect the amount and direction of capital flows. Among a set of developing countries, Lane (2004) also finds credit market frictions to be a determinant of debt flows during 1970–95.

These papers have not paid particular attention to the overall role institutions play in shaping long-term capital flows among a cross section of developed and developing countries. This is a task we started investigating in Alfaro, Kalemli-Ozcan, and Volosovych (2003; henceforth AKV). AKV find institutional quality to be a causal determinant of capital inflows, where current institutions are instrumented by their historical determinants.[3] In this

---

1. See Prasad et al. (2003) for an extensive review.
2. Wei and Wu (2002) also investigate the determinants of bilateral bank flows from thirteen industrialized source countries to eighty-three host countries, showing similar results.
3. Institutional quality is measured as a composite political safety index. It is the sum of all the components rated by an independent agency, the PRS Group, in the *International*

paper, we re-establish our results from AKV for a different sample using balance of payments (BOP) statistics from the International Monetary Fund (IMF).[4] We then extend our original analysis in significant ways by asking three main questions: Is there any direct effect of the legal system on foreign investments other than through its effect on institutions? Is there any role for policy over institutions? Does institutional quality influence the volatility of capital flows?

Our evidence shows that the historical legal origin of a country has a direct impact on capital inflows during 1970–2000. We interpret this finding as evidence that legal origins measure different components of institutional quality, such as investor protection. What about policies? There is an important distinction between policies and institutions. Institutions are sets of rules constraining human behavior.[5] Policies are choices made within a political and social structure that is, within a set of institutions. As mentioned, we find institutional quality to have a first-order effect over policies as a determinant of capital flows. Given this, it is important to know if there is any role left for policymaking. In order to investigate this question, we look at the changes in the level of capital inflows and regress them on the policy changes and institutional quality changes from the first half to the second half of the sample period. In those regressions, both changes in institutions and policy variables, such as inflation, capital controls, and financial development, are shown to have a role in explaining changes in capital inflows. This result has important policy implications in the sense that improving institutions and domestic policies can increase the inward foreign investment to a country over time.

Finally, we examine the determinants of the volatility of capital flows and study whether institutions and policies play a role in reducing the instability in the international financial markets. Theoretical research has linked capital flow volatility to periods of liberalization. One argument is that the unprecedented globalization of the securities market in the 1990s resulted in high volatility of capital flows.[6] Other researchers model how frictions in the international financial markets together with weak fundamentals lead to excessive volatility of capital flows.[7] The empirical work focuses more on financial crises. That literature shows that bad policies, such as fiscal deficits, inflation, and bank fragility, seem to matter for the finan-

---

Country Risk Guide (ICRG). The components are government stability, internal conflict, external conflict, no corruption, militarized politics, religious tensions, law and order, ethnic tensions, democratic accountability, and bureaucratic quality. See Acemoglu, Johnson, and Robinson (2001, 2002) for the historical determinants of current institutional quality.

4. AKV calculate inflows using data on foreign-owned stocks estimated by Lane and Milesi-Ferretti (1999, 2001) and Kraay et al. (2000), in addition to using BOP data from IMF.

5. See North (1994, 1995).

6. See Calvo and Mendoza (2000a, 2000b) and Bacchetta and van Wincoop (2000).

7. See Chari and Kehoe (2003).

cial crises, which may be regarded as episodes of extreme volatility.[8] Our evidence suggests that both low institutional quality and bad policies, in particular bad monetary policy, have played a role in the long-run volatility of capital flows during 1970–2000.[9]

The chapter is organized as follows. Section 1.2 presents a preliminary discussion on capital mobility, institutions, and policies. Section 1.3 presents extensive data and overviews the stylized facts related to capital flow mobility and the volatility of these flows during 1970–2000. Section 1.4 presents results on the determinants of capital flows, changes in capital flows over time, and capital flow volatility. Section 1.5 concludes.

1.2   Capital Flows and Institutions

Despite the surge in capital mobility over the last decade, capital flows from rich to poor countries have been at much lower levels than predicted by the standard neoclassical models.[10] This phenomenon is usually referred to as the "Lucas paradox."[11] Lucas (1990) examines international capital movements from the perspective of rich and poor countries. Under the standard assumptions—such as countries producing the same goods with the same constant returns to scale production function, the same factors of production, and the same technology—and where there is free capital mobility, new investment will occur only in the poorer economy, and this will continue to be true until the returns to capital in every location are equalized. Hence, Lucas argues that given the implications of the frictionless

8. See Frankel and Rose (1996), Kaminsky and Reinhart (1999), Corsetti, Pesenti, and Roubini (2001), Kaminsky (2003), and Frankel and Wei (2004). McKinnon and Pill (1996) model how financial liberalization together with distortions can make boom-bust cycles even more pronounced by fueling lending booms that lead to the eventual collapse of the banking system. Aizenman (2004) links financial crises to financial opening. Other researchers have found that stabilization programs cause large capital inflows at the early stages of the exchange rate stabilization reforms, followed by high capital flow reversals when the lack of credibility behind the peg fuels an attack against the domestic currency. See Calvo and Vegh (1999).

9. Eichengreen, Hausmann, and Panizza (2003) examine the relation between "original sin" (the inability of countries to borrow abroad in their own currencies) and capital flow volatility for thirty-three countries. The work by Gavin and Hausmann (1999) and Gavin, Hausmann, and Leiderman (1995) establishes the volatility patterns for Latin American countries up to the early 1990s and relates them to external shocks and internal policies; see also Inter-American Development Bank (1995).

10. Section 1.3 documents this and other facts related to international capital flows.

11. The Lucas paradox, the lack of flows from rich to poor countries, is related to some of the major puzzles in the literature: the high correlation between savings and investment in OECD countries (the Feldstein-Horioka puzzle), the lack of investment in foreign capital markets by home-country residents (the home bias puzzle), and the low correlations of consumption growth across countries (the lack of risk sharing puzzle). All of these puzzles deal with the question of the lack of international capital flows. See Obstfeld and Rogoff (2000) for an overview of the major puzzles in international economies.

neoclassical theory, the fact that more capital does not flow from rich countries to poor countries constitutes a paradox.

Lucas's work has spawned an extensive theoretical literature. Researchers, including Lucas himself, show that with slight modifications of the basic neoclassical theory, such as changing the production structure, adding an internationally immobile factor such as human capital, or deviating from perfect markets assumption, the paradox disappears. The main theoretical explanations for the Lucas paradox can be broadly grouped into two categories.[12] The first group includes differences in fundamentals that affect the production structure of the economy. Researchers have explored the role of omitted factors of production, government policies, institutions, and differences in technology.[13] The second group of explanations emphasizes international capital market imperfections, mainly sovereign risk and asymmetric information. Although capital is potentially productive and has a high return in developing countries, it does not flow there because of market failures.[14]

Empirical research on the Lucas paradox is rather limited. As far as indirect evidence goes, O'Rourke and Williamson (1999) find that before World War I British capital chased European emigrants, when both were seeking cheap land and natural resources. Clemens and Williamson (2004), using data on British investment in thirty-four countries during the nineteenth century, show that two-thirds of the historical British capital exports went to the labor-scarce New World and only about one-quarter to labor-abundant Asia and Africa for similar reasons. Direct evidence is provided by AKV, who investigate the role of the different explanations for the lack of inflows of capital (FDI, portfolio equity, and debt) from rich to poor countries—the "paradox." Using cross-country regressions, and paying particular attention to endogeneity issues, AKV show that during

12. For a recent overview of the different explanations behind the Lucas paradox, see Reinhart and Rogoff (2004).

13. For the role of different production functions, see King and Rebelo (1993); for the role of government policies, see Razin and Yuen (1994); for the role of institutions, see Tornell and Velasco (1992); for the role of total factor productivity (TFP), see Glick and Rogoff (1995) and Kalemli-Ozcan et al. (2005). Note that it is very difficult to differentiate both theoretically and empirically between the effect of institutions and the effect of TFP on investment opportunities, given that institutional quality is also a determinant of TFP. Prescott (1998) argues that the efficient use of the currently operating technology or resistance to the adoption of new ones depends on the "arrangements" a society employs. Kalemli-Ozcan et al. (2005) study capital flows between U.S. states, where there is a common institutional structure. They show these flows to be consistent with a simple neoclassical model with TFP that varies across states and over time and where capital freely moves across state borders. In this framework, capital flows to states that experience a relative increase in TFP.

14. Gertler and Rogoff (1990) show that asymmetric information problems might cause a reversal in the direction of capital flows relative to the perfect-information case. Gordon and Bovenberg (1996) develop a model with asymmetric information that explains the differences in corporate taxes and, hence, differences in real interest rates.

1970–2000 institutional quality is the most important causal variable explaining the Lucas paradox.

What about pre-1970 capital flows? Obstfeld and Taylor (2004) characterize four different periods in terms of the U-shaped evolution of capital mobility.[15] An upswing in capital mobility occurred from 1880 to 1914 during the gold standard period. Before 1914, capital movements were free and flows reached unprecedented levels. The international financial markets broke up during World War I. In the 1920s, policymakers around the world tried to reconstruct the international financial markets. Britain returned to the gold standard in 1925 and led the way to restoring the international gold standard for a short period. Capital mobility increased between 1925 and 1930. As the world economy collapsed into depression in the 1930s, so did the international capital markets. World War II was followed by a period of limited capital mobility. Capital flows began to increase starting in the 1960s, and further expanded in the 1970s after the demise of the Bretton Woods system. In terms of the Lucas paradox, Obstfeld and Taylor (2004) argue that capital was somewhat biased toward the rich countries in the first global capital market boom in pre-1914, but it is even more so today. In the pre-1914 boom, there was little difference between net flows and gross flows because most of the flows were unidirectional from the rich core to the periphery. Post-1970 gross flows (both inflows and outflows) relative to GDP increased tremendously. But net flows (inflows minus outflows) stayed constant at relatively low levels for the last thirty years. This is consistent with the fact that most flows are between rich countries (called north-north as opposed to north-south). Obstfeld and Taylor (2004) conclude that modern capital flows are mostly "diversification finance" rather than "development finance."

If the Lucas paradox was to a certain extent a feature of the pre-1914 global capital market boom, and even more so in the last thirty years, what is the explanation? We argue that it is differences in institutional quality among the poor and rich countries. Institutions are the rules of the game in a society. They consist of both informal constraints (traditions, customs) and formal rules (regulations, laws, and constitutions). They create the incentive structure of an economy. Institutions are understood to affect economic performance through their effect on investment decisions by protecting the property rights of entrepreneurs against the government and other segments of society and preventing elites from blocking the adoption of new technologies. In general, weak property rights owing to poor quality institutions can lead to lack of productive capacities or uncertainty of returns in an economy.

Lucas (1990) argues that "political risk" cannot explain the lack of flows before 1945 because during that time most poor countries were subject to

---

15. See also Eichengreen (2003) and O'Rourke and Williamson (1999).

European legal arrangements imposed through colonialism. He gives India as an example, arguing that investors in India were governed by the same rules and regulations as investors in the United Kingdom. However, the recent work on institutions and growth by Acemoglu, Johnson, and Robinson (2001, 2002) illustrates how conditions in the colonies shaped today's institutions. The British institutions in India do not necessarily have the same quality as the British institutions in the United States and Australia. They argue that it is not the legal origin or the identity of the colonizer that matters for shaping institutions, but whether the European colonialists could safely settle in a particular location. If the European settlement was discouraged by diseases or surplus extraction was beneficial via an urbanized and prosperous population, the Europeans set up worse institutions. This is also consistent with the argument of Reinhart and Rogoff (2004), who emphasize the relationship between sovereign risk and historical defaults and conclude that sovereign risk must be the explanation for the Lucas paradox. Historically bad institutions are strong predictors of sovereign risk and, hence, historical serial default.

In the next section we present an overview of the general patterns of international capital mobility and capital flow volatility over the last thirty years. These data show that, despite the dramatic increase in capital flows over the last two decades, most capital flows to rich countries.

1.3   International Capital Flows: 1970–2000

1.3.1   Data

We use data on annual capital flows from the *International Financial Statistics* (IFS) issued by the IMF. Although there are other data sources, the IFS provides the most comprehensive and comparable data on international capital flows.[16] These data are described in detail in appendix A.

One might expect that in the financial account (formerly called the capital account) of the BOP, changes in liabilities should be shown as positive entries (inflows) and changes in assets should be shown as negative entries (outflows). In practice, changes in both liabilities and assets are reported as net of any disinvestment, and consequently both can have any sign. In the BOP accounts, an increase (decrease) in liabilities to foreigners is entered as positive (negative), while an increase (decrease) in foreign assets held by

---

16. The balance of payments (BOP) statistics, also issued by the IMF, present the same data. There are two presentations of the BOP data: Analytical and Standard. IFS and BOP Analytical present the same data and report "exceptional financing" as a separate line. BOP Standard, on the other hand, does not report "exceptional financing" as a separate line and instead includes it in the "other investment" category (refer to IMF 1993). Items reported under "exceptional financing" vary from country to country and are described in the country profiles in the corresponding BOP manual.

locals is entered as negative (positive).[17] Following this convention, net flows of capital are calculated as the sum of the flows of foreign claims on domestic capital (change in liabilities) and the flows of domestic claims on foreign capital (change in assets) in a given year. Gross flows of capital are calculated as the sum of the absolute value of the flows of foreign claims on domestic capital and the absolute value of the flows of domestic claims on foreign capital in a given year. Hence, they are always positive.

The main categories of capital flows are FDI, portfolio equity investment, and debt flows. In what follows, we describe the definition and measurement of these categories in great detail.

Total Equity Flows

For FDI, we use direct investment abroad (IFS line 78bdd) and direct investment in reporting economy (line 78bed). These categories include equity capital, reinvested earnings, other capital, and financial derivatives associated with various intercompany transactions between affiliated enterprises. For portfolio equity investment, we use equity security assets (line 78bkd) and equity security liabilities (line 78bmd), which include shares, stock participation, and similar documents (such as American depository receipts) that usually denote ownership of equity.

Direct investments include greenfield investments and equity participation giving a controlling stake. When a foreign investor purchases a local firm's securities without exercising control over the firm, the investment is regarded as a portfolio investment. The IMF classifies an investment as direct if a foreign investor holds at least 10 percent of a local firm's equity while the remaining equity purchases are classified under portfolio equity investment. In the regression analysis, we do not distinguish between minority and majority shareholders, as this distinction is not important to our analysis. In addition, because of missing or insufficient portfolio data (some countries tend not to receive portfolio flows, due in part to lack of

---

17. The balance of payment is a record of a country's transactions with the rest of the world. The financial account within the balance of payments, broadly speaking, keeps track of transactions in financial assets. It reports changes in the asset position (assets and liabilities) of a country vis-à-vis the rest of the world. For example, if a U.S. firm imports goods from Switzerland for $10 million and pays with a check drawn on a U.S. bank, the corresponding transaction in the financial account is recorded as an increase in U.S. liabilities to foreigners (a credit of $10 million). If the payment is drawn against an account the U.S. firm has in a Swiss bank, the corresponding transaction in the financial account is recorded as a reduction in U.S. assets (a credit of $10 million). Note that a country's balance of payment record is kept according to the principles of double-entry bookkeeping. The corresponding balancing transaction would be a debit (–$10 million) in the current account (import of goods). A specific example is as follows: On September 1, 1998, as part of a broader set of policies to restrict capital outflows, the Malaysian government eliminated the offshore trading of the Malaysian ringgit by requiring all ringgit offshore to be repatriated within a month. By the end of 1998 the account "other investment" was –4,604 million U.S. dollars. This amount, among other transactions, reflects the repatriation of the ringgit, which will show as a reduction in Malaysian liabilities.

functioning stock markets), we prefer to use total equity flows in the analysis, which is the sum of flows of FDI and flows of portfolio equity.

Debt Flows

For debt flows, we use debt security assets (IFS line 78bld) and debt security liabilities (line 78bnd) as well as other investment assets (line 78bhd) and other investment liabilities (line 78bid). Debt securities include bonds, debentures, notes, and money market or negotiable debt instruments. Other investments include all financial transactions not covered in direct investment, portfolio investment, financial derivatives, or other assets. Major categories are trade credits, loans, transactions in currency and deposits, and other assets.

Data Issues

Although the IMF provides the most comprehensive data, there are several issues associated with the compilation of the BOP statistics, as discussed in greater detail by Lane and Milesi-Ferretti (2001). A substantial amount of data is missing for many countries, in particular for developing countries. In addition, some countries do not report data for all forms of capital flows. Unfortunately, it is difficult to verify whether the data are in fact missing as opposed to simply being zero. For example, portfolio equity data for most countries were negligible until recently. There are additional misreporting issues related to the fact that several countries tend to report data for liabilities only and not for assets. This is particularly the case for FDI flows. Some of these data, reported in the liability line, seem to correspond to net flows (i.e., liabilities minus assets). For debt data, there are additional issues. Consequent to the debt crisis there are a number of measurement problems related to different methodologies for recording nonpayments, rescheduling, debt forgiveness, and reductions.[18] Finally, the time coverage of the data varies substantially from country to country. Most developed countries begin reporting data in the early 1970s, and a substantial subset of developing countries in the mid-1970s. For other countries, data are not available until the mid-1980s or early 1990s.

Stocks versus Flows and Valuation Effects

The IFS reports BOP transactions as flows of equity and debt. In 1997, the IMF began to report international investment position for each country—that is, the stocks. However, stocks are not just cumulative flows; they also depend on capital gains, losses, and defaults—that is, on valuation adjustments. These stocks reported by the IMF are reported by countries

---

18. As noted by Lane and Milesi-Ferretti (2001), these issues create large discrepancies among debt data reported by different methodologies. We thank Gian Maria Milesi-Ferretti for pointing this out to us and helping us with the data in general.

themselves. Some calculate them in a pretty sophisticated fashion (with surveys, etc.), while others cumulate flows with valuation adjustments. Kraay et al. (2000; hereafter KLSV) and Lane and Milesi-Ferretti (1999, 2001; hereafter LM) construct consistent estimates of foreign assets and liabilities and their subcomponents for different countries in the 1970s, 1980s, and 1990s, paying particular attention to these valuation effects. LM estimate stocks of equity and FDI based on the IMF flow data adjusted to reflect changes in financial market prices and exchange rates. In order to estimate FDI stocks, the authors accumulate flows and adjust for the effects of exchange rate changes. For equity stocks, they adjust for changes in the end-of-year U.S. dollar value of the domestic stock market. KLSV argue against the valuation of stocks using financial market prices, maintaining that capital listed on the stock market and the corresponding share prices—especially in developing countries—are not representative of the stock of capital of a country or of the value of a firm. Instead, they use the price of investment goods in local currency, which is the investment deflator. They also adjust for exchange rate changes. LM found the correlation between the first difference of foreign claims on capital and current account to be generally high but significantly below unity for several countries, confirming the importance of valuation adjustments.

1.3.2   Some Stylized Facts

We express all flows in 1995 U.S. dollars using the U.S. consumer price index (CPI) taken from the World Bank's *World Development Indicators.* We divide these flows by the corresponding country's population, taken from the same source. We believe that data expressed as real dollars per capita are consistent with the neoclassical theory and provide a better picture of the evolution of the global capital markets over the last three decades. We exclude from the sample countries with populations of less than half a million, because very small countries in the sample tend to distort the pattern of capital flows per capita. We have data on 72 countries for FDI, 68 countries for portfolio equity, and 122 for debt flows.[19]

Total inflows of capital per capita as well as each of the components increased substantially throughout the sample period for most of our countries. Average inflows of capital per capita within our sample grew by 4.8 percent per year during the sample period. There is, however, variability in terms of the composition. Figure 1.1 plots the evolution of the composition of inflows of capital per capita for the countries in our sample.[20] The increasing role of FDI and portfolio flows is evident. Based on the sample of

19. In calculating total equity flows, we treat missing portfolio equity data as zero. We then add zero and FDI for that country. So we also have seventy-two countries for the total equity flows. The four countries with FDI data but no portfolio equity data are Bolivia, Central African Republic, Mauritius, and Papua New Guinea.

20. See appendix tables 1B.1 and 1B.2 for the list of countries.

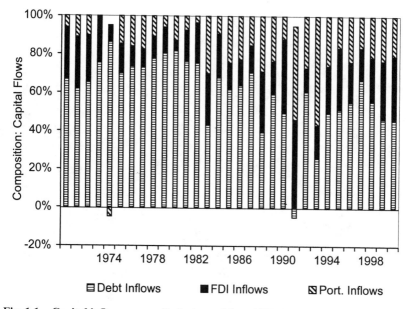

Fig. 1.1   Capital inflows per capita by type of flow, 1970–2000

Notes: Inflows represent inflows of FDI, portfolio equity investment, and debt divided by population based on IMF data in 1995 U.S. dollars. FDI data are available for 72 countries, portfolio data for 68 countries, and debt data for 122 countries. Inflows represent flows of foreign claims on domestic capital (liability). FDI inflows correspond to Direct Investment in Reporting Economy (IFS line 78bed), which includes equity capital, reinvested earnings, other capital and financial derivatives associated with various intercompany transactions between affiliated enterprises. Portfolio equity inflows correspond to Equity Liabilities (line 78bmd), which include shares, stock participations, and similar documents that usually denote ownership of equity. Data on inflows of debt include Debt Securities Liabilities (line 78bnd), which include bonds, notes, and money market, or negotiable debt instruments; and Other Investment Liabilities (line 78bid), which include all financial transactions not covered by direct investment, portfolio investment, financial derivatives, or other assets.

72 countries, average inflows of FDI per capita grew by 6.2 percent over the last thirty years and became the main source of private capital for developing countries during the 1990s. For our sample of 68 countries, average inflows of portfolio equity per capita grew by 9.3 percent. Finally, based on 122 countries, average inflows of debt per capita grew by 3.3 percent. Although their role is quite dominant, debt inflows clearly contracted following the 1980s' debt crisis. Figure 1.2 plots the evolution of the composition of the gross flows per capita. The patterns overall are similar to those in figure 1.1.

Figures 1.3, 1.4, and 1.5 plot the evolution of FDI, portfolio equity, and debt flows per capita, respectively. FDI flows remained relatively stable for most of the sample period, then increased steadily around the mid-1990s. Portfolio equity flows rose as well but fluctuated more. Debt flows also fluctuated, increasing during the 1970s, then crashing following the wake of

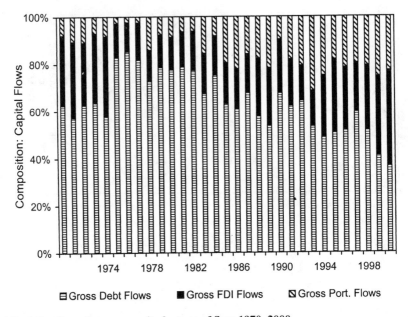

☐ Gross Debt Flows   ■ Gross FDI Flows   ☒ Gross Port. Flows

Fig. 1.2   Gross flows per capita by type of flow, 1970–2000

Notes: Gross flows represent gross flows of FDI, portfolio equity investment, and debt divided by population based on IMF data in 1995 U.S. dollars and correspond to the sum of the absolute value of the flows of assets (outflows) and liabilities (inflows). FDI data are available for 72 countries, portfolio data for 68 countries, and debt data for 122 countries. FDI assets and liabilities correspond respectively to Direct Investment Abroad (IFS line 78bdd) and Direct Investment in Reporting Economy (line 78bed) and include equity capital, reinvested earnings, other capital, and financial derivatives associated with various intercompany transactions between affiliated enterprises. Portfolio equity investment assets and liabilities correspond to Equity Securities Assets (line 78bkd) and Equity Securities Liabilities (line 78bmd) and include shares, stock participations, and similar documents that usually denote ownership of equity. Debt assets and liabilities include Debt Security Assets (line 78bld) and Debt Security Liabilities (line 78bnd), which include bonds and money market or negotiable debt instruments; Other Investment Assets (line 78bhd); and Other Investment Liabilities (line 78bid), which include all financial transactions not covered by direct investment, portfolio investment, financial derivatives, or other assets.

the 1980s debt crisis and reviving only in the 1990s. Figures 1.4 and 1.5 show that net portfolio and net debt flows become negative after 1995, a phenomenon driven mainly by industrial countries whose external asset holdings tend to exceed the liability holdings. With a few exceptions (in particular the United States), most of the developed countries have negative financial accounts. This is consistent with the results of Lane and Milesi-Ferretti (2001), which show net foreign asset positions on average to be increasing since 1995 for developed countries.

Panel A of figure 1.6 shows total equity inflows, which is the sum of inflows of FDI and inflows of portfolio equity investment, for twenty OECD and fifty-two developing countries. The difference between the two is a

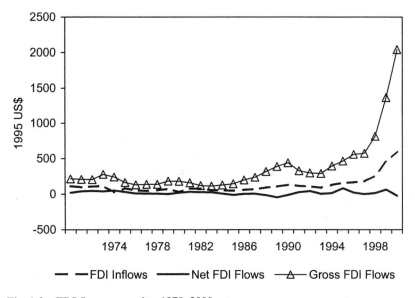

Fig. 1.3   FDI flows per capita, 1970–2000

Notes: Flows represent flows of FDI divided by population based on IMF data in 1995 U.S. dollars. Data are for 72 countries. Inflows represent flows of foreign claims on domestic capital (liability). Net flows are calculated as the difference between corresponding inflows (liabilities) and outflows (assets). Gross flows correspond to the sum of the absolute value of the flows of assets and liabilities. FDI assets and liabilities correspond, respectively, to Direct Investment Abroad (IFS line 78bdd) and Direct Investment in Reporting Economy (line 78bed) and include equity capital, reinvested earnings, other capital, and financial derivatives associated with various intercompany transactions between affiliated enterprises.

stark demonstration of north-north flows, or the Lucas paradox. Panel B of the figure shows the share of total equity inflows to total capital inflows for the OECD and developing countries. Since 1990, almost half of the total inflows were composed of FDI and portfolio equity investment for both rich and poor countries. Total equity flows are clearly an important part of the big picture, especially for poor countries.

Tables 1.1–1.4 present a variety of descriptive statistics on the various forms of capital flows for our sample of countries from 1970 to 2000. Table 1.1 provides descriptive statistics for inflows of capital per capita. Total capital inflows vary from –44.94 to 8320.9, with a mean of 406.29 dollars per capita. During the sample period, debt inflows averaged 284.07 dollars per capita, FDI inflows 169.44 dollars per capita, and total equity inflows 232.70 dollars per capita. Table 1.2 shows the increasing role of FDI and portfolio inflows per capita over debt inflows per capita for all regions (sub-Saharan Africa is the exception, where all types of inflows have a declining trend). These trends notwithstanding, the bulk of capital still flows to high-income countries, which attract 80 percent of all capital inflows.

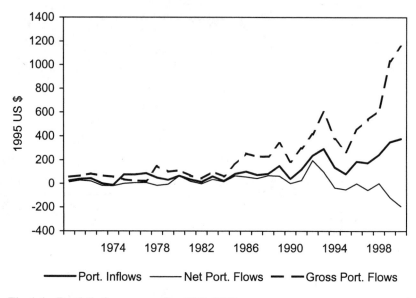

——— Port. Inflows ——— Net Port. Flows — —Gross Port. Flows

Fig. 1.4   Portfolio flows per capita, 1970–2000

Notes: Flows represent flows of portfolio equity investment divided by population based on IMF data in 1995 U.S. dollars. Data are for 68 countries. Inflows represent flows of foreign claims on domestic capital (liability). Net flows are calculated as the difference between corresponding inflows (liabilities) and outflows (assets). Gross flows correspond to the sum of the absolute value of the flows of assets and liabilities. Portfolio equity investment assets and liabilities correspond, respectively, to Equity Securities Assets (IFS line 78bkd) and Equity Securities Liabilities (line 78bmd) and include shares, stock participations, and similar documents that usually denote ownership of equity.

Table 1.3 presents summary statistics on the volatility of inflows of capital per capita. The volatility of inflows of capital is calculated as the standard deviation of the corresponding inflows per capita divided by the mean of gross flows over the sample period, which is the average of the absolute value of the inflows and the absolute value of the outflows per capita (hence always positive). Normalization prevents spuriously higher volatility in the recent period due to higher flow volume. Table 1.4 shows the volatility of the different forms of inflows of capital to have been lower during the 1990s. FDI flows are generally less volatile than portfolio flows as they tend to be driven by long-term considerations. Debt flows also exhibit higher volatility relative to FDI. Inflows of portfolio and debt experienced higher volatility during the 1980s consequent to the debt crises and the increasing role of portfolio flows in the aftermath of the crises. As expected, the volatility of each component of inflows of capital is lower for high-income countries than for developing countries. The volatility of inflows has remained relatively constant for South and Southeast Asian countries, with a slight increase during the 1990s driven by increased volatility of inflows of portfolio capital in the periods before and after the Asian crisis of the

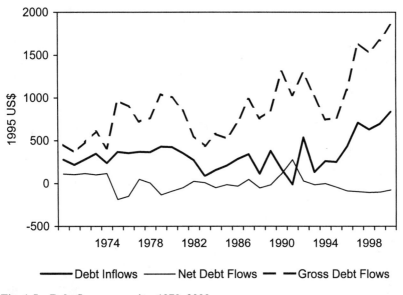

Fig. 1.5 Debt flows per capita, 1970–2000

Notes: Flows represent flows of debt divided by population based on IMF data in 1995 U.S. dollars. Data are for 122 countries. Inflows represent flows of foreign claims on domestic capital (liability). Net flows are calculated as the difference between corresponding inflows (liability) and outflows (asset). Gross flows correspond to the sum of the absolute value of the flows of assets and liabilities. Debt assets and liabilities include, respectively, Debt Securities Assets (IFS line 78bld) and Debt Securities Liabilities (line 78bnd), which cover bonds, notes, and money market or negotiable debt instruments; Other Investment Assets (line 78bhd); and Other Investment Liabilities (line 78bid), which include all financial transactions not covered by direct investment, portfolio investment, financial derivatives, or other assets.

late 1990s. Recently opened-up countries in Eastern Europe experienced a dramatic increase in the volatility of all forms of inflows of capital during the 1990s. For Latin America, on the other hand, the 1980s were turbulent years mostly driven by the debt crisis. The volatility of inflows of capital has declined during the 1990s. A similar pattern is observed for sub-Saharan Africa. The volatility of inflows of capital increased substantially in the 1990s for the Middle Eastern and North African countries.[21]

1.4 Empirical Analysis

1.4.1 Determinants of Capital Flows

For the regression analysis, we exclude countries with substantial missing data. In addition, there are various outliers in terms of capital flows per

21. Note that a very volatile form of foreign capital is foreign aid, which is driven by a host of factors, as shown by Alesina and Dollar (2000), and is not the focus of this study.

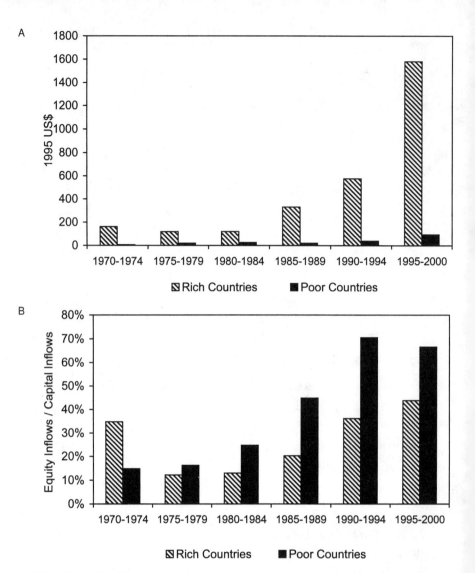

Fig. 1.6   *A,* **Total equity inflows to rich and poor countries, 1970–2000;** *B,* **ratio of total equity inflows to total inflows to rich and poor countries, 1970–2000**

Notes: Total equity inflows represent inflows of FDI and portfolio equity investment divided by population based on IMF data in 1995 U.S. dollars. Data are for 72 countries for which to-tal equity data are available and are averaged over five-year periods: FDI inflows correspond to Direct Investment in Reporting Economy (IFS line 78bed), which includes equity capital, reinvested earnings, other capital, and financial derivatives associated with various inter-company transactions between affiliated enterprises. Portfolio equity inflows correspond to Equity Liabilities (line 78bmd), which includes shares, stock participations, and similar doc-uments that usually denote ownership of equity. Rich countries denote high-income OECD countries; poor countries denote the remaining ones.

In panel B, Total inflows are the sum of total equity inflows and debt divided by population based on IMF data in 1995 US$. Data on inflows of debt include Debt Securities Liabilities (IFS line 78bnd), which cover bonds or negotiable debt instruments, and Other Investment Liabilities (line 78bid), which include all financial transactions not covered in direct invest-ment, portfolio investment, financial derivatives, or other assets.

Table 1.1   Descriptive statistics: Inflows of capital, 1970–2000 (per capita
                 U.S. dollars; sample: 122 countries)

	Mean	Standard deviation	Minimum	Maximum
FDI inflows	169.44	292.44	–122.51	1,723.78
Portfolio equity inflows	104.82	273.12	–2.17	1,769.21
Debt inflows	284.07	656.00	–83.56	4,827.94
Total equity inflows	232.70	487.09	–122.51	3,492.99
Total equity and debt inflows	406.29	1,012.32	–44.94	8,320.92

Notes: Inflows represent flows of foreign claims on domestic capital (liability) divided by population based on IMF data in 1995 U.S. dollars. FDI inflows correspond to Direct Investment in Reporting Economy (IFS line 78bed), which includes equity capital, reinvested earnings, other capital, and financial derivatives associated with various intercompany transactions between affiliated enterprises. Portfolio equity inflows correspond to Equity Liabilities (line 78bmd), which include shares, stock participations, and similar documents that usually denote ownership of equity. Data on inflows of debt include Debt Securities Liabilities (line 78bnd), which include bonds, notes, and money market or negotiable debt instruments; and Other Investment Liabilities (line 78bid), which include all financial transactions not covered by direct investment, portfolio investment, financial derivatives, or other assets. Inflows of total equity are the sum of FDI and portfolio equity investments. Total equity data are available for 72 countries; debt data are for 122 countries. See appendix tables 1B.1 and 1B.2 for countries in the sample.

capita. This, of course, should be considered in the econometric analysis. Table 1.5 lists the countries used in the regression analysis.[22]

The dependent variable is inflows of capital per capita, which is inflows of total equity (FDI and portfolio equity) investment averaged over the sample period. We prefer to abstract most of our analysis from debt flows since they tend to be shaped by government decisions to a greater extent

22. We keep track of the series of countries that have data throughout the whole sample period, as shown in appendix table 1B.3. The table provides descriptive statistics for a subsample of forty-seven countries for which there are data for both total equity and debt flows throughout the different decades. This subsample exhibits overall patterns similar to our regression sample. The forty-seven countries of this subsample are shown in boldface type in appendix table 1B.1. Unfortunately, we cannot use this sample in the regressions because there are several outliers. In addition, some of our independent variables do not exist for this subsample. Benelux and Singapore are outliers in terms of large inflows. Bahrain, Botswana, Gabon, Burkina Faso, and Niger do not have human capital data. Central African Republic, Fiji, Libya, Mauritius, Swaziland, and Chad are outliers in terms of other independent variables. This leaves us with a sample of thirty-four countries. In order to increase the number of observations we add the countries shown in italics. Although data for these countries start later in the sample period, there are enough data to construct averages over the period. Out of these twenty-three late starters, we cannot use Burundi, Switzerland, China, Kuwait, Latvia, Mauritania, Namibia, Slovenia, Trinidad and Tobago, and Uruguay. Switzerland and Kuwait are outliers in terms of large inflows. China is an outlier in terms of very low levels of GDP per capita. Latvia and Slovenia do not have human capital data. The rest are outliers for the other independent variables. So we add the remaining thirteen to our thirty-four and have our forty-seven-country sample for the regression analysis as shown in table 1.5. Ending up again with a sample of forty-seven is pure coincidence.

Table 1.2 **Inflows of capital by decade and region, 1970–2000 (per capita U.S. dollars; sample: 122 countries)**

	1970–2000	1970–1980	1981–1990	1991–2000
FDI inflows				
United States, Japan, Western Europe	348.93	115.73	170.23	684.52
Latin America and Caribbean	92.67	60.18	44.26	158.93
East Asia Pacific	247.90	115.38	208.70	419.82
South Asia	1.96	0.45	1.73	2.87
Europe and Central Asia	109.70	2.03	3.26	116.83
Sub-Saharan Africa	19.67	32.86	22.88	6.49
Middle East and North Africa	55.31	–114.64	29.13	128.67
Portfolio equity inflows				
United States, Japan, Western Europe	223.24	11.55	92.02	442.02
Latin America and Caribbean	9.06	–0.10	4.99	15.69
East Asia Pacific	33.93	24.72	54.59	53.98
South Asia	1.08	0.06	0.14	1.19
Europe and Central Asia	22.19	n.a.	1.11	22.26
Sub-Saharan Africa	7.91	3.49	–1.15	10.77
Middle East and North Africa	150.73	329.64	113.75	2.62
Debt inflows				
United States, Japan, Western Europe	1,136.02	845.29	1,048.38	1,462.65
Latin America and Caribbean	50.30	331.71	–62.97	39.55
East Asia Pacific	214.92	219.90	233.03	272.45
South Asia	12.05	11.14	15.19	9.59
Europe and Central Asia	124.95	30.83	–1.73	127.13
Sub-Saharan Africa	20.65	44.17	33.10	–5.29
Middle East and North Africa	204.00	382.60	–138.69	435.74
Total equity inflows				
United States, Japan, Western Europe	546.75	123.11	247.70	1,114.20
Latin America and Caribbean	84.05	65.86	38.08	139.61
East Asia Pacific	269.07	125.27	226.90	454.84
South Asia	4.00	1.00	2.80	6.39
Europe and Central Asia	128.01	2.03	3.37	136.07
Sub-Saharan Africa	23.99	33.21	22.61	13.16
Middle East and North Africa	77.86	54.20	32.59	129.51
Total equity and debt inflows				
United States, Japan, Western Europe	1,636.23	943.80	1,277.15	2,501.27
Latin America and Caribbean	82.66	348.16	–41.51	92.47
East Asia Pacific	376.36	324.29	384.29	545.35
South Asia	14.12	11.74	16.31	13.43
Europe and Central Asia	209.95	31.64	–0.60	229.18
Sub-Saharan Africa	30.23	56.37	42.61	0.17
Middle East and North Africa	258.08	417.04	–117.95	528.89

Notes: Inflows of each category correspond to foreign claims on domestic capital (liability) divided by population. Data are from IMF in 1995 U.S. dollars. Inflows of total equity represent the sum of FDI and portfolio equity investment. FDI data are for 72 countries; portfolio data are for 68 countries, and debt data are for 122 countries.

Table 1.3   Volatility of inflows of capital, 1970–2000 (per capita U.S. dollars; sample: 122 countries)

	Mean	Standard deviation	Minimum	Maximum
Volatility of FDI inflows	1.03	2.64	0.12	22.35
Volatility of portfolio equity inflows	0.78	0.43	0.16	2.29
Volatility of debt inflows	0.74	0.43	0.14	4.42
Volatility of total equity inflows	1.02	2.58	0.12	22.35
Volatility of total equity and debt inflows	0.75	0.68	0.07	7.26

Notes: Volatility of inflows is the standard deviation of the corresponding inflows per capita divided by the average of the absolute value of the inflows and outflows of capital per capita over time for each country. Data are from IMF in 1995 U.S. dollars. FDI inflows correspond to Direct Investment in Reporting Economy (IFS line 78bed), which includes equity capital, reinvested earnings, other capital, and financial derivatives associated with various intercompany transactions between affiliated enterprises. Portfolio equity inflows correspond to Equity Liabilities (line 78bmd), which includes shares, stock participations, and similar documents that usually denote ownership of equity. Data on inflows of debt include Debt Securities Liabilities (line 78bnd), which cover bonds, notes, and money market or negotiable debt instruments; and Other Investment Liabilities (line 78bid), which include all financial transactions not covered by direct investment, portfolio investment, financial derivatives, or other assets. Inflows of total equity are the sum of FDI and portfolio equity investments. FDI data are for 72 countries, portfolio data are for 68 countries, and debt data are for 122 countries.

than flows of equity.[23] On the other hand, we would like to capture market decisions.[24] Ideally, we would like to use all of the private capital flows and abstract from the public part of debt flows, but these data are not available. The IFS data include both private and public issuers and holders of debt securities. Although the data are further divided by monetary authorities, general government, banks, and other sectors, this information is unfortunately not available for most countries for long periods of time. In addition, it is difficult to divide the available data by private/public creditor and debtor.[25] On the other hand, one might fear that excluding debt inflows totally will reduce measures of capital inflows for countries with limited stock market development and/or for countries that receive low levels of FDI, which in turn might bias our results. We argue that the role of total equity (direct and portfolio) flows for the developing countries is not small at all. For the developing countries, average inflows of FDI per capita grew

23. Until the mid-1970s—following the shutting down of the international markets in the 1930s—debt flows to most developing countries were generally restricted to international organizations/government-to-government loans. During the late 1970s, banks replaced governments of industrial countries as lenders to developing countries. After 1982, following the debt crisis, official creditors once again dominated lending to developing countries.

24. In many countries bank loans have usually been intermediated through financial systems that often do not follow market incentives due to explicit or implicit government involvement. See Henry and Lorentzen (2003) and Obstfeld and Taylor (2004).

25. The World Bank's Global Development Finance database, which focuses on the liability side, divides debt data by the type of creditor (official and private) but not by the type of debtor. These data are available only for developing countries.

Table 1.4	Volatility of inflows of capital by decade and region, 1970–2000 (per capita U.S. dollars; sample: 122 countries)			
	1970–2000	1970–1980	1981–1990	1991–2000
Volatility of FDI inflows				
United States, Japan, Western Europe	0.58	0.30	0.33	0.39
Latin America and Caribbean	0.82	0.41	0.78	0.55
East Asia Pacific	0.61	0.41	0.48	0.41
South Asia	0.53	n.a.	0.34	0.44
Europe and Central Asia	0.69	0.35	0.63	0.57
Sub-Saharan Africa	2.41	0.63	0.78	0.78
Middle East and North Africa	0.86	0.64	0.83	0.66
Volatility of portfolio equity inflows				
United States, Japan, Western Europe	0.70	0.62	0.83	0.48
Latin America and Caribbean	0.92	0.70	3.85	0.74
East Asia Pacific	0.68	0.42	0.49	0.72
South Asia	0.77	n.a.	n.a.	0.77
Europe and Central Asia	0.75	n.a.	0.33	0.74
Sub-Saharan Africa	1.04	0.93	2.12	0.74
Middle East and North Africa	0.64	0.43	0.56	0.69
Volatility of debt inflows				
United States, Japan, Western Europe	0.57	0.41	0.50	0.43
Latin America and Caribbean	0.86	0.52	0.85	0.63
East Asia Pacific	1.04	0.35	0.64	0.53
South Asia	0.47	0.32	0.32	0.45
Europe and Central Asia	0.68	0.57	0.67	0.60
Sub-Saharan Africa	0.77	0.52	0.72	0.51
Middle East and North Africa	0.72	0.49	0.64	0.67
Volatility of total equity				
United States, Japan, Western Europe	0.62	0.32	0.42	0.38
Latin America and Caribbean	0.79	0.38	0.71	0.44
East Asia Pacific	0.60	0.42	0.48	0.42
South Asia	0.73	n.a.	0.41	0.58
Europe and Central Asia	0.64	0.35	0.58	0.53
Sub-Saharan Africa	2.39	0.62	0.77	0.71
Middle East and North Africa	0.81	0.65	0.79	0.64
Volatility of total equity and debt inflows				
United States, Japan, Western Europe	0.51	0.34	0.44	0.37
Latin America and Caribbean	0.86	0.44	0.98	0.62
East Asia Pacific	1.31	0.26	3.14	0.55
South Asia	0.46	0.31	0.31	0.44
Europe and Central Asia	0.63	0.72	0.66	0.52
Sub-Saharan Africa	0.76	0.45	0.79	0.52
Middle East and North Africa	0.76	0.48	0.62	0.68

Notes: Volatility of inflows is the standard deviation of the inflows per capita divided by the average of the absolute value of the inflows and outflows of capital per capita over time for each country. Data are from IMF in 1995 U.S. dollars. FDI data are for 72 countries; portfolio data are for 68 countries, and debt data are for 122 countries.

Table 1.5   **Sample of countries for the regression analysis, 1970–2000**

Argentina	Cyprus	Israel	Pakistan	Sri Lanka
Australia[a]	Czecy Republic[a]	Italy[a]	Papua New Guinea	Sweden[a]
Austria[a]	Denmark[a]	Japan[a]	Paraguay	Thailand
Bolivia	Egypt	Jordan	The Philippines	Tunisia
Brazil	Estonia	Kenya	Poland[a]	Turkey[a]
Cameroon	Finland[a]	Korea[a]	Portugal[a]	United States[a]
Canada[a]	France[a]	Morocco	Romania	United Kingdom[a]
Chile	Germany[a]	The Netherlands[a]	Senegal	
Colombia	Hungary[a]	New Zealand[a]	South Africa	
Costa Rica	India	Norway[a]	Spain[a]	

Note: Base sample of 47 countries for the regression analysis.
[a]OECD member country.

by 6.2 percent over the last thirty years and became the main source of private capital during the 1990s. Average inflows of portfolio equity per capita grew by 9.3 percent. Average inflows of debt per capita grew only by 3.3 percent. We nevertheless examine the role of debt inflows in our empirical analysis for robustness.

Table 1.6 provides descriptive statistics for our regression sample of forty-seven countries averaged over the sample period 1970–2000. Following AKV, we use the initial level of human capital (years of total schooling in total population) and institutional quality averaged over the sample period as independent variables to capture the fundamentals of the economy. We use the *International Country Risk Guide*'s (ICRG) political safety variables as our measure of institutional quality. This composite index is the sum of the indexes of government stability, internal conflict, external conflict, no corruption, nonmilitarized politics, protection from religious tensions, law and order, protection from ethnic tensions, democratic accountability, and bureaucratic quality.

In the empirical capital flow literature, distance has been used as a proxy for the international capital market failures, mainly asymmetric information.[26] We construct a variable called *distantness,* which is the weighted average of the distances from the capital city of a particular country to the capital cities of the other countries, using the gross domestic product (GDP) shares of the other countries as weights.[27]

We use additional variables on the right-hand side to capture domestic

---

26. Portes and Rey (2005) use a similar interpretation of distance in the context of bilateral capital flows, as do Wei and Wu (2002) in analyzing the determinants of FDI and bank lending. See also Coval and Moskowitz (1999, 2001).

27. We construct this variable following Kalemli-Ozcan, Sorensen, and Yosha (2003). We use Arcview software to get the latitude and longitude of each capital city and calculate the great arc distance between each pair. The GDP weights capture the positive relationship between trade volume and GDP.

Table 1.6   **Descriptive statistics**

	Sample	Mean	Standard deviation	Minimum	Maximum
Inflows of total equity per capita	47	173.81	199.93	1.68	697.97
Volatility of inflows of total equity per capita	47	1.50	0.57	0.71	3.14
Institutional quality	47	5.56	1.11	3.41	7.27
Human capital	47	4.65	2.64	0.54	9.55
Distantness (000 km)	47	7.64	2.48	5.13	14.06
Inflation volatility	47	0.90	0.71	0.30	4.64
Capital controls	47	1.53	0.26	1.00	1.96
GDP per capita ($000)	47	6.72	6.99	0.21	23.46
Bank credit ($ total credit)	45	83.49	11.95	54.34	98.50
Sovereign risk	36	6.69	5.06	1.00	13.86
Corporate taxes (%)	34	33.76	4.83	18.00	42.00
French legal origin	47	0.46	0.51	0.00	1.00
British legal origin	47	0.31	0.47	0.00	1.00

Notes: Inflows are calculated as net change in investment liabilities in a reporting economy. Total equity inflows are the sum of portfolio and foreign investment inflows. Volatility is calculated as the normalized standard deviation of the inflows. Normalization is performed by average gross flows. Institutional quality is represented by the composite political safety index calculated as the sum of all the rating components from *International Country Risk Guide* (PRS Group 2001), averaged from 1984 to 2000, divided by 10. The index takes values from 0 to 76 for each country, where a higher score means lower risk. Human capital is measured as the average years of total schooling over 25 years old in the total population, in 1970. Distantness is the weighted average of the distances in thousands of kilometers from the capital city of the particular country to the capital cities of the other countries, using the GDP shares of the other countries as weights, averaged from 1970 to 2000. Inflation volatility is the standard deviation of the annual CPI inflation over the 1970–2000 normalized by the average inflation for that period. Capital controls is an index calculated as the mean value of the four dummy variables—exchange arrangements, payments restrictions on current transactions, and capital transactions, repatriation requirements for export proceeds, averaged from 1971 to 2000; it takes a value between 1 and 2. GDP per capita is measured in per capita 1995 U.S. dollars. Bank credit is claims of deposit money banks on nonfinancial domestic sectors as share of claims of central bank and deposit money banks on nonfinancial domestic sectors, in percent, average from 1970 to 2000 (without outliers Bolivia and Hungary). Sovereign risk is an index based on Standard & Poor's long term foreign currency denominated sovereign debt ratings. Index ranges from 1, an obligor rated AAA, to 23, an obligor rated SD (selective default). Data are available for Argentina, Australia, Austria, Bolivia, Brazil, Canada, Chile, Colombia, Costa Rica, Denmark, Egypt, Finland, France, Germany, Great Britain, India, Israel, Italy, Jordan, Japan, Korea, Morocco, the Netherlands, Norway, New Zealand, Pakistan, Philippines, Portugal, Paraguay, South Africa, Spain, Sweden, Thailand, Tunisia, Turkey, and the United States. Corporate taxes represents the corporate income tax rate, single year value varying by country. Data are available for Argentina, Australia, Austria, Brazil, Canada, Chile, Colombia, Costa Rica, Czech Republic, Denmark, Egypt, Finland, France, Germany, Great Britain, Hungary, India, Israel, Italy, Japan, Korea, Morocco, the Netherlands, New Zealand, Norway, the Philippines, Poland, Portugal, South Africa, Spain, Sweden, Thailand, Tunisia, and the United States. French and British legal origin are dummy variables taking the value of 1 if a country's legal code can be traced to French civil law or British common law legal tradition.

distortions associated with government policies and also with the financial structure of the economy. These are inflation volatility, capital controls, sovereign risk, corporate tax, and bank credit, all averaged over the sample period. Inflation volatility captures macroeconomic instability. It is measured as the standard deviation divided by the mean of the inflation rate

Table 1.7   **Correlation matrix**

	Human capital	Distantness
Institutional quality	0.69	−0.41
Human capital		−0.19

	Inflation volatility	Capital controls	Bank credit	Sovereign risk ratings	Corporate tax
No. of observations	47	47	45	36	34
Institutional quality	−0.09	−0.64	0.61	−0.85	−0.20
Human capital	0.17	−0.51	0.37	−0.68	−0.18
Distantness	0.24	0.30	−0.43	0.53	0.16

Notes: Correlations are for the logarithm of the variables. Panel A reports the correlation matrix for the main regressions with the 47-country sample. Panel B reports the correlation between the main explanatory variables and the other independent variables. Sample sizes vary for these variables.

over the sample period. Normalization by mean is crucial given the differences in average inflation levels across time for the different countries. Our capital controls measure is the average of four dummy variables constructed using data collected by the IMF's *Annual Report on Exchange Arrangements and Exchange Restrictions* (AREAER). These dummy variables are exchange arrangements, payments restrictions on current transactions and on capital transactions, and repatriation requirements for export proceeds. Bank credit is the share of credit provided by deposit money banks, which include commercial banks and other financial institutions entitled to accept deposits from the public.[28]

It is clear that there is extensive cross-sectional variation on these variables. The institutional quality index varies from 3.4 to 7.3 with a mean of 5.5. Human capital varies from 1 to 10 years with a mean of 4.7 years. Table 1.7 presents the correlation matrix. Some of our independent variables are highly correlated, such as institutional quality and human capital, and sovereign risk and institutional quality. Hence, it is essential to employ a multiple-regression framework with many robustness tests.[29]

Table 1.8 shows the results. Institutional quality, human capital, and

28. In AKV we used a wider range of additional right-hand-side variables, such as GDP per capita, inflation, government consumption, government budget, trade openness (share of exports plus imports in GDP), restrictions on foreign investment, incentives on foreign investment, government infrastructure (percent of paved roads), stock market capitalization, reuters (number of times the country's name is mentioned in Reuters), foreign banks (share of foreign banks in total), and accounting (an index of accounting standards of corporate firms). In that work, out of all these variables only sovereign risk, corporate tax, and bank credit were significant depending on the specification. Hence, we check their role here again.

29. We refer the reader to AKV for a sensitivity analysis with a wider range of variables.

Table 1.8 OLS regression of capital inflows per capita

Dependent variable	Inflows of total equity and debt per capita (1)	Inflows of total equity per capita (2)	(3)	(4)	(5)	(6)	(7)
Countries	47	47	47	47	45	36	34
Institutional quality	16.18***	5.56***	5.29***	4.83***	5.83***	4.10**	6.30***
	(5.04)	(4.74)	(4.57)	(4.57)	(4.48)	(2.22)	(3.95)
Human capital	1.11*	0.57**	0.57**	0.42*	0.46*	0.70*	0.66**
	(1.79)	(2.00)	(2.40)	(1.85)	(1.81)	(1.88)	(2.00)
Distantness	−5.25**	−1.16**	−1.04*	−1.11**	−1.27**	−1.56	−1.37**
	(−2.87)	(−2.07)	(−1.92)	(−2.03)	(−2.03)	(−1.54)	(−2.06)
Inflation volatility			−0.36				
			(−1.29)				
Capital controls				−1.58			
				(−1.23)			
Bank credit					−0.36		
					(−0.36)		
Sovereign risk						−0.25	
						(−0.46)	
Corporate taxes							−0.75
							(−0.49)
R^2	0.60	0.63	0.64	0.64	0.63	0.66	0.62

Notes: All regressions include a constant and are estimated by OLS with White's correction of heteroskedasticity. *t*-statistics are in parentheses. All right-hand-side variables are in logs. Inflows of total equity include inflows of foreign and portfolio equity investment. Descriptive statistics for inflows of total equity and debt are as follows: mean 488.38, standard deviation 623.21, minimum 1.43, maximum 2552.43. The 45-country sample excludes outliers Bolivia and Hungary in terms of Bank Credit. The 36-country sample includes Argentina, Australia, Austria, Bolivia, Brazil, Canada, Chile, Colombia, Costa Rica, Denmark, Egypt, Finland, France, Germany, Great Britain, India, Israel, Italy, Jordan, Japan, Korea, Morocco, the Netherlands, Norway, New Zealand, Pakistan, the Philippines, Portugal, Paraguay, Spain, Sweden, Thailand, Tunisia, Turkey, the United States, and South Africa. The rest of the countries do not have data on sovereign risk. The 34-country sample includes Argentina, Australia, Austria, Brazil, Canada, Chile, Colombia, Costa Rica, Czech Republic, Denmark, Egypt, Finland, France, Germany, Great Britain, Hungary, India, Israel, Italy, Japan, Korea, Morocco, the Netherlands, Norway, New Zealand, the Philippines, Poland, Portugal, Spain, Sweden, Thailand, Tunisia, the United States, and South Africa. The rest of the countries do not have data on corporate taxes.

***Significant at the 1 percent level.

**Significant at the 5 percent level.

*Significant at the 10 percent level.

distantness are all important determinants of capital inflows.[30] This result holds regardless of including debt inflows on the left-hand side, as shown in columns (1) and (2). Other potential determinants turn out to be insignificant.[31] Sovereign risk is borderline significant when distantness is left out. Obviously, both are capturing information/market frictions. Figure 1.7 shows the partial correlation plot for the institutional quality variable for the regression shown in column (2) of table 1.8. The slope of the fitted line is 5.56, as shown in that column.[32] The strong positive relation between institutional quality and the inflows of capital per capita is evidently not due to the outliers.

What about endogeneity? It is possible that capital inflows affect the institutional quality of a country. More inflows can generate incentives to reform and create an investor-friendly environment by improving property rights. Moreover, because most institutional quality measures are constructed ex post, analysts might have a natural bias toward "assigning" better institutions to countries with higher capital inflows. One way to solve this problem is to find variables not subject to reverse causality that can account for the institutional variation.[33] AKV instrument institutional quality with its historical determinants mainly with settler mortality rates from Acemoglu, Johnson, and Robinson (2001, 2002; hereafter AJR) and show that the effect of institutional quality on capital inflows is causal.[34] AJR argue that the historical mortality rates of European settlers in colonized countries are a good instrument for current institutions of former colonies since if the European settlement there was discouraged by diseases then the Europeans set up worse institutions.

In this paper we investigate whether there is any direct effect of some other historical determinants of institutions, such as legal origins and legal system. La Porta et al. (1998) emphasize the importance of historical legal origins in shaping current financial institutions. They examine the effect of legal origin on the laws governing investor protection, the enforcement of these laws, and the extent of concentration of firm ownership across coun-

30. In AKV, we also explored the role of each of the components of the composite index that is used as a proxy for institutional quality. We find institutional quality indicators that are closer proxies of property rights protection, such as the no-corruption index and protection from expropriation, to be important determinants of capital inflows.

31. We also investigate the effect of the exchange rate regime. The results remain the same.

32. We first regressed inflows of capital per capita on human capital and distantness. We took the residuals and regressed them on the residuals from a regression of institutional quality on human capital and distantness. The Frisch-Waugh theorem says the coefficient from this regression is exactly the same as the one in the multiple regression. The figure plots these two sets of residuals against each other.

33. Another source of endogeneity can come from the possibility that both inflows and institutional quality might be determined by an omitted third factor. We believe the extensive robustness analysis that is undertaken in AKV shows that this is not the case.

34. AKV also use other instruments, such as historical indicators of regime type and political constraints to the executive power from the polity data set and the fraction of the population speaking English.

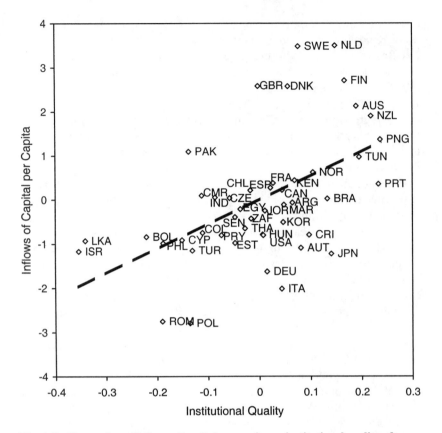

Fig. 1.7 Regression of inflows of capital per capita on institutional quality after controlling for other regressors

Notes: We first regressed the inflows of capital per capita on the regressors other than institutional quality and took the residuals, which we then regressed on the residuals from a regression of institutional quality on the other regressors (including a constant in both regressions). The coefficient on institutional quality is then exactly the same as the coefficient in the multiple regression. We plot the first set of residuals against the second set in the figure. Inflows of capital per capita include direct and portfolio investment.

tries. Most countries' legal rules, either through colonialism, conquest, or outright borrowing, can be traced to one of four distinct European legal systems: English common law, French civil law, German civil law, and Scandinavian civil law. These legal-origin variables have been adopted as exogenous determinants of institutional quality, in particular for financial institutions, in the economic growth literature. On the other hand, AJR claim that legal origin is a weak instrument for institutional quality, in particular for institutions that protect property rights. They claim it is hard to

Table 1.9   OLS regression of capital inflows per capita: Historical legal origins

	OLS (1)	OLS (2)	OLS (3)	OLS (4)	IV (5)	OLS (6)
Countries	47	47	47	47	21	21
Institutional quality	5.04***	5.39***			6.91***	4.77***
	(5.01)	(5.69)			(2.90)	(5.84)
Human capital	0.39*	0.45**	1.26***	1.39***	0.01	0.47*
	(1.90)	(2.32)	(5.96)	(5.99)	(1.40)	(1.70)
Distantness	−0.97*	−1.44***	−1.90***	−2.31***	−0.12	−0.28
	(−1.81)	(−2.77)	(−2.64)	(−3.34)	(−0.20)	(−0.34)
French legal origin	−0.56**		−0.57**			
	(−2.01)		(−1.99)			
British legal origin		0.84**		0.63*	0.94*	0.79***
		(2.51)		(1.64)	(2.27)	(2.50)
R^2	0.64	0.66	0.51	0.51	0.80	0.84

Notes: Dependent variable: inflows of total equity per capita. All regressions include a constant and are estimated by OLS with White's correction of heteroskedasticity. *t*-statistics are in parentheses. Inflows of total equity include inflows of foreign and portfolio equity investment. All right-hand-side variables are in logs except the legal origin variables.

***Significant at the 1 percent level.

**Significant at the 5 percent level.

*Significant at the 10 percent level.

make a case that legal origins do not have any direct effect on the relevant outcome variables such as income levels.[35] Thus we investigate whether legal origins have a direct effect on capital inflows in addition to their partial effect on institutional quality by adding legal origin as an additional right-hand-side variable.

Table 1.9 shows the results. As shown in columns (1)–(4), French legal origin has a negative significant effect and British legal origin has a positive significant effect. It seems these effects are first order in addition to institutions. If institutional quality is left out from the regressions, the British legal origin variable is significant only at the 10 percent level. We do not tabulate the details, but we found in our data that British legal origin is negatively correlated with institutions, and this leads to a downward bias in British legal origin when institutional quality is omitted. Column (5) displays an instrumental variables (IV) regression that instruments institu-

35. AJR stress that successful instruments have to be *theoretically* excludable from the empirical model used by the econometrician and that undertaking overidentification tests is not enough. In addition, overidentification tests have low power in general. AJR show that in their first-stage regression French legal origin is associated with worse institutions. But in their second-stage regression, where French legal origin is included as one of the explanatory variables and institutions are instrumented with settler mortality rates, French legal origin has a positive effect on income. The net effect of this variable on income (directly and indirectly via institutional quality) is positive.

tions with log settler mortality rates from AJR, which is only available for twenty-one ex-colonies in our sample.[36] If there is a direct effect of legal origin on capital inflows we expect it to be significant in this regression. We find this to be the case.[37] Column (5) also reestablishes the causal effect of institutions, which is already shown by AKV. Column (6) reports the corresponding ordinary least squares (OLS) regression for comparison. We only show the IV regression in column (5) with British legal origin since our sample is composed of *only* British and French legal origin countries. Thus, the corresponding IV regression with French legal origin is exactly the same as in column (5) with a reverse sign on the French legal origin variable.[38] We also investigated the direct effect of the variables proposed by La Porta et al. (1997, 1998) to capture investor protection, such as shareholder rights, and found similar results. The partial correlation plots given in figures 1.8 and 1.9 show that the significant effects of French and British legal origins are not due to the outliers but rather are driven by the countries one would expect, such as Turkey for French origin and Australia for British origin.

1.4.2   Determinants of Changes in Capital Flows

Our results thus far suggest that institutional quality has a first-order effect over policies in explaining the pattern of capital flows in the period 1970–2000. Is there any role left for policies? Can a country that improves its institutions or macroeconomic policies expect to receive more inflows? To investigate these questions we run change regressions. We calculate the change in inflows per capita as the difference between average capital inflows per capita over 1970–93 and average capital inflows per capita over 1994–2000. We did the same for the independent variables, and we regress changes on changes. The reason for this division of the sample is the fact that visible improvements, if any, in institutional variables occur in the late 1990s, as shown in figure 1.10.[39]

The results are given in table 1.10. We only consider the twenty-three developing countries out of our forty-seven-country sample, since for the OECD the institutional changes are basically zero and this distorts the picture. The results suggest that a country that improves institutions, decreases capital controls, and increases its growth is going to receive more capital in-

36. The corresponding first-stage regression reports a coefficient of –0.21 on settler mortality rates with a t-statistic of –4.09.

37. Note that this regression is an interpretable version of an overidentification test.

38. Institutional quality is estimated to have a higher coefficient in the IV regression since two-stage least squares (2SLS) regression corrects for the measurement error that causes attenuation bias in the OLS regression.

39. At first, we cut the sample in the middle and calculated the change from 1970–85 to 1986–2000. However, given the time-invariant nature of our variables, this way of dividing the sample does not provide us with much variation.

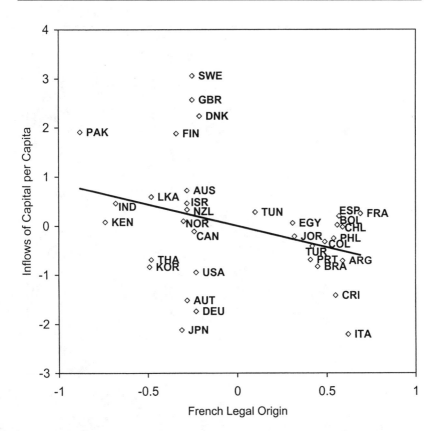

Fig. 1.8   Regression of inflows of capital per capita on French legal origin controlling for other regressors

Notes: We first regressed the inflows of capital per capita on the regressors other than French legal origin and took the residuals, which we then regressed on the residuals from a regression of French legal origin on the other regressors (including a constant in both regressions). The coefficient on the French legal origin is then exactly the same as the coefficient in the multiple regression. We plot the first set of residuals against the second set in the figure. Inflows of capital per capita include direct and portfolio investment.

flows.[40] The change in institutions is not always very significant, though. This is not surprising given the small sample size and low time variation in this variable. Of course, we have to interpret the results with caution since most of these right-hand-side variables are endogenous, such as the change in GDP per capita. An interesting result is the positive significant distant-

40. Note, however, that the IMF measure for capital controls does not control for the fact that legal restrictions are sometimes circumvented. See Edwards (2001) for criticisms to the use of this index.

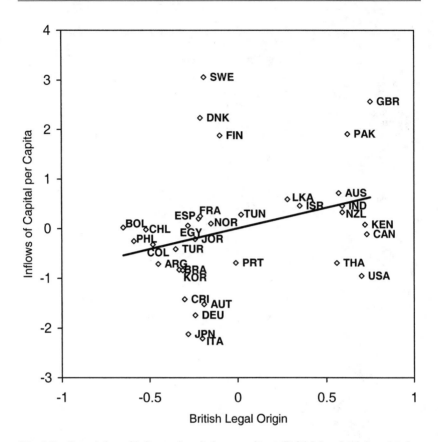

Fig. 1.9   Regression of inflows of capital per capita on British legal origin controlling for other regressors

Notes: We first regressed the inflows of capital per capita on the regressors other than British legal origin and took the residuals, which we then regressed on the residuals from a regression of British legal origin on the other regressors (including a constant in both regressions). The coefficient on the British legal origin is then exactly the same as the coefficient in the multiple regression. We plot the first set of residuals against the second set in the figure. Inflows of capital per capita include direct and portfolio investment.

ness. This variable enters in levels since differencing this variable is going to capture only the change in GDP weights. The result suggests that information frictions have become less important for capital inflows in the 1990s since even the "remote and distant countries" receive higher capital inflows in the 1990s, which is exactly what we expect to find. Overall, these results suggest that there is a role for improved policy and institutions.

1.4.3   Determinants of Capital Flow Volatility

A natural intermediate step toward understanding the link between capital flows and financial crises is to look at the determinants of volatility of

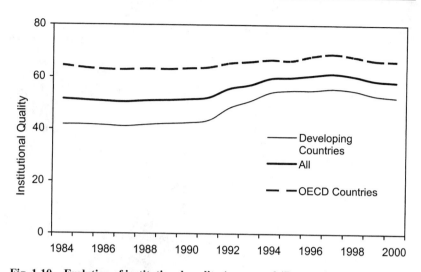

Fig. 1.10   Evolution of institutional quality (average of 47 countries)

Notes: Institutional quality index is a composite political safety index, which is the sum of all the rating components from *International Country Risk Guide* (PRS Group 2001). The components are as follows: Government stability is defined as the government's ability to carry out its declared programs and its ability to stay in office. It ranges from 0 to 12. Internal conflict is defined as the political violence in the country and its actual or potential impact on governance. It ranges from 0 to 12. External conflict is the risk to the incumbent government from foreign action, ranging from nonviolent external pressure to violent external pressure. It ranges from 0 to 12. Noncorruption is an index of the degree of the noncorruption within the political system. It ranges from 0 to 6. Militarized politics is the degree of protection from the military involvement in politics. It ranges from 0 to 6. A religious tension is the degree of the protection from religious tensions in the society. It ranges from 0 to 6. The law component of the law and order index is an assessment of the strength and impartiality of the legal system; the order component is the assessment of the popular observance of the law. It ranges from 0 to 6. Ethnic tensions are the degree of protection from the tensions attributable to racial, nationality, or language divisions in the society. It ranges from 0 to 12. Democratic accountability ranges from 0 to 6, where a higher score represents stable democracies and lower scores represents autocracies. Bureaucratic quality ranges from 0 to 4 and represents institutional strength and quality of the bureaucracy.

capital flows. There have not been many empirical papers that look at the determinants of capital flow volatility. As a preliminary investigation of the patterns in the data, we run cross-country regressions for the period 1970–2000. We measure volatility as the standard deviation of inflows of total equity per capita divided by the mean gross flows over the sample period.

Table 1.11 shows our results. We do find a significant effect of institutional quality on the volatility of the inflows of total equity. However, this effect is sensitive to inclusion of some other independent variables such as sovereign risk and capital controls. We also find the coefficient of inflation volatility to be positive and significant. It appears that countries with lower levels of inflation volatility tend to experience lower levels of uncertainty in terms of the inflows of external capital. Bank credit is positive and signifi-

Table 1.10   OLS regression of changes in capital inflows: Developing countries

	(1)	(2)	(3)	(4)
Countries	23	23	23	23
Δ Institutional quality	1.58*	2.27*	1.45	1.25
	(1.70)	(1.61)	(1.33)	(1.52)
Distantness	0.21***	0.21***	0.20***	0.21***
	(3.34)	(3.40)	(3.80)	(3.60)
Δ Capital controls	−0.19***	−0.21***	−0.22***	−0.20***
	(−4.73)	(−4.20)	(−4.41)	(−4.90)
Δ GDP per capita	0.81***	0.91***	0.84***	0.75***
	(3.68)	(3.14)	(4.18)	(3.19)
Δ Inflation volatility		0.17		
		(0.65)		
Δ Human capital			0.22	
			(1.27)	
Δ Bank credit				0.87
				(1.49)
R^2	0.71	0.75	0.75	0.79

Notes: Dependent variable: change in inflows of total equity per capita between the periods of 1994–2000 and 1970–93. All regressions include a constant and are estimated by OLS with White's correction of heteroskedasticity. t-statistics are in parentheses. Inflows of total equity include inflows of foreign and portfolio equity investment. The sample of 23 developing countries includes Argentina, Brazil, Chile, Cameroon, Colombia, Costa Rica, Egypt, Hungary, India, Jordan, Kenya, Sri Lanka, Morocco, Pakistan, Paraguay, the Philippines, Poland, Romania, Senegal, Thailand, Tunisia, Turkey, and South Africa (Bolivia, Cyprus, Israel, and South Korea are outliers and dropped). Δ represents the difference between the average value of the corresponding variable between the periods of 1994–2000 and 1970–93.
***Significant at the 1 percent level.
**Significant at the 5 percent level.
*Significant at the 10 percent level.

cant. This can be due to several reasons. First, as noted in the introduction to the chapter, the literature has related high volatility of capital flows and currency crisis to bank fragility. Financial liberalization, when not followed by proper regulation and supervision, can lead to both greater capital flows intermediated through banks and greater bank credit and later to abrupt reversals in capital flows.[41] Moreover, the positive correlation between bank credit and capital flow volatility might be due to cronyism in the banking sector.[42] We also control for stock market capitalization and trade openness, both of which come in as insignificant.[43]

41. Henry and Lorentzen (2003) argue that liberalization of debt flows exposes countries to the risk of crises stemming from sudden changes in investors' sentiments. Equity market liberalizations, on the other hand, have promoted growth in almost every liberalizing country.
42. This finding is consistent with Wei (2000) and Wei and Wu (2002). The authors show that corruption within a country increases the loan-FDI ratio.
43. Other measures of credit market and capital market development in general, such as liquid liabilities and total value traded, are also insignificant.

Table 1.11   **OLS regression of volatility of capital inflows**

	(1)	(2)	(3)	(4)	(5)	(6)	(7)	(8)
Countries	47	47	47	47	36	34	47	47
Institutional quality	-0.42**	-0.50*	-0.47**	-0.33	0.04	-0.47	-0.50*	-0.44**
	(-2.29)	(-1.76)	(-2.55)	(-1.55)	(0.14)	(-1.53)	(-1.76)	(-2.25)
Inflation volatility	0.24**	0.23**	0.25**	0.26**	0.19	0.26**	0.23**	0.24**
	(2.41)	(2.19)	(2.45)	(2.48)	(1.57)	(2.09)	(2.19)	(2.35)
Bank credit	0.37**	0.38**	0.36**	0.43**	0.42	0.62***	0.38**	0.38**
	(2.22)	(2.29)	(2.23)	(2.08)	(1.27)	(2.64)	(2.29)	(2.19)
Human capital		0.03						
		(0.44)						
Distantness			-0.10					
			(-0.87)					
Capital controls				0.21				
				(0.80)				
Sovereign risk					0.10			
					(1.53)			
Corporate taxes						-0.35		
						(-1.31)		
French legal origin							-0.07	
							(-0.91)	
British legal origin								-0.04
								(-0.48)
R^2	0.20	0.21	0.21	0.21	0.14	0.26	0.22	0.21

Notes: Dependent variable: volatility of inflows of total equity per capita. Volatility is calculated as normalized standard deviation of inflows. Normalization is performed by average gross flows. All regressions include a constant and are estimated by OLS with White's correction of heteroskedasticity. t-statistics are in parentheses. Inflows of total equity include inflows of foreign and portfolio equity investment. All right-hand-side variables are in logs except the legal origin variables. The 36-country sample includes Argentina, Australia, Austria, Bolivia, Brazil, Canada, Chile, Colombia, Costa Rica, Denmark, Egypt, Finland, France, Germany, Great Britain, India, Israel, Italy, Jordan, Japan, Korea, Morocco, the Netherlands, Norway, New Zealand, Pakistan, the Philippines, Portugal, Paraguay, South Africa, Spain, Sweden, Thailand, Tunisia, Turkey, and the United States. The 34-country sample includes Argentina, Australia, Austria, Brazil, Canada, Chile, Colombia, Costa Rica, Czech Republic, Denmark, Egypt, Finland, France, Germany, Great Britain, India, Israel, Italy, Japan, Hungary, Korea, Morocco, the Netherlands, New Zealand, Norway, the Philippines, Poland, Portugal, South Africa, Spain, Sweden, Thailand, Tunisia, and the United States.
***Significant at the 1 percent level.
**Significant at the 5 percent level.
*Significant at the 10 percent level.

Figures 1.11–1.13 show the partial correlation plots for institutions, inflation volatility, and bank credit with slopes –0.42, 0.24, and 0.37, respectively, as shown in column (1) of table 1.11. Clearly, these significant relations are not due to outliers and driven by volatile countries of Latin America and Asia. The last two columns investigate the role of legal origins, which turn out to be insignificant. This phenomenon might be due to the fact that they work their effect via institutions.

Table 1.12 looks at the issue of measuring volatility. Our results might be

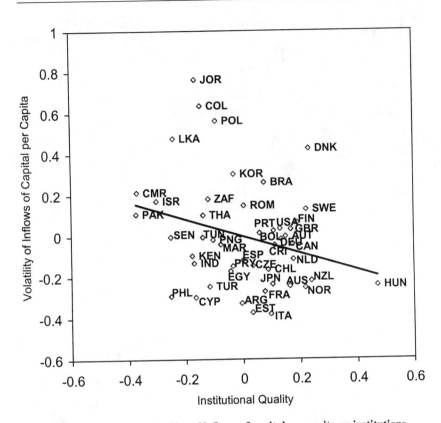

Fig. 1.11   Regression of volatility of inflows of capital per capita on institutions controlling for other regressors

Notes: We first regressed the volatility of inflows of capital per capita on the regressors other than institutional quality and took the residuals, which we then regressed on the residuals from a regression of institutional quality on the other regressors (including a constant in both regressions). The coefficient on the institutional quality is then exactly the same as the coefficient in the multiple regression. We plot the first set of residuals against the second set. Inflows of capital per capita include direct and portfolio investment.

due to the fact that some countries have liberalized their financial accounts over the last thirty years and received huge inflows. As a result, the measured volatility could increase because the volume and upward trend in capital inflows may not be captured by our benchmark normalization. We experiment with different ways to deal with these problems: we use standard deviation of inflows, standard deviation of detrended inflows, and normalized versions of these measures. In columns (1) and (3) volatility is measured as the standard deviation of inflows. In columns (2) and (4), it is normalized standard deviation of inflows. Normalization is performed by the average gross flows. In columns (5) and (7), it is the standard deviation of detrended inflows. Detrending is performed by regressing inflows on a constant and a linear trend and using residuals from that regression as a

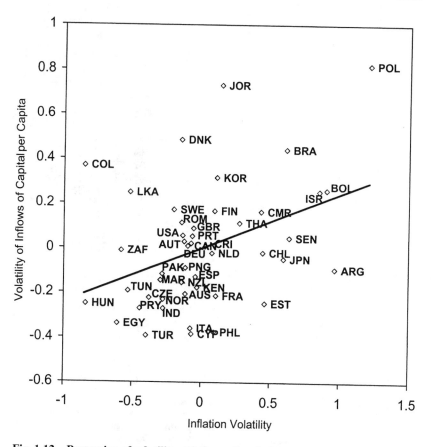

Fig. 1.12   Regression of volatility of inflows of capital per capita on inflation volatility controlling for other regressors

Notes: We first regressed the volatility of inflows of capital per capita on the regressors other than inflation volatility and took the residuals, which we then regressed on the residuals from a regression of inflation volatility on the other regressors (including a constant in both regressions). The coefficient on inflation volatility is then exactly the same as the coefficient in the multiple regression. We plot the first set of residuals against the second set in the figure. Inflows of capital per capita include direct and portfolio investment.

proxy for inflows. In columns (6) and (8) it is normalized standard deviation of detrended inflows. Normalization is performed by the average gross flows.[44] It is clear that detrending does not matter and what matters is normalization. Columns (3), (4), (7), and (8) control for the level of inflows on the right-hand side. The main conclusion is that normalization does a good job of controlling the volume and trend effects of the level of inflows. Figure 1.14 plots the partial correlation plot out of column (6), with slope −0.44. Although this is a tighter fit, there are no important differences rel-

44. We also investigated the effect of a quadratic trend. The results were similar.

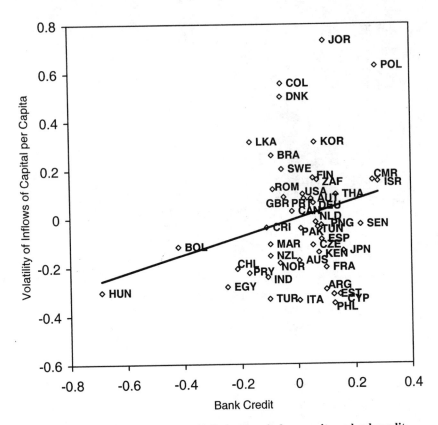

Fig. 1.13   Regression of volatility of inflows of capital per capita on bank credit controlling for other regressors

Notes: We first regressed the volatility of inflows of capital per capita on the regressors other than bank credit and took the residuals, which we then regressed on the residuals from a regression of bank credit on the other regressors (including a constant in both regressions). The coefficient on the bank credit is then exactly the same as the coefficient in the multiple regression. We plot the first set of residuals against the second set in the figure. Inflows of capital per capita include direct and portfolio investment.

ative to figure 1.11. Figure 1.15 plots the partial correlation from column (1), with slope 11.56. Scandinavian countries evidently have high volatility due to volume, and our normalization takes care of this.

Overall, the results suggest that institutional quality and macroeconomic policy play an important role for capital flow volatility. We should note, however, that we are establishing correlations more than causality. For example, inflation volatility is probably endogenous to the volatility of capital inflows and to institutional quality. Higher volatility can also cause an increase in bank credit or capital controls. Finding good instruments for the policy variables is a rather difficult task and not the focus of this study.

Table 1.12   OLS regression of volatility of capital inflows: Measurement issues

Volatility	St. Dev. (1)	St. Dev./Mean (2)	St. Dev. (3)	St. Dev./Mean (4)	St. Dev. (dt1) (5)	St. Dev. (dt1)/Mean (6)	St. Dev. (dt1) (7)	St. Dev. (dt1)/Mean (8)
Countries	47	47	47	47	47	47	47	47
Institutional	11.56***	−0.42**	−3.37***	−0.63***	8.54***	−0.44**	−2.81***	−0.69***
quality	(4.26)	(−2.29)	(−2.77)	(−2.99)	(4.01)	(−2.54)	(−2.68)	(−3.74)
Inflation	−0.22	0.24**	0.46*	0.25**	−0.21	0.13**	0.30	−0.15**
volatility	(−0.33)	(2.41)	(1.77)	(2.51)	(−0.43)	(2.03)	(1.45)	(−2.20)
Bank credit	0.61	0.37**	1.26	0.38**	0.30	0.29**	0.79	0.30**
	(0.30)	(2.22)	(1.45)	(2.30)	(0.21)	(2.15)	(1.32)	(2.18)
Inflows of			19.77***	0.28			15.04***	0.33*
total equity			(11.26)	(1.15)			(9.42)	(1.72)
R^2	0.44	0.20	0.89	0.22	0.40	0.16	0.85	0.19

Notes: Dependent variable: various estimates for volatility of inflows of total equity per capita. Volatility is calculated as follows: for columns (1) and (3), standard deviation of inflows; (2) and (4), normalized standard deviation of inflows; (5) and (7), standard deviation of detrended inflows divided by 100; (6) and (8), normalized standard deviation of detrended inflows divided by 100. All regressions include a constant and are estimated by OLS with White's correction of heteroskedasticity. t-statistics are in parentheses. Inflows of total equity include inflows of foreign and portfolio equity investment. All variables are in logs except for inflows of total equity per capita.
***Significant at the 1 percent level.
**Significant at the 5 percent level.
*Significant at the 10 percent level.

1.5   Conclusions

Over the last thirty years, international capital flows have experienced tremendous growth. The surge in capital flows and, in particular, the crises of the last decade have revived the debate over the merits of international capital mobility. Our objective in this paper has been to overview the main stylized facts behind capital flow mobility over the last thirty years and establish the empirical determinants of capital flows and capital flow volatility. We find institutional quality to be an important determinant of capital inflows. Historical legal origins have a direct effect on capital inflows during the period 1970–2000. Policy plays a significant role in explaining changes in the level of inflows and their volatility.

Appendix A

Data

Foreign direct investment: Direct Investment abroad (IFS line 78bdd) and Direct Investment in Reporting Economy (line 78bed) include equity capital, reinvested earnings, other capital, and financial derivatives associated

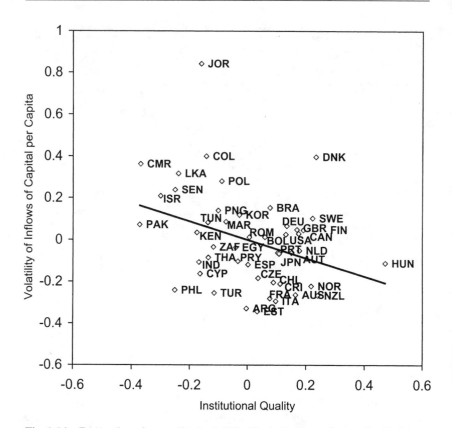

Fig. 1.14   Regression of normalized volatility (deviation from the trend) of inflows of capital per capita on institutions controlling for other regressors

Notes: We first regressed the volatility of net inflows of capital per capita on the regressors other than institutional quality and took the residuals, which we then regressed on the residuals from a regression of institutional quality on the other regressors (including a constant in both regressions). The coefficient on the institutional quality is then exactly the same as the coefficient in the multiple regression. We plot the first set of residuals against the second set in the figure. Inflows of capital per capita include direct and portfolio investment.

with various intercompany transactions between affiliated enterprises. Excluded are inflows of direct investment capital into the reporting economy for exceptional financing such as debt-for-equity swaps. We include only countries with data for both direct investment abroad and direct investment in the reporting economy.

Portfolio equity investment: Equity Securities Assets (IFS line 78bkd) and Equity Securities Liabilities (line 78bmd) include shares, stock participations, and similar documents (such as American depository receipts) that usually denote ownership of equity. These are divided into monetary authorities, general government, banks, and other sectors. We calculate

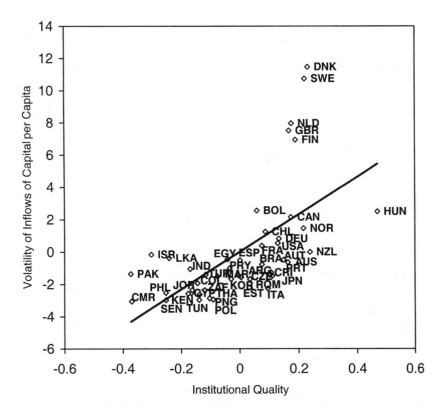

Fig. 1.15   Regression of volatility (not normalized) of inflows of capital per capita on institutions controlling for other regressors

Notes: We first regressed the volatility of net inflows of capital per capita on the regressors other than institutional quality and took the residuals, which we then regressed on the residuals from a regression of institutional quality on the other regressors (including a constant in both regressions). The coefficient on the institutional quality is then exactly the same as the coefficient in the multiple regression. We plot the first set of residuals against the second set in the figure. Inflows of capital per capita include direct and portfolio investment.

net portfolio equity flows only for countries with data for both equity securities assets and debt security liabilities.

Debt flows: Debt Securities Assets (IFS line 78bld) and Debt Securities Liabilities (line 78bnd) cover (a) bonds, debentures, notes, and so on (divided into monetary authorities, general government, banks, and other sectors) and (b) money market or negotiable debt instruments (divided into monetary authorities, general government, banks, and other sectors). Other investment assets (line 78bhd) and other investment liabilities (line 78bid) include all financial transactions not covered in direct investment, portfolio investment, financial derivatives, or other assets. Major categories are trade credits, loans (divided into monetary authorities, general government, and banks), transactions in currency and deposits (monetary authorities, general government, and banks), and other assets (monetary authorities, general government, and banks). We first calculate total debt assets as the sum of debt securities assets and other investment assets; total debt liabilities correspond to the sum of debt securities liabilities and other investment liabilities. We calculate net total debt flows only for countries that had information for both total debt liabilities and total debt assets.

Total equity flows: Sum of foreign direct investment and portfolio equity flows.

Volatility of inflows: Standard deviation of the corresponding inflows per capita divided by the average of the absolute value of the inflows and outflows of capital per capita.

Independent Variables

Bank credit, 1970–2000: Average value of claims of deposit money banks on nonfinancial domestic sectors as share of claims of central bank and deposit money banks on nonfinancial domestic sectors, in percent.

Capital controls, 1971–97: The mean value of four dummy variables: (a) exchange arrangements, separate exchange rates for some or all capital transactions and/or some or all invisibles; (b) payment restrictions, restrictions on payments for current transactions; (c) payment restrictions, restrictions on payments for capital transactions; and (d) surrender or repatriation requirements for export proceeds. From International Monetary Fund *Annual Report on Exchange Arrangements and Exchange Restrictions* (various issues).

Corporate taxes: Corporate tax rates from PricewaterhouseCoopers (PwC) for 1990–97, from Wei (2000).

Distance: Thousands of kilometers, from Arcview 3.x software.

GDP per capita, 1971–2000: Shown in 1995 U.S. dollars; from World Bank *World Development Indicators* (2002).

Human capital, 1970, 1975, 1980, 1985, 1990, 1995: Average years of secondary, higher, and total schooling in the total population over twenty-five years old. From World Bank (2002).

Legal origin: Origin of a country's formal legal code: English common law, French civil law, German civil law, and Scandinavian civil law. From La Porta et al. (1997, 1998).

Inflation rate: Annual CPI inflation (World Bank 2002).

Inflation volatility: Standard deviation of inflation rate over the sample period divided by the corresponding mean.

Institutional quality: Composite political safety, 1984–98: Sum of all the rating components from *International Country Risk Guide* except for socioeconomic conditions and investment profile. Average yearly rating from 0 to 76, with a higher score meaning lower risk. Data from the Political Risk Services (PRS) Group (2001).

Government stability, 1984–98: The government's ability to carry out its declared program(s), and its ability to stay in office. Average yearly rating from 0 to 12, with a higher score meaning lower risk. Data from PRS Group (2001).

Internal conflict, 1984–98: Political violence in the country and its actual or potential impact on governance. Average yearly rating from 0 to 12, with a higher score meaning lower risk. Data from PRS Group (2001).

External conflict, 1984–98: Assessment both of the risk to the incumbent government from foreign action, ranging from nonviolent external pressure (diplomatic pressures, withholding of aid, trade restrictions, territorial disputes, sanctions, etc.) to violent external pressure (cross-border conflicts to all-out war). Average yearly rating from 0 to 12, with a higher score meaning lower risk. Data from PRS Group (2001).

Noncorruption index, 1984–98: Assessment of corruption within the political system. Average yearly rating from 0 to 6, where a higher score means lower risk. Data from PRS Group (2001).

Nonmilitarized politics, 1984–98: Protection from the military involvement in politics. Average yearly rating from 0 to 6, with a higher score meaning lower risk. Data from PRS Group (2001).

Protection from religious tensions, 1984–98: Protection from the religious tensions in society. Average yearly rating from 0 to 6, with a higher score meaning lower risk. Data from PRS Group (2001).

Law and order, 1984–98: The law subcomponent is an assessment of the strength and impartiality of the legal system; the order subcomponent is an assessment of popular observance of the law. Average yearly rating from 0 to 6, with a higher score meaning lower risk. Data from PRS Group (2001).

Protection from ethnic tensions, 1984–98: Assessment of the degree of tension within a country attributable to racial, nationality, or language divisions. Average yearly rating from 0 to 12, with a higher score meaning lower risk. Data from PRS Group (2001).

Democratic accountability, 1984–98: Average yearly rating from 0 to 6, with a higher score meaning lower risk. In general, the highest number of risk points is assigned to alternating democracies, while the lowest number of risk points is assigned to autarchies. Data from PRS Group (2001).

Quality of bureaucracy, 1984–98: Institutional strength and quality of the bureaucracy is another shock absorber that tends to minimize revisions of policy when governments change. Average yearly rating from 0 to 4, with a higher score meaning lower risk. Data from PRS Group (2001).

Protection from government repudiation of contracts, 1982–95: Average yearly rating from 0 to 10, with a higher score meaning lower risk. Data from IRIS time series of PRS Group (2001).

Protection from expropriation, 1984–98: Average yearly rating from 0 to

10, with a higher score meaning lower risk. Data from IRIS time series of PRS Group (2001).

Sovereign risk: Index based on Standard & Poor's long-term foreign currency denominated sovereign debt ratings, average from 1971 to 1997. Index ranges from 1 (an obligor rated AAA) to 23 (an obligor rated SD [selective default]).

Appendix B

Table 1B.1   Sample countries: Total equity data

All countries	1970–1980	1981–1990	1991–2000
Algeria	Algeria	Algeria	Algeria
Argentina	Argentina	Argentina	Argentina
Australia	Australia	Australia	Australia
Austria	Austria	Austria	Austria
Bahrain	Bahrain	Bahrain	Bahrain
Bene-Lux	Bene-Lux	Bene-Lux	Bene-Lux
Bolivia	Bolivia	Bolivia	Bolivia
Botswana	Botswana	Botswana	Botswana
Brazil	Brazil	Brazil	Brazil
Burkina Faso	Burkina Faso		Burkina Faso
Burundi (starts 1989)			*Burundi*
Cameroon	Cameroon	Cameroon	Cameroon
Canada	Canada	Canada	Canada
Central African Republic	Central African Republic	Central African Republic	Central African Republic
Chad	Chad	Chad	Chad
Chile	Chile	Chile	Chile
China (starts 1982)		*China*	*China*
Colombia		Colombia	Colombia
Costa Rica	Costa Rica	Costa Rica	Costa Rica
Cyprus (starts 1985)		*Cyprus*	*Cyprus*
Czech Republic (starts 1993)			*Czech Republic*
Denmark	Denmark	Denmark	Denmark
Egypt, Arab Republic	Egypt, Arab Republic	Egypt, Arab Republic	Egypt, Arab Republic
Estonia (starts 1993)			*Estonia*
Fiji	Fiji	Fiji	Fiji
Finland	Finland	Finland	Finland
France	France	France	France
Gabon	Gabon	Gabon	Gabon
Germany	Germany	Germany	Germany
Hungary (starts 1992)			*Hungary*
India (starts 1993)			*India*
Israel	Israel	Israel	Israel
Italy	Italy	Italy	Italy
Japan	Japan	Japan	Japan
Jordan	Jordan	Jordan	Jordan

Table 1B.1 (continued)

All countries	1970–1980	1981–1990	1991–2000
Kenya	**Kenya**	**Kenya**	**Kenya**
Korea, Republic	**Korea, Republic**	**Korea, Republic**	**Korea, Republic**
Kuwait (starts 1993)			*Kuwait*
Latvia (starts 1992)			*Latvia*
Libya	**Libya**	**Libya**	**Libya**
Mauritania (not available for 1990s)	*Mauritania*	*Mauritania*	
Mauritius	**Mauritius**	**Mauritius**	**Mauritius**
Morocco (starts 1991)			*Morocco*
Namibia (starts 1989)			*Namibia*
Netherlands, The	**Netherlands, The**	**Netherlands, The**	**Netherlands, The**
New Zealand	**New Zealand**	**New Zealand**	**New Zealand**
Niger	**Niger**	**Niger**	**Niger**
Norway	**Norway**	**Norway**	**Norway**
Pakistan (starts 1984)		*Pakistan*	*Pakistan*
Papua New Guinea (not available after 1991)	*Papua New Guinea*	*Papua New Guinea*	
Paraguay	**Paraguay**	**Paraguay**	**Paraguay**
Philippines, The (starts 1993)		*Philippines, The*	
Poland	**Poland**	**Poland**	**Poland**
Portugal	**Portugal**	**Portugal**	**Portugal**
Romania (starts 1991)			*Romania*
Senegal	**Senegal**	**Senegal**	**Senegal**
Singapore	**Singapore**	**Singapore**	**Singapore**
Slovak Republic (starts 1992)		*Slovak Republic*	
Slovenia (starts 1992)			*Slovenia*
South Africa (starts 1985)		*South Africa*	*South Africa*
Spain	**Spain**	**Spain**	**Spain**
Sri Lanka (starts 1985)		*Sri Lanka*	*Sri Lanka*
Swaziland	**Swaziland**	**Swaziland**	**Swaziland**
Sweden	**Sweden**	**Sweden**	**Sweden**
Switzerland (starts 1982)		*Switzerland*	*Switzerland*
Thailand	**Thailand**	**Thailand**	**Thailand**
Trinidad and Tobago (starts 1983)		*Trinidad and Tobago*	*Trinidad and Tobago*
Tunisia	**Tunisia**	**Tunisia**	**Tunisia**
Turkey (starts 1987)		*Turkey*	*Turkey*
United Kingdom	**United Kingdom**	**United Kingdom**	**United Kingdom**
United States	**United States**	**United States**	**United States**
Uruguay (starts 1986)		*Uruguay*	*Uruguay*

Notes: Total equity data are the sum of foreign direct investment (FDI) and portfolio equity investment data. Countries for which either FDI or portfolio equity investment data are available are included in the sample. Countries in italics have data only for certain periods, as indicated in the table. Countries in bold have data for both equity and debt flows throughout the whole sample period. FDI data correspond to Direct Investments Abroad (IFS line 78bdd) and Direct Investments in Reporting Economy (line 78bed) and include equity capital, reinvested earnings, other capital, and financial derivatives associated with various intercompany transactions between affiliated enterprises. Portfolio equity investments correspond to Equity Security Assets (line 78bkd) and Equity Securities Liabilities (line 78bmd) and include shares, stock participations, and similar documents that usually denote ownership of equity. Data taken from IMF (2001).

Table 1B.2   Sample countries: Debt data

All countries	1970–1980	1981–1990	1991–2000
Albania (starts 1992)			*Albania*
Algeria (1977–91)	*Algeria*	*Algeria*	
Angola	Angola	Angola	Angola
Argentina	Argentina	Argentina	Argentina
Australia	Australia	Australia	Australia
Austria	Austria	Austria	Austria
Bahrain	Bahrain	Bahrain	Bahrain
Bangladesh	*Bangladesh*	*Bangladesh*	*Bangladesh*
Belarus (starts 1993)			*Belarus*
Bene-Lux	Bene-Lux	Bene-Lux	Bene-Lux
Benin	Benin	Benin	Benin
Bolivia	Bolivia	Bolivia	Bolivia
Botswana	Botswana	Botswana	Botswana
Brazil	Brazil	Brazil	Brazil
Bulgaria (starts 1980)		*Bulgaria*	*Bulgaria*
Burkina Faso		Burkina Faso	Burkina Faso
Cambodia	Cambodia	Cambodia	Cambodia
Cameroon	Cameroon	Cameroon	Cameroon
Canada	Canada	Canada	Canada
Central African Republic	Central African Republic	Central African Republic	
Chad	Chad	Chad	Chad
Chile	Chile	Chile	Chile
China (starts 1982)		*China*	*China*
Colombia	Colombia	Colombia	Colombia
Comoros (starts 1983)		*Comoros*	*Comoros*
Congo, Republic	Congo, Republic	Congo, Republic	Congo, Republic
Costa Rica	Costa Rica	Costa Rica	Costa Rica
Côte d'Ivoire	Côte d'Ivoire	Côte d'Ivoire	Côte d'Ivoire
Croatia (starts 1993)			*Croatia*
Cyprus	*Cyprus*	*Cyprus*	*Cyprus*
Czech Republic (starts 1993)			*Czech Republic*
Denmark	Denmark	Denmark	Denmark
Dominican Republic	Dominican Republic	Dominican Republic	Dominican Republic
Ecuador	Ecuador	Ecuador	Ecuador
Egypt, Arab Republic	Egypt, Arab Republic	Egypt, Arab Republic	Egypt, Arab Republic
El Salvador	El Salvador	El Salvador	El Salvador
Eritrea (starts 1992)			*Eritrea*
Estonia (starts 1992)			*Estonia*
Ethiopia	Ethiopia	Ethiopia	Ethiopia
Fiji	Fiji	Fiji	Fiji
Finland	Finland	Finland	Finland
France	France	France	France
Gabon	Gabon	Gabon	Gabon
Gambia	Gambia	Gambia	Gambia
Germany	Germany	Germany	Germany
Ghana	Ghana	Ghana	Ghana
Guatemala	Guatemala	Guatemala	Guatemala
Guinea (starts 1987)		*Guinea*	*Guinea*

Table 1B.2   (continued)

All countries	1970–1980	1981–1990	1991–2000
Guyana (starts 1992)			*Guyana*
Haiti	Haiti	Haiti	Haiti
Honduras	Honduras	Honduras	Honduras
Hungary (starts 1982)		*Hungary*	*Hungary*
India	India	India	India
Iran, Islamic Republic	Iran, Islamic Republic	Iran, Islamic Republic	Iran, Islamic Republic
Ireland	Ireland	Ireland	Ireland
Israel	**Israel**	**Israel**	**Israel**
Italy	**Italy**	**Italy**	**Italy**
Jamaica	Jamaica	Jamaica	Jamaica
Japan	**Japan**	**Japan**	**Japan**
Jordan	**Jordan**	**Jordan**	**Jordan**
Kenya	**Kenya**	**Kenya**	**Kenya**
Korea, Republic	**Korea, Republic**	**Korea, Republic**	**Korea, Republic**
Kuwait	Kuwait	Kuwait	Kuwait
Lao PDR (starts 1989)			*Lao PDR*
Latvia	Latvia	Latvia	Latvia
Lesotho	Lesotho	Lesotho	Lesotho
Libya	**Libya**	**Libya**	**Libya**
Lithuania (starts 1993)			*Lithuania*
Madagascar	Madagascar	Madagascar	Madagascar
Malawi	Malawi	Malawi	Malawi
Malaysia	Malaysia	Malaysia	Malaysia
Mali	Mali	Mali	Mali
Mauritania	Mauritania	Mauritania	Mauritania
Mauritius	**Mauritius**	**Mauritius**	**Mauritius**
Mexico	Mexico	Mexico	Mexico
Mongolia (starts 1990)			*Mongolia*
Morocco	Morocco	Morocco	Morocco
Namibia (starts 1990)	*Namibia*	*Namibia*	*Namibia*
Nepal	**Nepal**	**Nepal**	**Nepal**
Netherlands, The	**Netherlands, The**	**Netherlands, The**	**Netherlands, The**
New Zealand	New Zealand	New Zealand	New Zealand
Nicaragua (starts 1991)			*Nicaragua*
Niger	**Niger**	**Niger**	**Niger**
Nigeria	Nigeria	Nigeria	Nigeria
Norway	**Norway**	**Norway**	**Norway**
Oman	Oman	Oman	Oman
Pakistan	Pakistan	Pakistan	Pakistan
Panama	Panama	Panama	Panama
Papua New Guinea	Papua New Guinea	Papua New Guinea	Papua New Guinea
Paraguay	**Paraguay**	**Paraguay**	**Paraguay**
Peru (starts 1985)		*Peru*	*Peru*
Philippines, The	Philippines, The	Philippines, The	Philippines, The
Poland	**Poland**	**Poland**	**Poland**
Portugal	**Portugal**	**Portugal**	**Portugal**
Romania	Romania	Romania	Romania
Rwanda	Rwanda	Rwanda	Rwanda

(*continued*)

Table 1B.2 (continued)

All countries	1970–1980	1981–1990	1991–2000
Saudi Arabia	Saudi Arabia	Saudi Arabia	Saudi Arabia
Senegal	**Senegal**	**Senegal**	**Senegal**
Sierra Leone	Sierra Leone	Sierra Leone	Sierra Leone
Singapore	**Singapore**	**Singapore**	**Singapore**
Slovak Republic (starts 1993)			*Slovak Republic*
Slovenia (starts 1992)			*Slovenia*
South Africa	South Africa	South Africa	South Africa
Spain	**Spain**	**Spain**	**Spain**
Sri Lanka	Sri Lanka	Sri Lanka	Sri Lanka
Sudan	Sudan	Sudan	Sudan
Swaziland	**Swaziland**	**Swaziland**	**Swaziland**
Sweden	**Sweden**	**Sweden**	**Sweden**
Switzerland	Switzerland	Switzerland	Switzerland
Syria	Syria	Syria	Syria
Tanzania (starts 1993)			*Tanzania*
Thailand	**Thailand**	**Thailand**	**Thailand**
Togo	Togo	Togo	Togo
Trinidad and Tobago	Trinidad and Tobago	Trinidad and Tobago	Trinidad and Tobago
Tunisia	**Tunisia**	**Tunisia**	**Tunisia**
Turkey	Turkey	Turkey	Turkey
Uganda	Uganda	Uganda	Uganda
United Kingdom	**United Kingdom**	**United Kingdom**	**United Kingdom**
United States	**United States**	**United States**	**United States**
Uruguay	Uruguay	Uruguay	Uruguay
Zambia	Zambia	Zambia	Zambia
Zimbabwe	Zimbabwe	Zimbabwe	Zimbabwe

Notes: Countries in italics have data only for certain periods, as indicated in the table. Countries in bold have data for both equity (FDI and portfolio equity investments) and debt flows throughout the whole sample period. Debt data correspond to Debt Securities Assets (IFS line 78bld) and Debt Securities Liabilities (line 78bnd), which cover bonds, notes, and money market or negotiable debt instruments; other investment assets (line 78bhd); and other investments liabilities (line 78bid), which include all financial transactions not covered in direct investment, portfolio investment, financial derivatives, or other assets. Data taken from IMF (2001).

Table 1B.3   Descriptive statistics: Inflows of capital and volatility, 1970–2000 (per capita U.S. dollars)

	Mean	Standard deviation	Minimum	Maximum
Capital inflows				
FDI inflows	166.92	307.64	–122.51	1,723.78
Portfolio equity inflows	129.44	310.90	–2.17	1,769.21
Debt inflows	501.33	821.60	–84.65	4,827.94
Total equity inflows	287.47	562.50	–122.51	3,492.99
Total equity and debt inflows	795.40	1,363.66	–84.65	8,320.92
Volatility of inflows				
Volatility of FDI inflows	0.78	0.32	0.12	1.63
Volatility of portfolio equity inflows	0.80	0.47	0.16	2.29
Volatility of debt inflows	0.70	0.24	0.32	1.40
Volatility of total equity inflows	0.93	0.38	0.34	2.01
Volatility of total equity and debt inflows	0.62	0.24	0.13	1.38

Notes: Inflows represent flows of foreign claims on domestic capital (liability), divided by population based on IMF data in 1995 U.S. dollars. Volatility of inflows is the standard deviation of the corresponding inflows per capita divided by the average of the absolute value of the inflows and outflows of capital per capita. Data are for 47 countries out of the 122-country sample for which both equity and debt flows data are available throughout the whole sample period. FDI inflows correspond to Direct Investments in Reporting Economy (IFS line 78bed), which includes equity capital, reinvested earnings, other capital, and financial derivatives associated with various intercompany transactions between affiliated enterprises. Portfolio equity inflows correspond to Equity Liabilities (line 78bmd), which include shares, stock participations, and similar documents that usually denote ownership of equity. Data on inflows of debt include Debt Securities Liabilities (line 78bnd), which cover bonds and money market or negotiable debt instruments; and Other Investments Liabilities (line 78bid), which include all financial transactions not covered in direct investment, portfolio investment, financial derivatives, or other assets. Inflows of total equity are the sum of FDI and portfolio equity investments.

References

Acemoglu, Daron, Simon Johnson, and James A. Robinson. 2001. The colonial origins of comparative development: An empirical investigation. *American Economic Review* 91:1369–1401.

———. 2002. Reversal of fortune: Geography and institutions in the making of the modern world income distribution. *Quarterly Journal of Economics* 117:1231–94.

Aizenman, Joshua. 2004. Financial opening: Evidence and policy options. In *Challenges to globalization: Analyzing the economics,* ed. R. Baldwin and A. Winters. Chicago: University of Chicago Press.

Alesina, Alberto, and David Dollar. 2000. Who gives foreign aid to whom and why? *Journal of Economic Growth* 5:33–64.

Alfaro, Laura, Sebnem Kalemli-Ozcan, and Vadym Volosovych. 2007. Why doesn't capital flow from rich to poor countries? An empirical investigation. *Review of Economics and Statistics,* forthcoming.

Bacchetta, Philippe, and Eric van Wincoop. 2000. Capital flows to emerging markets: Liberalization, overshooting, and volatility. In *Capital flows and the emerging economies,* ed. S. Edwards. Chicago: University of Chicago Press.

Bhagwati, Jagdish. 1998. The capital myth. *Foreign Affairs* 77 (3): 7–12.

Calvo, Guillermo, Leonardo Leiderman, and Carmen Reinhart. 1996. Inflows of capital to developing countries in the 1990s. *Journal of Economic Perspectives* 10:123–39.

Calvo, Guillermo, and Enrique Mendoza. 2000a. Contagion, globalization, and the volatility of capital flows. In *Capital flows and the emerging economies,* ed. S. Edwards, 15–42. Chicago: University of Chicago Press.

———. 2000b. Regional contagion and the globalization of securities markets. *Journal of International Economics* 51:79–113.

Calvo, Guillermo, and Carlos Vegh. 1999. Inflation stabilization in chronic inflation countries. In *Handbook of macroeconomics 1C,* ed. J. B. Taylor and M. Woodford. Amsterdam: North-Holland.

Chari, Varadarajan V., and Patrick Kehoe. 2003. Hot money. Federal Reserve Bank of Minneapolis Staff Report no. 228. Minneapolis, MN: Federal Reserve Bank of Minneapolis.

Clemens, Michael, and Jeffrey G. Williamson. 2004. Wealth bias in the first global capital market boom, 1870–1913. *Economic Journal* 114 (127): 304–37.

Corsetti, Giancarlo, Paolo Pesenti, and Nouriel Roubini. 2001. Fundamental determinants of the Asian crisis: The role of financial fragility and external imbalances. In *Regional and global capital flows: Macroeconomic causes and consequences,* ed. T. Ito and A. Krueger. Chicago: University of Chicago Press.

Coval, Joshua, and Tobias J. Moskowitz. 1999. Home bias at home: Local equity preferences in domestic portfolios. *Journal of Finance* 54:2045–73.

———. 2001. The geography of investment: Informed trading and asset prices. *Journal of Political Economy* 109:811–41.

Edwards, Sebastian. 1991. Capital flows, foreign direct investment, and debt-equity swaps in developing countries. In *Capital flows in the world economy,* ed. Horst Siebert. Tubingen, Germany: J. C. B. Mohr.

———. 2001. Capital mobility and economic performance: Are emerging economies different? NBER Working Paper no. 8076. Cambridge, MA: National Bureau of Economic Research.

Eichengreen, Barry. 2003. *Capital flows and crises.* Cambridge, MA: MIT Press.

Eichengreen, Barry, Ricardo Hausmann, and Ugo Panizza. 2003. Currency mismatches, debt intolerance, and original sin: Why they are not the same and why it matters. NBER Working Paper no. 10036. Cambridge, MA: National Bureau of Economic Research.

Frankel, Jeffrey, and Andrew Rose. 1996. Currency crises in emerging markets: An empirical treatment. *Journal of International Economics* 41:351–66.

Frankel, Jeffrey, and Shang-Jin Wei. 2004. Managing macroeconomic crises. NBER Working Paper no. 10907. Cambridge, MA: National Bureau of Economic Research.

Gavin, Michael, and Ricardo Hausmann. 1999. Preventing crisis and contagion: Fiscal and financial dimensions. IADB Working Paper no. 401. Washington, DC: Inter-American Development Bank.

Gavin, Michael, Ricardo Hausmann, and Leonardo Leiderman. 1995. The macroeconomics of capital flows to Latin America: Experience and policy issues. IADB Working Paper no. 310. Washington, DC: Inter-American Development Bank.

Gertler, Mark, and Kenneth Rogoff. 1990. North-south lending and endogenous domestic capital market inefficiencies. *Journal of Monetary Economics* 26: 245–66.

Glick, Reuven, and Kenneth Rogoff. 1995. Global versus country-specific productivity shocks and the current account. *Journal of Monetary Economics* 35:159–92.

Gordon, Roger H., and A. Lans Bovenberg. 1996. Why is capital so immobile internationally? Possible explanations and implications for capital income taxation. *American Economic Review* 86:1057–75.

Henry, Peter B., and Peter L. Lorentzen. 2003. Domestic capital market reform and access to global finance: Making markets work. NBER Working Paper no. 10064. Cambridge, MA: National Bureau of Economic Research.

Inter-American Development Bank (IADB). 1995. Hacia una economia menos volatil. In *Economic and Social progress in Latin America,* 195–262. Washington, DC: Inter-American Development Bank.

International Monetary Fund (IMF). 1993. *Balance of payments manual.* 5th ed. Washington, DC: International Monetary Fund.

———. 2001. *International financial statistics.* CD-ROM. Washington, DC: International Monetary Fund.

———. Various issues. *Annual report on exchange arrangements and exchange restrictions.* Washington, DC: International Monetary Fund.

Kalemli-Ozcan, Sebnem, Bent Sorensen, and Oved Yosha. 2003. Risk sharing and industrial specialization: Regional and international evidence. *American Economic Review* 93:903–18.

Kalemli-Ozcan, Sebnem, Bent Sorensen, Ariell Reshef, and Oved Yosha. 2005. Capital flows and productivity: Evidence from U.S. states. NBER Working Paper no. 11301. Cambridge, MA: National Bureau of Economic Research.

Kaminsky, Graciella. 2003. Varieties of currency crises. NBER Working Paper no. 10193. Cambridge, MA: National Bureau of Economic Research.

Kaminsky, Graciella, and Carmen Reinhart. 1999. The twin crises: The causes of banking and balance of payment problems. *American Economic Review* 89:473–500.

King, Robert, and Sergio Rebelo. 1993. Transitional dynamics and economic growth in the neoclassical model. *American Economic Review* 83:908–31.

Kraay, Aart, Norman Loayza, Luis Serven, and Jaume Ventura. 2000. Country portfolios. NBER Working Paper no. 7795. Cambridge, MA: National Bureau of Economic Research.

Krugman, Paul. 1998. Saving Asia: It's time to get radical. *Fortune* 138 (5): 74–80.

La Porta, Rafael, Florencio Lopez-de-Silanes, Andrei Shleifer, and Robert Vishny. 1998. Law and finance. *Journal of Political Economy* 106:1113–55.

Lane, Philip. 2004. Empirical perspectives on long-term external debt. *Topics in Macroeconomics* 4:1–21.

Lane, Philip, and Gian Maria Milesi-Ferretti. 1999. The external wealth of nations: Measures of foreign assets and liabilities for industrial and developing countries. IMF Working Paper. Washington, DC: International Monetary Fund.

———. 2001. The external wealth of nations: Measures of foreign assets and liabilities for industrial and developing countries. *Journal of International Economics* 55:263–94.

Lucas, Robert. 1990. Why doesn't capital flow from rich to poor countries? *American Economic Review* 80:92–96.

McKinnon, Ronald, and Huw Pill. 1996. Credible liberalization and international capital flows: The overborrowing syndrome. In *Financial Deregulation and Integration in East Asia,* ed. T. Ito and A. Kruger, 7–51. Chicago: University of Chicago Press.

North, Douglass C. 1994. Economic performance through time. *American Economic Review* 84:359–68.

———. 1995. Institutions. *Journal of Economic Perspectives* 5:97–112.
Obstfeld, Maurice, and Kenneth Rogoff. 2000. The six major puzzles in international macroeconomics: Is there a common cause? In *NBER macroeconomics annual 2000,* ed. B. Bernanke and K. Rogoff, 339–90. Cambridge, MA: MIT Press.
Obstfeld, Maurice, and Alan M. Taylor. 2004. *Global capital markets: Integration, crisis, and growth.* Cambridge: Cambridge University Press.
O'Rourke, Kevin H., and Jeffrey G. Williamson. 1999. *Globalization and history: The evolution of a nineteenth-century Atlantic economy.* Cambridge, MA: MIT Press.
Political Risk Services (PRS) Group. 2001. *International country risk guide.* New York: PRS Group.
Portes, Richard, and Helene Rey. 2005. The determinants of cross-border equity transaction flows. *Journal of International Economics* 65:269–96.
Prasad, Eswar S., Kenneth Rogoff, Shang-Jin Wei, and M. Ayhan Kose. 2003. Effects of financial globalization on developing countries: Some empirical evidence. IMF Occasional Paper no. 220. Washington, DC: International Monetary Fund.
Prescott, Edward. 1998. Needed: A theory of total factor productivity. *International Economic Review* 39:525–52.
Razin, Assaf, and Chi-Wa Yuen. 1994. Convergence in growth rates: A quantitative assessment of the role of capital mobility and international taxation. In *Capital mobility: The impact on consumption, investment, and growth,* ed. Leonardo Leiderman and Assaf Razin, 237–57. New York: Cambridge University Press.
Reinhart, Carmen, and Kenneth Rogoff. 2004. Serial default and the "paradox" of rich to poor capital flows. *American Economic Review Papers and Proceedings* 94:52–58.
Rodrik, Dani. 1998. Who needs capital account convertibility? *Princeton Essays in International Finance* 207:55–65.
Tornell, Aaron, and Andres Velasco. 1992. Why does capital flow from poor to rich countries? The tragedy of the commons and economic growth. *Journal of Political Economy* 100:1208–31.
Wei, Shang-Jin. 2000. Local corruption and global capital flows. *Brookings Papers in Economic Activity,* Issue no. 2:303–46.
Wei, Shang-Jin, and Yi Wu. 2002. Negative alchemy? Corruption, composition of capital flows, and currency crises. In *Preventing currency crises in emerging markets,* ed. S. Edwards and J. Frankel, 461–501. Chicago: University of Chicago Press.
World Bank. 2002. *World development indicators.* CD-ROM. Washington, DC: World Bank.

Comment   Gerd Häusler

The paper notes in the introduction that there are two important facts about capital flows in the period 1970–2000:

Gerd Häusler is a vice chairman and a managing director at Lazard.

- Capital does not flow from rich to poor countries (the "Lucas paradox").
- In fact, net capital flows have been negative for emerging market (EM) countries in recent years, as noted in chapter 4 of the September 2004 issue of the *Global Financial Stability Report* of the International Monetary Fund. Rather, EM economies focused on reducing debt and building up reserves as a self-insurance against global factors. This risk appetite was also mirrored in the corporate sector, where corporations focused on repairing their balance sheet.

I would add that the period 1970–2000 was one that could be characterized by mature markets seeking to diversify rather than one of "development" finance (Obstfeld and Taylor 2004). But is the Lucas paradox—the fact that capital did not flow from rich to poor countries—really a paradox? I will return to this question.

On a different point, I would also like to note that the title of the paper is misleading in its generality. Although it is entitled "Capital Flows in a Globalized World," the paper does not cover debt flows, which is a very important asset class and component of capital flows. The authors focus on equity flows and argue about lack of quality in debt data. It is unclear to me if equity data are better. Moreover, as shown in the paper's figures 1.1 and 1.2, debt flows are a big—albeit declining in the late 1990s—part of the capital flows story. I should also point out here that Reinhart and Rogoff (2004) show that the Lucas paradox can be easily explained with credit and political risk—especially for countries that they describe as "serial defaulters."

Let me now turn to the main focus of my discussion. The Lucas paradox is not really a paradox at all. At a very basic level, what drives capital flows is one common criterion that banks and other lenders employ toward all types of borrowers. At times they are so risk averse that they flock toward the best risk.

An important element that is missing from the paper is a discussion of the behavior of the supply side:

- The authors' list of determinants of capital inflows focuses only on (recipient) country characteristics, not on changes in the supply of funds.
- A key change in the financial landscape over the past two decades has been the growth of institutional investors, which are missing from the paper (see fig. 1C.1).
- The activities of institutional investors (and the decline in banking activities) have been changing the supply of capital flows in fundamental ways:
  —For EM countries, there was a sharp shift in the investor base in the second half of the 1990s (as shown in the September 2003 *Global Financial Stability Report,* chap. 4).

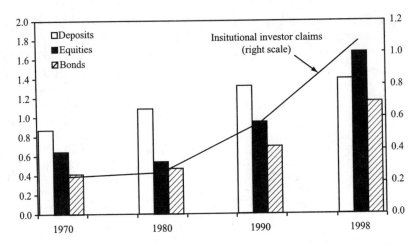

Fig. 1C.1   Group of seven: Financial instruments outstanding and institutional investor assets (percentage of GDP)

—For mature markets, the growing role of institutional investors is behind the "diversification" factors in determining capital flows rather than "development" finance. *Uncorrelated assets* is the catch-phrase here (more on this below).

—Diversification goes beyond mature markets: low returns in mature markets and demographic trends will lead to more rich-to-poor capital flows.

• Global financial assets held by private nonbank institutional investors have more than doubled in the past ten years and more than tripled in the past fifteen years, to reach about US$40 trillion in a handful of the largest mature markets. Capital funds are expected to continue to grow at a rapid pace (demographic trends necessitate pension reforms that are expected to create more and larger asset gatherers). One only needs to look at what is happening in Europe or Japan, or in the discussion on Social Security reform in the United States. Putting aside the policy debate for a moment on defined benefit versus defined contribution systems, in Europe informal systems are developing already as families accumulate additional savings to top off social security.

• Changes in the asset allocation decisions of institutional investors will have an increasingly important impact on capital flows across asset classes and across national borders, as well as asset prices. Sustained differences in growth rates—such as, for example, low rates for Europe and Japan while the United States and emerging Asia are growing at significantly faster rates—will drive asset allocation to the point where returns promise to be higher. Both institutional funds and personal savings will seek to maximize risk-adjusted returns in an increasingly globalized financial system by diversifying their holdings in uncorrelated assets and returns. I should note here that I use the phrase "institutional investors" loosely. The increase of personal savings will mostly be through institutional investors.

- One corollary to these developments is that a relatively small change in the asset allocation of funds—given their enormous relative size—may affect global financial stability and, more specifically, have a significant impact on the cost of external funding for EM countries.
- As EM countries mature, which includes opening their capital accounts over time, financial market integration will intensify, and these countries' growing financial sectors will increasingly compete for, open to, and receive from the global pool of capital.

As the global financial markets evolve in the context of demographic developments and regulatory changes, there will be some adjustment problems. As I already mentioned, aging societies will behave like rentiers.

Returning to my earlier comment, the need to diversify capital assets—which was a key driver during the period 1970–2000—is an even more significant factor in institutional investors' investing decisions today. As the globe becomes more and more integrated, asset prices become increasingly correlated, and investors, therefore, face a growing challenge in securing uncorrelated assets.

Pension funds, which, by their nature, are cautious in their investment decisions, will be slow to adopt the notion of the global asset allocation process that faces no national or asset class boundaries. It will eventually arrive, however, and the effects will be enormous given the size of pension funds. As this unfolds, we should not underestimate the role that financial consultants will play in influencing the nature and direction of capital flows.

A huge uncertainty in determining the nature, pace, and direction of the global asset allocation process as it goes forward will be estimating the "discount rate" of future developments in the real economy for the purpose of investing large funds.

References

Obstfeld, Maurice, and Alan M. Taylor. 2004. *Global capital markets: Integration, crisis, and growth.* Cambridge: Cambridge University Press.
Reinhart, Carmen, and Kenneth Rogoff. 2004. Serial default and the "paradox" of rich to poor capital flows. *American Economic Review Papers and Proceedings* 94: 52–58.

Capital Controls, Sudden Stops, and Current Account Reversals

Sebastian Edwards

2.1 Introduction

During the last few years a number of authors have argued that free capital mobility produces macroeconomic instability and contributes to financial vulnerability in the emerging nations. For example, in his critique of the U.S. Treasury and the International Monetary Fund (IMF), Stiglitz (2002) has argued that pressuring emerging and transition countries to relax controls on capital mobility during the 1990s was a huge mistake. According to him, the easing of controls on capital mobility was at the center of most (if not all) currency crises in the emerging markets during the last decade—Mexico in 1994, East Asia in 1997, Russia in 1998, Brazil in 1999, Turkey in 2001, and Argentina in 2002. These days, even the IMF seems to criticize free capital mobility and to provide (at least some) support for capital controls. Indeed, on a visit to Malaysia in September 2003 Horst Koehler, then the IMF's managing director, praised the policies of Prime Minister Mahathir, and in particular his use of capital controls in the aftermath of the 1997 currency crisis (Beattie 2003).

Supporters of capital controls have argued that restricting capital mobility has two important potential benefits: (a) it reduces a country's vulnerability to external shocks and financial crises; and (b) it allows countries that have suffered a currency crisis to lower interest rates, implement pro-

Sebastian Edwards is the Henry Ford II Professor of International Business Economics at the Anderson Graduate School of Management at the University of California, Los Angeles (UCLA), and a research associate of the National Bureau of Economic Research.

I am grateful to the participants in the Cambridge preconference meeting for their very helpful comments and suggestions. I thank Roberto Alvarez for his comments and excellent assistance. I am particularly grateful to my discussant, Alan Taylor, for his very useful comments.

growth policies, and emerge from the crisis sooner than they would have otherwise. According to this view, controlling capital outflows would give crisis countries additional time to restructure their financial sector in an orderly fashion.[1]

The evidence in support of these claims, however, has been mostly country specific, and not particularly convincing. Some authors have claimed that by restricting capital mobility Chile was able to avoid the type of macroeconomic turmoil that affected the rest of Latin America during the 1990s (Stiglitz 1999).[2] Also, it has been argued that Malaysia's imposition of controls on capital outflows in the aftermath of the Asian debt crisis helped the country rebound quickly and resume a growth path (Kaplan and Rodrik 2002). According to other authors, however, the experiences of both Chile and Malaysia with capital controls have been mixed at best (Dornbusch 2002; Johnson and Mitton 2001; De Gregorio, Edwards, and Valdes 2000). What is particularly interesting about this debate is that after many years it continues to be centered mostly on the experiences of a handful of countries, and that much of it has taken place at an anecdotal level. There have been very few studies that have provided multicountry evidence on whether capital controls indeed reduce vulnerability or reduce the costs of crises.[3] This paucity of multicountry studies is partially explained by the difficulties in measuring the degree of capital mobility across time and countries (Eichengreen 2001).

In this paper I use a broad multicountry data set to analyze the relationship between restrictions to capital mobility and external crises. The analysis focuses on two manifestations of external crises that have received considerable attention during the last few years: (a) sudden stops of capital inflows, and (b) current account reversals.[4] I am particularly interested in dealing with the following two specific questions:

- Do capital controls reduce the probability of a major external crisis (defined as a sudden stop or a current account reversal)?
- And, once a crisis has occurred, do countries that restrict capital mobility incur in lower costs—measured by reductions in growth—than countries that have a more open capital account?

---

1. Most well-trained economists would agree that there are trade-offs associated with the imposition of capital controls. Whether the costs offset the benefits is a complex empirical question, whose answer will depend on the specificities of each particular country. Doing a full-blown cost-benefit analysis is well beyond the scope of this paper, however.

2. See, however, De Gregorio, Edwards, and Valdes (2000). Some authors have also argued that the absence of crises in India and China is an indication of the merits of controlling capital mobility. It is difficult, however, to take these claims seriously.

3. There have been, however, a number of cross-country studies that have tried to determine whether capital controls have an effect on economic growth. For a survey, see Eichengreen (2001).

4. For a discussion of these two phenomena see, for example, Calvo, Izquierdo, and Mejía (2004) and Edwards (2004b).

In analyzing these issues I rely on two complementary approaches. First, I use a methodology based on the computation of nonparametric tests and frequency tables to analyze the incidence and main characteristics of both sudden stops and current account reversals in countries with different degrees of capital controls. And second, I use a regression-based analysis that estimates jointly the probability of having a crisis, and the cost of such crisis, in terms of short-term declines in output growth.

The rest of the paper is organized as follows. In section 2.2 I provide a selected survey of recent efforts to measure the degree of capital mobility. I review various indexes, and I discuss their strengths and weaknesses. In section 2.3 I deal with the evolution of capital account restrictions during the last thirty years. The section opens with an analysis of the evolution of capital account openness based on a new index, which I have constructed by combining three data sources: (a) the index developed by Quinn (2003); (b) the index by Mody and Murshid (2002); and (c) country-specific information obtained from various sources, including country-specific sources. Section 2.4 deals with the anatomy of sudden stops and current account reversals. I analyze their incidence and the extent to which these two phenomena are related. This analysis is performed for three groups of countries classified according to the degree of capital mobility: *Low* capital mobility, *Intermediate* capital mobility, and *High* capital mobility countries. My main interest in this analysis is to compare the two extreme groups: *Low* and *High* capital mobility. In section 2.5 I report new results on the costs of external crises characterized by sudden stops and/or current account reversals. I am particularly interested in determining if the cost of a crisis—measured in terms of lower growth—is different for countries with different degrees of capital mobility. I use *treatment regressions* to analyze whether restricting capital mobility reduces vulnerability and the costs of crises. Finally, in section 2.6 I provide some concluding remarks. The paper also has a data appendix.

Before proceeding it is important to stress that in this paper I do not provide a full-fledged cost-benefit analysis of capital controls. I deal in detail with two important aspects of the problem—capital controls and vulnerability, and the growth consequences of crises under different intensity of controls—but I don't cover all the consequences of control policies. In particular, I don't deal with many microeconomic consequences and costs of a policy of capital controls (see Forbes 2003 for this type of discussion).

2.2 Measuring the Degree of Openness of the Capital Account

Most analysts agree that during the last few decades there has been an increase in the degree of international capital mobility. There is less agreement, however, on the exact nature (and magnitude) of this phenomenon. The reason for this is that it is very difficult to measure in a relatively precise way a country's degree of capital mobility. Indeed, with the exception of the two extremes—absolute freedom or complete closeness of the capital account—it is not easy to provide effective measures that capture the extent of capital market integration. What has been particularly challenging has been constructing indexes that allow for useful comparisons across countries and across time. In this section I review a number of attempts at building *indexes* of capital mobility, and I propose a new measure that combines information from two of the better indexes with country-specific data. I then use this new index to analyze the evolution of capital account restrictions during the last three decades.

Historically, most emerging and transition countries have relied heavily on different forms of capital account restrictions. While throughout most of the post–World War II period these have been aimed at avoiding capital "flight," more recently countries have tried to avoid (or at least slow down) large inflows of capital (Edwards 1999). However, there has long been recognition that legal impediments on capital mobility are not always translated into actual restrictions on these movements. This distinction between *actual* and *legal* capital mobility has been the subject of policy debates, including the debate on the effectiveness of capital controls.

There is ample historical evidence suggesting that there have been significant discrepancies between the legal and the actual degree of capital controls. In countries with severe legal impediments to capital mobility—including countries that have banned capital movement—the private sector has traditionally resorted to the overinvoicing of imports and underinvoicing of exports to sidestep legal controls on capital flows (Garber 1998 discusses more sophisticated mechanisms). For example, the massive volumes of capital flight that took place in Latin America in the wake of the 1982 debt crisis clearly showed that, when faced with the "appropriate" incentives, the public can be extremely creative in finding ways to move capital internationally. The question of how to measure, from an economic point of view, the degree of capital mobility and the extent to which domestic capital markets are integrated to the world capital market continues to be the subject of extensive debate. (See Dooley, Mathieson, and Rojas-Suarez 1997 for an early and comprehensive treatment of the subject. See Eichengreen 2001 for a more recent discussion.)

In two early studies Harberger (1978, 1980) argued that the effective degree of integration of capital markets should be measured by the convergence of private rates of return to capital across countries. In trying to measure the effective degree of capital mobility, Feldstein and Horioka (1980) analyzed the behavior of savings and investments in a number of countries. They argue that if there is perfect capital mobility, changes in savings and investments will be uncorrelated in a specific country. That is, in a world without capital restrictions an increase in domestic savings will tend to "leave the home country," moving to the rest of the world. Likewise, if international capital markets are fully integrated, increases in domestic investment will tend to be funded by the world at large and not necessarily by domestic savings. Using a data set for sixteen Organization for Economic Cooperation and Development (OECD) countries, Feldstein and Horioka found that savings and investment ratios were highly positively correlated, and concluded that these results strongly supported the presumption that *long-term* capital was subject to significant impediments. Frankel (1991) applied the Feldstein-Horioka test to a large number of countries during the 1980s, including a number of Latin American nations. His results corroborated those obtained by the original study, indicating that savings and investment have been significantly positively correlated in most countries. In a comprehensive analysis of the degree of capital mobility, Montiel (1994) estimated a series of Feldstein-Horioka equations for sixty-two developing countries. Using the estimated regression coefficient for the industrial countries as a benchmark, he concluded that the majority of the Latin American nations exhibited a relatively high degree of capital mobility—indeed, much larger than what an analysis of legal restrictions would suggest.

In a series of studies Edwards (1985) and Edwards and Khan (1985) argued that degree of convergence of domestic and international interest rates could be used to assess the degree of openness of the capital account (see also Montiel 1994). The application of this model to the cases of a number of countries (Brazil, Colombia, Chile) confirms the results that, in general, the actual degree of capital mobility is greater than what the legal restrictions approach suggests. Haque and Montiel (1991), Reisen and Yèches (1993), and Dooley (1995) have provided expansions of this model that allow for the estimation of the degree of capital mobility even in cases when there are not enough data on domestic interest rates, and when there are changes in the degree of capital mobility through time. Their results once again indicate that in most emerging countries true capital mobility has historically exceeded the legal extent of capital mobility. Dooley, Mathieson, and Rojas-Suarez (1997) developed a method for measuring the changes in the degree of capital mobility in emerging countries that recognizes the costs of undertaking disguised capital inflows. The model is estimated using a Kalman filter technique for three countries. The results suggest that all three countries experienced a very significant increase in the degree of capital mobility between 1977 and 1989. Edwards (2000) used a "time-varying coefficients" variant of this approach to analyze the way in which Chile's *actual* degree of capital mobility evolved through time.

Some authors have used information contained in the IMF's *Exchange Arrangements and Exchange Restrictions* to construct indexes on capital controls for a panel of countries. Alesina, Grilli, and Milesi-Ferretti (1994), for example, constructed a dummy variable index of capital controls. This indicator—which takes a value of 1 when capital controls are in place and 0 otherwise—was then used to analyze some of the political forces behind the imposition of capital restrictions in a score of countries.[5] Rodrik (1998) used a similar index to investigate the effects of capital controls on growth, inflation, and investment between 1979 and 1989. His results suggest that, after controlling for other variables, capital restrictions have no significant effects on macroeconomic performance. Klein and Olivei (1999) used the IMF's *Exchange Arrangements and Exchange Restrictions* data to construct an index of capital mobility. The index is defined as the number of years in the period 1986 and 1995 that, according to the IMF, the country in question has had an open capital account.[6] In contrast to that of Rodrik, their analysis suggests that countries with a more open capital account have performed better than those that restrict capital mobility.[7] Leblang (1997), Razin and Rose (1994), and Chinn and Ito (2002) have also used indicators based on the IMF binary classification of openness. The standard approach is to use line E.2 of the annual summary published in the *Annual Report on Exchange Arrangements and Exchange Restrictions.* In an early attempt to use this IMF report, Edwards (1989) used the detailed information in the individual country pages to analyze the way in which restrictions on capital mobility changed in the period immediately surrounding a major exchange rate crisis.

A major limitation of these IMF-based binary indexes, however, is that they are extremely general and do not distinguish between different intensities of capital restrictions. Moreover, they fail to distinguish the type of flow that is being restricted, and they ignore the fact that, as discussed above, legal restrictions are frequently circumvented. For example, according to this IMF-based indicator, Chile, Mexico, and Brazil were subject to the same degree of capital controls in 1992–94. In reality, however, the three cases were extremely different. While in Chile there were restrictions on short-term inflows, Mexico had (for all practical purposes) free capital mobility, and Brazil had in place an arcane array of restrictions. Montiel and Reinhart (1999) have combined IMF and country-specific information to construct an index on the intensity of capital controls in fifteen countries during 1990–96. Although their index, which can take three values (0, 1, or 2) represents an improvement over straight IMF indicators, it is still rather general, and does not capture the subtleties of actual capital restrictions. These measurement difficulties are not unique to the capi-

5. Edison et al. (2002) provide a very useful summary (table 1 of their paper) of twelve different measures of capital account restrictions used in recent studies on the relationship between capital controls and economic performance.

6. A limitation with this indicator is that it does not say if the index's number (i.e., the percentage of years with restrictions) refers to most recent or most distant years in the time window being considered.

7. As Eichengreen (2001) points out, some authors supplement the information from the IMF's *Exchange Arrangements and Exchange Restrictions* with information on the extent of restrictions on current transactions. See also Frankel (1992).

tal flows literature, however. In fact, as Rodrik (1995) and Edwards (1998) have argued, the literature on trade openness and growth has long been affected by serious measurement problems.

In an effort to deal with these measurement problems, Quinn (1997) constructed a comprehensive set of cross-country indicators on the degree of capital mobility. His indicators cover twenty advanced countries and forty-five emerging economies. These indexes have two distinct advantages over other indicators. First, they are not restricted to a binary classification, where countries' capital accounts are either open or closed. Quinn uses a 0–4 scale to classify the countries in his sample, with a higher number meaning a more open capital account. Second, the Quinn indexes cover more than one time period, allowing researchers to investigate whether there is a connection between capital account *liberalization* and economic performance. This is, indeed, an improvement over traditional indexes that have concentrated on a particular period in time, without allowing researchers to analyze whether countries that open up to international capital movements have experienced changes in performance.[8] In an interesting exercise, Edison and Warnock (2003) compared Quinn's (1997) index with an index based on the number of years that, according to the *Exchange Arrangements and Exchange Restrictions,* a country has had a closed capital account. They found that for most (but not all) countries and periods there was a correspondence between the two indicators.

Chinn and Ito (2002) built a new index based on the IMF binary data. Their index is the average of the first standardized principal component of each of four categories of transactions considered by the IMF. Chinn and Ito consider their index to be in the spirit of the work by Edwards (2001) and Klein and Olivei (1999), and argue that, in contrast with the simple 0–1 IMF-based indexes, theirs is able to capture the intensity of capital restrictions. An advantage of this index constructed by Chinn and Ito is that it is available for 105 countries for the period 1977–97.

More recently, Quinn, Inclan, and Toyoda (2001) and Quinn (2003) used detailed data obtained from the IMF to develop a new index of capital mobility for fifty-nine countries. This index goes from 1 to 100, with higher values denoting a higher degree of financial integration. Thus, countries with stricter capital controls have a lower value of this index. For a small number of these countries the index is available for the period 1950–99; for most of them it is available for five years: 1959, 1973, 1982, 1988, and 1997. And for a core number of countries the index is available since 1890 (for details see Quinn 2003). Mody and Murshid (2002) also used IMF data as the bases for their index of financial integration. This index covers 150 countries for (most of) the period 1966–2000, and is tabulated from a value of 0

---

8. Note, however, that the basic information used by Quinn to construct this index also comes from the IMF's *Exchange Arrangements and Exchange Restrictions.*

to 4. This index takes the value of 0 in the case that a country has a closed capital account, has a closed current account, places restrictions on their exports receipts, and operates under multiple exchange rates. Both these new indexes (Quinn and Mody-Murshid) represent a significant improvement over previous attempts at measuring the variation across time and countries of capital restrictions.

In a recent paper Miniane (2004) has proposed a new measure based on detailed country-specific data compiled by the IMF. Since 1996 the IMF's *Annual Report on Exchange Rate Arrangements and Exchange Restrictions* has published a very detailed and disaggregated index of capital account restrictions that distinguishes between thirteen different categories. This level of disaggregation is a marked improvement over the pre-1996 *Annual Report* data, which considered only six categories—bilateral payment arrangements, restrictions on current account transaction payments, restrictions on capital account, import surcharges, advanced deposits on imports, and export proceeds surrendering. Miniane has extended the more detailed thirteen-category index backward to 1983 for thirty-four countries. He shows that this new measure is more accurate than the older, less detailed one.

Although these new indexes on capital restrictions represent a major improvement with respect to earlier indicators, they still have some limitations, including the fact that, in spite of the authors' efforts, the indexes do not distinguish sharply between different types of restrictions (i.e., controls on foreign direct investment versus portfolio flows; controls on inflows versus controls on outflows).[9] Second, these indexes tend to blur the distinction between exchange restrictions—including the required surrendering of exports' proceeds—and capital account restrictions. Third, they do not deal in a systematic way with the fact that many countries' controls are (partially) evaded. This means that an ideal index of capital account restrictions would make a correction for the effectiveness of the controls (see De Gregorio, Edwards, and Valdes 2000 for an attempt to deal with this issue for the case of Chile).

Most of the indexes discussed above have tried to capture the overall degree of capital mobility in particular countries at a particular moment in time. A number of authors, however, have concentrated on the degree of openness of the stock market. Most of these studies have tried to analyze the effect of the *opening* of the stock market on several macroeconomic and microeconomic variables. For this reason, these studies make a significant effort to date correctly different liberalization efforts. Early and ambitious efforts along these lines were made by Bekaert (1995), Bekaert and Harvey

9. The Quinn (1997) index considers separately capital account receipts and payments. The Johnston and Tamirisa (1998) paper is one of the few where an attempt is made to distinguish between controls on capital inflows and on various types of outflows. Their index, however, covers only one year. For related work see Tamirisa (1999).

(1995, 2000), and Bekaert, Harvey, and Lundblad (2001). An important point made by these authors is that using the official or legislative dates of stock market liberalization may be highly misleading. For this reason, the authors use data on actual net capital flows to date stock market liberalization episodes in a score of countries. More specifically, they argue that liberalization episodes may be dated by identifying *break points* in the net capital flows data.[10] In a recent study, Edison and Warnock (2003) have used data on stock markets compiled by the International Finance Corporation to construct a new index of restrictions on ownership of stock by foreigners. This index—which was constructed for twenty-nine countries— has a high degree of correlation with the index by Bekaert, Harvey, and Lundblad (2001).[11] Shatz (2000) has built an index on capital account restrictions on the basis of restrictions on foreign direct investment in fifty-seven countries. This index has been used by Desai, Foley, and Forbes (2004) in a study on the way in which multinational firms deal with capital controls.

The selective survey presented in this subsection vividly captures the difficulties that researchers have encountered in their efforts to measure the degree of capital mobility of particular countries at particular points in time. It also shows that this is a rapidly moving area of research, which is likely to continue to evolve in the future. Most recent efforts to improve measurement have focused on moving away from coarse "closed-open" binary indexes, and have dealt with two issues: (a) capturing the fact that when it comes to controls there are "grey areas," and that there are gradations of restrictions; and (b) allowing comparisons of the intensity of controls across countries and time. In both of these areas there have been considerable improvements in the last few years.

2.3   The Evolution of Capital Mobility in the World Economy: 1970–2001

In this section I analyze the evolution of capital mobility in a large number of countries—both advanced and emerging—during the last three decades. The first step is to discuss a new index on capital mobility; I then provide evidence of the extent to which countries have liberalized their capital account in the last ten years.

In order to analyze the evolution of capital account restrictions I constructed a new index on capital mobility that combines information from Quinn (2003) and Mody and Murshid (2002), with information from country-specific sources. In creating this new index I followed a three-step procedure. First, the scales of the Quinn and Mody and Murshid indexes were

10. See also Henry (2000).
11. See Edison et al. (2002) for a survey of studies on the effect of capital account restrictions on stock markets.

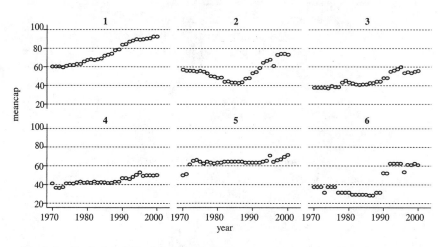

Fig. 2.1   Capital mobility index, 1970–2000

Note: Figure shows graphs by region code: 1 = industrial countries, 2 = Latin America and Caribbean, 3 = Asia, 4 = Africa, 5 = Middle East, 6 = Eastern Europe.

made compatible. The new index has a scale from 0 to 100, *where higher numbers denote a higher degree of capital mobility;* a score of 100 denotes absolutely free capital mobility. Second, I use Stata's "impute" procedure to deal with missing observations in the new index. In order to impute *preliminary* values to the missing observations I use data on the two original indexes (Quinn and Mody-Murshid), their lagged values, openness as measured by import tariff collections over imports, the extent of trade openness measured as imports plus exports over GDP, and GDP per capita.[12] In the third step, I use country-specific data to revise and refine the preliminary data created using the "impute" procedure discussed above. The new index covers the period 1970–2000, and has data for 163 countries (although not every country has data for every year). It is important to note that although this new index is a clear improvement over alternative indexes, it still has some shortcomings, including the fact that it does not distinguish very sharply between restrictions on capital inflows and restrictions on capital outflows.[13]

In figure 2.1 I present the evolution of the new index for six groups of countries: (a) industrial countries, (b) Latin America and the Caribbean, (c) Asia, (d) Africa, (e) the Middle East and North Africa, and (f) Eastern Europe. This figure clearly captures the fact that the degree of capital mobility has increased in every one of these six regions during the last three

12. See Aizenman and Noy (2004) on the relationship between trade account openness and capital account openness.

13. See the discussion in the preceding section for an analysis of the shortcomings of different indexes. See also Eichengreen (2001) and Edwards (1999).

decades. A comparison of the 1970–89 and 1990–2000 periods suggests that, on average, the industrial countries made the most progress in moving toward greater capital mobility; their average index went from 66.5 to 88.8. The Middle East and North African countries, on the other hand, experienced only moderate capital account liberalization. Their capital mobility index went from an average of 41.3 to 49.1. Figure 2.1 also shows that this process of financial openness has followed different patterns in the different regions. For instance, in the industrial countries it has been a relatively smooth process; in the Latin American countries, on the other hand, it is possible to see stricter capital account restrictions during the 1970s and 1980s, with an increase in the extent of capital mobility in the 1990s. In Asia, there was an increase in capital mobility during the early 1990s, followed by a somewhat abrupt imposition of controls after the 1997 crises. Since then, capital mobility has increased somewhat. Not surprisingly, Eastern Europe is the region that has experienced the greatest discrete jump in the degree of capital mobility.

As a way of gaining further insights into the evolution of capital mobility during the period 1970–2001, I used data on the new index on capital mobility to divide the sample into three equal-size groups depending on the extent of mobility. These groups have been labeled *High, Intermediate,* and *Low* mobility.[14] This three-way division of the sample clearly captures the fact that the degree of capital mobility has increased significantly during the last thirty years. In 1970, 44 percent of the observations corresponded to *Low* mobility; 26 percent to *Intermediate;* and 30 percent to *High* mobility. In the year 2000, in contrast, 24 percent of the observations corresponded to *Low* mobility; 25 percent to *Intermediate;* and 52 percent to *High* mobility. Table 2.1 contains summary data on the index of capital mobility for the *Low* and *High* mobility groups.[15] As may be seen, the mean and median values of the index are very different across groups. Indeed, a test with the equality of means indicates that the null hypothesis is rejected at a high degree of confidence (t-statistic = 136.9).

In order to illustrate which type of country belongs to each group, in table 2.2 I present a list of a subset of nations with *High* and *Low* capital mobility. These subsets focus on the extremes of the distributions and capture countries with *Very High* mobility (index value equal or higher than 87.5) and *Very Low* mobility (index value lower or equal to 12.5).[16] As may

14. Since the unit of analysis is a country-year observation, and there has been a trend toward higher capital mobility (see figure 2.1), most observations in the *High* mobility group correspond to recent country-year observations. Likewise, by construction most (but by no means all) observations in the *Low* mobility group correspond to early (1970s and 1980s) country-year observations.

15. In much (but not all) of the analysis that follows I will deal only with the *Low* and *High* restrictions groups. That is, in many of the results that follow the group of countries with *Intermediate* restrictions has been dropped.

16. These break points were selected in an arbitrary fashion.

Table 2.1 **Capital mobility index by group**

Group	Mean	Median	Standard deviation
Low capital mobility	30.0	37.5	9.9
High capital mobility	82.5	87.5	12.3

Table 2.2 **Countries with very high and very low capital mobility**

A. Very high capital mobility

1970–1979		1980–1989		1990–2000	
Bahrain	87.5	United States	95.0	Austria	87.5
The Gambia	87.5	Antigua and Barbuda	87.5	Belgium	96.6
Germany	96.3	Bahrain	87.5	Canada	100.0
Hong Kong, China	95.0	Germany	98.8	Denmark	100.0
Lebanon	87.5	Hong Kong, China	100.0	Estonia	87.5
Panama	100.0	Kuwait	87.5	Finland	95.4
Switzerland	93.8	Lebanon	87.5	France	90.9
United Arab Emirates	87.5	The Netherlands	92.5	Germany	100.0
		Panama	95.0	Guatemala	100.0
		Singapore	100.0	Hong Kong, China	100.0
		Switzerland	100.0	Ireland	93.1
		United Arab Emirates	87.5	Italy	96.6
		United Kingdom	100.0	Kuwait	87.5
		United States	100.0	Kyrgyz Republic	87.5
		Uruguay	95.0	Latvia	87.5
		Vanuatu	87.5	Lebanon	87.5
				Lithuania	87.5
				The Netherlands	100.0
				New Zealand	93.1
				Norway	100.0
				Singapore	97.7
				Sweden	87.5
				Switzerland	100.0
				United Arab Emirates	87.5
				United Kingdom	100.0
				United States	100.0
				Uruguay	93.1
				Vanuatu	87.5

B. Very low capital mobility

1970–1979		1980–1989		1990–2000	
China	0.0	Bangladesh	12.5		
Ethiopia	12.5	Iceland	12.5		
Iceland	12.5	Morocco	10.0		
Morocco	3.8	Sri Lanka	12.5		
South Africa	7.3				
Sri Lanka	12.5				

Notes: Very high capital mobility countries are those with average mobility index higher than or equal to 87.5. Very low capital mobility countries are those with average mobility index lower than or equal to 12.5.

Table 2.3   **Countries with major changes in capital mobility index**

A. *From high to low capital mobility*

1970–1974	1975–1979	1980–1984	1985–1989	1990–1994	1995–2000
	Uruguay	Barbados Grenada Haiti Mexico Nicaragua Paraguay			

B. *From low to high capital mobility*

		Australia Norway Uruguay	Portugal	Argentina Costa Rica El Salvador Grenada Hungary Mexico Paraguay Peru The Philippines Trinidad and Tobago	Colombia Ecuador Egypt Guyana Haiti Iceland Israel Jamaica Jordan Kenya Laos Mauritania Nicaragua Rwanda Uganda Zambia

Notes: Panel A shows countries with high capital mobility index in period $t - 1$ and low capital mobility index in period t. Panel B shows countries with low capital mobility index in period $t - 1$ and high capital mobility index in period t. Index is high if it is higher than 50, low if it is lower than 50.

be seen, while the number of countries with *Very High* capital mobility increased from decade to decade, the number with *Very Low* mobility declined, until in the 1990–2000 decade there were no nations with an index value below 12.5.

Finally, in table 2.3 I present a list of countries that during a five-year period experienced major changes in the extent of capital mobility. Panel A in table 2.3 lists countries that moved from *High* to *Low* mobility. As may be seen, there are relatively few nations that went through a rapid and extreme closing of the capital account. Interestingly, all cases correspond to countries in Latin America and the Caribbean, and took place during the first half of the 1980s when the region was going through the debt crisis. In panel B of table 2.3 I have listed countries that have gone through rapid capital account liberalizations—these are countries that within five years have gone from *Low* mobility all the way to *High* capital mobility—skipping, as it were, the adolescence stage of capital mobility. As may be seen, during the 1980s one emerging country (Uruguay) and three OECD countries—Australia, Norway, and Portugal—went through this rapid liberalization process. In contrast, during the 1990s an increasingly large number of emerging countries—including many in Latin America and Africa—liberalized their capital accounts rapidly.

2.4   The Anatomy of Current Account Reversals and Sudden Stops: Is There a Difference between High and Low Capital Mobility Countries?

Recent discussions on external crises have tended to focus on two related phenomena: (a) *sudden stops of capital inflows,* defined as situations in which the flow of capital coming into a country is reduced significantly in a very short period of time; and (b) *current account reversals,* or major reductions in the current account deficit that take place within a year or two.[17] In this section I analyze these two phenomena during the last thirty years, and I rely on nonparametric tests to investigate whether their incidence and main characteristics have been different for countries with *High* capital mobility and countries with *Low* mobility.

2.4.1   Incidence of Sudden Stops and Reversals

In this paper I have defined a "sudden stop" episode as an abrupt and major reduction in capital inflows to a country that up to that time had been receiving large volumes of foreign capital. More specifically, I imposed the following requirements for an episode to qualify as a sudden stop: (a) the country in question must have received an inflow of capital (relative to gross domestic product [GDP]) larger than its region's third quartile during the two years prior to the sudden stop; (b) net capital inflows must have declined by at least 5 percent of GDP in one year.[18] On the other hand, a "current account reversal"—reversal, in short—is defined as a reduction in the current account deficit of at least 4 percent of GDP in one year.[19]

17. The term "sudden stops" was introduced by Rudi Dornbusch and has been popularized by Guillermo Calvo and his associates. On sudden stops see, for example, Calvo, Izquierdo, and Mejía (2004) and Edwards (2004a, 2004b). On current account reversals see Milesi-Ferretti and Razin (2000), Edwards (2002, 2004a, 2004b) and Guidotti, Sturzenegger, and Villar (2003). See Taylor (2002) for a fascinating discussion of long-term trends in current account dynamics. On the long-term interplay between capital flows and the current account, see Obstfeld and Taylor (2004).

18. In order to check for the robustness of the results, I also used two alternative definitions of sudden stops, which considered a reduction in inflows of 3 and 7 percent of GDP in one year. Due to space considerations, however, I don't report detailed results using these definitions.

19. I also used an alternative definition. The qualitative nature of the results discussed below was not affected by the precise definition of reversals or sudden stops. See Edwards (2002).

Table 2.4   **Incidence of sudden stops**

Region	No sudden stop	Sudden stop
Industrial countries	96.3	3.7
Latin America and Caribbean	92.2	7.8
Asia	94.9	5.1
Africa	93.4	6.6
Middle East	88.7	11.3
Eastern Europe	93.7	6.4
Total	93.6	6.4
No. of observations	2,943	
Pearson		
Uncorrected χ^2 (5)	18.84	
Design-based $F(5, 14710)$	3.76	
p-value	0.002	

Table 2.5   **Incidence of current account reversals**

Region	No reversal	Reversal
Industrial countries	97.6	2.4
Latin America and Caribbean	84.0	16.0
Asia	87.9	12.1
Africa	83.4	16.6
Middle East	84.0	16.0
Eastern Europe	85.0	15.0
Total	87.2	12.8
No. of observations	2,975	
Pearson		
Uncorrected χ^2 (5)	77.88	
Design-based $F(5, 14870)$	15.57	
p-value	0.000	

Table 2.4 presents tabulation data on the incidence of sudden stops for the period under study; table 2.5 contains data on the incidence of current account reversals. In both tables I have considered six groups of countries—industrial countries, Latin America and the Caribbean, Asia, Africa, the Middle East and North Africa, and Eastern Europe. Each table also includes a Pearson test for equality of incidence across groups of countries. As may be seen, the total historical incidence of sudden stops has been 6.4 percent. Different countries, however, have experienced very different realities, with the incidence being highest in the Middle East (11.3 percent) and lowest in the industrial nations (3.7 percent). The tabulation on reversals in table 2.5 indicates that the aggregate incidence rate has been 12.8 percent; Latin America, Africa, and the Middle East have had the

highest incidence at 16 percent, and the industrial countries have had the lowest incidence at 2.4 percent.

From an analytical perspective sudden stops and reversals should be highly related phenomena. There is no reason, however, for their relationship to be one to one. Indeed, because of changes in international reserves it is perfectly possible that a country that suffers a sudden stop does not experience at the same time a current account reversal. In table 2.6 I present two-way frequency tables for the sudden stops and the current account deficit reversal, both for the complete sample and for the six regions. The table shows that for the complete sample (3,106 observations) 46.8 percent of countries subject to a sudden stop also faced a current account reversal. At the same time, 22.8 percent of those with reversals also experienced (in the same year) a sudden stop of capital inflows. The regional data show that joint incidence of reversals and sudden stops has been highest in Africa, where approximately 59.3 percent of sudden stops happened at the same time as current account reversals, and in Latin America, where 25 percent of reversals coincided with sudden stops. Notice that for every one of the regions, as well as for the complete sample, the Pearson χ^2 tests have very small p-values, indicating that the observed differences across rows and columns are significant. That is, these tests suggest that although there are observed differences across these phenomena, the two are statistically related. Interestingly, these results do not change in any significant way if different definitions of reversals and sudden stops are used, or if alternative configurations of lags and leads are considered.

2.4.2   Sudden Stops, Reversals, and Capital Controls

The tabulation results presented above on sudden stops and current account reversals (tables 2.5 and 2.6) did not group countries according to their degree of capital mobility. In table 2.7 I report the incidence of both sudden stops and current account reversals for the three categories of capital mobility defined above: *High, Intermediate,* and *Low* capital mobility. The table also presents the p-values for Pearson tests on the equality of incidence across regions, as well as t-statistics (and their p-values) on the equality of incidence under *High* mobility and *Low* mobility on the one hand, and equality of incidence under *High* mobility and *Intermediate* mobility, on the other hand (these tests are presented at both the country-group and aggregate levels). The results obtained may be summarized as follows:

- For the complete sample, the incidence of current account reversals is significantly lower for countries with *High* capital mobility than for countries with either *Intermediate* or *Low* mobility. This aggregate result is somewhat deceiving, however, since there are marked differ-

Table 2.6   **Incidence of current account reversals and sudden stops**

	All countries: Sudden stop		
Reversal	0	1	Total
0	2,587	107	2,694
	96.0	4.0	100.0
	89.1	53.2	86.7
1	318	94	412
	77.2	22.8	100.0
	11.0	46.8	13.3
Total	2,905	201	3,106
	93.5	6.5	100.0
	100	100	100
Pearson χ^2 (1)		209.65	
p-value		0.000	

	Industrial countries: Sudden stop			Latin America: Sudden stop		
	0	1	Total	0	1	Total
0	552	19	571	605	24	629
	96.7	3.3	100.0	96.2	3.8	100.0
	98.2	82.6	97.6	87.1	44.4	84.0
1	10	4	14	90	30	120
	71.4	28.6	100.0	75.0	25.0	100.0
	1.8	17.4	2.4	13.0	55.6	16.0
Total	562	23	585	695	54	749
	96.1	3.9	100.0	92.8	7.2	100.0
	100	100	100	100	100	100
Pearson χ^2 (1)		23.06			67.60	
p-value		0.000			0.000	

	Asia: Sudden stop			Africa: Sudden stop		
	0	1	Total	0	1	Total
0	328	12	340	689	22	711
	96.5	3.5	100.0	96.9	3.1	100.0
	87.7	60.0	86.3	85.2	40.7	82.4
1	46	8	54	120	32	152
	85.2	14.8	100.0	79.0	21.1	100.0
	12.3	40.0	13.7	14.8	59.3	17.6
Total	374	20	394	809	54	863
	94.9	5.1	100.0	93.7	6.3	100.0
	100	100	100	100	100	100
Pearson χ^2 (1)		12.32			68.85	
p-value		0.001			0.000	

(*continued*)

Table 2.6   (continued)

	Middle East: Sudden stop			Eastern Europe: Sudden stop		
	0	1	Total	0	1	Total
0	185	13	198	195	11	206
	93.4	6.6	100.0	94.7	5.3	100.0
	88.5	54.2	85.0	89.9	64.7	88.0
1	24	11	35	22	6	28
	68.6	31.4	100.0	78.6	21.4	100.0
	11.5	45.8	15.0	10.1	35.3	12.0
Total	209	24	233	217	17	234
	89.7	10.3	100.0	92.7	7.3	100.0
	100	100	100	100	100	100
Pearson χ^2 (1)		19.90			9.47	
p-value		0.000			0.002	

ences in incidence across groups of countries.[20] As may be seen from table 2.7, for industrial countries the incidence of reversals has been significantly smaller in countries with *High* mobility. In Asia, on the other hand, countries with *Low* mobility have had a significantly lower incidence of reversals than nations with *High* capital mobility. For the rest of the country groups there are no statistical differences in the incidence of reversals across degrees of capital mobility.

- For sudden stops, the results for the complete sample suggest that there are no statistical differences in incidence across countries with different degrees of capital mobility. At the country-group levels there are some differences, however. For industrial countries the incidence of sudden stops is smaller under *High* capital mobility; the opposite is true for the Asian and Eastern European countries. The *t*-statistics in table 2.7 indicate that for Latin America, Africa, and the Middle East there are no statistical differences in the incidence of sudden stops according to the degree of capital mobility.

The results presented in table 2.7 were obtained when the contemporaneous value of the index was used to classify countries as having a *High, Intermediate,* or *Low* degree of capital mobility. It is possible to argue, however, that what matters is not the degree of capital mobility in a particular year but the policy stance on capital mobility in the medium term. In order to investigate whether an alternative classification makes a difference, I reclassified countries as *High, Intermediate,* and *Low* capital mobility using the average value in the index in the previous five years. The results obtained are reported in table 2.8; as may be seen, the results are very similar to those reported in table 2.7.

20. Indeed, according to the Pearson test the null hypothesis of equality of incidence across country-group categories is strongly rejected.

Table 2.7 Incidence of current account reversals and sudden stops by categories of capital mobility (one-year average for capital mobility index)

	Current account reversals			t-test		Sudden stops			t-test	
	High	Intermediate	Low	H = I	H = L	High	Intermediate	Low	H = I	H = L
Industrial countries	1.1	3.5	16.7	1.71	6.40**	2.3	7.9	11.1	2.72**	3.01**
Latin America	14.6	18.2	15.9	1.04	0.44	7.2	7.1	8.9	0.05	0.72
Asia	16.1	18.0	7.3	0.35	2.65**	11.7	4.1	1.1	1.85	4.22**
Africa	14.3	19.7	15.0	1.31	0.18	5.9	8.1	5.5	0.80	0.16
Middle East	13.8	11.4	20.3	0.40	1.12	11.5	6.8	13.7	0.84	0.42
Eastern Europe	14.0	24.4	5.1	1.24	1.34	14.3	4.7	0.0	1.52	2.58**
Total	9.1	17.1	13.7	5.27**	3.45**	6.1	7.2	6.2	0.91	0.03
p-value	0.000	0.007	0.012			0.000	0.846	0.000		

Note: t-tests reported are absolute values.

**Significant at the 5 percent level.

Table 2.8   Incidence of current account reversals and sudden stops by categories of capital mobility (five-year average for capital mobility index)

	Current account reversals			t-test		Sudden stops			t-test	
	High	Intermediate	Low	H = I	H = L	High	Intermediate	Low	H = I	H = L
Industrial countries	1.0	3.4	18.8	1.91	6.86*	2.4	5.8	12.5	1.89	3.19*
Latin America	14.9	16.0	14.8	0.32	0.03	7.7	7.9	7.7	0.06	0.01
Asia	15.3	21.5	5.6	1.17	2.96*	11.9	6.7	0.6	1.23	4.51*
Africa	12.8	19.4	15.0	1.49	0.54	5.6	8.1	5.6	0.79	0.00
Middle East	15.1	8.5	22.8	1.19	1.16	12.7	8.5	12.5	0.77	0.03
Eastern Europe	10.0	18.8	0.0	0.58	1.65	20.0	6.3	3.7	1.05	1.63
Total	8.7	15.9	13.1	4.82*	3.07*	6.2	7.6	5.7	1.18	0.43
p-value	0.000	0.001	0.001			0.000	0.972	0.003		

Note: t-tests reported are absolute values.

**Significant at the 5 percent level.

2.4.3   Banking Crises

In this subsection I investigate whether sudden stops and current account reversals have historically been related to banking crises. A number of authors have argued that one of the costliest effects of external shocks is that they tend to generate banking crises and collapses. Most analyses on this subject have focused on the joint occurrence of devaluation crises and banking crises; see, for example, the discussion in Kaminsky and Reinhart (1999). In this subsection I take a slightly different approach, and I investigate whether sudden stops and major current account deficits—not all of which end up in devaluation crises, as established in Edwards (2004b)—have been associated with banking crises. I address this issue in tables 2.9 and 2.10, where I present two-way tabulations for current account reversals and a dummy variable that takes the value of 1 if in that year there has

Table 2.9   **Banking crises and current account reversals**

Reversal	Total sample: Banking crisis			High mobility: Banking crisis		
	0	1	Total	0	1	Total
0	2,443	118	2,561	956	59	1,015
	95.4	4.6	100.0	94.2	5.8	100.0
	87.1	86.1	87.0	90.7	92.2	90.8
1	363	19	382	98	5	103
	95.0	5.0	100.0	95.2	4.9	100.0
	12.9	13.9	13.0	9.3	7.8	9.2
Total	2,806	137	2,943	1,054	64	1,118
	95.3	4.7	100.0	94.3	5.7	100.0
	100.0	100.0	100.0	100.0	100.0	100.0
Pearson χ^2 (1)		0.10			0.16	
p-value		0.75			0.91	

	Intermediate mobility: Banking crisis			Low mobility: Banking crisis		
	0	1	Total	0	1	Total
0	608	22	630	879	37	916
	96.5	3.5	100.0	96.0	4.0	100.0
	83.0	75.9	82.7	86.3	84.1	86.2
1	125	7	132	140	7	147
	94.7	5.3	100.0	95.2	4.8	100.0
	17.1	24.1	17.3	13.7	15.9	13.8
Total	733	29	762	1019	44	1063
	96.2	3.8	100.0	95.9	4.1	100.0
	100.0	100.0	100.0	100.0	100.0	100.0
Pearson χ^2 (1)		0.98			0.17	
p-value		0.32			0.68	

Table 2.10   Banking crises and sudden stops

	Total sample: Banking crisis			High mobility: Banking crisis		
Sudden stop	0	1	Total	0	1	Total
0	2,587	128	2,715	980	59	1,039
	95.3	4.7	100.0	94.3	5.7	100.0
	93.4	93.4	93.4	93.6	92.2	93.5
1	182	9	191	67	5	72
	95.3	4.7	100.0	93.1	6.9	100.0
	6.6	6.6	6.6	6.4	7.8	6.5
Total	2,769	137	2,906	1,047	64	1,111
	95.3	4.7	100.0	94.2	5.8	100.0
	100.0	100.0	100.0	100.0	100.0	100.0
Pearson χ^2 (1)		0.00			0.20	
p-value		0.99			0.66	

	Intermediate mobility: Banking crisis			Low mobility: Banking crisis		
	0	1	Total	0	1	Total
0	688	28	716	919	41	960
	96.1	3.9	100.0	95.7	4.3	100.0
	92.7	96.6	92.9	93.8	93.2	93.8
1	54	1	55	61	3	64
	98.2	1.8	100.0	95.3	4.7	100.0
	7.3	3.5	7.1	6.2	6.8	6.3
Total	742	29	771	980	44	1024
	96.2	3.8	100.0	95.7	4.3	100.0
	100.0	100.0	100.0	100.0	100.0	100.0
Pearson χ^2 (1)		0.62			0.03	
p-value		0.43			0.87	

been a banking crisis (table 2.9), and for sudden stops and banking crises (table 2.10).[21] All panels in table 2.9 (see, in particular, the Pearson χ^2 tests for independence of rows and columns) show that there has not been a significant relationship between reversals and major banking crises. Interestingly, this is the case for all three capital mobility groups.

The results in table 2.10 refer to sudden stops and banking crises, and are very similar. They indicate that there has been no significant relationship—at any level of capital mobility—between sudden stops and banking crises (see the Pearson χ^2 tests for independence of rows and columns). It is important to note that this is the case independent of the lag-lead structure considered. In sum, the results reported in tables 2.9 and 2.10 indicate that,

21. The data on banking crises are from Glick and Hutchison (1999). When an alternative definition of reversals is used the results are similar to those reported in this section.

contrary to what some critics of capital account liberalization have argued, higher capital mobility has not been associated with a higher occurrence of banking crises; banking crises have occurred at the same rate in countries with *High, Intermediate,* and *Low* capital mobility.[22]

2.5 Capital Controls and the Costs of External Crises

According to the analysis presented in the preceding section, there is no clear evidence supporting the view that Low capital mobility countries— that is, countries that impose heavy restrictions (or controls) on the mobility of capital—have a significantly lower incidence of sudden stops or current account reversals. In this section I take the analysis a step further and investigate whether current account reversals and sudden stops have historically had significant costs in terms of lower GDP growth. More important in terms of the current paper, I analyze whether the (potential) costs of sudden stops and reversals have been different in countries with different degrees of capital mobility.

The section is organized as follows: I first present a preliminary analysis, where I compare growth before and after sudden stops and current account reversal episodes, for countries with different degrees of capital mobility. I then present results obtained from an econometric analysis that estimates jointly—using treatment regressions—the probability of having a crisis and the effect of the crisis on GDP growth. As pointed out, the main interest in this analysis is to determine whether the extent of capital mobility plays a role in explaining countries' propensity to having crises, and the costs associated with crises.

2.5.1 Sudden Stops, Current Account Reversals, Capital Controls, and Growth: A Preliminary Analysis

In table 2.11 I present a before-and-after analysis of GDP per capita growth for sudden stops and reversals. This analysis has been done for all countries, as well as for countries grouped according to their degree of capital mobility. The "before" data correspond to average GDP per capita growth during the *three years* before the crisis. I have computed two "after" rates of growth: (a) the year of the crisis, and (b) the average during three years after the crisis. Panel A in table 2.11 contains the results for one year after the crisis; panel B contains results for three years after the crisis. The first four columns in both panels of table 2.11 contain the average difference in the rate of growth per capita after and before the crisis. Column (1) is for all countries; columns (2) through (4) are for countries with *High, In-*

---

22. I also analyzed the incidence of sudden stops, current account reversals, and IMF programs. The results obtained indicate that there is no relationship between sudden stops and reversals on the one hand, and IMF programs on the other.

Table 2.11   GDP per capita growth: Before and after

Event	All (1)	High (2)	Intermediate (3)	Low (4)	High – Intermediate (5)	High – Low (6)
			A. Results for one year after crisis			
Reversal	-0.37	-0.54	0.75	-1.21	-1.29	0.67
	(1.07)	(0.71)	(1.54)	(2.18)**	(1.44)	(0.71)
Sudden stop	-0.88	-1.29	0.08	-1.27	-1.37	-0.02
	(1.84)	(1.60)	(0.09)	(1.52)	(1.17)	(0.02)
			B. Results for three years after crisis			
Reversal	-0.09	-0.25	0.75	-0.69	-1.00	0.44
	(0.34)	(0.51)	(2.12)**	(1.54)	(1.66)	(0.66)
Sudden stop	-0.61	-0.31	0.19	-1.55	-0.50	1.24
	(1.64)	(0.58)	(0.31)	(2.11)**	(0.62)	(1.36)

Notes: The "before" data correspond to average GDP per capita growth during the three years before the crisis. In panel A, "after" rate of growth is for year of the crisis. In panel B, "after" is average growth rate during three years after the crisis. *t*-tests reported (in parentheses) are absolute values.
**Significant at the 5 percent level.

termediate, and *Low* capital mobility. The numbers in parentheses are *t*-statistics for the null hypothesis that the "before" and "after" rates of growth are equal. The final two columns, columns (5) and (6), are difference-in-difference columns, which report the difference in the before and after growth rates for High and Intermediate and High and Low capital mobility; that is, the number in column (5) is equal to column (2) minus column (3). The number in parentheses is for the null hypothesis that this difference-in-difference is equal to zero.

As may be seen from table 2.11, these preliminary results suggest that, generally speaking, there are no significant differences in growth before and after the crises; this is the case for all categories of capital mobility. Notice that only three out of the twenty-four *t*-statistics in table 2.11 are significant at conventional levels. As emphasized above, however, these results are only preliminary, since no attempt has been made to control for other factors or to incorporate the determinants of the probability of a crisis.[23] In the subsection that follows I deal with these issues by using a treatment regression methodology.

2.5.2   An Econometric Analysis

In this subsection I present results from an econometric analysis that deals with two questions: (a) does a higher degree of capital mobility increase the probability of a crisis (defined as a sudden stop or as a current

23. Hong and Tornell (2005), however, have used a similar methodology and found that there are growth effects of crises. Their definition of crisis, however, is different from the two definitions I have used here.

account reversal), and (b) does the degree of capital mobility affect the cost of crises once they occur? The discussion proceeds as follows: I first present a simple analysis on the effects of sudden stops and current account reversals on growth (the following subsection); I then present results from the joint estimation of crises' probabilities and dynamics of growth equations (the succeeding subsection).

Growth Effects of Sudden Stops and Current Account Reversals: Preliminary Econometric Results

As in Edwards and Levy Yeyati (2005), the point of departure of the empirical analysis is a two-equation formulation for the *dynamics* of real GDP per capita growth of country *j* in period *t*. Equation (1) is the long-run GDP growth equation, while equation (2) captures the growth dynamics process.

(1) $g_j^* = \alpha + X_j \beta + R_j \theta + \omega_j.$

(2) $\Delta g_{tj} = \lambda(g_j^* - g_{t-1,j}) + \varphi v_{t,j} + \gamma u_{t,j} + \xi_{t,j}.$

I have used the following notation: g_j^* is the long-run rate of real per capita GDP growth in country *j*; X_j is a vector of structural, institutional, and policy variables that determine long-run growth; R_j is a vector of regional dummies; α, β, and θ are parameters; and ω_j is an error term assumed to be heteroskedastic. In equation (2), $g_{t,j}$ is the rate of growth of per capita GDP in country *j* in period *t*. The terms $v_{t,j}$ and $u_{t,j}$ are shocks, assumed to have zero mean, to have finite variance, and to be uncorrelated among them. More specifically, $v_{t,j}$ is assumed to be an external terms-of-trade shock, while $u_{t,j}$ captures other shocks, including sudden stops and current account reversals. $\xi_{t,j}$ is an error term, which is assumed to be heteroskedastic (see equation [3] below for details), and λ, φ, and γ are parameters that determine the particular characteristics of the growth process. Equation (2), which has the form of an equilibrium correction model (ECM), states that the actual rate of growth in period *t* will deviate from the long-run rate of growth due to the existence of three types of shocks: $v_{t,j}$, $u_{t,j}$ and $\xi_{t,j}$. Over time, however, the actual rate of growth will tend to converge toward its long-run value, with the rate of convergence given by λ. Parameter φ, in equation (2), is expected to be positive, indicating that an improvement in the terms of trade will result in a (temporary) acceleration in the rate of growth, and that negative terms-of-trade shocks are expected to have a negative effect on $g_{t,j}$.[24] The main interest from the perspective of the current paper is whether *sudden stops* and *current account reversals* have a negative effect on growth; that is, whether coefficient γ is significantly negative. In the actual estimation of equation (1), I used

24. See Edwards and Levy Yeyati (2005) for details.

Table 2.12   Current account reversals, sudden stops, and growth (GLS estimates)

	Eq. (1) R.E.	Eq. (2) F.E.	Eq. (3) R.E.	Eq. (4) F.E.	Eq. (5) R.E.	Eq. (6) F.E.
Constant	−0.15	−0.14	−0.27	−0.25	−0.14	−0.10
	(1.16)	(1.41)	(2.62)***	(2.44)**	(1.32)	(0.97)
Growth gap	0.82	0.86	0.81	0.87	0.82	0.88
	(42.10)***	(42.73)***	(40.18)***	(41.62)***	(40.76)***	(42.28)***
Change in terms of trade	0.06	0.07	0.07	0.07	0.08	0.08
	(12.65)***	(12.19)***	(11.31)***	(10.74)***	(12.18)***	(11.75)***
Reversal	−2.01	−2.10			−1.80	−1.97
	(6.64)***	(6.72)***			(5.50)***	(5.82)***
Sudden stop			−1.23	−1.25	−0.54	−0.60
			(2.82)***	(2.77)***	(1.19)	(1.31)
No. of observations	1,821	1,821	1,641	1,641	1,635	1,635
Countries	90	90	81	81	81	81
R^2	0.49	0.49	0.51	0.51	0.52	0.52

Notes: R.E. = random effect; F.E. = fixed effect; t-tests reported (in parentheses) are absolute values; country-specific dummies are included, but not reported.
***Significant at the 1 percent level.
**Significant at the 5 percent level.

dummy variables for sudden stops and reversals. An important question, and one that is addressed in detail in the subsection that follows, is whether the effects of different shocks on growth are different for countries with different degrees of capital mobility.

The system in equations (1) and (2) was estimated using a two-step procedure. In the first step I estimate the long-run growth equation (1) using a cross-country data set. These data are averages for 1974–2000, and the estimation makes a correction for heteroskedasticity. These first-stage estimates are then used to generate long-run predicted growth rates to replace g_j^* in the equilibrium error correction model in equation (2). In the second step, I estimated equation (2) using a generalized least squares (GLS) procedure for unbalanced panels; I used both random effects and fixed effects estimation procedures. The data set covers 157 countries, for the 1970–2000 period; not every country has data for every year, however. See the appendix for exact data definition and data sources.

The results from the first-step estimation of equation (1) are not reported due to space considerations.[25] Table 2.12 presents the results from the

25. In estimating equation (1) for long-run per capita growth, I follow the now standard literature on growth, as summarized by Barro and Sala-i-Martin (1995), and use average data for 1974–2000. In terms of the equation specification, I include the following covariates: the log of initial GDP per capita; the investment ratio; the coverage of secondary education; an index of the degree of openness of the economy; the ratio of government consumption relative to GDP; and regional dummies for Latin American, sub-Saharan Africa, and transition economies. The results are quite standard and support what has become the received wisdom on the empirical determinants of long-term growth.

second-step estimation of the growth dynamics equation (2). The first two equations refer to current account reversals, while the next two equations focus on sudden stops. Finally, in the table's equations (5) and (6) I included both the sudden stops and the reversals variables as regressors.

The estimated coefficient of $(g_j^* - g_{t-1,j})$ is, as expected, positive, significant, and smaller than 1. The point estimates are on the high side—between 0.81 and 0.88—suggesting that, on average, deviations between long-run and actual growth get eliminated rather quickly. For instance, according to equation (1) in table 2.12, after three years approximately 90 percent of a unitary shock to real GDP growth per capita will be eliminated. Also, as expected, the estimated coefficients of the terms-of-trade shock are always positive and statistically significant, indicating that an improvement (deterioration) in the terms of trade results in an acceleration (deceleration) in the rate of growth of real per capita GDP. As may be seen from equations (1) and (2) in the table, the coefficient of the current account reversals variable is significantly negative, indicating that reversals result in a deceleration of growth. The point estimate is –2.01, indicating that, with other things given, a reversal has on average resulted in a 2 percent reduction in short-term growth on average. The results from equations (3) and (4) in the table refer to sudden stops. They show that the estimated coefficients of the sudden-stop dummies are significantly negative, with a point estimate that ranges from –1.23 to –1.25. This suggests that while sudden stops also have a negative effect on per capita growth, their impact on growth has not been as severe as the impact of reversal episodes.

The results in the table 2.12 equations (5) and (6), where both the current account reversals and the sudden-stop dummies have been included, are particularly interesting: while the reversal dummies continue to be significantly negative, the coefficient for the sudden-stop dummy is not significant any longer. This suggests that what is costly—in terms of lower GDP per capita growth—is *not* a sudden stop per se. Indeed, according to these results, what is costly in terms of lower growth is a current account reversal. This is an important finding, since it suggests that countries that experience a sudden stop but are able to avoid a current account reversal, through the use of international reserves, will not face a significant decline in growth. Moreover, this result suggests that sudden stops have an indirect (negative) effect on growth. According to this conjecture, the occurrence of a sudden stop increases the probability of a current account reversal. The reversal, in turn, will have a negative impact on GDP per capita growth. I formally investigate this hypothesis in the subsection that follows.

Joint Estimation

I use a treatment effects model to estimate jointly an equation on real GDP growth and a probit equation on the probability that a country experiences a current account reversal. The base empirical treatment effects model is as follows:

(1′) $g_j^* = \alpha + \mathbf{X}_j\beta + \mathbf{R}_j\theta + \omega_j.$

(2′) $\Delta g_{t,j} = \lambda(g_j^* - g_{t-1,j}) + \varphi v_{t,j} + \gamma u_{t,j} + \theta(u_{t,j} \times \text{Openness}_{t,j}) + \xi_{t,j}.$

(3) $u_{t,j} = \begin{cases} 1 & \text{if } u_{t,j}^* > 0 \\ 0 & \text{otherwise} \end{cases}$

(4) $u_{t,j}^* = \mathbf{W}_{j,t}\alpha + \varepsilon_{j,t}.$

As before, equation (1′) is the long-term real growth equation, and equation (2′) is the growth dynamics equation, with $u_{j,j}$ a dummy variable (i.e., the treatment variable) that takes a value of one if country j in period t experienced a current account reversal, and zero if the country did not experience reversal. Accordingly, γ is the parameter of interest: the effect of the treatment on the outcome. Finally, the product $u_{t,j} \times \text{Openness}_{t,j}$ interacts $u_{t,j}$ with a measure of openness. The coefficient of this interactive variable θ will capture the effect of openness on the transmission of external shocks on growth. In the estimation I used two alternative measures of openness: the index of capital account openness presented in section 2.3 of this paper, and a measure of trade openness (defined as the ratio of exports plus imports over GDP).

According to equation (3), whether the country experiences a current account reversal is assumed to be the result of an unobserved latent variable $u_{j,t}^*$—which in turn is assumed to depend linearly on vector $\mathbf{W}_{j,t}$. In the estimation, one of the $\mathbf{W}_{j,t}$ variables is the degree of capital mobility, or financial openness. Some of the variables in $\mathbf{W}_{j,t}$ may be included in $\mathbf{X}_{j,t}$.[26] β and α are parameter vectors to be estimated; $\xi_{j,t}$ and $\varepsilon_{j,t}$ are error terms assumed to be bivariate normal, with a zero mean and a covariance matrix given by

(5) $$\begin{pmatrix} \sigma & \psi \\ \psi & 1 \end{pmatrix}$$

If equations (2′) and (3) are independent, the covariance term ψ in equation (5) will be zero. Under most plausible conditions, however, it is likely that this covariance term will be different from zero (see Wooldridge 2002 for details). The model in equations (1′)–(5) will satisfy the consistency and identifying conditions of mixed models with latent variables if the outcome variable $y_{j,t}$ is not a determinant of the treatment equation—that is, if y is

---

26. For details on the identification requirements for this type of models see, for example, Wooldridge (2002).

not one of the variables in **W** in equation (4).[27] As is clear in the discussion that follows, in the estimation of the model in equations (1′)–(5) we impose a number of exclusionary restrictions; that is, a number of variables in vector $\mathbf{W}_{j,t}$ are not included in vector $\mathbf{X}_{j,t}$.

The system in equations (1′)–(5) was estimated using a three-step procedure. The first step consists of estimating the long-run growth equation [1′]). The results from this estimation are used to compute the growth gap term $(g_j^* - g_{t-1,j})$. In the second step the treatment equation on the probability of having a current account reversal is estimated using a probit procedure. From this estimation a hazard is obtained for each j, t observation. In the third step, the outcome equation (2′) is estimated with the hazard added as an additional covariate; in this third step the outcome equation is estimated using fixed effects. From the residuals of this augmented outcome regression, it is possible to compute consistent estimates of the variance-covariance matrix, equation (4). (See Maddala 1983 and Wooldridge 2002 for details.)

The Treatment Equation. Following work by Frankel and Rose (1996), Milesi-Ferretti and Razin (2000), and Edwards (2002), among others, in the estimation of the first treatment (probit) I included the following covariates:

- The index of capital mobility discussed in section 2.3. If, as critics of capital mobility have argued, greater mobility increases countries' vulnerability to crises, the estimated coefficient should be significantly positive.
- The ratio of the current account deficit to GDP lagged one and two periods. It is expected that, with other things given, countries with a larger current account deficit will have a higher probability of experiencing a reversal. The best results were obtained when the one-year lagged deficit was included.
- A sudden-stop dummy that takes the value of one if the country in question has experienced a sudden stop in that particular year. Its coefficient is expected to be positive.
- An index that measures the relative occurrence of sudden stops in the country's region (excluding the country itself) during that particular year. This variable captures the effect of "regional contagion"; its coefficient is expected to be positive.
- The one-year lagged external debt–GDP ratio. Its coefficient is expected to be positive.
- An index that measures whether the country in question has been subject to a banking crisis during the year in question. Its coefficient will

27. Details on identification and consistency of models with mixed structures can be found in Maddala (1983). See also Heckman (1978) and Angrist (2000).

measure the extent to which banking and external (i.e., current account) reversals have tended to occur jointly.

- The ratio of net international reserves to GDP, lagged one year. Its coefficient is expected to be negative, indicating that, with other things given, countries with a higher stock of reserves have a lower probability of experiencing a current account reversal.
- Short-term (less than one-year maturity) external debt as a proportion of external debt, lagged one period. Its coefficient is expected to be positive.
- The one-year lagged rate of growth of domestic credit. Its coefficient is expected to be positive.
- The lagged ratio of external debt service to exports. Again, its coefficient is expected to be positive.
- The country's initial GDP per capita (in logs).
- Country fixed effect dummies.

In some of the probit regressions I also included an index that measures the extent of dollarization in the country in question. Also, in some specifications I included the ratio of foreign direct investment (FDI) to GDP, and the public-sector deficit (both lagged). Their coefficients were not significant, however. Since these three variables were available for a smaller number of observations than the other variables, they were not included in the final specification of the probit equations reported in this section.

In table 2.13 I summarize the basic results obtained from the estimation of number of treatment models for GDP growth (the coefficients of the country-specific fixed effect variables are not reported due to space considerations). The table contains two panels. Panel A includes the results from the growth outcome equation (2'); panel B contains the estimates for the treatment equation, or probit equation on the probability of experiencing a current account reversal. As pointed out above, the *treatment observations* correspond to current account reversal episodes, and the untreated group is comprised of all country-year observations where there have been no reversals.[28] Table 2.13 also includes the estimated coefficient of the hazard variable in the third-step estimation, as well as the estimated elements of the variance-covariance matrix, equation (5).

Probability of Experiencing a Current Account Reversal. The probit estimates are presented in panel B of table 2.13. I discuss first the results in equations (1) and (2), since they were estimated over a larger sample. As may be seen, the results are similar across models and are quite satisfactory. Most of the coefficients have the expected signs, and many of them are sta-

---

28. Naturally, countries and time periods included in the analysis are determined by data availability. For many countries there are no data on the (potential) determinants of the probability of a current account reversal, including data on external debt and its characteristics.

Table 2.13   **Growth, current account reversals, and sudden stops: Treatment effects model (three-step estimates)**

Variable	Eq. (1)	Eq. (2)	Eq. (3)
A. Results from growth equation			
Growth gap	0.87	0.87	0.86
	(32.63)***	(32.66)***	(25.76)***
Terms of trade	0.07	0.07	0.07
	(8.48)***	(8.43)***	(6.47)***
Reversal	−5.35	−3.93	−6.72
	(4.83)***	(2.86)***	(3.69)***
Reversal · openness	0.02	0.02	0.01
	(2.22)**	(2.38)**	(0.97)
Reversal · capital mobility		−0.03*	−0.005
		(1.70)	(0.19)
B. Results from treatment equation			
Capital mobility (−1)	−0.007	−0.007	−0.008
	(1.47)	(1.48)	(1.56)
Current account deficit to GDP (−1)	0.10	0.10	0.11
	(8.16)***	(8.16)***	(5.93)**
Sudden stop	0.67	0.67	0.63
	(3.09)***	(3.08)***	(2.26)**
Sudden stops in region	1.34	1.34	1.09
	(2.08)**	(2.08)**	(1.43)
Reserves to GDP (−1)	−16.95	−16.85	−5.47
	(1.87)*	(1.86)*	(0.40)
Domestic credit growth (−1)	0.0002	0.0002	0.0002
	(1.33)	(1.33)	(1.12)
Banking crisis	0.19	0.18	0.16
	(0.79)	(0.76)	(0.63)
External debt to GDP (−1)	0.004	0.004	0.004
	(2.11)**	(2.11)**	(1.47)
Short-term debt (−1)	−0.007	−0.007	−0.0001
	(0.75)	(0.77)	(0.00)
Debt services (−1)	−0.002	−0.002	−0.001
	(0.37)	(0.36)	(0.18)
Initial GDP per capita	−0.01	−0.01	−0.81
	(0.05)	(0.05)	(2.97)***
Dollarization			0.24
			(5.14)***
Hazard lambda	1.18	1.23	1.85
	(2.45)**	(2.56)**	(2.85)***
Rho	0.29	0.30	0.45
Sigma	4.11	4.11	4.11
Wald χ^2 (215)	1,190.70	1,190.74	786.2
No. of observations	1,071	1,069	647

Notes: Absolute values of z-statistics are reported in parentheses; (−1) denotes a one-period lagged variable; country-specific dummies are included but not reported.
***Significant at the 1 percent level.
**Significant at the 5 percent level.
*Significant at the 10 percent level.

tistically significant at conventional levels. A particularly interesting result is that in every equation the estimated coefficient of the capital mobility index was negative (although it was not significant at conventional levels). This was also the case when lagged values of this index were included in the estimation. These results suggest that, contrary to what has been argued by the critics of financial liberalization, a greater degree of capital account openness has not increased the degree of vulnerability in the world economy. If anything, these results provide some (preliminary and weak) evidence suggesting that countries with a higher degree of capital mobility have had a lower probability of experiencing a current account reversal. The results in panel B of table 2.13 also indicate that the probability of experiencing a reversal is higher for countries with a large (lagged) current account deficit and a high external debt ratio. Countries that have experienced a sudden stop also have a high probability of a current account reversal, as do countries that are in a region where many countries experience a sudden stop (i.e., there is evidence of regional contagion). The coefficient of net international reserves is negative, as expected, and it is significant at the 10 percent level in equations (1) and (2). The coefficients of the short-term debt and total debt service have the expected signs but tend not to be significant. The coefficients of initial GDP per capita are negative but not significant. Overall, when different lag structures of the regressors were considered, the nature of the results did not change.

An important policy issue has to do with the effects of dollarization and dollarized liabilities on macroeconomic vulnerability and on the costs of crises. If, as argued by Calvo, Izquierdo, and Talvi (2003), countries with dollarized financial systems are particularly vulnerable to external shocks, one would expect that dollarization would positively affect the probability of facing a reversal. Unfortunately, there are no extensive data sets on dollarization across countries and time. It is possible, however, to use a more limited data set—limited in terms of both year and country coverage—to further investigate this issue. I use the data set recently assembled by Reinhart, Rogoff, and Savastano (2003) that covers 117 countries for the period 1996–2001. This index goes from 1 to 30, with higher numbers indicating higher degrees of dollarization. The results obtained when this index is included in the treatment regression are reported in equation (3) of table 2.13. As may be seen, the estimated coefficient is positive and significant, indicating that a higher degree of dollarization increases the probability of a country experiencing a current account reversal.[29] This result supports findings by Edwards (2004b) and Calvo, Izquierdo, and Mejía (2004). Notice, however, that due to the limited nature of the dollarization data, the

---

29. The Reinhart, Rogoff, and Savastano (2003) dollarization index refers only to the period 1996–2002. I have assumed, however, that the extent of dollarization detected by Reinhart et al. applies to the 1976–2000 period. For this reason the results reported here should be taken with a grain of salt.

number of observations in regression (3) is significantly smaller than in the original regressions.

GDP Growth Models. The results from the estimation of the growth equation are reported in panel A of table 2.13. I discuss first the results from the first two equations that exclude the dollarization variable. As may be seen, the coefficient for the growth gap variable is significantly positive and smaller than one, as expected. The point estimates are similar to those reported in table 2.12. Also, as in table 2.12 the coefficients of the terms-of-trade shocks are significantly positive. The coefficient of the current account reversal variable is significantly negative, indicating that a current account reversal has a negative effect on growth.

Interestingly, in both equations (1) and (2) of table 2.13 the coefficient of the variable that interacts the reversal dummy and an index of trade openness are significantly positive. This means that the less open the country is to trade, the *higher* will be the cost of a current account reversal, in terms of lower growth. These results are consistent with a number of open economy macroeconomic models, which postulate that the costs of foreign shocks—including the costs of current account reversals—are inversely proportional to the country's degree of openness. In the Mundell-Fleming type of models, for example, the *expenditure reducing* effort, for any given level of expenditure switching, is inversely proportional to the marginal propensity to import. Recently, Calvo, Izquierdo, and Talvi (2003) developed a model where sudden stops result in abrupt current account reversals and in major real exchange rate depreciations. Depreciations, in turn, are contractionary, with the extent of the contraction depending inversely on the degree of trade openness of the economy. They argue that sudden stops and current account reversals will have a greater impact in closed economies, such as Argentina, than in more open ones, such as Chile.

In order to investigate how the degree of capital mobility affects the cost of an external crisis characterized by a current account reversal, in equation (2) of table 2.13 I also included a variable that interacts the current account reversal with the capital mobility index. As may be seen, the estimated coefficient is negative and significant at the 10 percent level. According to these results the growth effects of a reversal are given by the following expression:

(6)   Growth effect $= -3.93 + 0.02 \times$ Trade openness

$- 0.03 \times$ Capital mobility.

This means that, with other things given, the decline in GDP per capita growth will be more pronounced in a country with a higher degree of capital mobility that in one with a lower degree of capital mobility. Consider, for example, the case of two countries that have the same degree of trade openness—say, 60 percent. Assume further that while one country has a low degree of capital mobility (an index of 25), the other country has a high degree of mobility (index of 90). According to equation (6) the country with low capital mobility will experience a decline in growth of 3.48 percent as a consequence of the reversal. The country with high mobility, on the other hand, will experience a decline in growth of 5.43 percent.

Finally, in equation (3) of table 2.13 I included a dollarization index in the treatment equation. As discussed earlier, the estimated coefficient is positive and significant, indicating that countries with a higher degree of dollarization have a higher probability of experiencing a reversal. Notice that in the outcome equation on GDP growth, equation (3), the reversal coefficient is still significantly negative. The coefficients of the two interactive variables (reversal and trade openness, and reversal and capital mobility) are not significant any longer. This, however, is likely to be the result of using a much smaller and restricted data set than in the two base equations.

To summarize, the results reported in this section indicate that current account reversals are costly, in the sense that they result in a (temporary) reduction in GDP per capita growth. Notice that this contrasts with results reported by Milesi-Ferretti and Razin (2000), who argued that "reversals . . . are not systematically associated with a growth slowdown" (p. 303). The results reported in this paper also indicate that it is the reversals that are costly; once reversals are introduced into the analysis, the coefficient of sudden stops is not significant in the growth dynamics equations. The regression results reported in table 2.13 also indicate that the degree of capital mobility does not have a significant effect on the probability of a country facing a crisis. However, these results indicate that once a reversal has taken place, countries with a higher degree of capital mobility will experience a deeper drop in growth.

Endogeneity and Robustness

The results presented in table 2.13 assume that capital mobility is exogenous to the current account. In particular, it is assumed that the restrictions on capital mobility don't change if the probability of a reversal becomes higher. This, however, need not be the case. Indeed, some authors have argued that as a country's external position worsens, policymakers will have the temptation to heighten restrictions on capital mobility, and in particular on capital outflows.[30] If this is indeed the case, estimates that ignore potential endogeneity will be biased.[31] In order to address this issue I estimated the equation on the probability of experiencing a current account reversal using an instrumental variables probit procedure based on Amemiya's GLS estimators with endogenous regressors. In the estimation

---

30. See, for example, Edwards (1989).
31. Notice, however, that the results in table 2.13 use the lagged value of the capital mobility index.

Table 2.14   **Determinants of current account reversals: Instrumental variables probit model**

Variable	Set one	Set two
Capital mobility (–1)	–0.004	–0.002
	(0.42)	(0.19)
Current account deficit to GDP (–1)	0.064	0.065
	(8.06)***	(8.33)***
Sudden stop	0.868	0.861
	(4.74)***	(4.79)***
Sudden stops in region	1.761	1.771
	(3.13)***	(3.25)***
Reserves to GDP (–1)	–2.935	–4.437
	(0.56)	(0.84)
Domestic credit growth (–1)	0.0001	0.0001
	(0.66)	(0.60)
External debt to GDP (–1)	0.001	0.001
	(1.10)	(0.93)
Short-term debt (–1)	0.002	0.004
	(0.39)	(0.84)
Debt services (–1)	–0.008	–0.007
	(1.46)	(1.29)
Initial GDP per capita	0.094	0.065
	(0.86)	(0.58)
No. of observations	1,071	1,071

Notes: Absolute values of z-statistics are reported in parentheses; (–1) denotes a one-period lagged variable; country-specific dummies are included but not reported. For a list of the instruments used, see the text.
***Significant at the 1 percent level.

I used two alternative sets of instruments. The first set includes change in the terms of trade (as a measure of external real shocks), the world rate of interest (as a measure of external financial shocks), and a measure of trade openness obtained as the fitted value from a gravity model of bilateral trade.[32] In the second set of instruments, I added the three-year lagged current account balance to the first set of instruments. The results obtained under both sets of instruments are very similar; they are presented in table 2.14. As may be seen, by and large, these instrumental variables probit estimates confirm the results presented in panel B of table 2.13 for the treatment regressions. The signs of all coefficients have been preserved. It is important to notice, however, that the coefficients of international reserves and external debt, which were significant in table 2.13, are not statistically significant at conventional levels in table 2.14. More important for the subject of this paper, the coefficient of the capital mobility index continues to

32. As Aizenman and Noy (2004) have shown, there is a strong empirical connection between trade openness and the degree of capital mobility. The use of gravity trade equations to generate instruments in panel estimation has been pioneered by Jeff Frankel. See, for example, Frankel and Cavallo (2004).

be negative and insignificant, indicating that the probability of a current account reversal is not different for countries with a high degree of capital mobility than for countries with a low degree of capital mobility.

In order to investigate further the robustness of the results reported in tables 2.12 and 2.13 I analyzed the potential role of outliers, and I considered somewhat different samples, as well as different specifications. These robustness checks indicate that, from a qualitative point of view, the results discussed above are not affected by the choice of sample, specification, or outliers. Further research, however, should focus on generating more detailed and comprehensive indexes of capital mobility.

2.6   Concluding Remarks

In this paper I have used a broad multicountry data set to analyze the relationship between restrictions to capital mobility and external crises. The analysis focuses on two manifestations of external crises that have received considerable attention during the last few years: sudden stops of capital inflows, and current account reversals. I have tried to deal with two important policy-related issues: first, does the extent of capital mobility affect countries' degree of vulnerability to external crises, and second, does the extent of capital mobility determine the depth of external crises—as measured by the decline in growth—once the crises occur?

In analyzing these issues I relied on two complementary approaches. First, I used a methodology based on the computation of nonparametric tests and frequency tables to analyze the incidence and main characteristics of both sudden stops and current account reversals in countries with different degrees of capital controls. Second, I used a regression-based analysis that estimates jointly the probability of having a crisis, and the cost of such a crisis, in terms of short-term declines in output growth. Overall, my results cast some doubts on the assertion that increased capital mobility has caused heightened macroeconomic vulnerabilities. I have found no systematic evidence suggesting that countries with higher capital mobility tend to have a higher incidence of crises, or tend to face a higher probability of having a crisis, than countries with lower mobility. My results do suggest, however, that once a crisis occurs, countries with higher capital mobility tend to face a higher cost in terms of growth decline.

Appendix

Description of the Data

Variable	Definition	Source
Index of capital mobility	Index: 0 (low mobility) to 100 (high mobility)	Author's construction based on indexes of capital restrictions computed by Quinn (2003) and Mody and Murshid (2002), and on country-specific data
Current account reversal	Reduction in the current account deficit of at least 4% of GDP in one year, when initial balance is indeed a deficit	Author's construction based on data of current account deficit (World Development Indicators)
Sudden stop	Reduction of net capital inflows of at least 5% of GDP in one year, when the country in question received an inflow of capital larger than its region's third quartile during the previous two years prior to the sudden stop.	Author's construction based on data of financial account (World Development Indicators)
Banking crisis	Dummy variable for occurrence of a banking crisis	Glick and Hutchinson (1999)
Dollarization	Index: 0 (low dollarization) to 30 (high dollarization)	Reinhart, Rogoff, and Savastano (2003)
Terms of trade	Change in terms of trade as capacity to import (constant local currency units)	World Development Indicators
Openness	Trade openness: exports plus imports over GDP	World Development Indicators
Reserves to GDP	Net international reserves over GDP	World Development Indicators
Domestic credit growth	Annual growth rate of domestic credit	World Development Indicators
External debt to GDP	Total external debt over GDP	World Development Indicators
Short-term debt	Short-term debt as percentage of total external debt	World Development Indicators
Debt services	Total debt services as percentage of exports of goods and services	World Development Indicators
GDP per capita	GDP per capita in US$ (1995)	World Development Indicators

References

Aizenman, Joshua, and Ilan Noy. 2004. On the two way feedback between financial and trade openness. NBER Working Paper no. 10496. Cambridge, MA: National Bureau of Economic Research.

Alesina, Alberto, Vittorio Grilli, and Gian Maria Milesi-Ferretti. 1994. The political economy of capital controls. In *Capital mobility: The impact on consumption, investment and growth,* ed. L. Leiderman and A. Razin, 289–321. Cambridge: Cambridge University Press.

Angrist, Joshua. 2000. Estimation of limited dependent variable models with dummy endogenous regressors: Simple strategies for empirical practice. NBER Technical Working Paper no. 248. Cambridge, MA: National Bureau of Economic Research.

Barro, Robert J., and Xavier Sala-i-Martin. 1995. *Economic growth.* Cambridge, MA: MIT Press.

Beattie, Alan. 2003. IMF chief happy to gamble on debt-laden Argentina. *Financial Times.* September 15.

Bekaert, Geert. 1995. Market integration and investment barriers in emerging equity markets. *World Bank Economic Review* 9:75–107.

Bekaert, Geert, and Campbell R. Harvey. 1995. Time-varying world integration. *Journal of Finance* 50:403–44.

———. 2000. Capital flows and the behavior of emerging equity market returns. In *Capital flows and the emerging economies: Theory, evidence and controversies,* ed. S. Edwards, 159–94. Chicago: University of Chicago Press.

Bekaert, Geert, Campbell R. Harvey, and Christian Lundblad. 2001. Does financial liberalization spur growth? NBER Working Paper no. 8245. Cambridge, MA: National Bureau of Economic Research.

Calvo, Guillermo A., Alejandro Izquierdo, and Luis-Fernando Mejía. 2004. On the empirics of sudden stops: The relevance of balance-sheet effects. NBER Working Paper no. 10520. Cambridge, MA: National Bureau of Economic Research.

Calvo, Guillermo A., Alejandro Izquierdo, and Ernesto Talvi. 2003. Sudden stops, the real exchange rate, and fiscal sustainability: Argentina's lessons. NBER Working Paper no. 9828. Cambridge, MA: National Bureau of Economic Research.

Chinn, Menzie, and Hiro Ito. 2002. Capital account liberalization, institutional and financial development. NBER Working Paper no. 8967. Cambridge, MA: National Bureau of Economic Research.

De Gregorio, Jose, Sebastian Edwards, and Rodrigo Valdes. 2000. Controls on capital inflows: Do they work? *Journal of Development Economics* 63:59–83.

Desai, Mihir A., C. Fritz Foley, and Kristin J. Forbes. 2004. Financial constraints and growth: Multinational and local firm responses to currency crises. NBER Working Paper no. 10545. Cambridge, MA: National Bureau of Economic Research.

Dooley, Michael P. 1995. A survey of academic literature on controls over international capital transactions. IMF Working Paper no. 95/127. Washington, DC: International Monetary Fund.

Dooley, Michael, Donald Mathieson, and Liliana Rojas-Suarez. 1997. Capital mobility and exchange market intervention in developing countries. NBER Working Paper no. 6247. Cambridge, MA: National Bureau of Economic Research.

Dornbusch, Rudi. 2002. Malaysia: Was it different? In *Preventing currency crises in emerging markets,* ed. S. Edwards and J. Frankel, 441–54. Chicago: University of Chicago Press.

Edison, Hali, Michael W. Klein, Luca Ricci, and Torsten Sloek. 2004. Capital account liberalization and economic performance: Survey and synthesis. *IMF Staff Papers* 52 (1): 220–56.

Edison, Hali J., and Francis E. Warnock. 2003. A simple measure of the intensity of capital controls. *Journal of Empirical Finance* 10 (1/2): 81–103.

Edwards, Sebastian. 1985. Money, the rate of devaluation and interest rates in a semi-open economy: Colombia 1968–1982. *Journal of Money, Credit and Banking* 17 (1): 59–68.

———. 1989. *Real exchange rates, devaluation and adjustment.* Cambridge, MA: MIT Press.

———. 1998. Openness, productivity and growth: What do we really know? *Economic Journal* 108 (447): 383–98.

———. 1999. How effective are capital controls? *Journal of Economic Perspectives* 13 (4): 65–84.

———. 2000. Capital flows, real exchange rates and capital controls: Some Latin American experiences. In *Capital flows and the emerging economies,* ed. S. Edwards, 197–246. Chicago: University of Chicago Press.

———. 2001. Capital mobility and economic performance: Are emerging economies different? NBER Working Paper no. 8076. Cambridge, MA: National Bureau of Economic Research.

———. 2002. Does the current account matter? In *Preventing currency crises in emerging markets,* ed. S. Edwards and J. A. Frankel, 21–69. Chicago: University of Chicago Press.

———. 2004a. Financial openness, sudden stops, and current account reversals. *American Economic Review* 94 (2): 59–64.

———. 2004b. Thirty years of current account imbalances, current account reversals, and sudden stops. Fourth Mundell-Fleming Lecture. *IMF Staff Papers* 51 (Special Issue): 1–49.

Edwards, Sebastian, and Mohsin S. Khan. 1985. Interest rate determination in developing countries: A conceptual framework. *IMF Staff Papers* 32 (3): 377–403.

Edwards, Sebastian, and Eduardo Levy Yeyati. 2005. Flexible exchange rates as shock absorbers. *European Economic Review* 49 (8): 2079–2105.

Eichengreen, Barry J. 2001. Capital account liberalization: What do cross-country studies tell us? *World Bank Economic Review* 15:341–65.

Feldstein, Martin, and Charles Horioka. 1980. Domestic saving and international capital flows. *Economic Journal* 90 (June): 314–29.

Forbes, Kristin J. 2003. One cost of the Chilean capital controls: Increased financial constraints for smallest traded firms. NBER Working Paper no. 9777. Cambridge, MA: National Bureau of Economic Research.

Frankel, Jeffrey A. 1991. Quantifying international capital mobility in the 1980s. NBER Working Paper no. 2856. Cambridge, MA: National Bureau of Economic Research.

———. 1992. Measuring international capital mobility: A review. *American Economic Review* 82:197–202.

Frankel, Jeffrey A., and Eduardo Cavallo. 2004. Does openness to trade make countries more vulnerable to sudden stops, or less? Using gravity to establish causality. NBER Working Paper no. 10957. Cambridge, MA: National Bureau of Economic Research.

Frankel, Jeffrey A., and Andrew K. Rose. 1996. Currency crashes in emerging markets: An empirical treatment. *Journal of International Economics* 41 (November): 351–56.

Garber, Peter M. 1998. Buttressing capital account liberalization with prudential regulation and foreign entry. In *Should the IMF pursue capital-account convert-*

ibility? Essays in International Finance no. 207, ed. Stanley Fischer et al., 28–33. Princeton, NJ: Princeton University Press.

Glick, Reuven, and Michael Hutchison. 1999. Banking and currency crises: How common are twins? FRBSF Working Paper no. PB 99-07. San Francisco: Federal Reserve Bank of San Francisco.

Guidotti, Pablo, Federico Sturzenegger, and Agustín Villar. 2003. Aftermaths of current account reversals: Export growth or import contraction. Documento de Trabajo 06/2003. Universidad Torcuato Di Tella.

Haque, Nadeem U., and Peter Montiel. 1991. Capital mobility in developing countries: Some empirical tests. *World Development* 19 (10): 1391–98.

Harberger, Arnold C. 1978. Perspectives on capital and technology in less developed countries. In *Contemporary economic analysis,* ed. M. Artis and A. Nobay, 151–69. London: Croom Helm.

———. 1980. Vignettes on the world capital market. *American Economic Review* 70 (2): 331–37.

Heckman, James. 1978. Dummy endogenous variables in a simultaneous equation system. *Econometrica* 46:931–60.

Henry, P. B. 2000. Stock market liberalization, economic reform, and emerging market equity prices. *Journal of Finance* 55:529–64.

Hong, Kiseok, and Aaron Tornell. 2004. Recovery from a currency crisis: Some stylized facts. *Journal of Development Economics* 76 (1): 71–96.

Johnson, Simon, and Todd Mitton. 2001. Cronyism and capital controls: Evidence from Malaysia. NBER Working Paper no. 8521. Cambridge, MA: National Bureau of Economic Research.

Johnston, R. Barry, and Natalia T. Tamirisa. 1998. Why do countries use capital controls? IMF Working Paper no. 98-181. Washington, DC: International Monetary Fund.

Kaminsky, Graciela L., and Carmen M. Reinhart. 1999. The twin crises: The causes of banking and balance of payments problems. *American Economic Review* 89 (3): 473–500.

Kaplan, Ethan, and Dani Rodrik. 2002. Did the Malaysian capital controls work? In *Preventing currency crises in emerging markets,* ed. S. Edwards and J. Frankel, 393–431. Chicago: University of Chicago Press.

Klein, Michael W., and Giovanni Olivei. 1999. Capital account liberalization, financial depth and economic growth. NBER Working Paper no. 7384. Cambridge, MA: National Bureau of Economic Research.

Leblang, David A. 1997. Domestic and systemic determinants of capital controls in the developed and developing world. *International Studies Quarterly* 41 (3): 435–54.

Maddala, G. S. 1983. *Limited-dependent and qualitative variables in econometrics.* Cambridge: Cambridge University Press.

Milesi-Ferretti, Gian Maria, and Assaf Razin. 2000. Current account reversals and currency crises: Empirical regularities. In *Currency crises,* ed. P. Krugman, 285–323. Chicago: University of Chicago Press.

Miniane, Jacques. 2004. A new set of measures on capital account restrictions. *IMF Staff Papers* 51 (2): 276–308.

Mody, Ashoka, and Antu P. Murshid. 2002. Growing up with capital flows. IMF Working Paper no. WP/02/75. Washington, DC: International Monetary Fund.

Montiel, Peter. 1994. Capital mobility in developing countries: Some measurement issues and empirical estimates. *World Bank Economic Review* 8 (3): 311–50.

Montiel, Peter, and Carmen Reinhart. 1999. Do capital controls and macroeconomics policies influence the volume and composition of capital flows? Evidence from the 1990s. *Journal of International Money and Finance* 18 (4): 619–35.

Obstfeld, Maurice, and Alan Taylor. 2004. Global capital markets: Integration, crisis, and growth. Japan-U.S. Center Sanwa Monographs on International Financial Markets. Cambridge: Cambridge University Press.

Quinn, Dennis P. 1997. The correlates of changes in international financial regulation. *American Political Science Review* 91:531–51.

———. 2003. Capital account liberalization and financial globalization, 1890–1999: A synoptic view. *International Journal of Finance and Economics* 8 (3): 189–204.

Quinn, Dennis P., Carla Inclan, and A. Maria Toyoda. 2001. How and where capital account liberalization leads to economic growth. Paper presented at American Political Science Association annual convention. San Francisco, California.

Razin, Assaf, and Andrew K. Rose. 1994. Business cycle volatility and openness: An exploratory cross-section analysis. In *Capital mobility: The impact on consumption, investment and growth,* ed. L. Leiderman and Assaf Razin, 48–75. Cambridge: Cambridge University Press.

Reinhart, Carmen M., Kenneth S. Rogoff, and Miguel A. Savastano. 2003. Addicted to dollars. NBER Working Paper no. 10015. Cambridge, MA: National Bureau of Economic Research.

Reisen, Helmut, and Hélène Yèches. 1993. Time-varying estimates on the openness of the capital account in Korea and Taiwan. *Journal of Development Economics* 41 (2): 285–305.

Rodrik, Dani. 1995. The political economy of trade policy. In *Handbook of international economics,* vol. 3, ed. G. Grossman and K. Rogoff, 1457–94. Amsterdam: North-Holland.

———. 1998. Who needs capital-account convertibility? In *Should the IMF pursue capital-account convertibility?* Essays in International Finance no. 207, ed. Stanley Fischer et al., 55–65. Princeton, NJ: Princeton University Press.

Shatz, Howard J. 2000. The location of U.S. multinational affiliates. PhD diss., Harvard University.

Stiglitz, Joseph. 1999. Bleak growth prospects for the developing world. *International Herald Tribune.* April 10–11.

———. 2002. *Globalization and its discontents.* New York: W. W. Norton.

Tamirisa, Natalia T. 1999. Exchange and capital controls as barriers to trade. *IMF Staff Papers* 46 (1): 69–88.

Taylor, Alan. 2002. A century of current account dynamics. NBER Working Paper no. 8927. Cambridge, MA: National Bureau of Economic Research.

Wooldridge, J. M. 2002. *Econometric analysis of cross section and panel data.* Cambridge, MA: MIT Press.

Comment   Alan M. Taylor

This paper by Sebastian Edwards sheds light on one of the most heated policy questions in international macroeconomics: can capital controls help governments prevent crises? Although theory and introspection might provide an unambiguous positive answer to that question under laboratory

Alan M. Taylor is a professor of economics at the University of California, Davis, and a research associate of the National Bureau of Economic Research.

conditions, the real world does not always conform to the tidy assumptions of our toy models. Thus, the question is ultimately an empirical one, and the author is to be congratulated for bringing a formidable range of applied tools and new data to construct an answer. And the answer, subject to various qualifications, would seem to be negative. Across countries and across time there appears to be very little correlation between the intensity of capital controls and crisis events. The only qualification offered is that, once a crisis is underway, there is a risk of a greater output loss during the crisis when capital is more internationally mobile, a result that seems quite plausible.

There is not much to quibble with here. This is a clearly written and well-executed paper. Its results fall in line with, and lend additional weight to, an emerging empirical literature that challenges the standard prescriptions. In these comments I will review the approach of the paper, offer a few constructive criticisms, and try to suggest directions for future research.

The paper starts with a nice motivation: a brief history of the (so-called) Washington Consensus, or at least of how it has been interpreted on the issue of capital mobility.[1] It is a familiar tale, and need not be recounted at great length. In the early 1990s, several emerging-market countries elected to liberalize their capital markets in line with the then conventional wisdom. Starting in 1997 in Asia, some of these countries experienced crises. Soon alternative views started to be heard. Some suggested that the liberalization had been premature and inappropriate, and even that it had been done under pressure from identifiable external sources, conspiratorially termed the "[IMF–] Wall Street–Treasury complex" (Bhagwati 1998; Wade and Veneroso 1998). In this drama, the villains are top IMF officials, Treasury brass, and major investment banks. These critics, plus other noted economists like Krugman (1998), Rodrik (1998), and Stiglitz (2002), questioned the wisdom of a policy of international capital mobility in emerging markets. The media perceived that the IMF was "chastened" (Blustein 2001). The seemingly inevitable post–Cold War advance toward an ever more economically integrated new world order suddenly faltered as antiglobalization sentiment pushed back. In defense of the still-prevailing consensus within the profession, other leading economists and financiers such as Fischer (2004), Rogoff (2003), Rubin (2003), and Summers (2000) have stepped up to give their accounts of events. Still, no agreement between the two sides seems near.

Edwards steers us away from the heat in this debate and urges that we look systematically for some light. To that end, some well-defined and testable propositions must be teased out from the rhetoric of policy briefs,

1. I say "so-called" because, in fairness to John Williamson (1990), the originator of that buzzword, his original policy recommendations were a broad and coherent package and their references to capital mobility very carefully nuanced.

op-eds, and "airport economics." The antiglobalization position, insofar as it pertains to capital mobility, is summed up by Edwards in two propositions: capital controls can (1) reduce the risk of crisis and (2) reduce the impact of a crisis by enabling countercyclical monetary policy.

In theory, the first claim follows because if controls were literally impermeable, then they would forcibly prevent capital flight. A crisis, as conventionally defined, would then be impossible. Again in theory, the second claim follows since capital controls undo the forces of interest arbitrage and allow domestic interest rates to be set independently of world conditions. By resolving the classic trilemma in favor of autonomy, countries with "fear of floating" can both manage their exchange rates (to limit price volatility and to prevent damaging balance-sheet effects in the financial system) and yet still pull the levers of monetary policy in an attempt to revive their economy.

In reality, of course, controls are leaky and require adept implementation. Leakage would obviously compromise the two claims. As for implementation, policymakers may incline toward making hay while the sun shines. Hence, controls tend to be lifted when incipient flows are inward, as this flow helps the economy to grow. But controls may not be implemented in time to prevent a crisis event when the tide starts to ebb. If they are imposed too late, they will fail to stop the crisis and are likely to end up generating the reverse correlation in the data (i.e., crises would end up being associated with the *presence* of controls, not their absence). Less naively, if the risk of capital controls being implemented is anticipated, this could induce a crisis too (or, alternatively, discourage the capital inflow in the first place).

These numerous qualifications suggest an empirical investigation is needed, and Edwards assembles a formidable data set to address the questions. Data requirements are a binary variable that indicates the occurrence of a crisis; a measure of the cost of the crisis, such as an output loss; and a measure of capital controls.

The crisis indicator takes two forms: "sudden stop" or "current account reversal." These are fine choices, but not the only ones available in the literature. The emphasis here is on the balance of payments in the aggregate, not on official reserves. So we have to be aware that the object of study is balance-of-payments crises, not currency crises or financial crises. In essence we are looking at a quantity measure of the worsening of the country's external financing position, and the trigger is some threshold for size or change in the current account. The reversal measure seems quite robust to different thresholds; I worry a little more about the way sudden stops are defined, particularly with respect to the size of flows in the country's region. It is not clear to me why a country cannot be said to suffer a sudden stop if its flows fall off rapidly from a maximum level *for that country,* even if that country's flows never get large enough to be above the third quartile for the region. Perhaps the country has structural reasons (size? capital abundance? institutions?) that make it less of a target for flows on average, but it still might have a hard time if its inflows drop by 5 percentage points. That should also count as a sudden stop, I think. The one other sensitivity check worth investigating might be to allow for size-dependent hetero-skedasticity in the current account, and apply some rescaling based on GDP. Simply put, a 5 percentage point change is far out in the tails of the current account/GDP distribution for a large country (e.g., the United States) but not quite as much for a tiny country with a more volatile ratio of trade balance to GDP.

Overall, these definitions seem adequate for the task at hand, and my only anxiety is that the two variables are inherently highly—but not per-fectly—correlated with one another. This is not a problem if the analysis is just using two different measures for the same purpose as a robustness check. It might be a problem when we regress one variable on the other, as happens occasionally (table 2.12). If x is (almost) being regressed on x, the fit is likely to flatter, and we will have problems estimating the effects of other independent variables. I'd be happier if neither variable were used as an independent variable in this way, and both were just kept as variables to be explained.

The independent variable of most interest (as a cause of crises and their costs) is capital mobility, which is the most challenging variable to mea-sure. As is well known, there are few sources for these measures, and re-searchers have tended to rely on one of a few sources. The IMF's own data-base is widely used, but it suffers from a simple binary definition of capital mobility. This has been joined of late by the pioneering work of Quinn (2003), who has constructed a more refined annual index of current and capital account restrictions, a project that has now reached back a century or more. Authors such as Chinn and Ito (2002), Klein and Olivei (1999), Mody and Murshid (2002), and Miniane (2004) have also added their own measures to the literature. As Edwards notes, this is a rapidly evolving area of research, and we will doubtless see even more indexes soon. Not to be outdone, Edwards constructs his own index of capital mobility using Quinn plus Mody and Murshid, plus other country-specific sources. Like other measures it has weaknesses, but with the benefit of an algorithm to impute missing data, it offers very wide coverage by year and by country. For analytical purposes, the index is used to classify the country-year ob-servations into three subsets of equal size, referring to high, medium, and low capital mobility, respectively.

Estimating a crisis model is then a matter of using probit or other mod-els to figure out the determinants of crisis events. Estimating the cost of a crisis is a more routine matter in terms of variable definitions—we just look at the growth rate of GDP—but the way to actually extract the postcrisis effects on growth benefits from the use of a treatment effects model to sort out short-run and long-run growth effects and allow for a first-stage (probit) equation where the binary crisis event is predicted. This part of the paper should be a model for future researchers seeking to estimate these kinds of impacts.

The results presented (e.g., table 2.13) show that it is hard to find any evidence that restrictions on capital mobility lower the likelihood of a crisis event. However, conditional on a crisis event having occurred, restrictions on capital mobility do seem to limit the damage. As far as they go, the results are convincing. They are also consistent with other contemporary analyses showing an inverse correlation of various crises with capital controls (Glick and Hutchison 2005; Glick, Guo, and Hutchison 2004). I am particularly impressed by the rigor of the econometric analysis and the clarity with which it is presented. Let me simply offer a plea for more research, by Edwards or by others, to address some unresolved questions.

First, what about the type of controls? Can we obtain more indicators telling us what form controls actually take for each observation? We would like to know if these results hold up for controls on inflows versus controls on outflows. In light of the current fad for all things Chilean—wine, sea bass, capital controls, pension systems—it would be helpful to know if there is any sort of robust advantage to one type of control versus another. The same could be said for controls aimed at "hot" versus "cold" flows more generally; one might want to think about freeing FDI and long-term flows while limiting short-term bank flows (exactly the sorts of flows Fischer and others have highlighted as problematic in the Thai case, among others).

Second, what about temporary versus permanent controls? We might imagine that a regime committed to permanent controls would fare differently compared to a regime where policymakers are trying (succeeding? failing?) to time the application of controls to just stave off a crisis.

Third, what about contagion? Does the state of the global economy matter? Eichengreen and Leblang (2003) have found evidence of spillovers from international crises to the local economy. If you have controls, they can help insulate you from this type of event. Should some control for this type of channel be included in the regressions?

Finally, what about institutional quality? Recent work by Klein (2005) emphasizes that in an average period (including crisis and noncrisis) the effect of capital mobility is to raise the growth rate, but not in every developing country—only in emerging markets: countries that are poor enough to be considered capital scarce but that also maintain some minimum level of institutional quality (e.g., measured by corruption or rule of law). Could not a case be made that the incidence and impact of crises may also be affected by institutional quality?

It would be interesting to see institutional variables placed in the probit and growth regression models and interacted with capital mobility, because there are big questions to be answered. Do institutions matter? Do better institutions tame crises? Do they make capital mobility a safer bet? If so, this would be one more element in a newly forming consensus, a sort of Washington Consensus II.

In this view, policy reform without institutional reform is a dead end. This view is not universally embraced in the operational sphere—indeed, it would require the international financial institutions (IFIs) to try to make more objective, and more politically charged, distinctions between good and bad borrowers, something their governmental masters are probably loath to do. Yet these ideas might be seen as gaining some limited traction—for example, in the efforts by the World Bank under Wolfensohn to crack down on corrupt borrowers and better prioritize loans, or efforts by the IMF to increase transparency and exert (some) pressure on severe offenders like Zimbabwe.

We are beginning to recognize that opening up to the global capital market may have the potential to do either good or harm, depending on the circumstances. Recommending capital mobility for institutional basket cases is pointless, the argument goes: with their low productivity levels there isn't much to finance, and essentially there is no positive future growth path (Easterly 2001; Gourinchas and Jeanne 2003; Obstfeld and Taylor 2004). Moreover, countries with weak institutions may be more susceptible to crises (Acemoglu et al. 2003). According to this logic, when it comes to capital market liberalization, it is the emerging markets we need to focus on, countries that have taken the first step on the escalator of modern economic growth and now have improved growth prospects (and lower crisis risk) that justify the inflow of capital. If these arguments hold up, and we continue to find strong effects of institutions on growth and crises, the case for a more nuanced approach to capital mobility would be bolstered.

References

Acemoglu, Daron, Simon Johnson, James Robinson, and Yunyong Thaicharoen. 2003. Institutional causes, macroeconomic symptoms: Volatility, crises and growth. *Journal of Monetary Economics* 50:49–123.

Bhagwati, Jagdish. 1998. The capital myth: The difference between trade in widgets and dollars. *Foreign Affairs* 77 (May–June): 7–12.

Blustein, Paul. 2001. *The chastening: Inside the crisis that rocked the global financial system and humbled the IMF.* New York: Public Affairs.

Chinn, Menzie, and Hiro Ito. 2002. Capital account liberalization, institutional and financial development. NBER Working Paper no. 8967. Cambridge, MA: National Bureau of Economic Research.

Easterly, William. 2001. *The elusive quest for growth: Economists' adventures and misadventures in the tropics.* Cambridge, MA: MIT Press.

Eichengreen, Barry, and David Leblang. 2003. Capital account liberalization and growth: Was Mr. Mahathir right? *International Journal of Finance and Economics* 8 (3): 205–24.

Fischer, Stanley. 2004. *IMF essays from a time of crisis: The international financial system, stabilization, and development.* Cambridge, MA: MIT Press.

Glick, Reuven, Xueyan Guo, and Michael Hutchison. 2004. Currency crises, capital account liberalization, and selection bias. Federal Reserve Bank of San Francisco Working Paper no. 2004-15. San Francisco, CA: Federal Reserve Bank, June.

Glick, Reuven, and Michael Hutchison. 2005. Capital controls and exchange rate instability in developing economies. *Journal of International Money and Finance* 24 (3): 387–412.

Gourinchas, Pierre-Olivier, and Olivier Jeanne. 2003. The elusive gains from international financial integration. NBER Working Paper no. 9684. Cambridge, MA: National Bureau of Economic Research.

Klein, Michael W. 2005. Capital account liberalization, institutional quality and economic growth: Theory and evidence. NBER Working Paper no. 11112. Cambridge, MA: National Bureau of Economic Research.

Klein, Michael W., and Giovanni Olivei. 1999. Capital account liberalization, financial depth and economic growth. NBER Working Paper no. 7384. Cambridge, MA: National Bureau of Economic Research.

Krugman, Paul. 1998. Heresy time. http://web.mit.edu/krugman/www/heresy.html.

Miniane, Jacques. 2004. A new set of measures on capital account restrictions. *IMF Staff Papers* 51 (2): 276–308.

Mody, Ashoka, and Antu P. Murshid. 2002. Growing up with capital flows. IMF Working Paper no. WP/02/75. Washington, DC: International Monetary Fund.

Obstfeld, Maurice, and Alan M. Taylor. 2004. *Global capital markets: Integration, crisis, and growth.* Cambridge: Cambridge University Press.

Quinn, Dennis P. 2003. Capital account liberalization and financial globalization, 1890–1999: A synoptic view. *International Journal of Finance and Economics* 8 (3): 189–204.

Rodrik, Dani. 1998. Who needs capital-account convertibility? In *Should the IMF pursue capital-account convertibility?* Essay in International Finance no. 207, ed. Stanley Fischer et al., 55–65. Princeton, NJ: Princeton University, International Finance Section.

Rogoff, Kenneth. 2003. The IMF strikes back. *Foreign Policy* 134 (January–February): 38–46.

Rubin, Robert. 2003. *In an uncertain world.* New York: Random House.

Stiglitz, Joseph E. 2002. *Globalization and its discontents.* New York: W. W. Norton.

Summers, Lawrence H. 2000. International financial crises: Causes, prevention, and cures. *American Economic Review* 90 (2): 1–16.

Wade, Robert, and Frank Veneroso. 1998. The Asian financial crisis: The high debt model versus the Wall Street–Treasury–IMF complex. *New Left Review* 228 (March–April): 3–23.

Williamson, John. 1990. What Washington means by policy reform. In *Latin American adjustment: How much has happened?* ed. John Williamson, 7–20. Washington, DC: Institute for International Economics.

3

Currency Mismatches, Debt Intolerance, and Original Sin
Why They Are Not the Same and Why It Matters

Barry Eichengreen, Ricardo Hausmann, and
Ugo Panizza

3.1 Introduction

Recent years have seen the development of a large literature on balance sheet factors in financial crises.[1] The balance sheet approach focuses on the impact of disturbances on the assets, liabilities, and net worth of households, firms, government, and the economy as a whole and on the implications for growth and stability. Some studies focus on the net worth effects of shocks to the exchange rate in the presence of foreign currency–denominated liabilities. Others look at liquidity or interest rate shocks when the tenor of a bank, firm, or country's liabilities is shorter than the tenor of its assets. In some studies the propagation mechanism is the impact on consumption and investment of the change in net worth of households and nonfinancial firms. In others it is the impact on the liquidity and solvency of financial institutions and markets and hence on confidence in the financial system. In still others it is the impact on the sustainability of the public debt.

Recent contributions also differ in their assumptions about the distortion giving rise to these fragilities. Our own work focuses on problems with the structure of global financial markets that result in the inability of econ-

Barry Eichengreen is the George C. Pardee and Helen N. Pardee Professor of Economics and Political Science at the University of California, Berkeley, and a research associate of the National Bureau of Economic Research (NBER). Ricardo Hausmann is director of the Center for International Development and professor of the practice of economic development at the Kennedy School of Government, Harvard University. Ugo Panizza is a senior economist in the research department at the Inter-American Development Bank.

We are grateful to our conference discussant, Joshua Aizenman, for helpful comments.

1. See, for example, Krugman (1999), Razin and Sadka (1999), Aghion, Bacchetta, and Banerjee (2000), Céspedes, Chang, and Velasco (2002), and Jeanne (2002).

omies to borrow abroad in their own currencies.[2] Others focus on policy failures as a result of which governments fail to limit foreign currency and short-maturity borrowing to socially desirable levels and/or fail to insure adequately against its potentially destabilizing consequences.[3]

Hence, while all of these studies are concerned in a broad sense with open-economy balance sheet effects, the issues on which they focus are not the same. These different emphases lead to different perspectives on research and policy.

In section 3.2 we introduce several concepts that are widely used in the literature, describe how they differ, and explain why these differences matter. We distinguish between currency mismatches (differences in the currencies in which assets and liabilities are denominated), debt intolerance (the inability of emerging markets to manage levels of debt that are manageable for advanced industrial countries), and original sin (the difficulty emerging markets face when attempting to borrow abroad in their own currencies). We emphasize that the phenomena denoted by these terms are analytically distinct.

In section 3.3 we show that these distinctions matter empirically as well as conceptually. We analyze the impact of balance sheet variables on the volatility of output, the volatility of capital flows, the management of exchange rates, and creditworthiness of countries. We show that it is important when considering the behavior of such variables to clearly distinguish original sin, debt intolerance, and currency mismatches. Section 3.4 addresses a number of additional debates that have arisen in this context, after which section 3.5 summarizes our conclusions.

3.2 Currency Mismatches, Debt Intolerance, and Original Sin Are Not the Same

Three terms that are prevalent in this literature—currency mismatches, debt intolerance, and original sin—in fact refer to quite different phenomena.

3.2.1 Original Sin

Eichengreen, Hausmann, and Panizza (2005b) define original sin as *the inability of a country to borrow abroad in its own currency*.[4] This focus on ex-

---

2. See Eichengreen and Hausmann (1999) and Eichengreen, Hausmann, and Panizza (2005b).

3. See, for example, Goldstein and Turner (2004) and Reinhart, Rogoff, and Savastano (2003).

4. In earlier work, Eichengreen and Hausmann (1999) used the term to refer to both the difficulty that countries experience when attempting to borrow abroad in their own currencies and the difficulty they face when attempting to borrow at home at long maturities. In subsequent work we came to conclude that the first of these two problems is particularly difficult. While it is not easy to develop domestic bond markets—something that is the sine qua non of

ternal borrowing is motivated by the observation that, in the absence of other distortions, world welfare would be enhanced if capital flowed from capital-rich advanced countries to their more capital-poor emerging market counterparts. It would be further enhanced if countries could use the current account and the capital flows needed to finance it to stabilize the domestic economy when faced with shocks.[5]

One possible explanation for the failure of more capital to flow from rich to poor countries and the difficulty experienced by the latter in using the capital account to smooth consumption is their inability to borrow abroad in their own currencies. If a country's external debt is denominated in foreign currency, then real exchange rate depreciation, by reducing the purchasing power of domestic output over foreign claims, will make it more difficult to service that debt. Knowing that shocks affecting the real exchange rate can disrupt the country's ability to service its debt, foreigners may be rendered less willing to lend. And since the real exchange rate tends to strengthen in good times and weaken in bad times, foreign currency debt will be harder to service in bad times, reducing willingness to lend and thereby accentuating the procyclical nature of capital flows.

Aware of these dangers, a government may use macroeconomic and regulatory policies to limit foreign borrowing. But then capital still will not flow from capital-rich to capital-poor countries, nor will countries be able to cushion the effect of shocks through international borrowing. The government may accumulate foreign reserves to be used to intervene in the foreign exchange market in order to prevent the currency from moving and/or to enable it to act as debt servicer of last resort. But in this case, the country's gross foreign currency liabilities, accumulated by borrowing abroad, are matched by gross foreign currency assets that the government holds in the form of international reserves. If reserves equal gross foreign borrowing, then there will again be no capital transfer from capital-rich to capital-poor economies.

In part, debate on these questions revolves around the validity of the premise that other distortions are absent or at least that they are not the

---

facilitating the efforts of firms and governments to borrow at home at long maturities—a growing number of countries are showing an ability to do so. Chile, Hungary, India, and Thailand, among other countries, are able to borrow on domestic markets at fixed rates without indexing their bonds to the exchange rate, as documented in section 3.4. But these same countries are making less progress in developing the ability to borrow abroad in their own currencies. In Eichengreen, Hausmann, and Panizza (2005b) we have also devoted some attention to "the domestic aspect" of original sin. But because the constraints on borrowing abroad in one's own currency seem particularly intractable, we have made this the focus of our recent work and adopted a correspondingly narrower definition of original sin. We return to these issues in section 3.4.

5. That net capital flows from relatively capital-rich to relatively capital-poor countries are not larger is referred to as the "Lucas paradox" (after Lucas 1990). That capital flows are procyclical, exacerbating booms and recessions, has also been widely commented upon (see, e.g., Gavin, Hausmann, and Leiderman 1995).

main thing going on. A contrary view is that the inability of emerging markets to borrow abroad in their own currencies is simply a corollary of other distortions to their economies that remove the incentive for lending and borrowing. Weak policies and institutions in emerging markets so depress the marginal productivity of capital, in this view, that neither the welfare of these countries, nor that of the world as a whole, is enhanced by capital transfer. Foreigners are not inclined to invest in emerging markets, in this view, because productivity there is so low.

The intermediate position is that domestic policies and institutions are important for the ability of countries to borrow abroad in their own currencies, but so are factors largely beyond the control of the individual country.[6] Foreign investors may be reluctant to lend to a country in its own currency if the authorities are prone to manipulating the value of that currency. Institutional and policy reforms giving investors confidence that the value of the currency will be maintained may thus be necessary for a country to be able to borrow abroad in its own currency. But the evidence does not suggest that they are sufficient; too many countries with strong policies and institutions also suffer from original sin. Moreover, if the problem was fear of inflation, we should observe inflation-indexed local currency debts or contracts in the currencies of a variety of well-behaved countries. Instead, we observe a large concentration of debt denominated in a few major currencies.[7]

Chile is a favorite example of a country with increasingly strong institutions and policies. In terms of rule of law, the International Country Risk Guide (ICRG) gave Chile 5 of 6 possible points in 2001, compared to a Latin American average of 2.9 and a world average of 3.8. Chile has also done a good job of managing the risks associated with foreign borrowing, using capital account regulation, prudential supervision, transparency requirements for banks and firms, and flexible exchange rates to encourage prudent management of foreign currency exposures.[8]

One thing that these strengthened policies and institutions have not done, however, is to enable Chile to borrow abroad in its own currency. The consequences have been significant. In 1998 Chile was hit by an adverse

6. This is a fair summary of our view.

7. Of the nearly $5.8 trillion in outstanding securities placed in international markets in the period 1999–2001, $5.6 trillion was issued in five major currencies: the U.S. dollar, the euro, the yen, the pound sterling, and the Swiss franc. See Eichengreen, Hausmann, and Panizza (2005b). To be sure, the residents of the countries issuing these currencies (or, in the case of Euroland, the group of countries) constitute a significant portion of the world economy and hence form a significant part of global debt issuance. But while residents of these countries issued $4.5 trillion of debt over this period, the remaining $1.1 trillion of debt denominated in their currencies was issued by residents of other countries and by international organizations (which issued a total of $1.3 trillion of debt). The causes and consequences of this concentration of debt denomination in few currencies are the focus of the literature on original sin.

8. These policies are a reasonable approximation of the emerging consensus on how a prudent emerging market should manage the risks of external borrowing.

terms-of-trade shock. A country able to borrow abroad in its own currency, when hit by this temporary shock, would have eased monetary and fiscal policies, loosened the exchange rate, and financed its growing external deficit by borrowing abroad in order to smooth consumption and stabilize production. This is what Australia did, for example, when hit by the same global shock.[9] But Chile, rather than seeing capital inflows buffer its export shock, suffered a sudden stop in such flows, forcing it to cut its imports by fully 22 percent (nearly 6 percent of gross domestic product [GDP]) between 1997 and 1999. This entailed a collapse in GDP growth from 6.8 percent in 1997 to –0.8 percent in 1999.[10] These are large swings by the standards of the advanced industrial economies.

Why did Chile's performance resemble that of Latin American countries plagued by weak institutions rather than that of advanced countries with comparable institutional-quality ratings, like Australia? Original sin may be part of the answer. If Chile had pursued accommodative policies and allowed the real exchange rate to adjust, adverse balance sheet effects would have created doubts about its ability to service its debt, limiting the willingness of the foreign investors to fund the ensuing deficit. By opting for restrictive policies, the authorities curtailed the demand for foreign finance so as to limit the increase in country risk, but at the cost of a major recession.[11]

The Chilean authorities were not unaware of these dangers, but the ex ante policies available to limit the country's vulnerability to sudden stops had costs as well. Gallego and Hernandez (2003) show that the non-interest-bearing deposit requirement imposed on foreign borrowing in the 1990s increased the cost of external finance for Chilean firms. This does not mean that these policies were inadvisable; we have argued elsewhere that such costs were worth paying.[12] In effect they were optimal second-best policies—they were a sensible way of insuring against the risk of sudden stops given that external debt was denominated in foreign currency. But the distance to the first best was substantial because the policies in question entailed a trade-off between access to external finance on the one hand and financial stability on the other. Chile was able to attain a reasonable position on this frontier owing to the strength of its policies and institutions. Even better, of course, would have been the ability to push that frontier outward by acquiring the ability to borrow abroad in local currency.

9. This is the counterexample considered in Eichengreen and Hausmann (1999). This comparison is pursued by Caballero, Cowan, and Kearns (2003), whose interpretation differs.
10. Calculations based on data for imports and GDP from the Central Bank of Chile. For a discussion of the costs of sudden stop in capital flows see Calvo, Izquierdo, and Talvi (2002).
11. After 2000 and especially after 2002, policies became more accommodative and the real exchange rate was allowed to depreciate by 38.6 percent from its peak in 1997. However, capital inflows have yet to resume and growth has remained lackluster, as would be expected given the less expansionary effect of depreciations in countries that suffer from original sin.
12. See Hausmann and Gavin (1996) and Eichengreen (2002).

It is striking in this context that Chile, despite the strength of its institutions, has been unable to escape the problem of original sin that was a constraint on shifting that frontier. This is a specific example of the general point that the standard institution-strengthening measures appear to have relatively little ability over policy-relevant horizons to enable developing countries to acquire the capacity to borrow abroad in their own currencies.[13] The label "original sin" is designed to convey the possibility that the problem may not result only from the actions of the affected country but in addition may have something to do with factors largely beyond its immediate determination and control.[14]

3.2.2   Debt Intolerance

Reinhart, Rogoff, and Savastano (2003) define debt intolerance as *the inability of emerging markets to manage levels of external debt that are manageable for advanced countries.* They operationalize the concept as the relationship between a country's credit rating (also referred to as country risk) and its external debt. They report that ratings fall more rapidly with debt in emerging markets than advanced countries, as if the former have less debt management capacity.

Debt intolerance and original sin are not the same. The inability of a country to borrow abroad in its own currency is one potential explanation for why it may have trouble managing levels of debt that would be manageable for other countries. But no one to our knowledge has claimed that original sin is the only determinant of debt problems.[15]

Reinhart, Rogoff, and Savastano (2003) write that "a country's external debt intolerance can be explained by a very small number of variables related to its repayment history." They show that countries that defaulted in the past and have histories of inflation have lower credit ratings in the present. We endorse the insight that history can play an important role in shaping current outcomes. But a minimal condition for a theory of the historical determinants of current events is a transmission mechanism through which events in the past can influence outcomes in the present.[16] One

13. See section 3.3 for additional evidence.
14. We will have more to say about the specific nature of these factors below.
15. This point would not be worth making except that some contributors to the literature have referred interchangeably to countries' external debt problems in general (their "country risk" or "debt intolerance") and their inability to borrow abroad in their own currencies in particular ("original sin"). In our previous work and again below, we analyze the determinants of a country's debt problems, as measured by their credit ratings. We study the impact of original sin on credit ratings, controlling for several other potential determinants of ratings such as a country's per capita income and its overall indebtedness. This makes clear that we do not see original sin as the only determinant of country risk, although we do find that it is an important determinant.
16. There is now a large literature on this subject. See the discussion in David (2001). We endorse Joshua Aizenman's conjecture, in his comment on the present paper, that a history of macroeconomic and financial instability may weaken the social contract and impact in-

would also want evidence that this mechanism is at work, for otherwise one could not rule out that omitted factors associated with external debt–servicing difficulties in both the past and present explain the observed correlation, where in fact there is no causal mechanism linking past events to current outcomes.

Reinhart, Rogoff, and Savastano (2003) conjecture that default on external debt may weaken a country's financial system and that a weaker financial system increases the likelihood of subsequent default because countries with weaker financial systems suffer larger output losses when access to external finance is interrupted. They suggest that default on external debt may weaken a country's tax system by encouraging capital flight and tax avoidance, in turn making it harder to raise the revenues needed to service public debts. But they report no regressions relating the size of the financial system and the tax base to countries' histories of default, and no regressions relating current default to the size of the financial system and the tax base. They present no evidence of these or other mechanisms causally linking past defaults to current debt-servicing difficulties.[17]

That the same countries have defaulted in both the distant and the more recent past may in fact reflect other characteristics of those countries that are slow to change but that are omitted from this analysis of debt intolerance. Original sin may be one such characteristic. Elsewhere we have shown that the inability of countries to borrow abroad in their own currencies is persistent.[18] Similarly, that the commodity composition of exports renders some countries' terms of trade persistently more volatile than others may explain why some countries have more difficulty than others in coping with external debt.[19]

Reinhart, Rogoff, and Savastano (2003) regress credit ratings as a measure of debt-servicing prospects on the history of debt and inflation, using data for fifty-three advanced and developing countries. To determine whether developing countries are less able to manage debts that are manageable for advanced economies, they enter the ratio of debt to gross national product (GNP) separately for countries with high credit ratings (67.7 and above on the *Institutional Investor* 100-point scale) and low credit ratings (below 67.7).[20] In support of their hypothesis, they point to the fact

vestors' attitudes regarding a country's ability to service debts. But these ideas are not made explicit in the literature on debt intolerance.

17. In principle, empirical work along these lines should be feasible. We return to this in the concluding section of our paper.

18. Eichengreen, Hausmann, and Panizza (2005a) use the measures of original sin circa 1850 constructed by Flandreau and Sussman (2005) to document the correlation between original sin then and now.

19. Blattman, Hwang, and Williamson (2003) suggest that the commodity composition of exports and the resulting behavior of the real exchange rate have persistent implications for volatility and growth.

20. Some of their regressions also include the percentage of sample years in which the debt was in default or restructuring.

that the coefficient on the debt-GNP ratio is negative for countries with low ratings and positive for countries with high ratings and to the high R^2 of the regression.

We see three problems with this analysis. First is the omitted-variables problem described above.[21] Second, credit ratings appear on both sides of this equation, as a continuous variable on the left and a dummy for above or below 67.7 on the right (interacted with the debt ratio). This makes it hard to draw much comfort from the high R^2. Third, there is no separate intercept for countries with credit ratings below 67.7. Hence, all respects in which countries with low credit ratings differ from countries with high credit ratings are loaded into the interaction term between credit ratings and the debt-GNP ratio.

In table 3.1 we show the difference that this makes. The first regression relates credit ratings to debt-GDP separately for advanced and developing countries but does not include a separate intercept for the latter. Here we use Standard & Poor's (S&P) rating data instead of those from *Institutional Investor* in order to preserve comparability with our previous work and further results reported below.[22] Despite using slightly different country samples and data, we obtain the same result as Reinhart, Rogoff, and Savastano (2003)—namely, that the coefficient on the debt ratio is significantly larger for developing countries.[23] The second regression then shows that this result evaporates when a separate intercept is included.

In equation (3), we split the sample not into advanced and developing countries but into countries with high and low credit ratings, following Reinhart, Rogoff, and Savastano (2003). We generate a dummy variable

21. To put the same point another way, the authors put a structural interpretation on an extremely reduced-form relationship.

22. Our rating variable is from S&P and ranges between 0 and 19. (We converted the S&P rating into a numerical variable by adopting the following criteria: selective default = 0, C = 2, CC = 2.5, CCC = 3, B– = 4, and each extra upgrade = one point. A value of 19 corresponds to AAA.) We also adjust our classification for the outlook assigned by S&P to each country, and we increase the rating by 0.33 when the country has a positive outlook and decrease the rating by 0.33 when the country has a negative outlook. The rating variable used by Reinhart, Rogoff, and Savastano is from *Institutional Investor* and ranges from 0 to 100. We report regressions using this alternative measure below.

23. There are two additional differences between these regressions and the ones in Reinhart, Rogoff, and Savastano (2003). First, since our rating variable is censored at 19 (and more than 10 percent of observations are at the upper bound), we use a Tobit model instead of ordinary least squares (OLS). The results are robust to estimating these equations by OLS instead of Tobit. Second, we use averages over the 1993–99 period, while Reinhart et al. use averages for the 1979–2002 period. Finally, while the two samples have similar size (sixty-two countries in our sample, fifty-three in Reinhart et al.), they do not overlap perfectly. We do not know exactly which countries are included in the Reinhart et al. regressions. However, in appendix B1 of their paper, they list sixty-three countries for which they have information on credit rating. Presumably the fifty-three countries included in the regressions are a subset of this sample. There are twenty-three countries that are included in our sample but not in table B1 of Reinhart, Rogoff, and Savastano, and twenty-four countries included in their table B1 that are not in our sample (these countries are listed in the appendix).

Table 3.1 Credit rating in developing and advanced countries

	RATING I				RATING II		RATING II excluding South Korea
	(1)	(2)	(3)	(4)	(5)	(6)	(7)
Debt/GDP advanced	4.814 (2.30)**	-2.659 (1.24)					
Debt/GDP developing	-8.627 (4.96)***	-3.671 (2.34)**					
Developing		-9.027 (5.78)***					
Debt/GDP high rating			5.783 (3.10)***	-1.511 (0.83)	25.295 (2.46)**	1.597 (0.46)	1.597 (0.46)
Debt/GDP low rating			-9.207 (5.85)***	-4.438 (3.36)***	-32.386 (3.75)***	-12.266 (1.62)	-8.527 (1.18)
High rating				8.917 (6.60)***		33.811 (6.22)***	36.444 (6.98)***
Constant	13.999 (15.60)***	19.757 (15.27)***	14.138 (17.51)***	11.028 (15.03)***	58.449 (10.69)***	44.988 (9.03)***	42.355 (8.92)***
No. of observations	61	61	61	61	45	45	44
R-squared		0.705			0.53	0.73	0.76
DEG_DEV = DEG_ADV	$F(1,59) = 41.31$	$F(1,58) = 0.14$					
DEG_HR = DEG_LR			$F(1,59) = 62.7$	$F(1,58) = 1.69$	$F(1,42) = 72.9$	$F(1,41) = 2.77$	$F(1,40) = 1.69$
p	0.000	0.705	0.000	0.199	0.000	0.104	0.214

Notes: Tobit regressions shown in columns (1)–(4), and ordinary least squares (OLS) with robust standard errors in columns (5)–(7). Absolute value of t-statistics in parentheses.

***Significant at the 1 percent level.

**Significant at the 5 percent level.

that takes value 1 if a given country has a rating above the mean plus 1 standard deviation of our cross-country sample.[24] Column (3) reproduces their result: the coefficients on the debt ratios for high- and low-rated countries are significantly different from one another at standard confidence levels.[25] But when in column (4) we allow the two groups of countries to have a different intercept, the point estimate and the statistical significance of the difference in slope coefficients again collapse.

In the last three columns of the table we replace the Standard & Poor's rating variable used in the first four columns with the *Institutional Investor* rating (which varies from 0 to 100) used by Reinhart, Rogoff, and Savastano (2003). When we intersect the *Institutional Investor* rating with the sample of countries for which we have information on debt relative to GDP we are left with a sample of forty-five countries. We separate the sample into countries with high and low credit ratings using the same threshold used by Reinhart, Rogoff, and Savastano (67.7). Column (5) reproduces their result: the effect of debt-GDP is positive and significant in countries with high credit ratings and negative and significant in countries with low credit ratings. The difference between the two groups is also statistically significant. In column (6), we allow the two groups of countries to have different intercepts and find that the coefficients of debt over GDP are no longer significant in either group of countries.[26] Furthermore, the difference between the two coefficients is no longer significant at conventional confidence levels. The results are also sensitive to the inclusion of an outlier, South Korea, which has relatively low levels of debt and a high credit rating. If Korea is dropped (column [7]), the difference between the coefficients of high- and low-rated countries declines still further.[27]

3.2.3 Currency Mismatch

Original sin also differs from currency mismatches, defined as *differences in the values of the foreign currency–denominated assets and liabilities on the balance sheets of households, firms, the government, and the economy as a whole.* In the case of a bank, the concept of a currency mismatch is familiar: it is the difference between the value of the foreign currency–denomi-

---

24. Reinhart, Rogoff, and Savastano also separate their sample at the mean plus 1 standard deviation. On our numerical scale, this corresponds to a cutoff of 16.
25. That the results are very similar to the preceding set of regressions is not surprising. Only two countries that we classify as advanced have low ratings (Greece and Iceland), while just one country that we classify as developing has a high rating (Singapore).
26. The point estimates are also very different from those in the regressions omitting the additional intercept term.
27. If panel data methods are used instead of simple cross-country comparisons, the difference between the coefficients of high-rating and low-rating countries also remains statistically significant after controlling for country fixed effects. Fixed effect estimates may however be problematic (they amplify the ratio of noise to signal) in a setting where the fixed effects explain 90 percent of the variance of the dependent variable and 80 percent of the variance of the explanatory variable.

nated liabilities and assets (typically normalized by total assets, total domestic currency assets, or another appropriate scale variable). For a firm, the currency mismatch derives from the relationship between net foreign currency–denominated liabilities and the net present value of domestic currency–denominated cash flow. A firm with a currency mismatch will experience an adverse balance sheet effect if exchange rate depreciation raises the value of its net foreign currency–denominated liabilities relative to the net present value of its cash flow.[28]

When we aggregate this up to the national level, consolidating the foreign currency assets and liabilities of residents, we are left with the aggregate currency mismatch. This means that there will be an aggregate currency mismatch when there is a net debt to foreigners denominated in foreign currency. The implications for the country then parallel those for the firm: real exchange rate depreciation that raises the value of a country's external net debt in terms of the value of its national output will create adverse balance sheet effects.

However, the aggregate mismatch that exists when there is a net debt to foreigners denominated in foreign currency is different from original sin, defined as the inability of a country to borrow abroad in its own currency and measured as the ratio of foreign currency–denominated gross debt to foreigners as a share of total gross debt to foreigners. By definition, when banks, firms, or public agencies of a country suffering from original sin borrow abroad, they incur a gross foreign debt denominated in foreign currency. But the country may or may not also incur a currency mismatch, depending on how the authorities respond to that act of borrowing. One consequence of original sin is the tendency for countries afflicted by this problem to accumulate international reserves as a way of protecting themselves from potentially destabilizing financial consequences. We show in section 3.3 that countries with high levels of original sin do in fact hold significantly larger international reserves, other things being equal.

But where reserve accumulation is large, currency mismatches will be small. Thus, where an aggregate mismatch is one possible consequence of original sin, it is not a necessary one. While one possible consequence of original sin is a currency mismatch, another possible consequence is a large reserve accumulation. Either, or to some extent both, may occur.

Currency mismatches may have costs. But large reserve holdings may also have costs, since the yield on reserves is typically less than the cost of funds. If governments settle on an interior solution to their optimization problem, they are likely to accumulate reserves that offset some fraction less than one of gross foreign debt denominated in foreign currency. The re-

---

28. If depreciation is fully translated into higher prices for firms' output, as would happen with a small exporting firm or when there is a full pass-through of exchange rates into prices, there will be no change in the net worth of a company. But this is not the general case.

sulting currency mismatch will be smaller than the gross debt denominated in foreign currency, while reserve holdings will be larger than in a country that can borrow in domestic currency terms.

It thus makes no sense to criticize measures of original sin as poor measures of aggregate currency mismatches. Authors concerned with the two concepts are attempting to measure different things.

Currency mismatches may have other causes besides original sin. If banks are undercapitalized, with weak risk management and inadequate prudential supervision, moral hazard may tempt banks to fund themselves in foreign currency at low interest rates and on-lend in domestic currency at high rates, ignoring the fact that they incur a currency mismatch that leaves them vulnerable to exchange rate fluctuations.[29] Or a government may neglect the need to accumulate reserves as insurance against exchange rate shocks when foreign debt is denominated in foreign currency terms. Or the authorities may mislead banks and firms into believing that the exchange rate will remain pegged forever, encouraging them to underestimate exchange risk and hence the danger of open positions in foreign currency. Original sin may result in mismatches, depending on how the authorities manage its consequences. But we have never suggested that only original sin matters for currency mismatches, as is asserted in some discussions of our work.

Nor have we asserted that the strength of a country's institutions and policies is irrelevant for managing the consequences of original sin. In particular, countries with strong institutions, capable of running strong policies, are in the best position to cope with the potential mismatch problem. They can accumulate reserves. They can limit foreign borrowing. They can operate more flexible exchange rates. All of these steps may help to limit currency mismatches and financial fragility.[30] But these measures are second best. The first best would involve having the capacity to borrow from foreigners without incurring a currency mismatch.

This is just another way of saying that the measures that countries use to insure against mismatches are not without cost. Limiting access to foreign borrowing may limit investment. Reserve accumulation is costly. Flexible exchange rates are more problematic in countries with large shares of foreign currency–denominated debt. Thus, measures to limit the consequences of original sin taken by countries with the institutional capacity to implement them may come at a cost, as discussed above. This is the sense in which such measures may be incompletely successful at reconciling growth and stability.

---

29. This is an element of Goldstein's (1998) analysis of the Asian crisis.

30. Thus, where previous authors have said that in empirical work like that presented below we minimize the importance of macroeconomic and prudential policies for currency mismatches, they are confusing currency mismatches with original sin.

3.3   How These Differences Matter in Practice

We now show that these distinctions matter in practice. We start by constructing measures of original sin and presenting evidence of its consequences for policy, the volatility of growth and capital flows, and country creditworthiness.[31] We then repeat the exercise adding measures of aggregate currency mismatches and debt intolerance. The results suggest that the effects of original sin are the more statistically robust than those of these alternative concepts.

3.3.1   Original Sin

Our index of original sin is[32]

$$(1) \qquad \text{OSIN}_i = \max\left(1 - \frac{\text{Securities in currency } i}{\text{Securities issued by country } i}, 0\right)$$

The numerator includes all securities issued in currency i regardless of the nationality of the issuer. We adopt this formulation because if residents of countries different from i issue bonds in currency i, these bonds can then be used by residents of country i to swap their foreign currency obligations into domestic currency obligations. This opportunity to hedge would not be captured by an index that only includes local currency debt issued by residents. Although (Securities in currency i/Securities issued by country i) can be greater than 1 (for countries that issue currencies that are widely used by nonresidents), we bound OSIN at zero because countries cannot hedge more debt than they have.

This index includes bonded international debt but does not include cross-border bank loans, since the Bank for International Settlements (BIS) does not provide detailed currency breakdowns of international loans.[33] We therefore weight each observation in the regression analysis below by the share of securities in total foreign debt.[34]

Table 3.2 presents simple averages of OSIN for several groups of countries. The financial centers (United States, United Kingdom, Switzerland, and Japan) have the lowest levels of original sin (in an obvious sense since this is what defines them as financial centers). They are followed by the Euroland countries. Evidently, the advent of the euro (whose introduction provides the dividing point between the two periods in the table) led to a

---

31. This material is drawn from Eichengreen, Hausmann, and Panizza (2005b).

32. In Eichengreen, Hausmann, and Panizza (2005b), we develop some additional measures of original sin and discuss their strengths and weaknesses.

33. In Eichengreen, Hausmann, and Panizza (2005b) we construct an alternative measure that takes into account bank loans. However, in order to construct this index it is necessary to make assumptions about the currency composition of these loans.

34. The weight is equal to (total securities issued by country i)/(total bank loans + total securities issued by country i).

Table 3.2   Measures of original sin (OSIN) by country groupings (simple average)

	1993–1998	1999–2001
Financial centers	0.07	0.08
Euroland	0.53	0.09[a]
Other developed	0.78	0.72
Offshore	0.96	0.87
Developing	0.96	0.93
Latin America	0.98	1.00
Middle East and Africa	0.95	0.90
Asia and Pacific	0.99	0.94
Eastern Europe	0.91	0.84

Source: Authors' calculations.

[a]In the 1999–2001 period it is impossible to allocate the debt issued by nonresidents in euros to any of the individual member countries of the currency union. Hence, the number here is not the simple average, but is calculated taking Euroland as a whole.

drop in original sin in Euroland countries.[35] Developing countries have comparatively high levels of original sin, with Latin America having the most and Eastern Europe the least.

As argued above, we expect countries with original sin to be more inclined to accumulate international reserves and to use them to stabilize the exchange rate. Table 3.3 tests these hypotheses. All regressions in this table control for the level of development (proxied by the log of GDP per capita), openness, and foreign debt (total debt securities plus international loans) as a share of GDP. All variables are averages for the period 1993–98.[36]

Column (1) considers the choice of exchange rate regime. The dependent variable LYS is the de facto classification of Levy Yeyati and Sturzenegger (2000), which equals 1 for countries with floating exchange rates, 2 for countries with intermediate regimes, and 3 for countries with fixed rates. Since this measure increases with exchange rate inflexibility, we expect a positive relationship with original sin. The coefficient in question is positive and significant, indicating that countries with original sin float less freely.[37] The coefficient is also economically important. It suggests that moving OSIN from 1 to 0 is associated with a jump of one and a half points on the Levy Yeyati and Sturzenegger (2000) three-point scale. Countries previously inclined to peg will move to limited flexibility, while countries previously following policies of limited flexibility will be inclined to float. Original sin is one explanation, then, for the fear-of-floating phenomenon.

35. This is to be expected, since all of them, including a number of small ones that had not previously enjoyed the privilege, immediately became issuers of a major currency.
36. Since table 3.2 suggests a structural shift in 1999.
37. Since LYS is bounded at 1 and 3, we estimate the equation using double-censored Tobit. In Eichengreen, Hausmann, and Panizza (2005b) we explore whether this result could be due to reverse causality. We refer the reader to that paper for further discussion.

Table 3.3   Original sin and exchange rate volatility

	LYS (1)	RESM2 (2)	RVER (3)	LYS (4)	RESM2 (5)	RVER (6)
Original sin	1.503	0.248	−0.801	2.285	0.357	−1.034
	(3.56)***	(3.74)***	(2.02)**	(3.43)***	(4.01)***	(2.12)**
GDP per capita	0.302	−0.053	0.027	0.321	−0.047	0.014
	(2.89)***	(1.84)*	(0.61)	(2.53)**	(1.74)*	(0.31)
Openness	0.198	−0.014	1.018	0.129	−0.030	1.046
	(0.92)	(0.41)	(2.88)***	(0.60)	(0.89)	(2.99)***
External debt/GDP	0.290	−0.036	−0.570	0.622	0.005	−0.664
	(0.96)	(0.66)	(2.36)**	(1.13)	(0.09)	(2.55)**
Mismatch				−0.037	−0.037	0.084
				(0.35)	(2.09)**	(1.22)
Constant	−2.187	0.531	0.101	−3.094	0.399	0.394
	(1.94)*	(1.73)*	(0.17)	(2.14)**	(1.37)	(0.56)
No. of observations	75	65	65	59	64	64
R-squared		0.37	0.62		0.42	0.63

Notes: Equations (1) and (4) are estimated by weighted Tobit. All the other equations are estimated with weighted OLS with robust standard errors. Absolute value of t-statistics in parentheses.
***Significant at the 1 percent level.
**Significant at the 5 percent level.
*Significant at the 10 percent level.

Next we explore whether countries with high levels of original sin hold more reserves. As noted in section 3.2, this relationship sheds light on the connections between original sin and currency mismatches. Since reserves are often used to intervene in the foreign exchange market, their level may also shed light on the freedom of the float. The dependent variable here is international reserves normalized by M2 (denoted RESM2). Column (2) shows that the coefficient on OSIN is positive, as expected, and significant, as before. The estimated coefficient implies that the increase in reserves in a country where OSIN equals 1 instead of 0 is 25 percent of M2.

Following Bayoumi and Eichengreen (1998a, 1998b), we also define the freedom of the float as the volatility of exchange rates relative to the volatility of reserves (we denote the ratio as RVER). If countries with original sin are less inclined to float, we would expect a negative coefficient. Column (3) supports this hypothesis.

Next we consider the relationship between original sin and volatility of growth and capital flows.[38] There are at least three reasons why original sin may be positively correlated with volatility. First, it limits the authorities' capacity to undertake countercyclical policies. Second, dollar liabilities

38. Besides the independent variables included in table 3.3, we also control for the volatility of terms of trade. All equations are estimated by weighed OLS using robust standard errors.

Table 3.4   Original sin and GDP and capital flow volatility

	Growth (1)	Flows (2)	Growth (3)	Flows (4)
Original sin	0.011	7.069	0.016	9.139
	(1.87)*	(3.54)***	(1.49)	(1.53)
GDP per capita	−0.012	−3.242	−0.012	−3.265
	(2.19)**	(2.56)**	(2.03)**	(2.00)*
Openness	−0.001	−4.250	−0.002	−5.136
	(0.14)	(1.21)	(0.29)	(0.90)
Terms-of-trade volatility	−0.000	0.221	−0.000	0.201
	(0.90)	(1.08)	(0.82)	(0.73)
External debt/GDP	−0.014	0.212	−0.025	−2.747
	(1.67)*	(0.06)	(1.64)	(0.29)
Mismatch			−0.002	−0.655
			(1.18)	(1.29)
Constant	0.128	33.134	0.133	33.181
	(2.30)**	(2.40)**	(2.17)**	(1.91)*
No. of observations	77	33	63	23
R-squared	0.41	0.63	0.38	0.59

Note: Robust t-statistics in parentheses.
***Significant at the 1 percent level.
**Significant at the 5 percent level.
*Significant at the 10 percent level.

limit the central bank's ability to act as a lender of last resort. Third, dollar-denominated debt increases the costs of currency depreciations that, in the event of a currency crisis, may lead to large falls in output.

Table 3.4 confirms the existence of a positive and statistically significant relationship between original sin and macroeconomic volatility. The estimated coefficient implies that going from an OSIN of 0 to an OSIN of 1 raises the volatility of GDP growth by 1.1 percentage points. Given that the average volatility of GDP growth is 1.5 percent in industrial countries and 3.5 percent in developing countries, original sin may account for a significant part of the difference.

A final set of equations further explores the relationship between original sin and credit ratings (introduced in table 3.1 above). We expect original sin to be negatively related to ratings because it makes the cost of servicing debt dependent on a real exchange rate that is procyclical, increasing the states of the world in which payment is difficult.[39] We regress credit ratings on OSIN, several standard fiscal indicators (public debt over GDP,

39. Hausmann (2003) provides a value-at-risk model of credit ratings and shows that original sin makes debt service depend differently on the variances and covariances of output, the real exchange rate, and the real interest rate. Moreover, the arguments already presented explain why these variances and covariances are themselves different in countries with original sin.

Table 3.5   Original sin and credit ratings

	RATING					
	(1)	(2)	(3)	(4)	(5)	(6)
Original sin	−5.844	−5.642	−5.346	−7.202	−7.195	−4.949
	(4.07)***	(4.00)***	(4.08)***	(5.20)***	(5.05)***	(2.90)***
Debt/GDP	−2.426		−2.376	−3.721	−3.695	−2.358
	(2.51)**		(2.71)***	(3.79)***	(3.66)***	(2.31)**
Debt/revenues		−1.000				
		(2.49)**				
GDP per capita	2.917	2.670	2.758	1.618	1.636	2.992
	(8.47)***	(6.15)***	(8.65)***	(4.25)***	(4.12)***	(9.09)***
External debt ratio	2.184	2.784	1.390	3.546	3.617	5.309
	(1.43)	(1.52)	(0.99)	(2.11)**	(2.00)*	(2.85)***
Terms-of-trade volatility			−0.092		0.015	
			(2.49)**		(0.29)	
Real exchange rate volatility				−4.187	−4.229	
				(5.49)***	(4.50)***	
Mismatch						−2.928
						(3.65)***
Constant	−8.062	−5.962	−5.931	8.394	8.114	−9.000
	(2.12)**	(1.28)	(1.66)	(1.83)*	(1.69)*	(2.39)**
No. of observations	56	49	54	41	40	45

***Significant at the 1 percent level.
**Significant at the 5 percent level.
*Significant at the 10 percent level.

public debt over government revenues), the country's level of economic development (as proxied by per capita income), and the share of external debt in GDP. S&P rating data, adjusted as above, are used in what follows.

We find a strong negative correlation between original sin and credit ratings. Columns (1)–(5) of table 3.5 confirm that original sin is correlated with creditworthiness even after controlling for the level of development, total external debt, public debt relative to GDP or revenues, terms-of-trade volatility, and the real exchange rate volatility.[40] A drop in OSIN from 1 to 0 is associated with a five-notch improvement in credit ratings. This would push most countries in the sample above investment grade.

3.3.2   Currency Mismatches

Goldstein and Turner (2004) suggest that original sin has been improperly used as a proxy for aggregate currency mismatches. To this we would

40. The volatility of the real exchange rate may be persistent (depending on openness of the economy and the commodity composition of exports), and it is likely to be correlated with the probability of payment difficulties.

only say "not by us." They suggest that a measure of aggregate mismatches should take into account the currency composition of domestic debt. This is incorrect, since if that debt is domestically held, the assets and liabilities of residents cancel out in the aggregate. To the extent that domestically issued, foreign currency–denominated or linked debt is held by foreigners, that is another issue. Such debt falls conceptually under the heading of foreign currency–denominated external debt.

In practice, holdings of domestically issued, foreign currency debt owned by foreigners are not easy to track. Some information can be obtained by a report on the currency composition of all holdings by U.S. residents of foreign securities for 2001 issued by the U.S. Department of the Treasury. This report has the advantage that it includes holdings of locally issued instruments; its disadvantage is that it covers only the holdings of U.S. residents. These data, summarized in table 3.6, corroborate the idea that the global portfolio is concentrated in very few currencies and that, by implication, the issuers of other currencies suffer from original sin (in other words, that the claims they sell to foreigners are predominantly denominated in foreign currencies, whether these are issued on foreign markets or not). Of the $648 billion of financial claims on foreigners held by U.S. residents in 2001, $456 billion (fully 70 percent) were denominated in U.S. dollars. U.S. residents hold 50.9 percent of their claims on Euroland countries in euros and 22.5 percent of their claims on other advanced countries in the currencies of those countries but only 3.1 percent of their claims on developing countries in the currencies of those developing countries.[41]

Goldstein and Turner (2003) define their measure of aggregate effective currency mismatches (AECM) as

$$(2) \qquad AECM = \frac{NFCA}{EXP} \cdot FCSHARE,$$

where NFCA is net foreign currency assets, EXP is exports, and FCSHARE is the foreign currency share of total debt (both domestic and in-

---

41. Burger and Warnock (2003) look at these data from a different point of view, one that is entirely orthogonal to our point. They compare U.S. holdings of European bonds as a share of the total European market with U.S. holdings of Canadian (or emerging market) bonds expressed as a share of the Canadian (or emerging market) bond market. In Europe, where the overall bond market is much larger, they obtain a relatively small fraction. But this is due to the larger denominator. Consider a world in which the European economy and European bond market are many times larger than those of the United States. We would then see U.S. investors holding only a small fraction of total European bond issuance. But this would tell us nothing about Europe's susceptibility to original sin; it would only confirm that the European economy and bond market are very much larger than those of the United States. In addition, Burger and Warnock look at asset allocation by region of issuer rather than by currency composition, which is our concern. Thus, table 2 in their paper, cited by Goldstein and Turner (2004) as a criticism of the original-sin view, has no bearing on the question.

Table 3.6   Composition outstanding of international securities issued by non-U.S. residents and held by U.S. investors (2001)

	USD	EUR	JPY	GBP	OWN	Other	Total	Share of total	Share of international securities	Securities by currency	Currency share
Financial centers	137.4	5.1	32.5	16.1	0.1	0.3	191.6	29.57	19.45	511.8	79.00
Euroland	81.8	87.9	1.9	1.0	0.0	0.3	172.8	26.68	6.74	97.3	15.02
Other developed	115.3	1.0	0.7	0.5	34.1	0.3	151.8	23.44	29.91	34.1	5.26
Offshore	32.7	1.8	0.5	0.5	0.5	0.0	36.1	5.57	69.73	0.5	0.08
Developing	80.0	0.9	0.2	0.1	2.6	0.1	84.0	12.96	17.09	2.6	0.41
International organizations	9.0	0.6	0.8	0.6	0.0	0.6	11.5	1.78	3.05	0.0	0.00
Other and unallocated										1.5	0.23
Total	456.0	97.3	36.7	18.9	37.4	1.5	647.8	100	13.01	647.8	100

Source: Authors' calculations based on tables 16 and 17 in U.S. Treasury (2003).

Notes: USD = US. Dollar; EUR = euro; JPY = yen; GBP = British pound. The OWN currency column is set equal to zero for Euroland (everything is reported under the euro column) and, in the case of financial centers, for Japan and the United Kingdom. The value reported under OWN for financial centers corresponds to issues in Swiss francs. The "Share of International Securities" column shows the share held by U.S. investors over total international bonds issued in 2001 by non-U.S. residents. The "Securities by Currency" and "Currency Share" columns show international securities (and their share) held by U.S. investors in each of the currency groups. For instance, at the end of 2001 U.S. investors held US$97.3 billion worth of international securities denominated in euro; this corresponds to 15 percent of the total international securities held by U.S. investors.

ternational).[42] Unfortunately, the data do not exist to compute AECM for a substantial number of countries. In particular, information on net foreign currency assets beyond international reserves and on the currency composition of total debt (international and domestic) are available for a limited number of countries. For this reason, Goldstein and Turner restrict their sample to twenty-two countries.

It is possible to build a measure similar to AECM for a larger sample. Consider the following index:

$$(3) \qquad \text{MISMATCH} = \frac{\text{RES} - \text{DEBT}}{\text{EXP}} \cdot \text{OSIN},$$

where RES is international reserves, DEBT is international debt, and other variables are defined as above.[43] MISMATCH is not identical to AECM, but for the countries for which we have data on both the correlation of the two measures is 0.82 (p-value = 0.000).[44]

We now augment the preceding regressions with this measure.[45] To facilitate comparison we multiply MISMATCH by –1 so that a higher value indicates a higher mismatch.

Columns (4)–(6) of table 3.3 show that controlling for MISMATCH does not eliminate the correlation between original sin and our three measures of exchange rate flexibility. If anything, the effect of OSIN becomes stronger. MISMATCH has a significant effect on RESM2 (the ratio of reserves to M2), but this is to be expected because reserves are used in the construction of MISMATCH. There is no significant correlation between MISMATCH and either LYS or RVER, our two measures of exchange rate policy. Columns (3) and (4) of table 3.4 similarly show that MISMATCH is not significantly correlated with the volatility of growth or capital flows.[46]

The last column of table 3.5 checks whether controlling for MIS-

42. Goldstein and Turner suggest that this is a good measure of overall mismatches because, besides capturing both sides of the balance sheet and considering the currency denomination of total debt, it also has substantial volatility over time and hence the potential of being a useful leading indicator of currency crises. Note that since higher levels of AECM indicate lower mismatches, when NFCA is positive they replace exports with imports.

43. We could also measure mismatches as [RES – (DEBT · OSIN)]/EXP. This alternative definition makes more sense to us, but the one in the text is closer to that used by Goldstein and Turner. In practice, the two measures are highly correlated. The results discussed below do not change if we use one measure instead of the other.

44. In particular, MISMATCH does not capture net international assets or measure the currency composition of total debt.

45. The present expanded sample includes twenty of Goldstein and Turner's twenty-two countries. (Some of the data needed to construct the mismatch proxy for China and Taiwan are not available.)

46. Including this variable in the regressions also reduces the explanatory power of original sin; with a p value of 0.14, OSIN is no longer statistically significant at conventional levels. At the same time, controlling for MISMATCH substantially raises the point estimate of OSIN. This suggests that the drop in statistical significance is due to the fact we are now forced to use a smaller sample. If we estimate equations (1) and (2) on the same sample as equations (3) and (4) we find results similar to those of columns (3) and (4): the point estimates of original sin increase, but the coefficients are not statistically significant.

MATCH affects the relationship between original sin and credit ratings. The significance of MISMATCH indicates that countries with large stocks of international reserves and small international debts have better ratings, other things being equal, these variables providing widely utilized rules of thumb for the rating agencies. But controlling for MISMATCH leaves the point estimate and significance of the coefficient on OSIN unchanged. An interpretation is that credit ratings are sensitive to both whether a country can borrow abroad in its own currency and how effectively it manages any currency mismatches that result from its inability to do so.

3.3.3 Debt Intolerance

Recall that Reinhart, Rogoff, and Savastano (2003) define debt intolerance as the inability of emerging markets to manage external debts that are manageable for advanced countries. They operationalize it as the relationship of external debt (scaled by GDP or exports) to a measure of country risk (credit ratings).

We already included the debt-GDP and debt-revenue ratios in the credit rating regressions reported earlier in this section, along with OSIN. There we found that both original sin and debt ratios matter for credit ratings.[47] We can generalize this analysis by allowing the debt ratio to have a different impact on credit ratings in advanced and developing countries. Let DE_GDP · IND and DE_RE · IND denote the effect of the debt-GDP and debt–tax revenue ratios in the advanced economies and DE_GDP · DEV and DE_RE · DEV the effect of these same ratios in developing countries. Table 3.7 shows that the impact of original sin on credit ratings is robust to this extension. When we add a separate intercept for developing countries to avoid loading all other respects in which advanced and developing countries differ into the DE_GDP · DEV and DE_REV · DEV terms, original sin remains significant and important, while there is again no difference in the elasticity of credit ratings with respect to the external debt ratio in developing versus advanced economies.

We constructed two alternative measures of debt intolerance and checked whether adding them to our regressions for exchange rate flexibility diminishes the impact of original sin. The first measure, DI1, is nonofficial external debt (scaled by GDP) relative to RATING.[48] The second one, DI2, is the domestic and external public debt (again scaled by GDP) relative to RATING. Table 3.8 asks whether controlling for debt intolerance, so measured, affects the correlation between original sin and exchange rate flexibility.[49] It turns out that these proxies for debt intolerance have little

---

47. As does MISMATCH—again, see table 3.5.
48. Our measure differs from that of Reinhart, Rogoff, and Savastano in that we include both public and private debt while excluding official instead of concessional debt.
49. When we use DI1, we run regressions both including and excluding external debt over GDP from some specifications on the grounds that this variable is in the numerator of DI1.

Table 3.7   Original sin and credit rating in developing and industrial countries

	RATING			
	(1)	(2)	(3)	(4)
Original sin	−5.100	−5.385	−4.751	−5.101
	(3.38)***	(3.46)***	(3.32)***	(3.53)***
DE_GDP · IND	−1.553		−2.451	
	(1.31)		(2.05)**	
DE_GDP · DEV	−3.557		−2.475	
	(2.66)**		(1.84)*	
DE_RE · IND		−0.860		−1.354
		(1.57)		(2.45)**
DE_RE · DEV		−1.113		−0.847
		(2.22)**		(1.79)*
GDP per capita	2.663	2.575	1.936	1.729
	(6.71)***	(5.12)***	(4.00)***	(3.01)***
External debt/GDP	2.252	2.799	1.751	2.015
	(1.50)	(1.54)	(1.22)	(1.17)
Developing			−3.004	−3.226
			(2.38)**	(2.52)**
Constant	−6.314	−5.288	1.606	4.085
	(1.58)	(1.06)	(0.32)	(0.69)
No. of observations	56	49	56	49

Notes: Table shows weighted Tobit estimations. Absolute value of t-statistics in parentheses.
***Significant at the 1 percent level.
**Significant at the 5 percent level.
*Significant at the 10 percent level.

additional impact on exchange rate flexibility, while the results for original sin are basically unchanged.[50]

Table 3.9 examines the implications of adding these alternative measures of debt intolerance to our analysis of the volatility of growth and capital flows. Their addition does not diminish the impact of original sin on the volatility of either GDP growth or capital flows. In contrast, neither measure of debt intolerance has a significant impact on the volatility of GDP growth.

There is some evidence that debt intolerance is significantly correlated with the volatility of capital flows. But when we separate the variable into its two components (debt ratio and credit rating), we find that most of the explanatory power resides with the denominator (see columns [9]–[11] of table 3.9). Total external debt over GDP and government debt over GDP are never statistically significant (total debt also has the wrong sign). This

50. The debt intolerance measure has additional impact on exchange rate flexibility only in two specifications.

Table 3.8   Original sin, debt intolerance, and exchange rate volatility

	LYS			RESM2			RVER		
	(1)	(2)	(3)	(4)	(5)	(6)	(7)	(8)	(9)
Original sin	1.737	1.886	1.738	0.271	0.247	0.271	-0.843	-0.136	-0.809
	(3.74)***	(3.89)***	(3.85)***	(4.09)***	(3.61)***	(4.11)***	(2.18)**	(0.76)	(2.02)**
GDP per capita	0.259	0.220	0.259	-0.034	-0.044	-0.034	0.124	0.033	-0.001
	(1.94)*	(1.69)*	(2.39)**	(1.12)	(1.72)*	(1.57)	(1.78)*	(1.66)	(0.03)
Openness	0.208	0.391	0.208	0.007	0.079	0.007	0.990	-0.057	1.052
	(0.84)	(0.86)	(0.85)	(0.22)	(1.20)	(0.22)	(4.37)***	(0.68)	(3.70)***
External debt/GDP	-0.004	0.069		0.001	-0.050		-1.603	0.072	
	(0.01)	(0.20)		(0.00)	(0.62)		(2.85)***	(0.80)	
DI1	2.435		2.377	-1.012		-1.006	17.456		2.368
	(0.19)		(0.43)	(0.43)		(0.83)	(2.52)**		(0.83)
DI2		-1.849			-0.766			0.299	
		(0.74)			(1.70)*			(1.26)	
Constant	-2.033	-1.817	-2.030	0.338	0.415	0.337	-0.825	0.002	0.151
	(1.48)	(1.26)	(1.66)	(1.12)	(1.47)	(1.41)	(1.07)	(0.01)	(0.24)
No. of observations	59	51	59	53	46	53	52	45	52
R-squared				0.34	0.40	0.34	0.73	0.25	0.69

Notes: Equations (1)–(3) are estimated with weighted Tobit model. All the other equations are estimated with weighted OLS with robust standard errors.

***Significant at the 1 percent level.

**Significant at the 5 percent level.

*Significant at the 10 percent level.

Table 3.9   Original sin, debt intolerance, and GDP and capital flow volatility

	Growth (1)	Flows (2)	Growth (3)	Growth (4)	Flows (5)	Flows (6)	Flows (7)	Flows (8)	Flows (9)	Flows (10)	Flows (11)
Original sin	0.013	0.015	0.013	0.015	5.271	9.163	6.693	8.959	3.155	5.630	5.547
	(2.45)**	(2.84)***	(2.46)**	(2.77)***	(2.77)**	(4.48)***	(3.15)***	(4.19)***	(1.82)*	(2.35)**	(2.15)**
GDP per capita	-0.007	-0.008	-0.007	-0.009	-1.234	-2.173	-3.041	-2.340	2.012	1.469	1.240
	(2.04)**	(2.65)**	(2.98)***	(2.85)***	(1.13)	(2.43)**	(2.58)**	(2.48)**	(1.16)	(0.99)	(0.87)
Openness	0.002	-0.005	0.002	-0.006	-1.606	-1.918	-6.413	-3.357	3.139	3.948	2.243
	(0.41)	(0.50)	(0.50)	(0.65)	(0.35)	(0.44)	(1.67)	(0.91)	(1.10)	(1.22)	(0.79)
Terms-of-trade volatility	0.000	0.000	0.000	0.000	0.145	-0.159	0.217	-0.137	0.100	-0.224	-0.197
	(0.23)	(0.13)	(0.37)	(0.24)	(0.59)	(1.65)	(1.03)	(1.55)	(0.49)	(1.86)*	(1.59)
External debt/GDP	-0.008	-0.005			-20.531	-2.797			-0.616	-3.093	
	(0.42)	(0.65)			(1.83)*	(1.14)			(0.23)	(1.10)	
DI1	-0.026		-0.109		355.751		57.418				
	(0.09)		(0.81)		(1.76)*		(0.75)				
DI2		-0.075		-0.078		52.839		52.850			
		(1.19)		(1.21)		(4.85)***		(4.87)***			
Rating									-1.494	-1.337	-1.316
									(2.54)**	(2.51)**	(2.44)**
Public debt/GDP										1.686	1.839
										(0.60)	(0.66)
Constant	0.078	0.093	0.082	0.097	13.241	22.635	31.258	23.906	5.858	9.169	10.562
	(2.35)**	(2.80)***	(3.01)***	(2.94)***	(1.03)	(2.36)**	(2.37)**	(2.39)**	(0.58)	(0.91)	(1.08)
No. of observations	62	54	62	54	29	26	29	26	29	26	26
R-squared	0.38	0.35	0.38	0.35	0.64	0.75	0.60	0.74	0.68	0.73	0.73
Sum of coefficients evaluated at the mean									DEBT + RATING	DEBT + RATING + DE_GDP	RATING + DE_GDP
									-20.58	-18.84	-17.16
Test									$F(1,22) = 6.1$	$F(1,18) = 6.0$	$F(1,19) = 6.5$
p									0.022	0.025	0.020

Note: Robust t-statistics in parentheses.

***Significant at the 1 percent level.

**Significant at the 5 percent level.

*Significant at the 10 percent level.

is telling us that countries with low credit ratings have relatively volatile capital flows, which is not surprising given the bidirectional causality between the variables.[51]

3.4 Additional Issues

In this section we consider a number of additional issues arising from the recent literature related to this paper.

3.4.1 Hedging

Efforts to measure an economy's vulnerability to balance sheet effects using the value of securities issued abroad that are denominated in foreign currencies can mislead if swaps and other derivative transactions are used to hedge currency exposures.[52] The limited availability of information on derivative transactions is thus an impediment to empirical work in this area.[53]

Of course, if foreigners hold no financial claims on a country that are denominated in its own currency (the extreme form of original sin that appears to afflict fully half of the countries considered in the appendix to Eichengreen, Hausmann, and Panizza 2005b), then its *aggregate* foreign currency exposure cannot be hedged as a matter of definition.[54] For residents of the country to swap out of their aggregate currency mismatch, there must be someone on the other side of the swap. If foreigners are unwilling to hold local currency exposure, they will be unwilling to purchase swaps, and the issuing country will be unable to hedge its aggregate foreign currency exposure. Firms can use hedges to pass around foreign currency exposure like a hot potato, but as a group they cannot shed it if foreign investors are unwilling to hold it.[55] If that exposure is reallocated domesti-

---

51. In addition, we reject the null that the two coefficients enter with equal and opposite signs, as suggested by the debt intolerance hypothesis. This is shown in the last two rows, which check whether the sum of the rating and debt coefficients (evaluated at the mean of the respective variables) is equal to zero and strongly reject the hypothesis.

52. Simply tabulating the value of foreign currency–denominated securities sold to foreigners will not produce a measure of gross foreign currency exposure, for example, if domestic issuers use derivative transactions to swap out of the foreign currency.

53. To put the point another way, the difficulty of tracking off-balance-sheet transactions creates problems for the balance sheet approach.

54. Goldstein and Turner (2004) state that the "original sin hypothesis" assumes that all emerging markets are alike in terms of their ability to hedge foreign exposures. If they are alluding to our work, then this description is erroneous. To the contrary, we emphasize that those countries with the most severe cases of original sin (i.e., when all of the country's debt to foreigners is denominated in foreign currency) are by definition unable to hedge their exposures in the aggregate, while others may be able to do so to some extent.

55. Alternatively, the government can assume the risk. Bonomo, Martins, and Pinto (2003) suggest that after the Brazilian devaluation of 1998 the government became the ultimate source of hedging. In this case, then, the mismatch was transferred from the private to the public sector.

cally in efficient ways—if it is transferred at a price to firms in the strongest position to manage the associated risks (from firms producing nontradables to firms producing tradable goods, for example)—then the effects of original sin may be mitigated.[56] But the effects are analytically distinct from the phenomenon itself.[57]

3.4.2   Measuring Currency Mismatch

In the case of aggregate currency mismatches, it is important to net a country's international reserves and other foreign currency–denominated financial assets from gross external liabilities denominated in foreign currency. It may or may not be important to also include domestic debts denominated in foreign currency. If there is no foreign participation in domestic debt markets, then the currency denomination of domestic debts has no bearing on calculations of the aggregate currency mismatch, insofar as one resident's domestic dollar (peso) liability is another resident's domestic dollar (peso) asset.[58]

With the growing participation of foreign investors in local emerging bond markets, it becomes increasingly problematic to neglect the currency denomination of issues on the latter. But it cannot simply be assumed that all local currency issues are local currency denominated. Burger and Warnock (2003, n. 9) observe that "BIS data on domestic bonds is not collected at the security level but *should* contain only local-currency denominated bonds placed locally; for Argentina and Peru, however, it contains some foreign currency issues" (emphasis added). Burger and Warnock recategorize the relevant bonds for these two countries. Unfortunately, it is probable that there also exist other foreign currency issues in the BIS data. There is also the fact that some fraction of emerging market debt securities placed locally is indexed to the exchange rate rather than denominated in foreign currency, creating the same problems as foreign currency–denominated debt from the point of view of the balance sheet literature.

Concentrating solely on the currency composition of financial assets

56. Goldstein and Turner (2004) criticize our OSIN measure for failing to distinguish the allocation of currency risk between traded and nontraded goods–producing sectors. This confuses the effects of OSIN with its magnitude (in effect, it fails to distinguish between the left- and right-hand-side variables in our regression equations). We return to this point below. It also confuses their concern, currency mismatches, with ours, the currency composition of the gross external debt. This criticism is also disingenuous because Goldstein and Turner themselves have no information on the distribution of aggregate currency exposures between the traded and nontraded goods–producing sectors for the sample of twenty-two countries.

57. If hedging had been important in the sample period for mitigating the *effects* of original sin, we of course would not find the strong correlation between original sin, fear of floating, capital flow and output volatility, and credit ratings that we document in the previous section.

58. The currency denomination of domestic debts may still have important implications for the financial vulnerability of individual firms and banks, as noted above (if, for example, foreign currency net liabilities are concentrated among producers of nontradables). But this vulnerability will not be picked up by aggregate measures of the currency mismatch.

and liabilities also ignores natural hedges. The same exchange rate change that increases the cost of servicing foreign currency–denominated external obligations may increase the demand abroad for the exports of the indebted country and hence its capacity to meet its debt service obligations. This observation has encouraged some students of currency mismatches to normalize net foreign currency–denominated financial debt by exports, as we saw in equation (2) above.

But normalizing by exports, whether gross or net, confuses stocks with flows.[59] What is relevant when the exchange rate changes is the (increase in the) flow of export revenues relative to the (increase in the flow of) debt service costs, not a comparison of stocks of financial assets with flows of export receipts. Comparing the flow of export receipts with the flow of interest payments on foreign currency–denominated financial assets would be more appropriate in this context.[60]

Normalizing the stock of net external debt denominated in foreign currency by exports also conflates the extent of the mismatch with its effects. A country that exports less will almost certainly find it harder to undertake the macroeconomic adjustment needed to contend with the adverse balance sheet effects of exchange rate depreciation. But the impact of an exchange rate change when there is a currency mismatch is different from the size of the mismatch.[61] A measure like equation (2) might be defended as a leading indicator of the potential severity of potential mismatch problems, but this would be quite different from saying that it is an adequate measure of the extent of mismatches.

3.4.3 The Domestic Dimension

Eichengreen and Hausmann (1999) used original sin to refer to both the difficulty emerging markets have in borrowing abroad in their own currencies and the difficulty that many of them also experience in borrowing at home, in local currency terms, at long maturities and fixed rates. Countries suffering from both problems will find it particularly difficult to cope with adverse shocks. If they allow the currency to depreciate in response, they will be hammered by the balance sheet effects of the aggregate currency mismatch. But if they attempt to support the currency by raising interest

59. At the level of abstraction, Goldstein and Turner (2004) distinguish a flow measure of mismatches from a stock measure of mismatches, but this distinction is not maintained when they turn to empirics and develop the measure reproduced in equation (2) above.

60. In addition, the same distinction between gross and net foreign currency–denominated financial obligations emphasized elsewhere applies to exports as well; the (increase in) export revenues should presumably be net (of the increase in import spending) rather than gross.

61. In a regression framework, an appropriate way of controlling for the fact that the same currency mismatch may have larger effects on macroeconomic variables in less open economies is to interact the mismatch variable with a measure of openness (also controlling separately for openness, since openness may also affect those macroeconomic variables through non–balance sheet channels), not to construct a variable that conflates the extent of the mismatch with the likely magnitude of its effects.

rates, firms and banks will have their financial situation destabilized by the rise in the short-term interest rate, given the absence of long-term fixed-rate debt.[62]

In subsequent work we narrowed our definition, focusing on the difficulty that emerging markets experience in borrowing abroad in their own currencies, reflecting evidence that, with sufficient time and effort, it has become possible for some of them to develop the capacity to place longer-term domestic currency issues with local residents. The International Monetary Fund (IMF; 2003) reports that local corporate bond issues in emerging markets grew by a factor of 10 between 1997–99 and 2000–2001 and that local bond markets have been the dominant source of funding for the public sector in emerging markets as a class. The role of domestic bond issues in corporate funding has been particularly important in Latin America, where local bond issues nearly equaled the sum of international issues of bonds, equities, and syndicated lending in the period 1997–2001.

At the same time, a substantial number of domestic bond placements are indexed to the exchange rate, as noted above, rendering them indistinguishable from a currency-risk point of view from foreign currency–denominated issues. A substantial share of the remainder is indexed to the short-term interest rate, thereby providing no protection from interest rate hikes. Still, emerging markets, especially in Asia, have made some progress in issuing long-dated bonds that, when indexed at all, are indexed to slowly moving variables like inflation rather than to financial variables like exchange rates and short-term interest rates that respond instantaneously to shocks.[63]

Figure 3.1 shows a scatter plot of our original sin measure (OSIN) versus a measure of the ability to issue domestic currency long-term fixed-rate debt, or "domestic original sin" (DSIN), for all countries for which we have been able to construct both measures. Our main source of information on domestic original sin is JPMorgan's (1998, 2000, 2002) *Guide to Local Markets,* which reports detailed information on domestically traded public debt for twenty-four emerging market countries. We divide outstanding government bonds into five categories: (a) long-term domestic currency fixed rate (DLTF); (b) short-term domestic currency fixed rate (DSTF); (c) long-term (or short-term) domestic currency debt indexed to interest rate (DLTII); (d) long-term domestic currency debt indexed to prices (DLTIP); and (e) foreign currency debt (FC). We define domestic original sin as

---

62. This was the situation in which Asian banks that had funded themselves by incurring short-term obligations found themselves in 1997; it is also the reason the dilemma of whether to let the exchange rate go or to defend it with interest rate hikes was a no-win situation.

63. Thus, in our empirical work we classify countries as not suffering from the domestic aspect of original sin only when they have issued significant amounts of domestic currency debt that is not floating rate, short term, or dollar indexed. In one of our measures, we include debt that is indexed to the consumer price index, a more slowly moving nonfinancial variable.

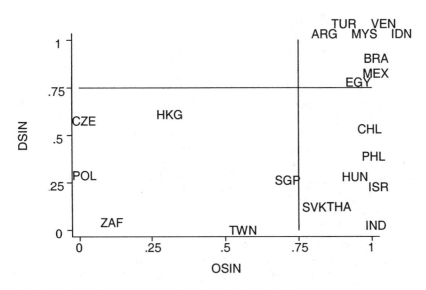

Fig. 3.1   Domestic versus international original sin (2001)

$$DSIN = \frac{FC + DSTF + DLTII}{FC + DLTF + DSTF + DLTII + DLTIP}$$

This definition focuses on both foreign currency debt and domestic currency short-term debt (or long-term but indexed to the interest rate).[64] Note that there are a number of countries with low levels of DSIN but high levels of OSIN, such as Chile, Israel, India, Hungary, and Thailand. Contrary to the conjecture of Reinhart, Rogoff, and Savastano (2003), it is not obvious that the domestic and international aspects of original sin are determined by identical sets of factors.[65]

There is now a substantial literature on the development of domestic bond markets and on the relevant policy initiatives (see Harwood 2000; Herring and Chatusripitak 2000). Steps for developing domestic bond markets include running stable macroeconomic policies, strengthening

64. We only have information on traded debt (and mostly public debt). Hence, if a country has a market for long-term fixed-rate bank loans but no market for long-term fixed-rate debt instruments, our indexes may overestimate original sin. If, on the other hand, a country has a market for long-term fixed-rate debt instruments but no market for long-term fixed-rate bank loans, our indexes will provide a lower bound for original sin. The data in figure 3.1 are for December 2001, with the exception of Argentina (where the data refer to 1998) and Egypt (where the data refer to 2000).

65. On the other hand, there are no countries with high levels of DSIN and low values of OSIN. This supports the idea that resolving the domestic aspects of original sin is a necessary condition for addressing the international aspect. Hausmann and Panizza (2003) show that the determinants of DSIN and OSIN are empirically quite different, with inflation history and institutions playing a larger role in the former and country size playing an important and robust role in the latter.

payment and settlement systems, and using regulation to encourage transparency on the part of market participants. But what is striking is that the same emerging markets that have made progress in these areas and thus have been rewarded with faster domestic bond market development have made less progress in acquiring the capacity to borrow abroad in their own currencies. This is the observation that led us to more narrowly focus our definition of original sin. It is what has led us to conjecture that something about the structure of foreign demand for claims denominated in the local currency is contributing to the problem of original sin.[66]

Even if domestic reforms that help to promote the development of local markets do not eliminate original sin, might they not eliminate the main reason for worrying about it by eliminating the need for countries to borrow abroad? With well-developed domestic financial markets, the argument might run, it will become possible to finance domestic investment out of domestic savings, with no need for recourse to foreign finance. However, such a conclusion would minimize the benefits of international borrowing (and lending) for smoothing consumption, diversifying risk, and augmenting investment where appropriate. Countries like the United States with well-developed domestic financial markets still make use of the capital account for these purposes. It is not obviously the case, in other words, that well-developed domestic financial markets render the foreign finance superfluous.[67] To the contrary, the case for having safe access to international finance remains compelling.

The question is what safety requires. Potential borrowers must pursue macroeconomic, financial, and institutional reforms in order to be able to deploy foreign funding productively and become attractive destinations for international capital flows. But potential borrowers and lenders must also be able to address the sources of the reluctance of foreign investors to hold claims denominated in the currencies of emerging markets in order to create an attractive balance between the risks and returns of borrowing abroad. It is to this problem that we now turn.

3.4.4   Reflections on Causes

In Eichengreen, Hausmann, and Panizza (2005a) we examine several potential explanations for original sin. Although level of development, monetary credibility, and quality of institutions may play a role, the evidence there suggests that these variables by themselves cannot account for the

66. We consider this possibility more systematically below.
67. Goldstein and Turner (2004, p. 21) write that they find unpersuasive "the view (implicit in the OSH [original sin hypothesis]) that any analysis of the path to reduced financial fragility and higher economic growth in emerging markets should concentrate exclusively on external sources of finance." This position is certainly not implicit in our work. Rather, our position is that domestic bond market development does not eliminate the argument for international finance. If we have focused on measures to enhance access to international finance, this is because this aspect of the problem is particularly difficult to solve (as is explained in the text).

widespread nature of the phenomenon. Country size is the only variable analyzed that is both statistically and economically significant as a determinant of original sin. It is this finding that leads us to formulate an explanation for original sin based on the costs and returns to portfolio diversification at the global level.

Here we summarize our previous empirical analysis and consider some additional wrinkles.[68] Country size is measured as the principal component of the log of total GDP, log of total trade and the log of total domestic credit. Column (1) of table 3.10 shows that country size is negatively related to original sin. A variety of sensitivity analyses support the conclusion that size is important in regressions seeking to explain original sin. We therefore control for country size in all of the empirical analysis that follows.

Table 3.2 above suggested that original sin varies between financial centers, the Euroland countries, other advanced economies, and developing countries. In the analysis that follows we therefore control for membership in these country groups by including a vector of country-group variables (where developing country is the omitted alternative). Table 3.2 shows that these fixed effects are quite important.[69]

In column (2) of table 3.10 we add per capita GDP as a measure of economic development. Both this variable and country size are negatively correlated with original sin, although only size is significantly different from zero at standard confidence levels.

In column (3) we consider inflationary history as a measure of monetary credibility. Our variable is constructed as the average of log inflation over the last twenty years in an effort to capture any lingering effects of policies long past. While countries with histories of more inflation appear to have more original sin, the effect does not approach statistical significance at standard confidence levels.[70]

---

68. Since our dependent variable ranges between 0 and 1, all the regressions are estimated by weighted Tobit. In Eichengreen, Hausmann, and Panizza (2005a) we show that the results are robust to alternative estimation techniques. As before, all variables are measured as 1993–98 averages (except where explicitly noted to the contrary).

69. Not including these fixed effects, which subsequent analysis shows to be important, may therefore bias our results. Doing so may attribute to a country's policies the effects of its status as a financial center. Or it may attribute to, say, inflation the effect of all the characteristics of a country that are associated with its industrial-country status. In the interest of completeness, we show below how the results change when we omit these country-group fixed effects and provide an interpretation of the differences. It turns out that they do not change very much.

70. Shorter lags of inflation only strengthen this result. This finding is also robust to a variety of sensitivity analyses. When we replace average inflation with the log of maximum inflation over the period, we again find no significant relationship with original sin. To test potential nonlinearities in the relationship between inflation and original sin, we also experimented with both the average log of inflation and its square. In this case, neither of the coefficients on inflation is significant. Alternatively, we use the principal component of average inflation and maximum inflation and again find no significant correlation with original sin (results are reported in the appendix of Eichengreen, Hausmann, and Panizza 2005a).

Table 3.10 The causes of original sin

	OSIN (1)	OSIN (2)	OSIN (3)	OSIN (4)	OSIN (5)	OSIN (6)	OSIN (IV) (7)	OSIN (IV) (8)	OSIN (9)	OSIN (10)	OSIN (IV) (11)
Size	-0.562 (6.16)***	-0.310 (3.37)***	-0.318 (3.57)***	-0.350 (3.71)***	-0.330 (3.60)***	-0.323 (3.53)***	-0.318 (3.54)***	-0.345 (2.07)**	-0.365 (2.13)**	-0.290 (3.22)***	-0.270 (2.64)**
GDP per capita		-0.142 (1.59)									
AV_INF			0.307 (1.19)								
DE_GDP				-0.073 (0.50)							
DE_GDP · DEV					0.247 (0.88)						
DE_GDP · IND					-0.186 (1.13)						
Institutions						-0.050 (0.46)	0.158 (0.50)	-0.226 (0.68)	-0.041 (0.36)		
DC_GDP										-0.332 (1.49)	-1.568 (0.95)
FIN_CENTER		-0.679 (1.99)*	-0.866 (2.88)***	-0.825 (2.72)***	-0.645 (2.01)**	-0.883 (2.65)**	-1.179 (2.16)**			-0.753 (2.40)**	0.239 (0.19)
EUROLAND		-0.125 (0.61)	-0.304 (2.11)**	-0.344 (2.61)**	-0.155 (0.84)	-0.326 (1.80)*	-0.553 (1.50)			-0.226 (1.37)	0.488 (0.53)
OTH_DEVEL		0.007 (0.03)	-0.200 (1.47)	-0.275 (2.18)**	-0.094 (0.53)	-0.203 (1.03)	-0.501 (1.05)			-0.224 (1.75)*	-0.016 (0.05)
DEVELOPING								0.049 (0.09)	0.409 (1.38)		
Constant	1.388 (13.14)	2.526 (3.40)***	1.277 (10.87)***	1.426 (11.99)***	1.260 (8.00)***	1.388 (13.18)***	1.343 (11.64)***	1.224 (2.29)**	0.931 (2.64)**	1.521 (10.13)***	2.119 (2.65)***
No. of observations	75	75	74	64	64	75	75	29	29	74	74

Notes: Table shows weighted Tobit estimations. Absolute value of *t*-statistics in parentheses.

***Significant at the 1 percent level.

**Significant at the 5 percent level.

*Significant at the 10 percent level.

Columns (4) and (5) test the hypothesis that original sin is the consequence of debt-intolerant countries borrowing too much.[71] Regressing original sin on the public debt–GDP ratio, we find that the coefficient on the latter is insignificantly different from zero. To capture the possibility that the impact of the same debt-GDP ratio is greater in developing countries, column (5) allows the impact of debt to differ between them (where DE_GDP · DEV is the debt-GDP ratio interacted with a developing-country dummy and DE_GDP · IND is the same ratio interacted with an industrial-country dummy, as before). While we obtain a positive coefficient on debt-GDP for developing countries and a negative coefficient for the advanced countries, neither coefficient differs significantly from zero at standard confidence levels.

Columns (6)–(9) consider institutional quality (using the index of rule of law developed by Kaufmann, Kraay, and Zoido-Lobaton 1999). The Tobit regression in column (6) produces a negative effect of institutions on original sin, but one that is again statistically insignificant at standard confidence levels. Recent papers (e.g., Sachs 2001; Hall and Jones 1999; Acemoglu, Johnson, and Robinson 2001) suggest focusing on geography and colonial settlement patterns as ways of identifying the exogenous component of institutions. When we instrument institutions with distance from the equator (column [7]), we find that the former is still not statistically significant. When we instrument institutions with the log of settler mortality (column [8]), there again appears to be no effect. Column (9), where we estimate this equation by OLS but use the same sample as in column (8), suggests that this is not due to the limited number of countries for which we have data on settler mortality.

In column (10) we consider the role of financial development.[72] We find a negative but not statistically significant relationship between original sin and financial development as measured by the ratio of domestic credit to GDP. To control for the endogeneity of financial development, we next instrument the domestic credit–GDP ratio with the origin of the legal system. We follow La Porta et al. (1998), using a dummy variable that takes a value of 1 in countries that follow the French civil law tradition. Column (11) shows that controlling for endogeneity does not affect the result.

Column (1) of table 3.11 includes all of these variables in the same equation. We consider these to be the definitive hypothesis tests. Again, we find that the coefficient on SIZE is negative and significantly different from zero at conventional confidence levels. In addition, GDP per capita and institutions are also statistically significant. But while GDP per capita has the expected negative sign, institutions have a positive coefficient, as if coun-

71. This would make debt intolerance the fundamental cause of the financial fragility problem and original sin one of its symptoms.
72. Tirole (2002) provides a political economy explanation for a possible relationship between original sin and the development of the domestic financial system.

Table 3.11   The causes of original sin: Encompassing tests

	OSIN			OSIN (IV)
	(1)	(2)	(3)	(4)
Size	−0.302	−0.325	−0.326	−0.333
	(3.32)***	(3.48)***	(3.50)***	(3.52)***
GDP per capita	−0.262	−0.127		
	(2.08)**	(1.31)		
AV_INF	0.288	0.150	0.070	−0.060
	(0.89)	(0.49)	(0.29)	(0.14)
DE_GDP	−0.003	−0.102	0.044	−0.059
	(0.02)	(0.60)	(0.26)	(0.28)
Institutions	0.305		0.091	−0.120
	(1.88)*		(0.70)	(0.33)
DC_GDP	−0.313	−0.173	−0.403	−0.319
	(1.05)	(0.59)	(1.38)	(1.19)
FIN_CENTER	−0.492	−0.453	−0.680	−0.479
	(1.45)	(1.31)	(2.06)**	(0.91)
EUROLAND	0.032	0.010	−0.220	−0.074
	(0.15)	(0.04)	(1.18)	(0.22)
OTH_DEVEL	−0.053	0.030	−0.299	−0.072
	(0.24)	(0.14)	(1.55)	(0.17)
DEVELOPING				
Constant	3.506	2.505	1.516	1.618
	(3.54)***	(3.22)***	(7.66)***	(4.89)***
No. of observations	63	63	63	63

Notes: Table shows weighted Tobit estimations. Absolute value of *t*-statistics in parentheses.
***Significant at the 1 percent level.
**Significant at the 5 percent level.
*Significant at the 10 percent level.

tries with worse institutions suffer less from original sin. This appears to be due to the high correlation between GDP per capita and rule of law (0.83). A Wald test suggests that the two variables are not jointly significant (*p*-value = 0.14), and when they are entered one at a time (in columns [2] and [3]) neither of them is statistically significant. The last column shows that the results do not change if we instrument institutions with latitude.[73]

Tables 3.10 and 3.11 thus suggest that original sin is robustly related to country size and to countries' status as financial centers, advanced economies, or emerging markets but that it is only weakly related to institutional variables like rule of law and measures of policy like inflation and fiscal history.

When we eliminate the country-group dummies, in table 3.12, inflation

73. When we instrument institutions with settler mortality, none of the explanatory variables matters (which presumably reflects the limited sample size).

Table 3.12 The causes of original sin omitting country-group fixed effects

	OSIN (1)	OSIN (2)	OSIN (3)	OSIN (4)	OSIN (5)	OSIN (IV) (6)	OSIN (IV) (7)	OSIN (8)	OSIN (9)	OSIN (IV) (10)
SIZE	-0.415 (4.51)***	-0.495 (5.71)***	-0.555 (5.92)***	-0.414 (4.54)***	-0.480 (5.32)***	-0.487 (4.58)***	-0.358 (2.17)**	-0.435 (2.97)***	-0.399 (4.47)***	-0.84 (0.38)
GDP per capita	-0.170 (3.00)***									
AV_INF		0.610 (2.20)**								
DE_GDP			0.050 (0.31)							
DE_GDP · DEV				0.421 (2.04)**						
DE_GDP · IND				-0.210 (1.24)						
INSTITUTIONS					-0.182 (2.33)**	-0.196 (1.19)	-0.309 (1.92)*	-0.202 (1.96)**		
DC_GDP									-0.554 (2.99)***	-3.22 (1.52)
Constant	2.835 (5.47)***	1.226 (11.08)***	1.374 (11.66)***	1.224 (11.01)***	1.486 (12.33)***	1.483 (10.62)***	1.382 (7.66)***	1.429 (7.82)***	1.636 (11.32)***	3.046 (2.74)***
No. of observations	75	74	64	64	75	75	29	29	74	74

Notes: Table shows weighted Tobit estimations. Absolute value of t-statistics in parentheses.

***Significant at the 1 percent level.

**Significant at the 5 percent level.

*Significant at the 10 percent level.

Table 3.13   The causes of original sin: Encompassing tests omitting fixed effects

	OSIN (1)	OSIN (IV) (2)	(3)
SIZE	−0.352	−0.366	−0.700
	(3.88)***	(3.43)***	(2.10)**
GDP per capita	−0.248	−0.156	−0.269
	(2.30)**	(0.52)	(0.71)
AV_INF	0.274	0.164	0.775
	(0.88)	(0.32)	(0.84)
DE_GDP	−0.002	−0.050	−0.893
	(0.01)	(0.26)	(1.09)
DC_GDP	−0.291	−0.286	2.897
	(1.25)	(1.08)	(0.91)
INSTITUTIONS	0.255	0.092	−0.546
	(1.61)	(0.15)	(0.83)
Constant	3.437	2.785	2.546
	(4.03)***	(1.31)	(1.22)
No. of observations	63	63	63

Notes: Table shows weighted Tobit estimations. Absolute value of *t*-statistics in parentheses.
***Significant at the 1 percent level.
**Significant at the 5 percent level.
*Significant at the 10 percent level.

history matters when entered by itself, as in column (2). There is also some evidence of an effect of institutions (whether modeled as exogenous or instrumented using settler mortality) in columns (5) and (7). There is more evidence of the importance of financial development (see column [9]), although the correlation between financial development and original sin is not robust to instrumenting financial development with the origin of the legal code (see in column [10]).

But when we include proxies for the competing hypotheses simultaneously, in table 3.13, the results are essentially identical to before. Column (1) shows that SIZE and GDP per capita are statistically significant. Column (2) allows institutions to be endogenous (we use latitude as an instrument) and shows that only size remains statistically significant. Column (3) treats both rule of law and domestic credit over GDP as endogenous (again we instrument domestic credit over GDP with the origin of the legal code). Once more, only SIZE enters with a coefficient that is statistically distinguishable from zero at standard confidence levels.[74]

---

74. If one ignores the fact that the coefficients on the policy and institutional variables go to zero when they are included in the equation simultaneously (which will be comfortable only for readers with strong priors), then the contrast between tables 3.11 and 3.12 would suggest an interpretation like the following. When the fixed effects for financial centers, advanced economies, and emerging markets are included in the equation, they absorb the cross-group

What might account for the fact that it is mainly large countries that seem to be able to issue foreign debt in their own currencies and for the concentration of the world's portfolio in a few currencies? While each additional currency adds opportunities for diversification, it does so with decreasing marginal benefits. In a world with transaction costs (which increase with the number of currencies in which investors take positions), the optimal portfolio will therefore have a finite number of currencies.

Imagine the following situation.[75] There are two countries: one has N trees while the other has one tree. All trees are identical in their expected income and its variance; the large country just has more of them. Shocks to each tree are uncorrelated. Assume that the exchange rate moves with the realization of relative output. If there were no transaction costs of investing abroad, then it would be optimal to hold a globally diversified portfolio: the large country would invest $1/(N + 1)$ of its wealth in the small country, while the latter would invest $N/(N + 1)$ in the large country. Now introduce costs to international transactions. If all countries were of size 1, then the presence of transaction costs would not affect the composition of the world portfolio. But if country size differs, then the benefits of international diversification will be greater for the small country than for the large one. There will be less appetite in the large country to hold the currency of the small country, while there will still be a large appetite for the small country to hold the assets of the large one. This is to say, large countries offer significant diversification possibilities, while small countries do not. If the transaction costs associated with international diversification are the same for investors in both countries, then the world will choose to invest in a few large currencies. Notice that this is through no fault of the small country, but a consequence of the existence of cross-border costs and asymmetries in size and diversification.

An implication of this view is that even if we identify characteristics that have allowed a few small countries to issue external debt in their own currencies—like, say, South Africa, New Zealand, or Poland—it would be a fallacy of composition to assume that if other small countries acquired those same characteristics then they too would make it into the world port-

variation in the data. The coefficient on a variable like, say, inflation or rule of law then picks up only the within-group variation. This is telling us that if we could transform Colombia into Canada and give the former the more favorable policy history and institutions of the latter overnight (along with its greater proximity to large markets, etc.), then we would also give it a greater ability to borrow abroad in its own currency. On the other hand, transforming Colombia into Chile (in terms of the quality of policies and institutions) would do little to enhance its ability to borrow abroad in its own currency. This is not to reject the importance of sound policies and institutional development. But it does suggest that the standard advice to this effect is not going to solve the problem of original sin that plagues emerging markets any time soon.

75. We are indebted to Roberto Rigobon for yet unpublished joint work on this idea.

folio. Each successful country may limit the chances of the others, given declining marginal benefits of diversification.

A further implication of this approach is that country size matters for original sin. Some countries have an advantage in shedding original sin because the large size of their economies and currency issue makes them attractive as components of the world portfolio. In contrast, the currencies of small countries add few diversification benefits relative to the additional costs they imply.

Country size can explain why large countries like the United States and Japan do not suffer from original sin. But what about Switzerland and, for that matter, the United Kingdom? Note that the financial-center dummy remains large and significant even after controlling for country size. This is another way of saying that the United Kingdom and Switzerland have become immune to the problem. But if becoming a financial center is evidently another way of shedding original sin, this is easier said than done. Clearly, countries that either are or were major commercial powers (e.g., the United States, Britain in the past) have a leg up. In addition, some countries have been able to gain the status of financial centers as a quirk of history or geography.[76] Network externalities giving rise to historical path dependence have worked to lock in their currencies' international status: once the Swiss franc was held in some international portfolios and used in some international transactions, it became advantageous for additional investors and traders to do likewise. And because Britain was the world's leading industrial, trading, and lending nation once upon a time, the pound sterling acquired its position as a prominent currency for the denomination of international claims—a luxury that the country enjoys to this day, albeit to a lesser and declining extent. These observations are related to the literature on the determinants of key currency status (Kiyotaki, Matsuyama, and Matsui 1992), which explains the dominance of a small number of currencies in international markets as a function of network externalities and transaction costs. This literature does not deny that additional countries can gain admission to this exclusive club, but it suggests that they face an uphill battle.

All this suggests that the global portfolio may be concentrated in a very few currencies for reasons beyond control—at least, beyond that of the excluded countries.

3.4.5   Borio and Packer

Since the first draft of this paper was circulated as an NBER working paper, Borio and Packer (2004) have sought to replicate and extend its regressions for credit ratings and the causes of original sin. Their tests differ

---

76. For example, Switzerland, a mountainous country at the center of Europe that was hard to take over and also small enough to retain its neutrality, became a convenient destination for foreign deposits.

slightly from ours in their particulars. Thus, they use a slightly different measure of original sin (also drawn from the appendix in Eichengreen, Hausmann, and Panizza 2005b). They attempt to adjust for hedging by interacting our measures of original sin and currency mismatches with the BIS's data on total foreign exchange spot and derivatives transactions. They use a different measure of credit ratings (an average of Moody's and S&P ratings, in contrast to the S&P measure utilized here). In some of their work they add measures of corruption and country risk constructed from indexes provided by Transparency International and the ICRG, respectively. They measure debt intolerance in the same manner as Reinhart, Rogoff, and Savastano (2003; in addition to including the external debt ratio as a regressor, interacting this with a dummy variable for emerging markets), and also model it as the interaction of the debt-GDP ratio with measures of recent default history and inflation history. And their analysis of the causes of original sin pools the data for different years rather than using cross-section averages as in subsection 3.4.4 above.

Despite these changes, their results for credit ratings are similar to our own. Original sin continues to affect credit ratings at the 99 percent level despite the use of a longer list of controls, although their point estimate is somewhat smaller than our own. They also find a significant effect for currency mismatches, as do we in table 3.5 above. Their debt intolerance proxies are significant about half the time.

Some of their findings regarding the causes of original sin are also consistent with ours. They too report a significant positive coefficient on country size. Our measure of the importance of inflation (average inflation over the last twenty years) and their measure of strength of institutions (the Kaufmann, Kraay, and Zoido-Lobaton 1999 measure of rule of law) never approach statistical significance at standard confidence levels.[77] Where their results appear to differ is where they obtain a positive coefficient on an alternative measure of inflation (share of the last forty years when inflation exceeded 40 percent) and on the ICRG measure of political risk, suggesting that past policies and current institutions do in fact affect the incidence of original sin.

There is some evidence that these findings are sensitive to the particulars of specification and estimation. Borio and Packer's (2004) regressions appear to be estimated on pooled data, but the measure of inflation (the share of the last forty years when inflation exceeded 40 percent) does not have any within-country variation. In pure cross-section estimates (which seem more appropriate given the lack of time variation in the key independent variable) the significance of this variable declines significantly (as it does when we adjust the standard errors for clustering). In addition, their re-

77. They also obtain, counterintuitively, a negative coefficient on corruption, suggesting that more corrupt countries find it easier to borrow abroad in their own currency.

gressions do not include the dummy variables for country groups; adding them, as in our table 3.12, causes the significance of this variable to disappear. We also worry about their use of data for the years 2000–2003 for the Euroland countries, when the advent of the euro made the concept of original sin much less relevant for them. Recall that we limit our own analysis to data through 1998, with precisely this problem in mind. And when we instrument the ICRG index of institutions (as in subsection 3.4.4), the significance of this variable also evaporates.

3.5 Conclusion

In this paper we have contrasted three concepts widely utilized in the recent literature on emerging market debt. Two of the terms—original sin and debt intolerance—attempt to explain the same phenomenon, namely the volatility of emerging market economies and the difficulty that these countries have in servicing and repaying their external debts. The debt intolerance school traces the problem to institutional weaknesses of emerging market economies that in turn lead to weak and unreliable policies. It suggests that these countries' histories have bequeathed a situation where they find it difficult to run strong policies.

The original-sin school traces the problem instead to the structure of global portfolios and international financial markets. It suggests that emerging market economies are volatile because they find it difficult to denominate their obligations in units that better track their capacity to pay, such as the domestic currency or the domestic consumption basket. It suggests that this constraint derives in part from the structure of international portfolios and the operation of international financial markets. It points to forces that concentrate international portfolios and markets in a few major currencies—the dollar, euro, yen, pound, and Swiss franc—and to the evidently limited appetite of international investors for adding additional currencies to their portfolios.

In contrast, the literature on currency mismatches, as we read it, is concerned with the consequences of these problems. It emphasizes balance sheet mismatches that may arise either from the weak policies pointed to by the debt intolerance literature or from the difficulty emerging markets experience when attempting to place domestic currency–denominated debt with foreign investors pointed to by work on original sin. It is concerned with how these consequences are managed by the macroeconomic and financial authorities.

Thus, these terms should not be used interchangeably. The hypotheses and problems to which they refer are distinct. Using them synonymously is an unnecessary source of confusion.

We close with suggestions for investigators concerned with currency mismatches, debt intolerance, or original sin. For those concerned with currency mismatches, the challenge is to show that mismatches can be measured with the precision needed to systematically test hypotheses regarding their causes and consequences. Absent comprehensive information on the currency denomination of assets, liabilities, swaps, and other derivatives, it is difficult to reliably measure the currency composition of a country's external assets and liabilities. The same problem follows from the absence of information on foreign holdings of domestic placements and on the presence or absence of exchange rate indexation clauses in those holdings. Once the concept is adequately operationalized, the challenge will be to model its determinants as well as its consequences—since the extent of the mismatch is a choice variable of, among others, the government, which chooses whether to restrict foreign borrowing and to insure against the consequences by accumulating reserves—and to analyze the two aspects in a consistent way.

For those concerned with debt intolerance, the challenge is to establish the existence of links between past policies and current outcomes and to document the mechanisms through which they act. Reinhart, Rogoff, and Savastano (2003) suggest that the fact that the same countries have defaulted repeatedly over a period of centuries reflects the corrosive impact of past policies on their financial markets and tax systems today and, through that channel, on their current management of external obligations. A correlation between past defaults and current defaults is insufficient to establish this case. That correlation could reflect any omitted variable that matters persistently for debt-servicing difficulties and is slow to change over time.[78] The challenge is thus to show that past default plays a causal role in the development of financial markets and tax systems, after controlling adequately for other determinants of their development, and that the structure of fiscal and financial systems in turn matters for current debt-servicing outcomes, after similarly controlling for their other determinants.

For those concerned with original sin, the challenge is to document the distortions in global financial markets that make it difficult to get international investors to add more currencies to their portfolios. In previous work we speculated that most of the benefits of international portfolio diversification can be obtained by building portfolios limited to a handful of currencies. If there are fixed transaction and management costs associated with including additional currencies, then the diversification benefits of adding more may be dominated by these costs. Here, shedding light on the

---

78. As we noted above, two candidates are the commodity composition of exports, which affects the volatility of the terms of trade, and the persistent difficulty that the same relatively small, less developed countries have had in getting their currencies added to the global portfolio.

obstacles to getting international investors to hold additional currencies in their portfolios is the principal challenge to research.

Appendix

Countries included in table 3.1 of this paper but not included in table B1 of Reinhart, Rogoff, and Savastano (2003): Austria, Barbados, Belgium, Belize, China, Cyprus, Estonia, Germany, Iceland, Kazakhstan, Latvia, Lebanon, Luxembourg, Malta, Mongolia, Oman, Russian Federation, Slovak Republic, Slovenia, Switzerland, Tunisia, and the United Kingdom.

Countries included in table B1 of Reinhart, Rogoff, and Savastano (2003) but not included in table 3.1 of this paper: Algeria, Ecuador, Egypt, Ethiopia, Ghana, Hong Kong, Ireland, Japan, Kenya, Mali, Malaysia, Nepal, New Zealand, Nigeria, Portugal, Romania, Saudi Arabia, Sri Lanka, Swaziland, Tanzania, Uruguay, Venezuela, and Zimbabwe.

References

Acemoglu, Daron, Simon Johnson, and James Robinson. 2001. The colonial origins of economic development: An empirical investigation. *American Economic Review* 91:1361–1401.

Aghion, Philippe, Philippe Bacchetta, and Abhijit Banerjee. 2000. Currency crises and monetary policy in an economy with credit constraints. University College London, Department of Economics. Mimeograph.

Bayoumi, Tamim, and Barry Eichengreen. 1998a. Exchange rate volatility and intervention: Implications from the theory of optimum currency areas. *Journal of International Economics* 45:191–209.

———. 1998b. Optimum currency areas and exchange rate volatility: Theory and evidence compared. In *International trade and finance: New frontiers for research*, ed. Benjamin Cohen, 184–215. Cambridge: Cambridge University Press.

Blattman, Christopher, Jason Hwang, and Jeffrey Williamson. 2003. The terms of trade and economic growth in the periphery, 1870–1938. NBER Working Paper no. 9940. Cambridge, MA: National Bureau of Economic Research, September.

Bonomo, Marco, Betina Martins, and Rodrigo Pinto. 2003. Debt composition and exchange rate balance sheet effects in Brazil: A firm-level analysis. *Emerging Markets Review* 4:368–96.

Borio, Claudio, and Frank Packer. 2004. Assessing new perspectives on country risk. *BIS Quarterly Review* 2004 (December): 47–65.

Burger, John, and Francis Warnock. 2003. Diversification, original sin, and international bond portfolios. International Finance Discussion Paper no. 755. Washington, DC: Board of Governors of the Federal Reserve System.

Caballero, Ricardo, Kevin Cowan, and Jonathan Kearns. 2003. Reducing external vulnerability through financial development: Lessons from Australia. MIT, Inter-American Development Bank, and Reserve Bank of Australia. Unpublished manuscript.

Calvo, Guillermo, Alejandro Izquierdo, and Ernesto Talvi. 2002. Sudden stops, the real exchange rate and fiscal sustainability. Research Department Working Paper no. 469. Washington, DC: Inter-American Development Bank.

Céspedes, Luis Felipe, Roberto Chang, and Andrés Velasco. 2002. IS-LM-BP in the Pampas. Harvard University, Department of Economics. Unpublished manuscript.

David, Paul. 2001. Path dependence, its critics and the quest for "Historical Economics." In *Evolution and path dependence in economic ideas: Past and present,* ed. Pierre Garrouste and Stavros Ionnides, 15–40. Cheltenham: Edward Elgar.

Eichengreen, Barry. 2002. *Financial crises and what to do about them.* Oxford: Oxford University Press.

Eichengreen, Barry, and Ricardo Hausmann. 1999. Exchange rates and financial fragility. In *New challenges for monetary policy,* 329–68. Kansas City, MO: Federal Reserve Bank of Kansas City.

Eichengreen, Barry, Ricardo Hausmann, and Ugo Panizza. 2005a. The mystery of original sin. In *Other people's money: Debt denomination and financial instability in emerging-market economies,* ed. Barry Eichengreen and Ricardo Hausmann, 233–65. Chicago: University of Chicago Press.

———. 2005b. The pain of original sin. In *Other people's money: Debt denomination and financial instability in emerging-market economies,* ed. Barry Eichengreen and Ricardo Hausmann, 13–47. Chicago: University of Chicago Press.

Flandreau, Marc, and Nathan Sussman. 2005. Old sins. In *Other people's money: Debt denomination and financial instability in emerging-market economies,* ed. Barry Eichengreen and Ricardo Hausmann, 154–89. Chicago: University of Chicago Press.

Gallego, Francisco, and Leonardo Hernandez. 2003. Microeconomic effects of capital controls: The Chilean experience during the 1990s. *International Journal of Finance and Economics* 8:225–54.

Gavin, Michael, Ricardo Hausmann, and Leonardo Leiderman. 1995. The macroeconomics of capital flows to Latin America: Experience and policy issues. Working Paper no. 310. Washington, DC: Inter-American Development Bank.

Goldstein, Morris. 1998. *The Asian financial crisis.* Washington, DC: Institute of International Economics.

Goldstein, Morris, and Philip Turner. 2004. *Controlling currency mismatches in emerging market economies: An alternative to the original sin hypothesis.* Washington, DC: Institute for International Economics.

Hall, Robert, and Charles Jones. 1999. Why do some countries produce so much more output per worker than others? *Quarterly Journal of Economics* 114:83–116.

Harwood, Alison, ed. 2000. *Building local currency bond markets: An Asian perspective.* Washington, DC: International Finance Corporation.

Hausmann, Ricardo. 2003. Good credit ratios, bad credit ratings: The role of debt structure. In *Rules-based fiscal policy in emerging markets: Background, analysis and prospects,* ed. G. Kopits, 30–52. London: Macmillan.

Hausmann, Ricardo, and Michael Gavin. 1996. Securing stability and growth in a shock-prone region: The case of Latin America. In *Securing stability and growth in Latin America: Policy issues and prospects for shock-prone economies,* ed.

R. Hausmann and H. Reisen, 23–64. Paris: Organization for Economic Cooperation and Development.

Hausmann, Ricardo, and Ugo Panizza. 2003. The determinants of original sin: An empirical investigation. *Journal of International Money and Finance* 22:957–90.

Herring, Richard J., and Nathporn Chatusripitak. 2000. The case of the missing market: The bond market and why it matters for financial development. ADB Institute Working Paper no. 11. Manila, Spain: Asian Development Bank, July.

International Monetary Fund (IMF). 2003. *Global financial stability report.* Washington, DC: International Monetary Fund, March.

Jeanne, Olivier. 2002. Monetary policy and liability dollarization. Washington, DC: International Monetary Fund. Unpublished manuscript.

JPMorgan. Various years. *Guide to local markets.* New York: JPMorgan.

Kaufmann, Daniel, Aart Kraay, and Pablo Zoido-Lobaton. 1999. Aggregating governance indicator. World Bank Policy Research Working Paper no. 2195. Washington, DC: World Bank.

Kiyotaki, Nobu, Kiminori Matsuyama, and Akihiko Matsui. 1992. Toward a theory of international currency. *Review of Economic Studies* 60:283–307.

Krugman, Paul. 1999. Balance sheets, the transfer problem, and financial crises. Massachusetts Institute of Technology, Department of Economics. Unpublished manuscript.

La Porta, Rafael, Florencio Lopez de Silanes, Andrei Shleifer, and Robert Vishny. 1998. Law and finance. *Journal of Political Economy* 106 (6): 1113–55.

Levy Yeyati, Eduardo, and Federico Sturzenegger. 2000. Classifying exchange rate regimes: Deeds vs. words. Universidad Torcuato di Tella, Department of Economics. Unpublished manuscript.

Lucas, Robert. 1990. Why doesn't capital flow from rich to poor countries? *American Economic Review Papers and Proceedings* 80 (May): 92–96.

Razin, Assaf, and Efraim Sadka. 1999. Country risk and capital flow reversals. Tel Aviv University, Department of Economics. Unpublished manuscript.

Reinhart, Carmen, Kenneth Rogoff, and Miguel Savastano. 2003. Debt intolerance. *Brookings Papers on Economic Activity,* Issue no. 1:1–74.

Sachs, Jeffrey. 2001. Tropical underdevelopment. NBER Working Paper no. 8119. Cambridge, MA: National Bureau of Economic Research, February.

Tirole, Jean. 2002. Inefficient foreign borrowing. Invited lecture at Latin American and Caribbean Economic Association meeting. 11–13 October, Madrid.

U.S. Treasury. 2003. Report on U.S. holdings of foreign securities as of December 31, 2001. http://www.treas.gov/tic/shc2001r.pdf.

Comment   Joshua Aizenman

This is a comprehensive paper, which provides an overview of a large body of research. The purpose of the paper is to compare and contrast three approaches dealing with balance sheet factors in emerging markets: original sin (OS), debt intolerance (DI), and currency mismatches (CM).

Joshua Aizenman is a professor of economics at the University of California, Santa Cruz, and a research associate of the National Bureau of Economic Research.

Synopsis of the Paper

As the paper's title highlights, it shows that the OS, DI, and CM hypotheses, and problems with which these three approaches deal, are analytically distinct. Both OS and DI seek to explain the volatility of emerging markets (EM) and their difficulty in servicing debts. The DI school argues that institutional weaknesses of EM economies lead to weak and unreliable policies. In contrast, the OS school focuses on the structure of global portfolios and international financial markets. The CM concept deals with the consequences of these problems. The authors point out that OS differs from CM. By definition, OS implies a gross foreign debt denominated in foreign currency. But the country may or may not also incur CM, depending on how the authorities respond to the act of borrowing.

Debt intolerance is reflected in the EMs' inability to manage levels of external debt that are manageable for OECD countries. As was shown by Reinhart, Rogoff, and Savastano (2003), credit ratings fall more rapidly with debt in EMs than in advanced countries, indicating that the former have less debt management capacity. Possible interpretations of DI include institutional weaknesses of EM economies which lead to weak and unreliable policies. Countries' histories have bequeathed a situation where they find it difficult to run strong policies. The Eichengreen, Hausmann, and Panizza paper questions the validity of the debt intolerance tests implemented by Reinhart, Rogoff, and Savastano, raising several robustness concerns.

The authors illustrate the issues at hand by asking in section 3.2 why Chile's performance resembled that of Latin America and not Australia. Original sin is part of the answer. Chile is a favorite example for economists of a country with increasingly strong institutions and policies. Standard institution strengthening measures have not impacted the capacity to borrow abroad in an EM's own currency, over policy-relevant horizons. The OS approach views this inability as a key shortcoming, explaining the problems facing EMs.

A key part of the paper is section 3.3, where the authors run an implicit horse race, contrasting OS versus CM and DI. They start by showing that countries with high levels of OS hold more reserves, are less inclined to float, and are characterized by higher macro volatility and lower credit ratings. The authors repeat the exercise adding measures of aggregate CM and DI. The results suggest to the authors that the effects of OS are more statistically robust than those of these alternative concepts.

Comment 1: The Costs and Benefits of External Borrowing

Original sin presumes that external borrowing is beneficial. This presumption is not supported by the data of recent years.

The authors state early in section 3.2 that OS is defined as "the inability of a country to borrow abroad in its own currency." They add that the "focus on external borrowing is motivated by the observation that, in the absence of other distortions, world welfare would be enhanced if capital flowed from capital-rich advanced countries to their more capital-poor emerging market counterparts."

Had OS been the only distortion, then removing it would have been welfare improving. Yet, in practice, developing countries are struggling with a large number of distortions. Hence, the welfare effect of removing one distortion is ambiguous. Specifically, if removing the OS would increase the volume of other distortion activities, it may be welfare reducing.

Unlike the authors, I argue that external borrowing, as a source of financing growth, is overrated. To illustrate this, I rely on results reported in Aizenman, Pinto, and Radziwill (2004). Using the World Development Indicators data, we construct there a self-finance measure, indicating the stock of tangible capital supported by actual national past saving, relative to the actual stock of capital.[1] We found that, in the 1990s, 90 percent of the stock of tangible capital of a typical developing country was self-financed, and that higher self-financing ratios were associated with higher growth. Alternatively, in recent years, countries that relied more on external finance, including external borrowing, grew at a slower rate. The data are also consistent with the notion that the surge in capital inflows in the aftermath of financial liberalization funds capital outflows, with little impact on self-financing ratios.

These findings are consistent with several interpretations.

- *Habit formation:* A takeoff triggered by relaxing a state's attitude toward private saving and investment increases both saving and investment. If saving and investment increased at the same rate, we would observe a self-financed higher growth rate, as has been the case in

---

1. The ideal self-financing would be obtained by unbounded backward discounting, had we all the past information:

$$\hat{f} = \frac{\sum_{i=1}^{\infty} S_{t-i}(1 - d)^{i-1}}{\sum_{i=1}^{\infty} I_{t-i}(1 - d)^{i-1}},$$

where d is the depreciation rate of tangible capital, I_t and S_t are gross investment and national saving at time t, in constant purchasing power parity, respectively. A value of 1 of the self-financing measure would correspond to an economy where the entire stock of domestic capital is self-financed. A self-financing ratio below 1 indicates reliance on foreign saving; $1 - \hat{f}_t$ is the foreign-financing ratio, measuring the fraction of domestic capital that was financed by foreign saving. In practice, the unbounded backward discounting is not feasible due to scarcity of data. This limitation induces us to rely on approximated measures of self-financing. As is illustrated in Aizenman, Pinto, and Radziwill (2004), the approximated self-financing measure deviates from the ideal financing measure by second-order magnitude. An alternative strategy is to construct self-financing ratios using gross domestic saving instead of national saving (the gap between the two is the net current transfers from abroad). This does not affect the main results inferred by relying on the self-financing ratio.

China, India, and other countries in recent years (see Carroll, Overland, and Weil 2000 for further discussion).
- *Collateral to induce FDI* (Dooley, Folkerts-Landau, and Garber 2004): Countries may accumulate foreign assets to signal their soundness, in order to attract FDI.
- Most capital flows are *gross, with little net effect* (Dooley 1988). This is consistent with response to differences in risk perceived by residents and nonresidents.

Comment 2: Limited Ability to Test Which Approach—OS, DI, or CM— Is Most Important

Some of the methodological concerns are generic and may apply equally well to all tests of balance sheet problems; short of conducting controlled experiments, available empirical procedures have limited power in identifying the independent roles of OS, DI, and CM. More specific concerns:

- Original sin measures of most developing countries are practically the same (one for most external OS measures, as can be seen in figure 3.1 in the paper). This suggests a censoring problem.
- Theory predicts a nonlinear interaction between OS, DI, and CM. It may be hard to pick up such nonlinearity in a log linear model, especially if one is not testing a tightly specified model.
- The background literature suggests several variables that are omitted in the present study, like polarization, political instability, and distribution of income.

All the above suggest that more insight can be gained by looking at case studies.

Comment 3: Is OS the Key for Explaining Problematic Performance? Not Necessarily

A possible clue to the issues at hand is that there is very little variation in the OS measures across countries, yet there is large variation in performance. This observation suggests that countries may take off without solving OS and without solving "institutional weaknesses." Such a takeoff may be accomplished by relaxing the grip of the state on the private sector, encouraging, instead of penalizing, entrepreneurship (as has apparently been the case of China, India, etc.). Hence, prolonged growth acceleration may happen without dealing with constraints imposed by OS, or the constraints imposed by existing institutions.

Comment 4: Are Institutional Weaknesses the Key to DI?

An alternative interpretation is that the key to DI is deeper structural factors, including polarization, distribution of income, and political instability. More generally, DI may be related to the ability of the social contract to deal with shocks. History impacts investors' priors about these concerns. All the above may explain the root sources of EM vulnerability, as has been articulated in past contributions (see Alesina and Tabellini 1989; Cukierman, Edwards, and Tabellini 1992; Rodrik 1999).

Comment 5: Second-Best Effects of Relaxing OS Constraints

For countries characterized by overborrowing, relaxing the OS constraints without dealing with the overborrowing bias would increase excessive borrowing by weak regimes, reducing welfare. This is another example of the second-best situation confronting most developing countries.

Comment 6: Chile versus Australia Is a Prime Example of OS

The latest World Development Indicators reveals that the real GDP per capita growth rate of Chile was double that of Australia during 1986–2003 (0.04 versus 0.02). This may suggest that OS is not the major obstacle to growth. It is also consistent with the findings of Caballero, Cowan, and Kearns (2005), who contrasted country trust versus currency trust, arguing that the lack of country trust is a more fundamental and serious problem behind sudden stops. They point out that Chile needs external insurance more than Australia does, precisely because its terms-of-trade shocks are amplified by the resulting contraction in the supply of external funds. So OS is a greater problem for Chile than for Australia. "But importantly," Caballero et al. add, "OS is not the primitive problem behind the need for substantial insurance; the problem is a lack of country-trust." This is vividly illustrated by the observation that Australia's inflation was 4 percent since federation (about 102 years ago), exceeding 20 percent in only one year. In contrast, Chile's inflation exceeded 20 percent in approximately half the years during that period. Australia has a long history with no default by the federal or state governments. Australia's trust was generated by experiencing several substantial negative external shocks without defaulting, unlike most Latin American countries.

To conclude: the authors are making a strong case that OS, CM, and DI are distinct hypotheses, dealing with related but different issues. The empirical evaluation of the relative merits of OS, CM, and DI remains debatable—there is no clean test that can do the job. The authors' presumption underlying the focus on OS—that foreign borrowing is welfare enhancing—is debatable. Original sin is only one of the distortions EMs grapple with, and potentially not the most important one. Removing OS, without dealing with the other distortions, may be welfare reducing.

References

Aizenman, J., B. Pinto, and A. Radziwill. 2004. Sources for financing domestic capital: Is foreign saving a viable option for developing countries? *Journal of International Money and Finance.* Forthcoming.

Alesina, A., and G. Tabellini. 1989. External debt, capital flight, and political risk. *Journal of International Economics* 27:199–220.

Caballero R., K. Cowan, and J. Kearns. 2005. Fear of sudden stops: Lessons from Australia and Chile. *Journal of Policy Reform* 8 (4): 313–54.

Carroll C., J. Overland, and D. N. Weil. 2000. Saving and growth with habit formation. *American Economic Review* 90 (3): 341–90.

Cukierman, A., S. Edwards, and G. Tabellini. 1992. Seigniorage and political instability. *American Economic Review* 82 (3): 537–55.

Dooley, M. 1988. Capital flight: A response to differences in financial risks. *IMF Staff Papers* 35 (September): 422–36.

Dooley, M., D. Folkerts-Landau, and P. M. Garber. 2004. The U.S. current account deficit and economic development: Collateral for a total return swap. NBER Working Paper no. 10727. Cambridge, MA: National Bureau of Economic Research.

Reinhart, C., K. Rogoff, and M. Savastano. 2003. Debt intolerance. *Brookings Papers on Economic Activity,* Issue no. 1:1–74.

Rodrik, Dani. 1999. Where did all the growth go? External shocks, social conflict and growth collapses. *Journal of Economic Growth* 4 (4): 385–412.

4

The Microeconomic Evidence on Capital Controls
No Free Lunch

Kristin J. Forbes

4.1 Introduction

The free movement of capital can have widespread benefits. Capital inflows can provide financing for high-return investment, thereby raising growth rates. Capital inflows—especially in the form of direct investment—often bring improved technology, management techniques, and access to international networks, all of which further raise productivity and growth. Capital outflows can allow domestic citizens and companies to earn higher returns and better diversify risk, thereby reducing volatility in consumption and income. Capital inflows and outflows can increase market discipline, thereby leading to a more efficient allocation of resources and higher productivity growth. In order to obtain these widespread benefits of free capital flows, most developed countries and many developing countries have lifted most of their capital controls.

In the spring of 1997 there was such widespread support for free capital flows that the International Monetary Fund (IMF) Interim Committee suggested amending the IMF's Articles of Agreement to extend its jurisdiction to include capital movements and make capital account liberalization a purpose of the IMF.[1] Soon after this recommendation was announced, however, a series of financial crises spread across Asia and disproportionately affected countries that had recently liberalized their

Kristin J. Forbes is an associate professor of international economics at the Sloan School of Management, Massachusetts Institute of Technology, and a research associate of the National Bureau of Economic Research (NBER).

Thanks to Charles Calomiris and participants in the NBER conference for helpful comments and suggestions. Further thanks to Peter Kenen for inspiring the title of this paper.

1. The IMF's charter requires that member countries have convertible currencies for the purposes of current account transactions, but not capital account transactions.

capital accounts. In contrast, several Asian countries that had maintained more stringent capital controls—such as China and India—emerged from the crisis relatively unscathed. These experiences caused a reassessment of the desirability of capital controls, especially for emerging markets and developing economies.

In a sharp sea change, many policymakers and leading economists now support the use of capital controls, especially taxes on capital inflows, in some circumstances. For example, former U.S. Treasury Secretary Robert Rubin, who actively encouraged emerging markets to open their capital accounts in the mid-1990s, has expressed support for controls on capital inflows.[2] A series of reports by the Group of Twenty-Two (G22) in 1998 raised concerns about capital account liberalization and cautiously endorsed taxes on capital inflows.[3] Even the *Economist* magazine, traditionally a supporter of the free movement of goods and capital, wrote: "some kinds of restriction on inflows (not outflows) of capital will make sense for many developing countries. . . . Chile's well-known system . . . was a success worth emulating" (*Economist* 2003). Possibly even more surprising, senior officials from the IMF, formerly the bastion of capital market liberalization, have expressed support for taxes on capital inflows. For example, Stanley Fischer, former first deputy managing director of the IMF, stated: "The IMF has cautiously supported the use of market-based capital inflow controls, Chilean style" (Fischer 2001).

One of the most common justifications for this sea change in attitudes and the recent support for capital controls is the lack of empirical evidence on the benefits of capital account liberalization. If lifting capital controls does yield net benefits, then these benefits should be measurable and identifiable in empirical analysis. Although an extensive literature has attempted to measure the macroeconomic effects of capital account liberalization, this literature is generally interpreted as being inconclusive. For example, a recent survey of the empirical literature on capital controls by authors in the IMF research department concludes: "if financial integration has a positive effect on growth, there is as yet no clear and robust empirical proof that the effect is quantitatively significant" (Prasad et al. 2003). Similarly, Eichengreen (2001) writes: "Capital account liberalization, it is fair to say, remains one of the most controversial and least understood policies of our day. . . . Empirical analysis has failed to yield conclusive results."

This interpretation that the empirical evidence on capital controls is inconclusive, however, overlooks a number of recent studies using microeconomic data. These studies provide persuasive evidence on the different

2. For example, see Rubin and Weisberg (2003, p. 257).
3. See the G22 reports released in 1988: *Report of the Working Group on Transparency and Accountability, Report of the Working Group on Strengthening Financial Systems,* and *Report of the Working Group on International Financial Crises.*

effects of capital controls and capital account liberalization. The studies cover a variety of countries and periods, use a range of approaches and methodologies, and build on several different literatures. By focusing on individual experiences and/or specific effects of capital controls, this microeconomic approach can yield more concrete and robust evidence than the cross-country macroeconomic studies that assume that capital controls have similar effects across countries and periods. Granted, this microeconomic approach has the disadvantage that it is difficult to generalize from individual countries' experiences. It also has the disadvantage that it is difficult to aggregate the different microeconomic results to capture the macroeconomic effects of capital controls. Nonetheless, this new series of microeconomic studies provides compelling and robust evidence of the pervasive effects of capital controls.

This paper surveys these diverse microeconomic studies and attempts to develop a more coherent picture of the microeconomic evidence on capital controls. Several key themes emerge. First, capital controls tend to reduce the supply of capital, raise the cost of financing, and increase financial constraints—especially for smaller firms and firms without access to international capital markets. Second, capital controls can reduce market discipline in financial markets and the government, leading to a more inefficient allocation of capital and resources. Third, capital controls significantly distort decision making by firms and individuals as they attempt to minimize the costs of the controls or even evade them outright. Fourth, the effects of capital controls can vary across different types of firms and countries, reflecting different preexisting economic distortions. Finally, capital controls can be difficult and costly to enforce, even in countries with sound institutions and low levels of corruption.

Although this literature examining the microeconomic effects of capital controls is only in its infancy and much more careful analysis remains to be done, the combination of results is compelling. These papers use diverse methodologies to examine very different aspects of capital controls in a range of countries and time periods, yet most find a consistent result: capital controls have pervasive effects, yield many unexpected costs, and can distort the allocation of resources, all of which can hinder market efficiency. Granted, capital controls may also have some costs and benefits that are not addressed in these microeconomic papers—such as reducing a country's vulnerability to currency crises.[4] Moreover, in the presence of existing market distortions, capital controls can be a second-best policy.[5] Therefore, this survey is not, in any way, a full cost-benefit analysis of capital controls. Countries evaluating whether to impose capital controls or

4. See Block and Forbes (2004) for an evaluation of the various costs and benefits of capital controls.

5. For example, if capital market inefficiencies allow companies to overborrow, capital controls that limit the supply of loans may minimize the initial distortion.

liberalize their capital accounts need to consider factors other than this microeconomic evidence. The results in this paper do clearly suggest, however, that capital controls (including taxes on capital inflows) create substantial microeconomic distortions. The recent sea change in views supporting capital controls (bolstered by the inconclusive macroeconomic evidence) appears to be premature. The microeconomic evidence on capital controls presents a clear picture: capital controls have pervasive effects and can generate substantial, unexpected costs. Capital controls are no free lunch.

The remainder of this paper is organized as follows. Section 4.2 discusses reasons why the macroeconomic evidence on capital controls has been inconclusive to date. Section 4.3 surveys the microeconomic evidence on how capital controls affect the supply and cost of capital. Section 4.4 reviews the evidence on how controls affect market discipline and the allocation of capital. Section 4.5 describes how controls can affect the behavior and actions of firms and individuals. Section 4.6 briefly discusses the challenges to implementing and enforcing capital controls. Section 4.7 concludes.

4.2   Inconclusive Macroeconomic Evidence on Capital Controls

The macroeconomic literature has had limited empirical success to date in providing robust evidence on the benefits of capital account liberalization.[6] Most papers in this literature use a variant of the standard cross-country growth regression developed by Robert Barro to test if the presence of capital controls or capital account liberalization is correlated with higher economic growth. Prasad et al. (2003) provide a detailed survey of this literature and argue that the results are inconclusive. More specifically, of the fourteen recent papers they examine, three find a positive effect of financial integration on growth, four find no effect, and seven find mixed results. The only consistency in the papers surveyed is that none find evidence that capital account liberalization significantly reduces growth. Prasad et al. (2003) also perform their own analysis, whose key result is replicated in figure 4.1. They find no significant relationship between financial openness and growth in real per capita income across countries— even after controlling for standard variables in this literature.[7]

There are several possible explanations for these conflicting results and the lack of consensus in the macroeconomic literature.[8] First, it is ex-

6. For excellent surveys of this literature, see Edison et al. (2002), Eichengreen (2001), or Prasad et al. (2003).
7. The control variables include initial income, initial schooling, average investment/gross domestic product (GDP), political instability, and regional dummies.
8. For a more thorough discussion of these challenges, see Eichengreen (2003, chap. 3), Prasad et al. (2003), or Magud and Reinhart (2004).

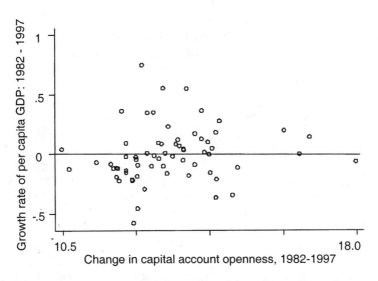

Fig. 4.1   Conditional relationship between financial openness and growth
Source: Prasad et al. (2003).
Notes: Growth is measured by growth in real per capita GDP. Conditioning variables are initial income, initial schooling, average investment/GDP, political instability, and regional dummies.

tremely difficult to accurately measure capital account openness.[9] Many studies use rough numerical indexes of different policies and regulations, but even the more carefully constructed measures cannot capture the complexity and effectiveness of a country's liberalization. Due to these problems, other studies have used de facto measures of integration (such as capital flows or foreign asset holdings). These are also problematic, since some countries with large capital inflows still maintain relatively strict capital controls (such as China), while other countries with relatively unrestricted capital accounts receive little foreign capital (such as many African nations). Still other studies have examined market comovement to measure integration with international markets, but these studies face the challenge of controlling for other factors that could cause markets to comove—such as global shocks or similar asset structures. A final approach has been to study onshore-offshore interest rate differentials. This approach is also problematic since not only are these differentials only available for a limited set of countries, but also interest rate differentials could move due to a number of factors other than capital account liberalization.

Second, different types of capital flows and capital controls may have

---

9. See Edison et al. (2002) for an excellent discussion of different measures of capital account openness.

different effects on growth and other macroeconomic variables. For example, recent work suggests that the benefits of foreign direct investment (FDI) may be greater than those of other types of capital flows. Reisen and Soto (2001) examine the impact of six different types of capital flows on growth and find that only two—FDI and portfolio equity flows—are positively associated with growth. Henry and Lorentzen (2003) argue that equity market liberalizations are more likely to promote growth than debt market liberalizations. Other papers argue that controls on capital inflows may be less harmful than controls on capital outflows, because controls on inflows may be viewed as a form of prudential regulation, while controls on outflows may be viewed as a lack of government commitment to sound policies. For example, Rossi (1999) finds that controls on capital inflows reduce the risk of a currency crisis, while controls on capital outflows heighten the risk. Moreover, even the sequence in which different types of capital controls are removed may determine the aggregate impact. For example, lifting restrictions on offshore bank borrowing before freeing other sectors of the capital account may increase the vulnerability of a country's banking system (as seen in Korea in the mid-1990s).

Finally, the impact of removing capital controls could depend on a range of other, hard-to-measure factors that are difficult to capture in simple cross-country regressions, such as a country's institutions or corporate governance. For example, Chinn and Ito (2002) show that financial systems with a higher degree of legal and institutional development benefit more, on average, from liberalization.[10] Gelos and Wei (2002) show that countries with greater transparency are not only more likely to attract international equity investment but less vulnerable to herding and capital flight during crises. A closely related factor is that there may be "threshold effects" that are difficult to capture in linear regressions. More specifically, countries may need to attain a certain level of financial market integration or overall economic development before attaining substantial benefits from lifting capital controls. For example, Klein and Olivei (1999) find that capital account openness only stimulates financial development in Organization for Economic Cooperation and Development (OECD) countries. Moreover, most countries that remove their capital controls simultaneously undertake a range of additional reforms and undergo widespread structural changes. Therefore, it can be extremely difficult to isolate the specific impact of removing capital controls during these transition periods.

Given all of these challenges to measuring the impact of capital controls, it is not surprising that the empirical literature has had difficulty documenting the effect of capital controls on growth at the macroeconomic

10. Aghion, Bacchetta, and Banerjee (2001) develop a theoretical model of why financial development is a key variable determining the impact of capital account liberalization.

level. Moreover, to put these challenges in perspective, the current status of this literature is similar to the earlier literature on how trade liberalization affects growth. Economists generally believe that trade openness raises economic growth, but most of the initial work on this topic (which used the same cross-country framework as these studies of capital account openness) also reached inconclusive results. In some cases trade liberalization appeared to have a positive correlation with economic growth, but in most cases these results were not robust to sensitivity testing. Stanley Fischer (2003) recently made this point: "With regard to empirical evidence on the benefits of capital account liberalization, I believe we are roughly now where we were in the 1980s on current account liberalization—that some evidence is coming in, but that it is at this stage weak and disputed" (p. 14). Since accurately measuring capital account liberalization and its interactions with other key variables may be even more difficult than for trade liberalization, it is not surprising that the initial work in this area has generated mixed results to date.

Although the macroeconomic empirical evidence on how trade openness affects growth took years to develop, at a much earlier date several papers using microeconomic data and case studies found compelling evidence that trade liberalization raises productivity and growth. Similarly, recent work using microeconomic and case study evidence has been much more successful than the macroeconomic literature in documenting the costs of capital controls. Although case studies have shortcomings, such as the difficulty of controlling for other simultaneous events and generalizing to different countries and experiences, this microeconomic approach can avoid many of the problems with the macroeconomic, cross-country literature. Moreover, this microeconomic approach can facilitate a much more detailed measurement of exactly how capital account liberalization affects the allocation of resources and market efficiency.

4.3   Capital Controls and the Supply and Cost of Capital

Lifting capital controls should allow capital to flow where it can earn the highest expected rate of return. Since capital is relatively scarce in low-income, labor-intensive economies, the return to capital would be expected to be higher, on average, than in capital-abundant, wealthy countries. Therefore, standard economic theory suggests that when emerging markets lift their capital controls, capital should tend to flow in from wealthier countries. Capital inflows could generate substantial benefits, such as providing capital for investment, making advanced technology available, and spurring competitiveness.

This simple prediction, however, does not hold for many countries. Most capital currently flows from developing to developed countries or between developed countries—not from developed to developing countries. Figure

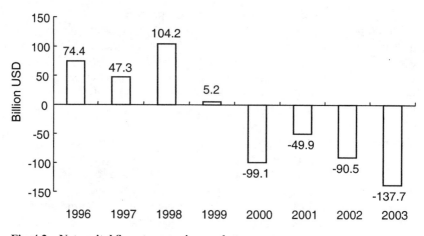

Fig. 4.2   Net capital flows to emerging markets
Source: IMF *Global Financial Stability Report.*
Note: Emerging market countries are those included in the EMBI and/or EMBI+.

4.2 shows that emerging markets have been net exporters of capital, instead of net importers, since 2000. Even before 2000 when emerging markets were net capital importers, their volume of capital inflows was much lower than might be expected given their relative scarcity of capital. One reason why capital inflows to developing countries may be so low is the greater prevalence of capital controls in these markets. Some low- and middle-income countries that have lifted their capital controls, however, still experience net capital outflows.

There are a number of reasons why capital might flow from capital-scarce to capital-rich countries, even in the absence of capital controls. First, the enforceability of property rights is weak in most developing countries. Second, informal administrative barriers (such as corruption, the absence of transparent rules for investment, and the scarcity of trained, professional civil servants) can discourage foreign investment in developing countries. Third, lower levels of human capital in developing countries can reduce productivity.[11] Finally, many developing countries have a history of default and substantially higher credit risk (Reinhart and Rogoff 2004). All of these factors can reduce the expected return to capital in developing countries, despite their relative scarcity of capital. For all of these reasons, if emerging markets lift their capital controls, capital could actually flow out of, instead of into, the country. As a result, it is difficult to predict, a priori, how lifting capital controls will affect the supply of capital in a country.

Moreover, lifting capital controls can affect the cost of capital not only

11. See Lucas (1990).

by affecting the supply of capital but also by allowing investors to expand their portfolio of asset holdings to better diversify risk. Since asset returns in an individual country are not perfectly correlated with global asset returns (or returns in any other individual country), removing capital controls can facilitate international risk sharing. A greater diversification of risk will reduce the volatility of expected portfolio returns, thereby reducing the cost of capital.[12]

4.3.1 The Cross-Country Evidence

Several microeconomic studies address these issues by assessing how lifting capital controls affects equity markets, the cost of capital, and financial constraints for different types of firms. Chari and Henry (2004b) examine the impact of removing controls on stock market investment on different types of firms in eleven emerging markets. They find that when publicly listed firms become eligible for foreign ownership, they experience an average stock price revaluation of 15.1 percent and a significant fall in their average cost of capital (with the risk-free rate of return falling between 5.9 percent and 9.1 percent, depending on the specification).[13] The impact on the expected returns of individual firms is directly proportional to the firm-specific changes in systematic risk resulting from the liberalization. These affects are also greater for stocks that become "investible" (i.e., that can be purchased by foreigners after liberalization) as compared to firms that are "noninvestible" (i.e., that remain off-limits for foreign investment). These results suggest that the supply of capital increases and the cost of capital decreases after capital controls on equity investment are removed, although the effects will vary across different types of firms.

A number of studies assess the impact of removing capital controls on the supply and cost of capital by using a different approach—measuring how capital controls affect the financing constraints of different types of companies. Financing constraints are generally measured as the sensitivity of investment to cash flow, while controlling for a number of firm-level variables (including investment opportunities). Harrison, Love, and McMillan (2004) follow this approach and use an extensive cross-country, time-series, firm-level data set.[14] Their study finds that restrictions on capital account transactions tend to increase firms' financing constraints. These financial

---

12. See Bekaert and Harvey (2003) for a formal model and more detailed discussion of this effect.

13. These results are supported by several macroeconomic studies of how liberalizations affect equity markets. For example, Henry (2000) shows that the mean growth rate of private investment increases by about 22 percentage points over the three years after liberalizations in emerging markets. Bekaert and Harvey (2000) show that the cost of capital decreases by between 5 and 75 basis points after liberalizations.

14. Capital controls are measured using different dummy variables for the five categories of capital controls in the IMF's *Trade and Exchange Restrictions*. This measure of capital controls is imprecise, and its problems are discussed in the literature surveyed in section 4.2.

constraints are greater for firms that are domestically owned (as compared to those with either foreign ownership or assets), which the authors interpret as being "consistent with the hypothesis that foreign investment is associated with a greater reduction in the credit constraints of firms which are less likely to have access to international capital markets" (Harrison, Love, and McMillan 2004, p. 272). Restrictions on capital flows other than capital account transactions—such as on import surcharges or surrender requirements for exporters—have no impact on firms' financial constraints. The study also finds that increased FDI is associated with reduced firm financing constraints—although a number of factors other than lifting controls on capital inflows will determine FDI flows.

Several studies use broader measures of liberalization and also find that greater liberalization decreases financial constraints in a panel of firms and countries. One of the most common measures of liberalization is financial liberalization—which generally includes lifting controls on foreign investment in the financial sector, as well as lifting controls on interest rates and reducing directed-credit programs. For example, Laeven (2003) constructs a new measure of banking-sector liberalization that includes several factors in addition to removing barriers to bank entry by foreign investors. Using this measure, Laeven's study finds that financial liberalization significantly reduces financing constraints for small firms, with an 80 percent average reduction in the sensitivity of investment to cash flow. Laeven (2003) also finds that large firms tend to be less financially constrained before liberalization and are less likely to experience a reduction in financial constraints afterward. There is even some evidence that large firms may experience an increase in financial constraints after bank liberalizations. The study suggests this may reflect that "in many developing countries, large firms had access to preferential (directed) credit during the period before financial liberalization. This form of favoritism is likely to decrease during financial liberalization" (Laeven 2003, p. 25).

Other papers expand beyond the banking sector and use even broader measures of financial liberalization to examine the microeconomic impact on firm financing constraints.[15] For example, Love (2003) uses an index of financial development that includes market capitalization, value traded, and the share of credit going to the private sector. Although this study does not explicitly test the relationship between this measure of financial development and capital account liberalization, other work shows that capital account liberalization tends to significantly increase financial market development.[16] Love (2003) finds a strong negative relationship between fi-

15. In a closely related study, Demirguc-Kunt and Maksimovic (1998) show that firms in countries with a more active stock market and large banking sector grow faster than they could using only internally generated funds.
16. For example, see Klein and Olivei (1999). Also see Bekaert and Harvey (2003) for an excellent survey of this literature.

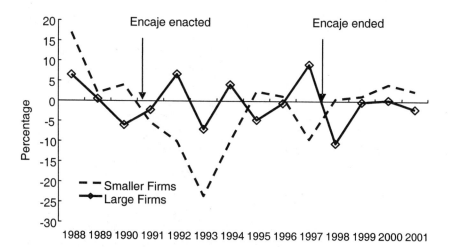

Fig. 4.3   Growth in investment-capital ratios for Chilean firms
Source: Forbes (2003).

nancial market development and financing constraints for all types of firms. Her study also finds that smaller firms have significantly greater financial constraints than larger firms in less financially developed countries.

4.3.2   Evidence from Individual Countries

This series of studies using a range of different statistics to measure capital account liberalization and its impact on firm financing constraints has utilized cross-country, firm-level data. Although cross-country data have the obvious advantage of being able to test for common relationships across different countries, they have the disadvantage of aggregating across very different liberalization experiences and relying on more limited data that are only available across countries. In order to avoid these problems, several studies have focused on individual countries' experiences with capital account liberalization and firm financing constraints.

One country that has received substantial attention is Chile. Chile enacted taxes on capital inflows (the *encaje*) from 1991 to 1998. This experience is useful for case studies not only because it is generally cited as one of the most successful examples of capital controls, but also since the enactment and then removal of the tax provides a useful time-series dimension to assess its impact.[17] Forbes (2003) examines how the *encaje* affected investment and financial constraints for different types of publicly traded firms in Chile. Figure 4.3, which is replicated from the paper, shows that in-

---

17. See Forbes (2003) for more information on the *encaje* and the literature assessing the impact of these capital controls.

vestment growth was higher for smaller, publicly traded firms than larger firms both before and after the *encaje* (which is a standard result in the finance literature). During the period that the capital controls were in place, however, investment growth plummeted for smaller companies and was generally lower than for larger companies. A more formal empirical analysis in the study that controls for a range of variables confirms these results and indicates that the *encaje* significantly increased financial constraints for smaller, publicly traded companies, but not for larger firms.

Gallego and Hernández (2003) use a different estimation technique to examine the impact of capital controls in Chile, but they find similar results. Their study shows that the *encaje* significantly increased the cost of external funding for Chilean firms, although the average effect was small in magnitude. These effects also vary substantially across different types of firms. For example, the impact of the *encaje* on financing costs for smaller firms was about 60 basis points higher than for firms that could issue securities abroad. Gallego and Hernández (2003) also examine the impact of lifting restrictions on capital outflows in Chile. In contrast to the effect of the *encaje,* lifting controls on capital outflows increases the cost of funding for all types of firms, although the magnitude of the effect is small. The paper states that controlling capital outflows by "keeping national savings 'captive' in the local market may have resulted in an artificially lower cost of borrowing for firms" (Gallego and Hernández 2003, p. 243).

Although most other countries do not provide as clear a natural experiment to test the impact of capital account liberalization as the Chilean *encaje,* other studies have focused on how broader measures of financial liberalization affect firm financing constraints. For example, Gelos and Werner (2001) examine the impact of widespread financial market liberalization in Mexico in the late 1980s on fixed investment in Mexican manufacturing firms.[18] Their study finds that after financial market liberalization, financial constraints were significantly eased for smaller companies, although not larger companies. Liberalization may not have reduced financial constraints for larger companies, for two reasons. First, larger companies had much lower financial constraints before liberalization. Second, larger companies were more likely to have stronger political connections that provided better access to directed credit at preferential rates before liberalization.

Other studies examine the impact of broader financial market liberalizations in other Latin American countries. Gallego and Loayza (2000) focus on Chilean firms between 1985 and 1995 and find that firms were financially constrained before liberalization (during the period from 1985 to 1990), and these constraints were significantly reduced after liberalization

---

18. This study uses an innovative approach to address a censoring problem in investment data by using real estate as collateral.

(from 1991 to 1996). The paper does not test for the impact of the *encaje* (which was enacted midway through the later period) or differentiate between large and small firms.[19] Jaramillo, Schiantarelli, and Weiss (1996) focus on Ecuadorian firms in the 1980s and find that capital market imperfections caused smaller and younger firms to be more financially constrained than older firms. Financial constraints do not fall significantly after liberalization (even for small firms), but the authors admit that since financial reform was an ongoing process, it is difficult to clearly identify the pre- and postreform episodes. They also admit that this time-series analysis is complicated by several macroeconomic events during this period, including severe inflation in 1988, a major earthquake, loose fiscal policy, and a sharp reduction in credit provided by the central bank.

A final country study of the impact of financial market liberalization on financial constraints is Harris, Schiantarelli, and Siregar (1994). This study examines Indonesian manufacturing establishments and suffers from similar time series identification problems as Jaramillo, Schiantarelli, and Weiss (1996). With this caveat, the study finds that liberalization improves access to financing for all types of firms, but may increase borrowing costs, especially for smaller firms. The study suggests that the movement from preferential credit to lending based on market mechanisms can increase the overall availability of financing, but it may simultaneously raise the cost of capital for individual firms that previously benefited from preferential access to credit.

4.3.3 Summary

This series of cross-country and individual case studies on the impact of capital controls, capital account liberalization, and broader financial market liberalization on the supply and cost of capital has several key themes. First, liberalization tends to reduce the cost of capital and ameliorate financial constraints, on average, two effects that are consistent with liberalization's increasing the supply of capital. Second, smaller firms and companies that did not previously have access to international capital markets are more likely to experience these benefits of liberalizations. Third, certain types of firms in several countries may have benefited from capital controls and more restricted financial markets, possibly through preferential lending agreements. These companies were less likely to benefit from reduced financial constraints after liberalizations, and may even face a higher cost of capital. This set of microeconomic results clearly suggests that capital controls can reduce the supply and increase the price of capital, making it

---

19. Gallego and Loayza (2000) find evidence, however, that firms eligible for investment in pension funds (pension fund management company [PFMC]–grade firms) were less financially constrained than non PFMC-grade firms before 1990. Since PFMC-grade firms tend to be larger than the average Chilean firm, this is consistent with the hypothesis that smaller firms were more financially constrained than larger firms during this period.

more difficult for many firms to obtain financing for productive investment. Although experiences vary across countries, these effects are generally greatest for smaller firms, firms in less distorted financial markets, and firms without access to international capital markets or preferential lending arrangements. This impact of capital controls on small firms could be particularly important for emerging markets in which small and new firms are often important sources of job creation and economic growth.

4.4   Capital Controls and Market Discipline

Capital controls can not only reduce the supply and increase the cost of capital, but they can insulate an economy from competitive forces, reducing market discipline and allowing capital to be allocated inefficiently. Some of the results discussed in the last section were consistent with this effect—although none of the studies tested it explicitly. An additional series of microeconomic papers, however, tests whether capital controls affect market discipline through three closely related channels: through the efficiency with which capital is allocated, through the government's ability to channel resources inefficiently, and through the information content in asset prices.

4.4.1   Capital Controls and the Allocation of Capital

Chari and Henry's study (2004a) is the most careful study directly testing for the impact of capital controls on the allocation of capital. This study examines how stock market liberalizations in emerging markets affect investment and the return to capital for different types of firms. It finds that firms with better fundamentals before liberalization have a greater increase in capital investment after liberalization. Moreover, this effect of firm characteristics on the allocation of investment can outweigh the average effects on all equities from liberalization. For example, the paper's baseline estimates show that a 1 percentage point increase in a firm's expected future cash flow (indicating stronger fundamentals) predicts a 4.1 percentage point increase in its investment ratio after liberalization. In comparison, the country-specific impact of liberalization on the cost of capital predicts only a 2.3 percentage point increase in investment. The authors conclude that stock market liberalizations do "not constitute a wasteful binge" and that the "invisible hand" is "discerning" in its ability to allocate capital to firms with higher expected returns after liberalizations.

A number of studies focus on how liberalizations in areas other than equity markets affect the allocation of investment across firms. Galindo, Schiantarelli, and Weiss (2006) assess if banking-sector liberalizations (which include reducing barriers to foreign investment as well as other reforms) improve the efficiency with which investment is allocated in twelve developing countries. The study measures the efficiency of the allocation of capital using an index measuring whether investment funds go to firms with a higher marginal return to capital. The return to capital is measured using panel estimates of a Cobb-Douglas production function. Results show that liberalizations increase the efficiency of the allocation of investment in the majority of emerging markets in their sample. Jaramillo, Schiantarelli, and Weiss (1992) focus on a broader definition of financial market liberalization (including the banking sector as well as other financial markets) and only include firms in Ecuador during its period of liberalization in the 1980s. They also find that liberalization increases credit flows to more "technically efficient" firms, although the time series framework in this study has several problems (as discussed in section 4.3.2).

Several microeconomic studies have also tested for a relationship between the allocation of capital and overall financial development, as measured by the size of a country's equity and credit markets relative to GDP. This measure has a positive relationship to capital controls, although an even weaker one than measures of financial market liberalizations (as discussed above). Nonetheless, the results from these studies are consistent with the results on how capital controls affect the allocation of capital. For example, Wurgler (2000) uses industry-level data to show that investment growth is more closely associated with the growth in value added (a measure of the return to capital) in countries with more developed financial systems. Rajan and Zingales (1998) show that industries that are more reliant on external financing grow faster in more financially developed countries, suggesting that financial development reduces firms' costs of external finance.[20] These results suggest that capital is allocated more efficiently in countries with more developed or deeper financial markets.

Abiad, Oomes, and Ueda (2004) also examine the relationship between financial markets and the allocation of capital, but they explicitly test for differences in the relative importance of financial liberalization (the focus of the papers at the beginning of this section) and of overall financial development (the focus of the papers in the previous paragraph). The Abiad et al. study also develops a new method for measuring the efficiency of the allocation of capital. More specifically, it uses the dispersion in Tobin's q in a given country and year (after controlling for other factors) to proxy for the variation in expected returns. A lower variation in returns is interpreted as indicating that capital is allocated more efficiently, because if a country removes its capital controls, then credit should be reallocated from firms with lower expected returns to firms with higher expected returns, thereby raising expected returns for the former group and reducing them for the latter. The study finds that financial liberalization (which includes entry

20. Reliance on external financing is measured by the industries' reliance on external financing in the United States.

barriers for banks, restrictions on international financial transactions, credit and interest rate controls, privatization, and other regulations) improves the allocation of credit across firms. In contrast, financial deepening (which is measured by the volume of credit being intermediated in financial markets) affects firms' access to finance but is a less important determinant of the allocation of capital.

4.4.2   Capital Controls and Government's Allocation of Resources

In developed countries, the allocation of capital and investment is largely determined by financial markets. In emerging markets and developing countries, however, the government often plays a more important role. Moreover, capital controls can insulate governments from market discipline, giving government agencies greater freedom to allocate capital based on factors other than the expected returns to investment. Therefore, instead of testing for the general impact of capital account liberalization on the allocation of a capital, an alternate approach is to test whether liberalization affects the government's ability to allocate capital to preferred companies.

One paper that uses this approach is Johnson and Mitton (2002). This study examines how the Asian crisis and the announcement of Malaysia's capital controls affected stock returns for individual Malaysian companies. It splits the sample into firms with political connections to senior government officials (such as Prime Minister Mahathir) and those without political connections. The paper finds that in the initial phase of the crisis (before the capital controls were enacted), politically connected firms experienced a greater loss in market value than firms without political connections. When the controls were put into place, politically connected firms experienced a relatively greater increase in market value. These results suggest that the Asian crisis initially increased financial pressures on Malaysian firms, improving market discipline and reducing the expected ability of the government to provide subsidies for favored firms. When the capital controls were put into place, however, investors expected that the Malaysian government would have more freedom to help favored firms, thereby reducing market discipline.

Moreover, the empirical estimates in Johnson and Mitton (2002) suggest that this effect of the Malaysian capital controls on expected market discipline was substantial. In the initial phase of the crisis (from July 1997 to August 1998), politically connected firms lost about $5.7 billion in market value due to the fall in the expected value of their connections. When the controls were enacted in September 1998 (and market values were substantially lower), politically connected firms gained about $1.3 billion in market value due to the increased value of their connections. Another calculation indicates that at the end of September 1998, after the capital controls had reduced market discipline, political connections were worth about 17 percent of the total market value for connected firms.

4.4.3   Capital Controls and Asset Market Pricing

Capital controls can also impact the allocation of capital by affecting the liquidity of asset markets and the efficiency of asset market pricing. Controls on capital inflows can make it more difficult for foreigners to invest in domestic financial markets, therefore reducing a valuable source of investment and liquidity. On the other hand, controls on capital outflows could increase liquidity by keeping funds inside the country. Similarly, restrictions on domestic companies' ability to raise financing abroad could foster the development and liquidity of domestic financial markets. Controls on either capital inflows or outflows, however, could reduce competitive pressure and market discipline, thereby reducing the information content of asset prices. This effect could be particularly important in less developed financial markets, where foreign investors can have greater experience valuing assets and therefore provide more reliable pricing information. Therefore, the impact of capital account liberalization on asset market liquidity and pricing efficiency must be resolved empirically. This is an important issue not only in and of itself but also because stock market mispricing can affect a number of firm-level variables, such as the cost of debt, total investment, FDI, and merger and acquisition activity.[21]

Li et al.'s (2004) study provides evidence on how capital account liberalization could affect the efficiency of asset pricing. This study examines the extent to which individual stock prices move up and down together in specific countries—what is also called "synchronicity." High levels of comovement and low levels of firm-specific variation in prices suggest that stock prices are less efficient. In other words, when stock prices are driven more by aggregate, country-level news instead of by firm-specific variables and information, there is less market discipline. The Li et al. paper uses several different measures to show that greater openness in capital markets (but not in goods markets) is correlated with greater firm-specific content in stock prices. Therefore, greater openness in capital markets is associated with more market discipline and more efficient stock market pricing. This relationship is magnified in countries with strong institutions and good governance.

One set of results in the working-paper version of the study by Li et al. (2004) is particularly relevant to the previous discussion of the impact of the Asian crisis and Malaysian capital controls on stock market prices.[22] Around the time of the Asian crisis, the firm-specific variation in stock

21. Different studies in this literature find different effects. See Baker, Foley, and Wurgler (2004) for an overview.
22. These results were removed from the published version of the paper but are included in the working-paper version prepared for the conference on Global Linkages held at the IMF on January 30–31, 2003. The paper is available at http://web.mit.edu/kjforbes/www/GL-Website/GL-Conference.htm.

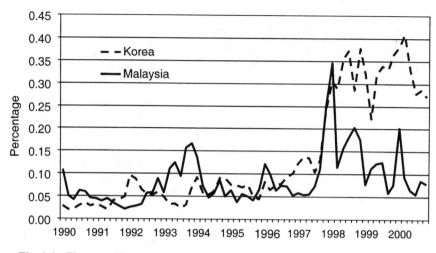

Fig. 4.4   Firm-specific variation in stock prices

Source: Based on data from Li et al. (2004).

Notes: Higher levels of firm-specific variation in stock prices indicate greater pricing efficiency.

prices increased significantly in most Asian countries and remained high for an extended period. This pattern is graphed for Korea in figure 4.4, and it is typical of most open economies in the region. In Malaysia, the firm-specific component of stock prices also increased significantly after the Asian crisis, but it then fell sharply after capital controls were imposed (as also shown in fig. 4.4). Although not a definitive test, this comparison supports the claim that the Asian crisis increased market discipline and the firm-specific content in stock prices, while the Malaysian capital controls suppressed market discipline and reduced the efficiency of stock market prices.

Several studies have focused on an even narrower aspect of the relationship between capital controls and asset pricing by examining the impact of firms' "migrating" abroad (i.e., of cross-listing on foreign stock markets, issuing depositary receipts, or raising capital directly in international markets). Capital controls can limit—or even restrict entirely—the ability of firms to access international capital markets through these channels. An extensive literature evaluates the impact of migration on firms that access international markets, as well as the corresponding impact on domestic firms that do not migrate. Bekaert and Harvey (2003) include a summary of this literature. Firms that access international capital markets generally attain a lower cost of capital and greater trading liquidity. Levine and Schmukler (2006), however, show that migration reduces the trading activity and liquidity of domestic firms that do not raise capital internationally. Migration not only shifts some trading activity abroad; it also shifts trading activity within the domestic market away from purely domestic firms to the "migrated" firms.

4.4.4   Summary

This series of cross-country and case studies on the impact of capital controls, capital account liberalization, and broader financial market development on market discipline and the allocation of capital provides several insights. First, capital controls can reduce market discipline and insulate the economy from competitive forces. Second and closely related, financial development, and especially capital market liberalization, leads to a more efficient allocation of capital across firms. Third, these effects of capital controls work through a number of different channels—including effects on stock market valuations, access to financing, the government's ability to channel resources inefficiently, and the efficiency of stock market pricing. Therefore, capital controls appear to have widespread effects on market discipline and the allocation of capital across firms, effects that are likely to reduce productivity and growth.

4.5   Capital Controls and the Behavior of Firms and Individuals

Capital controls can cause firms and individuals to alter their behavior to minimize the costs created by the controls. This modification in behavior can result from the explicit tax imposed by the capital controls, as well as from the impact of capital controls on the supply and allocation of capital. In some cases, this modification of behavior can involve inaccurate or dishonest reporting or accounting in order to evade the controls outright. These types of attempts by firms and individuals to minimize the costs of capital controls can create additional distortions in an economy.

4.5.1   Capital Controls and Firm Behavior

One careful study of how capital controls affect firm behavior focuses on U.S. multinationals. Desai, Foley, and Hines (2004) show that U.S. multinationals adjust their trade patterns, profits, and dividend repatriations in order to evade capital controls in other countries. For example, their study estimates that multinational affiliates are about 10 percent more likely to remit dividends to parent companies in the presence of capital controls, and that the distortions to profitability from capital controls are comparable to a 24 percent increase in the corporate tax rate. It also shows that the cost of borrowing is higher in countries with capital controls, and when this effect is combined with the other steps multinationals take to evade the controls, this reduces the size of foreign investment by multinationals by 13 percent to 16 percent. Therefore, not only can capital controls create widespread distortions in how foreign companies behave in countries with controls, but they also reduce the total amount of FDI available to host countries.

Another study that examines the effect of capital controls on firm behavior focuses on local firms instead of multinational affiliates. Schmukler and Vesperoni (2001) use firm-level data from East Asia and Latin America for the 1980s and 1990s to examine how leverage ratios, debt maturity structures, and financing sources change when countries increase their integration with international equity and bond markets and undergo financial liberalization. The study finds that, on average, debt maturity tends to shorten but debt-equity ratios do not increase. It also finds that domestic firms that participate in international markets obtain better financing opportunities and extend their debt maturities. Also, firms in economies with more developed domestic financial systems are less affected by liberalization. These results suggest that some, although not all, firms may have expanded financing opportunities when countries lift their capital controls and increase their integration with global financial markets.

Instead of focusing on a cross section of countries, several studies examine how capital controls affect firm behavior in an individual country. Forbes (2003) shows that the *encaje* (the Chilean tax on capital inflows discussed in section 4.3) caused companies to adjust their financial structure in a number of ways. For example, immediately after the *encaje* was enacted, there was a sharp increase in the number of firms choosing to issue stock that could then be cross-listed in the United States as American Depositary Receipts (ADRs). Individuals trading stock listed as secondary ADRs could avoid paying the *encaje*. In 1995, however, the Chilean government closed this loophole and included ADRs under the *encaje*. The number of Chilean firms issuing stock plummeted. Figure 4.5 shows these distortions to Chilean stock listings created by the *encaje* and changes in its coverage. Cifuentes, Desormeaux, and González (2002) also discuss how changes in this ADR loophole affected the evolution of the Chilean stock market. Their paper argues that the extension of the *encaje* to include secondary ADRs significantly reduced financial liquidity, transactions, and investment in the domestic stock market—a reduction that persisted even after the *encaje* was lifted.

Gallego and Hernández (2003) perform an even more detailed empirical analysis of how the *encaje* affected the financial decisions of Chilean firms. Their study finds that the *encaje* caused firms to reduce their leverage ratios and paid capital, and increase their reliance on retained earnings. This suggests that the capital controls raised the cost of borrowing and of issuing equity, although the average magnitudes of these effects were fairly small. The study also finds that the *encaje* shortened the maturity of debt, while reducing the relative importance of short-term financial debt, indicating that firms shifted to other sources of short-term funding to avoid the tax (such as delaying tax payments and obtaining credit from suppliers). Moreover, one fairly consistent finding throughout the study is that estimates of the average effects of the capital controls mask significant differ-

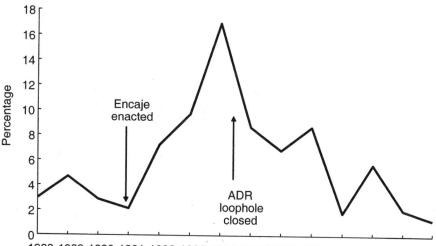

Fig. 4.5   **Stock issuance/capital for Chilean firms**
Source: Data from Forbes (2003).

ences across firms (as was found in the work discussed in section 4.3 on the impact of the *encaje* on firm financing constraints). Firms that were larger, belonged to a conglomerate, or were able to issue securities abroad were more likely to respond to the capital controls by reducing their leverage through increases in their capital base (instead of resorting to retained earnings). Other firms, and especially smaller firms, were more likely to respond to the capital controls by resorting to retained earnings for financing and increasing their reliance on short-term debt.

Other than the cross-country and Chilean studies on how capital controls affect firm behavior, most other evidence relies on anecdotes instead of formal empirical analysis. Several of these case studies, however, provide more concise descriptions of exactly how companies adapt their behavior in order to avoid capital controls. Many of these mechanisms are difficult to test empirically—but they could explain some of the more general effects discussed throughout this paper. One such study by Loungani and Mauro (2001) focuses on Russia.[23] This paper provides a detailed description of different strategies followed by Russian firms to evade capital controls. For example, in order to take money out of the country, firms would overstate import payments, by means that included the use of fake import contracts for goods and services. Companies would also create enterprises with the sole purpose of presenting fake import contracts requiring ad-

23. Also see Tikhomirov (1997) for an excellent description of different methods used to evade capital controls in Russia.

vance payments, and then the enterprises would be dissolved once the funds had been transferred out of the country. Companies would also misrepresent export earnings, by means such as under-invoicing exports or exporting via an offshore subsidiary with a low recorded transfer price (so that the margin between the transfer and market prices could be deposited offshore). All Russian firms, however, were not equally adept at circumventing the controls, which contributed to uneven competitive conditions and distorted the allocation of resources. The study presents evidence that firms' ability to evade the capital controls was widespread and that, as a result, capital controls increased corruption and lowered economic efficiency in Russia.

4.5.2   Capital Controls and Individual Behavior

Individuals, as well as firms, can modify their behavior to minimize the cost of capital controls—or even evade them outright. One compelling example is how individuals responded to the *"corralito"* enacted by Argentina at the end of 2001. The *corralito* restricted capital outflows and withdrawals from the banking system. During this period the stock market rose dramatically, despite a sharp economic contraction, a plummeting peso, and a banking system on the verge of collapse. Auguste et al. (2002) explain this apparent discrepancy. Investors dodged the capital controls by purchasing Argentine stocks for pesos, converting the stocks into ADRs, and then selling the ADRs in New York for dollars that could be deposited in U.S. bank accounts. The study estimates that the capital outflow through this single loophole was between $835 million and $3.4 billion in just the four months starting in December 2001. Investors were willing to pay a substantial premium to evade the *corralito*—with some ADRs trading at a discount of over 40 percent. Once the conversion of Argentine shares into ADRs was prohibited, the premium returned to nearly zero. Figure 4.6 (replicated from the Auguste et al. paper) shows these trends for one Argentine stock. Melvin (2003) also studies the same episode and reaches similar conclusions. The surge in the ADR premium during the period of the *corralito* reflects what investors were willing to pay to avoid the Argentine capital controls.

Several papers also describe how investors adjusted their behavior to avoid capital controls in Russia. For example, Tikhomirov (1997) provides a number of examples—including how Russian citizens would hold foreign currency funds in banks abroad so that they could invest and utilize these resources more freely. Abalkin and Whalley (1999) discuss how Russian citizens would convert local currency holdings and bank deposits into dollars, partially to facilitate evasion of the controls.

4.5.3   Summary

This series of microeconomic studies suggests that capital controls can cause widespread distortions in the behavior of firms and individuals. U.S.

Fig. 4.6   Argentine and U.S. prices and premia for Perez Companc
Source: Auguste et al. (2002, fig. 6).

multinationals adjust their trade patterns, profits, and dividend repatriations to evade the controls. Domestic companies adjust their debt maturities and financing structures when capital controls are lifted. Individuals are willing to pay a substantial premium for a financial transaction that allows them to evade controls. Companies and individuals adopt numerous accounting gimmicks—including creating temporary corporations—simply to dodge the controls. These widespread distortions to firm and individual behavior resulting from the capital controls are likely to be inefficient.

4.6   The Enforcement of Capital Controls

Since firms and individuals will respond to capital controls by adjusting their behavior, enforcing the controls and ensuring that they are effective can not only be a challenge but also involve substantial administrative costs. Implementing capital controls is often a dynamic process. After a system of controls is specified, firms and individuals often find ways to evade the controls, diminishing their effectiveness over time. Governments that do not wish to see the effectiveness of the controls weakened will need to constantly adopt new controls and regulations in order to close loopholes and respond to the adjustments in behavior that resulted from the initial controls. Countries with weak institutions, especially a weak rule of law and high levels of corruption, are even less likely to be able to implement and enforce capital controls. Moreover, by providing an opportunity for government officials to collect rents, capital controls can increase incentives for corruption and undermine institutions.

There is extensive anecdotal evidence from different countries on the difficulty faced by governments that attempt to enforce capital controls and the link between capital controls and corruption. For example, Tikhomirov (1997) provides a fairly detailed account of the attempts by the Russian government to limit illegal capital flight. Despite the continual passing of new rules and regulations in order to improve the government's control over capital flows, many of these rules were highly ineffective and capital flight was extensive. Different sources suggest that capital flight from Russia between 1990 and 1995 was somewhere in the very wide range of $35 billion to $400 billion. The study asserts that "instead of cutting profits from the illegal transfer of foreign currency funds abroad, these measures [the controls] spread the corruption from the foreign trade sector to the bureaucracy and, later, to the banking sector" (Tikhomirov 1997, p. 595). Russia's challenges in enforcing capital controls, however, could result partially from the weak institutions in the country during the period of this study.

The Chilean experience with the *encaje* (discussed above) therefore provides a useful contrast. Chile has sound institutions, a strong rule of law, and low levels of corruption. Despite these advantages, the government was constantly modifying the *encaje* in order to close new loopholes that were discovered by firms and investors. These changes included everything from the types of inflows covered, to the currency with which to pay the tax, to restrictions on rolling over maturing investments.[24] Moreover, despite Chile's constant attempts to raise the amount of the tax, tighten the capital controls, and close loopholes, there is some evidence that the effectiveness of the controls may still have declined over time.[25] Central bank data show that in 1992 the *encaje* covered about half of total gross capital inflows, but in subsequent years coverage declined to only 24 percent of inflows (Gallego, Hernández, and Schmidt-Hebbel 1999). Despite these challenges of enforcing the capital controls, however, the Chilean government still collected substantial revenues under the tax, which suggests that it still maintained some degree of effectiveness.[26]

---

24. See Simone and Sorsa (1999) or Ariyoshi et al. (2000) for detailed information on this evolution of capital account restrictions in Chile over the 1990s.

25. For example, Cowan and de Gregorio (1998) calculate the "power" of the controls and argue that their power declined between 1995 and 1997 as evasion increased. Other studies, however, argue that the power of the controls increased steadily over time until they were removed in 1998. For example, see Gallego, Hernández, and Schmidt-Hebbel (1999) and Valdés-Prieto and Soto (1998). Also see Simone and Sorsa (1999) for an overview of work on the evasion of the *encaje*.

26. Gallego, Hernández, and Schmidt-Hebbel (1999) report that between June 1991 and September 1998, the *encaje* increased central bank reserves by an average of 2 percent of GDP, or 40 percent of the average capital account surplus.

Moreover, as new financial instruments continue to be developed and investors and firms become more adept at transferring capital across borders, it will become even more difficult to enforce capital controls. The recent case of Argentine investors using ADRs to evade the *corralito* provides a clear example of this challenge. After studying this experience, Auguste et al. (2002) suggest that once countries allow financial market development, "it may be difficult if not impossible to reverse the process of capital market integration with (even draconian) capital controls" (p. 4).

4.7   Conclusions

Although the cross-country macroeconomic evidence on how capital account liberalization affects growth has yielded mixed results to date, a series of microeconomic papers provides far more persuasive evidence on the diverse effects of capital controls and capital account liberalization. The studies surveyed in this paper present compelling empirical evidence that capital controls can affect the supply and cost of capital, market discipline, the allocation of resources, and the behavior of firms and individuals. Several studies also find that the effects of capital account liberalization vary across types of firms, reflecting different preexisting distortions under capital controls. For example, although lifting capital controls tends to reduce financial constraints for most firms, it can have no effect (or even increase financial constraints) for firms that received preferential treatment under the controls or had already found ways to evade them.

This microeconomic research on the impact of capital controls, however, is only in its infancy. Much more careful analysis is needed to better understand why capital account liberalization can have varied effects in different countries, and especially on what variables determine the success of liberalizations. For example, what are the microeconomic consequences of different sequencing when lifting capital controls? What are the microeconomic linkages between trade liberalizations and capital account liberalizations? How do different institutions interact with the microeconomic effects of capital controls? And are the benefits of capital account liberalization usually level effects or growth effects?

Moreover, although this paper discusses how capital controls and financial liberalizations directly affect a series of microeconomic variables, it does not address a number of additional channels by which capital controls could affect key macroeconomic variables (such as exchange rates, the financial system, and/or monetary policy), which could, in turn, have additional effects on firms and individuals. For example, controls on capital outflows could reduce pressure on a currency to depreciate, and controls on capital inflows could reduce pressure on a currency to appreciate. Controls on capital outflows could help support a weak financial system, while controls on capital inflows could hinder the development of a deeper and more efficient financial market. Controls on capital inflows and outflows could create a wedge between domestic and foreign interest rates, thereby providing a country with more flexibility to follow an independent monetary policy. Changes in exchange rates, the financial system, and interest rates will, in turn, affect a range of microeconomic variables in the economy.[27] The paper also does not make any attempt to address the political economy of capital controls, such as what factors determine whether a country is more likely to adopt controls or liberalize its capital account.[28]

Although this survey does not address a number of questions, largely due to the limited microeconomic evidence that currently exists on these issues, it does present a series of convincing results on the effects of capital controls and benefits from capital account liberalizations. Although some specific effects vary across country experiences, capital controls generally reduce the supply of capital, increase the price of capital, and increase financial constraints, especially for smaller firms, firms in less distorted financial markets, and firms without access to international financial markets or preferred access to credit. Capital controls can insulate an economy from competitive forces, reducing market discipline and hindering the efficient allocation of capital through several channels. Capital controls can also cause widespread distortions in behavior, affecting multinationals, domestic companies, and individuals. Moreover, administering capital controls requires a recurrent cost by the government, especially to enforce the regulations and update rules to close loopholes. These widespread effects of capital controls suggest that even though they may yield limited benefits in certain circumstances, they also have substantial and often unexpected economic costs. Capital controls are no free lunch.

References

Abalkin, A., and John Whalley. 1999. The problem of capital flight from Russia. *World Economy* 22 (3): 412–44.

Abiad, Abdul, Nienke Oomes, and Kenichi Ueda. 2004. The quality effect: Does financial liberalization improve the allocation of capital? IMF Working Paper no. WP/04/112. Washington, DC: International Monetary Fund.

Aghion, Philippe, Philippe Bacchetta, and Abhijit Banerjee. 2001. Currency crises and monetary policy in an economy with credit constraints. *European Economic Review* 45:1121–50.

Ariyoshi, Akira, Karl Habermeier, Bernard Laurens, Inci Otker-Robe, Jorge Iván Canales-Kriljenko, and Andrei Kirilenko. 2000. Capital controls: Country expe-

---

27. For example, see Forbes (2002a, 2002b) for a literature review and analysis of just the single topic of how depreciations affect different measures of firm performance.

28. For a discussion of these political economy questions, see Johnston and Tamirisa (1998).

riences with their use and liberalization. IMF Occasional Paper no. 190. Washington, DC: International Monetary Fund.

Auguste, Sebastian, Kathryn Dominguez, Herman Kamil, and Linda Tesar. 2002. Cross-border trading as a mechanism for capital flight: ADRs and the Argentine crisis. NBER Working Paper no. 9343. Cambridge, MA: National Bureau of Economic Research.

Baker, Malcolm, C. Fritz Foley, and Jeffrey Wurgler. 2004. The stock market and investment. NBER Working Paper no. 10559. Cambridge, MA: National Bureau of Economic Research.

Bekaert, Geert, and Campbell Harvey. 2000. Foreign speculators and emerging equity markets. *Journal of Finance* 55 (2): 565–614.

———. 2003. Emerging markets finance. *Journal of Empirical Finance* 10:3–55.

Block, William, and Kristin Forbes. 2004. Capital flows to emerging markets: The myths and realities. Paper presented at Federal Reserve Bank conference "Myths and Realities of Globalization." 4 November, Dallas, Texas.

Chari, Anusha, and Peter Blair Henry. 2004a. Is the invisible hand discerning or indiscriminate? Investment and stock prices in the aftermath of capital account liberalizations. NBER Working Paper no. 10318. Cambridge, MA: National Bureau of Economic Research.

———. 2004b. Risk sharing and asset prices: Evidence from a natural experiment. *Journal of Finance* 59 (3): 1295–1324.

Chinn, Menzie, and Hiro Ito. 2002. Capital account liberalization, institutions and financial development: Cross country evidence. NBER Working Paper no. 8967. Cambridge, MA: National Bureau of Economic Research.

Cifuentes, Rodrigo, Jorge Desormeaux, and Claudio González. 2002. Capital markets in the Chilean economy: From financial repression to financial deepening. Santiago, Chile: Central Bank of Chile. Mimeograph.

Cowan, Kevin, and José De Gregorio. 1998. Exchange rate policies and capital account management: Chile in the 1990s. In *Managing capital flows and exchange rates: Perspectives from the Pacific Basin,* ed. Reuven Glick, 465–88. Cambridge: Cambridge University Press.

Demirguc-Kunt, Asli, and Vojislav Maksimovic. 1998. Law, finance, and firm growth. *Journal of Finance* 53 (6): 2107–31.

Desai, Mihir, C. Fritz Foley, and James Hines. 2004. Capital controls, liberalizations, and foreign direct investment. NBER Working Paper no. 10337. Cambridge, MA: National Bureau of Economic Research.

Economist. 2003. A slightly circuitous route. May 1.

Edison, Hali, Michael Klein, Luca Ricci, and Torsten Sloek. 2002. Capital account liberalization and economic performance: Survey and synthesis. NBER Working Paper no. 9100. Cambridge, MA: National Bureau of Economic Research.

Eichengreen, Barry. 2001. Capital account liberalization: What do cross-country studies tell us? *World Bank Economic Review* 15 (3): 341–65.

———. 2003. *Capital flows and crises.* Cambridge, MA: MIT Press.

Fischer, Stanley. 2001. Exchange rate regimes: Is the bipolar view correct? Distinguished Lecture in Economics and Government, delivered at the meeting of the American Economic Association. 6 January, New Orleans, Louisiana.

———. 2003. Globalization and its challenges. *American Economic Review* 93 (2): 1–30.

Forbes, Kristin. 2002a. Cheap labor meets costly capital: The impact of devaluations on commodity firms. *Journal of Development Economics* 69 (2): 335–65.

———. 2002b. How do large depreciations affect firm performance? *IMF Staff Papers* 49:214–38.

———. 2003. One cost of the Chilean capital controls: Increased financial constraints for smaller traded firms. NBER Working Paper no. 9777. Cambridge, MA: National Bureau of Economic Research.

Galindo, Arturo, Fabio Schiantarelli, and Andrew Weiss. 2006. Does financial liberalization improve the allocation of investment? Micro evidence from developing countries. *Journal of Development Economics,* forthcoming.

Gallego, Francisco, and Leonardo Hernández. 2003. Microeconomic effects of capital controls: The Chilean experience during the 1990s. *International Journal of Finance and Economics* 8 (3): 225–53.

Gallego, Francisco, Leonardo Hernández, and Klaus Schmidt-Hebbel. 1999. Capital controls in Chile: Effective? Efficient? Working Paper no. 59. Santiago, Chile: Central Bank of Chile.

Gallego, Francisco, and Norman Loayza. 2000. Financial structure in Chile: Macroeconomic developments and microeconomic effects. Working Paper no. 75. Santiago, Chile: Central Bank of Chile.

Gelos, R. Gaston, and Shang-Jin Wei. 2002. Transparency and international investor behavior. NBER Working Paper no. 9260. Cambridge, MA: National Bureau of Economic Research.

Gelos, R. Gaston, and Alejandro Werner. 2001. Financial liberalization, credit constraints, and collateral: Investment in the Mexican manufacturing sector. *Journal of Development Economics* 67 (1): 1–27.

Harris, John, Fabio Schiantarelli, and Miranda Siregar. 1994. The effect of financial liberalization on the capital structure and investment decisions of Indonesian manufacturing establishments. *World Bank Economic Review* 8 (1): 17–47.

Harrison, Ann, Inessa Love, and Margaret McMillan. 2004. Global capital flows and financing constraints. *Journal of Development Economics* 75 (1): 269–301.

Henry, Peter. 2000. Do stock market liberalizations cause investment booms? *Journal of Financial Economics* 58 (October): 301–34.

Henry, Peter, and Peter Lorentzen. 2003. Domestic capital market reform and access to global finance: Making markets work. NBER Working Paper no. 10064. Cambridge, MA: National Bureau of Economic Research.

Jaramillo, Fidel, Fabio Schiantarelli, and Andrew Weiss. 1992. The effect of financial liberalization on the allocation of credit: Panel data evidence for Ecuador. World Bank Policy Research Department Working Paper no. WPS 1092. Washington, DC: World Bank.

———. 1996. Capital market imperfections before and after financial liberalization: An Euler equation approach to panel data for Ecuadorian firms. *Journal of Development Economics* 51 (2): 367–86.

Johnson, Simon, and Todd Mitton. 2002. Cronyism and capital controls: Evidence from Malaysia. *Journal of Financial Economics* 67:351–82.

Johnston, R. Barry, and Natalia Tamirisa. 1998. Why do countries use capital controls? IMF Working Paper no. WP/98/181. Washington, DC: International Monetary Fund.

Klein, Michael, and Giovanni Olivei. 1999. Capital account liberalization, financial depth and economic growth. NBER Working Paper no. 7384. Cambridge, MA: National Bureau of Economic Research.

Laeven, Luc. 2003. Does financial liberalization reduce financing constraints? *Financial Management* 32 (1): 5–34.

Levine, Ross, and Sergio Schmukler. 2006. Migration, spillovers, and trade diversion: The impact of internationalization on domestic stock market activity. *Journal of Banking and Finance,* forthcoming.

Li, Kan, Randall Morck, Fan Yang, and Bernard Yeung. 2004. Firm-specific variation and openness in emerging markets. *Review of Economics and Statistics* 86 (3): 658–69.

Loungani, Prakash, and Paolo Mauro. 2001. Capital flight from Russia. *World Economy* 24 (5): 689–706.

Love, Inessa. 2003. Financial development and financing constraints: International evidence from the structural investment model. *Review of Financial Studies* 16 (3): 765–91.

Lucas, Robert. 1990. Why doesn't capital flow from rich to poor countries? *American Economic Review, Papers and Proceedings* 80 (May): 92–96.

Magud, Nicolas, and Carmen Reinhart. 2004. Controls on international borrowing: An evaluation of alternative measures used to restrict capital inflows. Paper presented at the National Bureau of Economic Research conference on International Capital Flows. 17 December, Santa Barbara, California.

Melvin, Michael. 2003. A stock market boom during a financial crisis? ADRs and capital outflows in Argentina. *Economic Letters* 81:129–36.

Prasad, Eswar, Kenneth Rogoff, Shang-Jin Wei, and M. Ayhan Kose. 2003. Effects of financial globalization on developing countries: Some empirical evidence. IMF Occasional Paper no. 220. Washington, DC: International Monetary Fund.

Rajan, Raghuran, and Luigi Zingales. 1998. Financial dependence and growth. *American Economic Review* 88 (3): 559–86.

Reinhart, Carmen, and Kenneth Rogoff. 2004. Serial default and the "paradox" of rich to poor capital flows. *American Economic Review* 94:52–58.

Reisen, Helmut, and Marcelo Soto. 2001. Which types of capital inflows foster developing-country growth? *International Finance* 4 (Spring): 1–14.

Rossi, Marco. 1999. Financial fragility and economic performance in developing economies: Do capital controls, prudential regulation and supervision matter? IMF Working Paper no. 99/66. Washington, DC: International Monetary Fund.

Rubin, Robert, and Jacob Weisberg. 2003. *In an uncertain world: Tough choices from Wall Street to Washington.* New York: Random House.

Schmukler, Sergio, and Esteban Vesperoni. 2001. Globalization and firms' financing choices: Evidence from emerging economies. World Bank Policy Research Working Paper no. 12323. Washington, DC: World Bank.

Simone, Francisco Nadal De, and Piritta Sorsa. 1999. A review of capital account restrictions in Chile in the 1990s. IMF Working Paper no. 99/52. Washington, DC: International Monetary Fund.

Tikhomirov, Vladimir. 1997. Capital flight from post-Soviet Russia. *Europe-Asia Studies* 49 (4): 591–616.

Valdés-Prieto, Salvador, and Marcelo Soto. 1998. The effectiveness of capital controls: Theory and evidence from Chile. *Empirica* 25 (2): 133–64.

Wurgler, Jeffrey. 2000. Financial markets and the allocation of capital. *Journal of Financial Economics* 58 (1): 187–214.

Comment   Charles W. Calomiris

Kristin Forbes offers a compelling case for the proposition that capital controls generally impose significant economic costs, and more—she pro-

Charles W. Calomiris is the Henry Kaufman Professor of Financial Institutions in the Graduate School of Business, Columbia University, and a research associate of the National Bureau of Economic Research.

vides an illuminating review of the microeconomic empirical literature that nicely summarizes the various channels through which capital controls harm the economy. Forbes does not argue against potential benefits from capital controls, but rather cautions against advocating capital controls only on the basis of arguments or evidence suggesting that they may have gross benefits.

The various channels she describes remind us that financial-sector policies alter economic outcomes not only through their immediate effects on the flow of investment, but also through important indirect effects on the productivity of investment, which operate through market competition and discipline, political economic outcomes, and the costs firms expend to avoid financial constraints. The methodological point of the paper—that macroeconomic studies of capital controls using cross-country aggregate data are prone to error because of difficulties of measurement—bears emphasis, as do the unambiguous results of the microeconomic empirical literature, which does not suffer similar measurement problems.

Some of the evidence summarized by Forbes does not directly address the consequences of capital controls, but rather examines the effects of financial controls of many kinds on financial and real outcomes at the firm level. But there are many studies that do bear directly on the question of the costliness of capital controls.

Chari and Henry (2004) find that equity market liberalizations (the removal of capital controls relating to equity markets) are associated with very large positive price effects on domestic stock prices, which are especially large for those in which foreigners are able to invest. Related macroeconomic work by Bekaert, Harvey, and Lundblad (2004, 2005), finds that equity market liberalizations spur economic growth and reduce consumption volatility; significantly, they show that these positive effects associated with international liberalization of equity markets are not explained by other (potentially correlated) financial reforms.

Harrison, Love, and McMillan (2004) find that capital account restrictions increase firms' financing constraints, especially for domestically owned firms. Similarly, Forbes (2003) and Gallego and Hernández (2003) show that Chile's *encaje* reduced the use of debt finance, increased firms' reliance on retained earnings and costly equity offerings, and reduced investment growth, particularly for smaller firms (those most likely to face external financing constraints). Johnson and Mitton (2002) show that Malaysia's capital controls favored politically connected firms by removing the discipline of the marketplace that would otherwise have steered resources elsewhere. Desai, Foley, and Hines (2004) show that, on average, capital controls raise the cost of funds and reduce investments by multinational firms in a manner comparable to a 24 percent increase in the corporate tax rate.

The notion that capital controls are costly also finds support from other studies, especially the economic history literature, which emphasizes the positive effects of Western European capital outflows (largely from Great Britain) in promoting global economic growth in the pre-World War I era (see Calomiris 2005 for a review). From the perspective of the unambiguously favorable macroeconomic historical evidence on capital mobility, the ambiguity of the macroeconomic evidence from the post-World War II era is quite revealing.

In my view, that difference points to incentive problems in financial regulation in the current era (especially generous safety nets for domestic banks) as the main problem in need of a policy remedy, rather than capital flows per se. Emerging market financial crises (in which so-called sudden stops of capital can be an important exacerbating influence) have been associated with overreliance on short-term, dollar-denominated debt inflows—a form of international financial flow that reflects a weak domestic financing system, and a form of capital inflow that was extremely uncommon historically. In part, the absence of such destabilizing capital flows historically reflected the fact that historical banking systems, even in emerging market countries, largely avoided incentive problems from government protection.

Is it possible to avoid the costs of destabilizing capital flows without giving up the advantages of accessing foreign capital? Yes. Rather than employing costly limits on capital inflows to emerging market countries, policy should instead focus on ways to improve the underlying problem of weak domestic bank regulation and thus overcome perverse incentives created by government policies that encourage the reliance on destabilizing forms of foreign capital.

References

Bekaert, Geert, Campbell R. Harvey, and Christian Lundblad. 2004. Growth volatility and financial liberalization. NBER Working Paper no. 10560. Cambridge, MA: National Bureau of Economic Research.

———. 2005. Does financial liberalization spur growth? *Journal of Financial Economics* 77 (1):3–55.

Calomiris, Charles W. 2005. Capital flows, financial crises, and public policy. In *Globalization: What's new,* ed. Michael Weinstein, 36–76. New York: Columbia University Press.

Chari, Anusha, and Peter Blair Henry. 2004. Risk sharing and asset prices: Evidence from a natural experiment. *Journal of Finance* 59 (3): 1295–1324.

Desai, Mihir, C. Fritz Foley, and James Hines. 2004. Capital controls, liberalization, and foreign direct investment. NBER Working Paper no. 10337. Cambridge, MA: National Bureau of Economic Research.

Forbes, Kristen. 2003. One cost of the Chilean capital controls: Increased financial constraints for smaller traded firms. NBER Working Paper no. 9777. Cambridge, MA: National Bureau of Economic Research.

Gallego, Francisco, and Leonardo Hernández. 2003. Microeconomic effects of capital controls: The Chilean experience during the 1990s. *International Journal of Finance and Economics* 8 (3): 225–53.

Harrison, Ann, Inessa Love, and Margaret McMillan. 2004. Global capital flows and financing constraints. *Journal of Development Economics* 75 (1): 269–301.

Johnson, Simon, and Todd Mitton. 2002. Cronyism and capital controls: Evidence from Malaysia. *Journal of Financial Economics* 67:351–82.

5

The International Exposure of U.S. Banks
Europe and Latin America Compared

Linda S. Goldberg

5.1 Introduction

As a major player in international capital markets, the United States often receives attention as a source of global macroeconomic fluctuations and, more recently, a destination for global savings resources. Since banks play a central role in the financial systems of many economies, they may be active in transmitting these fluctuations. Within banking, recent years have been marked by the dramatic rise in foreign ownership of banks, especially in emerging market economies. This compositional shift has raised questions about associated bank claims altering the extent of financial-sector depth in markets, expanding opportunities for international risk sharing and consumption smoothing in response to idiosyncratic country shocks, leading to altered international transmission of disturbances, and altering the institutions in the source and destination markets. Supporters see the foreign banks as key sources of otherwise scarce capital, with broader positive spillovers on the stability and efficiency of local financial markets. Critics of industrialized-country banks participating in emerging markets sometimes argue that these banks are unstable lenders that undermine local financial markets. The debate on whether foreign lenders are fickle con-

Linda S. Goldberg is vice president and head of the International Research Function at the Federal Reserve Bank of New York, and a faculty research fellow of the National Bureau of Economic Research (NBER).

The views expressed in this paper are those of the author and do not necessarily reflect the position of the Federal Reserve Bank of New York or the Federal Reserve System. This paper benefited from the comments of Matias Braun, Kenneth Lamar, Leon Taub, and participants in the NBER conference on international capital flows, December 2004. Eleanor Dillon provided diligent research support. Richard Molloy and Alex Santana provided valuable data assistance.

tinues to rage (Galindo, Micco, and Powell 2004) and underscores the importance of fact finding and communications on the international lending practices of industrialized-country banks.

This paper explores patterns in U.S. bank claims on foreign partners. U.S. banks have emerged as key participants in international banking and are particularly active in European and Latin American countries, with the latter group having faced tumultuous periods in recent decades. This motivates our contrast between the determinants and trends in international capital flows from U.S. banks to European and Latin American counterparties. As in Goldberg (2002), these capital flows are analyzed using data from a time series panel of individual U.S. banks that report exposures to foreign markets. These reports are filed quarterly by each U.S. bank (or bank holding company) to support the bank supervisory process of the Federal Reserve, Federal Depository Insurance Corporation, and Office of Comptroller of the Currency. The banks report the country-by-country distribution of their foreign exposures, the form of these exposures (cross-border claims and local claims—i.e., claims extended by the affiliates of U.S. banks located in foreign markets), valuations of derivative positions held, some maturity composition details, and broad categories of recipients of U.S. claims by destination market.[1]

Four interesting findings arise in our current examination of data, which extends through mid-2004. First, claims extended by larger U.S. reporting banks tend to be less volatile than claims by smaller U.S. banks. Second, while there have been some declines in cross-border flows to Latin American counterparties, larger U.S. banks have had robust trend growth in local claims on Latin America. Third, local claims tend to be more stable than cross-border claims. Finally, there is at best mixed evidence in support of the idea that U.S. international claims are cyclically driven, where cyclical forces are proxied by gross domestic product (GDP) growth rates and interest rates. While U.S. bank cross-border claims on European counterparties tend to expand with European growth performance, these sensitivities are not robust, and the explanatory power of these forces is low. We do not observe stable transmission of U.S. or destination market cycles into either Latin American or European partners, in either cross-border or local claims.[2]

These findings build on Goldberg (2002), wherein it was observed that the U.S. banks engaged in international lending had become more diverse

---

1. The term "U.S. banks" in this paper generally includes U.S.-owned banks, bank holding companies, and U.S. subsidiaries of foreign banks. The reported data also are combined with similar data from other countries to form the consolidated data on international bank lending reported by the Bank for International Settlements (BIS).

2. BIS (2004) provides a thoughtful overview of issues from the perspective of source and host countries of financial-sector FDI. Goldberg (2007) surveys the host-country implications of financial-sector foreign direct investment and draws parallels between the effects of financial-sector FDI and FDI in manufacturing and extractive resource industries.

since the 1980s, with fewer banks overall, and the remaining banks becoming increasingly polarized in terms of size and portfolio allocations. By the late 1990s, while a substantial share of the U.S. banks reporting foreign exposures were smaller banks, the vast majority of U.S. exposures were nonetheless attributable to a few large banks. Lending by the larger banks is less volatile than lending by the smaller banks.

Our findings of weak and variable cyclical transmission from the U.S. banks contrast with stronger results by Peek and Rosengren (1997, 2000a) on Japanese business-cycle transmission to the United States. Our results also contrast with those of Van Rijckeghem and Weder (2001), who find more transmission when banks have a presence across multiple markets.[3] U.S. banks do not appear particularly fickle in emerging markets, in contrast to some of the conclusions on international banks of Galindo, Micco, and Powell (2004). Indeed, while our results support the view that foreign banks *can* transmit international business cycles into host-country financial markets, this result is neither strong or robust. U.S. banks also may reduce the extent to which locally sourced real shocks and interest rates (i.e., local business cycles) are amplified by banking intermediaries. Consequently, the U.S. banks engaged in this type of credit extension abroad may reduce the highly procyclical credit cycles in some foreign markets.[4]

Section 5.2 of this paper discusses the U.S. bank foreign exposure data and provides background on the extensive changes that have occurred since 1986 in U.S. bank lending abroad and in the form and scale of their exposures. Data on the relative importance of U.S. bank and other foreign bank claims relative to GDP across European and Latin American countries provide context for the importance of this financial activity. Section 5.3 econometrically explores the volatility of the panel data on U.S. bank international claims. We contrast the cyclical properties of claims on industrialized countries in Europe versus on Latin American countries. Section 5.4 discusses the implications of our results, on balance emphasizing that foreign banks may contribute to aggregate stability in emerging markets.

5.2 Broad Patterns in U.S. Bank Foreign Exposures

The Federal Financial Institutions Examinations Council (FFIEC) Country Exposure Report (FFIEC 009) must be filed by every U.S. chartered, insured, commercial bank in the United States, including the District of Columbia, Puerto Rico, and U.S. territories and possessions, or its

---

3. See also Goldberg (2002), Dages, Goldberg, and Kinney (2000), and Peek and Rosengren (2000b).
4. Galindo, Micco, and Powell (2004) argue that foreign banks may be fickle lenders in times of local crisis, sharply reducing credit extension to local markets. We do not find general support for this argument in U.S. bank data.

holding company, provided that the bank (or holding company) has, on a fully consolidated bank basis, total outstanding claims on residents of foreign countries exceeding $30 million in aggregate. In these reports, bank claims are itemized by country and separately encompass claims on banks, public entities, and other recipients, including individuals and businesses. In addition to direct international flows, bank claims include the fair value of interest rate, foreign exchange, equity, commodity, and other derivative contracts. Banks provide some details on time remaining to maturity of claims (one year and under, one to five years, and over five years) as well as on direct claims versus ultimate risk claims. Other quarterly reports filed by banks contain information on bank total assets located in the United States and abroad. Some reporting conventions have changed over time, but much of this confidential data has been consistently filed by banks since 1986.

5.2.1   Foreign Claims Relative to Local Economies

Foreign lending can constitute a substantial fraction of claims in recipient countries. In this context, foreign claims are the sum of cross-border claims and local claims denominated in both foreign and local currencies. As shown in the first data column of table 5.1 and indicated by values exceeding one, European countries often have total foreign claims in excess of 100 percent of their GDP. This large fraction in part reflects volumes of back-and-forth financial flows across borders, heavy use of banking-sector finance, and the role of European financial centers in intermediation of some flows. For Latin American countries, foreign claims represent a much smaller share of GDP: across the region, the ratio of foreign claims to country GDP is closer to 70 percent.

As shown in the second data column, the United States accounts for a relatively small portion of the foreign claims on European countries, typically close to 6 percent overall. Intra-European flows dominate the foreign claims on European countries. By contrast, U.S. banks account for a large portion of overall foreign claims on Latin American countries. There is considerable cross-country variation in the share of the United States within these foreign claims, from Costa Rica, at less than 20 percent of total foreign claims, to Mexico, where this ratio exceeds 95 percent.

5.2.2   Consolidation in U.S. Banks with Foreign Exposures

Industry consolidation, observed elsewhere across banking and financial services industries, is clearly evident in the changing number of banks (or bank holding companies) with exposures to foreign markets. Figure 5.1 shows the number of U.S. banks that have filed foreign exposure reports each quarter since 1986. Starting from a high of 185 reporting banks in the mid-1980s, the number of U.S. banks with foreign exposures declined to 140 by the mid-1990s and further declined to 75 banks by 2004.

As the number of banks declined, the size distribution of remaining banks changed considerably over time. Figure 5.2 shows the share of re-

Table 5.1 U.S. and other foreign bank claim shares in local economies, 2003

	Ratio of total foreign claims to country GDP	Ratio of U.S. claims to total foreign claims	Ratio of total U.S. claims to country GDP
Europe	6.37	0.06	0.26
Austria	2.25	0.05	0.12
Belgium	3.87	0.06	0.22
Denmark	2.12	0.09	0.19
Finland	1.46	0.04	0.06
France	1.83	0.05	0.10
Germany	1.90	0.08	0.15
Greece	2.31	0.07	0.15
Iceland*	2.24	0.02	0.04
Ireland	8.45	0.03	0.24
Italy	1.85	0.05	0.09
Luxembourg	61.80	0.03	1.94
Netherlands	4.89	0.06	0.30
Norway*	1.36	0.11	0.14
Portugal	4.48	0.02	0.08
Spain	1.59	0.05	0.08
Sweden*	1.42	0.07	0.11
Switzerland	5.90	0.04	0.26
United Kingdom	4.97	0.08	0.40
Latin America	0.68	0.40	0.24
Argentina	0.84	0.28	0.24
Brazil	0.71	0.27	0.19
Chile	1.15	0.39	0.44
Colombia*	0.50	0.36	0.13
Costa Rica	0.84	0.18	0.15
Ecuador	0.30	0.27	0.08
Jamaica*	0.53	0.66	0.31
Mexico	0.41	0.97	0.40
Peru	0.32	0.40	0.13
Uruguay	1.02	0.43	0.44
Venezuela*	0.83	0.22	0.18

Source: BIS *Quarterly Review,* BIS Consolidated Banking Statistics for all reporting banks; and BIS Consolidated Banking Statistics for U.S.-owned bank claims.

Notes: 2003 data, except where indicated by an asterisk. Venezuela data are 2002 for all ratios; Sweden data are 2000 for total foreign claims ratios only; and Iceland, Norway, Colombia, and Jamaica data are 2002 for total foreign claims ratios only. For this table we use the BIS definition of foreign claims, meaning the sum of cross-border claims and local claims in both foreign currency and domestic currency.

porting banks in five different asset size ranges, contrasting size distributions for 1986:Q1 and 2004:Q1.[5] In the 1980s banks were broadly distributed across small, medium, and large asset ranges. By 2004 the distribution was more bimodal. Currently more than 30 percent of banks have assets

5. The ranges use 2003Q1 dollars as the base year.

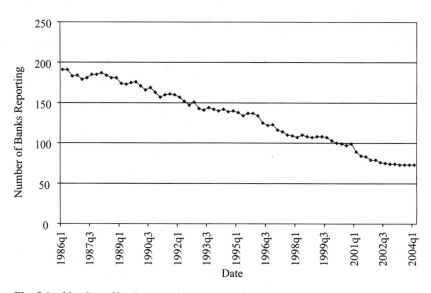

Fig. 5.1   Number of banks reporting exposure data 1986–2004

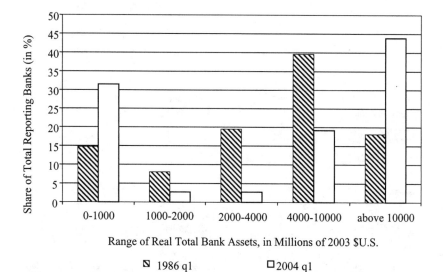

Range of Real Total Bank Assets, in Millions of 2003 $U.S.

◨ 1986 q1   □ 2004 q1

Fig. 5.2   Size distribution of U.S. banks reporting foreign exposures

well under $1 billion, while more than 40 percent of banks have total assets in excess of $10 billion.

As the total number of banks declined, so did the number of U.S. banks with exposures across different foreign regions. Among Europe, Canada, Asia and the Middle East, Africa, and Latin America, Latin America has

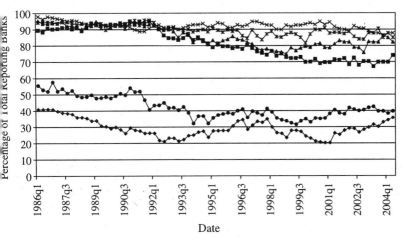

Fig. 5.3   Percent of total reporting banks that report exposure to each region

the most U.S. banks reporting exposure (sixty-six banks in mid-2004), with similar numbers participating in European and Canadian markets. Asia and the Middle East have fifty-six banks, while about thirty U.S. banks have some claims on Africa and other countries.

As a share of all banks reporting these foreign exposures, a similarly large proportion of banks—over 90 percent—maintained positions in Latin America, Canada, Europe, and Asia and the Middle East in the 1980s through the early part of the 1990s. As shown in figure 5.3, the 1990s was a decade of increasing differentiation across U.S. banks in terms of their regional exposures. While participation of U.S. banks in Canadian and in Latin American markets remained high, participation rates in Asia and the Middle East and Europe declined. By 2004, some of this differentiation was reduced: participation in European markets recovered to over 80 percent of reporting banks, and the share of banks participating in Latin American countries declined from highs observed prior to the Argentine crisis. During this period, the proportion of reporting banks with Asia/Middle East exposure stayed at near 70 percent.

Very few banks have foreign exposures in only one region. The number of banks exclusively focused on Latin America was three or four through the 1980s, rising to eight sporadically in the early 1990s, and declining again to a few specialty operations. Typically, between one and three banks specialize in other regions, generally in claims on either Europe or Asia. Banks with this sort of regional specialization are usually within the smallest quartile of banks by asset size.

5.2.3   Magnitudes of U.S. Bank Foreign Claims

The trend toward consolidation in the banking sector has not led to a decline in the total foreign exposures across U.S. banks. The increasing values over past decades of total foreign exposure of U.S. banks (in 2003 dollars) are depicted in figure 5.4 for cross-border claims and figure 5.5 for local claims. After sharp declines over the late 1980s, U.S. bank foreign exposures had persistent expansion from 1993 through 2004. This growth occurred both in total cross-border claims and in total local claims, even when evaluated relative to the growth in total assets of U.S. banks reporting foreign exposures.

These observations are drawn from data aggregated across all U.S. banks reporting foreign exposures. Next, we instead utilize the source data, at the level of individual reporting banks, and construct bank-specific measures of foreign exposure–to-asset position. We then average this foreign exposure ratio across all individual reporting banks. The resulting averages, shown in figure 5.6, are unweighted by bank size and therefore place greater (relative) weight on the exposures of smaller banks. Trend increases in average foreign exposure ratios occurred through late 1998, driven strongly by growth in U.S. average ratios of bank claims on Latin America.

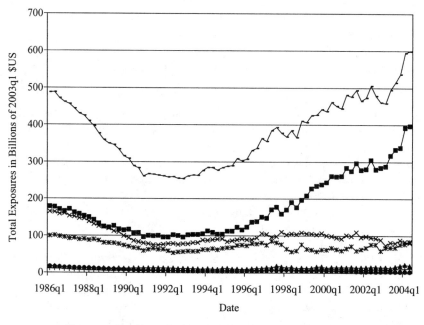

Fig. 5.4   Total value of U.S. bank cross-border claims, by region

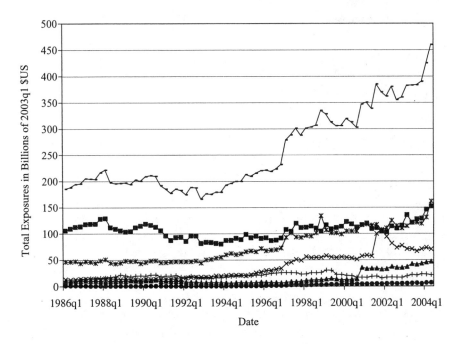

Fig. 5.5   Total value of U.S. bank local claims, by region

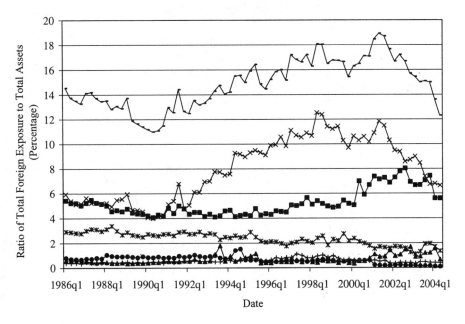

Fig. 5.6   Average bank-specific ratios of regional foreign exposure to bank total assets

These average claims on Latin American counterparties fluctuated substantially through 2000 before sharply declining between mid-2001 and 2004 when our data end. These ratios shown in figure 5.6 contrast sharply with patterns in total flows from all U.S. banks reporting foreign exposures. The difference demonstrates that smaller U.S. banks with foreign exposures both had higher-than-average exposures to Latin America and reduced these exposures (relative to their asset bases) more dramatically than their larger bank counterparts.

Our examination of U.S. bank exposure data leads to more nuanced conclusions than some other studies of international capital flows that argue that the 1999 to 2000 credit crunch was common throughout Latin America. Braun and Hausmann (2002), for example, using data through 2001, find that bank credit in many Latin American countries collapsed in the aftermath of the Asian and especially the Russian crises. The strong rates of real credit growth, sometimes described as credit booms, that characterized the early and mid-1990s generally decreased since 1998 and stayed at lower levels through 2001. We find that this type of credit crunch in claims on Latin American countries was more a feature of the cross-border flows than of the local claims of U.S.-owned banks. Moreover, this credit crunch seems to better describe banks other than the largest U.S. banks with foreign exposures to countries in the region. This interesting set of observations may be relevant for discussions of overall banking-sector stability. Crystal, Dages, and Goldberg (2001) argue that the mix of foreign versus domestically owned banks within Latin America was important for the growth rates and stability of credit flows: credit growth and credit stability were enhanced when strong foreign partners were participating in local markets. Here we confirm this finding, and extend it with the observation that the size as well as the form of foreign bank claims on a market also may matter for sustained intermediation by the banking sector.

5.2.4 The Composition of U.S. Bank Foreign Clients

The exposure data show the relative importance of banks, public-sector borrowers, and all other borrowers in U.S. bank cross-border claims on each country. Figures 5.7 and 5.8 show these broad details for cross-border claims on Europe and Latin America, respectively. In U.S. bank cross-border claims on Europe, the share of public-sector borrowers was in the area of 10 percent since the 1980s, rising as high as 14 percent in the early 1990s and again in 1998, but recently falling to below 7 percent. Other private-sector borrowers became increasing active in total cross-border claims on Europeans over the past two decades, ultimately rising to be comparable in size to bank borrowers.

U.S. bank cross-border claims on Latin American counterparties were also characterized by a declining relative importance of bank-to-bank lending. Even more dramatic were the reductions in the share of cross-

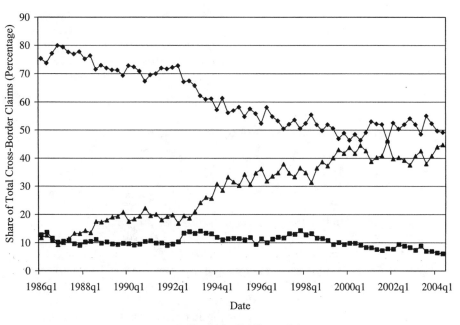

Fig. 5.7   Breakdown of European cross-border claims by client

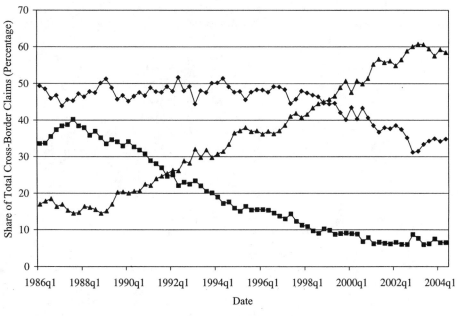

Fig. 5.8   Breakdown of Latin American cross-border claims by client

border claims accounted for by the public sector, moving from 40 percent in the late 1980s to under 10 percent in 2004. The share accounted for by nonbank private borrowers has continued to rise over past decades, reaching almost 60 percent in 2003 and 2004. By 1999 private nonbank activity displaced bank-to-bank lending as the primary client in U.S. bank cross-border claims on Latin American customers.

5.3   U.S. Bank Foreign Exposures and Business-Cycle Transmission

International banks entering into local markets can potentially change the transmission of international shocks to local markets (Peek and Rosengren 1997, 2000a) and spur contagion across markets (Van Rijckeghem and Weder 2001). These banks can also have different risk management systems and sources of funds, raising the prospect that they may change the typically procyclical response of the host-country banking system to local shocks. In this section we provide evidence relevant for the debate on shock transmission by exploring the sensitivity of U.S. bank foreign exposures to local country and U.S. business-cycle variables. In order to have a benchmark for comparison, we contrast the patterns in U.S. bank claims on European countries with the patterns in U.S. bank claims on Latin American countries. Delving further into this issue, we ask whether larger banks—here taken to be the five largest money center banks—are more stable in credit extension and differ from smaller banks in the sensitivity of this credit to business-cycle variables.[6] Some of the analysis uses aggregated claims across banks, while other parts of our analysis exploit the rich time series panel nature of the bank exposure data.[7]

5.3.1   Exposures to European and Latin American Countries

Europe accounts for 40 percent of total U.S. bank foreign exposures (table 5.2), with U.S. bank cross-border claims three times as large as U.S. bank local claims (i.e., claims extended by their branches and subsidiaries abroad). The United Kingdom, Germany, France, and the Netherlands account for most of the U.S. bank claims on Europe. Latin American coun-

6. The top five money center banks are Bank of America Corp., Bank One Corp., Taunus Corp., JPMorgan Chase Bank, and Citigroup. Taunus is the U.S. holding company subsidiary of Deutsche Bank. These banks are formed in part by smaller banks that consolidated. Thus, for each of these five large money center banks we create *a synthetic construct going back in time that includes the exposures of smaller banks that eventually merged together into the current five money center banks.* This approach may impart a survivorship bias to the empirical results that follow. Note that Taunus is not domestically owned. An alternative group of large banks could be geared toward large domestic lenders and be broader. Such a grouping could include Citigroup Inc., Bank of America Corp., JPMorgan Chase and Co., Wells Fargo and Co., Wachovia Corp., Bank One Corp., U.S. Bancorp, National City Corp., and Suntrust Banks, Inc.

7. See also recent work by Santor (2004) applying portfolio theory to Canadian bank exposure data.

Table 5.2   **Foreign exposure of U.S. reporting banks, 2004:Q1 (country share in total U.S. bank foreign exposures)**

	Cross-border claims	Local claims	Total		Cross-border claims	Local claims	Total
Europe	25.55	8.91	39.98	*Latin America*	2.77	4.69	7.57
Austria	0.39	0.01	0.47	Argentina	0.19	0.22	0.42
Belgium	0.78	0.26	1.15	Brazil	0.67	0.82	1.54
Denmark	0.64	0.01	0.70	Chile	0.21	0.34	0.57
Finland	0.23	0.00	0.27	Colombia	0.08	0.07	0.15
France	2.72	0.11	3.35	Costa Rica	0.04	0.01	0.04
Germany	4.62	1.58	7.23	Ecuador	0.02	0.01	0.03
Greece	0.15	0.17	0.37	Jamaica	0.03	0.02	0.05
Iceland	0.00	0.00	0.00	Mexico	1.32	3.06	4.41
Ireland	0.47	0.07	0.65	Peru	0.04	0.07	0.12
Italy	1.63	0.42	2.58	Uruguay	0.04	0.04	0.08
Luxembourg	0.57	0.07	0.86	Venezuela	0.13	0.03	0.16
The Netherlands	2.45	0.02	2.93				
Norway	0.49	0.02	0.57				
Portugal	0.09	0.04	0.17				
Spain	0.75	0.40	1.29				
Sweden	0.56	0.04	0.66				
Switzerland	1.12	0.12	1.62				
United Kingdom	7.89	5.57	15.10				

Note: The total exposure column includes derivative positions, and typically exceeds the sum of cross-border and local claims.

tries account for less than 8 percent of the total foreign exposures of U.S. banks. In contrast to the pattern vis-à-vis Europe, where cross-border claims dominate, U.S. bank exposures to Latin American countries now occur more through local claims, by a ratio of nearly two to one. Looking across countries, the largest U.S. banks with foreign exposures typically dominate local claims more than they dominate cross-border claims. In some Latin American countries, most notably Costa Rica, Ecuador, Jamaica, and Uruguay, smaller U.S. banks account for more of the cross-border claims than do the larger U.S. banks (appendix table 1).

To gain perspective on the fluctuations in different types of U.S. bank foreign exposures, we construct volatility measures by country and across types of claims (cross border, local). "Volatility" is the standard deviation of these claims on each country (summed across banks), normalized by the associated mean U.S. bank claims on that country. As shown in table 5.3, the volatility of cross-border claims in recent data (2000:Q1 through 2004:Q2) is similar for Europe and Latin American regions.[8] Iceland and

8. This time frame both captures the dynamics surrounding the Argentine crisis and has the technical advantage of minimizing the adjustments to account for bank mergers needed as the analysis goes further back in time.

Table 5.3   Volatility of foreign exposures of U.S. banks

	Cross-border claims	Local claims	Total		Cross-border claims	Local claims	Total
Europe	0.15	0.11	0.13	*Latin America*	0.17	0.23	0.15
Austria	0.22	1.11	0.19	Argentina	0.51	0.62	0.57
Belgium	0.20	0.17	0.16	Brazil	0.21	0.19	0.19
Denmark	0.18	0.47	0.17	Chile	0.15	0.06	0.06
Finland	0.27	1.16	0.23	Columbia	0.31	0.17	0.25
France	0.24	0.38	0.15	Costa Rica	0.11	0.26	0.09
Germany	0.15	0.14	0.10	Ecuador	0.25	0.44	0.15
Greece	0.18	0.34	0.21	Jamaica	0.15	0.14	0.11
Iceland	0.54	3.74	0.51	Mexico	0.11	0.54	0.37
Ireland	0.32	0.20	0.25	Peru	0.35	0.08	0.17
Italy	0.16	0.13	0.10	Uruguay	0.35	0.32	0.31
Luxembourg	0.32	0.37	0.29	Venezuela	0.20	0.34	0.21
The Netherlands	0.16	0.46	0.14				
Norway	0.30	0.22	0.27				
Portugal	0.16	0.49	0.16				
Spain	0.22	0.09	0.10				
Sweden	0.16	0.35	0.11				
Switzerland	0.25	0.15	0.20				
United Kingdom	0.25	0.14	0.19				

Notes: Standard deviation of total U.S. bank foreign exposures in each category (cross-border claims, local claims, or total claims) divided by the average value of those foreign exposures. Data used for 2000:Q1–2004:Q2, in 2003:Q1 millions of U.S. dollars.

Argentina had similar and particularly high coefficients of variation in the cross-border claims. While the average variation in local claims appears higher for countries in Latin America compared with Europe, this observation masks the high volatility of claims on some individual European countries with relatively small volumes of such claims. Finally, abstracting from Mexico, where local claim volatility is driven by recent purchases of Mexican banks, and Argentina, which was in crisis during part of this period, local claims issued by U.S. banks have tended to be more stable than cross-border claims in most Latin American countries.

The next pair of tables compares patterns in the foreign claims of larger versus smaller U.S. banks reporting foreign exposures. For these calculations, we sum across the claims of larger U.S. reporting banks (five money center) vis-à-vis individual countries and compare these sums with similar constructs using data summed across all other banks reporting foreign exposures. We compute the relative coefficients of variation across large versus smaller banks for a specific type of claim and for a specific country or region. In the results reported in each cell of table 5.4 a value greater than 1 can be interpreted as showing that claims extended by larger U.S. banks were relatively more volatile than claims extended by smaller U.S. banks. Analogously, a cell value less than 1 implies relatively less volatil-

Table 5.4   Relative volatility of U.S. bank foreign exposures: Top five U.S. banks and other U.S. reporting banks compared, 2000:Q1–2004:Q2

	Cross-border claims	Local claims	Total		Cross-border claims	Local claims	Total
Europe	0.84	0.38	0.60	*Latin America*	1.30	0.42	0.96
Austria	1.17	0.46	0.97	Argentina	0.79	0.52	0.88
Belgium	0.67	0.05	0.42	Brazil	0.82	0.12	0.60
Denmark	1.34	2.24	1.17	Chile	0.66	0.09	0.33
Finland	0.83	0.22	0.63	Colombia	2.69		2.05
France	1.44	0.64	0.58	Costa Rica	1.01	0.09	0.97
Germany	0.57	0.28	0.35	Ecuador	4.03		2.11
Greece	0.86	0.08	0.98	Jamaica	0.56		0.44
Iceland	0.55	1.03	0.53	Mexico	1.80	1.54	4.08
Ireland	0.93	0.74	0.64	Peru	1.14		0.48
Italy	0.66	0.06	0.52	Uruguay	2.77	0.47	1.53
Luxembourg	0.24	0.31	0.26	Venezuela	3.89		3.77
The Netherlands	0.59	0.67	0.45				
Norway	1.31	5.28	1.45				
Portugal	0.96		0.90				
Spain	0.56	0.06	0.22				
Sweden	0.35	1.09	0.34				
Switzerland	2.14	0.23	0.78				
United Kingdom	1.65	0.53	1.04				

Note: Mexican local claims appear more volatile due to acquisition events during this interval.

ity in the foreign exposures of the larger U.S. banks vis-à-vis a particular country.

The preponderance of cells with values less than 1 in the leftmost panel of table 5.4 suggests that, on average, the cross-border and local claims on European countries by larger U.S. banks are less volatile than the claims extended by smaller U.S. banks. There is clearly country-specific variation, with larger U.S. banks having higher volatility of claims than smaller U.S. banks in their transactions with financial centers such as Switzerland and the United Kingdom. Differences across larger and smaller U.S. banks are most pronounced in local claims in both European countries and Latin American countries (right panel): the claims by larger banks tend to be substantially less volatile than the claims by smaller banks. Evidence on cross-border claims to Latin American countries is mixed. For Argentina, Brazil, Chile, and Jamaica, cross-border claims from larger banks clearly were more stable, contrasting with patterns for Colombia, Ecuador, Mexico, and Uruguay.

5.3.2 Foreign Exposures of U.S. Banks and Business Cycles

As another window into the volatility of U.S. bank foreign exposures, we conduct regression analysis starting from a model of a bank's exposure to any country as dependent on local business-cycle variables (real local interest rates, i^c_t, and real GDP growth rates, $GGDP^c_t$) and U.S. business-cycle variables (U.S. real interest rates, i^{US}_t, and U.S. real GDP growth, $GGDP^{US}_t$).[9] The (log) exposure of bank i to country c at time t, Exp^{ic}_t, is expressed as

(1) $Exp^{ic}_t = a^i_0 + a^i_1 t + a^r + a^r_2 t + b \cdot i^c_t + c \cdot i^{US}_t + d \cdot GGDP^c_t$
$+ e \cdot GGDP^{US}_t,$

plus a random error term. In this specification the terms a^i_0 and $a^i_1 t$ allow for bank-specific variation in mean and trend growth in their foreign exposures. The terms a^r and $a^r_2 t$ introduce region-specific variation and allow for the possibility that, regardless of the role of other observable fundamentals, some regions are more popular destinations for U.S. bank foreign exposures.

To reduce estimation problems arising from unit root properties of GDP growth, real interest rates, and U.S. bank external exposures, we first-difference equation (1). The bank and region constant terms drop out, leaving equation (2) specified in log-differences with bank-specific and region-specific fixed effects to capture trends in claims on specific countries (and with a random error term assumed).

(2) $\Delta Exp^{ic}_t = a^i_1 + a^r_2 + b \cdot \Delta i^c_t + c \cdot \Delta i^{US}_t + d \cdot \Delta GGDP^c_t + e \cdot \Delta GGDP^{US}_t$

This basic testing specification states that the percentage change in a U.S. bank's claims on any country has the following: a bank-specific component common across all regions, a region-specific component shared by banks, components correlated with changes in foreign and U.S. real interest rates, and components correlated with changes in foreign and U.S. GDP growth rates. Regression specifications are run over quarterly data for the period 1986:Q1 to 2004:Q2 using percent changes in the bank exposures against changes in interest rates and against percent changes in real GDP growth rates.

As detailed in table 5.5, we performed many variations on this basic specification. Many regression results were starkly different for the full data period compared with a sample break at 2001:Q2. To capture the flavor of these changes, we present the earlier and latter results for contrast, fully aware of the limitations of using a small number of quarters in the latter period. Some regressions use data on claims aggregated across U.S. banks. Other regressions take greater advantage of the rich data of indi-

Table 5.5   Estimation intervals, data types, and parameter stability tests

Sample periods	Types of foreign exposure	Parameter tests
1986:Q1 through 2004:Q2	Total foreign exposure	Equality across types of banks (five money center vs. all others)
1986:Q1 through 2001:Q2	Cross-border claims	Equality across destination markets (European vs. Latin American countries)
2001:Q3 through 2004:Q2	Local claims	Latin American Sample, with and without Mexico included
		Equality across by bank type and destination market
		Random effects estimators versus fixed effects estimators
		Claims aggregated across banks, versus disaggregated by bank

vidual bank exposures, alternatively applying fixed effects estimators or random effects estimators to time-series panels. Hausmann tests favor the random coefficients model over fixed effects estimators. Other specifications compare the growth in U.S. bank foreign exposures across "crisis" versus "normal" periods.[10] We have run the regression specification with and without regional trend terms, with different intervals specified, and with cross-border claims aggregated across all reporting banks, disaggregated to larger versus smaller reporting banks, and as robustness checks, containing adjustments for the ultimate counterparty on transactions instead of just direct counterparties and excluding either U.S. GDP or U.S. interest rates from the regressions. Only a subset of our findings is reported in the tables of this section. Distinctions in the results generated across specifications are discussed if these are statistically or economically important.

Regression Results

Table 5.6 presents regression results using aggregates across all U.S. banks in their foreign exposures to individual countries. Panel A presents findings for cross-border claims. Panel B presents findings for the local claims of U.S. banks. There are eighteen European countries and eleven Latin American countries represented in each data quarter. Panel A shows that macroeconomic variables are significant drivers of U.S. bank *cross-border* claims on European countries. More specifically, these claims exhibit procyclicality vis-à-vis U.S. GDP growth and negative correlations with destination market interest rates (as indicated by boldface type).

10. For these regressions, crisis dates include the following: the exchange rate mechanism (ERM) crisis, 1992:Q3–1993:Q1; Tequila crisis, 1994:Q4–1995:Q1; Asia crisis, 1997:Q3–1997:Q4; Russian default, 1998:Q3–1998:Q4; and Argentine crisis dated here at 2001:Q4–2002:Q1.

Table 5.6   **Regressions on U.S. bank foreign exposures, with exposures aggregated across all U.S. reporting banks**

	Trend	Country real GDP	U.S. real GDP	Country real interest rate	U.S. real interest rate
A. Elasticities of response of cross-border claims					
1986:Q1–2001:Q2					
European countries	1.02	0.00	**2.6****	**–1.27*****	–0.60
	(0.94)	(0.24)	(1.16)	(0.43)	(1.14)
		0.02	**3.50*****	**–1.27*****	–0.88
		(0.24)	**(0.82)**	(0.43)	(1.11)
Latin American countries	–2.11	0.10	2.08	0.00	–1.41
	(1.30)	(0.19)	(1.61)	(0.00)	(1.58)
		0.08	0.19	0.00	–0.86
		(0.19)	(1.12)	(0.00)	(1.54)
2001:Q2–2004:Q2					
European countries	**5.12****	**1.27****	–0.79	–1.13	2.42
	(2.18)	(0.59)	(2.41)	(1.87)	(2.22)
		1.35**	**3.42****	–0.43	0.40
		(0.59)	(1.61)	(1.86)	(2.06)
Latin American countries	–2.83	0.20	0.66	0.08	3.90
	(3.07)	(0.4)	(3.41)	(0.31)	(2.95)
		0.14	–1.64	0.06	**4.89***
		(0.40)	(2.34)	(0.31)	(2.77)
B. Elasticities of response of local claims					
1986:Q1–2001:Q2					
European countries	7.82	–0.93	9.81	2.49	5.93
	(4.9)	(1.32)	(6.03)	(2.45)	(6.0)
		–0.61	**16.55*****	2.51	3.83
		(1.31)	(4.31)	(2.45)	(5.86)
Latin American countries	10.77	–1.05	1.50	0.00	3.55
	(6.73)	(0.98)	(8.35)	(0.00)	(8.11)
		–0.91	**11.24****	0.00	0.81
		(0.98)	(5.72)	(0.00)	(7.94)
2001:Q2–2004:Q2					
European countries	11.7	0.22	–4.77	4.03	–13.46
	(9.31)	(2.52)	(10.26)	(8.33)	(9.71)
		0.46	4.84	6.34	**–18.46****
		(2.51)	(6.83)	(8.12)	(8.85)
Latin American countries	7.48	–1.01	–6.54	–0.34	5.72
	(12.7)	(1.66)	(14.11)	(1.28)	(12.21)
		–0.85	–0.46	–0.27	3.12
		(1.64)	(9.62)	(1.27)	(11.39)

Notes: In panel A, 1986:Q1–2001:Q2 period, observations = 1,492, adjusted R^2 = 0.012, adjusted R^2 (no trend) = 0.015; in 2001:Q2–2004:Q2 period, observations = 309, adjusted R^2= 0.039, adjusted R^2 (no trend) = 0.031. In panel B, 1986:Q1–2001:Q2 period, observations = 1425, adjusted R^2 = –0.001, adjusted R^2 (no trend) = 0.009; in 2001:Q2–2004:Q2 period, observations 299, adjusted R^2 = –0.015, adjusted R^2 (no trend) = –0.005.

***Significant at the 1 percent level.

**Significant at the 5 percent level.

*Significant at the 10 percent level.

However, these cyclical forces have low explanatory power for the overall regression analysis, and they are particularly weak as determinants of the pattern of cross-border flows from U.S. banks to their Latin American counterparties.

In panel B of table 5.6, regression results for U.S. bank *local claims* on European and Latin American countries also show very low overall explanatory power of these macroeconomic forces. Additionally, the estimated relationships are not robust over time. Local claims of U.S. banks were procyclical with U.S. GDP in the data extending through 2000 or 2001 (as in Goldberg 2002), but these procyclical patterns are not sustained in 2001 through 2004.

In other regression specifications we explore whether these cyclical forces play different roles in the foreign exposures of larger U.S. banks versus smaller U.S. banks. Recall that claims from larger U.S. reporting banks tend to be less volatile than claims from smaller U.S. banks, and local claims tend to be more stable than cross-border flows. Tables 5.7 and 5.8 explore this theme for cross-border claims and local claims, respectively, using ordinary least squares regressions. As in the prior sections, the aggregate called "larger banks" is the sum of foreign exposures across five money center banks. The aggregate called "smaller banks" consists of the sum across all other banks of claims on each country at each date.[11] In these regressions the i superscript from equation (2) covers two aggregates, larger and smaller banks, while the regional superscript distinguishes between the regional location of the twenty-nine countries in the regression each quarter and spanning European and Latin American countries.

The relationships between business cycle variables and U.S. bank foreign exposures appear unstable over time and differentiated by region. U.S. bank claims on Europe exhibit positive growth in the cross-border and local claim components, with this growth alternatively attributable to trend or to U.S. GDP cyclical transmission. Cyclical transmission to European countries, to the extent to which it is present, is more robustly a feature of larger bank lending. Other cyclical variables do not enter these regressions with consistent signs or significance ranges. Larger U.S. banks had robust trend growth *in local claims* on Latin American countries across the different subperiods of our sample, including in the period following the Argentine crisis. These trends likely reflect strategic expansions by the U.S. banks that entered local markets by setting up branches and subsidiaries. Quarterly cyclical fundamental variables explain very little of the patterns of

---

11. Appendix tables 2 and 3 explore similar concepts but individually introduce individual bank claims on individual countries in the regressions, instead of claims aggregated by type of bank. While we report specifications using random effects estimators, we also have performed fixed effect regressions, with fixed effects defined over individual banks, yielding similar results. The random effects estimators provide a better description of the trend differences across banks in their claims on different regions.

Table 5.7   Regressions on U.S. bank cross-border claims, sum across larger banks and sum across smaller banks

	Trend	Country real GDP	U.S. real GDP	Country real interest rate	U.S. real interest rate
A. Elasticities of response of cross-border claims, 1986:Q1–2001:Q2					
On Europe, smaller banks	5.52***	0.04	−1.19	−0.95*	−0.98
	(1.27)	(0.33)	(1.57)	(0.58)	(1.54)
		0.22	3.62***	−0.93	−2.45*
		(0.33)	(1.11)	(0.58)	(1.51)
On Latin America, smaller banks	−1.44	0.20	1.50	0.00	0.96
	(1.75)	(0.25)	(2.17)	(0.00)	(2.13)
		0.18	0.20	0.00	1.34
		(0.25)	(1.51)	(0.00)	(2.09)
On Europe, larger banks	0.94	0.17	3.62**	−0.92	0.36
	(1.26)	(0.33)	(1.56)	(0.58)	(1.54)
		0.20	4.45***	−0.91	0.11
		(0.33)	(1.10)	(0.58)	(1.51)
On Latin America, larger banks	9.28**	−0.20	−5.05	−0.99	−5.44
	(3.77)	(0.83)	(4.67)	(1.31)	(4.59)
		0.10	3.04	−0.95	−7.93*
		(0.83)	(3.28)	(1.31)	(4.49)
B. Elasticities of response of cross-border claims, 2001:Q2–2004:Q3					
On Europe, smaller banks	3.04	1.27*	4.67	−0.71	4.19
	(2.85)	(0.77)	(3.13)	(2.44)	(2.89)
		1.32*	7.17***	−0.29	2.99
		(0.77)	(2.09)	(2.42)	(2.68)
On Latin America, smaller banks	−0.80	0.77	−0.71	−0.12	1.72
	(4.00)	(0.52)	(4.44)	(0.40)	(3.84)
		0.75	−1.36	−0.13	2.00
		(0.52)	(3.05)	(0.40)	(3.61)
On Europe, larger banks	9.01***	0.92	−3.52	−0.58	3.83
	(2.85)	(0.77)	(3.13)	(2.44)	(2.89)
		1.06	3.89*	0.65	0.26
		(0.77)	(2.09)	(2.42)	(2.68)
On Latin America, larger banks	−3.61	0.77	12.69	−0.65	7.78
	(8.52)	(1.87)	(9.42)	(5.48)	(8.46)
		0.71	9.72	−1.06	9.18
		(1.88)	(6.37)	(5.44)	(7.88)

Notes: In panel A, observations = 2,985, adjusted R^2 = 0.007, adjusted R^2 (no trend) = 0.009; In panel B, observations = 618, adjusted R^2 = 0.023, adjusted R^2 (no trend) = 0.024.

***Significant at the 1 percent level.

**Significant at the 5 percent level.

*Significant at the 10 percent level.

Table 5.8   **Regressions on U.S. bank local claims, sum across larger banks and sum across smaller banks**

	Trend	Country real GDP	U.S. real GDP	Country real interest rate	U.S. real interest rate
A. Elasticities of response of local claims, 1986:Q1–2001:Q2					
On Europe, smaller banks	52.29***	−3.76	−34.94**	6.95	33.74**
	(12.91)	(4.32)	(15.9)	(9.37)	(15.64)
		−1.04	9.64	7.06	17.51
		(4.28)	(11.52)	(9.4)	(15.17)
On Latin America, smaller banks	0.10	−6.06	43.17*	0.00**	−37.30
	(19.73)	(4.3)	(24.6)	(0.00)	(22.45)
		−6.06	43.27***	0.00**	−37.32
		(4.28)	(16.7)	(0.00)	(22.16)
On Europe, larger banks	7.98	−0.70	10.39	2.38	5.87
	(8.88)	(2.40)	(10.93)	(4.44)	(10.88)
		−0.37	17.26**	2.39	3.73
		(2.38)	(7.84)	(4.46)	(10.65)
On Latin America, larger banks	107.3***	−1.82	−121.97***	11.53	102.4**
	(35.83)	(10.11)	(44.34)	(19.27)	(42.63)
		3.44	−29.95	11.72	69.34
		(10.03)	(31.31)	(19.33)	(41.64)
B. Elasticities of response of local claims, 2001:Q2–2004:Q3					
On Europe, smaller banks	121.64***	8.23	−84.32**	10.75	−22.61
	(33.56)	(8.38)	(37.2)	(27.93)	(34.99)
		9.84	16.94	33.8	−75.07**
		(8.45)	(24.79)	(27.46)	(32.17)
On Latin America, smaller banks	−23.44	−1.28	7.41	0.21	12.72
	(74.78)	(14.69)	(97.29)	(4.64)	(78.11)
		−1.72	−12.56	0.01	20.32
		(14.77)	(74.25)	(4.65)	(74.99)
On Europe, larger banks	8.39	−1.90	0.79	−1.12	−7.20
	(30.67)	(8.24)	(33.67)	(27.25)	(31.78)
		−1.73	7.68	0.47	−10.78
		(8.3)	(22.56)	(26.88)	(29.25)
On Latin America, larger banks	266.7**	18.60	−184.08	22.05	−44.69
	(112.98)	(24.39)	(135.15)	(62.47)	(116.65)
		22.26	38.32	66.83	−156.53
		(24.55)	(97.42)	(61.48)	(109.7)

Notes: In panel A, observations = 2,079, adjusted R^2 = 0.003, adjusted R^2 (no trend) = 0.004; in panel B, observations = 490, adjusted R^2 = −0.006, adjusted R^2 (no trend) = −0.014.

***Significant at the 1 percent level.

**Significant at the 5 percent level.

*Significant at the 10 percent level.

foreign exposure expansions in recent years. While cross-border claims have a greater tendency toward comovement with the U.S. cycle, this pattern is not robust across larger and smaller U.S. banks, and we do not observe stable rates of transmission of U.S. or destination market cycles in cross-border or local claims.

As further robustness checks, we consider whether simultaneously including U.S. real GDP and U.S. real interest rates in specifications biases each individual term toward insignificance. Such misspecification might arise, for example, because U.S. real interest rates are endogenous to the business cycle, following a policy reaction function, or because interest rates play a role in investment growth, a key component of GDP fluctuations. Alternative regression specifications using either but not both of the country fundamentals (not shown) do not qualitatively change our conclusions. Likewise, our qualitative findings are robust to the choice of different break point dates post-2000:Q1 and are robust across regression specifications using individual bank data instead of data aggregated across groups of banks.

5.4   Concluding Remarks

This paper has explored recent patterns in the international exposures of U.S. banks. Despite continued consolidation in the financial services industry, reflected in the sharply reduced total number of U.S. banks with foreign exposures, the total foreign exposure of these banks has continued to grow. U.S. bank claims represent a large fraction of foreign claims on Latin American countries, as well as being large relative to local GDP. This role is stronger than in individual European countries, where other European banks tend to dominate foreign claims. Public-sector recipients of these claims account for less than 10 percent of the total cross-border claims on European countries, consistent with how bank lending has been allocated in Europe in recent decades. While a similar ratio now applies for Latin American countries, this represents a sharp departure from allocations in the early 1990s, when the public debt share exceeded 30 percent of U.S. bank claims on the region.

The largest U.S. banks increasingly dominate the total volumes of foreign transactions of U.S. banks, with the composition of transactions evolving differently for larger banks than smaller banks involved in foreign exposures. Cross-border claims have soared with respect to European counterparts but more recently have been flat or declining in the Latin American region. Instead of representing declines in the related foreign exposures of larger U.S. banks, these cross-border claims have been replaced by claims from U.S. bank branches and subsidiaries located in Latin American markets. Such local claims soared after 1997 and later stabilized at high levels, even in the aftermath of the Argentine crisis. Postcrisis declines in U.S. bank positions in Latin America were more heavily concentrated among the smaller U.S. banks with foreign exposures. Smaller banks' positions have been concentrated in cross-border claims, with these claims exhibiting slower and more volatile overall credit growth than claims emanating from the largest banks.

The final empirical section of the paper uses data on individual U.S. bank foreign exposures to investigate the claim that such banks may be highly cyclical lenders and transmit foreign shocks to local markets. We find evidence of procyclical cross-border flows from U.S. banks to European markets. However, U.S. bank claims on Latin American countries tend to have weak and unstable relationships with both U.S. business-cycle variables and local business variables. We do not present a structural model of portfolio theory as a determinant of the behavior of U.S. banks in selecting markets for extending claims and for determining quantities of these claims. However, our regression results do not bode well for such an application, especially if the application will rely on U.S. and counterpart country GDP growth rates and interest rates.

Overall, we find that cyclical variables explain very little of the movements observed in cross-border claims or the growth in local claims. The evidence certainly does not support strong U.S. business-cycle transmission. Indeed, the lack of importance of local business-cycle variables as determinants of U.S. bank foreign exposures may have direct policy relevance. These claims of foreign banks may dampen the strong procyclicality of overall credit issuance by local financial systems, ultimately reducing the amplitude of local cycles. This hypothesis is worth future investigation. U.S. banks, and in particular the larger U.S. banks that have been heavily involved in local claims, may play a role in stabilizing the business cycles of the foreign host markets.

Appendix A

Data

Banking Exposure Data

U.S. FFIEC 009 and 009a reports are filed quarterly by all U.S. banks with significant exposures.

Background

The FFIEC report was initiated in 1977 as the Federal Reserve (FR) 2036 report and was used to collect data on the distribution, by country, of claims on foreigners held by U.S. banks and bank holding companies. The

Table 5A.1   Data sources

Countries	Source	Type	Currency
GDP			
All but those below	IFS	Nominal	Millions of local currency
The Euro-zone countries, Denmark, Iceland	OECD	Nominal	Millions of local currency
Jamaica (1986)	IFS	Real	Millions of local currency
Argentina (1993), Brazil (1990), Chile (1996), Colombia (1994), Ecuador (1975)	INTL	Real	Millions of local currency
Venezuela	INTL	Nominal	Millions of local currency
Interest rates			
All other countries	IFS	Lending rate (60p)	
Denmark, Finland, Germany, Spain	IFS	Money market rate (60b)	
Argentina, Brazil, Mexico, Greece	IFS	Deposit rate (60l)	
Sweden	IFS	Repurchase rate (60a)	
Austria, Luxembourg	EuroStat	Government long-term Interest rate	
Portugal	OECD	Government long-term Interest rate	
CPI			
All countries	IFS		

FDIC and OCC collected similar information from institutions under their supervision. In March 1984, the FR 2036 became an FFIEC report and was renumbered FFIEC 009. It was revised in March 1986 to provide more detail on guaranteed claims. In 1995, the report was revised to add a schedule for the fair value of derivative contracts, and several items were combined.

Respondent Panel

The panel consists of U.S. commercial banks and bank holding companies holding $30 million or more in claims on residents of foreign countries. Respondents file the FFIEC 009a if exposures to a country exceed 1 percent of total assets or 20 percent of capital of the reporting institution. FFIEC 009a respondents also furnish a list of countries in which exposures were between .75 percent and 1 percent of total assets or between 15 and 20 percent of capital. Participation is required.

Appendix B

Table 5B.1 **Value of foreign exposures of five money center banks relative to the value of foreign exposures of all other U.S. banks, 2004:Q1**

	Cross-border claims	Local claims	Total		Cross-border claims	Local claims	Total
Europe	4.2	3.1	4.1	*Latin America*	3.3	233.6	10.2
Austria	0.9		1.3	Argentina	5.7		13.5
Belgium	1.3	322.8	2.3	Brazil	2.8		7.6
Denmark	0.8	5.5	1.0	Chile	1.8		6.3
Finland	10.7	12.20	11.7	Colombia	3.8		8.2
France	6.9	7.4	5.8	Costa Rica	0.7		1.0
Germany	4.4	379.2	6.2	Ecuador	0.4		1.2
Greece	8.7		22.8	Jamaica	0.9		1.9
	0.7		1.2	Mexico	5.0	160.8	17.5
Ireland	1.9	0.9	2.0	Peru	2.8		9.6
Italy	19.2	313.9	22.2	Uruguay	0.7	37.2	2.2
Luxembourg	32.4	4.5	25.3	Venezuela	1.9		2.5
The Netherlands	5.1	14.6	5.0				
Norway	10.7	2.4	10.5				
Portugal	2.1		4.5				
Spain	10.8	42.3	14.9				
Sweden	2.4	9.7	2.7				
Switzerland	5.7	174.4	5.0				
United Kingdom	3.6	1.7	2.8				

Appendix C

Regressions Using Individual U.S. Bank Data (Bank-Specific Random Effects, Maximum-Likelihood Estimation)

Table 5C.1   Elasticities of response of cross-border claims, 1986:Q1–2001:Q2

	Trend	Country real GDP	U.S. real GDP	Country real interest rate	U.S. real interest rate
On Europe, smaller banks	46.02***	0.79	7.32	2.78	0.25
	(4.52)	(1.09)	(4.64)	(1.99)	(4.49)
		1.72	27.75***	2.94	−6.37
		(1.09)	(4.15)	(1.99)	(4.44)
On Latin America, smaller banks	11.21***	0.37	−0.08	0.00**	−6.87
	(4.71)	(0.6)	(5.14)	(0.00)	(4.87)
		0.29	−5.99	0.00**	−5.17
		(0.6)	(4.25)	(0.00)	(4.8)
On Europe, larger banks	16.79*	−0.94	5.32	−0.83	−3.66
	(9.89)	(1.79)	(8.29)	(3.19)	(8.22)
		−0.7	11.57	−0.79	−5.55
		(1.78)	(7.3)	(3.2)	(8.14)
On Latin America, larger banks	65.51***	2.27	11.78	6.4	8.15
	(14.73)	(3.2)	(17.81)	(5.11)	(17.39)
		3.9	45.17***	6.67	−2.87
		(3.19)	(12.98)	(5.11)	(17.02)

Notes: Positive trend growth to Europe, with even higher trend growth to Latin America. Procyclical lending with U.S. GDP, but not significant. Low interest rates in United States increase claims abroad, but not with statistical significance. In general, destination country interest rates economically unimportant for claims. While statistically significant differences are often observed across banks, we focus our attention on the elasticities reporting instead of the differences reporting. Number of observations = 34,650; number of groups = 89. With constant, log-likelihood = −248690.9, pseudo R^2 = 0.000; without constant, log-likelihood = −248735.4; pseudo R^2 = 0.000.

***Significant at the 1 percent level.
**Significant at the 5 percent level.
*Significant at the 10 percent level.

Table 5C.2   Elasticities of response of cross-border claims, 2001:Q3–2004:Q2

	Trend	Country real GDP	U.S. real GDP	Country real interest rate	U.S. real interest rate
On Europe, smaller banks	66.82***	11.17*	27.35	−20.54	−3.99
	(26.12)	(6.19)	(25.24)	(20.14)	(23.7)
		11.93**	67.2***	−11.73	−24.36
		(6.19)	(19.38)	(19.84)	(22.22)
On Latin America, smaller banks	14.38	0.36	−4.73	−0.28	1.48
	(27.91)	(3.46)	(28.58)	(2.45)	(24.89)
		0.38	−3.60	−0.27	0.81
		(3.45)	(21.37)	(2.44)	(23.55)
On Europe, larger banks	171.19***	12.49	−109.2***	58.84*	36.48
	(52.45)	(10.89)	(45.36)	(35.59)	(42.3)
		14.41	−20.3	76.74**	−7.99
		(10.88)	(37.17)	(35.22)	(40.27)
On Latin America, larger banks	−46.11	9.41	172.93*	−99.62*	−42.51
	(91.33)	(18.58)	(99.05)	(54.11)	(89.11)
		7.88	116.3*	−100.42*	−18.1
		(18.52)	(68.31)	(53.35)	(82.65)

Notes: Larger banks reversed their trend of cross-border credit growth to Latin America, while cross-border flows from smaller banks had more pronounced trends. Slowdowns in the United States reinforced this pattern with respect to Latin America, but cross-border claims accelerated instead with respect to European countries. Number of observations = 6,844; number of groups = 62. With constant, log-likelihood = −55020.58, pseudo R^2 = 0.000; without constant, log-likelihood = −55029.28, pseudo R^2 = 0.000.

***Significant at the 1 percent level.
**Significant at the 5 percent level.
*Significant at the 10 percent level.

Table 5C.3   Elasticities of response of local claims, 1986:Q1–2001:Q2

	Trend	Country real GDP	U.S. real GDP	Country real interest rate	U.S. real interest rate
On Europe, smaller banks	−0.82	0.53	13.12	2.38	4.71
	(8.85)	(3.86)	(11.01)	(5.33)	(10.39)
		0.47	12.43	2.39	4.94
		(3.8)	(8.09)	(5.33)	(10.09)
On Latin America,	−1.02	−1.27	27.57	0.00	−24.61
smaller banks	(16.28)	(3.43)	(20.16)	(0.00)	(19.06)
		−1.30	26.64**	0.00	−24.37
		(3.41)	(13.81)	(0.00)	(18.69)
On Europe, larger banks	5.58	0.22	6.59	1.50	3.00
	(5.37)	(1.74)	(6.53)	(3.15)	(6.46)
		0.60	11.25***	1.46	1.51
		(1.7)	(4.75)	(3.15)	(6.30)
On Latin America,	1.51	2.48	11.47	3.27	41.63
larger banks	(25.98)	(8.73)	(32.18)	(11.13)	(30.57)
		2.13	13.28	3.31	41.34
		(8.60)	(22.85)	(11.13)	(29.82)

Notes: None of the portfolio terms appear statistically significant in the local claims regressions for the first fifteen years of the data sample. Number of observations = 5,501; number of groups = 25. With constant, log-likelihood = −36787.49, pseudo R^2 = 0.000; without constant, log-likelihood = −36788.48, pseudo R^2 = 0.000.

***Significant at the 1 percent level.

**Significant at the 5 percent level.

Table 5C.4   Elasticities of response of local claims, 2001:Q3–2004:Q2

	Trend	Country real GDP	U.S. real GDP	Country real interest rate	U.S. real interest rate
On Europe, smaller banks	110.16***	0.75	–59.58	10.17	–15.49
	(44.21)	(10.2)	(37.96)	(30.19)	(34.97)
		2.55	–8.24	18.72	–41.66
		(10.19)	(32.76)	(30.06)	(33.57)
On Latin America, smaller banks	–27.14	1.19	8.59	0.28	10.76
	(96.58)	(16.22)	(118.04)	(6.63)	(93.41)
		0.98	–20.81	–0.11	21.27
		(16.25)	(94.32)	(6.56)	(91.58)
On Europe, larger banks	7.71	–2.92	35.26	11.26	–4.55
	(43.46)	(9.53)	(30.13)	(24.81)	(28.25)
		–2.78	38.92	12.17	–6.45
		(9.53)	(25.66)	(24.53)	(27.12)
On Latin America, larger banks	238.14*	2.95	–135.57	8.5	–47.01
	(135.6)	(28.25)	(149.28)	(65.73)	(125.22)
		6.5	–11.15	25.04	–106.19
		(28.23)	(117.71)	(65.35)	(120.56)

Notes: Number of observations = 1,154; number of groups = 18. With constant, log-likelihood = –8446.80, pseudo R^2 = 0.000; without constant, log-likelihood = –8449.85, pseudo R^2 = 0.000.
***Significant at the 1 percent level.
*Significant at the 10 percent level.

References

Bank for International Settlements (BIS), Committee on the Global Financial System. 2004. Foreign direct investment in the financial sector of emerging market economies. Basel, Switzerland: Bank for International Settlements.

Braun, Matias, and Ricardo Hausmann. 2002. Financial development and credit crunches: Latin America and the world. In *Latin American competitiveness report 2001–2002,* ed. J. Vial and P. K. Cornelius, 98–120. New York: Oxford University Press.

Crystal, Jennifer, B. Gerard Dages, and Linda Goldberg. 2001. Does foreign ownership contribute to sounder banks in emerging markets? The Latin American experience. In *Open doors: Foreign participation in financial systems in developing countries,* ed. R. Litan, P. Masson, and M. Pomerleano, 217–66. Washington, DC: Brookings Institution Press.

Dages, B. Gerard, Linda Goldberg, and Daniel Kinney. 2000. Foreign and domestic bank participation in emerging markets: Lessons from Mexico and Argentina. *Economic Policy Review* 6 (3): 17–36.

Galindo, Arturo, Alejandro Micco, and Andrew Powell. 2004. Loyal lenders or fickle financiers: On the role of foreign banks in Latin America. IADB Working Paper no. 529. Washington, DC: Inter-American Development Bank.

Goldberg, Linda. 2002. When is foreign bank lending to emerging markets volatile?

In *Preventing currency crises in emerging markets,* ed. Sebastian Edwards and Jeffrey Frankel, 171–91. Chicago: University of Chicago Press.
————. 2004. Financial sector foreign direct investment: New and old lessons. *Economic Policy Review.* Forthcoming.
Peek, Joe, and Eric Rosengren. 1997. The international transmission of financial shocks: The case of Japan. *American Economic Review* 87 (4): 495–505.
————. 2000a. Collateral damage: Effects of the Japanese bank crisis on real activity in the United States. *American Economic Review* 90 (1): 30–45.
————. 2000b. Implications of the globalization of the banking sector: The Latin American experience. *New England Economic Review* 2000 (September/October): 45–62.
Santor, Eric. 2004. Contagion and the composition of Canadian banks' foreign asset portfolios: Do crises matter? Ottawa: Bank of Canada. Unpublished manuscript.
Van Rijckeghem, Caroline, and Beatrice Weder. 2001. Sources of contagion: Is it finance or trade? *Journal of International Economics* 54 (2): 293–308.

Comment   Matías Braun

Linda Goldberg presents an interesting analysis of the international exposure of U.S. banks since the mid-1980s. The very rich data set allows a more direct look at how this key component of cross-country flows behaves across a number of important dimensions. Touching upon the debate over the costs and benefits of foreign lending, special attention is paid to the cyclical properties of these exposures. Her stylized facts of U.S. banks' foreign claims may be summarized as follows:

- Across countries, U.S. banks' foreign claims are concentrated in Europe, where they primarily take the form of cross-border claims. Claims on Latin American countries, where the local component is much larger than in Europe, comprise a much smaller fraction of total exposures. Foreign claims in Latin America are dominated by U.S. banks' claims.
- Foreign exposures have been growing strongly since the early 1990s, even relative to total banking system assets in the United States. As time passes, bank-to-bank and public borrowing are being displaced by lending to nonbank borrowers. During the first half-decade of the twenty-first century, claims of small banks on Latin America, particularly the cross-border component, exhibited large reductions.
- Claims of large banks and local claims tend to be relatively more

Matías Braun is an assistant professor of economics and finance at the Anderson School at the University of California, Los Angeles, and a professor of economics at the Universidad Adolfo Ibáñez.

stable. The volatility of claims does not appear to be much larger in Latin America than in Europe.

- U.S. banks' foreign claims are not robustly related to either U.S. or client country business cycle variables such as GDP growth and interest rates. This pattern does not seem to be significantly different when comparing across regions, bank size, and type of claims. If anything, claims on Latin American countries tend to be *less procyclical* than those on European nations.

The background question of this paper may be what role foreign bank lending plays in the transmission and amplification of shocks. The major strengths of the paper are, first, that it addresses the issue by taking a *direct* look at what very rich data on U.S. bank foreign claims can say, and second, that it does do so in a relatively model-free way. The analysis shows that the volatility and cyclical properties of foreign bank lending are not at all easy to explain. In particular, the findings contrast sharply with the idea that foreign lending is critical in the understanding of the high volatility present in emerging markets. Given the nature of the data and the simple approach, the results are hard to pass by, opening the door for new, interesting questions that the microdata approach may be able to answer.

International capital integration remains a contentious issue within both the academic and the policy communities. The evidence of a positive effect of capital account openness on growth is far from unquestionable. On the one hand, Quinn (1997), Klein and Olivei (2000), Edwards (2001), and Bekaert, Harvey, and Lumsdaine (1999) have all argued that an empirical link between growth and openness is indeed present and relevant in economic terms. However, Grilli and Milesi-Ferretti (1995), Rodrik (1998), and Kraay (1998) have questioned this finding. Even if capital account openness turns out to be positively associated with *average* growth rates and causality can be established, allowing free flow of capital may not be welfare enhancing if it brings about instability and the possibility of serious crises. While Demirguc-Kunt and Detragiache (1999) argue that this is indeed the case empirically, Glick and Hutchison (2005) not only cast doubt on that finding but argue that the data actually show that openness helps avoid crises. Also, the effect that capital flows may have on the recipient countries seems to be quite heterogeneous. Of course the discussion is not limited to academia. The potential effect of cross-country capital flows on volatility and the deepening of internal disequilibria has been one of the reasons capital controls were imposed in otherwise liberal, outward-oriented countries such as Chile.

This is, of course, not the first time the role of foreign lending has been studied. The effects of foreign bank lending on the host country have attracted a lot of attention in academic and policy circles. On the bright side, aside from being a source of scarce capital, foreign banks are viewed as helping to smooth country-specific shocks, and even changing local institutions in a way that improves the efficiency of credit allocation (Levine 1996). On the negative side, they are seen as conduits for the amplification and international transmission of shocks. This last mechanism seems to be real, at least in some contexts. Peek and Rosengren (2000), Van Rijckeghem and Weder (2001), and Galindo, Micco, and Powell (2004) provide interesting empirical evidence in this respect. Studies like these, however, have important shortcomings in that in general they either represent very particular situations in which the aggregate magnitude of the effects is unclear or base their conclusions on indirect evidence. One of the biggest strengths of Goldberg's paper is to tackle the issues at hand by taking a direct look at the microdata and asking how foreign banks (in this case, U.S.-based ones) actually behave. To this purpose the author has compiled (in Goldberg 2002) a very rich set of data consisting of a time series panel of individual U.S. banks that report exposures to foreign markets to U.S. regulators. Without getting into a particular mechanism the paper asks very generally whether the behavior of the claims of these banks on Latin America differ from those on European countries in terms of volatility and cyclicality. The evidence turns out to be unsupportive of the view that foreign lending has an important role in explaining the higher volatility that Latin American economies exhibit. None of the patterns one would expect under that view seem to be found in the data in a clear or robust way. Foreign exposures on Latin American countries are not significantly more volatile than those on European ones, nor are cross-border claims relative to local ones. It is not clear that smaller, supposedly less informed banks exhibit higher volatility either. In terms of cyclical behavior, foreign claims on Latin America (especially of the cross-border type) are not more procyclical with respect to local factors.

Given the generality of the analysis and the data used, it is difficult to argue against these findings. However, this generality does not come for free, in the sense that it can mask important features of the credit market that average out in the portfolio-type specification used. Consider, for instance, the effect of foreign lending in the local credit market, depicted in figure 5C.1.

In an integrated market, agents face a perfectly elastic supply of funds at the global real interest rate. Changes in the local demand for credit or investment opportunities trigger quick and large responses in the form of foreign capital flows. In this case, foreign claims would be procyclical with respect to GDP growth if this is thought to be a proxy for the state of the demand for credit. Unless one is prepared to argue that these changes in the demand for credit do not reflect fundamentals in a consistent way (not an uncommon assertion), it is clear that volatility per se is not necessarily bad, since swings in foreign claims reflect rapid adjustment to new fundamentals rather than fickle reactions. Even if that were the prevalent case,

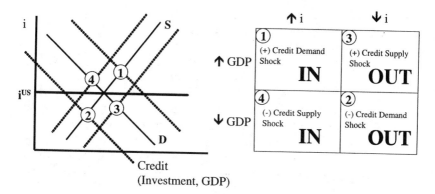

Fig. 5C.1   Foreign lending and the local credit market

one still needs to consider that the reaction of foreign capital to local credit supply shocks also manifests itself as volatility. In this case the counter-cyclical nature would actually reduce overall volatility.

The paper bases most of its conclusions on the comparison between the behaviors of claims on European vis-à-vis Latin American countries. A more primitive question to ask is whether foreign lender claims are different from domestic lender ones in any significant dimension. Figure 5C.1 suggests that a more appropriate benchmark would be the behavior of local banks in each country. The point is that one can explore further the main issues in this paper by distinguishing credit supply from credit demand shocks, and by looking at how foreign claims correlate with local credit (or GDP growth) under different states. The simplest extension of the empirical model in the paper would be to allow the coefficients of GDP growth to vary with the level of (risk-adjusted) local interest rates via the inclusion of interactive terms. A second step would allow for asymmetries in the effect of each variable. Extensions such as these could shed greater light on the desirability of foreign participation in local credit markets under different assumptions about the extent to which local market conditions reflect fundamentals rather than *animal spirits*. For instance, it could be the case that foreign claims are only responsive to positive credit demand shocks (box 1 in second panel of figure 5C.1). Under the assumption that those situations reflect primarily credit booms, the evidence would be supportive of the negative view of foreign bank participation. The conclusions and policy implications would be quite different if foreign flows were particularly responsive to local supply shocks (boxes 3 and 4) and there was indication that these are the result of deficiencies in local institutions.

Other (small) issues in the paper deserve some attention. First, the dependent variable is not net capital flows; it also includes revaluations. Under interest rate parity, movements of interest rates and exchange rates are linearly related. This implies a mechanical relationship between the dependent and independent variables in the paper's empirical model. Also, deviations from interest parity are probably not unrelated to the volatility or cyclicality of foreign claims, which makes interpretation of differences across Europe and Latin America troublesome. Allowing for a richer dynamic structure in the empirical model could be helpful. The static approach runs into some difficulties. For instance, while interest rates are forward looking, GDP growth is not. Also, only unexpected movements should matter, unless there are important adjustment costs.

When the claims of all banks are aggregated, the endogeneity of local GDP and interest rates makes it even more problematic to interpret the results in a causal way. Once the analysis focuses on bank-level data (particularly for small banks), the interpretation of the results can shift from simple correlations to causality. When computing significance levels, the potential correlation of the many observations for each bank and country should be taken into account.

Finally, the micro approach Goldberg's paper suggests opens a number of ways in which the literature on capital flows and capital controls can be expanded and deepened. Exploring specific mechanisms in the context of bank-level data allows easing the endogeneity and omitted-variable bias concerns typically present in macro studies. For instance, the within-country, cross-bank dimension of the data should be informative of whether herd behavior is indeed a typical outcome, as would be expected under informational asymmetries. Contagion may be assessed by exploiting the within-bank, cross-country data. Bank characteristics can inform on learning and its effect on the decision to focus or diversify operations. The interaction of these characteristics with the host-country dimension of the data speaks to the importance of relationships, and the choice of whether to lend across borders or to set up local operations.

References

Bekaert, Geert, Campbell R. Harvey, and Robin Lumsdaine. 1999. The dynamics of emerging market equity flows. NBER Working Paper no. 7219. Cambridge, MA: National Bureau of Economic Research, July.

Demirguc-Kunt, Asli, and Enrica Detragiache. 1999. Financial liberalization and financial fragility. World Bank Policy Research Working Paper no. 1917. Washington, DC: World Bank.

Edwards, Sebastian. 2001. Capital mobility and economic performance: Are emerging economies different? NBER Working Paper no. 8076. Cambridge, MA: National Bureau of Economic Research.

Galindo, Arturo, Alejandro Micco, and Andrew Powell. 2004. Loyal lenders or fickle financiers: On the role of foreign banks in Latin America. Washington, DC: Inter-American Development Bank. Working paper.

Glick, Reuven, and Michael Hutchison. 2005. Capital controls and exchange rate instability in developing economies. Journal of International Money and Finance 24 (3): 387–412.

Goldberg, Linda. 2002. When is foreign bank lending to emerging markets volatile? In *Preventing currency crises in emerging markets,* ed. Sebastian Edwards and Jeffrey Frankel, 171–96. Chicago: University of Chicago Press.

Grilli, Vittorio, and Gian Maria Milesi-Ferretti. 1995. Economic effects and structural determinants of capital controls. *IMF Staff Papers* 42 (September): 517–51.

Klein, Michael, and Giovanni Olivei. 2000. Capital account liberalization, financial depth and economic growth. Tufts University and Federal Reserve Bank of Boston. Manuscript, April.

Kraay, Aart. 1998. In search of the macroeconomic effects of capital account liberalization. Washington, DC: World Bank. Working paper.

Levine, Ross. 1996. Foreign banks, financial development, and economic growth. In *International financial markets: Harmonization versus competition,* ed. Claude E. Barfield, 224–54. Washington, DC: AEI Press.

Peek, J., and E. S. Rosengren. 2000. Collateral damage: Effects of the Japanese bank crisis on real activity in the United States. *American Economic Review* 90 (1): 30–45.

Quinn, Dennis. 1997. The correlates of change in international financial regulation. *American Political Science Review* 91 (3): 531–51.

Rodrik, Dani. 1998. Who needs capital-account convertibility? In *Should the IMF pursue capital account mobility?* Princeton Essays in International Finance no. 207, ed. S. Fischer et al., 55–65. Princeton, NJ: Princeton University.

Van Rijckeghem, Caroline, and Beatrice Weder. 2001. Sources of contagion: Is it finance or trade? *Journal of International Economics* 54 (2): 293–308.

II

Country Studies

6

International Borrowing, Capital Controls, and the Exchange Rate
Lessons from Chile

Kevin Cowan and José De Gregorio

6.1 Introduction

This paper discusses Chile's experience with international borrowing over the last two decades. This period allows us to contrast the Chilean experience during two recent episodes of capital flows to Latin America: the late 1970s and the 1990s. The first episode ended in disaster for Chile, with a balance-of-payments and financial crisis, and huge costs in terms of output and employment. Unlike those of other countries in the region, the crisis was not caused by fiscal imbalances but was triggered by a deteriorating international environment, a misaligned exchange rate, and a weak financial system. Indeed, it started before Mexico announced that it could not meet its foreign obligations, which ignited the debt crisis. In many aspects the Chilean crisis of the early 1980s resembles the more recent Asian crises and the so-called twenty-first-century crises.

During the second episode of capital inflows Chile fared much better, and managed to avoid the large financial collapses that afflicted many other emerging economies during this period. Following the 1980s crisis Chile experienced a sharp recovery, and between 1990 and 1997 was the recipient of massive capital inflows. During this period, and in order to stem net inflows, avoid a large appreciation, and keep control of monetary policy,

Kevin Cowan is an economist at the Central Bank of Chile. José De Gregorio is vice-governor of the Central Bank of Chile.

We thank (without implicating) Ricardo Caballero, Guillermo Calvo, Arturo Galindo, Alejandro Micco, Luis Oscar Herrera, and Aaron Tornell for helpful comments on a previous version of this paper. We are also very grateful to Erwin Hansen, Danielken Molina, and Marco Nuñez for excellent research assistance. The views expressed in this paper are our own and do not necessarily represent those of the institutions with which we are affiliated. This paper was written while Kevin Cowan was at the Inter-American Development Bank (IADB).

the authorities implemented capital controls on inflows and liberalized outflows. The most widely cited control was the unremunerated reserve requirement (URR) on capital inflows, the *encaje*.[1] Because of the resiliency of the Chilean economy to the events following the Tequila crisis in Mexico and the Asian-Russian crisis of the late 1990s this policy has received a lot of attention in both academic and policy circles. Finally, after mounting currency pressures in 1998 and a recession in 1999, capital controls were eliminated.

The late 1970s and early 1980s provide a good control group against which to evaluate the financial integration and macroeconomic developments of the Chilean economy during the 1990s. For a start, capital controls on inflows were much stricter before the 1982 crisis than during the 1990s. In addition, financial regulation requiring banks to match the currency composition of their income and liabilities to avoid exposure to exchange rate risk was very similar in 1982 to that in place in the 1990s. Neither avoided the collapse of the corporate sector, which in turn contaminated the financial system. Clearly, explanations for the lower vulnerability of the Chilean economy must lie beyond capital controls and mismatch regulation.

In this paper we argue that the resilience of the Chilean economy during the 1990s was mainly due to (a) changes in banking regulation that promoted a solid financial system (in particular, changes in regulation for related lending) and (b) the absence of currency risk guarantees to the private sector. These in turn induced more prudent indebtedness policies by corporations, which as a result were well equipped to tolerate the exchange rate fluctuations of the late 1990s. We argue in the paper that a rigid exchange rate system contributes to capital inflows by reducing the risk of arbitraging existing interest rate differentials. There is no evidence that capital controls were able to reduce these inflows, although there is evidence that they had a limited effect on the composition of these flows.

In a nutshell, we conclude that flexibility in exchange rate management and a sound financial system are more important than capital controls in protecting the economy from external shocks and fluctuations in the availability of international capital.

There are additional characteristics of Chile's international borrowing that are worth examining. One of these is the secondary role played by the banking sector in intermediating foreign credit. In contrast to other countries with similar levels of economic development, nonfinancial corporations did most of the international borrowing in Chile during the 1990s. We do not have arguments to say whether this is a positive or negative development. On the one hand, it isolates the financial system from financial

---

1. We use the terms URR and *encaje* interchangeably.

turmoil. On the other hand, it limits the access of smaller firms to foreign funds. This second aspect becomes more important in the presence of a solid financial system.

Finally, there is the issue of whether Chile can introduce capital controls after signing a free trade agreement with the United States. Although there is some loss of degrees of freedom to apply controls, the option, although limited, still remains.

The paper proceeds as follows. The second section describes foreign debt and the international investment position for Chile over the last quarter century. Section 6.3 discusses the issue of capital controls, focusing on the effects of the unremunerated reserve requirement, the *encaje*. We explore a new issue, namely the composition between financial and nonfinancial borrowing. We show, from an international perspective, that while capital controls were in place in Chile the composition of external debt tilted toward the nonfinancial sector. Then, section 6.4 follows with a discussion on banking regulation and international borrowing. As we argue, the exchange rate regime is the key, and the effects of exchange rate regimes on debt inflows in the 1990s are discussed in section 6.5, while section 6.6 focuses on currency mismatches. Section 6.7 discusses the implications for Chile of the recently signed free trade agreement with the United States. Finally, section 6.8 analyzes the Chilean experience following the Asian-Russian crisis, where we dispute the view that Chile had a sudden stop. As we discuss in the section, Chile had a current account reversal due to an initially large current account deficit and a negative terms-of-trade shock, which induced the authorities to follow a very tight monetary policy and a strong defense of the peso. We conclude that from the capital account point of view, the reversal was a sudden start of outflows rather than a sudden stop of capital inflows. Section 6.9 concludes.

6.2   Stylized Facts

In this section we provide an overview of the evolution of Chilean international borrowing and capital flows. We start with the early 1980s, as this period provides a good (or a bad) benchmark against which to evaluate the evolution of international financial integration during the 1990s.

6.2.1   The Evolution of External Debt

Prior to the debt crisis of 1982 Chile's external debt was approximately $14 billion, slightly less than 50 percent of gross domestic product (GDP; figures 6.1 and 6.2). Then, between 1982 and 1985, external debt grew moderately in dollar terms, but sharply in terms of GDP, as a result of the depreciation of the Chilean peso and a large fall in output during the debt crisis. External debt peaked at 120 percent of GDP in 1986. In the second half of the 1980s Chile's external debt remained relatively stable in dollar

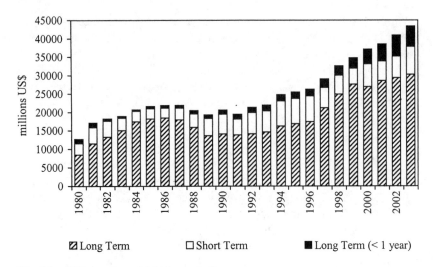

Fig. 6.1   Chile's external debt by maturity

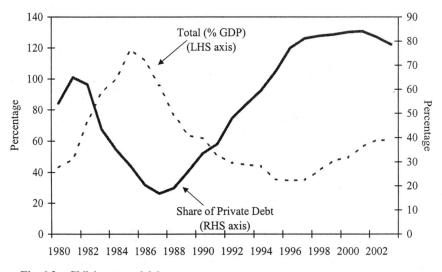

Fig. 6.2   Chile's external debt
Source: Central Bank of Chile.

terms, while output growth helped bring the debt-GDP ratio down to 60 percent of GDP by 1989.

As a result of renewed access to international capital markets external debt went from $21 billion at the beginning of the 1990s to $35 billion in 1999. Most of this growth took place in the second half of the decade. In recent years, debt has continued to grow in dollar terms, reaching $43 billion in December 2003. Although foreign debt has doubled in dollar terms since 1990 as a fraction of GDP, it still remains below its 1989 level.

Prior to the debt crisis, most of Chile's external debt was private (about 60 percent). Following the crisis, and in order to successfully renegotiate external debt, private debt received public guarantees. In addition, most new foreign borrowing was done by the public sector. This caused a large drop in the share of private debt, which bottomed out at 17 percent of total external debt in 1987. Later, Chile's return to international financial markets and voluntary lending combined with sound public finances (the fiscal accounts were in surplus until 1999) drove the share of the private sector in total external debt up to 84 percent in 2000. Subsequently, as a result of the slowdown in economic activity and mild fiscal deficits, the share of public debt has increased slightly, rising from 16 percent of the total stock in 2000 to 20 percent in 2003.

Another characteristic of Chilean private-sector external debt is that most of it is nonfinancial (figure 6.3)—that is, not intermediated by the domestic financial system. Firms borrow directly from abroad, skipping the domestic financial system. Caballero, Cowan, and Kearns (2005) stress this point when comparing Australia and Chile and their relative resilience to external shocks. In the case of Australia, banks do most of the foreign borrowing, which is then intermediated to the domestic economy. Accordingly, Caballero, Cowan, and Kearns (2005) argue that international borrowing done by banks allows access to international capital markets to a broader set of borrowers, which may in turn explain Australia's different response to the large negative terms-of-trade shocks following the Asian crisis.

This has not always been the case. In 1975, as Chile began opening to international capital markets, private debt was only $786 million. Because of severe restrictions on foreign borrowing by domestic banks (discussed in

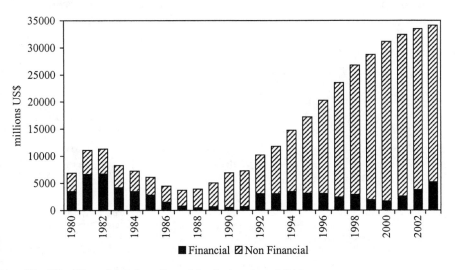

Fig. 6.3   **Financial and nonfinancial private external debt**

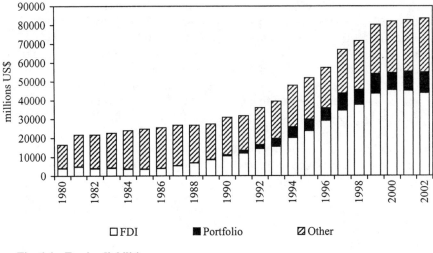

Fig. 6.4   Foreign liabilities
Source: Central Bank of Chile.

detail below), only 20 percent of this private debt was financial. Restrictions on international borrowing for domestic banks were gradually lifted during the late 1970s and early 1980s, and private debt grew massively, especially banking debt. In 1981 private external debt was close to $10 billion, two-thirds of which was owed by the banking system.

Foreign borrowing by the domestic banking system and the mismatches it generated were at the center of the financial crisis of 1982. Interestingly, it was not the banks that were mismatched but their corporate borrowers. Banks were forced to lend in foreign currency all that they had borrowed in foreign currency (Edwards and Cox-Edwards 1991). The result was large dollar-denominated bank debts in the balance sheets of domestic firms, many of which operated in the nontradable sector.

6.2.2   The Evolution of the International Investment Position

Chile's foreign liabilities in 1980 were about $16.5 billion, of which $12.7 billion corresponded to external debt and the rest to foreign direct investment (FDI; figure 6.4 and table 6.1).[2] Most of the liabilities were in the form of external debt, the standard pattern of capital flows prior to the debt crisis. The composition of foreign liabilities started to change in the late 1980s and early 1990s, when foreign direct investment started to play a much more

2. The International Monetary Fund separates liabilities into three categories in their international investment position statistics: FDI, portfolio, and other investment. Although most of Chilean external debt is in the "other investment" category, there is also some portfolio debt (bonds) and some debt contracted by Chilean subsidiaries with their foreign owners (FDI).

Table 6.1   International investment position (in US$ millions)

	1980	1985	1990	1995	1999	2000	2001	2002
Net international investment position								
(assets minus liabilities)	−7,402	−16,447	−14,988	−23,471	−28,729	−29,314	−29,510	−27,981
Percent GDP	25.1	90.3	44.7	32.6	39.4	39.0	43.1	41.5
Assets	9,080	8,264	15,898	28,517	51,502	52,569	53,137	55,490
Foreign direct investment	56	103	137	2,460	9,000	11,154	11,905	12,389
Portfolio investment	0	0	0	52	11,402	9,876	10,662	12,988
Other investment (debt)	4,587	4,954	8,687	10,782	16,154	16,429	16,169	14,762
International reserves	4,436	3,206	7,074	15,224	14,946	15,110	14,400	15,351
Liabilities	16,482	24,711	30,887	51,989	80,231	81,883	82,647	83,471
Foreign direct investment	3,982	3,527	10,539	23,656	43,498	45,418	45,082	43,861
Portfolio investment	107	232	598	6,167	10,611	9,187	10,302	11,079
Other investment (debt)	12,393	20,952	19,750	22,165	26,122	27,278	27,263	28,531
Memorandum item[a]								
External debt	12,697	21,656	20,655	25,505	34,758	37,177	38,538	40,956

Source: Central Bank of Chile.

[a]In the international investment position statistics external debt is mostly included in the "other investment" category, although some debt is also distributed in other categories, as described in the text.

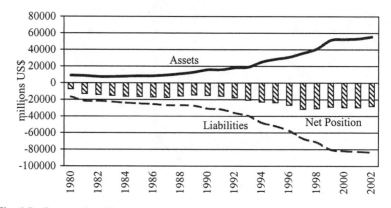

Fig. 6.5   International investment position

important role. While in 1985 total foreign direct investment represented 15 percent of total liabilities, in 1990 its share was up to 34 percent, and currently it represents 53 percent. External debt, in contrast, has reduced its importance, falling from close to two-thirds in 1990 to less than half in 2002. Portfolio investment makes up only 13 percent of total liabilities.

From 1990 to 2002 total external liabilities increased from $31 to $84 billion. As shown in figure 6.5, foreign assets also increased significantly during this period, rising from $16 to $56 billion. As a result, the net position has grown by considerably less than total foreign liabilities, remaining between 35 and 45 percent of GDP since 1990. On the other hand, financial integration (measured as the sum of assets and liabilities over GDP) has increased substantially during the 1990s, rising from 140 percent of GDP in 1990 to 206 percent in 2002.

An important development regarding Chile's international investment position is the increased relevance of pension funds in international assets. Pension funds have gradually been allowed to increase the foreign share of their portfolio, so that currently about 30 percent of total pension funds are invested abroad (figure 6.6). Because of the size of the accumulated savings in the funds—about 50 percent of GDP—this has made a significant difference in the composition of the country's international assets, which shows up in portfolio investment in the asset section of table 6.1. The logic for the gradual opening up of investment abroad by pension funds was twofold. On the one hand, lifting restrictions allowed for greater portfolio diversification. On the other hand, it was initially meant to encourage capital outflows in a period of continuous real exchange rate appreciation.[3]

---

3. The exchange rate pressures of the outflows of pension funds have been minor, since by regulation they must have low currency exposure, so that in practice they have been investing abroad, fully hedging their currency exposure. This is one of the factors behind the development of the foreign exchange derivative market in Chile (De Gregorio and Tokman 2004).

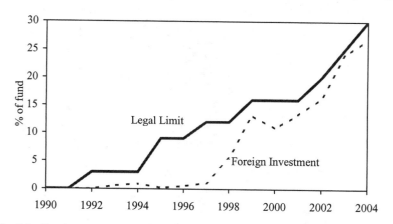

Fig. 6.6   Foreign assets in pension fund portfolios
Sources: Central Bank of Chile, Pension Fund Superintendency (SAFP).

Although its net international investment position is similar to that of other emerging markets, Chile is more financially integrated (figure 6.7). In terms of composition of assets, Chile has more portfolio investment than other emerging markets, mainly because of the activity of pension funds. It has also more reserves. In terms of liabilities, the share of FDI in Chile is one of the largest among emerging markets and high-income economies. External debt as fraction of GDP is slightly larger than that of emerging markets and significantly less than that of advanced economies. Another important characteristic of Chile's recent international borrowing is that foreign companies owe most external debt. Indeed, in 2002 foreign companies owed 57 percent of total private debt. This shows that degrees of vulnerability of Chile are much less than those indicated by external debt figures.[4]

6.3   Capital Controls: The *Encaje*

Following the surge in capital flows to emerging markets in the early 1990s, Chilean authorities imposed controls on capital inflows while gradually liberalizing capital outflows.[5] The stated purpose of this policy was to reduce net inflows and stem the appreciation of the Chilean peso.

The main instrument used to limit inflows, widely discussed in policy circles, was an unremunerated reserve requirement known as the *encaje*. The *encaje* required that a fraction of the capital inflow be deposited in a

---

4. For further details see Jadresic et al. (2003).
5. As part of the effort to increase outflows, the years required for foreign investors to remit capital and profits were slowly reduced and finally eliminated. Pension fund limits to investing abroad were also widened. For details on the main measures taken since 1990 see appendix A. See also Gallego, Hernández, and Schmidt-Hebbel (1999).

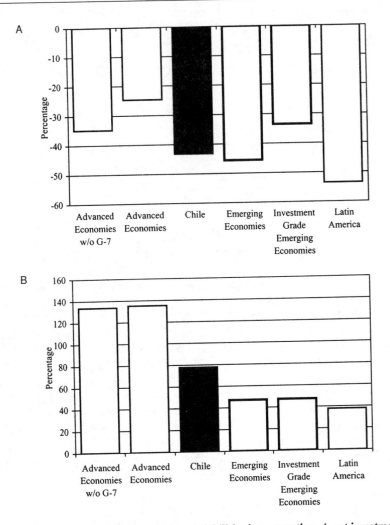

Fig. 6.7   Chile's international assets and liabilities in perspective: *A,* **net investment position (% GDP);** *B,* **foreign assets (% GDP);** *C,* **foreign liabilities (% GDP);** *D,* **international financial integration (% GDP)**
Source: Jadresic et al. (2003)

non-interest-bearing account in the Chilean central bank. The *encaje* was introduced in June 1991 and was expanded and extended various times in the following years. Initially, it was set at 20 percent of the inflow, for a period from three months to twelve months depending on the maturity and the nature of the credit. Trade credit was excluded from the *encaje*.[6] Later,

---

6. De Gregorio, Edwards, and Valdés (2000) argue that the *encaje* gradually lost power, as markets came up with ways to circumvent it. The most obvious way to overcome the *encaje*, frequently cited but not quantified, was to register short-term credit as trade credit.

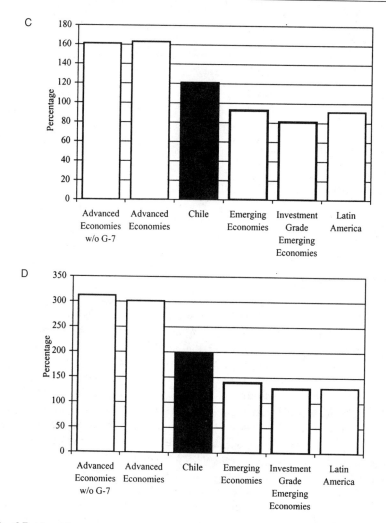

Fig. 6.7   **(cont.)**

in 1992 and then in 1995, the base was broadened to include foreign currency deposits and the proceeds from the issuance of American depository receipts (ADRs), the rate was increased to 30 percent, and the period was set at twelve months regardless of the term of the credit. The *encaje* was reduced in 1998 and finally eliminated in 2001.[7]

Several reasons were given for introducing the *encaje*. The most prominent was the need to reduce net capital inflows to prevent an appreciation of the Chilean peso. Indeed, a depreciated real exchange rate was considered a key factor behind the successful recovery of the economy that had

---

7. Before its elimination the rate of the reserve requirement was set to zero.

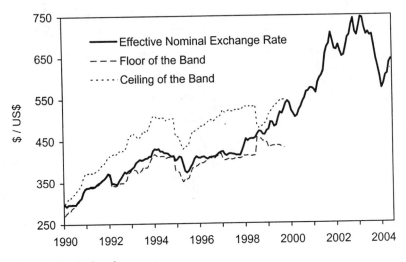

Fig. 6.8   Nominal exchange rate

taken place since the mid-1980s. In addition, it was argued that capital controls would allow for some degree of monetary policy independence in the context of a managed exchange rate, which for most of the 1990s was an exchange rate band with adjustable width and a crawling central parity (figure 6.8). Finally, since the cost of the *encaje* was proportionally higher for short-term inflows, it was argued that it would reduce the vulnerability of the economy to "hot capital."

An assessment of the macroeconomic consequences of the *encaje* requires looking at its effect on interest rates, the level and composition of capital flows, and the exchange rate.[8] We review existing evidence on the effects of the *encaje* on all of these variables in this section.

6.3.1   Macroeconomic Effects

Interest Rates

In theory the existence of an *encaje* should allow for differences between domestic and foreign interest rates without inducing capital flows to restore a nonarbitrage condition. Assuming full compliance, and an international interest rate of 7 percent, a 30 percent *encaje* for a year leads to a differential of about 3 percentage points on a one-year inflow. In practice, however, the impact on interest rates is likely to be considerably smaller, as agents switch to longer maturities or find ways of circumventing the *encaje*.

---

8. The review of the evidence is mainly focused on De Gregorio, Edwards, and Valdés (2000). See also Soto and Valdés-Prieto (1996), Edwards (1999), Gallego, Hernández, and Schmidt-Hebbel (1999), and Nadal De Simone and Sorsa (1999).

What then are the empirical estimates of the effect of the *encaje* on domestic interest rates? Using a vector autoregression (VAR) framework, De Gregorio, Edwards, and Valdés (2000) found that the effect on the interest rate was both small and short lived. In the first six months after a change in the *encaje* regulation—which the authors interpret as closing an existing loophole—they find effects that range between 90 and 150 basis points for a 30 percent *encaje*. This effect dies out slowly over a twelve-month horizon. This result lies at the upper range of the estimated effects of the controls on interest rates in Chile. Smaller effects are reported in Edwards (1999), while Gallego, Hernández, and Schmidt-Hebbel (1999) found no effects whatsoever.

Level of Inflows

The Chilean economy received massive capital inflows during the 1990s, and there is no solid evidence showing that they would have been substantially larger if the *encaje* had not been implemented. Indeed, most existing empirical studies find no effects of the *encaje* on the level of capital inflows. The only exception is a study by Gallego, Hernández, and Schmidt-Hebbel (1999), who find that a 100 basis point increase in the cost of the *encaje* reduces total capital inflows by 1 percent of GDP. In addition, they find that those flows directly affected by the *encaje* would decline by 2 percent of GDP, which indicates that the composition across maturities of international borrowing was affected. It is important to note that this effect is computed for the stock of foreign liabilities. Given that the total cost of the *encaje,* using the estimates of Gallego, Hernández, and Schmidt-Hebbel (1999), was on average between 100 and 200 basis points, the reserve requirement reduced total inflows by at most 2 percent of GDP. This is relatively small, considering that total net inflows during the whole period from 1991 until 1997 were approximately 27 percent of GDP.

Composition of Inflows

One would expect that taxing short-term flows more heavily would increase the maturity of capital inflows. Indeed, existing evidence shows that the *encaje* led to longer-term external debt. As column (1) in table 6.2 shows, in the mid-1990s, as capital controls were tightened, short-term debt declined sharply as percentage of total debt. According to De Gregorio, Edwards, and Valdés (2000), the total effect of the *encaje* on short-term debt would have been between 0.5 and 1 percentage points of GDP, which would have resulted in a lower stock of short-term debt (about $600 million).

From a vulnerability perspective it usually makes sense to look at trade credit separately from other forms of short-term credit, as trade credit consists of advances on exports and is therefore less volatile. In the Chilean case, however, this distinction may be blurred by the fact that short-term debt was

Table 6.2   Short-term external debt

	Narrow definition		New definition		Debt maturing within a year	
	US$ millions (1)	% total debt (2)	US$ millions (3)	% total debt (4)	US$ millions (5)	% total debt (6)
1991	2,199	11.3	4,346	22.3	5,658	29.0
1992	3,475	16.3	5,841	27.3	7,239	33.9
1993	3,487	15.9	5,769	26.3	7,353	33.5
1994	3,865	15.6	6,859	27.7	8,541	34.5
1995	3,431	13.5	6,891	27.0	8,636	33.9
1996	2,635	10.0	7,045	26.8	8,862	33.7
1997	1,287	4.4	5,522	19.0	7,829	27.0
1998	1,610	4.9	5,130	15.7	7,672	23.5
1999	1,171	3.4	4,317	12.4	7,145	20.6
2000	2,531	6.8	6,172	16.6	10,236	27.5
2001	2,051	5.3	5,290	13.7	9,944	25.8
2002	2,324	5.7	5,823	14.2	11,591	28.3

Source: Central Bank of Chile.

registered as trade credit as a way of evading the *encaje.* With this in mind, column (3) shows the evolution of an expanded definition of short-term debt that includes trade credit. Here the effects of the *encaje,* mentioned above, are not that clear. Most of the decline in short-term debt takes place between 1997 and 1999, a couple of years after the *encaje* was tightened.

Exchange Rate

During most of the 1990s, the nominal exchange rate in Chile was allowed to fluctuate within a band. On several occasions the width as well as the center of the band was adjusted (figure 6.8). The first change was the widening of the band from ±5 percent to ±10 percent. Later, in 1997, it was widened again to ±12.5 percent. The center of the band was adjusted several times; most notably, it was revalued in early 1992, late 1994, and early 1997. Finally, on the eve of the Asian crisis and due to fear of floating (Calvo and Reinhart 2002), the band was narrowed. Several changes finally led to the elimination of the band and a move to a flexible exchange rate regime in December 1999.[9]

Both the exchange rate policy and the *encaje* tried to avoid an appreciation in the context of massive capital inflows. Casual observation suggests that they failed to do so (figure 6.9). From 1990 until late 1997 the real exchange rate appreciated persistently. The most appreciated level occurred in 1997, a year in which net capital inflows, excluding reserves, were 9.1 percent of GDP, accumulation of reserves amounted to 3.3 percent of GDP, and the *encaje* was in full application.

Of course, the correct counterfactual is to determine the marginal effect

9. For further details see De Gregorio and Tokman (2004).

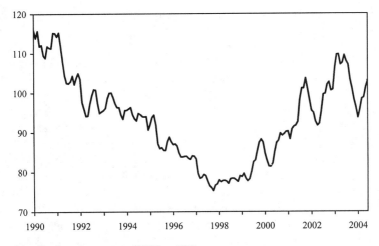

Fig. 6.9   Real exchange rate (1986 = 100)
Source: Central Bank of Chile.

of the *encaje* on the real exchange rate. We turn to this next. The first empirical study on the effects of the *encaje* (Soto and Valdés-Prieto 1996), as well as most subsequent work, has focused on determining whether it was effective in avoiding an appreciation of the peso. All of the existing studies mentioned so far in this section—spanning a broad set of measures, periods, and empirical specifications—fail to find an effect of the *encaje* on the path of the real exchange rate.

Financial Vulnerability

In 1998 the Chilean peso suffered three rounds of speculative attacks. These turbulences were fought off with large hikes in interest rates and massive intervention in the foreign exchange market. As a result of this intervention and a series of negative external shocks, in 1999 the economy suffered its first recession in many years. However, the fall in output was small in comparison to other countries that also experienced sudden stops in capital inflows in the late 1990s. Furthermore, Chile in 1999 did not face a financial crisis. This has led many observers to argue that the presence of the *encaje* reduced Chile's external vulnerability and was central to the mild recession. After all, it reduced the share of short-term debt, a variable that many authors have singled out as an important source of financial vulnerability.[10]

---

10. A recent literature, motivated by events in East Asia, has argued that short-term external debt may be an important source of macroeconomic vulnerability. Proponents of this view include Radelet and Sachs (1998) and Chang and Velasco (1999), who argue that excessive reliance on short-term debt leaves emerging market corporations vulnerable to "financial panic" as in the stylized model of Diamond and Dybvig (1983). In this context, policies like the *encaje* have the potential to reduce vulnerability by lengthening the tenor of the external debt contracts.

The problem with this view is that the magnitude of the estimated effects of the *encaje* on the level and composition of capital flows during the 1990s makes it hard to believe that capital controls were central to Chile's economic success during the 1990s. Furthermore, Chile's experience in the early 1980s shows that, even if capital controls are effective in limiting the share of short-term debt, this certainly does not provide a guarantee against currency crises.

The Chilean 1982 crisis was a full-blown twin crisis (currency and financial). Starting from a closed capital account, legislation passed early in 1974 allowed Chilean nonfinancial firms and individuals to borrow abroad. However, inflows were restricted to maturities greater than six months. In April 1976, concerned with the destabilizing effects of short-term capital inflows, Chilean authorities further lengthened this minimum maturity to two years. The minimum maturity restriction was to stay in place up to the debt crisis in 1982. In 1979 an additional restriction on short-term debt was introduced: a URR (an *encaje*) was put in place on all foreign loans shorter than sixty-five months.[11] As a result of these stringent controls, short-term debt in 1981 was only 19 percent of total debt. This did not prevent a severe crisis, however, with output declines of 13.6 percent in 1982 and 2.8 percent in 1983.[12]

6.3.2   Microeconomic Effects

The available evidence shows that, at best, the effects of the *encaje* on capital inflows, interest rates, and the exchange rate are small. Furthermore, the estimated magnitudes and the events of 1982 suggest that it is no panacea against currency and financial crisis. So much for the benefits. What about the costs?

Differential Effects across Firm Size

The microeconomic distortions that the *encaje* introduces are an issue frequently ignored in the evaluation of capital controls in Chile. If and when the *encaje* worked, its main effect was to push the domestic cost of capital—in particular short-term capital—above its international opportunity cost. This presumably had differential effects across firms depending on their ability to obtain long-term financing abroad. Forbes (2003) takes this issue to the data by analyzing the investment behavior of publicly listed companies. She shows that during the period that the *encaje* pre-

---

11. This reserve requirement ranged from 25 percent, for loans shorter than thirty-six months, to 10 percent for loans between forty-eight and sixty-five months in maturity. Trade credit was excluded. See Edwards and Cox-Edwards (1991).

12. One of the reasons behind the collapse was the weakness of corporate-sector balance sheets to tolerate a massive exchange rate adjustment, which ultimately contaminated a poorly regulated banking system. We will return to this issue with further details in section 6.6.

vailed, smaller firms faced a higher cost of capital and less investment. She interprets this as a cost of the *encaje*.

Although suggestive, we believe that this result must be interpreted cautiously. Although the *encaje* was clearly a variable that distinguished the periods analyzed, there are other factors that could also explain the differences in firm behavior across size. One of these was restrictions placed on international bond issuance. During the 1990s, regulations requiring a minimum size and credit rating for international bond issues effectively excluded many smaller firms from the international bond market.[13] These limits were gradually relaxed, so that in 1998 the minimum rating was lowered to BBB- and the minimum size reduced to $5 million.

Differential Effects on the Financial Sector

As mentioned in section 6.2, an interesting characteristic of the Chilean economy in the 1990s is the direct external indebtedness of corporations, with domestic banks playing a minor role in intermediating international debt. To see whether this is Chilean quirk or a feature common to other emerging economies, we explore whether banks in Chile intermediate a relatively low share of international debt in comparison to other economies at similar levels of development. To do so we look at the behavior of bank and nonbank debt inflows for a sample of capital-importing countries during the 1990s. For each country we calculate the average ratio of bank inflows over total debt inflows over two periods: 1990–96 and 2000–2003. We exclude the period 1997–99, as it is a period of substantial changes in the regulations affecting the Chilean capital account, and also a period of substantial instability in aggregate capital flows. We then regress the ratio of bank inflows to total debt inflows against a broad measure of development, the log of GDP per capita (purchasing power parity at the beginning of each period). We also include a dummy for Chile, an interaction of the Chile dummy with a dummy for the second period, and the second-period dummy itself.

The results are shown in table 6.3. The basic result of column (1) shows that the estimated coefficient on the income variable is positive and significant: banks play a larger role in intermediating capital inflows in high-income economies (which we interpret as countries with more highly developed financial systems). More important, the Chilean dummy is negative, significant, and sizable. The share of bank inflows in total debt inflows in Chile is 20 percent lower than the level predicted by its income level in the period 1990–96. This difference disappears in the latter period, as indicated by the positive and significant coefficient on the interaction between the Chile dummy and the second-period dummy. This result is ro-

---

13. Corporations required a rating equal to or more than sovereign risk, and the minimum size of borrowing was set at $50 million.

Table 6.3   The role of banks in capital inflows: Is Chile atypical?

Independent variables	Dependent variable: Bank inflows/total debt inflows			Dependent variable: Bank inflows/total non-FDI inflows		
	(1)	(2)	(3)	(4)	(5)	(6)
log (GDP per capita PPP) beginning of period	0.152 (0.016)***	0.161 (0.013)***		0.142 (0.016)***	0.145 (0.013)***	
I(year > 2000)	0.006 (0.038)	0.034 (0.038)	-0.003 (0.051)	-0.003 (0.038)	0.012 (0.036)	-0.013 (0.051)
Chile dummy	-0.218 (0.027)***	-0.229 (0.024)***	-0.242 (0.033)***	-0.212 (0.027)***	-0.219 (0.024)***	-0.238 (0.033)***
Chile dummy × I(year > 2000)	0.222 (0.039)***	0.189 (0.037)***	0.256 (0.053)***	0.281 (0.039)***	0.264 (0.035)***	0.315 (0.053)***
Bank credit over GDP beginning of period			0.004 (0.001)***			0.004 (0.001)***
No. of observations	149	198	106	149	198	106
R^2	0.35	0.34	0.23	0.32	0.31	0.21
Sample	Net capital importers	All	Net capital importers	Net capital importers	Net capital importers	Net capital importers

Source: Authors' calculations based on International Financial Statistics (IFS) data.

Note: Robust standard errors in parentheses.

***Significant at the 1 percent level.

bust to changes in the sample (column [2]), using a direct measure of financial development (bank credit over GDP, again at the beginning of each period, in column [3]) and an alternative measure of capital inflows (columns [4]–[6]).

A possible explanation of this finding is that closely monitored banks found it harder to avoid paying the *encaje* than corporations, so that the effective cost of foreign credit for banks was higher. If this were the case, the *encaje* would have had important distributional effects across firms. Small firms (reliant on short-term bank credit) would have borne the brunt of the *encaje*, while large firms (able to borrow in international markets or to evade the *encaje*) would have been relatively unaffected.

An alternative explanation is in the recent development of the Chilean derivatives market. As we mentioned above, Caballero, Cowan, and Kearns (2005) find that in Australia a large share of foreign debt is intermediated by banks. They also find that banks lend most of these funds in Australian dollars and use the derivatives market to hedge their positions. Indeed, banks in Australia are the largest holders of net currency derivative positions. This being the case, the development of the Chilean derivatives markets in the last few years is a possible explanation for the increased role of banks in international debt flows.

Finally, changes in capital account regulations after 1998 (discussed in the appendix), in particular those changes pertaining to bond issue, may also have played a part in switching the mix away from direct international borrowing toward bank-intermediated foreign borrowing. Currently, as a result of some combination of market development, the consolidation of a flexible exchange rate regime, and further liberalization of bank borrowing, the composition of Chile's private external debt is not significantly different from what would be predicted according to international patterns.

6.4   Bank Regulations, International Borrowing, and Financial Crises

We show above that banks in Chile during the 1990s intermediated a relatively low share of international debt inflows, with most international borrowing done directly by corporations. We also show that in the years after the capital account was fully liberalized and the exchange rate floated, banks have begun playing a significantly larger role in debt inflows. There are two opposing views on the benefits and risks of this increased participation of banks in international capital flows. On the one hand, Caballero, Cowan, and Kearns (2005) have argued that the larger role that banks in Australia play in international borrowing vis-à-vis Chilean banks allows the economy greater resilience to external demand shocks by enhancing access to international capital, especially to firms and consumers that do not have direct access to the international capital markets. The Chilean experience in 1982, on the other hand, suggests exactly the opposite: large foreign liabilities on bank balance sheets can become a source of vulnerability. If currency risk is not correctly managed by the banking system, a large devaluation can lead to a financial crisis.[14]

We think that both arguments have a case. The optimality of increased intermediation of capital flows by domestic banks depends crucially on the incentives banks have for correctly managing aggregate risk—in particular exchange rate risk—and the tools available for the banks to manage such risks. Banking regulation and macroeconomic policy both have a direct impact on banks' incentives to hedge against exchange rate uncertainty. The ability to contract foreign debt in the domestic currency, a well-developed domestic currency debt market that is liquid and covers a broad range of maturities, and the development of a derivatives market are all tools that allow banks to take on foreign debt without necessarily taking on exchange rate risk.[15] In this section we concentrate on the importance of bank regulation. In the following section we turn our attention to exchange rate policy and its effect on debt inflows.

Banking regulation has played a key role in determining the size and nature of capital inflows to Chile. As mentioned above, capital controls in Chile in the early 1980s were more stringent than those in the mid-1990s. Bank regulation, however, was radically different. In what follows of this section, we look at bank regulation in the early 1980s and argue that it played an important part in the large capital inflows, mostly banking, of the period and the resulting financial crisis.[16]

Following a period of state control and financial repression, a series of measures thrust the Chilean financial system into the free market arena in the second half of the 1970s. In May 1974 *financieras* (finance houses) were authorized to operate and to freely fix interest rates. Commercial banks, mostly state controlled, still had fixed rates and quantity controls. Then, in April 1975, banks were allowed to freely determine interest rates. During this year, over 86 percent of state-owned banks were privatized. Hence, by the time of full capital account opening in April 1980, Chilean banks had been operating in a free market system for no more than five years. In Chile domestic financial liberalization happened before international financial opening, but the former was far from well done, as we discuss below.

Initially there was no explicit deposit insurance in Chile, and authorities advocated a market-oriented banking system in which depositor monitor-

14. For recent discussion on the negative affects of international borrowing in the context of a fragile banking system see Soto (2000).
15. A series of papers addressing the issue of domestic financial dollarization have also made this point. This literature emphasizes the interactions between exchange rate regimes and bank regulations in determining the share of domestic bank contracts denominated in foreign currencies. IADB (2005) contains a recent survey.
16. For a recent discussion on the development of the Chilean financial market since the 1980s, see Cifuentes, Desormeaux, and Gónzalez (2002).

ing would avoid excessive risk taking by banks. However, in December of 1976, a series of *financieras* defaulted on their deposits. This led to the intervention of the Banco Osorno, which was at the center of a large business group. The government bailed out 100 percent of the deposits of the troubled *financieras*. In addition, an explicit deposit guarantee of approximately US$2500 per depositor was put in place. A series of authors have argued that the bailout of the *financieras* led to the belief that all deposits would be guaranteed (see Arellano 1983; Velasco 1991; and De la Cuadra and Valdés-Prieto 1992). There were also official statements from authorities that reinforced this idea. This belief would explain why, despite repeated problems with banks and *financieras* in the late 1970s, there never was a substantial run on deposits in Chile (Velasco 1991).

Rules setting prudential constraints on lending and investment portfolios and those forcing the timely disclosure of accurate information evolved slowly over the period 1975–82. In addition, the government recognized its limited enforcement capacity, so many rules (in particular those regulating related lending) were poorly enforced. Early legislation (1975) setting a maximum individual holding of bank property at 3 percent was discarded after extensive abuse. As a result, recently privatized banks were purchased by existing and new *grupos* (conglomerates). It was only after three large banks and a series of *financieras* (which together made up 8 percent of deposits) went into crisis in late 1981 that limits on related lending were introduced. However, no consideration was made in these limits for firm ownership structure, so that binding limits on related lending were really only introduced in 1982. The result was highly concentrated lending. For example, Arellano (1983) argues that one of the causes of the Fluxa group intervention was the high concentration of assets, mostly to related companies (see also Moulian and Vergara 1979).

Evaluating the health of a bank therefore required information not only on the bank itself but also on the financial health of the conglomerate. Information available to depositors was also limited by the slow implementation of loan risk classification rules by regulators. Although the Chilean Bank Superintendency (SBIF) was authorized to classify loans by risk as early as January 1978, it did not issue specific rules for this classification until February 1980 and did not fully enforce classification until 1982.

At the same time as cross-ownership and the lack of risk classification mechanisms made private monitoring extremely costly, the growing belief of full deposit insurance lowered the incentives for this monitoring. Compounding the problem, legislation setting prudential constraints on lending and investment portfolios evolved slowly and in some cases was weakly enforced by the government. The presumption was that private monitoring and legislation classifying managers' actions as fraud (punishable by prison terms) were enough to limit excessive risk taking by banks. As argued by Barandiarán and Hernández (1999), the government was keen for the financial sector to help reactivate the economy; hence, "rules on collateral were simple and many loans were not properly secured, rules on non-performing loans and loss provisions were below international standards, rules for asset classification were only implemented gradually." Capital adequacy ratios existed (5 percent of liabilities), but their effectiveness was limited by a weak asset classification system.

Another factor that was indicative of the great distress that was incubating in the financial system was the high interest rates, as well as spreads between lending and borrowing rates. At the time of the liberalization real loan rates climbed to more than 60 percent, which by 1980 had declined to 12 percent. But as the crisis was emerging, real loan rates increased sharply, to 39 percent in 1981 and 35 percent in 1982, even with a fully open capital account. One could think that there could be an overshooting at the early stages of the financial liberalization (De la Cuadra and Valdés-Prieto 1992). Although it is not easy to rationalize the magnitudes in Chile, it is more difficult to argue that such overshooting was the case in the early 1980s. Nor can one explain the high rates as a peso problem.[17] The most likely factor was the rollover of bad loans made by banks, which was due to the expected bailout that banks perceived as financial fragility was growing, a problem that was exacerbated by related lending.

All in all, it is not possible to determine how much of the ensuing credit growth was the result of "excessive" risk taking by banks. What is clear, however, is that the incentives for risky behavior by banks were present and that prudential regulation was weak and unable to prevent this conduct. Legislation had to be modified continuously as regulators became aware of highly concentrated lending patterns and risky loans. This was not a healthy financial system that collapsed because of the large external shocks that hit the economy in the early 1980s: prior to 1983, the country had already seen two episodes of substantial banking distress.

The flip side of the lending boom was large capital inflows to the banking sector. As we mentioned above, international borrowing financed a substantial share of bank lending in the early 1980s. After 1980, banks had open access to international capital markets. With their funding base suddenly expanded, banks intermediated large volumes of foreign debt—all of which was denominated in dollars. By regulation, banks were required to match the currency composition of their liabilities with their assets, and hence they lent sizable amounts to local firms in dollar-indexed debt. This matching did not mean, however, that banks were not exposed to large systemic risks due to currency exposure. It simply meant that the risk was shifted to the corporate balance sheets. Banks traded currency risk for systemic default risk. We return to the evidence on mismatch in section 6.7.

Even if they were aware of this risk, bank regulators had a limited abil-

---

17. See Velasco (1991) for further discussion and additional references.

ity to deal with it because of the existing exchange rate system. How could banks set provisions or cap exposure for exchange rate risk if central bank authorities (by fixing the exchange rate) were committing to eliminating this risk completely?

In the end, some combination of excessive idiosyncratic risk (due to bank moral hazard) and systemic risk (due to large exchange rate exposure) precipitated the financial crisis. The interaction of a poor financial regulation and the systemic risk generated by a fixed exchange rate was a key determinant of this outcome.

6.5   Exchange Rate Regimes and International Borrowing

An interesting fact about the Chilean experience is that the large inflows of 1996–97 occurred in the presence of massive reserve accumulation, a commitment to a (relatively) stable exchange rate, and capital controls. As discussed above, existing evidence indicated that capital controls did not have a major impact on these inflows. In this section we turn to another aspect of the Chilean policy mix that we argue did play a central role in the Chilean international borrowing experience: the exchange rate regime.

Standard approaches to international capital flows assume risk neutrality across the board and therefore focus exclusively on uncovered interest parity (or the failure of it) as an explanation for capital movements. However, if borrowers in emerging markets are risk averse, then the decision to borrow from abroad will depend not only on the expected interest rate differential between domestic and foreign loans, but also on the variance of debt service payments in the domestic currency. All else being equal, a more volatile nominal exchange rate (or real exchange rate if the relevant variance is of real peso values of debt payments) will make dollar borrowing relatively less attractive to risk-averse local borrowers whose income is denominated in the local currency. The role of the "currency mismatch" implicit in this argument has received extensive attention in the recent literature on the balance sheet effects of currency mismatches and their role in recent financial crises. Firms or consumers faced with a large depreciation and unhedged dollar liabilities experience a negative net worth shock, which leads to lower output, investment, or consumption.[18]

All else being equal, we should expect firms and consumers to take these balance sheet effects into consideration when choosing the level and currency composition of their foreign debt. If currency composition is not a choice, as is indeed the case for most emerging market economies (see Eichengreen, Hausmann, and Panizza 2004), then for a given expected in-

---

18. Krugman (1999a, 1999b) presents a stylized version of this effect, while Aghion, Bacchetta, and Banerjee (2001) and Céspedes, Chang, and Velasco (2004) incorporate this mechanism into more fully articulated models.

terest rate differential between foreign and domestic debt, the level of foreign debt will be decreasing in the expected variance of the exchange rate. This implies that countries with credible fixed or managed exchange rates should, all else being equal, experience larger debt inflows. Furthermore, even if the fixed exchange rate is not credible, it may still have a positive effect on inflows if agents believe that an exchange rate precommitment makes a government bailout in the case of a devaluation more likely or prevents banking regulation from explicitly addressing exchange rate risk. In the previous section we discussed how this might have operated in the banking system in Chile in the early 1980s, where regulators had their hands tied when it came to regulating the risks arising from dollar lending. Similar concerns have been expressed for the case of Argentina, where dollarization also extended to domestic debt contracts. Beyond the banking system, the preferential exchange rate agreements put in place after the Chilean crisis in 1982 are one form of such a bailout: dollar-indebted firms were allowed to buy discounted dollars with which to pay off their dollar debts. If indeed firms in Chile in the early 1980s believed that the government would bail them out in the event of depreciation, they were ultimately proven right by the events that unfolded after the peg was abandoned.

In this section we want to test this hypothesis empirically so as to determine to what extent the exchange rate regime may have played an important part in Chile's international borrowing experience. However, the many policies and external conditions prevailing in Chile at the time make it impossible to separate the effects of the exchange rate regime from those of capital controls on the evolution of capital inflows. Because of this, we estimate the effects of capital controls and the exchange rate regime on capital inflows using cross-country regressions. We examine the period of large capital inflows from 1991 to 1997 to explore the effects of capital controls and the exchange rate regime on the speed of inflows. Our dependent variable is the increase in external debt. For this variable we use two measures: the increase in the ratio of external debt to GDP and the rate of growth of external debt.

We estimate regressions for the increase in debt on the exchange rate regime and the extent of capital controls, and other control variables that may affect international borrowing. The other control variables are exchange rate volatility, the rate of growth of the economy, and the initial ratio of external debt to GDP.

We compute the volatility of the exchange rate during the period, as the volatility of the monthly exchange rate, to control for fluctuations in the exchange rate. Perhaps what makes a difference regarding the volume of capital inflows is the actual fluctuation of the exchange rate rather than the declared exchange rate regime. A highly volatile exchange rate may prevent investors from taking advantage of arbitrage opportunities to avoid losses from exchange rate risk. However, from the point of view of expectations

of market participants it is essential to understand the logic of the authorities when intervening in the foreign exchange market, and hence volatility
could exacerbate flows under the presumption that authorities will intervene as a result of fear of floating. For this reason we still think that the
declared exchange rate regime is relevant. The impact of exchange rate
volatility on capital inflows is different if volatility happens in a fixed or
floating exchange rate regime.

Growth is clearly endogenous, and what should affect the increase in
borrowing is the growth potential. For this reason, the predicted value of
growth for the period 1990–95 from cross-country growth regressions,
from De Gregorio and Lee (2004), was used as an exogenous variable. This
variable should proxy for the potential of the economy and, hence, for the
demand for international borrowing.

We also consider the initial level of external debt to GDP.[19] This variable
could have either a positive or a negative effect on indebtedness. The negative effect could come from the fact that a high initial level of debt may indicate that the economy may be closer to a point where solvency could be
questioned, which could slow down the availability of debt. However, we
could observe a positive sign, when a large level of foreign debt may be a
signal that the country is less liquidity constrained, and so it has more
funds available to borrow.

To proxy for capital controls we use the index constructed by Chinn and
Ito (2002). This index is based on four dummy variables. One indicates
whether the country has multiple exchange rates; the second indicates the
existence of restrictions on current account transactions; the third is based
on restriction on capital accounts transactions; and the last one is based on
the requirement of the surrender of export receipts. The global index on
capital control intensity is the first standardized principal component of
the four indexes. Chinn and Ito (2002) are interested in the effects of financial integration, so their measure takes a higher value the more open the
country is to cross-border transactions; hence, this is an index increasing
in financial integration. In contrast, we are interested in the extent of capital controls, and for this reason we multiply the Chinn-Ito index by –1 to
have an index increasing in capital controls. Therefore, we would expect
that when capital controls are effective, an increase in the index (more controls) should result in a decline of international borrowing, and hence the
coefficient should be negative. We also used the proxy constructed by
Quinn (2003), and the results are basically the same, although in that case
we had fewer observations.

To control for the exchange rate regime we use the index constructed by
Levi Yeyati and Sturzenegger (2005). We consider their de jure and de facto

---

19. We could also have controlled for initial GDP, as proposed by Lane (2004), but this is
in the growth forecast and also related to the initial level of debt.

definitions for their three-way classification (fixed, managed, and floating). To initiate our investigation we include the intermediate regime together with the fixed. Later on, we separate the three regimes.

We construct a cross section of countries with an initial sample of eighty middle- and high-income countries, but because of data availability we end up reporting regressions for twenty-six to fifty-seven observations. This will also help us check the robustness of the results to changes in the sample.

The first set of regressions is presented in table 6.4, where fixed and managed exchange rate regimes are put together. The dependent variable is the change in the debt-output ratio. Regressions (1) to (4) present the de jure classification, and (5) to (8) the de facto one. The coefficient on the exchange rate regime appears with a positive sign and is always significant at conventional significance levels. This evidence confirms that countries with fixed or managed exchange rate regimes experienced a larger increase in external debt. The coefficient on the volatility of the exchange rate is always not significantly different from zero.

Regarding capital controls, the coefficient of the proxy for capital controls is only marginally significant, and with the wrong sign, when the exchange rate regime variable is based on the de facto classification and the growth forecast is excluded (regression [6]). The result could be due to correlations between the exchange rate regime and the pervasiveness of capital controls. In fact, it is expected that the more controlled the exchange rate regime is, the more likely is the prevalence of capital controls. However, the correlation between the de jure classification and the index of capital controls is zero, and with the de facto classification the correlation is only 0.25 in our sample, so the insignificance of the capital controls variable does not stem from the correlation of controls with the exchange rate regime.

For the other two variables used in the regressions we found that growth forecast has the expected sign, although it is insignificant in all the specifications. On the other hand, the initial level of debt with respect to GDP is negative, consistent with the idea that as debt increases borrowing constraints in international financial markets may become more relevant.

As a final check to examine whether the irrelevance of some variables is due to possible correlations with the exchange rate regime, regression (9) excluded the exchange rate regime altogether from the regression. As the table shows, the insignificance of exchange rate volatility, capital controls, and the growth forecast remains.

We run the same regressions for the percent change in external debt, and the results are similar, although the exchange rate regime is not significant in some of the regressions. The problem may be due to the fact that the fixed exchange rate regime is classified together with the intermediate. For this reason, in tables 6.5 and 6.6 we separate the three exchange rate

Table 6.4   Regression results (dependent variable: Change in debt-GDP ratio, 1991–97)

Independent variables	Classification de jure					Classification de facto			
	(1)	(2)	(3)	(4)	(5)	(6)	(7)	(8)	(9)
Fixed and managed exchange rate	0.170**	0.166***	0.148**	0.095*	0.181**	0.169	0.184**	0.135**	
	(0.068)	(0.065)	(0.071)	(0.059)	(0.074)	(0.067)	(0.074)	(0.063)	
Exchange rate volatility	0.111	0.216	0.050	0.255	−0.268	−0.206	−0.350	−0.074	−0.018
	(0.391)	(0.389)	(0.412)	(0.417)	(0.390)	(0.382)	(0.405)	(0.413)	(0.039)
Capital controls	0.035	−0.029			0.050	0.052*			0.028
	(0.032)	(0.028)			(0.033)	(0.029)			(0.033)
Growth forecast 1990–95	0.553		1.011		0.445		0.965		0.995
	(1.413)		(1.391)		(1.443)		(1.479)		(1.442)
External debt–GDP 1990	−0.029***	−0.474***	−0.360***	−0.595	−0.385***	−0.521***	−0.390***	−0.617***	−0.356***
	(0.087)	(0.076)	(0.116)	(0.059)	(0.090)	(0.069)	(0.122)	(0.390)	(0.109)
R^2	0.49	0.58	0.42	0.84	0.49	0.61	0.47	0.86	0.38
No. of observations	27	37	29	56	26	34	27	47	31

Notes: All regressions estimated with ordinary least squares (OLS). Robust standard errors in parentheses.

***Significant at the 1 percent level.

**Significant at the 5 percent level.

*Significant at the 10 percent level

Table 6.5   Regression results (dependent variable: Change in debt-GDP ratio, 1991–97)

Independent variables	Classification de jure						Classification de facto			
	(1)	(2)	(3)	(4)	(5)	(6)	(7)	(8)	(9)	(10)
Fixed exchange rate	0.268***	0.249***	0.171*	0.274***	0.274***	0.215	0.327***	0.162	0.287***	0.287***
	(0.099)	(0.064)	(0.103)	(0.042)	(0.042)	(0.145)	(0.078)	(0.143)	(0.059)	(0.058)
Managed exchange rate	0.08	0.158**	0.091	0.239***	0.242***	0.184*	0.242***	0.177*	0.323***	0.317***
	(0.086)	(0.076)	(0.099)	(0.066)	(0.065)	(0.102)	(0.082)	(0.106)	(0.059)	(0.055)
Floating exchange rate	−0.013	0.05	−0.018	0.17***	0.181***	0.011	0.108	−0.011	0.169***	0.169***
	(0.080)	(0.071)	(0.093)	(0.060)	(0.057)	(0.096)	(0.070)	(0.100)	(0.057)	(0.057)
Exchange rate volatility	0.21	0.242	0.071	0.264		−0.232	−0.116	−0.366	−0.128	
	(0.361)	(0.387)	(0.414)	(0.420)		(0.419)	(0.395)	(0.427)	(0.430)	
Capital controls	0.499*	0.034				0.053	0.059*			
	(0.029)	(0.028)				(0.350)	(0.030)			
Growth forecast 1990–95	−0.423		0.832			−0.36***		1.023		
	(1.364)		(1.408)			(0.128)		(1.563)		
External debt–GDP 1990	−0.358***	−0.473***	−0.363***	−0.594***	−0.594***		−0.512***	−0.384***	−0.615***	−0.615***
	(0.100)	(0.075)	(0.116)	(0.037)	(0.037)		(0.080)	(0.130)	(0.039)	(0.039)
R^2	0.59	0.60	0.44	0.84	0.85	0.50	0.62	0.47	0.86	0.87
No. of observations	27	37	29	56	56	26	34	27	47	47

Notes: All regressions estimated with ordinary least squares (OLS). Robust standard errors in parentheses.

***Significant at the 1 percent level.

**Significant at the 5 percent level.

*Significant at the 10 percent level

Table 6.6 Regression results (dependent variable: Percent change in external debt, 1991–97)

Independent variables	Classification de jure						Classification de facto			
	(1)	(2)	(3)	(4)	(5)	(6)	(7)	(8)	(9)	(10)
Fixed exchange rate	1.31***	1.058***	1.128***	0.985***	0.988***	0.724	1.034***	0.87*	0.927***	0.927***
	(0.958)	(0.244)	(0.343)	(0.257)	(0.255)	(0.516)	(0.284)	(0.474)	(0.348)	(0.344)
Managed exchange rate	0.955***	0.909***	0.925***	1.133***	1.17***	1.193***	1.377***	1.242***	1.407***	1.404***
	(0.340)	(0.290)	(0.332)	(0.369)	(0.349)	(0.365)	(0.300)	(0.350)	(0.349)	(0.326)
Floating exchange rate	0.63*	0.594**	0.605*	0.858**	0.867**	0.746**	0.938***	0.757**	0.711**	0.711**
	(0.318)	(0.270)	(0.310)	(0.405)	(0.400)	(0.342)	(0.254)	(0.330)	(0.340)	(0.336)
Exchange rate volatility	0.752	0.867	0.777	0.882		-0.889	-0.569	-0.625	-0.06	
	(1.433)	(1.466)	(1.382)	(2.588)		(1.493)	(1.443)	(1.416)	(2.553)	
Capital controls	-0.062	-0.056				-0.101	-0.037			
	(0.118)	(0.106)				(0.126)	(0.111)			
Growth forecast 1990–95	1.744		3.677			5.623		4.471		
	(5.417)		(1.382)			(5.547)		(5.174)		
External debt–GDP 1990	-0.759*	-0.683**	-0.747*	-0.532**	-0.532**	-0.735	-0.898***	-0.818*	-0.502**	-0.502**
	(0.399)	(0.286)	(0.389)	(0.230)	(0.229)	(0.452)	(0.294)	(0.429)	(0.232)	(0.229)
R^2	0.34	0.23	0.29	0.10	0.31	0.34	0.28	0.33	0.15	0.35
No. of observations	27	37	29	56	56	26	34	27	47	47

Notes: All regressions estimated with ordinary least squares (OLS). Robust standard errors in parentheses.

***Significant at the 1 percent level.

**Significant at the 5 percent level.

*Significant at the 10 percent level

regimes using dummy variables. Both tables report the same regressions, and the only difference is in the dependent variable. Table 6.5 presents the results for the change in the external debt–GDP ratio, and table 6.6 the results for the percent change of external debt.

The results are similar to those of table 6.4. The volatility of the exchange rate and the growth forecast are generally insignificant. Capital controls only appear marginally significant in two regressions of table 6.5, and again with the wrong sign. On the other hand, the ratio of initial external debt to GDP is always negative and significant at conventional levels.

The regressions show that external debt grew more in countries with fixed and managed exchange rates than in countries with flexible exchange rates. This is valid for the de jure and the de facto classifications, and for the two alternative measures of the dependent variables, as can be seen in both tables. These results also hold for the regressions that include all the controls as well as those that only have the exchange rate regime, and therefore they hold for the more restricted sample of twenty-six observations and the enlarged one with fifty-six observations. The only exception is regression (6) of table 6.6, where we do not find a significant coefficient for fixed exchange rates, but inflows are larger in countries with a managed exchange rate than floating.

Moreover, an interesting result that appears in almost half of the regressions is that the increase in debt is higher in countries with managed exchange rates than in countries with flexible exchange rates. This can be seen in the regressions that have a larger sample, (4), (5), (9), and (10) in both tables, as well as (6)–(8) of table 6.6. In the more restricted sample, the largest increase is in countries with a fixed exchange rate. Although the results still confirm that the lowest increase in debt is in countries with flexible exchange rates, the results are less definite when comparing fixed versus managed exchange rates.

This last result may be explained by the fact that managed exchange rate regimes may be, in some instances, more prone to investors' speculating against the exchange rate regime. As long as managed exchange rates, such as the one in Chile in the 1990s, imply a limited defense on the exchange rate, investors may speculate against the authority capabilities to defend the currency, and hence the results should not be a surprise. This could lend support to the bipolar view on exchange rate regimes, namely that it is better to have fully fixed or floating exchange rate regimes, and middle grounds are dominated by the extremes.

Several other estimations were done to check robustness. First, as the dependent variable we also used the average balance in the financial account over GDP during 1991–97, as well as the average change in net foreign assets as reported by Lane and Milesi-Ferretti (2001). The exchange rate regime was never significant. We interpret this as an indication that the flow that is actually affected by the exchange rate regime is debt, rather than portfolio flows or FDI. We also made some changes to the sample, excluding highly indebted countries and countries with less than $1,000 of per capita GDP. These changes reduced the sample by between two and four in the regressions with twenty-six observations and by up to ten observations in the enlarged sample. There were no changes in the results with those modifications of the sample.

Overall, the international evidence reported here shows those countries with fixed and managed exchange rates are more prone to increases in external debt, and capital controls do not play a significant role in reducing debt inflows. The best way to prevent excessive borrowing is to let the exchange rate fluctuate rather than to use capital controls. More work could be done to check the robustness of our results, but the evidence presented here is already very persuasive.

6.6   International Borrowing and Currency Mismatches

Much recent discussion has emphasized that the currency mismatches that may arise from international borrowing are an important source of international vulnerability. Firms and consumers holding dollar-denominated debt but whose income is not highly correlated with the exchange rate see the local currency value of their debt expand relative to their income and assets following depreciation. This deterioration in their balance sheet reduces, or may even reverse, the expansionary effect a depreciation is assumed to have. With this in mind, this section presents evidence on the extent of currency mismatches in Chile in both the banking and corporate sectors.

We start with data on currency mismatches in 1982. Figure 6.10 shows the mismatch between assets and liabilities denominated in dollars in the banking system. As expected, there were no mismatches in the early 1980s, as regulation forced all domestic loans in dollars to be fully backed by liabilities in dollars.[20] It is clear, therefore, that the currency mismatch that existed in the Chilean economy in 1982 was not on the balance sheets of the banks but in the corporate sector.

There are no detailed data on currency mismatches in the corporate sector during this period. However, some sense of the existing currency imbalances can be obtained by looking at the sectoral composition of the foreign currency lending of the banking system. That there was a currency

20. In Chile regulation regarding currency exposure of the banking system is dictated by the central bank. The first change occurred with the debt crisis in August 1982, when banks were allowed to have a maximum exposure to foreign currency of 20 percent of basic capital (capital plus reserves). Regulation has been basically the same until today. However, in August 1998 the global limit was maintained, but the computation of mismatches distinguished among currencies. The weighting of each currency, which assigns factors of 1, 1.5, and 5, was based on the risk classification of countries of origin.

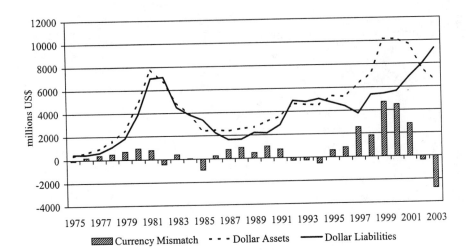

Fig. 6.10   Currency mismatch in the banking system
Sources: Herrera and Valdés (2004), Central Bank of Chile, and IFS.

Table 6.7   Financial system lending by sector in 1981 (in US$ millions)

	Chilean currency	Foreign currency
Agriculture	2,667	647
Mining	292	165
Industry	2,421	1,839
Construction	2,262	908
Commerce	3,995	1,427
Transportation and telecommunications	641	174
Financial services	4,744	453
Nonfinancial services	1,487	n.a.

Source: Arellano (1983).
Note: n.a. = not available.

mismatch problem in the corporate sector is evident in table 6.7. Considering the first three sectors as tradable and the rest as nontradable, the figures show that 53 percent of total loans in foreign currency went to nontradable sectors. We do not have information on the hedging practices of corporations in Chile, but the large devaluation of June 1982 caused the bankruptcy of the banking system, triggered by insolvencies at the corporate level.

Figure 6.10 shows that by the mid-1990s the total dollar value of foreign currency exposure of banks increased. However, as figure 6.11 shows, the magnitudes are small relative to total assets and therefore do not constitute a major source of vulnerability in the banking system. On the whole, the Chilean banking system of the late 1990s is not highly dollarized, a marked

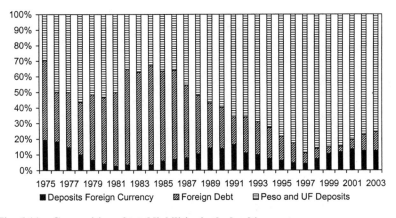

Fig. 6.11   Composition of total liabilities in the banking sector
Sources: Herrera and Valdés (2004), Central Bank of Chile, and IFS.

contrast with the early 1980s. In 1981, about 70 percent of total liabilities were composed of dollar deposit and foreign debt. In contrast, in 2003 this was only 24 percent, and regulation insured that mismatches were within safe limits given banks' levels of capitalization.

As we argue above, a large share of Chilean foreign debt is not intermediated by the banking sector but is held directly by firms. The picture painted by the bank data in figures 6.10 and 6.11 may therefore provide a partial view of total foreign debt in the economy. In addition, as we mentioned above, it is not dollar debt that matters for financial vulnerability but currency mismatches. It is therefore important to know not only how much foreign debt there is, but also who holds the debt—in particular, whether firms whose income is more correlated with the exchange rate are those firms that hold higher foreign liabilities. To do this we turn to firm-level data on the currency composition of firm liabilities.

Our data consist of firm-level accounting information for nonfinancial corporations in Chile for the period 1993 to 2002. In addition, we have data on firm exports and sectors in which the firms operate. Our main source of information is the Ficha Estadistica Codificada y Uniforme (FECU) database of the Superintendencia de Valores y Seguros (SVS).[21] Data on the currency composition of liabilities and assets are not recorded directly in the FECU database but are reported in the notes attached to each firm's annual financial statistics. These notes are neither standardized nor available in an electronic format. Because of this, we start with the data on for-

---

21. The FECU database (available on request from the SVS) has standardized accounting data for all firms categorized as Sociedades Anonimas Abiertas. By law these firms must disclose their accounting information using a standardized format (the FECU). We use nonconsolidated data, so that investments in subsidiaries are reported in a separate account and not as a part of the aggregate stock of fixed assets.

Table 6.8   Distribution of dollar debt, 1993–2002

	1993–1998	1999–2002
Dollar debt (% total liabilities)		
Full sample	23.6	20.5
Nontradable sectors	13.9	12.8
Tradable sectors	34.3	29.2
No exporters ($X < 10\%$ sales)	19.4	15.5
Exporters ($X > 10\%$ sales)	47.7	42.4
Small firms (assets < median)	12.2	8.8
Big firms (assets > median)	35.0	32.1
No dollar assets (<5% assets)	17.7	12.9
Dollar assets (>5% assets)	51.6	45.8
Currency mismatch (% total assets)		
Dollar debt	8.8	8.3
Dollar debt net of derivative position	8.5	7.0
Dollar debt net of derivative position		
and dollar assets	3.1	0.0

Source: Authors' calculations based on SVS data.

eign currency liabilities assembled by Benavente, Johnson, and Morandé (2003).[22] We then input data on foreign currency assets and derivatives collected from each of the notes mentioned above.[23] For our estimates, we use a sample restricted to the nonfinancial firms for which foreign currency data are available. The size of the sample changes as new firms are incorporated into the SVS database, but it consists of about 150 firms.

The distribution of dollar debt is presented in table 6.8, where we separate the entire period in two subperiods: the 1993–98 period of managed exchange rate and capital controls, and the 1999–2002 post–Asian crisis period with flexible exchange rate. The table shows that dollar debt is less than 25 percent of total liabilities over 1993–98 and that this share declines slightly in the second subperiod. The table also shows that firms (and/or lenders) take into account the elasticity of their income to the real exchange rate when choosing currency composition of liabilities, as exporters and firms in the tradable goods sector have a larger share of their liabilities in dollar debt.

In addition, large firms also hold more dollar debt. This has three possible explanations: fixed costs in accessing international capital markets, the size restrictions mentioned in section 6.4, and lower costs of a mismatch, since we would expect that large firms suffer less from fluctuations in their accounting net worth. Finally, firms that hold foreign assets, an-

22. This database is part of a broader effort by the IADB to put together data on firm-level currency composition of liabilities. For more details see Galindo, Panizza, and Schiantarelli (2003).
23. This data set is also used in Cowan, Hansen, and Herrera (2005).

other proxy for the elasticity of income to the real exchange rate, hold more dollar debt. Therefore, as expected or desired, firms that are less vulnerable to exchange rate fluctuations are also those that hold more dollar debt.

The final panel of table 6.8 presents simple measures of currency mismatch. Starting with the ratio of total dollar debt to total assets, we then subtract the net currency derivative position of the firm, and then in turn subtract dollar-indexed assets. Once assets and derivative positions are considered, average currency mismatches for Chilean corporations are below 5 percent of total assets in the first period, and close to zero in the second period.

Cowan, Hansen, and Herrera (2005) confirm that it is this currency mismatch—or exposure—that makes firms financially vulnerable to a depreciation and not dollar debt. Using firm-level data, they fail to find a differential effect of depreciations on firms with higher levels of dollar debt in Chile.[24] In other words, Chilean firms with higher dollar debt do not invest less than their peso-indebted counterparts following depreciation. Cowan and coauthors argue that this result does not invalidate the balance sheet mechanism but that instead it shows the importance of using measures of currency mismatch instead of debt measures to determine vulnerability. Indeed, as we discussed above, the fact that Chilean corporations match the currency composition of their liabilities with that of their incomes means that negative balance sheet effects are offset by positive competitiveness gains, so that dollar debt is a poor measure of mismatch.

The fact that even before the floating of the exchange rate and the elimination of capital controls currency mismatches in Chilean corporations were minor lends support to the idea that firms had a prudent attitude toward exchange rate changes even before the exchange rate was allowed to float. This suggests, in turn, that the exchange rate band did not provide full implicit insurance to those holding unhedged foreign debt and that a sharp exchange rate adjustment before 1999 would not have resulted in serious financial problems for the corporate sector. In addition, more instruments to hedge currency exposure have become available to Chilean firms since the peso started to float, as the foreign exchange derivative market has deepened significantly (De Gregorio and Tokman 2004).

6.7   The United States–Chile Free Trade Agreement

Chile signed a free trade agreement with the United States in 2003. This agreement involved some commitments in terms of capital flows, and a relevant issue is whether Chile could reimpose capital controls, in particular

---

24. These are in line with previous results by Bleakley and Cowan (2002) for five Latin American countries and with more recent results for eight East Asian economies by Luengnaruemitchai (2004).

on inflows. The agreement's chapter on financial services considers the free mobility of capital with no provisions. However, annex 10-C to the chapter on investment establishes some margins to the application of capital controls by establishing the legal actions that investors can take against Chilean authorities in case of disputes regarding controls on capital movements.[25]

In terms of capital controls on outflows, Chile has not used them since the crisis of the 1980s, and even when pressures on the peso were at their maximum in 1998 they were not used. But annex 10-C says that Chile will not incur liabilities for costs arising from the imposition of restrictions on outflows as long as they are not applied for more than a year and the restrictions do not "substantially impede transfers." Therefore, restrictive and focalized measures for up to a year are still possible. But the agreement explicitly excludes transfers from FDI and external debt payments, as agreed in the original terms of the loan, from the one-year restriction on submitting claims.

The most relevant issue is restrictions on capital inflows. Investors may take legal action when they are impeded from investing in Chile. However, there are constraints on these actions. Chile should not be subject to claims from losses incurred within one year from the date restrictions are imposed. The first year can be applied along the same principles as outflows. The treaty also establishes that a claim can be submitted only after one year has elapsed from the loss incurred by the investor, which in fact would result in submission two years after the application of the restriction. In addition, the loss that can be claimed is limited to interest losses only, and no other costs, such as loss of profits or business. There is no class action, and therefore all investors should submit claims independently. Therefore, Chile could still impose capital controls on inflows, although for a shorter period and with less freedom than in the 1990s.

However, the main limit to the application of capital controls in Chile was their workings itself. In order to encourage domestic investors to invest abroad during the application of the *encaje,* most investment abroad was guaranteed the ability to return without having to pay the *encaje.* This amount is large, and current estimates indicate that about $27 billion could return free of *encaje.* Therefore, these investments have plenty of arbitrage opportunities in case Chile reimposes the reserve requirement.

Therefore, Chile's ability to apply capital controls is more limited than in the past. In particular, the ability to impose controls for a year is more relevant for outflows than inflows. The historical experience suggests that transitory controls are more important to outflows, to prevent them during a speculative attack, than to inflows, which require a longer-term application. The limitations of Chile to impose capital controls is the com-

---

25. This annex is reproduced in appendix B of this paper.

bined result of the Free Trade Agreement with the United States and, more important, the same regulations and guarantees granted during the period of capital inflows. Regardless the feasibility of application of controls, the relevant question is their desirability. In the case of Chile, the financial system is strong, there is a credible flexible exchange rate regime—with minimal reasons for fear of floating (De Gregorio and Tokman 2004)—and inflation is low. Therefore, the arguments used to impose capital controls in the 1990s are much less important today, and, in addition, as argued in this paper, it is not clear that the controls were even effective.

6.8   Why Did Chile Not Have a Sudden Stop?

Following the Asian-Russian crisis Chile experienced a sharp reversal in net capital flows, which has led many observers to use it as example of sudden stops in capital inflows. Total net inflows fell from over $6 billion in 1997 to $0.5 billion per year during 1999–2000. As seen in table 6.9, this drop is comparable to, and in some cases larger than, that experienced by other emerging economies that underwent capital account reversals during the 1990s. These events raise the question of Chile's external vulnerability. Why, despite relatively low levels of foreign debt, low currency mismatches,

Table 6.9   **Sudden stops in emerging economies**

	Δ net inflows (% GDP)	% explained by inflows
Argentina 1995	−6.0	64.0
Argentina 2001	−15.1	92.1
Colombia 1998	−6.9	95.6
Ecuador 1999	−48.3	84.8
Mexico 1995	−10.5	91.5
Peru 1997	−8.8	94.3
Indonesia 1998	−9.5	102.7
Korea 1998	−6.1	177.2
The Philippines 1997	−18.5	6.8
Thailand 1997	−19.8	100.3
Turkey 1994	−7.3	147.7
Turkey 1998	−11.4	103.8
Turkey 2001	−11.7	106.5
Average (no Chile)	−13.8	97.5
Chile 1982	−24.5	109.3
Chile 1998	−7.6	−39.1

Sources: Authors' construction based on IFS data. Sudden-stop episodes are from Calvo, Izquierdo, and Mejía (2004).

Notes: Δ net inflows correspond to the difference between the maximum value of net inflows in $[t-3, t]$ and the minimum value in $[t, t+3]$, where t is the year of the sudden stop. Δ net inflows are scaled by $t-1$ (GDP).

and relatively high levels of (allegedly) safe foreign direct investment, was Chile vulnerable to a capital account reversal of this magnitude? In this section we argue that the negative shock to the supply of international capital played a minor role in the collapse of net capital flows to Chile. Indeed, the size of the international liquidity shock, the causes of the adjustment, and the mechanism through which the different shocks were amplified set Chile apart from other emerging economies that experienced sudden stops in the late 1990s. We argue that in Chile an initial large current account deficit, a sharp decline in the terms of trade, a contractionary monetary policy, and the defense of the currency were the factors that triggered the adjustment in capital flows. In fact, Chile's situation is better understood as a current account reversal combined with a sudden start in capital outflows by domestic residents than a sudden stop in the inflows by nonresidents.

The main lesson from this experience is (once again!) that consistent macroeconomic policy matters, irrespective of the structure of gross foreign liabilities. As we documented above, despite controls on capital inflows Chile had grown increasingly integrated into international capital markets (a point also made recently by Milesi-Ferretti and Lane 2005). As a consequence of this integration—and in much the same way as in Europe in the early 1990s—inconsistent macro policy led to large net capital movements despite the high share of "safe" FDI in Chilean international liabilities. An additional lesson is that recent attention to the third-generation currency crisis is justified by what happened in Asia, but not in Chile. Indeed, as financial integration increases, previous varieties of crisis may become more likely in emerging market economies.

6.8.1   Sudden Stop or Sudden Start?

In the later part of the Asian-Russian crisis and its immediate aftermath, the period 1998–99, net capital inflows to Chile dropped by close to 8 percent of GDP. At the same time, the external financing conditions for Chile deteriorated, pushing up the cost of international borrowing. Figure 6.12 shows the spread between the returns on Chilean corporate and public bonds and the rates on U.S. treasury bills. Between 1997 and 1999, the spread on Chilean corporate bonds doubled. Data for public bonds suggest a similar pattern for sovereign spreads. The timing of the rising spread on Chilean bonds coincides with large hikes in the spread on bonds from other emerging market economies, as measured by the spread aggregate emerging markets bond index. The rise of corporate and sovereign spreads in 1998, and their failure to drop to initial levels even after the current account deficit was closed in 2000, is evidence that, along with many other emerging markets, Chile experienced a negative shock to the supply of international savings.

Despite similar patterns on spreads and the net capital account, Chile is

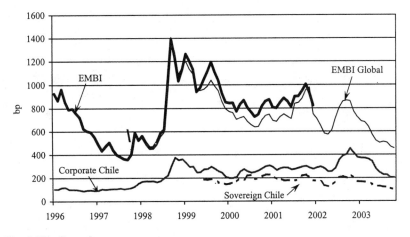

Fig. 6.12 Spreads
Sources: Merrill Lynch and JPMorgan.
Note: Sovereign spread corresponds to EMBI global Chile.

different from other countries that experienced sudden stops in the late 1990s. The first is in the level of country risk measured by the bond spreads. Even at its peak, risk premia on Chilean corporate bonds was lower than the average emerging market risk before the Asian crisis (see figure 6.12). Moreover, there are episodes where the corporate bond spread has been even higher, such as the second semester of 2002, and the domestic consequences were much smaller than during the Asian-Russian crisis, additional evidence that the problem was not mainly with foreign lending but with other factors.

Second, Chile ranks low in many of the variables that Calvo, Izquierdo, and Mejía (2004) identify as determinants of sudden stops, a point made originally by Calvo and Talvi (2005). According to Calvo, Izquierdo, and Mejía (2004), sudden stops are usually the result of an international credit shock that is amplified by the interaction between currency mismatches and a real depreciation. Faced with restricted access to international credit, currencies are forced to depreciate to close the gap between the current and capital accounts, with the size of depreciation depending on the relative size of the tradable sector. For those countries with large unhedged foreign currency liabilities, this depreciation causes large negative balance sheet effects that amplify the initial shock and lead to further reductions in output and expenditure. In Chile, dollar liabilities in the banking sector are small, and the corporate sector is relatively well hedged, as shown in section 6.6. Mismatches in the public sector are also small, even before including copper revenues in the picture (Ministerio de Hacienda 2006).

The behavior of gross capital flows sheds light on what was happening with capital flows in Chile at the time of the sudden stop. Figure 6.13 shows

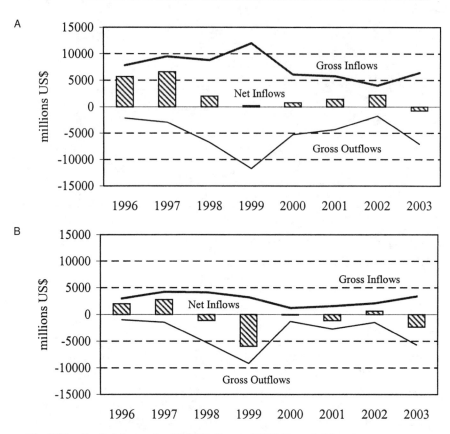

Fig. 6.13   Capital flows: *A,* with FDI; *B,* net of FDI (financial flows)
Source: IFS.

the path of gross inflows and outflows for Chile over 1996–2003. Following the Asian-Russian crisis, total gross inflows into Chile actually increased, while non-FDI gross inflows remained virtually unchanged. Gross outflows, on the other hand, increased substantially, peaking at over $10 billion during 1999. There is no clear evidence that access to foreign capital was curtailed, as gross outflows explain the bulk of the collapse in net inflows.

The relative importance of gross inflows and outflows in the Chilean episode is atypical within sudden-stop episodes in emerging economies. The last column of table 6.9 shows the share of the net capital reversal during the sudden-stop episodes in emerging markets that is explained by changes in gross inflows. In the average sudden-stop episode experienced by emerging economies 98 percent of the net capital flow reversal can be explained by changes in gross inflows—that is, by stops or reversals in the flow of funds from nonresidents. Since inflows actually increased in Chile

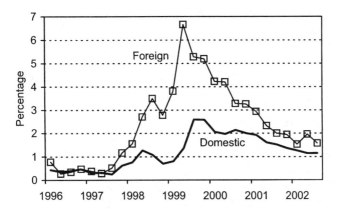

Fig. 6.14   Bank assets and currency mismatches, foreign assets (% total assets)
Sources: Caballero, Cowan, and Kearns (2005), Bank Superintendency of Chile, and IFS.
Notes: Dollar assets were calculated as the sum of dollar-denominated loans and foreign assets, and dollar liabilities as the sum of dollar-denominated deposits and foreign liabilities. Foreign banks are those in which more than 50 percent of equity is owned by nonresidents. Foreign assets are cash in foreign currency, offshore deposits, and offshore investments.

in 1998–99, the share explained by gross inflows is negative. Chile experienced more of a sudden start in outflows than a sudden stop in inflows in this period!

The behavior of two groups of institutional investors explains a large share of the total gross outflows from Chile in this period: pension fund management companies (AFPs) and banks.[26] Pension funds increased the share of foreign assets in their portfolio from close to 1 percent in 1997 to above 10 percent in 1999. This corresponds to capital outflows on the order of 5 percent of GDP. As this rising share of assets coincided with a widening of the legal investment limits on foreign asset holdings for AFPs it is hard to determine whether the outflow was driven by the macroeconomic events of this period or was simply an easing of a binding regulatory constraint.

The behavior of banks is more interesting. Banks contributed to capital outflows by substantially increasing the share of foreign assets in their portfolios. Starting from less than 1 percent in 1997, the ratio of foreign assets to total assets peaked at over 6 percent in 1999 (figure 6.14). This corresponds to an outflow of close to 5 percent of GDP. As shown in the figure, banks also increased their net dollar asset position over this period, taking on more exchange rate risk. This suggests that these outflows were not solely the response of banks looking to hedge rising dollar deposits. Interestingly, the share of foreign assets in total assets declined after the peso

26. See Caballero (2002) and Caballero, Cowan, and Kearns (2005) for a more detailed discussion of this point.

was floated in 1999, but well before country risk returned to its precrisis levels. Both the rising net asset position and the timing of the foreign asset spike suggest that banks took on a net dollar position to take advantage of arbitrage opportunities that arose prior to the currency being floated in 1999. In effect, Chilean residents were betting against an exchange rate policy that tried to minimize depreciations, while in fact the large negative external shocks pushed the equilibrium real exchange rate upward. The position against the peso that was taken by banks and the fear of floating on the part of the authorities induced the central bank to severely tighten liquidity in the interbank market in 1998.[27]

Finally, the timing of events also sets Chile apart from countries that experienced sudden stops. The Chilean peso came under severe pressure in January 1998. This led to an immediate monetary tightening, which successfully fended off a depreciation (during 1998 the peso only depreciated 8 percent). The international liquidity shock, evident in the evolution of spreads (figure 6.12), only began in July-August 1998. Therefore, in terms of timing, the original shock came from the exchange rate and monetary policy response.

6.8.2   Exchange Rate Policy

Following the Asian crisis in 1997 Chile's terms of trade deteriorated significantly, pushing up the equilibrium real exchange rate. Concerned with the effects of a nominal depreciation on inflation, and the loss of credibility that this would entail if the fixed annual inflation target was not met, the Chilean central bank set out to minimize the nominal devaluation and rein in nominal demand. To do so it implemented a contractionary monetary policy (figure 6.15).[28] In part the monetary contraction was also aimed at closing a large current account deficit. Since mid-1997 the current account deficit had been increasing, reaching a peak of about 8 percent of GDP in 1998, which authorities believed was unsustainable (figure 6.16). Simultaneously the Central Bank intervened in the foreign exchange market, selling close to $2 billion in reserves in 1998 alone.

The combination of a negative terms-of-trade shock, rising international interest rates, and contractionary domestic monetary policy led to a substantial slowdown in economic activity. Output growth fell from over 6 percent in 1997 and 1996 to 3 percent in 1998, and then it declined by 1 per-

27. De Gregorio and Tokman (2004) argue that there were no reasons for fear of floating since balance sheet effects were not sufficient to cause serious financial distress and the pass-through from exchange rate to prices was relatively low to instill fear of an outburst of inflation.

28. These are monthly figures. Daily figures show more clearly the extent of the domestic liquidity squeeze. In January 1998 rates went up to 100 percent in one day, and in July and September it reached almost 60 percent. The figure shows up to July 2001, since until then the policy interest rates, and most market rates, were set in terms of the UF (a Chilean unit of account indexed to the price level).

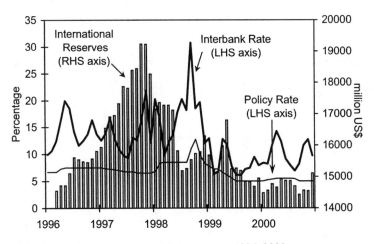

Fig. 6.15   International reserves and interest rates 1996–2000
Source: Central Bank of Chile.

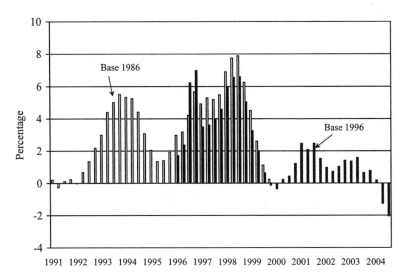

Fig. 6.16   Current account deficit (% GDP)
Source: Central Bank of Chile.

cent in 1999. Simultaneously, unemployment rose from 5 percent to over 8 percent in 1999 (figure 6.17). As in the Obstfeld (1996) currency crisis model (second generation), the rising output cost of the currency defense pushed up depreciation expectations, which in turn made the defense of the currency increasingly costly. This resulted in capital outflows of agents (banks in particular!) wishing to cash in on arbitrage opportunities from the gradual depreciations during 1998 and 1999. As we argued before, a

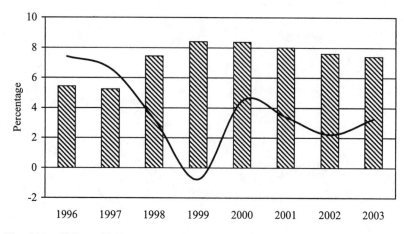

Fig. 6.17   Chilean GDP growth and unemployment rate
Source: Central Bank of Chile.

gradually appreciating exchange rate induces inflows. This experience reinforces that argument by showing that gradual depreciations promote outflows. Capital outflows by the banks, the portfolio recomposition by the AFPs, and a contractionary monetary policy all combined to generate a severe credit crunch, depressing consumption and investment and leading to a large reduction in the current account.

Overall, the Chilean experience was the result of a reversal in the current account, induced primarily by a very tight monetary policy and domestic liquidity squeeze, a sharp decline in terms of trade, and a strong defense of the peso. The pressures on the peso were caused by international turmoil and a change in the equilibrium exchange rate of Chile, after the deterioration of external conditions. In contrast, the international liquidity shock that caused a sudden stop in many emerging markets played a secondary role.

6.9   Conclusions

What then are the lessons from the Chilean experience with international borrowing?

The first is that domestic financial regulations, in particular regarding the financial system, play a crucial role in determining the level and composition of capital inflows. Despite a more restrictive *encaje* in the early 1980s than in the 1990s, and regulations limiting bank balance sheet currency mismatches, poor regulation of the banking system in Chile led to large inflows of debt, a substantial part of which was on-lent to the nontradable sector. The resulting corporate mismatch and additional problems such as asset concentration due to related lending and expectations of bank bailout contributed to the deep financial crisis that Chile experienced in 1982.

The second, and perhaps more important, lesson is that the exchange rate regime plays an important role in determining debt inflows, currency mismatches, and financial vulnerabilities. Fixed exchange rates, such as the one Chile had between 1979 and 1982, provide an implicit guarantee to borrowers and lenders alike. As long as the regime holds, borrowers and lenders are protected from exchange rate volatility. If, on the other hand, the currency depreciates, agents believe that they are entitled to transfers and bailouts from the government, leading to excessive risk taking ex ante. Ex post they have usually been proven right, as in the case of preferential exchange rate deals in Chile or, more recently, the pesification in Argentina. A fixed exchange rate regime also makes it very complicated to introduce prudential regulation for currency mismatches into banking legislation. How can you ask banks to insure against an event you are guaranteeing will never happen? But the real problem lies beyond banks, and therefore policies must be consistent with incentives for corporations to avoid excessive mismatches and banks for monitoring it, which requires careful rules to regulate related lending and implicit massive guarantees on the banking system.

More generally, rigidities in the exchange rate system may amplify shocks to the supply of international capital. In good periods, a rigid exchange rate regime provides implicit insurance to borrowers, reducing the risks of interest rate arbitrage. The risk of postponing an adjustment—that is, allowing the exchange rate to appreciate during a surge of capital inflows—is an incentive for further capital to flow in while assets still remain undervalued, putting additional pressures on an appreciation of the currency. In bad periods, delaying depreciations amplifies external shocks by piling higher depreciation expectations onto an already higher risk premium.

Finally, the *encaje* played at most a small role in the size and nature of debt inflows to Chile. Most studies show that it did have an effect on the maturity composition of inflows but that the magnitude of this effect was small. On the other hand, there is little evidence that it had a significant effect on total inflows or on the real exchange rate. Moreover, the proper functioning of restrictions, which attempted to deter flows in and encourage flows out, has its drawbacks. In the Chilean case there is an important stock of investment that left the country when the *encaje* was in place, and in order to encourage the outflow, they were insured to be able to return without the imposition of controls, which limits the scope for restrictive measures.

This paper also raises a series of additional issues regarding the Chilean experience. The first is the role of banks in intermediating capital inflows. Up to 1999, banks in Chile intermediated very little international debt.

Since 1999, this seems to be changing. One explanation for this is the *encaje*. An alternative explanation is the recent development of the derivatives market, which allows banks to borrow abroad without burdening themselves or their borrowers with currency risk. For the development of this market in turn, the internationalization of pension funds and the volatility that the flexible exchange rate regime has brought have been very important.

The second issue is currency mismatches. Using firm-level data for the late 1990s we show that currency exposure in Chilean corporations was low and that it fell after 1999. Bank-level data from 1982, on the other hand, suggest that mismatches in the corporate sector prior to the crisis in 1983 were sizable. Again, the commitment to a fixed exchange rate coupled with weak regulation induces mismatches.

Third, Chile experienced a substantial slowdown in capital inflows in the late 1990s. We argue that the exogenous international credit shock played a minor role in this reversal. Most of the action came from a sudden start of outflows, not from a sudden stop of inflows. Therefore, the Chilean case is better described with second-generation currency crisis models than with more recent models that center on balance sheet effects. In Chile, a negative terms-of-trade shock and an initially large current account deficit were amplified by a sharp tightening of monetary policy and an inconsistent exchange rate policy. The current account reversal that took place was accompanied not by a sudden stop of inflows in the capital account but by a sudden start of outflows. Consistent with the fact that a gradually appreciating currency encourages inflows, a gradually depreciating currency promoted outflows.

Appendix A

Main Capital Controls and Exchange Regulations, 1990–2004

Unremunerated Reserve Requirement

1991 June

A 20 percent reserve requirement is applied to foreign loans. The reserve is for a minimum period of ninety days and a maximum of one year. Prepayments (merchandise must be shipped within six months) and charges are exempt.

1992 January

The 20 percent reserve requirement on foreign loans is extended to commercial banks' sight and term deposits in foreign currency.

June

The reserve required is increased from 20 percent to 30 percent. The reserve period for chapter XIV loans is uniformly set at one year, and, in the case of banks, the days are counted as consecutive days instead of bank working days. A liquidity credit line in dollars is established to constitute the reserve.

1995 July

Secondary ADRs and investments not destined for the formation or increase of a local company's social capital are now subject to a reserve requirement in order to broaden the productive capacity of goods or services, excluding straightforward financial flows.

1996 March

Foreign loans entirely destined for the prepayment of foreign loans that were duly authorized and registered with the central bank are excluded from the reserve requirement, while the weighted average terms of the new loan and the remaining original loan remain similar.

September

The reserve required on firms' foreign loans contracted by way of bond issues is eliminated when the financing thus obtained is to finance investment abroad or to refinance liabilities of the firm's agents or affiliates abroad.

October

A reserve is established for portfolio investment made according to the stipulations of chapter XIV of the Compendium of Foreign Exchange Regulations (CNCI) even when this investment is to constitute or increase the capital of firms already established in the country if it is not made to increase productive capacity of goods and services or to contribute to the firms' productive operation. The reserve requirement is still excepted in the case of investment made to acquire first-issue shares on the grounds of an ADR convention.

December

Loans, capital contributions, and investment for amounts less than US$200,000 are exempt from the reserve requirements, but the same agent must not have exceeded US$500,000 in the past twelve months. This measure is eliminated in 1997.

1998 June

The reserve rate on foreign loans, capital contributions, and investment is lowered from 30 percent to 10 percent for the first year. Short-term banking system liabilities (credit lines and the public's cash deposits) remain subject to the 30 percent reserve, but two-thirds of the reserve will be remunerated.

August

The reserve requirement is lifted from capital inflows destined for ADR arbitrage transactions in the secondary market.

September

The exchange reserve is reduced to zero on all capital inflows. At the same time, the reserve rate on foreign currency sight and term deposits and loans is reduced to make the reserve cost in foreign currency the same as in local currency.

2001 April

The 0 percent reserve requirement on incoming capital is eliminated.

Loans, Investment, and Capital Contributions from Abroad

1993 April

The minimum period that capital contributions entering Chile under the stipulations of chapter XIV of the CNCI must remain in the country is reduced from three years to one year.

2000 May

The minimum period of one year that investments and capital contributions must remain in the country, as stipulated in chapter XIV of the CNCI, is eliminated.

2001 April

The capital account is completely freed by eliminating all remaining restrictions but keeping the requirement that financial-type exchange transactions must be channeled through the formal exchange market and the central bank informed of those exchange operations that it decides. Consequently, prior authorization is no longer needed for capital inflows associated with foreign loans, investment, and capital contributions, the same as for capital outflows associated with capital returns, dividends, and other benefits relating to capital contributions and investments and prepayments of foreign loans. The obligation of selling and/or buying foreign currency on the formal exchange market is also eliminated, as well as the restrictions on the currency in which foreign loans may be granted or taken.

2002 January

Financing obtained from foreign loans, investments, and capital contributions may be freely used abroad, including the capitalization of any outstanding debt abroad.

2003–2004

More simple requirements are set regarding information on all exchange matters regulated by the CNCI.

Bond Issues Abroad

1992 May

Residents in Chile are authorized to obtain foreign loans by placing bonds abroad. Bond issuers must have an A rating from the Risk Classifying Commission of the pension fund administrators.

1994 April

Solvency levels required for banks and nonbanking companies are lowered to BBB and BBB+, respectively. Moreover, nonbanking companies' minimum amount requirement is lowered from US$50 million to US$25 million, stays at US$50 million for banks, and the need for the central bank's express authorization is eliminated.

1995 November

Funding obtained from bond issues abroad no longer has to be brought back to Chile. It can be held in a bank account abroad and used to pay back foreign loans or imports that have been approved and registered with the central bank, or it can be invested in foreign instruments abroad.

1998 April

Minimum amount requirements for bond issues abroad are eliminated, and the required international risk classification of the issuing company is lowered. The weighted average term of subordinated bond issues made by banking companies is lowered from ten to five years to come into line with the new Bank Act. The issue of bonds abroad denominated in Chilean pesos or in UF is authorized, but these cannot be traded or offered in Chile and must be disbursable and payable in foreign currency.

1998 June

Funding generated by bond issues, under the stipulations of chapter XIV, can be put to wider uses, thereby allowing for the issue of bonds for infrastructure.

1999 April

Nonbanking debtors can issue bonds at maturities of less than four years, and the risk classification required for longer-term bonds is lowered.

2000 May

Bonds denominated in Chilean pesos or in UF can now be accepted as liabilities payable in foreign currency. Interest paid on these bonds is thus subject to the same tax rate as traditional bonds denominated in foreign currency (4 percent).

2001 April

Capital inflows obtained from bond issues are no longer restricted by requirements of prior authorization. Also, the requirements of minimum risk classification of the issuing company and minimum weighted term of the bond issues are eliminated.

ADR Issues

1990 April

ADR trading is introduced by which residents abroad can acquire shares in Chilean corporations. Companies must meet requirements with respect to the minimum amount of the issue and risk classification of the firm, differentiating between banking and nonbanking companies.

1998 April

The minimum amount requirement for issuing ADRs is eliminated, and the minimum level of international risk classification is lowered.

August

To simplify capital movements, the reserve requirement on incoming capital for ADR arbitrage operations in the secondary market is eliminated.

2000 April

Chapter XXVI of the CNCI is broadened to allow securities to be issued in stock exchanges abroad by way of instruments other than the ADRs on the New York Stock Exchange. It also allows company development funds and real estate investment funds to issue quotas abroad.

2001 April

Restrictions on ADR issues are eliminated.

Investment Abroad

1991 April

To widen investment opportunities, individuals' own foreign currency or currency that they have acquired on the informal exchange market can now be invested abroad, the central bank being duly informed.[29]

1997 April

Regulation on Chilean residents' investment abroad is changed, mainly in that (a) prior authorization is no longer required, (b) investment permitted abroad of foreign currency acquired through the formal exchange market is widened to include granting loans and buying physical assets, and (c) remittances must be made through the formal exchange market with the due central bank notification.

1998 June

The investment options abroad for foreign currency not acquired on the formal exchange market are now the same as those authorized for foreign currency acquired on the formal exchange market.

1999 November

Chapter XII of the CNCI is modified to contain the regulation on foreign currency remittances or availability of funding for amounts over US$10,000 or the equivalent in other currencies.

2001 April

All remaining restrictions are eliminated, but transactions must still be carried out through the formal exchange market and reported to the central bank.

Exchange Regulations on Institutional Investors

1992 January

Pension fund administrators (AFPs) are allowed to invest a maximum of 1.5 percent of the total value of the fund in securities approved by the Risk Classifying Commission. This limit is gradually increased until, in January 1999, it reaches 16 percent and the limit on investment in variable-income instruments is 10 percent. At the same time, the minimum risk classification of the investment instruments is also gradually lowered.

---

29. The law distinguishes between "formal" and "informal" foreign exchange markets. The formal market is constituted by banks, and the rest comprises the informal sector. The main difference has been only the information requirements.

1994 November

Insurance companies are authorized to invest abroad in financial investments (10 percent of their resources in the case of life insurers and 15 percent in the case of general insurers) and in nonresidential urban property (up to 3 percent). Mutual funds are also allowed to invest abroad (up to 30 percent of their resources).

1996 October

Mutual funds are authorized to invest abroad using foreign currency obtained in the formal exchange market, and the 30 percent limit is increased to 100 percent of their total assets.

1999 February

Insurance companies' limit on financial investment abroad is increased from 15 percent to 20 percent in the case of general insurers and from 10 percent to 15 percent in the case of life insurers.

2003 May

The limit on AFPs' investment abroad is raised to 25 percent; in 2004 it is raised again to 30 percent.

Appendix B

Annex 10-C of the Free Trade Agreement between Chile and the United States

Special Dispute Settlement Provisions: Chile

1. Where a claimant submits a claim alleging that Chile has breached an obligation under Section A, other than Article 10.3, that arises from its imposition of restrictive measures with regard to payments and transfers, Section B shall apply except as modified below:
   (a) A claimant may submit any such claim only after one year has elapsed since the events giving rise to the claim;
   (b) If the claim is submitted under Article 10.15(a)(b), the claimant may, on behalf of the enterprise, only seek damages with respect to the shares of the enterprise for which the claimant has a beneficial interest;
   (c) Loss or damages arising from restrictive measures on capital inflows shall be limited to the reduction in value of the transfers and shall exclude loss of profits or business and any similar consequential or incidental damages;

(d) Paragraph 1(a) shall not apply to claims that arise from restrictions on:
   (i) transfers of proceeds of foreign direct investment by investors
       of the United States, excluding external debt financing covered
       in subparagraph (d)(ii), and excluding investments designed
       with the purpose of gaining direct or indirect access to the fi-
       nancial market; or
   (ii) payments pursuant to a loan or bond issued in a foreign mar-
       ket, including inter- and intra-company debt financing between
       affiliated enterprises made exclusively for the conduct, opera-
       tion, management, or expansion of such affiliated enterprises,
       provided that these payments are made in accordance with the
       maturity date agreed on in the loan or bond agreement;
(e) Excluding restrictive measures referred to in paragraph 1(d), Chile
    shall incur no liability, and shall not be subject to claims, for dam-
    ages arising from its imposition of restrictive measures with regard
    to payments and transfers that were incurred within one year from
    the date on which the restrictions were imposed, provided that such
    restrictive measures do not substantially impede transfers;
(f) A restrictive measure of Chile with regard to payments and trans-
    fers that is consistent with this Annex shall be deemed not to con-
    travene Article 10.2 provided that, as required under existing
    Chilean law, it does not discriminate among investors that enter into
    transactions of the same nature; and
(g) Claims arising from Chile's imposition of restrictive measures with
    regard to payments and transfers shall not be subject to Article
    10.24 unless Chile consents.
2. The United States may not request the establishment of an arbitral
   panel under Chapter Twenty-Two (Dispute Settlement) relating to
   Chile's imposition of restrictive measures with regard to payments and
   transfers until one year has elapsed since the events giving rise to the dispute.
3. Restrictive measures on payments and transfers related to claims under
   this Annex shall otherwise be subject to applicable domestic law.

References

Aghion, P., P. Bacchetta, and A. Banerjee. 2001. Currency crises and monetary policy in an economy with credit constraints. *European Economic Review* 45 (7):
   1121–50.
Arellano, J. P. 1983. De la liberalización a la intervención: El mercado de capitales
   en Chile 1974–83. *Colección Estudios CIEPLAN* 11:9–37.
Barandiarán, E., and L. Hernández. 1999. Origins and resolution of a banking crisis: Chile 1982–86. Working Paper no. 57. Santiago, Chile: Central Bank of
   Chile.

Benavente, J. M., C. Johnson, and F. Moránde. 2003. Debt composition and balance sheet effects of exchange rate depreciations: A firm-level analysis for Chile. *Emerging Markets Review* 4 (4): 397–416.

Bleakley, H., and K. Cowan. 2002. Dollar debt and devaluations: Much ado about nothing? Working Paper no. 02-5. Boston: Federal Reserve Bank of Boston, December.

Caballero, R. 2002. Coping with Chile's external vulnerability: A financial problem. Working Paper no. 154. Santiago: Central Bank of Chile.

Caballero, R., K. Cowan, and J. Kearns. 2005. Reducing external vulnerability through financial development: Lessons from Australia and Chile. *Journal of Policy Reform* 8 (4): 313–54.

Calvo, G., A. Izquierdo, and L. F. Mejía. 2004. On the empirics of sudden stops: The relevance of balance-sheet effects. Research Working Paper no. 509. Washington, DC: Inter-American Development Bank.

Calvo, G., and C. Reinhart. 2002. Fear of floating. *Quarterly Journal of Economics* 177:379–408.

Calvo, G., and E. Talvi. 2005. Sudden stop, financial factors and economic collapse in Latin America: Learning from Argentina and Chile. NBER Working Paper no. 11153. Cambridge, MA: National Bureau of Economic Research.

Céspedes, L. F., R. Chang, and A. Velasco. 2004. Balance sheets and exchange rate policy. *American Economic Review* 94 (4): 1183–93.

Chang, R., and A. Velasco. 1999. Liquidity crises in emerging markets: Theory and policy. NBER Working Paper no. 7272. Cambridge, MA: National Bureau of Economic Research.

Chinn, M., and H. Ito. 2002. Capital account liberalization, institutions and financial development: Cross country evidence. NBER Working Paper no. 8967. Cambridge, MA: National Bureau of Economic Research.

Cifuentes, R., J. Desormeaux, and C. Gónzalez. 2002. Capital markets in Chile: From financial repression to financial deepening. Documento de Política Económica no. 4. BIS Paper no. 11. Basel, Switzerland: Bank for International Settlements.

Cowan, K., E. Hansen, and L. O. Herrera. 2005. Currency mismatches, balance sheet effects and hedging in Chilean non-financial corporations. IADB Working Paper no. 521. Washington, DC: Inter-American Development Bank.

De Gregorio, J., S. Edwards, and R. Valdés. 2000. Controls on capital inflows: Do they work? *Journal of Development Economics* 63 (1): 59–83.

De Gregorio, J., and J. W. Lee. 2004. Growth and adjustment in East Asia and Latin America. *Economia* 5 (1): 69–134.

De Gregorio, J., and A. Tokman. 2004. Overcoming fear of floating: Exchange rate policies in Chile. Working Paper no. 302. Santiago, Chile: Central Bank of Chile, December.

De la Cuadra, S., and S. Valdés-Prieto. 1992. Myths and facts about financial liberalization in Chile: 1974–1983. In *If Texas were Chile*, ed. P. Brock, 11–101. San Francisco, CA: Institute for Contemporary Studies Press.

Diamond, D. W., and P. H. Dybvig. 1983. Bank runs, deposit insurance, and liquidity. *Journal of Political Economy* 91 (3): 401–19.

Edwards, S. 1999. How effective are capital controls? *Journal of Economic Perspectives* 13 (4): 65–84.

Edwards, S., and A. Cox-Edwards. 1991. *Monetarism and liberalization: The Chilean experiment.* Second ed. with a new afterword. Chicago: University of Chicago Press.

Eichengreen, B., R. Hausmann, and U. Panizza. 2004. The pain of original sin. In

Other people's money: Debt denomination and financial instability in emerging market economies, ed. Barry Eichengreen and Ricardo Hausmann. Chicago: University of Chicago Press.

Forbes, K. 2003. One cost of the Chilean capital controls: Increased financial constraints for smaller traded firms. NBER Working Paper no. 9777. Cambridge, MA: National Bureau of Economic Research.

Galindo, A., U. Panizza, and F. Schiantarelli. 2003. Debt composition and balance sheet effects of currency depreciation: A summary of the micro evidence. *Emerging Markets Review* 4 (4): 330–39.

Gallego, F., L. Hernández, and K. Schmidt-Hebbel. 1999. Capital controls in Chile: Effective, efficient? Working Paper no. 59. Santiago, Chile: Central Bank of Chile.

Herrera, L. O., and R. Valdés. 2004. Dedollarization, indexation and nominalization: The Chilean experience. *Journal of Policy Reform* 8 (4): 281–312.

Inter-American Development Bank (IADB). 2005. Unlocking credit: The quest for deep and stable bank lending. http://www.iadb.org/res/ipes/2005/index.cfm.

Jadresic, E., S. Lehman, A. Rojas, J. Selaive, and A. Naudon. 2003. Análisis del balance financiero externo de Chile. Documento de Política Económica no. 7. Santiago, Chile: Central Bank of Chile.

Krugman, P. 1999a. Analytical afterthoughts on the Asian crisis. http://web.mit.edu/krugman/www.

———. 1999b. Balance sheets, the transfer problem, and financial crises. *International Tax and Public Finance* 6 (4): 459–72.

Lane, P. 2004. Empirical perspectives on long-term external debt. *Topics in Macroeconomics* 4 (1): 1152.

Lane, P., and G. Milesi-Ferretti. 2001. The external wealth of nations: Measures of foreign assets and liabilities for industrial and developing countries. *Journal of International Economics* 55 (December): 263–94.

Levy Yeyati, E., and F. Sturzenegger. 2005. Classifying exchange rate regimes: Deeds vs. words. *European Economic Review* 49 (6): 1603–35.

Luengnaruemitchai, P. 2004. The Asian crises and the mystery of the missing balance sheet effect. University of California, Berkeley, Department of Economics. Mimeograph.

Milesi-Ferretti, G. M., and P. Lane. 2005. Financial globalization and exchange rates. IMF Working Paper no. 05/3. Washington, DC: International Monetary Fund.

Ministerio de Hacienda. 2006. Informe de estadísticas de la deuda pública: Junio 2006. http://www.hacienda.gov.cl.

Moulian, T., and P. Vergara. 1979. Coyuntura economica y reacciones sociales: Las fases de la política económica en Chile 1973–78. Apuntes CIEPLAN no. 22. Santiago, Chile: CIEPLAN.

Nadal De Simone, F., and P. Sorsa. 1999. Capital account restrictions in Chile in the 1990s. IMF Working Paper no. 52. Washington, DC: International Monetary Fund.

Obstfeld, M. 1996. Models of currency crises with self-fulfilling features. *European Economic Review* 40:1037–48.

Quinn, D. 2003. Capital account liberalization and financial globalization, 1890–1999: A synoptic view. *International Journal of Finance and Economics* 8 (3): 189–204.

Radelet, S., and J. D. Sachs. 1998. The East Asian financial crisis: Diagnosis, remedies, prospects. *Brookings Papers on Economic Activity,* Issue no. 1:1–74.

Soto, M. 2000. Capital flows and growth in developing countries: Recent empirical evidence. Development Center Technical Paper no. 160. Paris: Organization for Economic Cooperation and Development.

Soto, M., and S. Valdés-Prieto. 1996. ¿Es el control selectivo de capitales efectivo en Chile? Su efecto sobre el tipo de Cambio Real. *Cuadernos de Economía* 33 (98): 77–104.

Velasco, A. 1991. Liberalization, crisis, intervention: The Chilean financial system 1975–1985. In *Banking crises: Causes and issues,* ed. V. Surandarajan and T. Baliño, 113–74. Washington, DC: International Monetary Fund.

7

International Borrowing and Macroeconomic Performance in Argentina

Kathryn M. E. Dominguez and Linda L. Tesar

7.1 Introduction

In the early 1990s Argentina was the darling of international capital markets and viewed by many as a model of reform for emerging markets. Early in his presidency, Carlos Menem embarked on a bold set of economic policies, including the adoption of a currency board that pegged the Argentine peso to the dollar, a sweeping privatization program for state-owned enterprises, an overhaul of the banking system, and privatization of the public pension system. The business press marveled over the rapid turnaround in the Argentine economy. Although there were some concerns about the appropriateness and sustainability of the dollar anchor and whether the fiscal reforms were more rhetoric than reality, the policies appeared to have conquered inflation and set the country on a course of steady economic growth.

By the end of the 1990s, however, Argentina's situation had dramatically changed. The country had weathered the financial crises in Mexico and Asia, and, despite the volatility of capital flows, Argentina's currency board remained intact and forecasts of future growth were relatively positive. The turning point for Argentina came with the Russian default in

Kathryn M. E. Dominguez is a professor of public policy and economics at the University of Michigan and a research associate of the National Bureau of Economic Research. Linda L. Tesar is a professor of economics at the University of Michigan and a research associate of the National Bureau of Economic Research.

We thank Ron Alquist for excellent research assistance. We are grateful for comments and suggestions from Nicolas Magud, Juan Carlos Hallak, Alan Taylor, Martin Feldstein, Barry Eichengreen, Charlie Calomiris, Sebastian Edwards, and an anonymous referee. The views expressed in this document are the authors' and do not necessarily reflect those of the National Bureau of Economic Research.

August 1998, which caused international investors to pull out of all emerging markets, seemingly with little regard for country-specific economic conditions. More bad luck followed in January 1999 when Brazil, Argentina's major trading partner, devalued its currency, further weakening the competitiveness of Argentine exports. Economic growth stalled, and unemployment remained high. Despite the lowering of world interest rates, which helped reduce the cost of external borrowing, the economy was teetering on the brink of default. In 2001 the economy spiraled downward, and depositors scrambled to pull their savings out of the banking system. In a desperate attempt to stave off disaster, the government imposed sweeping capital controls. By 2002, Argentina was in complete political and economic collapse. The currency board was abandoned, the exchange rate was devalued, and eight years of growth in gross domestic product (GDP) were lost.

Argentina's situation cannot be attributed solely to a run of bad luck. Policy decisions made during the 1990s—and, just as important, policy *indecision*—made the country vulnerable to the kinds of shocks that affected all emerging markets. The inability to bring fiscal policy under control, the incomplete reforms of the banking sector, and rigidities in the economy ultimately left the country with no good solutions. What the currency board required—constraints on fiscal policy and complete abdication of monetary policy—proved to be beyond the political capacity of the Argentine government.

Much has been written about what happened to Argentina, why the crisis happened when it did, and what might have been done to prevent it. Although views differ about the relative importance of the various factors leading up to the collapse, there is general consensus that peso-dollar convertibility was a double-edged sword: it effectively bought the country credibility and eradicated inflation, but at too high a price. Argentina's experience reveals two major problems with currency boards. The first is reflected in the relationship between the credibility of the currency board and capital flows. Argentina inadvertently entered into a vicious circle with financial markets, one in which it felt compelled to raise the exit costs from the currency board in order to maintain the regime's credibility. The Argentine government raised exit costs by issuing its own debt in dollars and by facilitating dollarization in the private sector (for example, by adopting prudential norms in the banking system that biased deposits and loans toward dollars rather than pesos). As exit costs mounted, financial markets became increasingly concerned about the dire implications of a devaluation, which in turn compelled the government to raise exit costs further.

A second, related issue has to do with the inescapable link between fiscal and monetary policy. In retrospect, it now seems clear that the lack of coordination between the fiscal policies of the central government and the provinces played a critical role in bringing about the failure of the currency board. By 1999, the economy was in a deep recession, with low growth and high unemployment, and required some sort of stimulus—either a loosening of monetary policy (i.e., a devaluation) or fiscal stimulus. But either spelled disaster. A devaluation would clearly undermine the currency board, and a rise in government debt would raise suspicions that it would eventually be monetized, further undermining the value of the peso. Ultimately, fears of a devaluation resulted in more dollarization and more strain on the banking sector. The added pressure of capital outflow, first by international investors and then by the withdrawal of deposits from the Argentine banking system, eventually tipped the scales.

The purpose of this paper is to provide an overview of the major economic events in Argentina from the adoption of the Convertibility Plan in 1991 to the collapse of the exchange rate regime in 2001. Section 7.2 reviews the key components of the Convertibility Plan and the responses of financial markets and the macroeconomy to the economic and financial reforms embodied in the plan. Section 7.3 describes the set of external shocks that buffeted the economy between 1994 and 1999. Section 7.4 reviews the set of policy decisions and reforms that took place over that period. Section 7.5 examines the unwinding of these reforms: the imposition of capital controls, channels used by Argentines to evade controls, and the consequent collapse of the Convertibility Plan and the economy in 2001. An epilogue follows in section 7.6, and a chronology of economic and political events in Argentina from 1989 through 2005 is provided in the appendix.

7.2   The Convertibility Plan

On July 9, 1989, Carlos Menem assumed the Argentine presidency in the first peaceful transfer of power from one democratically elected leader to another since 1928.[1] He assumed the office six months ahead of schedule, however, due to the social and economic crisis that engulfed the country. The Austral Plan, adopted in May 1985, had replaced the peso with a new currency, and prices, wages, and utility rates had been frozen in an attempt to stabilize inflation. Figure 7.1 shows monthly inflation and annual real GDP, two key barometers of the health of the Argentine economy over the 1980–2004 period. The Austral Plan had temporarily slowed inflation but did little to spur economic growth. During the period 1981–89, average real GDP growth was negative at –0.7 percent, and real income in 1989 had slid to 90 percent of its 1980 level.[2] In the spring of 1989, inflation spiraled out of control, and the Alfonsin government violently repressed mobs of angry rioters and looters.

After eighteen months in office, the Menem government, under the guid-

---

1. For a historical perspective on Argentina, see della Paolera and Taylor (2001, 2002, 2003b), Romero and Brennan (2002), Randall (1978), and Taylor (1998).
2. Growth in real GDP based on data from the IMF's *International Financial Statistics*.

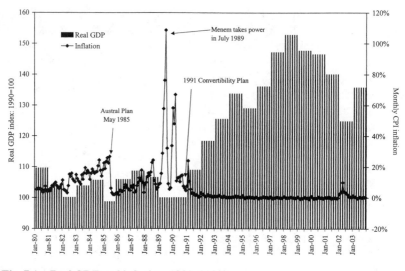

Fig. 7.1   Real GDP and inflation, 1980–2003
Source: IMF *International Financial Statistics.*

ance of Domingo Cavallo as minister of the economy, implemented far-reaching economic reforms. The capstone of the reform package was the Convertibility Plan, which was designed to eliminate Argentina's chronic inflation and restore credibility to the Argentine peso.[3] The plan pegged the peso at a one-to-one parity with the U.S. dollar and required that two-thirds of the monetary base be backed by international reserves. The remaining third could be backed by dollar-denominated Argentine central bank securities at market prices, but holdings of those securities could not expand by more than 10 percent per year.[4] The plan effectively converted the central bank into a currency board that could issue domestic currency only in exchange for foreign currency at a fixed rate. The government encouraged dollarization by making it legal to write contracts in foreign currencies and allowing foreign currencies to be used as an alternative means of payment. By 1994, over 60 percent of time deposits and 50 percent of loans to the private sector were denominated in dollars.

Until the 1990s, trade barriers and restrictions on international investment had insulated the country from international markets. Another important component of the plan was the reduction in tariffs and other barriers to trade in goods and the flow of capital. Restrictions on the entry of foreign banks were lifted. The banks faced high reserve requirements, and

3. See Cavallo and Cottani (1997) and Cavallo (2003).
4. See Pou (2000) for a detailed description of the Convertibility Plan and the central bank charter.

to minimize moral hazard, deposit insurance was eliminated. Effectively, monetary policy for Argentina was set by the U.S. Federal Reserve, and the Argentine central bank had very limited scope to operate as a lender of last resort. Implications of this new role for the central bank are discussed in more detail in section 7.4.2.

The Menem government also proceeded with the privatization of state-owned firms and the deregulation of a number of industries, particularly in the petroleum and gas, electricity, and communications sectors. According to a study by Galiani et al. (2005), privatization dramatically increased the profitability, sales, and efficiency of nonfinancial as well as financial firms. One of the negative consequences of the increase in efficiency, however, was employee layoffs. Galiani et al. (2005) estimate employment reductions of about 40 percent as a result of privatization. One of the positive benefits, and the likely motivator for the privatization program, was the revenue accrued by the central government. Some of the revenue from privatization was used to finance another of the Menem government's reforms: the transition from a pay-as-you-go social security system to privately managed retirement saving accounts.

An additional benefit of the privatization program was the jump start it provided to financial markets. Figure 7.2 shows the value of mergers and acquisitions of Argentine companies from 1990 through 2003. In the first mergers and acquisitions boom, in 1992, some $8 billion in assets changed hands, over 90 percent of which were in the electricity, gas, petroleum, and telecommunications industries. The second boom occurred in 1997–99, when a much larger fraction of Argentine assets was sold to foreign residents.

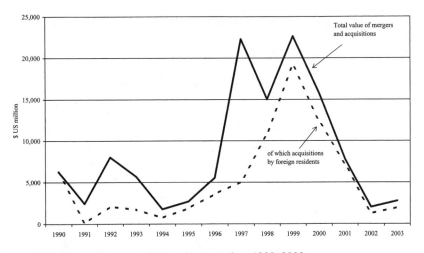

Fig. 7.2   Mergers and acquisitions in Argentina, 1990–2003
Source: Securities Data Corporation (SDC) Thompson's International Mergers and Acquisitions database.

The government also took some initial steps toward addressing the fiscal imbalances between the provincial and central government. Under the system of fiscal federalism in Argentina, the bulk of revenue is raised by the central government, while the provincial governments retain a large degree of autonomy in allocating expenditures. Expenditures are covered through a complicated system of intergovernmental transfers from the central government to the various provinces. Provincial governments also retained some authority to issue bonds, effectively backed by the central bank. In 1991–92, the Menem government was able to lower the transfer payments to the provinces to help cover the costs of the pension reform.[5]

The market response to the economic reforms was swift and dramatic. Table 7.1 provides summary statistics of Argentina's macroeconomic performance, government budget balance, and its balance of payments. GDP growth picked up in 1991 and continued at levels above those of the rest of Latin America through 1994. The currency board was effective in taming inflation—the mean level of inflation dropped from nearly 400 percent per annum to a little under 10 percent in 1991–94 to almost zero in 1995–98. The economic boom was fueled by increases in private consumption and investment.

The lifting of controls also had a positive effect on capital inflows and on financial markets. The U.S. investment position in Argentine equity rose from virtually nothing in the 1980s to around $5 billion by end 1994, roughly 14 percent of Argentine market capitalization. Figure 7.3 shows the volume of capital inflow by type (portfolio equity flows, long-term debt, short-term debt, and foreign direct investment [FDI]) into Argentina from 1986 through 2002. The country was effectively in financial autarky prior to the Menem reforms, with the exception of sovereign borrowing. That situation changed markedly in the 1990s. Capital inflows generally increased in the 1990s, with some ups and downs in the 1994–99 period. The cost of capital reflected in the Emerging Market Bond Index (EMBI) spread for Argentina hovered between 400 and 600 basis points from late 1993 through mid-1994.

The Convertibility Plan was far-reaching in scope and clearly had a positive impact on the economy. However, even at the time of its implementation, critics were quick to point out that it failed to grapple with some structural problems. First, the plan failed to consolidate the budget constraint for the central government and the provinces. Second, there were concerns that the banking reforms were not as deep as they needed to be given the lack of a national lender of last resort. Third, labor market rigidities slowed the economy's response to reforms. Fourth, the question remained whether pegging to the dollar was a feasible long-term anchor for the Argentine economy, particularly given that only a small share of

5. See Tommasi (2006).

Table 7.1   Economic performance, 1990–2002

	1990	1991	1992	1993	1994	1995	1996	1997	1998	1999	2000	2001	2002	1985–1990	1991–1994	1995–1998	1999–2002
National income accounts and macroeconomic indicators (1)																	
Real GDP	100.0	108.9	118.3	125.5	133.8	129.0	136.1	147.2	152.9	147.7	146.5	140.1	124.8	103.3	121.6	141.3	139.8
GDP growth (%)	0.1	8.5	8.3	5.9	6.4	-3.6	5.4	7.8	3.8	-3.4	-0.8	-4.5	-11.5	0.2	5.3	4.3	-4.1
Consumption growth (%)	0.8	14.4	10.6	-14.9	6.7	-4.9	5.3	9.0	3.4	-1.9	-2.0	-5.1	-22.3	0.4	0.6	4.5	-7.1
Investment growth (%)	-12.1	14.5	22.3	18.8	10.2	-13.5	6.2	14.7	6.7	-13.6	-11.5	-17.8	-28.5	-4.0	13.7	7.1	-13.5
Export growth (%)	-23.5	-19.6	-6.3	9.3	14.2	22.0	12.9	9.0	2.4	-9.4	9.8	1.2	76.1	-2.2	4.4	6.3	24.3
Import growth (%)	-36.9	37.9	39.6	17.1	18.6	-8.0	14.8	22.1	5.0	-14.9	-9.0	-16.6	11.1	-5.2	20.7	11.0	-1.6
Investment (% GDP)	14.0	14.6	16.7	19.1	19.9	17.9	18.1	19.4	19.9	18.0	16.2	14.2	12.0	17.0	17.6	18.8	15.1
Current account (% GDP)	2.3	-0.9	-3.1	-3.3	-4.1	-2.0	-2.5	-4.2	-4.9	-4.2	-3.2	-1.4	2.9	-1.4	-2.9	-3.4	-1.5
Unemployment rate (11)	9.2	6	7	9	12	16	16.56	13.41	12.1	13.48	14.65	18.06	17.5		8.5	14.5	15.9
Inflation, interest rates, and financial markets																	
CPI inflation (1)	318.4	99.9	22.2	10.1	4.1	3.3	0.2	0.5	0.9	-1.2	-0.9	-1.1	23.0	396.3	9.5	0.4	5.4
M3 growth (%) (2)						-4.4	18.2	23.8	9.8	2.3	4.3	-25.6				13.0	-7.1
Average EMBI+ index (3)				100.0	88.6	82.9	112.1	140.9	148.4	155.2	175.3	153.7	57.4		94.3	121.1	135.4
International Reserves (ARP millions) (4)					17,938	16,749	17,738	18,463	19,775	19,151	18,775	19,792	35,231		17,938	18,181	23,237
Real effective exchange rate (5)	100.0	35.6	39.5	76.3	103.1	105.1	112.4	122.5	133.1	148.5	167.0	129.6	44.8		63.6	118.3	122.5
Merval Index (6)	316.9	798.2	427.4	582.8	460.0	519.0	649.0	687.0	429.0	550.0	417.0	295.0	155.0		567.1	571.0	354.3
Peso (prime) loan rate (1)					10.1	17.8	10.5	9.2	10.6	11.0	11.1	27.7	51.7			12.1	25.4
Spread between peso and US$ interest rates (basis points) (1)		6,564.7	1,158.6	328.5	345.3	362.6	93.0	117.3	145.9	202.4	191.1	2,101.1	3,968.4		2,099.3	179.7	1,615.8
JPMorgan Sovereign Bond Spread (basis points) (3)								456.0	596.9	720.4	667.9	1,481.7	5,795.1			526.4	2,166.3

(continued)

Table 7.1 (continued)

	1990	1991	1992	1993	1994	1995	1996	1997	1998	1999	2000	2001	2002	1985–1990	1991–1994	1995–1998	1999–2002
Fiscal measures																	
Government deficit (% GDP) (1)	-0.3	-0.5	0.0	-0.6	-0.7	-0.6	-1.9	-1.5	-1.4	-2.9	-2.4	-3.3	-1.1	-2.1	-0.5	-1.3	-2.4
Public debt (% GDP) (2)	-9.4	-10.2	-11.5	-12.5	-12.4	-12.7	-11.9	-11.8	-12.4	-13.7	-13.5	-14.5	-11.6	-9.4	-11.6	-12.2	-13.3
External debt																	
Debt (US$ millions) (8)	62,233	65,406	68,345	64,718	75,139	98,802	111,380	128,410	141,550	145,290	145,880	136,710		58,030	68,402	120,036	142,627
Debt (% exports) (8)	373.7	405.4	385.3	341.1	327.9	336.0	338.9	352.2	379.4	426.6	377.6	373.7		535.9	365.0	351.6	392.7
Privatization revenue (ARP millions) (9)				523.3	732.9	1,171.2	374.9	21.5	96.3	2,579.1	144.7	60.2	4.5			416.0	697.1
IMF loans (US$ millions) (1)	-257.3	-589.8	-73.0	1,211.2	455.3	1,924.1	367.3	-37.6	-654.3	-826.5	773.1	9,334.9	-739.3	173.7	250.9	399.9	2,135.6
Banking-sector figures (10)																	
Lending to private sector/GDP (%)					17.5	18.1	18.8	20.5	22.4	23.0	21.8	18.7				20.0	21.2
Lending to public sector/GDP (%)					1.9	2.2	2.3	2.4	3.1	4.2	5.3	8.1	19.1			2.5	5.9
AARP deposits/GDP (%)					8.0	7.4	9.0	10.9	11.7	11.5	11.3	7.0				9.7	12.2
US$ deposits/GDP (%)					8.7	9.1	10.4	12.5	14.0	16.2	18.3	17.4	0.3			11.5	13.0

Sources and notes: (1) Della Paolera and Taylor (2003b), IMF (various issues); and authors' calculations; (2) Argentina Ministry of Economy and Production (average M3 growth for 1999–2002 is through 2001 only); (3) Data Resources International (average EMBI+ figures for 1991–94 include data from 1993–94 include data from 1995–98 includes data from 1997–98 only); (4) Central Bank of Argentina (figures for 1991–94 are from 1994 only); (5) Dubas, Lee, and Nelson (2004) (an increase indicates a peso appreciation); (6) Argentina Ministry of Economy and Production (index is in U.S. dollars; year-end figures); (7) Argentina Ministry of Economy and Production (1997–2002 data are provisional); (8) World Bank *Global Development Finance* (average for 1999–2002 includes data for 1999–2002 includes data through 2001 only); (9) Argentina Secretariat of Treasury and Ministry of Economy and Production; (10) Central Bank of Argentina (year-end figures); (11) IMF (various issues).

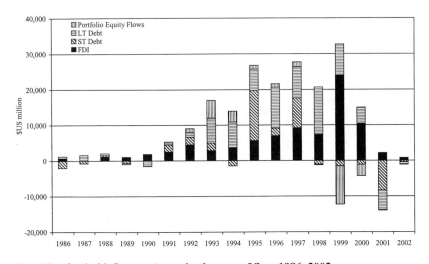

Fig. 7.3   Capital inflows to Argentina by type of flow, 1986–2002
Source: World Bank, *Global Development Finance.*

Argentine trade was with the United States. And finally, the plan, almost by design, did not specify an exit strategy from the peg, if it were found to be unsustainable in the long run. These issues would resurface precisely when the Argentine economy weakened and would contribute to the currency board's eventual collapse.[6]

7.3   External Shocks: Weathering the Storm, 1994–99

With hindsight it is easy to see that Argentina's boom in the early 1990s, with inflation under control and GDP growth on an upward path, was in fact on precarious footing. Like that of many other Latin American countries, the Argentine savings rate was low, and with Argentine government deficits rising, Argentina was especially dependent on foreign capital to finance new investments. Argentina's vulnerability to shifts in external capital flows was first apparent in the aftermath of the Tequila crisis, and this became especially worrisome by 1999, when Brazil devalued the real, and foreign capital again abruptly stopped flowing. The 1990s saw a number of "star" emerging markets falter, Argentina among them. The ultimate causes of the economic crises that shook Mexico in 1994, East Asia in 1997, Russia in 1998, and Brazil in 1999 are still under debate, but what is clear is that each of the crises took its toll on Argentina.

6. See, among others, Bleaney (2004), Calvo and Reinhart (2002), Edwards (2002), Feldstein (2002), Gurtner (2004), and Hausmann and Velasco (2002).

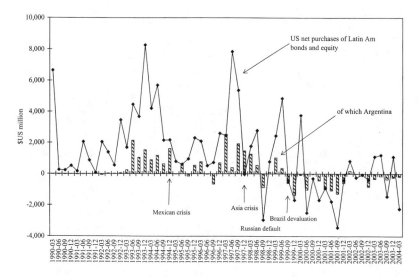

Fig. 7.4   Quarterly U.S. net purchases of bonds and equity in Latin America
Source: Treasury International Capital (TIC) system, U.S. Treasury Department.

7.3.1   The Tequila Financial Crises

The start of the so-called Tequila crisis is typically dated December 20, 1994, when the Mexican central bank was forced to widen its peso bands in reaction to massive capital outflows, leading to an immediate 15 percent devaluation of the peso relative to the dollar and further reserve outflows. Two days later the peso was officially allowed to float, and it continued to lose value while peso interest rates sharply increased. The peso deprecia-tions led to concern that the Mexican government would default on Tesobonos (short-term government bonds denominated in pesos but in-dexed to the dollar) and Mexican banks would fail (due to the large and growing proportion of nonperforming floating interest rate loans).

These fears led to a chaotic exit of foreign and domestic investors, not only from Mexico, but from most of Latin America.[7] Figure 7.4 shows U.S. net purchases of Latin American stocks and bonds, as well as net pur-chases of Argentine securities. Two things stand out from the figure. First, U.S. net purchases are highly correlated across Latin American countries. Second, U.S. net purchases, which reflect a large fraction of total flows to

7. On February 1, 1995, the IMF approved an external aid package for Mexico (which in-cluded $20 billion from the United States, $18 billion from the IMF, $10 billion from the Bank of International Settlements and $2 billion from commercial banks) which restored investor confidence in the Mexican government's ability to honor the Tesobono contracts. Mexico an-nounced a stringent austerity package in early March, and by July it reentered international capital markets and sold $11 billion in two-year dollar-denominated notes at 11 percent, an interest rate well below the rates of 20+ percent on Tesobonos sold in January 1995.

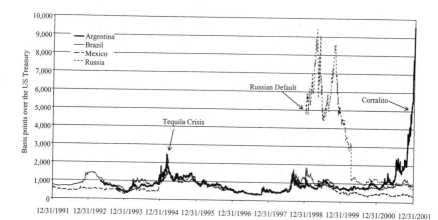

Fig. 7.5   Emerging Market Bond Index spreads, 1992–2001
Source: JPMorgan (http://www.jpmorgan.com/MarketDataInd/EMBI/).

this region, are highly volatile and are responsive to financial crises in Latin America as well as in other regions. The Tequila crisis led to a fall in Brady bond prices and stock exchange indexes in most Latin American countries. Figure 7.5 shows the increase in the EMBI spread, which jumped to nearly 2,000 basis points.

Argentina and Brazil were particularly hard hit by the exit of international investors from Latin America. The Argentine Merval index fell 33 percent between December 1, 1994, and January 10, 1995, and Argentine banks experienced significant peso deposit withdrawals and substitutions from peso to dollar accounts.[8] Total (peso and dollar) deposits had increased dramatically in Argentina between March 1991 and November 1994 as Argentines became more confident about the viability of the new economic regime. At the end of 1994 the value of peso deposits in Argentina was just 9 percent lower than the value of dollar deposits. During the Tequila crisis, total deposits in the Argentine banking system fell for the first time since the establishment of the Convertibility Plan, with the decline falling disproportionately on peso deposits. After the Tequila crisis, the dollarization of deposits steadily increased, so that by 2001 over 80 percent of time deposits were denominated in dollars.[9] A further indication of the impact of the Tequila crisis on the Argentine banking system is apparent in M3 (currency in pesos and deposits of pesos and dollars) growth, which fell by 4.4 percent in 1995. Peso prime loan rates rose from 10.1 in

---

8. See De La Torre, Levy Yeyati, and Schmukler (2003) for a detailed description of the reactions of Argentine depositors and the banking sector to the Tequila crisis.

9. Demand deposits remained largely denominated in pesos, while approximately 40 percent of savings deposits were dollarized in the 1990s. The large increase in deposit dollarization occurred in time deposits, which were already 60 percent dollarized in 1992.

1994 to 17.8 percent in 1995, and spreads between the peso interest rate and dollar interest rate widened by over 50 basis points. Argentine central bank international reserves fell by 18 percent in the first six months of 1995.

The Argentine government responded to the deterioration of its financial markets by putting in place a number of banking-sector reforms.[10] On December 28, 1994, it reduced reserve requirements on dollar deposits in order to provide more liquidity to the banking system. In mid-January reserve requirements on peso deposits were also lowered. A special security fund managed by Banco Nacion (the largest government bank), made up of five private institutions and two public banks and funded with reserve requirements, was set up to assist institutions that suffered high deposit withdrawals. (Recall that the Argentine central bank could not serve as a lender of last resort under the convertibility law.) In February 1995 the Trust Fund for Provincial Development was set up to help support the provincial banks. In March a similar Trust Fund for Bank Capitalization was established, and changes were made to the central bank charter to allow it to use repurchases and rediscounts to help troubled banks. In the same month, Argentina entered into new loan agreements with the International Monetary Fund (IMF), the World Bank, and the Inter-American Development Bank and issued new bonds (for a total of $7 billion) to increase international reserves and to fund the trust funds. In April a deposit insurance network was put in place, which covered up to $20,000 per person (later raised to $30,000) for certain bank deposits.

In the midst of the aftershocks of the Tequila crisis, President Menem won reelection in May 1995, and the run on Argentina's banks ended. Argentina's recovery from 1995 to 1996 was remarkably swift. GDP growth rallied from –3.6 percent in 1995 to 5.4 percent in 1996, led by investment and exports. However, this new growth did little to improve the fiscal situation; the government deficit as a percentage of GDP remained stable at 1.3 percent over this period, and the ratio of external debt to exports stayed at just under 340 percent (see table 7.1).

While the Tequila crisis and its implications for capital flows were clearly unlucky for Argentina, the crisis was followed by some good luck in the form of U.S. and Brazilian policy spillovers. The Federal Reserve shifted toward more expansionary monetary policy in early 1995, leading to a fall in U.S. interest rates and a sharp depreciation in the U.S. dollar, in turn improving Argentine competitiveness in world markets. At the same time Brazil, Argentina's main trading partner, experienced a rise in the value of the real, further strengthening Argentina's relative position. These good external shocks allowed Argentina to recover much more quickly than

---

10. See Dabos and Gomez-Mera (1998) for a detailed description of the post–Tequila crisis banking reforms.

many had anticipated, and perhaps lulled Argentine policymakers and investors into a false sense of security. Mussa (2002) goes so far as to suggest that "were it not for the substantial improvements in bank soundness and for the external good luck, the Convertibility Plan might not have survived the Tequila crisis" (p. 21).

7.3.2   The Asian Crisis

There is little evidence of spillover from the Asian crisis to Latin America until October 1997 after the attack on the Hong Kong dollar. International bond issues from Latin America declined to less than $4 billion in the fourth quarter of 1997, compared to $20 billion during the previous quarter. Figure 7.4 shows that U.S. net purchases of stocks and bonds in Latin America plummeted from a peak of $8 billion in the summer of 1997 to zero in the fourth quarter. U.S. net purchases in Argentina, however, remained positive. Stock indexes fell throughout the emerging markets, with Brazil being the hardest hit, apparently because of its large current account deficit and overvalued currency. At the same time, Argentina was considered doubly vulnerable because of its fixed exchange rate and its dependence on Brazil as a trading partner. Portfolio equity flows to Argentina fell 380 percent, and FDI flows fell by 23 percent between 1997 and 1998, although the net flow of long-term debt increased by 47 percent. Overall, net capital flows to Argentina over this period actually rose by 5 percent, because the sharp decline in portfolio and FDI investment was outweighed by the increase in long-term debt, which accounted for a larger share of the total. The Argentine government's only policy reaction to the Asian crisis was the introduction of the "antibubble" rule, which increased the capital requirement for new mortgage loans when a nationwide real estate price index surpassed certain thresholds.

7.3.3   The Russian Default

Just as emerging markets were beginning to recover from the Asian crisis, news that Russia would default on its sovereign bonds in August 1998 sent markets reeling once again. Few investors imagined that Russia would not be bailed out, and investors quickly realized that if Russia was to default, other vulnerable emerging markets would likely follow. The news from Russia was a disaster for stock market investors in Argentina, as the Merval plummeted 40 percent between August and September 1998. Private capital inflows to Argentina, which had already slowed in the aftermath of the Asian crisis, now turned negative in the fourth quarter of 1998. From July to August 1998, the spread on Argentine sovereign bonds almost tripled. Throughout the fall, the spread remained about 400 basis points higher than the spread that prevailed in July 1998, and this, in turn, led domestic peso and dollar interest rates to rise sharply.

Calvo, Izquierdo, and Talvi (2003) suggest that the dramatic stop in international capital flows to emerging markets that followed Russia's partial foreign debt repudiation provides strong evidence in favor of contagion-based (and against traditional fiscal-based) explanations for financial flows. Countries that had little or no financial or trading ties to Russia, such as Argentina and Brazil, found that their access to external capital had suddenly been cut off.

7.3.4 Brazilian Devaluation

While Argentina was badly affected by the general exit of investors from emerging markets, Brazil—already hard hit by the Asian crisis—was dealt a knockout blow.[11] On January 13, 1999, Gustavo Franco, the governor of the Brazilian central bank, resigned; and the government announced a widening of the fluctuation band for the real. This was tantamount to a devaluation of the real of 8 percent. The financial reaction in Argentina to the Brazilian devaluation was immediate. Argentine interest rates rose sharply, the Merval plummeted, and Argentina was effectively shut out of global financial markets.

Many observers, at least with hindsight, date the beginning of the Argentine economic crisis in 2001 to the Brazilian devaluation (which, in turn, may have been set off by the Russian default). Brazil was Argentina's major trading partner, and the combination of Brazil's economic woes, which would surely reduce its import demand from Argentina, and the exit of international capital flows from the region had serious implications for Argentina.

Returning to figure 7.3, we see that that short-term lending and portfolio equity flows to Argentina—whose trend had generally been rising throughout the 1990s, with short-term reversals after the Mexican and Asian crises—sharply plummeted in 1999. Total capital flows into Argentina remained positive, primarily because of an unprecedented inflow of FDI. Interestingly, 64 percent of the inflow of FDI in that year is due to the acquisition of a single company, YPF, by Repsol, a Spanish company (see figure 7.6). Netting out the YPF transaction, capital inflows would have remained positive in 1999 but would drop to $5 billion from $20 billion.

In a series of papers Guillermo Calvo and various coauthors make the case that severe capital flow reversals, such as that experienced by Argentina in 1999–2000, can be triggers of subsequent economic crisis.[12] Further, Calvo suggests that three factors in particular exacerbate an econ-

11. While portfolio flows to all emerging market countries fell dramatically after the Russia default, FDI flows were less uniform. Noteworthy in this regard is the fact that FDI flows to Brazil rose substantially in dollar terms from mid-1998 to mid-2001. Calvo, Izquierdo, and Talvi (2003) suggest that it was in part these FDI flows that allowed Brazil to recover so quickly from the Russian crisis–induced sudden stop. Other factors in Brazil's favor were the facts that its public debt was only partially dollarized and that substantial fiscal retrenchment was politically feasible.

12. See, for example, Calvo (1998), Calvo, Izquierdo, and Talvi (2003), and Calvo, Izquierdo, and Mejia (2004).

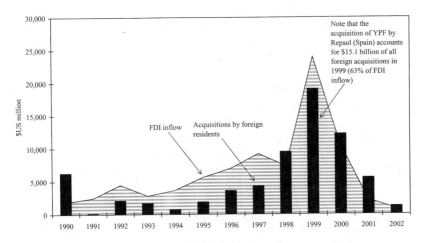

Fig. 7.6   FDI inflow and foreign acquisitions of Argentine companies
Source: FDI data from Global Development Finance, World Bank. Mergers and acquisitions data from SDC Thompson's International Mergers and Acquisitions database.

omy's vulnerability to "sudden stops":[13] the pre-stop level of indebtedness, the degree of domestic liability dollarization, and the dependence on financing from abroad to pay for imports. Calvo, Izquierdo, and Talvi (2003) argue that the Argentine economy in the 1990s had just the characteristics that would lead it to be hard hit in the advent of a sudden stop. Calvo, Izquierdo, and Mejía (2004) date Argentina's sudden stop as starting in May 1999.

The sudden-stop literature suggests that it is the capital flows (or lack thereof) themselves that are pivotal. In theory, a sudden stop in capital flows could arise from external factors, such as contagion or margin calls that arise from economic crises that are unrelated to the country in question.[14] Internal factors can either mitigate or magnify the effects of the sudden stop on the economy. In countries like Argentina, with a small share of tradable goods output relative to domestic absorption of tradable goods, a sudden stop in capital flows requires a sharp increase in the equilibrium real exchange rate to transform the current account deficit into a surplus.[15]

13. Calvo, Izquierdo, and Mejia (2004) define a sudden stop as a sharp decline in capital flows that meets the following three criteria: (a) it contains at least one observation where the year-on-year fall in capital flows lies at least 2 standard deviations below its sample mean; (b) it ends once the annual change in capital flows exceeds 1 standard deviation below its sample mean; and (c) the start is determined by the first time the annual change in capital flows falls 1 standard deviation below the mean.

14. For a further discussion of the potential role of margin calls in sudden stops see Mendoza and Smith (2002).

15. Calvo, Izquierdo, and Talvi (2003) calculate that Argentina would have needed to depreciate its equilibrium real exchange rate by a whopping 46 percent in 1998 in order to bring its current account into balance.

If the country also has large financial currency denomination mismatches (for example, liability dollarization), the real depreciation will in turn lead to a weakening of corporate—and, in the case of Argentina, government—balance sheets.[16]

Argentina's experience immediately following the Russian default closely follows the sudden-stop logic. With the falloff in capital inflows, investors and (perhaps most important) official creditors realized that the sustainability of Argentina's fiscal situation, though still not dramatically different from what it had been a year previous, was precarious. Calvo, Izquierdo, and Talvi (2003) estimate that "once all the elements triggered by the sudden stop are factored in (valuation effects, interest rate increases, growth slowdown, and emergence of contingent liabilities from the private sector), the primary fiscal balance needed to regain sustainability would have exceeded 3% of GDP" in 1998 (p. 32). The political economy implications of this for the Menem government, which was in its final year, were dire.

7.3.5   Reduction in World Interest Rates

Argentina was on the brink of economic collapse in early 1999, but just as had been the case after the Tequila crisis, Argentina was dealt a positive shock in the second half of 1999 that allowed it to make another surprising, even if temporary, recovery.

In this case Argentina's rescue came from an unusual source: conditions in European financial markets. As European governments strove to meet the Mastricht criteria in the run-up to the establishment of the euro, interest rates—which had been relatively high in a number of European countries—converged downward. This sent investors seeking higher yields to alternative markets. Argentina recognized this potential market niche and successfully floated (high-yield) sovereign debt denominated in euros during this period. As Mussa (2002) points out, "the success of Argentina in floating substantial amounts of sovereign debt in global credit markets during much of 1999 and the first half of 2000 testifies both to the special conditions in those markets and to Argentine authorities' particularly deft management of public debt" (p. 25).

---

16. Calvo, Izquierdo, and Talvi (2003) estimate that Argentina had an extremely high degree of public-sector debt mismatch in 1998. Their calculation for Argentina was 0.01 on a 1–0 scale with 1 representing a perfect match and zero representing the highest degree of mismatch. Given this level of currency mismatch, the authors indicate that had there been a real depreciation of 46 percent (the amount needed to balance the current account), Argentina would have had a debt-GDP ratio of just under 50 percent assuming no increase in interest rates and no fall in growth rates. If the contingent liabilities of the public sector that arose out of the (also highly dollarized) corporate and banking sectors are included, the debt-GDP ratio rises to well over 50 percent.

Government policy can, in principle, offset the negative effects of a sudden stop–induced real appreciation on corporate balance sheets by providing the private sector with additional collateral. Korea, with the help of the IMF, was able to mitigate the effects of the Asian crisis–induced sudden stop in this manner.

7.4   Internal Policy Mistakes

At the same time that Argentina was buffeted, in both positive and negative directions, by external shocks, internal policies had a major influence on the economy. The role of fiscal policy in the lead-up to Argentina's economic collapse is perhaps the most controversial. Mussa (2002) and the IMF (2003, 2004) emphasize failure in fiscal policy as the root cause of the crisis. Others suggest that fiscal policy was either less crucial or, in some views, irrelevant. Another area of controversy is the role of the banking sector in the ultimate collapse of the economy, and in particular the currency mismatches between dollar deposits and peso-denominated assets.

7.4.1   Untamed Fiscal Policy

Out of context, Argentina's fiscal numbers do not suggest much reason for concern. In 1993 public debt was 28 percent of GDP, inflation was under control, and GDP growth could arguably have been expected to continue at 6–7 percent. It was in this seemingly robust fiscal environment that the Argentine government decided to privatize its social security system, which produced an extra annual bill equal to 1.5 percent of GDP (roughly $2 billion based on GDP in 1995), although in the long run the privatization was expected to save the government money. Other privatization efforts in the period 1993–98 resulted in $2.9 billion in nonrecurring revenues. By 1998 the Argentine public debt had risen to $112 billion (the ratio of public debt to GDP had risen to 37 percent), which in a broader context might still be considered moderate.

Mussa (2002) points out, however, that this rise in public debt should have been worrisome because it occurred during a period of relatively high economic growth, it included a number of one-off revenue increases due to privatizations, and it would have looked worse but for the fact that Brady bond restructuring in 1993 involved substantial back-loading of interest payments, and "a good deal of public sector borrowing was not included in the budget" (Mussa 2002, p. 16).[17] An assessment of the Argentine fiscal situation is further complicated by the role of provincial government spending, which is not subject to a balanced-budget rule. While provincial expenditures generally totaled less than 12 percent of GDP per year, the system of Argentine fiscal federalism provided little incentive for provinces to reduce spending.[18]

17. Perry and Serven (2003) show that if an equilibrium real exchange rate (rather than the one-for-one peso-dollar rate) is used in the calculation, the public-sector debt-GDP ratio in 2001 rises by 24 percent.

18. Expenditures in the provinces rose steadily in the late 1990s, while transfers from the central government remained fixed as a constant proportion of tax revenue, which led to widening provincial deficits. See Cuevas (2003) for a discussion of reforming intergovernmental transfers.

Reinhart, Rogoff, and Savastano (2003) describe Argentina, which has defaulted on its debts five times since 1820, as a "serial defaulter." They show that serial defaulters can develop debt intolerance, where the risk of default begins to skyrocket at debt levels that might be quite manageable for countries with less checkered credit records. Argentina appears, in their calculations, to hit debt intolerance at debt-GDP ratios of only 25–30 percent, so that alarm bells should have been ringing well before 1998.

It is also worth remembering that Argentina's public debt during the 1990s was almost entirely denominated in foreign currencies, reflecting its limited ability to issue long-term debt in its own currency, itself a reflection of the fact that the convertibility regime encouraged dollar-denominated debt.[19] As with other emerging market economies, Argentina could borrow only at sizable spreads over U.S. treasuries, and a negative shift in market sentiment generally resulted in higher interest rates, creating potentially explosive debt dynamics even at relatively modest levels of debt.[20]

At the same time that debt-GDP ratios should have sounded alarms (and, indeed, seem not to have sounded alarms at the IMF until it was too late), Argentina's debt-export ratio should also have provided cause for concern. One of the costs of the currency board was a chronic overvaluation of the peso. Figure 7.7 shows that in the period 1991–93 the real effective peso exchange rate appreciated by almost 25 percent.[21] Between 1996 and 1997 the world price of Argentina's commodity exports fell by 20 percent, followed by a further decline of equal size in 1998.[22] By the end of 1998 Argentina's debt-export ratio was at 379 percent, and debt service payments alone absorbed the majority of annual export earnings. In 1999, in the wake of the Brazilian devaluation, export growth fell by over 9 percent, and the debt-export ratio rose to 427 percent.

Finally, the Convertibility Plan did not stop the Argentine government

19. The Argentine government did not issue peso-denominated debt, both because peso debt was more expensive (peso interest rates were always higher than dollar interest rates) and to avoid the appearance of hedging against the collapse of the Convertibility Plan. Eichengreen, Hausmann, and Panizza (2003) suggest that the difficulty emerging market economies face in issuing debt in local currency can be traced to one of two (similar though distinct) phenomena: original sin or debt intolerance. Original sin implies that the problem arises externally, with the structure of global portfolios and international financial markets, while debt intolerance implies that the problem arises internally, with weak institutions. In either case, the authors term the consequence of these problems "currency mismatches." See also Bordo, Meissner, and Redish (2004) and Rigobon (2002).

20. See, for example, Caballero and Krishnamurthy (2003), Cespedes, Chang, and Velasco (2004) and Galiani, Levy Yeyati, and Schargrodsky (2003).

21. See Dubas, Lee, and Mark (2005).

22. Another aspect of Argentina's trade patterns that increased its vulnerability was the fact that Mercosur, established in 1991 (which created a free-trade zone among Argentina, Brazil, Paraguay, Uruguay, Chile, and Bolivia), probably led to trade diversion and a less diversified trade market. Argentina went from trading around 20 percent with Mercosur partners in 1991 to 45 percent in 1998 (with the bulk of exports going to Brazil).

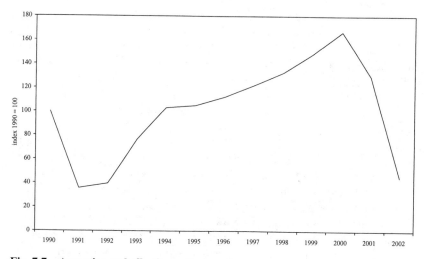

Fig. 7.7   Argentine real effective exchange rate
Source: Dubas, Lee, and Nelson (2004).
Note: An increase indicates a peso appreciation relative to a trade-weighted basket of currencies.

from attempting to monetize its debts. Once foreign capital had been exhausted, the Argentine government, though unable to directly print pesos, did the next best thing by issuing small-denomination federal bonds redeemable for federal tax payments. These bonds were called "lecop" (for *letras de cancelación de obligaciones provinciales*) and were considered quasi-money. Many of the provinces followed the federal government's lead and printed their own versions of quasi-money to pay for fiscal deficits. For example, the province of Buenos Aires issued "Patacón," and Córdoba issued "Lecor." In December 2001 quasi-monies issued by the federal government and the provinces exceeded 24 percent of pesos in circulation.

7.4.2   The Role of the Banks

The convertibility regime required an especially strong banking and financial system because restrictions on monetary policy prevented the central bank from acting as a lender of last resort through money creation.[23] In the aftermath of the Tequila crisis, when banks experienced massive deposit outflows, the Argentine government put in place a number of banking reforms to strengthen domestic banks, at the same time encouraging

---

23. There was a proviso in the Convertibility Plan law that allowed up to one-third of international reserves to be made up of internationally traded, dollar-denominated Argentine sovereign bonds, valued at market prices. This allowed a very limited "lender of last resort" role since the central bank could provide the banking system with pesos in exchange for sovereign Argentine bonds (rather than dollars).

foreign banking institutions to enter the Argentine market.[24] By the end of the 1990s, Argentina was considered a model for other emerging market economies in the area of banking supervision and prudential policy. Banking system assets doubled from only 20 percent of GDP in 1991 to 40 percent of GDP in 1999.

At the same time that the Argentine government was instituting important banking-sector reforms, it was also saddling its banks (and especially public banks) with public-sector debt. Banking system exposure to the public sector rose from about 10 percent of total assets in 1995 to more than 20 percent by 2001. In April 2001 alone the government placed $2 billion of its debts with banks in Argentina, at the same time that the central bank charter was amended in order to allow unlimited lender-of-last-resort liquidity with the backing of government securities.[25] The IMF (2003) was concerned by this growing exposure, and writes that in the 1990s the Argentine "banking system was vulnerable to three forms of shocks, all of which eventually materialized: economic downturn, devaluation of the exchange rate, and default by the public sector."

Under the currency board the Argentine banking system was heavily exposed to a devaluation of the peso against the U.S. dollar.[26] While most bank assets and liabilities were matched in terms of their currency of denomination, many dollar-denominated bank loans went to Argentine companies and households that had earnings in pesos. A large devaluation would make repayment of those loans difficult.[27]

Wealthy Argentine residents have long kept bank accounts outside of Argentina in case of economic crisis. It is estimated that Argentines held over $100 billion abroad in the 1990s, which suggests that they considered the risk of crisis (and presumably expropriation) to be substantial. Related to this is the fact that credit from the banking system to the private sector, which is generally low in Latin America, was particularly so in Argentina, where bank loans to the private sector were only 23 percent of GDP at their peak in 1999.

24. Foreign-owned banks presumably contribute to a strengthening of the banking system, because they are less tied to the domestic economy (and politics). In 1994 only 15 percent of total Argentine banking system assets were held in foreign banks; this increased to 55 percent in 1998 and 73 percent in 2000 (De La Torre, Levy Yeyati, and Schmukler 2003, p. 50). In the midst of the Argentine crisis, however, foreign banks reacted to the increased financial risk by reducing their exposure, so their presence did little to improve the situation.

25. This amendment, ironically put in place by Domingo Cavallo, effectively dismantled the money-issuance rule under the Convertibility Plan. Cavallo had hoped that renewing the central bank's ability to serve as a lender of last resort would encourage banks to extend credit, but it seemed to have only further weakened the credibility of the banking system.

26. It is worth noting, however, that prior to the imposition of capital controls in 2001 dollarization in the banking system was concentrated in longer-term bank deposits and loans. Demand deposits (which were presumably used for transaction purposes) were largely denominated in pesos throughout this period.

27. See De Nicolo, Honohan, and Ize (2003) and della Paolera and Taylor (2003a) for further discussion of the dollarization of the banking system.

7.5   The Unwinding of Reforms

In December 1999, Fernando de la Rua was elected president and inherited a public debt in excess of $100 billion. The new government made the decision to tighten fiscal policy with a series of tax increases, in the hope that this would further reassure investors and help to lower interest rates. But the tax increases only served to push a recovering economy back into recession. The country teetered on the edge of default throughout 2000, but once again a good external shock in early 2001 steadied the Argentine economy. U.S. monetary policy loosened, leading to lower U.S. interest rates and a weaker dollar. This in turn resulted in lower spreads on Argentina's bonds over U.S. treasuries and gave a boost to Argentina's exports.

De la Rua's contractionary fiscal policy received the endorsement of the IMF. In March 2000, a three-year standby arrangement for $7.2 billion was agreed to, and in January 2001 this was augmented by $13.7 billion. At the same time, additional financing of $39 billion was arranged from official and private sources. In September 2001, the IMF increased its loans to Argentina by $22 billion, with up to $3 billion to be used in support of a possible debt-restructuring operation.

However, it was too little and already too late. Argentines had begun to shift from peso to dollar deposits starting in February 2001, and this trend sharply increased during the fall of 2001, when outright withdrawals of deposits were observed throughout the banking sector. De la Torre, Levy Yeyati, and Schmukler (2003) document that by November 2001, forty-seven of the top fifty banks had suffered major withdrawals. Between July and November 2001, Argentines withdrew over $15 billion from banks: on November 30, 2001, alone, banks saw withdrawals of $1.3 billion.

On December 3, 2001, in a desperate effort to prevent further massive capital outflows and to halt the run on banks, the government imposed a set of draconian financial controls. The capital control regime, termed the *Corralito* (literally, "little corral," but also "playpen"), limited withdrawals from bank accounts to 250 pesos per week per account, but depositors could access their accounts to transfer funds within the banking system.[28] Wire transfers required central bank approval, foreign currency futures transactions were prohibited, and in effect all investors, foreign and domestic, were prohibited from transferring funds abroad. Depositors could exchange dollars for government bonds, but few chose to do so. The restrictions were announced as temporary measures that would remain in place until the danger of the speculative attack had

---

28. Perhaps unsurprisingly, there was a sudden increase in the number of new bank accounts in early December. The government promptly changed the regulations so that the deposit limits applied per person rather than per account. According to the press, some 500,000 accounts were opened in the two days following the imposition of bank restrictions.

passed.[29] The scheduled program review by the IMF was not completed, and IMF support of Argentina was effectively withdrawn. (A detailed time line of the economic and political events that occurred during the *Corralito* is provided in the appendix.)

On December 19, the ministers in President de la Rua's cabinet resigned, and the following day the president himself resigned.[30] Ramon Puerta assumed the presidency in the interim as Argentine country risk skyrocketed (see figure 7.5, where the EMBI spread for Argentina rises from 4,000 in November to just under 10,000 at the end of December 2001). Foreign exchange trading was suspended on December 21. A new interim president, Rodriguez Saa, was named on December 23. Saa promptly declared a moratorium on the country's $155 billion public foreign currency debt, making it the largest sovereign debt default in history. Saa resigned after just one week, and President Eduardo Duhalde assumed power on December 30.

In January the Argentine peso was officially devalued, and all bank deposits and debts were "pesofied." Dollar deposits were converted at 1.4 pesos to the dollar, while dollar loans were subject to one-to-one conversions, effectively imposing the bulk of the costs of pesofication on the banks rather than depositors. The situation of the banks was made worse by the fact that they remained exposed to foreign exchange risk on foreign liabilities, which were not pesofied. Gutierrez and Montes-Negret (2004) estimate that the banking system had a negative net worth of at least $32 billion in January 2002. To compensate the banks, the government issued new bonds called BODENs, which to date are illiquid (and their economic value is contingent on future debt restructuring and the government's fiscal sustainability).

Given the political and economic chaos, the payment system ceased to function. Citizens took to the streets in protest of the economic conditions, and the foreign banks became a focus for their rage. The number of reported bankruptcies by firms and individuals reached record proportions. Growth in real GDP, consumption, and investment turned sharply negative, and the current account deficit as a percentage of GDP swung from –1.4 percent in 2001 to 2.9 percent in 2002.

The one market in Argentina that did not collapse amid the economic crisis was the stock market. Indeed, the Argentine stock market expanded by 50 percent immediately following the imposition of capital controls. One potential explanation of the stock market boom in Argentina is that investors viewed the likely devaluation of the peso as beneficial for firms,

29. Some of the original withdrawal limits were eventually modified, although the main restrictions on capital outflow remained in place until December 2, 2002 (exactly one year after they were first introduced).

30. The resigning cabinet ministers included Domingo Cavallo, who had left public office in 1996 and returned to the position of economic minister with the de la Rua administration.

although in other countries such crises are generally harmful. A more plausible explanation is that the idiosyncratic reaction of the Argentine stock market was due largely to the specific restrictions in the *Corralito* that allowed investors to use their frozen bank deposits to purchase Argentine stocks, and inadvertently provided a legal mechanism for avoiding the capital controls through the purchase of Argentine stocks that were cross-listed in the United States, termed American depository receipts (ADRs).[31]

Auguste et al. (2006) document how the ADR loophole worked in practice. Under the *Corralito,* Argentine residents were allowed to use bank deposits in excess of the $1,000 monthly ceiling to purchase Argentine stocks. If a stock happened to be cross-listed in the United States, those shares could be legally converted from Argentine shares into ADRs. The ADRs could then be sold in the United States and the dollar proceeds deposited in a U.S. account. Under normal circumstances an ADR sale would result in Argentina experiencing a capital inflow, as U.S. residents have acquired claims on Argentine firms. Under the *Corralito,* however, the capital inflows did not occur, and the dollars and/or shares remained outside of Argentina. In effect, the ADR loophole allowed Argentines to transfer monies abroad, but the transactions did not result directly in a fall in Argentina's international reserves (or a fall in Argentine bank deposits). ADR conversions, however, did reduce the number of (underlying) shares available on the local stock exchange in Buenos Aires, La Bolsa.

Auguste et al. (2006) examine local share prices relative to their corresponding ADRs over the period when capital controls were in place. They find that Argentine investors were willing to pay a substantial price to move their deposits out of Argentina through ADR conversions. At their peak, some ADRs were trading at a discount of in excess of 40 cents on the dollar.

The existence of ADRs not only allowed Argentines to circumvent the capital controls put in place by the government during the economic crisis in 2001, but they also provided a shadow foreign exchange market during a period when the official foreign exchange market was closed. Auguste et al. (2006) estimate that the average expected devaluation of the peso implicit in ADR prices in January 2002 did a good job predicting the magnitude of the official devaluation, which was 40 percent.

Transaction data can be used to estimate the volume of wealth transfer from Argentina to the United States via ADRs. The most accurate measure would be to use the volume of ADR conversions that occurred after the imposition of the *Corralito.* The New York Stock Exchange collects the number of ADR conversions on a quarterly basis, which unfortunately

---

31. See Levy Yeyati, Schmukler, and van Horen (2003) for a further discussion of the stock market boom during the *Corralito.*

makes it impossible to back out the number of conversions during the peak period of December 2001 and January 2002. The data suggest that between the end of December 2001 and the end of March 2002, approximately 26 million shares of Argentine stock were converted to ADRs. Since we do not know in which month those shares were converted, and because share prices changed dramatically in this period, it is difficult to assign a value to this flow.

An alternative measure of the volume of wealth transfer is the post-*Corralito* cumulated volume of sales of Argentine ADRs in New York, under the assumption that all ADR sales reflect cashing out by Argentine investors. This figure comes to $835 million.[32] This is likely to be an underestimate of the volume of outflow, since many investors may simply hold the stock rather than sell at depressed prices. Another measure is the cumulated volume of purchases of local stocks with associated ADRs in Buenos Aires over this period. Under the assumption that all these purchases are intended for ADR conversion, the value of wealth transfer comes to $3.4 billion. This is probably an overestimate, since Argentines may have had other reasons for purchasing these stocks besides ADR convertibility.

On the one hand, a capital flow of even $3.4 billion is small given the magnitude of the crisis and the desire of Argentines to find a way to move wealth abroad. On the other hand, the fact that the volume is small is consistent with the fact that, unlike many unofficial channels for capital outflow, the value of the ADR loophole was priced by the market. It appears that the increase in local share prices effectively choked off the flow. This may have been why, in the midst of all of the other events taking place during the *Corralito,* the government did not appear to be much concerned about closing the ADR loophole.

ADRs were not the only legal means by which Argentines could circumvent the *Corralito.* CEDEARs (certificados de depositos Argentinos) are shares of non-Argentine firms (mostly U.S. firms) that are cross-listed on the Argentine exchange and sold for pesos. Before the imposition of the *Corralito* Argentine investors should have preferred to hold foreign stocks directly (and in dollars) rather than as a CEDEAR in pesos, especially given that they had to pay high conversion fees for the CEDEARs. However, after the imposition of the *Corralito* we might have expected Argentine demand for CEDEARs to have increased because underlying CEDEAR assets are denominated in dollars (although CEDEARs are priced in pesos), and because holding shares of non-Argentine firms would serve as a better means of hedging against the looming economic crisis. The supply of CEDEARs, however, did not immediately pick up, in large part because Argentine brokers were initially not able to send dollars abroad to buy the underlying stocks and convert them to CEDEARs, and

32. This is the cumulated sum between December 1, 2001, and May 31, 2002.

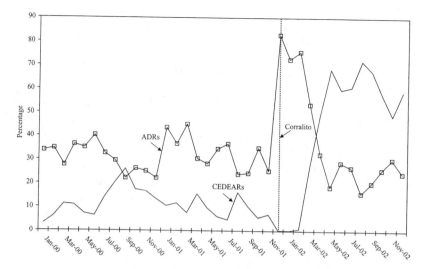

Fig. 7.8   Trading volume in ADRs and in CEDEARs as a percentage of total trading volume
Source: Bolsar (http://www.bolsar.com).

there was little incentive for investors outside of Argentina to convert U.S. stocks into peso-denominated CEDEARs before the devaluation.[33]

Figure 7.8 indicates that starting in late February 2002, however, liquidity in CEDEAR stocks gradually increased (just as trading in ADRs starts to fall off). Discussions with brokers in Argentina suggest that the increase in CEDEAR liquidity came from two sources. First, using operations called "via cable," brokers bought foreign bank checks that allowed them to purchase the underlying U.S. shares, convert these into CEDEARs, and then sell the CEDEARs (at a premium) in Argentina for pesos.[34] Second, mutual funds, pension funds, and other institutional investors are required to hold assets rated above BBB, and at this time all Argentine stocks and bonds were below the minimum ranking, forcing these funds to purchase non-Argentine securities. Since the *Corralito* disallowed direct purchases of foreign assets, CEDEARs were among the few assets that they could acquire.

Once liquidity in the CEDEAR market was established, investors had an alternative means of escaping the *Corralito,* by purchasing CEDEARs in Argentina for pesos, converting them back to the underlying dollar de-

33. Traders had little incentive to convert U.S. stocks into CEDEARs prior to the devaluation, both because of peso value uncertainty and because the *Corralito* restricted repatriation of any peso returns.

34. Another way that CEDEARs may have been created is through a practice termed pre-releasing, where the depositary bank lends out the underlying securities that make up the CEDEAR to brokers in the market. The brokers then sell the CEDEARs to investors who pay in pesos and then request that the broker convert the CEDEARs back into the underlying U.S. shares (and sell them in New York for dollars).

nominated stocks, and selling them in New York for dollars (that then were deposited in dollar accounts).[35] The transaction costs of CEDEAR conversion are similar to those in the ADR market, and the increased demand for CEDEARs in Argentina led to similar price spreads on CEDEARs in Argentina relative to the underlying prices of the stocks in New York. Before the *Corralito,* the mean CEDEAR discount was approximately zero, but during the period March 2002 through September 2002 the average discount increased to 3.3 percent (excluding transaction costs) with a maximum increase of 13 percent.[36]

There is clear indication that the Argentine government understood that CEDEARs were serving a purpose similar to that of ADRs in allowing investors to transfer funds (legally) outside of Argentina. On March 25, 2002, a report in the official central bank press communication suggests that the government considered adopting new measures to avoid capital outflows using ADR and CEDEAR transactions. However, no restrictions were imposed at that time. In September 2002, regulations were changed that increased the cost and difficulty of CEDEAR conversions.[37] CEDEAR discounts increased substantially after September 2002, which reflects the increased costs associated with shifting capital abroad through this mechanism.

Argentina appears to be a unique case in which a country with a significant number of cross-listed stocks and relatively well-integrated financial markets subsequently attempted to close its financial borders. The unusual set of circumstances in Argentina gave cross-listed shares (ADRs and CEDEARs) a new, and previously unstudied, role as a mechanism for capital flight. Further, the Argentine case suggests that, once having established ADRs and other kinds of contractual arrangements across markets, it may be difficult if not impossible to reverse the process of capital market integration with (even draconian) capital controls.

7.6   Epilogue

The *Corralito,* which officially ended on December 2, 2002, with its abrogation of individual and corporate property rights, resulted in a massive

35. Investors also purchased (in pesos) dollar-denominated Argentine government bonds (specifically Global 2008s) and resold them in New York (for dollars) for similar reasons. It is interesting to note that the two most frequently traded CEDEARs in the post-*Corralito* period, Lockheed and Avon, were rarely traded before the capital controls were imposed. The apparent reason for this shift in preference is that they both have low conversion ratios and high dollar prices (for the underlying shares) in the United States, which in turn meant that these securities sold at high prices in pesos in Argentina. Higher nominal peso prices meant that fewer of these CEDEARs had to be acquired to transfer a given amount of funds (and with fewer transactions, investors incur lower conversion costs).

36. Liquidity for many of the CEDEARs in Buenos Aires remained low even after March 2002. In our calculations we include the 15 most frequently traded CEDEARs (out of the 216 listed CEDEARs), and we calculate the discount for each of the CEDEARs only on the days when there was a closing price in both markets. The index is then the average of the daily premia.

37. See the entry for September 2002 in the appendix.

redistribution of wealth between depositors, lenders, and financial institutions. Not surprisingly, the question of who owed what to whom became a matter for the courts and left the economy in a state of limbo. The courts issued a number of injunctions to savers who demanded that their dollar deposits be paid at the market exchange rate rather than the rate decreed by the government of 1.4 pesos to the dollar, plus inflation. Honoring these injunctions cost the banks an extra 7 billion pesos. The Supreme Court finally ruled in October 2004 that the pesofication of dollar deposits that took place in 2001 was legal, relieving the banks of large potential losses from further injunctions.[38] As a consequence of this recent history, most bank deposits in Argentina are short term, which in turn limits the scope for banks to lend long term. In early 2004, credit to the private sector amounted to only 8 percent of GDP.

In May 2003 Nestor Kirchner, a populist nationalist, was sworn in as president on a pointedly anti-IMF platform. In September, a day after Argentina missed a $2.9 billion payment to the IMF (the single largest nonpayment of a loan in the IMF's history), Argentina signed a three-year agreement with the IMF, which included a fiscal target of a primary surplus of 3 percent of GDP in the first year (coincidentally, exactly the number Calvo, Izquierdo, and Talvi [2003] calculated as needed in 1998 to regain sustainability). In return the IMF agreed to lend Argentina $12.5 billion, the amount that was due to the IMF over the period 2003–6.[39] In 2005 Argentine GDP finally surpassed its previous precrisis peak. In the summer of 2005 Argentina suspended its agreement with the IMF and introduced a massive debt swap that involved an exchange for new bonds worth roughly 35 cents on the dollar.[40] In December 2005 Kirchner said his government would repay early its entire $98.8 billion debt to the IMF in order to be free of "further IMF restraint on Argentina's policies."[41]

38. The Supreme Court approved the conversion of fixed-term savings in dollars to pesos—known as "pesofication"—by five to one on October 26, 2004. The president of the court, Enrique Petracchi, abstained from voting because his savings were caught in the freeze on bank accounts when the crisis broke out.
39. The IMF's lending to Argentina makes up roughly 15 percent of its total loans, giving Argentina quite a bit of leverage.
40. In September 2003 the Kirchner government made an offer to bondholders that involved writing down 75 percent of the value of the defaulted debt, nonpayment of interest arrears, and the issuance of new low-interest bonds, amounting to a cut of up to 90 percent in the net present value of the bonds. The Argentine Bondholders' Committee made a counteroffer that accepted a write-off of 35 percent in the nominal value of the defaulted debt and required payment of overdue interest payments. The 2005 agreement is virtually identical to the terms of this counteroffer.
41. See the *Economist* (2005) for further description of the current economic and political situation in Argentina.

Appendix

Argentina's Financial Market Event Time Line

1989

July 9	Carlos Menem assumes the Argentine presidency in the first peaceful transfer of power from one democratically elected leader to another since 1928.
November	New Foreign Investment Regime put into place. All legal limits on foreign investment abolished. Capital gains and dividends can now be repatriated freely. No need for previous approval of transactions. No legal limits regarding type or nature of foreign investment. Introduction of a free exchange rate regime. Bekaert and Harvey identify this as the official liberalization date.
December	The exchange system is again unified for all dealings under a free-floating rate and the currency unit depreciated. Dual export rates still exist.

1990

March	Currency made fully convertible. Foreign portfolio investment by Argentine residents now possible.
November	Menem extends value added tax to services, implements tax on fixed assets.

1991

March 22	Export taxes are eliminated, abolishing the dual export rates.
April 1	Argentina's Congress enacts the Convertibility Law, which legally adopts the currency board guaranteeing the convertibility of peso currency to dollars at a one-to-one fixed rate and limiting the printing of pesos to only an amount necessary to purchase dollars in the foreign exchange market. Effectively, each peso in circulation is backed by a U.S. dollar, and monetary policy is forcibly constrained to uphold that promise.
August	Law protecting dollar-denominated deposits enacted.
October	Argentina Fund begins. This fund marks the first time U.S. investors can invest in a mutual fund that represents a broad part of the market. Deregulation decree reforms domestic industry, external trade, and capital markets. The deregulation decree eliminates capital gains taxes for foreigners.

1992

	Argentina enjoys strong economic growth, and the currency board is considered highly successful.

January	Austral replaced by peso. All transactions in currency can now be made on the free market at free negotiated rates.
July	Moody's upgrades Argentina's sovereign debt rating from B3 to B1.
1993	The economy soars, at an annual growth rate above 5.5 percent, as inflation subsides and the government embarks on an ambitious program of deregulation, lowering trade barriers and privatizing state-owned enterprises including oil, telephones, and power.
March	Social security reform (announcement of creation of private pension fund system to begin operation in future). Argentina's Comission de Valores stipulates that only financial intermediary firms belonging to self-regulating organizations can participate in public offering of securities. This move attempts to cut down on insider trading on the Buenos Aires exchange.
April 7	Swaps of bonds for eligible debts agreed to under the Brady Plan by Argentina and foreign creditor banks begins to take place in accordance with the debt and debt service reduction operations.
May	Import tariffs on capital goods abolished and a 15 percent tax reimbursement to capital goods producers established.
August	Standard & Poor's (S&P) assigns first-time rating of BB– to sovereign debt.
1994	
March 28	Swaps of bonds for eligible debts agreed to under the Brady Plan by Argentina and foreign creditor banks are completed.
August	First T-bill auction in twenty years held.
December 20	Mexican peso devaluation followed by a withdrawal of foreign investors from Latin American countries, leading to banking crises: eight banks are suspended and three banks collapse. Events weaken position of wholesale banks that have significant inventories of government securities on which they are incurring capital losses due to the increase in interest rates. Nonfinancial firms are affected as well. Central bank provides emergency liquidity assistance.
December 28	Reserve requirements reduced on dollar deposits in order to provide more liquidity to the banking system.
1995	Following Mexico's December 1994 peso devaluation, capital flows out of emerging markets. Argentina's GDP declines by 2.8 percent.

January 1	The Treaty of Asuncion (1991), establishing the Southern Core Common Market (Mercosur), becomes effective.
January 15	Reserve requirements on peso deposits lowered and a special security fund managed by Banco Nacion set up to assist institutions that suffered high deposit withdrawals.
February	Trust Fund for Provincial Development set up to help support provincial banks.
March	Tax of 3 percent reimposed on all imports, with the exception of capital goods, fuel, and goods produced in the paper, computer, and telecommunications sectors. All goods imported from the member countries of Mercosur are also exempt. Trust Fund for Bank Capitalization established; changes made to the central bank charter to allow it to use repurchase agreements and rediscounts to help troubled banks. New loan agreements made with the IMF, World Bank, and IBD; issuance of new bonds to increase international reserves and fund the trust funds.
April	A limited system of deposit insurance is introduced in response to the banking crisis. Provincial sales tax considered in exchange for lower social security contributions.
May	New rules for bank reserve requirements implemented. President Menem is reelected after convincing Congress to change electoral laws that prohibit a second term.
August	Bank reserve requirement for checking and savings accounts lowered from 33 percent to 30 percent; the 2 percent reserve requirement for time deposits eliminated.
1996	The central bank announces the creation of a $6 billion emergency fund to strengthen the banking sector. Labor reform allows companies to reduce payroll expenses by firing workers without severance pay.
July 26	Finance Minister Domingo Cavallo is dismissed.
August	Tax increases on fuel and public transportation. Government announces plans to increase personal asset tax on holdings over $100,000 to 1 percent.
September	Economic hardship leads to a general strike.
1997	Removal of most entry barriers and branching restrictions of the banking sector.
April	S&P raises sovereign debt rating to BB and upgrades thirteen private companies to investment grade.
July	East Asian financial crisis begins.
1998	Argentina enters prolonged recession in third quarter; unemployment begins to rise.
February	The IMF approves a three-year $2.8 billion line of credit to support Argentina's economic reform program. The

major tax package would reduce by 50 percent the value added tax (VAT) on basic consumer goods. The top corporate tax rate would rise to 35 percent from 33 percent and reduce by 10 percent the social security contributions by employees.

August   Russia announces a partial default on its sovereign bonds.

1999

January 13   Brazil devalues its currency.

September   The Argentine Congress passes the Fiscal Responsibility Law, committing to large reductions in both federal and provincial government spending.

October 24   Fernando de la Rua of the Radical Civic Union (UCR), the opposition coalition candidate, running on a platform to end corruption (under Menem) and the recession, defeats Peronist candidate Eduardo Duhalde for president. De la Rua inherits $114 billion public debt.

December 10   De la Rua is inaugurated president of Argentina and shortly thereafter seeks assistance from the IMF.

2000   Strikes and fuel tax protests. Beef exports slump after an outbreak of foot-and-mouth disease. Soy exports suffer from concerns over the use of genetically modified varieties.

March 10   The IMF agrees to three-year $7.2 billion standby arrangement with Argentina conditioned on a strict fiscal adjustment and the assumption of 3.5 percent GDP growth in 2000 (actual growth was 0.5 percent).

May 29   The government announces $1 billion in budget cuts in hopes that fiscal responsibility will bring renewed confidence to economy.

December 18   The de la Rua government announces a $40 billion multilateral assistance package organized by IMF.

2001

January 12   Argentina's continued poor economic performance prompts the IMF to augment the March 10, 2000, agreement by $7.0 billion as part of a $40 billion assistance package involving the Inter-American Development Bank, the World Bank, Spain, and private lenders. The agreement assumes that GDP will grow at a rate of 2.5 percent in 2001 (versus actual decline of 5.0 percent).

March 19   Domingo Cavallo, minister of economy under Menem and architect of the currency board ten years earlier, replaces Ricardo Lopez Murphy, who resigns as minister of economy.

March 26–28	Risk rating agencies lower Argentina's long-term sovereign rating (S&P from BB to B+ and Moody's from B1 to B2).
March 28	Minister Cavallo secures "emergency powers" from Congress. Cavallo announces economic program comprising a tax on bank transactions, changes in other taxes and tariffs, and sectoral "competitiveness plans."
April	Central bank reduces liquidity requirements and allows banks to include government securities up to 2 billion pesos among liquidity requirements.
May 8	S&P lowers Argentina's long-term sovereign rating further from B+ to B.
June 3	Authorities announce the completion of the "megaswap." Government bonds with a face value of $29.5 billion are voluntarily exchanged for longer-term instruments.
June 15	Minister Cavallo announces package of tax and trade measures, including a trade compensation mechanism for exporters and importers of nonenergy goods.
June 16–17	The de la Rua government announces a $29.5 billion voluntary debt restructuring in which short-term debt is exchanged for new debt with longer maturities and higher interest rates.
June 19	The peso exchange rate for merchandise trade is priced at a fifty-fifty dollar-euro peg, effectively allowing a 7 percent devaluation for foreign trade in hopes of improving Argentina's international competitiveness. Many analysts raise concerns over the effects on the credibility of the convertibility regime.
July	Much of the country is brought to a standstill by a general strike in protest against proposed government spending cuts. Risk rating agencies lower Argentina's long-term sovereign rating further (S&P from B to B– and Moody's first from B2 to B3 and then from B3 to Caa1).
July 10	Government pays yield of 14.1 percent to place $827 million of ninety-day paper.
July 11	Minister Cavallo announces drastic program of fiscal adjustment aimed at eliminating the federal government deficit from August 2001 onward (the "zero-deficit plan").
July 30	Senate approves the zero-deficit plan (lower house of Congress had approved it on July 20).
August 21	IMF announces likely $8 billion augmentation of Argentina's standby credit.

September 7	IMF approves augmentation of standby credit to about $21.6 billion and completes Fourth Review.
September 20	The central bank activates the contingent repurchase facility with international banks, boosting gross reserves by about $1.2 billion ($500 million was disbursed in October).
October 9–12	Risk rating agencies lower Argentina's long-term sovereign rating further (S&P from B– to CCC and Moody's from Caa1 to Caa3).
October 16	Preset date for Congressional elections. The Peronist opposition takes control of both houses of Parliament. Cavallo and financial markets (erroneously) expect that a fiscal deal can be worked out after the elections (on the 17th).
October 28	Minister Cavallo starts negotiations with the IMF and the U.S. Treasury to purchase collateral for new Argentine bonds to be issued in an exchange for the nearly $100 billion of local and external debt.
October 29	Cavallo defines the debt exchange operation as voluntary. The old debt would exchange for bonds paying 7 percent per year and be guaranteed by tax revenues. The IMF and U.S. Treasury require compliance with a zero deficit and an agreement with the provinces on tax revenue sharing before any kind of financial support is given.
October 30	S&P lowers Argentina's long-term sovereign rating from CCC+ to CC.
November 1	The authorities announce a new fiscal package, including a new batch of competitiveness plans, the rebate of VAT payments on debit card transactions, a temporary reduction in employee social security contributions, a corporate debt restructuring scheme, and a tax amnesty that writes off interest and penalty obligations accrued through the end of September 2001.
November 6	S&P lowers Argentina's long-term sovereign rating from CC to SD (selective default). Argentina conducts a second debt swap, exchanging $60 billion of bonds with an average interest rate of 11–12 percent for extended maturity notes carrying only a 7 percent interest rate. International bond rating agencies consider it an effective default.
November 19	The IMF announces it will not make any new disbursements without being satisfied that Argentina has secured the goals previously designated.

November 23	The central bank introduces an effective cap on bank deposits, by imposing a 100 percent liquidity requirement on deposits paying an interest rate more than 1 percentage point above average of all local banks.
November 30	End of a debt swap with local banks and pension funds for more than $55 billion (over a total public debt of $160 billion). The authorities announce completion of the local leg of the debt restructuring. Government bonds with a face value of $41 billion at the federal level and $10 billion at the provincial level are "voluntarily" exchanged.
December	Economy Minister Cavallo announces sweeping restrictions to halt an exodus of bank deposits. The IMF stops $1.3 billion in aid.
December 2	The government announces temporary capital control regime (termed *Corralito*) involving bank withdrawal limits and limits on dollar transfers abroad as a last-ditch effort to fend off a devaluation and prevent a major banking crisis. Withdrawals are limited to 250 pesos (dollars) per week per account. Depositors, however, may still access funds for larger purchases through checks or debit cards and transfer their money among banks. Holders of deposits may also exchange them for federal bonds (BODENs) maturing in 2005, 2007, or 2012 in a Canje exchange. No limits are placed on domestic payments made with checks, credits, debit cards, and electronic MEP (*metodo electronico de pagos*) payments.
December 3	The capital control measures announced on December 2 come into full effect through Decree 1570-01 on December 3:

- Wire transfers suspended except with prior central bank approval.
- Cash withdrawals from the banking system limited to $1,000 per month.
- Argentine financial institutions prohibited from foreign currency futures transactions.
- Argentine financial institutions prohibited from issuing new bank loans denominated in Argentine pesos. All new loans must be issued in U.S. dollars, and existing peso loans must be converted to U.S. dollar loans at a one-to-one rate.
- Foreign investors trading in the Argentine Securities Market subject to repatriation restrictions. Funds related to securities transactions must remain in the

country until government approval is obtained or the measure is officially revoked.

December 5   The IMF withholds $1.24 billion loan installment, citing Argentina's repeated inability to meet fiscal targets.

December 7   Argentina announces it can no longer guarantee payment on foreign debt.

December 10   The central bank imposes a 98 percent reserve requirement on deposit increases after December 1, 2001, aimed at limiting flight to quality within the system.

December 13   A twenty-four-hour general strike is held in protest at curbs on bank withdrawals, delayed pension payouts, and other measures. Phase one of the government debt exchange is completed.

December 19   State of emergency is declared to stop protests against Minister Cavallo's economic policies. The lower house of Congress repeals the special legislative powers granted to Cavallo.

December 20   President De la Rua and Minister Cavallo resign after days of riots and protests that leave over twenty demonstrators dead. A banking holiday is declared for December 21, extended through December 26. Moody's lowers Argentina ratings to Ca from Caa3. Ramon Puerta becomes interim president. Country risk reaches 4,618 points. Global (sovereign) bond yields reach their historical maximum of 49 percent annual return in dollars.

December 21   The official Foreign Exchange Rate market is closed.

December 23   Rodriguez Saa becomes the new interim president for sixty days. He declares the suspension of external debt payments for at least sixty days, totaling $166 billion in federal and provincial debt.

December 24   The government announces that a new fiat currency (i.e., without foreign currency backing) will be created (the argentino).

December 26   The liquidity standards for banks are relaxed. Rodriguez Saa announces a new economic plan based on (a) suspension of payments on public debt, (b) new job creation program, and (c) creation of new currency (the argentino) to begin circulating in January 2002 and not to be convertible to the U.S. dollar.

December 30   President Saa resigns after his emergency policies are rejected by the Peronist governors.

2002

January 1   Congress elects Peronist Senator Eduardo Duhalde as caretaker president.

January 3	Senator Duhalde is sworn in as president with a mandate to conclude the remaining period of the de la Rua presidency; President Duhalde announces the end of convertibility and the introduction of a dual foreign exchange regime.
January 4	Leak reported in the financial press suggests that a 40 percent devaluation is imminent.
January 5	The Argentine stock market is closed.
January 6	The Argentine Congress votes to establish the Law of Economic Emergency and abolish the Convertibility Law. After the Argentine Congress passes necessary legislation, President Duhalde announces the end of the currency board and a plan to devalue the peso by 29 percent (to 1.4 to the dollar) for major foreign commercial transactions, with a floating rate for all other transactions. Other elements of economic plan include converting all debts up to $100,000 to pesos (passing on devaluation cost to creditors), capital and bank account controls, a new tax on oil to compensate creditors for the losses that will ensue, renegotiation of public debt, and a balanced budget.
January 7	The new minister of finance, Lenicov, announces the devaluation of the peso and the establishment of a new dual foreign exchange rate regime, to be implemented on January 9, 2002.
January 10	Government announces it will guarantee dollar deposits, but to curtail bank runs, the $1,000 (1,500 peso) limit on monthly withdrawals is maintained and all checking and savings accounts with balances exceeding $10,000 and $3,000, respectively, will be converted to certificates of deposit and remain frozen for at least one year. Smaller deposits have the option of earlier withdrawal by moving to peso-denominated accounts at the 1.4 exchange rate.
January 11	After several delays, the exchange rate market reopens, and the new dual exchange rate system is put in place: • 1 Argentinean peso = 1 U.S. dollar parity (Convertibility Plan) is abolished. • All debts (capital and interest) in Argentine currency with financial entities—converted into U.S. dollars according to Decree 1570-01—will be reconverted into the original currency (pesos). • The official, fixed conversion rate of 1 U.S. dollar = 1.4 pesos is relevant for foreign trade operations. The free

	or floating rate is relevant for all other transactions and freely determined by the market.
January 16	The IMF approves request for one-year extension of $936 million payment due January 17, keeping Argentina from falling into arrears.
January 17	Argentine stock market reopens. The government announces that dollar-denominated loans exceeding $100,000 will be converted to pesos at 1.4 for fixed rate, deepening the balance sheet mismatch of banks.
January 19–20	Duhalde reverses his decision to guarantee dollar deposits, which will be converted to pesos at some undefined devalued exchange rate.
January 21	The government announces the easing of bank withdrawal restrictions:

- Up to 7,000 pesos can be withdrawn from term deposits in pesos (transferring that money to a checking account)
- Up to $5,000 can be withdrawn from term deposits in dollars (transferring that money to a checking account at the official exchange rate, 1.4).
- Up to $5,000 in a savings account can be pesofied at the official exchange rate.

January 23	The Argentine Senate passes bankruptcy law that would use capital controls to restrict foreign private debt payments through December 2003.
January 24	Utility tariffs are frozen indefinitely.
January 30	Argentina's Chamber of Deputies passes controversial bankruptcy law, stripping it of the Senate provision prohibiting foreign debt payments, but other capital controls remain in effect. The law retains language allowing conversion of dollar-denominated debt below $100,000 to pesos at one-to-one rate (benefitting debtors) and suspending creditor action on loan debt defaults for 180 days.
February 3	Lenicov announces an asymmetric pesofication and the end of the dual exchange rate regime:

- All dollar deposits are pesofied at 1.4 pesos per dollar.
- Corporate and consumer debts are also pesofied, but at the exchange rate prevailing during the Convertibility Plan period. Both deposits and credit will be indexed to inflation.
- The dual exchange rate regime is replaced by a unified floating exchange rate determined by market forces.

- The right is granted to withdraw wage and pension income from the *Corralito* without any amount restrictions (before, workers could only extract up to 1,500 pesos). *Corralon* starts, which freezes bank term deposits (holders of term deposits have the option to convert them into CEDROs or BODENs maturing in 2007 or 2012 in a Canje exchange).

February 4   The government decrees the unification of the exchange rate regime and the asymmetric pesofication of bank balance sheets (assets at one-to-one rate and liabilities at 1.4 pesos to dollar). The official foreign exchange market is closed.

February 11   The central bank establishes a new unified free foreign exchange market, which replaces the two markets—official and free—implemented in January. The exchange rate market reopens, and the floating dollar exchange rate reaches 2.1 pesos, well below the devaluation expectations built into asset prices.

February 27   The federal government and the provincial governors reach agreement on a temporary revenue-sharing arrangement that abolishes the minimum floor on transfers to the provinces in exchange for (a) the broadening of the coparticipation base to include the financial transactions tax, and (b) better terms for their debt servicing. The provinces commit to reducing fiscal deficits by 60 percent in 2002 and achieving balance in 2003.

March 5   Export taxes of 10 percent and 5 percent are imposed on primary products and process agricultural and industrial products, respectively.

March 8   The pesofication of government debt under Argentine law is decreed.

March 13   A voluntary bond swap (Swap I) is decreed authorizing the exchange of reprogrammed time deposits for government bonds. The decree also authorizes issuance of bonds to banks in compensation for the asymmetric pesofication of their balance sheets.

March 25   The peso exchange rate reaches a peak of 4 pesos per dollar. To contain the depreciation of the currency, the authorities intervene heavily in the foreign exchange market ($800 million in March), tighten access to central bank liquidity assistance (a matching dollar from the parent now being requested as a condition for assistance to foreign banks), and introduce a variety of exchange regulations affecting banks, foreign exchange bureaus, and exporters. Thirteen new regulations are issued on March 25 alone, bringing the total for the month of March to about fifty.

March 26 The central bank announces new measures related to foreign exchange transactions and ADR-CEDEAR conversions aimed at improving the functioning of the foreign currency market and regulating the buying and selling of foreign currency by order and for the account of the central bank. The press communication also mentions that there will be coordination between the Comision Nacional de Valores (CNV) and the Bolsa de Comercio de Buenos Aires (BCBA) in order to adopt new measures to regulate capital outflows via ADR and CEDEAR transactions.

April Banking and foreign exchange activity suspended; Duhalde says the financial system may collapse.

April 9 Export taxes on agricultural primary products increased to 20–23.5 percent.

April 19 The central banks suspends Scotiabank Quilmes for thirty days. A bank holiday is declared until Congress approves a solution to the problem of judicial injunctions (amparos) releasing bank deposits. The authorities begin working on a plan (the so-called BONEX II plan) to convert reprogrammed time deposits into government bonds.

April 20 Economy Minister Remes Lenicov presents to congress the BONEX II plan; the draft law is rejected, and Minister Remes resigns.

April 23 President Duhalde reaches agreement with provincial governors on a fourteen-point Federal-Provincial Pact.

April 25 Congress approves the Ley Tapón to ease pressure from the amparos. The law modifies court procedures and states that depositors can only access funds once the judicial process is over; in the meantime funds are deposited in an escrow account.

May 6 Congress approves the February Federal-Provincial Pact.

May 15 Congress approves law that reverses the most harmful provisions of the January emergency law and makes limited improvements to the insolvency law.

May 30 The Economic Subversion Law is repealed.

May 31 In order to tighten control over the sale of export receipts, the central bank announces that dollar export revenues in excess of $1 million will have to be sold directly to the central bank. Buenos Aires and the federal government sign full-fledged text of bilateral agreement. Agreement on the annexes (quarterly fiscal targets and calendar for disbursement) is reached in June.

June 1   President Duhalde signs the Options Plan on reprogrammed deposits, a revised version of former Minister Remes's BONEX II Plan, giving depositors the option to exchange deposits into bonds.

June 18   The minimum level of export proceeds that should be surrendered to the central bank lowered from $1 million to $500,000.

July   Duhalde calls early elections for March 2003, later put back to April, to try to win public support for the government's handling of the economic crisis.

July 9   In response to a class action suit lodged by the country's ombudsman on behalf of all depositors, a federal court declares the deposit freeze and pesofication unconstitutional.

July 24   The government issued a decree suspending court-ordered withdrawals of frozen bank deposits for 120 business days.

July 25   The decree suspending deposit withdrawals obtained through court orders is declared partially unconstitutional by a federal judge.

July 26   Following a demand by the national ombudsman, a judge rules unconstitutional the government decree suspending lawsuits on December's bank curbs for 120 business days.

July 29   A panel of monetary policy experts makes public several proposals to resolve the country's financial crisis, including a monetary policy anchor, an independent central bank, the ending of peso-printing deficit financing, and an end to the use of quasi-currencies by the provinces. The report calls for a floating exchange rate and urges Argentina to stop using international reserves to support the peso.

August 15   Congress approves a bill extending for ninety days (through mid-November 2002) the provision that suspends certain kinds of creditor-initiated nonbankruptcy law enforcement actions. Congress also approves a bill extending for sixty days (through end September 2002) the application of price indexation to loans.

August 22   The Supreme Court declares unconstitutional the 13 percent salary cut for federal government workers and pensioners, implemented from July 2001.

August 26	The government issues a resolution to allow the issuance of bank compensation bonds for the asymmetric pesofication.
August 28	A federal court establishes that parent banks should be fully responsible for the liabilities of subsidiaries in Argentina.
September	The central bank passes a very restrictive regulation (circular 3723) that mandates that every stock be traded in its underlying currency. After intense opposition from the financial community, the central bank rescinds 3723 and instead passes a resolution (circular 3727) that forbids "contra cable" operations. These operations allow brokers to sell stocks purchased in Buenos Aires instantaneously in New York (or any foreign market) using the Merval as a clearinghouse. Under 3727 it is still possible for investors in Argentina to convert CEDEARs and sell them in New York, but this new restriction significantly increases the transaction costs of doing so.
September 3	The government introduces new exchange controls in an attempt to boost international reserves and defend the peso: • The limit for exporters' foreign exchange surrender to the central bank is reduced from $500,000 to $200,000. • The minimum maturity of external debt contracted by private nonfinancial entities is set to ninety days. • Exchange bureaus are required to deposit with the central bank foreign exchange holdings exceeding $1.5 million on a daily basis. • The net dollar positions held by exchange dealers operating on behalf of the central bank are reduced by an average 40 percent.
September 5	The federal administrative dispute chamber, an appellate court, rules that the decrees establishing the *Corralito* and pesofication were unconstitutional. The ruling applies to only one case, but it opens the door for further similar rulings.
September 9	Further tightening of foreign exchange controls: prior authorization from the central bank is required for dollar purchases exceeding $100,000 for portfolio and other financial investments abroad, as well as for the purchase of foreign banknotes.
September 13	The Federal Court of Appeals declares the *Corralito,* pesofication, and the 120 days' suspension of executions

	against the *Corralito* unconstitutional; the decision allows depositors to claim their deposits in court immediately. The 2003 budget is submitted to Congress.
September 17	The government issues a decree that extends the negotiation period for utility tariffs for another 120 days with the possibility of a further 60-day extension.
September 20	The government launches a second swap of bonds for frozen deposits and announces the easing of restrictions on frozen time deposits of up to 7,000 pesos.
October 31	The monthly cash withdrawal limit on the *Corralito* raised to 2,000 pesos from 1,200 pesos.
November	Argentina defaults on an $800 million debt repayment to the World Bank, having failed to resecure IMF aid. The World Bank says it will not consider new loans for the country.
November 11	After discussions with the government, the banks announce a voluntary seventy-five-day stay on foreclosures.
November 14	The government fails to fully meet an $809 million World Bank debt payment; only $79.2 million in interest is paid. President Duhalde signs a decree lowering the VAT rate by 2 percentage points.
November 15	A lower court suspends the public hearings designed to grant a tariff increase to the privatized utility companies.
November 18	President Duhalde signs a twelve-point agreement with provincial governors and some key legislators over the new election timetable and the government's economic policies.
November 21	The Senate approves President Duhalde's plans for delaying the presidential election by a month to April. The first round of presidential elections is scheduled to be held on April 27, 2003, and will be followed by a second round on May 10 if necessary.
November 22	The government announces that it will lift the remaining *Corralito* restrictions on sight accounts effective December 2. Term deposits (the corralon) remain frozen. Minister Lavagna submits a draft decree to President Duhalde lifting the tariff rates on electricity and natural gas. On average, electricity rates will rise 9.0 percent and natural gas 7.2 percent.
November 27	An executive decree is issued authorizing court-imposed stay on foreclosures for thirty business days, during which time mediation is required.
December 2	*Corralito* rescinded.
December 9	The resignation of Central Bank President Pignanelli is accepted by President Duhalde.

| December 10 | President Duhalde appoints Alfonso Prat Gay to be central bank president. Legislation eliminating the ability of the executive to grant tax amnesties becomes effective. |
| December 11 | A court order reverses the decreed increases in electricity and gas tariffs. |

2003

March 9	The Supreme Court rules that conversion to pesos was illegal. According to the central bank, approximately $8,760 million is at stake.
May	Nestor Kirchner sworn in as president. Former President Carlos Menem gains most votes in first round of elections but pulls out before second round.
September 10	Argentine finance officials reach an agreement with the IMF for a three-year $12.6 billion standby credit. Under the terms of the new arrangement, the government pledges to raise the consolidated primary fiscal surplus from 2.5 percent of GDP this year to 3.0 percent next year.

2004

April 9	Argentina decides to make a $3.1 billion payment to the IMF, a retreat from a vow by Buenos Aires that it would not pay up unless the IMF signaled that it would approve an upcoming report on Argentina's economic progress as part of the 2003 accord.
July 2	Argentina files a shelf registration statement with the U.S. Securities and Exchange Commission, completing the documentation needed to seek regulatory approval in the United States for a debt exchange to restructure some $100 billion in defaulted debt.
August	Argentina suspends its agreement with the IMF but continues to repay its debts as they come in.
October 26	The Supreme Court rules that the conversion of fixed-term savings in dollars to pesos—known as pesofication—was legal, relieving the banks of large potential losses from further injunctions.

2005

| February | A majority of Republic of Argentina bondholders surrender their claims in exchange for new bonds worth roughly thirty-five cents on the dollar. |
| December | Kirchner says his government will repay its entire $9.8 billion debt to the IMF early—before the end of 2005. |

Sources: Ambito Financiero (http://www.ambitoweb.com), *La Nacion* (http://www.lanacion.com.architecture), *Clarin* (http://www.clarin.com), Pictet (http://www.pictet.com), BBC News (http://www.news.bbc.co.uk), IMF (2003), and Bekaert and Harvey (2003).

References

Auguste, S., K. Dominguez, H. Kamil, and L. Tesar. 2006. Cross border trading as a mechanism for capital flight: ADRs and the Argentine crisis. *Journal of Monetary Economics* 53:1259–95.

Bekaert, G., and C. Harvey. 2003. Chronology of economic, political and financial events in emerging markets: Argentina. Campbell R. Harvey's home page. http://www.duke.edu/~charvey/Country_risk/chronology/argentina.htm.

Bleaney, M. 2004. Argentina's currency board collapse: Weak policy or bad luck? *World Economy* 27 (5): 699–714.

Bordo, M. D., C. Meissner, and A. Redish. 2004. How "original sin" was overcome: The evolution of external debt denominated in domestic currencies in the United States and the British dominions 1800–2000. In *Other people's money*, ed. Barry Eichengreen and Ricardo Hausmann, 122–53. Chicago: University of Chicago Press.

Caballero, R., and A. Krishnamurthy. 2003. Excessive dollar debt: Financial development and underinsurance. *Journal of Finance* 58 (2): 867–93.

Calvo, G. 1998. Capital flows and capital-market crises: The simple economics of sudden stops. *Journal of Applied Economics* 1 (1): 35–54.

Calvo, G., A. Izquierdo, and L. Mejía. 2004. On the empirics of sudden stops: The relevance of balance-sheet effects. NBER Working Paper no. 10520. Cambridge, MA: National Bureau of Economic Research.

Calvo, G., A. Izquierdo, and E. Talvi. 2003. Sudden stops, the real exchange rate and fiscal sustainability: Argentina's lessons. NBER Working Paper no. 9828. Cambridge, MA: National Bureau of Economic Research.

Calvo, G., and C. Reinhart. 2002. Fear of floating. *Quarterly Journal of Economics* 17 (2): 379–408.

Cavallo, D. 2003. Exchange rate regimes. In *Economic and financial crises in emerging market economies*, ed. M. Feldstein, 78–81. Chicago: University of Chicago Press.

Cavallo, D., and J. Cottani. 1997. Argentina's convertibility plan and the IMF. *American Economic Review* 87 (2): 17–22.

Cespedes, L., R. Chang, and A. Velasco. 2004. Balance sheets and exchange rate policy. *American Economic Review* 94 (September): 1183–93.

Cuevas, A. 2003. Reforming intergovernmental fiscal relations in Argentina. IMF Working Paper no. 03/90. Washington, DC: International Monetary Fund.

Dabos, M., and L. Gomez-Mera. 1998. The Tequila banking crisis in Argentina. University of San Andres, Department of Economics. Mimeograph, September.

della Paolera, G., and A. Taylor. 2001. *Straining at the anchor: The Argentine currency board and the search for macroeconomic stability, 1880–1935.* Long-Term Factors in Economic Development Series. Chicago: University of Chicago Press.

———. 2002. Internal vs. external convertibility and emerging-market crises: Lessons from Argentine economic history. *Explorations in Economic History* 39:357–89.

———. 2003a. Gaucho banking redux. *Economia* 3 (2): 1–42.

———, eds. 2003b. *A new economic history of Argentina.* Cambridge: Cambridge University Press.

de la Torre, A., E. Levy Yeyati, and S. Schmukler. 2003. Living and dying with hard pegs: The rise and fall of Argentina's currency board. *Economia* 3 (2): 43–107.

De Nicolo, G., P. Honohan, and A. Ize. 2003. Dollarization of the banking system: Good or bad? IMF Working Paper no. WP/03/146. Washington, DC: International Monetary Fund.

Dubas, J., B. Lee, and N. Mark. 2005. Effective exchange rate classifications.

NBER Working Paper no. 11272. Cambridge, MA: National Bureau of Economic Research.

Eichengreen, B., R. Hausmann, and U. Panizza. 2003. Currency mismatches, debt intolerance and original sin: Why they are not the same and why it matters. NBER Working Paper no. 10036. Cambridge, MA: National Bureau of Economic Research.

The Economist. 2005. Argentina's economy. December 20.

Edwards, S. 2002. The great exchange rate debate after Argentina. NBER Working Paper no. 9257. Cambridge, MA: National Bureau of Economic Research.

Feldstein, M. 2002. Argentina's fall: Lessons from the latest financial crisis. Foreign Affairs 81 (2): 8–14.

Galiani, S., P. Gertler, E. Schargrodsky, and F. Sturzenegger. 2005. The benefits and costs of privatization in Argentina: A microeconomic analysis. In Privatization in Latin America: Myths and realities, ed. A. Chong and F. Lopez-de-Silanes, 67–116. Stanford, CA: Stanford University Press.

Galiani, S., E. Levy Yeyati, and E. Schargrodsky. 2003. Financial dollarization and debt deflation under a currency board: The case of Argentina. Emerging Market Review 4 (4): 340–67.

Gurtner, F. 2004. Why did Argentina's currency board collapse? World Economy 27 (5): 679–97.

Gutierrez, J., and F. Montes-Negret. 2004. Argentina's banking system: Restoring financial viability. World Bank Working Paper no. 2/04. Washington, DC: World Bank.

Hausmann, R., and A. Velasco. 2002. Hard money's soft underbelly: Understanding the Argentine crisis. In Brookings trade forum 2002, ed. S. Collins and D. Rodrik, 59–104. Washington, DC: Brookings Institution Press.

International Monetary Fund (IMF). 2003. Lessons from the crisis in Argentina. http://www.imf.org/external/np/pdr/lessons/100803.pdf.

———. 2004. The IMF and Argentina, 1991–2001. Washington, DC: Independent Evaluation Office.

———. Various issues. International financial statistics. Washington, DC: International Monetary Fund.

Levy Yeyati, E., S. Schmukler, and N. van Horen. 2003. The price of inconvertible deposits: The stock market boom during the Argentine crisis. Economics Letters 83 (1): 7–13.

Mendoza, E., and K. Smith. 2002. Margin calls, trading costs, and asset prices in emerging markets: The financial mechanics of the "sudden stop" phenomenon. NBER Working Paper no. 9286. Cambridge, MA: National Bureau of Economic Research.

Mussa, M. 2002. Argentina and the Fund: From triumph to tragedy. Washington, DC: Institute for International Economics.

Perry, G., and L. Serven. 2003. The anatomy of a multiple crisis: Why was Argentina special and what can we learn from it? World Bank Policy Research Working Paper no. 3081. Washington, DC: World Bank.

Pou, P. 2000. Argentina's structural reforms of the 1990s. IMF Finance and Development 37, no. 1 (March), http://www.imf.org/external/pubs/ft/fandd/2000/03/pou.htm.

Randall, L. 1978. An economic history of Argentina in the twentieth century. New York: Columbia University Press.

Reinhart, C., K. Rogoff, and M. Savastano. 2003. Debt intolerance. NBER Working Paper no. 9908. Cambridge, MA: National Bureau of Economic Research.

Rigobon, R. 2002. The curse of non-investment grade countries. Journal of Development Economics 69 (2): 423–49.

Romero, L. A., and J. Brennan. 2002. *A history of Argentina in the twentieth century*. University Park, PA: Penn State University Press.

Taylor, A. M. 1998. Argentina and the world capital market: Saving, investment and international capital mobility in the twentieth century. *Journal of Development Economics* 57 (October): 147–84.

Tommasi, M. 2006. Federalism in Argentina and the reforms of the 1990s. In *Federalism and economic reform: International perspectives*, ed. J. Wallack and T. N. Srinivasan, 25–84. Cambridge: Cambridge University Press.

Comment   Nicolas Magud

This paper does a stupendous job of describing in a detailed but concise way the reforms that took place in Argentina during the 1990s. It then draws on this description to narrate the incredibly fast unfolding of the reforms that occurred during the first years of the 2000s, emphasizing the capital controls episode that took place during December 2001–December 2002, known as the "corralito." Let me succinctly provide a summary of the paper, along with some comments on the facts and implemented (or not) policies, as well as the authors' explanation of them.

During the 1990s Argentina moved from being a hyperinflationary country to being the darling of international capital markets, to return later—by the end of the 1990s and the early 2000s—to being the spoiled one once again. The authors thoroughly describe the set of reforms put into place during these years. They then ask the question: was it bad luck, or bad policies? And they answer that both were responsible for the observed facts. I definitely agree with them, but I will disagree in some of the bad, or should I say *missing,* policies prior to the fall of the convertibility plan, and after the capital controls in which it ended.

The authors correctly ascertain that the currency board is partly guilty because, as they say, it is a double-edged sword: it buys low inflation and credibility, but at a potentially very high price (should you not accompany it with the corresponding fiscal soundness). For the convertibility plan to be effective (i.e., credible), it required increasing escape clause costs. This generated an increasing degree of liability dollarization (dollar-denominated debts), facilitating the dollarization of the private sector, and leaving the economy with a question: what if the exchange rate depreciates? In a sense, these high escape clause costs were just necessary for the convertibility plan to be successful.

A related question is why the peso was anchored to the dollar, given that Argentina's share of trade with the United States is small compared to Brazil and the EU. And for this I have a nonacademic explanation. The

Nicolas Magud is an assistant professor of economics at the University of Oregon.

representative Argentine agent saves in dollars, no matter what (at least, it used to until recently). Let me offer support—loosely speaking—by way of a personal anecdote, since I am from Argentina. When I was young, my father taught me that if I was ever able to save any money, I should *never* deposit that money into a savings or checking account. I should go to the exchange market, buy dollars, and put those dollars into a safe box. Clearly, this is not an academic explanation, but it works as a good example of Argentine thinking. As of the early 1990s the representative Argentine saved in dollars, so the convertibility plan was nothing but an exchange rate–based stabilization plan using the currency that Argentines used as a store of value as the anchor of the system.

But, again, the fiscal part of the story is crucial to an understanding of the path of events in Argentina. The country historically experienced a lack of coordination between the national government and provincial governments. Traditionally, most provincial governments spend as much as they can (many of them mainly in public servants), and then they require more funds to keep on operating.[1]

On top of this, the second half of the 1990s experienced another phenomenon, but of a political rather than an economic nature. During these years, Eduardo Duhalde, the governor of Buenos Aires, wanted to run for president in the 1999 election. For this purpose, he started spending big to gain political support among voters, many times spending money on white elephants. At the same time, President Carlos Menem wanted to get a third presidency—despite its being unconstitutional—and in order to secure the support of most of the other provinces, he also started to spend big. At the same time, he did not want to appear fiscally irresponsible. In table 7.1 of the paper, we can observe that the national government fiscal balance was apparently under control. But, interestingly, the provincial fiscal accounts were experiencing high deficits.

Related to the fiscal problem, some commentators argued that, in response to the mounting recession in 1999, expansionary fiscal policy could have been used as countercyclical policy. But there is also good empirical evidence documenting the expansionary effects of contractionary fiscal policy (see Alesina and Perotti 1997, among others). A highly indebted country (which is an idiosyncratic measure, as documented by Reinhart and Rogoff 2004), can reduce domestic market interest rates by reducing its fiscal deficit and consequently its financing needs: demand for credit decreases, thus increasing investment (see Magud 2002). In this case, a possible mistake of President Fernando de la Rua's government was not to implement contractionary fiscal policy during 1999–2000, but rather not to

---

1. It is commonly remarked that many times the job of a provincial finance minister is to try to spend as much as possible and, when funds run out, call Buenos Aires to ask the national government for more money.

do as much as necessary for it to be expansionary (if private investors perceive the fiscal consolidation as being insufficient, investment does not "take off"). Furthermore, given that the country was just getting out of a recession, it could have been more expansionary to reduce public expenditures instead of increasing taxes, so as not to reduce the private-sector demand for goods and services (which is the exact point made by Alesina and Perotti). Also, reducing public expenditures reduces the demand for nontradable goods—public expenditures are mostly in nontradables—and thus helps depreciate the real exchange rate, boosting net exports.

Other criticisms of the convertibility plan were that it failed to (1) consolidate the budget constraint of central and provincial governments, (2) provide deep banking system regulations, and (3) reduce labor market rigidities. It was also blamed for lacking an exit strategy, and there also existed doubts about its long-run feasibility. All these points are valid, but it is worth mentioning that this is asking one instrument to perform many activities at the same time. And we know that that does not work. The sole objective of the convertibility plan was to reduce high inflation rates, which it did. There were, as the paper thoroughly documents, many other parallel reforms to account for these other problems. As the facts showed, some of these reforms were not as successful as expected. And, once more, the lack of an exit strategy is a tricky point. Had one existed, credibility issues could have been raised that would probably have undermined most of the inflation reduction effects that the convertibility plan brought about.

As stated above, the authors claim that Argentina's problems were both the existence of external shocks and the lack of adaptive policies. I definitely agree with them. But I will claim that the lack of adaptive policies was more important during the second half of the 1990s than after 1999, as the authors highlight. And for this purpose I will first refer to table 7.1 in the paper. We can observe that Argentina's external debt increased throughout the 1990s (which relates to the "debt intolerance" in Reinhart, Rogoff, and Savastano 2003). During the first half of the decade, we can attribute this in part to the recognition of previously floating debt—trade credit that the government was not paying and that the government put in written terms to enhance the credibility of the plan—and to the privatization of the social security system, which is expansionary for any economy that is not dynamically inefficient, like Argentina. Also, de Pablo (2005) shows that once the floating debt is included, during the first half of the 1990s the debt level actually decreases, contrary to what most people think!

But more can be extracted from table 7.1 in the paper. Looking at the real effective exchange rate series, a continuous appreciation is observed (see also figure 7.7 in the paper), especially during the late 1990s—and particularly when external shocks took place: 1997–2000. Wasn't this a good opportunity to reduce government expenditures, thus contributing to increased sustainability of the fiscal sector, as well as reducing pressures on the real exchange rate appreciation? However, what we see is that the fiscal imbalance increased instead of decreasing during these years (despite a growing economy during 1991–98, so it was not taxes—at least those directly due to a markedly lower revenue—that was driving the deficit). And here both the central government and the provinces are to blame. Although it is a counterfactual, these years could have been very good times to perform a sharp fiscal adjustment, especially during 1996 and 1997, when the economy growth rate was still high (and in 1998, although it was not as big, the growth rate was still decent).

The 1990s brought a very good thing to the Argentine economy: an increase in the debt maturity profile. As of September 1999, of an external debt of $118.8 billion, 97 percent was long term. However, 8.7 percent of that long-term debt was due in 2000! (See figure 7C.1.) Furthermore, the amortization schedule of Argentina's public debt included heavy payments during 2000–2005, as can be seen in figure 7C.2. So, in a sense, the bomb was already there.

And then came the Duhalde administration (January 2002), probably the worst of all of them, and deserving more attention than it attracted in this paper. Capital controls were imposed by late 2001, originally for ninety days only. But these controls enabled people to make transactions through the banking system. The Duhalde administration not only made the capital controls regime last longer than originally planned (if it was such a bad thing, why didn't his administration levy it right away?); it also did not allow transactions to use money through the banking sector. All in all, it just

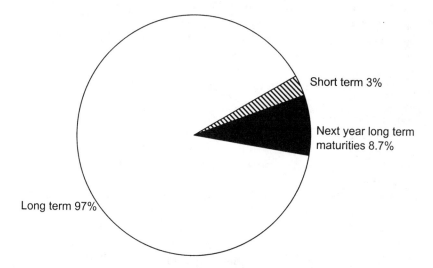

Fig. 7C.1   **Maturity structure of Argentine public debt as of September 30, 1999: $118.8 billion**

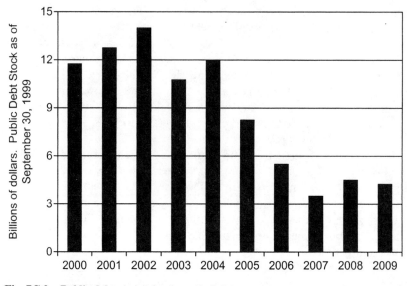

Fig. 7C.2   Public debt: Amortization schedule

made the capital controls more stringent than under president de la Rua's government.

Moreover, the short-lived government of Rodriguez Saa (which only lasted for the final week of December 2001) defaulted on its sovereign debt. So when the Duhalde administration devalued the currency, there was not a marked increase in exports, simply because there was no credit to finance export operations. On top of this, taxes on exports were raised, curbing a sharp increase in exports (so what was the devaluation for?). Furthermore, the way out of convertibility was astonishingly disordered, as the authors document in their appendix. First, the currency was devalued to 1.4 pesos per dollar, there were multiple exchange rates, and then the exchange rate was allowed to float, in just a couple of months, generating speculative behavior. *Clarin,* one of the most important newspapers in the country, reported in early 2002 in an interview with Finance Minister Remes Lenicov that those were days of a trial-and-error policy (no wonder the finance minister did not last long in office). During those days, it was commonly observed that the government was thinking of implementing some measures, which were made public, but many times after a couple of meetings, they were not. This raised many time inconsistency problems at the time.

The experience in Argentina during 1991–2004 is a clear case of policy reversals. It shows how even deep reforms can be rapidly undone, and it demonstrates the consequences that they bring. During 2002, the government claimed that its policy was against the financial system—which accounted for everything that happened in Argentina in the late 1990s, according to the administration's message—and for the "productive" sector. The government pushed a "buy Argentine" policy: consumers should buy domestically produced goods regardless of their price.

On the other hand, the 2002–3 administration was just a transition one, not elected by popular vote. One of its duties, then, should have been to put the country in order to facilitate the task of the following elected president. That was not observed. There seemed not to be any plan during this administration. For instance, nothing was done in regard to debt restructuring after the sovereign default. It was still not finished by the end of 2004, even though the finance minister was the same one who took office in early 2002, after Remes Lenicov left (and even though international interest rates were rising).

The newly elected government (which took office in May 2003) also contributed to undoing all the market-oriented reforms of the 1990s, leading the economy toward a populist path. Current economic policies lean toward a state-led economy, trying to move the economy away from the experience of the 1990s, probably reducing Argentina's long-term growth and—to be optimistic—just stabilizing it in the bad equilibrium. A process of re-statization of firms is underway, which is even absorbing firms that were never state owned before! But, contrary to their pledge, public debt is still in the banking system, and international borrowing has not stopped. Moreover, despite high tax revenues—the direct consequence of an artificially depreciated exchange rate and high export taxes—government expenditures are rising (and for 2007 this can be expected to increase further if the president aims at maintaining power, either through his reelection or if one of his close aides retains the presidency). The latter circumstance is also related to a debt swap that the Argentine government carried out in early 2006, through which it reduced its indebtedness to the IMF, issuing bonds that pay a higher interest rate, as the authors mention—as if this would reduce the need for fiscal adjustment! Coupled with a monetary expansion to keep the exchange rate undervalued and lack of sufficient investment—many times resulting from a government's failure to respect contracts—this raises concerns about the inflation rate starting to pick up again. The inflation rate for 2005 actually rose above 12 percent—compared to an estimated rate of 8 percent in the federal budget. As of the time of this writing, February 2006, the prospects seem the same for this year; I would be tempted to say that the president is comfortable with an inflation rate in the 10–15 percent range, as far as this makes the economy grow in case he is looking to remain in power somehow. But from there to a new high inflation process, things may turn kind of dangerous—not to mention that it is not clear how accountable to Congress the government is for spending revenues above what was forecast. So far the government has used light price controls against inflation. Eventually, we know, if investment does not increase, the latter will prove useless or even worse, given that they might generate some repressed inflation. In a sense, being forward looking, it looks like this government prefers big booms and recession instead of smooth growth—which does not sound very welfare improving.

To wrap up, I think that the paper does a superb job of describing the facts during the 1991–2001 period. A future task will be to analyze in more detail what happened after that, and what the short-run and long-run effects were of the convertibility plan and the corralito (the capital controls episode). More could be said on the missing fiscal adjustment and lack of corrective policies after the convertibility plan was ended, especially after the corralito. And a final message from the Argentina experience can be extracted by paraphrasing George Santayana: Those who do not learn from the past are doomed to repeat it. Let's hope we learned from this experience.

References

Alesina, Alberto, and Roberto Perotti. 1997. Fiscal adjustments in OECD countries: Composition and macroeconomic effects. *IMF Staff Papers* 44 (2): 210–48.

de Pablo, Juan Carlos. 2005. *La economía Argentina en la ultima mitad del siglo XX.* Buenos Aires, Argentina: Editorial La Ley.

Magud, Nicolás. 2003. On asymmetric business cycles, and the effectiveness of counter-cyclical fiscal policies. University of Oregon, Department of Economics. Manuscript, revised 2005.

Reinhart, Carmen, and Kenneth Rogoff. 2004. Serial default and the "paradox" of rich to poor capital flows. *American Economic Review* 94:52–58.

Reinhart, Carmen, Kenneth Rogoff, and Miguel Savastano. 2003. Debt intolerance. *Brookings Papers on Economic Activity,* Issue no. 1:1–74.

Capital Flows and Controls in Brazil
What Have We Learned?

Ilan Goldfajn and André Minella

8.1 Introduction

In the last few years, there has been a revival of the notion that capital controls may be a necessary evil. The main argument is that, although capital controls may introduce some economic distortions, excess capital mobility is partially responsible for financial crises (and macroeconomic instability) in emerging market economies (Stiglitz 2002). Capital controls, goes the argument, provide emerging market economies the means to prevent these unpleasant consequences. However, recent papers (e.g., Edwards 2005) have found no systematic evidence suggesting that countries with higher capital mobility tend to have a higher incidence of crises.

Detailed case studies may provide evidence for this debate. The Brazilian case provides an interesting example. Although Brazil still adopts a complex web of bureaucratic controls on capital flows, in the last fifteen years it has been more financially open than other large emerging market economies, in particular China and India. The analysis of Brazil, a large

Ilan Goldfajn is a professor in the Department of Economics at the Pontifical Catholic University of Rio de Janeiro (PUC-Rio) and a partner at Ciano Investmentos. André Minella is an economist at the Central Bank of Brazil.

We thank Edmar Bacha, Sebastian Edwards, Tricia Kissinger, and the participants in the International Capital Flows Conference and seminar at the Instituto de Estudos de Política Econômica, Casas das Garças, of Brazil for useful comments; Fernando Rocha and Fernando Lemos of the Balance of Payments Division of the Central Bank of Brazil for valuable explanations of the balance of payments statistics; and José Maria de Carvalho, Maria do Socorro Rebouças, and Luciana de Oliveira of the Exchange and Foreign Capital Regulation Executive Office (Gence) of the Central Bank of Brazil for precious and detailed comments on capital control issues. We are also grateful to Érica Diniz Oliveira and Eurípides de Freitas Neto for excellent assistance with data. The views expressed here are those of the authors and do not necessarily reflect those of the Central Bank of Brazil.

sub-investment-grade emerging market economy, which is relatively integrated to the financial world and has suffered from both financial crises and macroeconomic volatility, could shed further light on the capital controls issue. This chapter details the experience of Brazil with capital mobility and controls.

Macroeconomic performance in Brazil has indeed been quite volatile over the last thirty years. Part of this volatility can be traced to a sequence of financial crises and sudden stops and a boom-and-bust pattern of current account deficits and capital flows. Brazil experienced two large cycles of current account deficits: one in the 1970s, which lasted until the debt crisis of the early 1980s, and the second in the 1990s, which ended with an abrupt reversal of the current account deficit after the 2002 electoral crisis.

In 2004 Brazil ran a current account surplus of almost 2 percent of gross domestic product (GDP), receiving approximately 2 percent of GDP in net foreign direct investment (FDI); and since the beginning of the 2000s, for the first time in decades, Brazil has been reducing its external debt. In this environment, one wonders whether this performance is the sign of a new trend or the beginning of yet another cycle that eventually will reverse course. The issue is whether a regime based on a floating exchange rate, inflation targeting, fiscal responsibility, and a relatively more open financial account induced a structural change. It is difficult to judge at this point. However, the combination of a few factors suggests a new trend. First, the floating exchange rate regime is providing more incentives for borrowers to better assess risk, in particular in the nontradable sector. Second, exports are increasing in a magnitude not seen before, leading to a record low ratio (although still high by international comparison) of external debt to exports. Third, the larger role of net direct investment in the latest surge in capital flows is encouraging from a debt accumulation perspective. Nevertheless, more analysis is needed. From a historical perspective, a relevant question is how the current phase compares to the previous adjustment undertaken after the debt crisis of the 1980s. It is important to look at the past experience in Brazil.

In the last fifteen years Brazil has also started liberalizing its capital account. The liberalization was a gradual process of establishing new rules on capital inflows and outflows. The result of the liberalization process was (a) reduction or elimination of taxes on foreign capital financial transactions and of minimum maturity requirements on loans; (b) elimination of quantitative restrictions on investments by nonresidents in financial and capital markets securities issued either domestically or abroad; (c) permission for residents to issue securities abroad, including debt, without prior approval by the Central Bank; (d) more freedom for residents to invest in FDI and portfolio abroad; and finally (e) the introduction of currency convertibility, initially through the mechanism of "international transfers in reais," whereby residents could transfer their resources abroad through the use of nonresident accounts. Since March 2005 a more direct procedure has been in place.

In spite of the liberalization, the resulting system does not mean unrestricted freedom or free convertibility.[1] Export proceeds still are required to be converted into domestic currency ("export surrender"), and there are limits on foreign currency deposits. Current currency convertibility is based on the monetary authority's rules instead of laws. Therefore, these rules can be lifted at any time. In addition, public opinion still associates transfers abroad with illicit or antipatriotic practices. Also, notwithstanding the efforts to consolidate the exchange and capital account rules, regulation is still fragmented and involves rules set in different contexts and driven by various motivations.

A consolidation of the whole regulation in a unified law approved by Congress is necessary. Reduction in bureaucratic requirements is needed as well. The rules would become clearer and less uncertain. These changes would facilitate a change in the mentality that originated back in the capital flight period, when transfers abroad were necessarily associated with illicit or antipatriotic practices.

The great volatility of capital flows has been one of the main arguments of those that oppose complete liberalization of capital movements. Since liberalization in Brazil has occurred in parallel to a period of higher macroeconomic volatility, one could wonder whether the case of Brazil reinforces the argument. The key points of the chapter, summarized in the following list, do not point in this direction:

1. The debt accumulation pattern changed substantially after the liberalization of the capital account and, especially, after the floating of the currency. The private sector decreased significantly its issuance of external debt. The reduction in private debt resulted partly from the abrupt interruption of access during the crises but also from the floating of the currency, which ended a period of implicit guarantees that included a fixed parity for borrowers.

2. The profile of external financing has also changed since liberalization and the floating regime. After a period based on portfolio investment, FDI replaced it as the main financing source. Since 1998, net direct investment has comprised more than 100 percent of net private capital flows. In general, FDI flows tend to be more stable and less correlated with other flows. Long-term debt flows worked as a stabilizing factor during external crises, but behaved procyclically during domestic crises.

3. Net financial flows have, in general, financed current account deficits. Some differences emerge over time. Net financial flows financed (a) a

---

1. The complete set of existing capital controls is presented in appendix A.

strong accumulation of international reserves between 1992 and 1996; (b) a large expansion of the current account deficit from 1995 to 1997, representing a growth of both investment and consumption; and (c) an increase in the current account deficit from 1998 to 2001, resulting from a higher deficit in net income from abroad.

4. Following capital account liberalization, consumption—its growth rate and share in GDP—has been more stable than in the 1980s. In comparison to the 1990s growth episodes, economic growth in 2000–2001 and at the time of this writing (2004) took place in a different context. First, net capital flows have been of a lower magnitude and have been dominated by FDI. There has been no significant surge of short-term flows or portfolio investment. Second, the expansions have been accompanied by a more favorable situation in the trade balance. Third, one could argue that fundamentals improved with the change in the fiscal policy regime and the adoption of inflation targeting.

5. Sudden stops are more pronounced when the crisis is mostly domestically driven. Analysis using a vector autoregressive (VAR) estimation indicates that shocks to the country risk premium (measured by the Emerging Markets Bond Index [EMBI]) have the clearest effect on macroeconomic performance. Higher country risk levels induce greater interest rates, a more depreciated exchange rate, a reduction in capital inflows, and lower output. This leads us to the importance of building up good fundamentals in the economy.

These key points lead us to conclude that, notwithstanding the financial crises and macroeconomic volatility of the recent past, capital account liberalization has led to a more resilient economy. Therefore, further capital account liberalization should be considered. Liberalization should be accompanied by a broad range of reforms to improve and foster stronger institutions—such as approval of de jure (not only de facto) central bank independence—establish a longer track record of responsible fiscal policy (under the fiscal responsibility law), and reduce microeconomic inefficiencies and contractual uncertainties.

This chapter is organized as follows. The next section provides the balance-of-payment stylized facts of the last three decades (current account cycles, capital flow cycles and composition, and debt accumulation). Section 8.3 describes the evolution of capital controls in Brazil and evaluates the benefits and costs of further capital account liberalization. Section 8.4 examines the volatility of capital flows in general and the behavior of the flows during financial crises. Section 8.5 analyzes the relationship between capital flows and macroeconomic performance in Brazil, evaluating what capital flows have financed, the recent growth pattern, and whether there is more consumption smoothing. In addition, we conduct some estimations on the determinants of capital flows and develop a structural VAR to estimate the relationship between capital flows and macroeconomic performance. The final section presents the main conclusions.

8.2 Stylized Facts

Macroeconomic performance in Brazil has been volatile. Part of this volatility can be traced to the boom-and-bust pattern in the balance of payments. In fact, there have been long and pronounced cycles of current account deficits that ended abruptly. Each cycle had its own history: different types of capital flows financed the boom, sudden stops had different characteristics, and policy behavior was distinct.

After the confidence crisis in 2002, Brazil entered a postadjustment period, running both trade and current account surpluses. How does this phase compare to the previous adjustment after the debt crisis?

This section provides the stylized facts of the main components of the balance of payments in the last decades, starting with the current account cycles but then focusing on capital flows and the accumulation of external debt.

8.2.1 Current Account Cycles

In the last decades, Brazil experienced two large cycles of current account deficits, one in the 1970s, which lasted until the debt crisis of the early 1980s, and the second in the 1990s, punctuated by the crises of the last few years. Figure 8.1 shows the behavior of the current account and private capital account, defined as the capital and financial accounts minus official

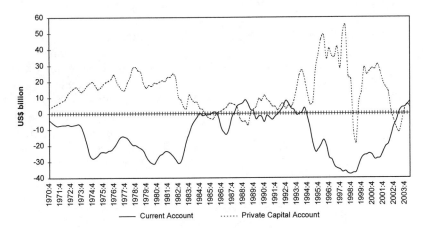

Fig. 8.1 **Current account and private capital account (four-quarter cumulative balance, 1970:Q4–2004:Q2, at 2003 prices)**

agency–related loans.[2] These long periods of current account deficits were financed by voluntary capital flows. The first period was also a period of high average GDP growth, but this was not the case in the second period. Tables 8.1 and 8.2 show annual values and period averages for broad categories of the balance of payments as a percentage of GDP as well as for GDP growth rate.

The behavior of the current account has been, in general, dominated by the dynamics of the trade balance, whose deficit cycles are financed by large expansions of capital inflows. Figure 8.2 depicts the path of the trade balance and income balance (net remittances abroad of wages, profits, dividends, and interests), which are the main components of the current account.[3]

To analyze the current account performance in a broader macroeconomic context, internationally as well as domestically, including the effect of policy decisions, we subdivide the current account performance into five phases since the mid-1970s, described in the following list.

1. *1974–82: The second National Development Plan (PND II) and external debt accumulation.* The economy presented large trade deficits from 1974 through 1980—averaging 1.6 percent of GDP—as a result of the heavy investments under the PND II and the two oil price shocks (1973 and 1979). The current account deficit was also exacerbated by the increase in U.S. interest rates in 1979. The deficits were financed basically by syndicated loans, in the context of a large expansion of international financial market liquidity. The external financing and investments under the PND II supported maintenance of high economic growth—GDP growth averaged 7.0 percent in the 1974–80 period—despite the oil crisis. The inflation rate was also increasing, rising from 15.5 percent in 1973 to 110.2 percent in 1980 (measured by the General Price Index [IGP-DI]). However, external debt reached high, unsustainable levels, leading to the 1982 external debt crisis.

2. *1983–94: External debt renegotiation, current account adjustment, and high inflation.* With the interruption of voluntary capital flows, the economy had to generate trade surpluses to finance the income account deficits. In fact, after the 1981–83 adjustment—maxidevaluation of the domestic currency and tightness of macroeconomic policy—the economy generated large trade surpluses from 1983 through 1994 (averaging 4.0 percent of GDP). In 1984, the trade surplus peaked at 6.9 percent of GDP. The current account balance

2. See appendix C for a more detailed explanation of the capital flows variables used in the text. The figures in the text are either shown as percentage of GDP or based on constant 2003 U.S. dollars.

3. Current account balance ≡ trade balance + balance of services + income balance + current transfers balance.

Table 8.1   Balance of payments (% of GDP) and GDP growth

	Current account	Trade balance	Capital and financial account	Private capital account	International reserves: Liquidity concept	GDP growth rate (%)	Per capita GDP growth rate (%)
1970	−1.97	0.54	3.01	1.75	2.79	10.40	7.20
1971	−3.31	−0.70	4.42	3.14	3.50	11.34	8.42
1972	−2.87	−0.41	6.46	5.53	7.12	11.94	9.05
1973	−2.48	0.01	4.89	3.91	7.63	13.97	11.07
1974	−6.80	−4.25	5.92	4.82	4.77	8.15	5.45
1975	−5.39	−2.73	4.91	4.14	3.11	5.17	2.58
1976	−4.17	−1.46	5.52	4.93	4.25	10.26	7.60
1977	−2.72	0.05	3.47	2.78	4.09	4.93	2.45
1978	−3.47	−0.51	5.91	5.17	5.91	4.97	2.54
1979	−4.79	−1.27	3.41	2.87	4.34	6.76	4.34
1980	−5.36	−1.19	4.04	3.56	2.91	9.20	6.80
1981	−4.53	0.47	4.93	4.36	2.90	−4.25	−6.34
1982	−6.00	0.29	4.46	1.95	1.47	0.83	−1.34
1983	−3.57	3.42	3.92	3.29	2.41	−2.93	−4.99
1984	0.05	6.90	3.44	0.96	6.32	5.40	3.20
1985	−0.12	5.91	0.09	−0.91	5.50	7.85	5.64
1986	−2.06	3.22	0.56	0.35	2.62	7.49	5.35
1987	−0.51	3.96	1.15	1.35	2.64	3.53	1.56
1988	1.37	6.28	−0.69	−1.09	2.99	−0.06	−1.88
1989	0.25	3.88	0.15	0.42	2.33	3.16	1.36
1990	−0.81	2.29	0.98	1.72	2.13	−4.35	−5.95
1991	−0.35	2.61	0.04	0.78	2.32	1.03	−0.66
1992	1.58	3.93	2.57	0.60	6.13	−0.54	−2.15
1993	−0.16	3.10	2.44	2.85	7.50	4.92	3.26
1994	−0.33	1.93	1.60	1.86	7.15	5.85	4.20
1995	−2.61	−0.49	4.12	4.33	7.35	4.22	2.62
1996	−3.03	−0.72	4.38	4.46	7.75	2.66	1.10
1997	−3.77	−0.84	3.19	3.07	6.46	3.27	1.72
1998	−4.24	−0.83	3.77	2.37	5.66	0.13	−1.36
1999	−4.72	−0.22	3.23	2.26	6.77	0.79	−0.71
2000	−4.02	−0.12	3.21	4.40	5.48	4.36	2.82
2001	−4.55	0.52	5.31	3.75	7.04	1.31	−0.17
2002	−1.66	2.86	1.74	−0.92	8.23	1.93	0.45
2003	0.82	4.89	1.01	0.50	9.73	0.54	−0.92
2004	1.94	5.60	−1.22	0.07	8.80	4.94	3.44

Sources: Central Bank of Brazil, IBGE, and authors' calculations.

stood at around zero, except for the deficits at the end of 1986 and beginning of 1987, as a result of the Cruzado Plan. GDP growth fell significantly, averaging 2.0 percent from 1983 through 1992, reaching negative values in four of these years. It was also a period of high inflation, which peaked at 82.4 percent per month in March 1990 and 47.4 percent in June 1994 (measured by the Broad National Con-

Table 8.2   Balance of payments (% of GDP) and GDP growth: Period averages

	Current account	Trade balance	Capital and financial account	Private capital account	International reserves: Liquidity concept	GDP growth rate (%)	Per capita GDP growth rate (%)
1974–1982	−4.80	−1.18	4.73	3.84	3.75	5.03	2.59
1983–1994	−0.39	3.95	1.35	1.01	4.17	2.54	0.68
1995–1998	−3.41	−0.72	3.87	3.56	6.80	2.56	1.01
1999–2001	−4.43	0.06	3.91	3.47	6.43	2.14	0.63
2002–2004	0.37	4.45	0.51	−0.11	8.92	2.45	0.97

Sources: Central Bank of Brazil, IBGE, and authors' calculations.

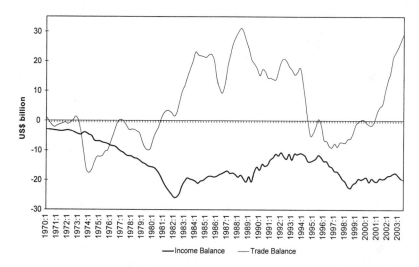

Fig. 8.2   Trade balance and income balance (four-quarter cumulative balance, 1970:Q4–2004:Q2, at 2003 prices)

sumer Price Index [IPCA]). Several stabilization programs tried to curb inflation, but achieved only temporary success. The end of the high-inflation period came with the Real Plan, launched in July 1994. The process of external debt renegotiation underwent several phases, eventually concluding with the conversion of the loans into debt securities under the Brady Plan in April 1994.[4] From 1992 through mid-

4. In 1991, the Brazilian government and the creditor private bank committee renegotiated the delayed interest payments of 1989 and 1990, and in the following year they agreed on a term sheet that set some principles for the negotiation. At end 1993, a final agreement was reached, under the guidelines of the Brady Plan, by which the loans were converted into sovereign bonds, some of them having U.S. Treasury bonds as collateral. The conversion occurred in April 1994. For an institutional description of the process of renegotiation, see Cerqueira (2003).

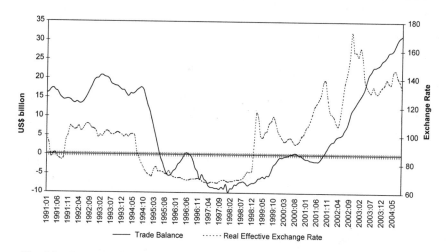

Fig. 8.3   Real effective exchange rate and cumulative twelve-month trade balance (January 1991–September 2004)

1994, exchange rate policy, under a managed system, basically aimed to keep constant the purchasing power of the domestic currency, as we can see in figure 8.3, which shows the real effective exchange rate and the trade balance.

3. *1995–98: New cycle of trade deficits, low inflation, and financial crises.* The revival of capital flows to emerging market economies at the beginning of the 1990s, the regulation changes in the capital account, and the external debt restructuring ended the external financing restrictions of the 1980s. Moreover, for the first time in more than three decades, the economy enjoyed a low-inflation environment. In 1995, inflation fell to 22.4 percent, and in 1998 it reached 1.7 percent. The stability brought by the Real Plan was also accompanied by a relatively short economic growth cycle, as depicted in figure 8.4. In the initial months after the launch of the Real Plan, a floating system was adopted, followed the next year by a crawling band, which increasingly turned into a crawling peg. Figure 8.5 shows the steady and low rate of adjustment in the nominal exchange rate, which led to a substantial appreciation of the real effective rate (figure 8.3). As a consequence of the surge in capital inflows, exchange rate overvaluation, and higher economic growth, large trade deficits emerged from 1995 through 1998 (averaging 0.7 percent of GDP, which is a value largely underestimated by the increase in dollar-denominated GDP resulting from the exchange rate overvaluation). The capital inflows that financed the deficits were predominantly portfolio investment (equity and debt securities) until 1996–97, when FDI started to assume greater significance. The economy was hit by external financial crises

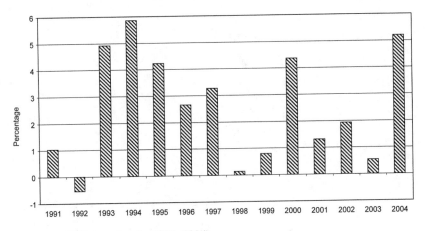

Fig. 8.4   GDP growth rate (1991–2004)

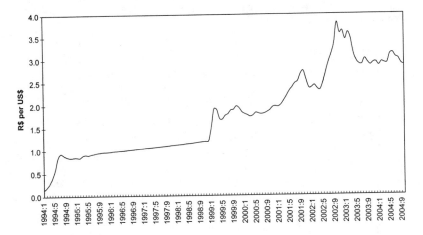

Fig. 8.5   Nominal exchange rate (January 1990–October 2004)

(Mexican, Asian, and Russian) and faced the domestic exchange crisis in 1998, which ended with the collapse of the exchange regime in January 1999.

4. *1999–2001: Floating exchange system, inflation targeting, sound fiscal policy, and reversal of trade balance deficits.* Economic policy had to deal with the exchange rate crisis and undertake a substantial change in the fiscal regime. A floating exchange rate system and an inflation-targeting regime were adopted, and substantial primary surpluses generated. Public-sector primary surplus rose from 0.0 percent of GDP in 1998 to 3.2 percent in the following year, reaching 4.4 percent in 2003. The exchange rate depreciated from 1.22 Brazilian reais (R$) to the U.S. dollar in mid-January 1999 to R$/US$ 2.16 at the begin-

ning of March. In June 1999, inflation targets were announced for that year and the following two years. It was a period of transition in terms of current account adjustment. The trade deficit fell from 0.8 percent of GDP in 1998 to 0.2 percent in 1999, turning into a surplus of 0.5 percent in 2001.

5. *2002 to the present: Confidence crisis and large current account adjustment.* Throughout 2002, with the electoral uncertainties, the economy faced a confidence crisis. Country risk premiums and the exchange rate rose sharply. After the transition of the prior years, large trade surpluses solidified from 2002 onward. The surpluses are a consequence of significant exchange rate depreciation, strong world economic growth, and a few specific bilateral trade agreements. In 2003 and 2004, the trade surplus reached 5.0 percent and 5.6 percent of GDP (US$24.8 billion and US$33.7 billion), respectively, leading to a current account surplus of 0.8 percent and 1.9 percent of GDP. The positive results in the trade balance have been accompanied by both export and import growth. In 2004, exports and imports reached US$96.5 billion and US$62.8 billion, respectively, representing an increase of 32.0 percent and 30.0 percent in relation to the previous year. In fact, as we can see in figure 8.6, the degree of trade openness of the economy—measured by the ratio of exports plus imports to GDP—has reached the record level of 26.5 percent, in sharp contrast to a 14.0 percent average in the 1990s.

Therefore, after the confidence crisis, Brazil entered a postadjustment period, running both trade and current account surpluses. How does this phase compare to the previous adjustment after the debt crisis? In both

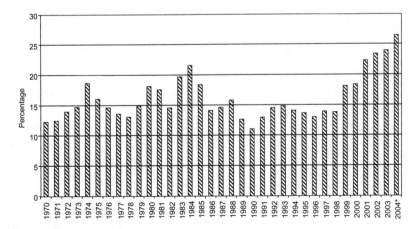

Fig. 8.6   Ratio of exports plus imports to GDP (1970–2004)
Note: GDP for 2004 is estimated.

cases, there was a strong reversion of the trade deficit cycle. The trade balance rose from –1.2 percent of GDP in 1980 to 6.9 percent in 1984, and from –0.8 percent in 1998 to 5.6 percent in 2004. Similarly, the trade adjustment was stimulated by a substantial exchange rate devaluation, which simultaneously generated significant inflationary pressures. However, the two adjustments present some important differences. First, the economic slowdown in the 1980s adjustment was substantially higher than in the 2000s. GDP accumulated a contraction of 6.3 percent in the 1981–83 period. In the recent adjustment, the higher troughs, considering four-quarter cumulative GDP, were of –0.5 percent in 1999:Q3, 0.0 percent in 2002:Q2, and 0.5 percent in 2003:Q4. Second, the exchange rate movement was higher in the recent adjustment. The real effective exchange rate rose by 35 percent in the months following the maxi-devaluation of February 1983 in comparison to the previous months. In 1999, the increase was around 47 percent, and it accumulated 66 percent until 2001. Third, the 1980s adjustment affected imports more intensely than exports. In 1984, imports fell by 39.4 percent relative to 1980, while exports increased 34.1 percent. The reduction in imports accounted for 56.8 percent of the change in the trade balance. In contrast, the recent adjustment has been incurred mainly by exports. In relation to 1998, exports grew 42.9 percent and 88.6 percent in 2003 and 2004, respectively, and imports fell by 16.3 percent in 2003 and grew by 8.8 percent in the following year. As a consequence, although also a reflection of changes in dollar-denominated GDP, the increase in the degree of openness has been substantially higher recently. Exports plus imports as a percentage of GDP rose from 18.1 percent to 21.6 percent between 1980 and 1984, whereas it went from 13.8 percent in 1998 to 26.5 percent in 2004. Fourth, in the 1980s, the country was excluded from international capital flows, whereas, since the 1990s, it has been integrated in the financial markets. Fifth, the level of import tariffs is lower currently than in the 1980s. Sixth, macroeconomic regimes are completely different: low inflation, sound fiscal policy, and better monetary institutions in the 2000s versus high inflation, unsound fiscal policy, and weak monetary institutions in the 1980s.

Although the trade balance has played the main role in the current account boom-and-bust cycles, the income balance has undergone important changes as well. Since 1998, the income deficit has reached a higher level (1998–2003 annual average of 3.4 percent of GDP), as a result of the surge in capital inflows, which increased nonresident-owned assets in the economy. As a consequence of the external debt conversion under the Brady Plan and the change in the pattern of capital inflows—from loans to direct and portfolio investment—the composition of the income balance has changed significantly since the 1990s, as we can see in figure 8.7. The deficit in portfolio investment income, rather than the deficit in other investment income, has become the main component since 1997, accounting for 46.8

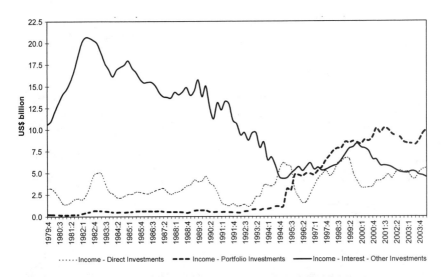

Fig. 8.7   Income account deficit (four-quarter cumulative balance, 1979:Q4–2004:Q2, at 2003 prices)

percent of the investment income deficit from 2000 through 2003. The share of the income deficit attributable to direct investments rose to 22.6 percent, whereas the share of the deficit attributable to other investment income decreased to 30.6 percent.

8.2.2   Capital Flow Cycles and Their Composition

Although current account cycles have a corresponding capital flow financing, it is not necessarily the case that capital flows behave in the same manner in each cycle. In fact, there are major differences in the composition of capital flows across the current account cycles—private versus public, portfolio, or FDI—that we opted to subdivide capital flow behavior into three longer periods (instead of the five above). We detail the methodological decomposition of capital flows into six categories in appendix C. Figures 8.8 and 8.9 show the path of the main categories.

1. *1970s–1982: Loan flows and external debt accumulation.* In the context of a significant liquidity expansion in international financial markets, Brazil received massive capital inflows. Table 8.3 shows, for each period, the average of different flows (as a percent of GDP). The private capital account balance averaged 3.8 percent of GDP from 1974 through 1982. As recorded in figure 8.9, the majority of capital inflows were loans, comprising 74.3 percent of the private capital balance. In contrast, portfolio investment was minimal (a 5.4 percent share in the flows). As a result, gross external debt, as a percentage of

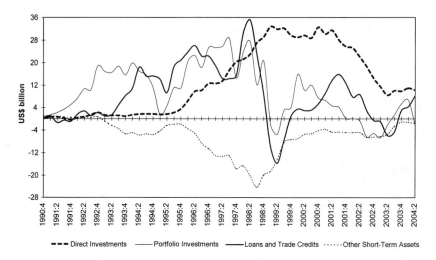

Fig. 8.8 Direct investments, portfolio investments, loans and trade credits, and other short-term assets (four-quarter cumulative balance, 1990:Q4–2004:Q2, at 2003 prices)

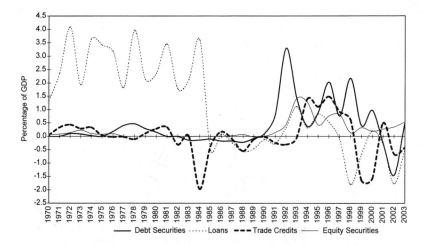

Fig. 8.9 Debt securities, loans, trade credits and equity securities: Ratio to GDP (1970–2003)

GDP, from 16.8 percent in 1970, reached 31.5 percent in 1982, and peaked at 53.8 percent in 1984 (new flows in the context of debt renegotiation, and maxi-devaluation of domestic currency reducing dollar-denominated GDP).

2. *1983–91: Shortage of capital flows.* The external debt crisis and debt renegotiation—extended until 1994—dominated the period. The scarce capital flows were basically part of debt renegotiation. The

Table 8.3   **Net capital flows by groups: Ratio to GDP**

	Direct investment	Equity securities	Debt securities	Loans	Trade credits	Other short-term assets	Official agencies	Other items
1974–1982	0.56	0.03	0.17	2.86	0.07	0.20	0.53	−0.04
1983–1991	0.20	0.02	−0.02	0.40	−0.36	0.12	0.11	0.40
1992–2004	2.27	0.56	0.77	−0.18	0.08	−0.91	0.42	−0.40
1992–1996	0.53	0.86	1.61	0.62	0.72	−0.61	0.16	−1.14
1997–2004	3.36	0.36	0.25	−0.68	−0.31	−1.10	0.59	0.07

Sources: Central Bank of Brazil and authors' calculations.
Note: The values of debt securities, portfolio investment, and loans exclude the values related to the debt conversion under the Brady Plan.

private account balance averaged 1.7 percent of GDP in the period (declining to 1.0 percent when excluding 1983–84). In 1983 and 1984, the country still received positive loan flows, but under the debt renegotiation. In fact, the loan flow balance remained negative for one decade (1985–94). Likewise, the negligible positive portfolio investment turned into (negligible) negative flows. Net direct investment was affected as well. As a percentage of GDP, it fell from 0.6 percent of GDP, in the previous period, to 0.2 percent.

3. *1992 to the present: Financial openness, reintegration in the international financial markets, and large swings of capital flows.* The country was reintegrated into cross-border flows. The resumption of capital flows to Brazil was associated with several factors: (a) increase in international liquidity and expansion of pension and hedge funds; (b) the process of capital account liberalization; (c) high-yield differentials between domestic and foreign bonds; (d) the end of the external debt restructuring period; and (e) higher macroeconomic stability with the launch of the Real Plan. The three main characteristics of capital flows in this period were the following: (a) the important role played by portfolio investment; (b) large swings in capital flows ("sudden stop" crises); and (c) the increasing role of FDI.

The resumption of capital flows was dominated by portfolio investment.[5] Except for brief pauses during the Mexican and Asian crises, portfolio inflows increased systematically and reached a four-quarter cumulative average of US$20 billion between 1996 and mid-1998. Portfolio investment accounted for 73.0 percent of the private capital account balance between 1992 and 1998, averaging 2.3 percent of GDP. In general,

---

5. The category portfolio investment follows the IMF's definition. It is represented by cross-border investment in equity securities that is not classified as direct investment, and debt securities. This category includes securities negotiated in Brazil and abroad.

debt security flows were larger than equity flows. The expansion of debt securities was reinforced by the return of the government to the international financial markets after the debt restructuring, with the first issuance of sovereign bonds taking place in mid-1995.

Portfolio investment also played an important role in the large capital flow swings associated with the financial crises, more intensely in the domestic crises (the exchange crisis in 1998–99 and the confidence crisis in 2002). The net portfolio balance amounted to –$11.2 billion from 1998:Q3 through 1999:Q1, and to –$7.6 billion in the last three quarters of 2002 (in U.S. dollars).

The other component that played a key role during the sudden-stop crises was "other short-term assets." These flows are, in general, negative because they basically refer to transfers of domestic currency abroad. As with portfolio investment, the main negative peaks of this group were associated with the financial crises. The higher trough took place in the exchange crisis, when its negative balance summed to –$15.2 billion (in U.S. dollars) in the last three quarters of 1998. These outflows were associated with growing doubts about the sustainability of the exchange rate regime and the corresponding expectations of currency devaluation. It was a way of protecting asset values in foreign currency and having capital gains in domestic currency. For those who had issued foreign currency–denominated or linked debt, it represented a way of hedging against prospective devaluation. After the devaluation in January 1999, these outflows fell significantly and were increasingly lower, except during the confidence crisis, when they reached a balance of –$5.6 billion (in U.S. dollars) in the last three quarters of 2002.

The main change in the profile of capital flows in the second half of the 1990s was the increasing role played by FDI. In fact, since 1998, net direct investment has become the main inflow group. These inflows followed a cycle of expansion, from the mid-1990s through 2002, peaking in 1999 and 2000. The expansion was stimulated by the improvement in domestic macroeconomic conditions with the Real plan, the lifting of restrictions on foreign investments in some sectors, and the wave of privatizations. The change to a low-inflation environment has reduced the level of uncertainty in the economy and ended the distortions brought about by high inflation. Furthermore, the passage to a more solid macroeconomic regime in 1999 has built a better economic environment.

Privatization was not, however, the main component of net FDI (figure 8.10). From 1997 through 2000, privatization accounted for 25.0 percent of net FDI. These data, however, tend to underestimate the contribution of privatization because they do not include additional capital inflows in the form of investment following privatization. In spite of the reduction in FDI, the levels have been relatively high. Net FDI stood at US$10.1 billion and US$18.2 billion in 2003 and 2004, representing 2.1 percent and 3.0

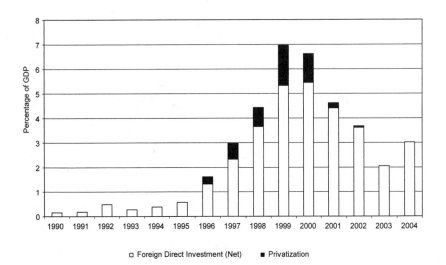

□ Foreign Direct Investment (Net)   ■ Privatization

Fig. 8.10   Net foreign direct investment and privatization as a proportion of GDP (1990–2004)

percent of GDP, respectively.[6] Therefore, in recent years, the pattern of external financing has shifted from debt inflows to direct investment. Moreover, as we can see in figure 8.8, net direct investment was much less affected than the other components during the crises.

Flows related to official agencies have demonstrated large increases when there was a sharp reduction in private capital flows, working clearly as compensatory flows. Figure 8.11 shows the balance of the private capital account and the official agency–related loans. The role of these flows is evident during both domestic crises. Between 2002:Q2 and 2003:Q3, net credits from the International Monetary Fund (IMF) reached US$22.7 billion (a gross credit of US$33.6 billion). The correlation coefficient between the two groups is –0.17 (1992:Q2–2004:Q2).

Using the definition of short- and long-term flows described in appendix C, figure 8.12 shows that short-term debt flows were preponderant between 1993 and 1996, and were clearly affected by the crises. Long-term debt flows, in turn, fell significantly during the domestic crises. Therefore, it seems that short-term flows were more sensitive to contagion crises than long-term flows, but the latter did not work as a factor of stability during domestic crises.

8.2.3   The Stocks: Has the Accumulation of External Debt Been Halted?

The revival of capital flows to Brazil was accompanied by an increase in external debt, mainly in the second half of the 1990s. Figure 8.13 shows

6. The 2004 figures include large operations involving a single firm.

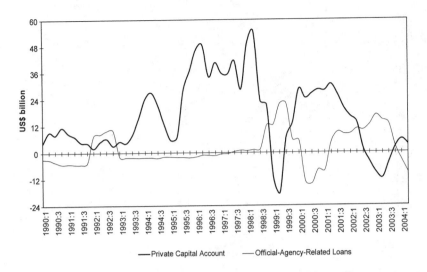

Fig. 8.11   Private capital account and official-agency-related loans (four-quarter cumulative balance, 1990:Q1–2004:Q2, at 2003 prices)

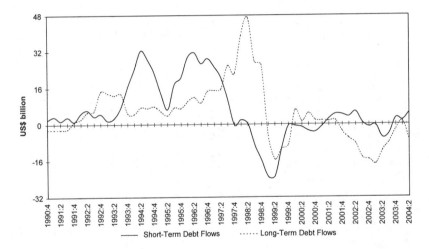

Fig. 8.12   Short- and long-term debt net flows (four-quarter cumulative balance, 1990:Q1–2004:Q2, at 2003 prices)

gross and net external debt as a proportion of GDP.[7] This ratio, however, is largely affected by the effect of exchange rate variations on GDP measured

7. Net external debt is obtained by subtracting reserves, commercial banks' assets, and Brazilian credits abroad from gross debt. Following IMF's recommendations, intercompany loans are excluded from external debt (starting in 1992 as data on these loans are not available previously).

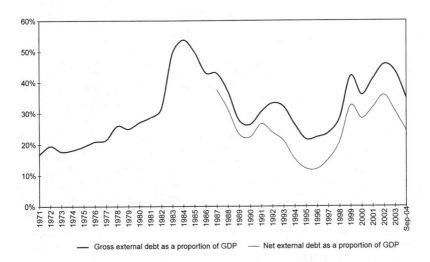

Fig. 8.13   Gross and net external debt as a proportion of GDP (1971–2004)

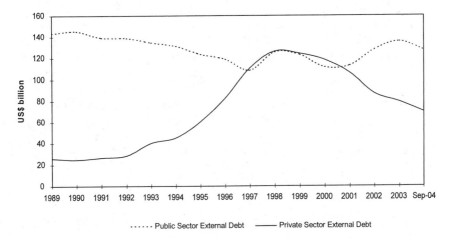

Fig. 8.14   Public and private external debt (1989–2004, at 2003 prices)

in dollars. Considering the debt level at constant prices, figure 8.14 shows the path of both public and private external debt.

The debt accumulation in the second half of the 1990s was primarily undertaken by the private sector. The lower interest rates on external debt relative to domestic debt, the stability of the exchange rate, and the associated implicit guarantee of exchange rate system continuity worked as important stimuli for the issuance of external debt, in the context of abundant international liquidity. Private external debt was rapidly increasing between 1992 and 1998, rising from US$21.9 billion to US$112.3 billion. As a consequence, the share of private-sector debt in total external debt rose from 17.0 percent to 50.2 percent.

The debt accumulation pattern has changed substantially after the float and large depreciation of the currency. The private sector significantly decreased its issuance of external debt, leading to a strong decline in private external debt, from US$111.6 billion in 2000 to US$71.7 billion in September 2004. The abrupt reduction in the first quarter of 2001 reflects an important data revision that excluded debt that was already paid but was not registered as such. This means that part of the debt decline of 2001 actually occurred in the previous years. Nevertheless, our assessment is that there was a continuing decline in external debt. The reduction in private debt resulted partly from the abrupt termination of access during the crises, but also from the increased uncertainty that a floating exchange regime introduces to borrowers. For agents that do not have dollar revenues, it is highly risky to issue foreign currency debt. Thus, the trend is for firms in the nontradable sector to repay their debts.

The public sector has also changed its behavior after the float of the currency. Brazil returned to issuing sovereign bonds in 1995, but, since 1998, issuance of public external debt has been dominated by compensatory flows. After a downward trend until 1997, the growth of public-sector debt resumed during the crises under IMF programs. IMF debt rose from nearly zero in 1997 to US$8.8 billion in 1999, falling back in the following year with the repayments. However, in the subsequent programs, debt owed to the IMF debt resumed an upward trend, peaking at US$33.5 billion in the third quarter of 2003. Between end 2000 and the third quarter of 2003, the IMF accounted for 90.1 percent of the US$35.2 billion increase in public external debt. The repayments to the IMF in 2004 reduced total public-sector debt by US$9.3 billion between the third quarters of 2003 and 2004. Overall, private debt was partly replaced by public debt.

In the aggregate, however, the total external debt level has been decreasing since 2000. After peaking around US$225 billion in 1998–99, it reached US$202.2 billion in September 2004. As a proportion of GDP, after reaching 45.9 percent of GDP in 2002, total external debt decreased to 34.9 percent in September 2004. The ratio of net external debt to GDP fell from 35.9 percent to 24.9 percent in the same period.

With the large expansion in exports in recent years, the ratio of gross external debt to twelve-month exports has declined substantially, as we can see in figure 8.15, reaching 2.2 in September 2004, the lowest value in the last thirty years, and 1.6 when considering net debt. Likewise, the proportion of interest payments to exports has declined steadily. It reached 15.9 percent in September 2004, which also represents one of the lowest values in the last three decades, as recorded in figure 8.16.

One wonders whether the remarkable decrease in debt since 2000 is the sign of a new trend or the beginning of yet another cycle that eventually will

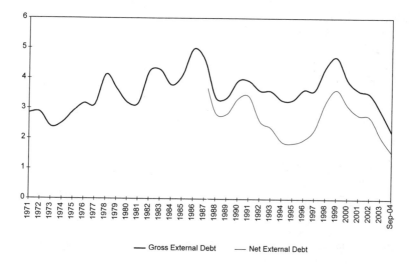

Fig. 8.15   Ratio of gross and net external debt to exports (1971–2004)

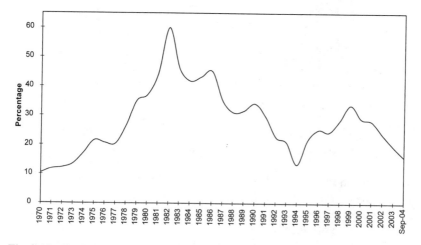

Fig. 8.16   Ratio of interest payments to exports (1970–2004)

reverse its course. It is difficult to judge at this point. However, the combination of a few factors suggests a new trend. First, more incentives are being provided by the floating regime for borrowers to better assess risk, in particular in the nontradable sector. Second, exports are increasing in a magnitude not seen before, leading to a record low ratio (although still high by international comparison) of external debt to exports. Third, the larger role provided by net direct investment in the latest surge in capital flows is encouraging from a debt accumulation perspective.

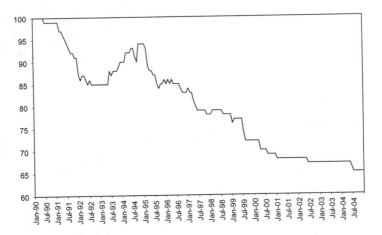

Fig. 8.17   Cumulative index of capital control: Normalization December 1989 = 100 (January 1990–December 2004)

Note: Elaborated by the authors using the chronology in appendix B. We have normalized December 1989 equal to 100 and have assigned –1 to each liberalizing measure and +1 to each restrictive one. Thus, the lower the index value, the lower the level of capital control.

8.3   Capital Controls

During the 1990s, Brazil liberalized its capital account, in parallel to the process of trade liberalization and the surge in capital inflows. The capital account liberalization was a gradual process of establishing new rules on capital inflows and outflows. Figure 8.17 shows an index of capital control estimated for 1990–2004: the lower the index, the more liberalized is the capital account.[8] The list of liberalization measures is vast, mostly adopted in the first half of the decade. Appendix A shows the current major restrictions, and appendix B presents a chronology of the main changes in capital account regulation in the 1990–2004 period.

The result of the liberalization process was the following: (a) reduction or elimination of taxes on foreign capital financial transactions as well as of minimum maturity requirements on loans; (b) elimination of quantitative restrictions on investments by nonresidents in financial and capital market securities issued domestically or abroad; (c) permission for residents to issue securities abroad, including debt, without prior approval by the Central Bank; (d) more freedom for residents to invest in FDI and portfolio abroad; and finally (d) introduction of currency convertibility through the mechanism of international transfers in reais, whereby residents could transfer their resources abroad through the use

8. The index was elaborated using the chronology in appendix B. We have normalized December 1999 equal to 100 and assigned –1 to each liberalizing measure and +1 to each restrictive one.

of nonresident accounts. Since March 2005 a more direct procedure has been in place.

This liberalization process occurred, however, without the necessary changes in the overall legislation. Each new liberalizing rule was inserted at the margin of the existing legislative framework, resulting in a complex web of regulations. The present set of regulations comprises different types of rules (laws, decree-laws, resolutions, memos, etc.) established in different contexts and driven by diverse motivations.

The existing legislative framework dates back as early as the 1930s. It was originally based on less liberal principles and was implemented before financial integration was an important consideration. The most important pillar of the existing legislation is that the domestic currency is the only legal tender; that is, payments in foreign currency are not allowed.[9] Moreover, banking deposits in foreign currency are usually not allowed.[10] The second pillar is that export proceeds are required to be converted into domestic currency (export surrender; Decree 23,258, 10.19.33). Furthermore, the netting of payments is not allowed; for example, exporters cannot use their proceeds to pay for an import or an external debt before converting them into domestic currency (Decree-Law 9,025, 2.27.46).

However, the most important pieces of capital flow legislation were introduced in the 1960s to regulate FDI and loans (Laws 4,131 [9.3.62] and 4,390 [8.29.64], and Decree 55,762 [2.17.65]). According to that regulation, foreign capital inflows should be registered (and income tax paid) in order to obtain permission for associated outflows (profits, interests, royalties, and repatriation). This basic legislation has remained in place without major changes.[11] The legislation also laid the groundwork for the existence of two separate exchange markets.

The 1960s legislation was enacted in the context of the Bretton Woods system when private capital flows were scarce and dominated by direct investment. Domestically, financial markets were underdeveloped, currency was weak—reflecting the effects of inflation—and import substitution policies at their peak. The basic idea was to control and limit currency convertibility. Access to foreign currency was restricted to imports—heavily taxed—and remittances, within certain limits, were associated with previ-

---

9. Decree 23,501, 11.27.33, was replaced by Decree-Law 857, 9.11.69 (the exception was given for some cases, such as contracts related to imports and exports, exchange contracts, and debt involving nonresidents as creditor or debtor). Law 10,192, 2.14.01 (previously Provisory Measure 1,053, 6.30.95) reaffirmed those restrictions, also making clear that the restriction involves indexation to a foreign currency.

10. There are few exceptions. Currently, foreign currency deposits are allowed for embassies, international organisms, oil and electric energy companies, insurance companies, institutions operating in the floating exchange market, foreigners temporarily in Brazil, Brazilians living abroad, the Brazilian postal service (ECT), and foreign cargo companies.

11. The main changes were the end of restrictions on investments in some sectors and a lower tax burden.

ous registered inflows. This legislation survived the next couple of decades, when the scenario was dominated by the debt crisis and unstable macroeconomy.

Nevertheless, the strong capital controls system did not prevent capital flight. The "parallel" (or black) exchange market gained importance. The exchange rate spread over the official exchange rate averaged 40 percent over the 1980s, peaking at 170 percent in May 1989 (Ipeadata, http://www.ipeadata.gov.br). The high spread of the exchange rate over the official market encouraged import overinvoicing and export underinvoicing. Even individuals who traveled abroad had to resort to the (illegal) parallel market because of the extremely low limits on the amount of foreign currency that they were allowed to buy in the official market.

The first change in the regulation occurred in 1987, when portfolio inflows were allowed through the establishment of foreign capital investment companies, foreign capital investment funds, and stock and bond portfolios (the so-called Annexes I to III). Other changes followed. An important reference point was the liberalization of the securities market to foreign institutional investors in 1991, with the so-called Annex IV. Other important measures that stimulated foreign capital flows at the beginning of the 1990s were the following: (a) reduction in the tax on remittances abroad of profits and dividends; (b) authorization for conversion of external debt instruments of the federal public sector, bonds, and deposits denominated in foreign currency for use in the National Privatization Program; (c) authorization for foreign investors represented by funds, investment companies, and institutional investors to operate in the options and futures markets for securities, exchange, and interest rates; and (d) authorization for the issuance abroad of convertible debentures and of depository receipts representing Brazilian securities, such as the American depository receipts (ADRs).

The creation of the floating exchange rate market—also called the "dollar-tourism market"—at end 1988, alongside the commercial or free exchange rate market, was another important reference point in the process of capital account liberalization. The goal was to bring exchange operations that were conducted in the parallel market into a regulated market (Central Bank of Brazil 1993). Increasingly, the regulation broadened the operations that could go through the new market. As a consequence, the parallel market lost its economic significance, as reflected in the spread, which decreased significantly, averaging 14 percent and 4 percent in the first and second halves of the 1990s. The rates in the floating and free exchange markets were aligned in 1996, and the markets were in practice unified in 1999 (Resolution 2,588, 1.25.99).

The floating exchange rate market allowed further liberalization of residents' outflows. The main change was to broaden the possibility of conversion of domestic into foreign currency through the nonresident accounts (the so-called CC5 accounts), starting at the end of 1988 and developing further in the following decade.[12] The 1960s legislation determines that nonresidents could transfer abroad, regardless of any authorization, the balance not withdrawn coming from foreign exchange sales or money orders in foreign currency. However, it did not establish what would happen to resources from other sources. At the end of the 1980s and the beginning of the 1990s, the Central Bank extended the possibility of transferring abroad, giving a "general and public authorization" for transfers from nonresident financial institutions, as pointed out in Central Bank of Brazil (1993), an important official text that clarified the changes in the exchange regime. Any transfers above US$10,000.00 (afterward changed to R$10,000.00), however, should be identified and registered in the Central Bank Information System (Sisbacen).

This transfer mechanism through the nonresident account was named "international transfers in reais" (TIR). In practice, residents in Brazil could deposit in a nonresident bank's account held in a domestic bank that could convert domestic into foreign currency. In other words, residents could transfer money abroad by making these deposits and asking the nonresident financial institution to buy foreign currency to make the deposit in an account abroad.[13] This mechanism has represented a crucial change in the capital account regulation: from a system based on strict limits to currency conversion—restricted only to nonresidents and outflows related to previous inflows—to a much broader scope, extended in practice also to residents. As stressed in Franco and Pinho Neto (2004), this rule represented the introduction of de facto convertibility.

Convertibility was enhanced by the authorization for nonfinancial resident firms to invest abroad up to US$1 million each twelve months—later expanded to US$5 million—without prior authorization. When above this limit, investors had to provide information to the Central Bank thirty days ahead of the exchange transaction.[14] These investments were conducted in the floating exchange rate market.[15]

From 1993 to 1996, however, capital inflows reached levels that prompted the monetary authorities to adopt restrictive measures, some of which were temporarily relaxed after the Mexican crisis.[16] The vast liquidity in international markets, the more open capital account, and the inter-

12. See the section on resident and nonresident accounts in appendix B for the specific regulation.

13. For a more recent explanation of the international transfers in reais, see Schwartsman (2004).

14. See the "Brazilian capital abroad" section in appendix B for more details.

15. From 1988 through 1992, Brazilian investment abroad was required to be compensated by a sale to the Central Bank of gold bought in the domestic market for a value equivalent to the investment.

16. See Ariyoshi et al. (2000), Cardoso and Goldfajn (1998), Garcia and Barcinski (1998), and Garcia and Valpassos (1998).

est differential between domestic and foreign interest rates led to a surge of capital inflows that pressured the exchange rate and the money market.[17] In fact, the restrictive measures were motivated by concerns regarding the amount of sterilization operations—with their fiscal cost associated with the yield differentials—and the short-term tenor of a significant portion of the inflows.

The restrictive measures involved quantitative and price-based measures, which constantly evolved as market participants found ways to circumvent them, as shown in Garcia and Valpassos (1998) and Carvalho (2005).[18] The regulatory changes discouraging capital inflows included (a) an increase in the financial transaction tax on capital inflows, in particular for shorter-term flows; (b) increases in the minimum maturity requirements for capital inflows; and (c) further quantitative restrictions on several portfolio investment instruments. For example, foreign investment under Annexes I to IV was prohibited from channeling resources to fixed-yield bonds and debentures (although partially compensated by the creation of specific foreign capital fixed-income funds [FRF-CE]). These prohibitions were gradually expanded over the period 1993–95, with successive measures restricting investment in derivatives markets—unless as an explicit hedge of existing contracts—certificates of privatization and related securities, Financial Investment Funds (FAF), futures and options markets, and finally other specific debt securities.

Measures aimed at stimulating outflows, such as the permission for prepayment of foreign borrowing and import financing, were also adopted. New channels for Brazilian investment abroad were established, such as the Brazilian depositary receipts (BDRs) regulation, which allowed residents to purchase securities of nonresident companies in Brazil, and the creation of Foreign Investment Funds, which facilitates purchases of debt securities by residents in international markets.

The measures easing outflows make it clear that the overall objective was to reduce net inflows without affecting the trend toward greater integration with international financial markets. In fact, the restrictive measures did not reverse the liberalization trend, but represented a cycle of restrictions around that trend, as we can see in figure 8.17. Furthermore, figure 8.18 decomposes the index into controls on outflows and inflows, showing that the focus of the measures was inflows.

The restrictive capital inflow measures did not involve FDI. On the contrary, the liberalization trend continued through the mid-1990s. The constitutional distinction between Brazilian firms—licensed under Brazilian

17. Cardoso and Goldfajn (1998) and Garcia and Barcinski (1998) have shown that capital flows to Brazil responded to interest rate differentials. Our estimations also provide evidence that domestic interest rates have stimulated capital flows.
18. Carvalho (2005) presents different strategies used by market agents to circumvent the regulation.

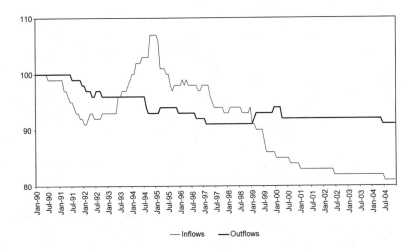

Fig. 8.18   Cumulative index of capital control on inflows and outflows: Normalization December 1989 = 100 (January 1990–December 2004)
Note: See figure 8.17 notes.

laws and with headquarters and administration in the country—and Brazilian firms of national capital—restricted to those under the control of residents—were removed. Likewise, new opportunities for investment in public utilities were opened with the Concession Law, as well as with the increase in the ceiling for nonresidents' ownership of financial institutions. Moreover, the income tax on remittance of profits and dividends abroad was removed.

The motivation for the restrictions adopted in this period stands in sharp contrast to that of the 1960s legislation. The latter was established in the context of a scarcity of foreign resources in order to prevent capital outflows—so-called capital flight. The objective was to restrict currency convertibility to avoid pressures on the exchange rate—and their consequences on inflation and import costs—and try to preserve the demand for domestic currency. In contrast, the 1993–96 restrictions were aimed at reducing capital inflows and easing outflows. In fact, as shown in Cardoso and Goldfajn (1998), capital controls were endogenous. The government reacted strongly to capital flows by increasing controls on inflows when these were booming and relaxing them in moments of distress. However, Cardoso and Goldfajn (1998) also show that, although the volume and composition of capital flows responded to the restrictive measures, these measures were ineffective in the long run.

Starting in 1997, capital controls on inflows were again relaxed with the outbreak of the Asian and Russian crises, and later on with the Brazilian exchange crisis. The measures from 1997 through 1999 included reduction and later elimination of both the minimum average maturity for external loans and the financial transaction tax on capital inflows, and elimination of the restrictions on investments under Annexes I to IV.[19] In 1999, the 1993–96 restrictive measures had all been lifted. The greater capital account openness culminated in Brazil accepting the obligations of IMF Article of Agreement VIII in November 1999.[20]

In the first five years of the twenty-first century, under the new floating exchange regime adopted in 1999, nonresidents were finally allowed to invest in the same instruments in the financial and capital markets that residents do. In addition, the prepayment of external debt was allowed, and the conditions for the issuance of Brazilian real–denominated external debt were set. Also, an important development of that period was the elimination of prior approval of external loans by the Central Bank of Brazil. In effect, the current registration process for capital flows has become a documentary requirement instead of part of an active authorization process.

More recently, at the beginning of March 2005, the Central Bank announced the unification of the exchange markets and clearer rules concerning the conversion of domestic currency into foreign currency. For example, the international transfer mechanism through deposits in accounts of nonresident financial institutions was replaced by a more direct procedure.

In spite of the substantial liberalization of the 1990s, Arida, Bacha, and Lara-Resende (2005) point out that the resulting system does not mean unrestricted or free convertibility. The authors list several limits of the current system, including the fact that current convertibility is based on the monetary authority's rules instead of laws, and these rules can be lifted at any time. In addition, public opinion still associates transfers abroad with illicit or antipatriotic practices.[21]

In fact, notwithstanding some efforts to consolidate the exchange and capital account rules, regulation is still fragmented and involves rules set in different contexts and driven by various motivations. A consolidation of the whole regulation in a unified law is necessary. Reduction in bureaucratic requirements is needed as well. The rules would become less uncertain and clearer. These changes would facilitate the change in mentality, which originated back in the capital flight period, that associates transfers abroad with illicit or antipatriotic practices.

19. A 5 percent tax is applied to inflows related to external loans with a minimum coverage maturity of up to ninety days.

20. This article precludes the country members from imposing restrictions without the approval of the IMF on the making of payments and transfers for current international transactions. It also forbids discriminatory currency arrangements or multiple currency practices. Previously, Brazil availed itself of the transitional arrangements of Article XIV, which allows exchange restrictions but requires countries to take measures toward acceptance of Article VIII as soon as conditions permit.

21. See Gleizer (2005) for a collection of papers on exchange arrangements and capital flow regulation in Brazil.

A further step could be adopted. Arida (2003a, 2003b, 2004) defends a change in legislation to assure unrestricted convertibility. He argues that the introduction by law of free convertibility—defined as the absence of any restriction on the exchange between foreign and domestic currencies, although keeping the domestic currency as the only means of domestic payments—would give a positive signal. Arida (2003a, 2004) stresses that free convertibility should not be adopted immediately, but should be announced beforehand and implemented gradually, accompanying some macroeconomic indicators and institutional changes, such as central bank independence.[22]

Our view is that much can and should be done in order to simplify and consolidate current exchange regulations. The system is excessively bureaucratic and complicated, as a consequence of the patchwork way it was created as macroeconomic conditions evolved and ideology changed. At this juncture the advances of the last decade should be unified in a consolidated and simple law. Further liberalization steps beyond consolidation will need to be accompanied by additional institutional developments such as establishing central bank autonomy, solidifying the fiscal responsibility law and the need for a mature fiscal policy, reaching a stronger consensus about the necessity of lower inflation, and implementing judiciary reform and further microeconomic reforms. Complete freedom of capital flows should emerge as a "natural" consequence of improvements and maturity in institutions.

The history of capital controls in Brazil can be summarized thus: (a) liberalization has advanced significantly since the 1990s; (b) the restrictive measures of the 1993–96 period were mostly aimed at reducing large capital inflows and did not reverse the liberalization trend; (c) currency convertibility has increased significantly; (d) the current situation calls for a simplification of the exchange market and elimination of existing bureaucracy; and (e) the advances achieved in the last decade (through several rules) should be consolidated into a simple law approved by Congress.

8.4 Volatility of Capital Flows and Financial Crises

The great volatility of capital flows has been one of the main arguments for those who oppose complete liberalization of capital movements. Is the volatility of capital flows in Brazil a permanent feature? Is the volatility sizable across the different types of flows?

Besides the normal volatility analysis, it is important to verify the behavior of capital flows in periods of stress, such as in financial crises. This provides more qualitative information regarding the whole distribution of

---

22. Arida's proposal has generated some controversy. An opposite view can be found in Ferrari Filho et al. (2005).

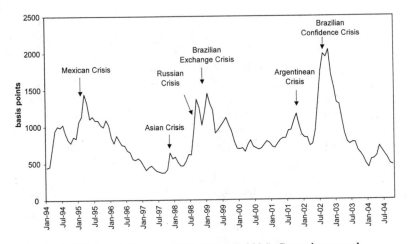

Fig. 8.19   EMBI Brazil (January 1994–October 2004): Sovereign spread

the flows. The Brazilian economy was affected by four external and two domestic crises in the last twelve years: (a) the Mexican crisis, in late 1994; (b) the Asian crisis, in the last quarter of 1997; (c) the Russian crisis, in the third quarter of 1998; (d) the Brazilian exchange crisis, in late 1998 to early 1999; (e) the Argentinean crisis, in the second half of 2001; and (f) the Brazilian confidence crisis, in the last three quarters of 2002. Figure 8.19 depicts monthly averages of the EMBI+ Brazil, whose peaks reflect the crises.[23] In this section we conduct some basic estimates of volatility of capital flows and assess their behavior during the crises.

8.4.1   Volatility of Capital Flows

The results on volatility are shown in table 8.4 for the 1992:Q1–2004:Q2 period (quarterly data). Considering the coefficient of variation (ratio of standard deviation to average), net direct investment is the less volatile group, in line with the results of Prasad et al. (2003), who use a data set of seventy-six industrial and developing countries to show that bank borrowing and portfolio flows are substantially more volatile than FDI. Portfolio investment is the most volatile group. The standard deviation and coefficient of variation of portfolio investment are 1.3 and 2.0 times higher than those for direct investment. Note that loans are extremely volatile as well. Thus, according to these indicators, financing through debt securities is not more volatile than via loans. Furthermore, the variance of direct investment is actually underestimated because its average in the second half

23. The series refers to the sovereign spread of the EMBI until December 1997 and of the EMBI+ thereafter. For simplicity, we call it EMBI throughout the text.

Table 8.4 Volatilities of net capital flows (quarterly data, 1992:Q1–2004:Q2, in US$ millions at 2003 prices)

	Direct investment	Equity securities	Debt securities	Portfolio investment	Loans	Trade credit	Other short-term assets	Short-term flows	Long-term flows
Standard deviation	3,077	1,668	3,718	4,084	2,813	2,284	1,799	4,582	5,166
Mean	3,717	947	1,559	2,488	–100	2,601	–1,712	1,645	1,102
Variation coefficient	0.83	1.76	2.39	1.64	–28.12	0.88	–1.05	2.78	4.69

Sources: Central Bank of Brazil and authors' calculations.
Note: See table 8.3 note.

Table 8.5 Volatilities of inflows and outflows (quarterly data, 1992:Q1–2004:Q2, in US$ millions at 2003 prices)

	Foreign direct investment	Foreign portfolio investment	Brazilian company equity	Debt securities	Other long-term loans	Long-term suppliers' trade credits	Long-term buyers' trade credits
Inflows							
Standard deviation	3,852	5,007	3,112	2,916	846	893	1,006
Mean	5,253	10,046	5,356	4,690	1,027	693	952
Variation coefficient	0.73	0.50	0.58	0.62	0.82	1.29	1.06
Outflows							
Standard deviation	965	4,310	2,719	2,731	649	677	927
Mean	1,287	7,371	4,268	2,343	1,051	722	1,116
Variation coefficient	0.75	0.58	0.64	1.17	0.62	0.94	0.83

Sources: Central Bank of Brazil and authors' calculations.
Note: See table 8.3 note.

of the sample is substantially higher than in the first half. For the 1997:Q1–2004:Q2 sample, its variation coefficient decreases to 0.5, whereas that of portfolio investment rises to 3.0.

When we use net flows, however, the variation coefficient is sensitive to averages close to zero. To minimize this problem, we estimate separately the volatility for inflows and outflows, which are shown in table 8.5. Similar to net flows, inflows and outflows of portfolio investment present a standard deviation significantly higher than that for FDI.[24] Likewise, contrary to expectations, the item "other long-term loans," when compared to the

24. Although the variation of coefficient of inflows and outflows of portfolio investments is lower than that of FDI, when we consider the 1997:Q1–2004:Q2 period, the result is reversed. Furthermore, under the point of view of pressures on the balance of payments, the standard deviation measure seems to be more relevant because it captures the absolute amount of change in the flows.

Table 8.6   Correlations across capital flows (quarterly data, 1992:Q1–2004:Q2, at 2003 prices)

	Equity securities	Debt securities	Loans	Trade credit	Portfolio investment	Direct investment
Equity securities	1.00	0.27	0.34	0.43	0.48	−0.28
Debt securities	0.27	1.00	0.36	0.15	0.97	−0.11
Loans	0.34	0.36	1.00	0.15	0.41	−0.38
Trade credit	0.43	0.15	0.15	1.00	0.24	0.16
Portfolio investments	0.48	0.97	0.41	0.24	1.00	−0.17
Direct investments	−0.28	−0.11	−0.38	0.16	−0.17	1.00

Sources: Central Bank of Brazil and authors' calculations.
Notes: See table 8.3 note.

group portfolio investment, does not present higher volatility.[25] Note also that trade credits present a high variation coefficient.

The literature has emphasized the volatility of short-term flows and their role during financial crises. The figures on the greater stability of FDI flows support this analysis. However, the same does not apply when we compare short- versus long-term debt flows. Long-term debt flows present a higher standard deviation and coefficient of variation. On the other hand, when including the groups "other short-term assets" and net direct investment in the short- and long-term flows, respectively, the volatility is significantly lower in the latter. Nevertheless, as we can see in figure 8.12, net short-term debt flows have been relatively more stable since mid-1999 when compared to the previous period.

We also conduct some basic analysis of the correlation between selected groups (table 8.6). The groups equities, debt securities, loans, and trade credits are positively correlated, although the correlation coefficients are not large.[26] Net direct investment, in turn, usually presents negative correlation with those groups. The correlation between short- and long-term flows (not shown) is significantly higher, mainly when we use annual data (correlation coefficient of 0.73). This result strengthens the previous findings concerning similar volatilities of short- and long-term debt flows.

8.4.2   Capital Flows during Crises

Sudden stops were more intense during the domestic crises than during the external ones. Table 8.7 shows net flows previous to and during the

25. Although other long-term loan inflows present a higher coefficient of variation than that of portfolio investment, when considering outflows they present similar coefficients. Furthermore, in both cases the standard deviation of other long-term loans is lower than that of portfolio investment.
26. Bosworth and Collins (1999) have found no or very low correlation between FDI, portfolio investment, and loans for a sample of fifty-eight developing countries.

Table 8.7 Private capital account balance in Brazil and crises (in US$ millions at current prices)

| | | Private capital account balance | | |
| | | Four-quarter average before the crisis (A) | Quarterly average during the crisis (B) | Difference (A) – (B) |
Crisis	Period			
Mexican	1994:Q4–1995:Q1	4,242	196	4,046
Asian	1997:Q4	9,000	1,364	7,636
Russian	1998:3	12,014	–17,290	29,304
Exchange crisis	1999:1	4,662	–5,499	10,161
	1998:3–1999:1	12,014	–7,724	19,738
Argentinian	2001:4	6,264	1,454	4,810
Confidence crisis	2002:3–2002:4	3,271	–6,363	9,634
	2002:2–2002:4	3,918	–3,045	6,962

Sources: Central Bank of Brazil and authors' calculations.

crises. In the domestic crises, the expectation of a change in regime and depreciation of domestic currency stimulated capital outflows and discouraged capital inflows significantly. Net flows during the Mexican and Asian crises were negative only for one or two quarters, and recovered quickly—four-quarter cumulative flows remained positive. In contrast, during the exchange crisis (1999)—considering also the Russian crisis period—and the confidence crisis (2002), the reversal of flows was large and lasted at least three quarters. From 1998:Q3 through 1999:Q1, the cumulative private capital account balance stood at –$23.2 billion (in U.S. dollars), after having accumulated US$48.1 billion in the previous four quarters. In the second half of 2002, flows reached –$12.7 billion, following US$13.1 billion accumulated in the previous four quarters.

The reversal in capital flows in the exchange crisis was higher than in the confidence crisis for the following reasons. (a) The economy was receiving large inflows, in part because of the huge spread between domestic and foreign interest rates. (b) In mid-1998, despite FDI growth, most of the flows consisted of portfolio investment, loans, and trade credits, which tend to respond more quickly and intensely to crises. In contrast, FDI comprised a large part of the flows when the confidence crisis took place. (c) After some point in time most agents considered the collapse of the exchange regime unavoidable, with the corresponding strong devaluation of domestic currency, and remaining doubts were mainly about when it would take place. In this context, protection of asset values meant large positive net capital outflows. In contrast, the confidence crisis occurred in a different regime, and was reversed as the elected government displayed some strong signs of continuity in macroeconomic policy. (d) The exchange depreciation during the confidence crisis, after some point in time, tended to discourage outflows and stimulate inflows. In the exchange crisis, the decision of sticking to the pegged system did not allow this mechanism.

In general, the literature has emphasized the role of short-term flows during the financial crises. In fact, in Brazil, FDI has been more stable than other flows. Nevertheless, debt securities, loans, and trade credits with maturity superior to 360 days—classified as long-term flows—have exerted an important role during the crises as well. In the moments of crisis, long-term debt inflows tended to decline as much as short-term inflows. Actually, they may fall more, as their horizon is longer and therefore they are more sensitive to uncertainties. The difference, of course, is that, with longer-term debt, outflows are better distributed over time—lower repayments and pressure for debt rollover—tending to reduce net outflows in the short run. However, the long-term category of the balance-of-payments statistics includes flows as short as one year, which are not enough to allow great extension of maturity.

The group "other short-term assets" exerted an important role, mainly in the exchange crisis. In fact, 44.3 percent of the deficit of US$25.1 billion in the private capital balance from 1998:Q8 through 1999:Q1 consisted of this category, which is related to the so-called CC5 (Circular Letter 5) accounts.

Sudden stops involve both the interruption of capital inflows and an increase in outflows. Figure 8.20 shows the behavior of inflows and outflows of foreign investments in Brazilian corporate equities, debt securities, and long-term loans. In general, both inflows and outflows have played an important role. Outflows of investments in equities closely followed inflows, placing in evidence their short-term nature. The reduction in inflows was substantially higher in the exchange crisis and took place before any increase in outflows, which actually started declining as inflows reduced. In the case of debt securities, the fall in inflows was large during both domestic crises. Since outflows depend on the due dates, a decrease in inflows took place before an increase in outflows for both debt securities and long-term loans.

In sum, we find in this section that in general FDI flows tend to be more stable and less correlated to the other flows. Long-term debt flows worked as a stabilizing factor during external crises but behaved procyclically during domestic crises. Moreover, sudden stops are more pronounced when the crisis is mostly domestically driven.

8.5   Capital Flows and Macroeconomic Performance

The analysis of capital flows in Brazil naturally brings up a set of important questions. What has been the role of capital flows in Brazil? What have

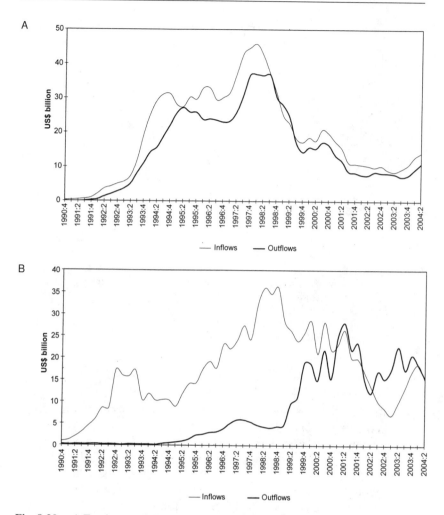

A

B

— Inflows   — Outflows

Fig. 8.20   *A,* **Foreign portfolio investment, Brazilian company equities: Inflows versus outflows (four-quarter cumulative balance, 1990:Q4–2004:Q2, at 2003 prices);** *B,* **foreign portfolio investment, debt securities: Inflows versus outflows (four-quarter cumulative balance, 1990:Q4–2004:Q2, at 2003 prices);** *C,* **other foreign investments: Other long-term loans, inflows versus outflows (four-quarter cumulative balance, 1990:Q4–2004:Q2, at 2003 prices)**

capital flows financed? What is the relationship with other macroeconomic variables? This section deals with these questions.

Initially, we investigate whether capital flows have financed a change in reserves or the capital account balance. Thereafter, using the national accounts, we examine whether current account deficits have financed consumption or investment or even reflected greater deficit in income account.

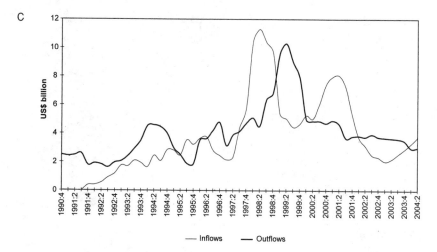

C

Fig. 8.20   (cont) *A,* Foreign portfolio investment, Brazilian company equities: In-flows versus outflows (four-quarter cumulative balance, 1990:Q4–2004:Q2, at 2003 prices); *B,* foreign portfolio investment, debt securities: Inflows versus outflows (four-quarter cumulative balance, 1990:Q4–2004:Q2, at 2003 prices); *C,* other for-eign investments: Other long-term loans, inflows versus outflows (four-quarter cu-mulative balance, 1990:Q4–2004:Q2, at 2003 prices)

8.5.1   What Have Capital Flows Financed? International Reserves versus Current Account Balance

Capital flows can be associated with the current account balance or changes in international reserves. In particular, positive net flows can be used to finance reserve accumulation or current account deficits. Figure 8.21 shows that short movements in capital flows have implied changes in reserves, whereas movements of lower frequency are associated with cur-rent account deficits. Using quarterly data, table 8.8 records the correla-tion of private capital account with the current account balance and re-serve changes for different periods. Private capital account and reserve changes are highly correlated contemporaneously. As expected, this corre-lation is higher in the 1992–98 period—dominated by managed exchange systems—than in the floating exchange rate period. As reserves respond less, the contemporaneous correlation between capital flows and current account deficits is higher in the latter period. Likewise, the lagged and lead-ing correlations are higher in the recent period. These results indicate that, during the floating exchange regime, capital flows have been associated with quicker and larger changes in the current account.

To have some indication of when net capital flows financed reserve ac-cumulation versus current account deficits, we have calculated, for each year, the ratios of both reserve change and current account deficit to the capital and financial account balance (including errors and omissions).

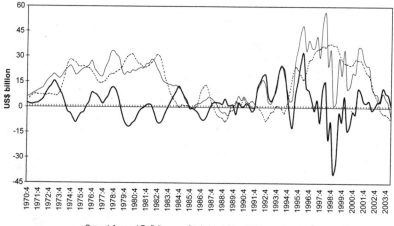

Fig. 8.21 **Capital and financial account, current account deficit and reserve changes (four-quarter cumulative balance, 1970:Q4–2004:Q2, at 2003 prices)**

Table 8.8   Correlation between private capital account and the items current account and change in reserves

	Private capital account			
	1974:Q1–1991:Q4	1992:Q1–2004:Q2	1992:Q1–1998:Q4	1999:Q1–2004:Q2
Current account				
lag (−4)	−0.178	0.005	0.039	−0.216
lag (−3)	−0.320	−0.190	−0.193	−0.312
lag (−2)	−0.334	−0.238	−0.267	−0.365
lag (−1)	−0.384	−0.284	−0.280	−0.501
Contemporary	−0.367	−0.262	−0.148	−0.544
lead (+1)	−0.351	−0.235	−0.130	−0.501
lead (+2)	−0.442	−0.338	−0.361	−0.460
lead (+3)	−0.458	−0.381	−0.353	−0.507
lead (+4)	−0.486	−0.418	−0.316	−0.454
Change in reserves,				
Contemporary	0.329	0.704	0.766	0.427

Sources: Central Bank of Brazil and authors' calculations.
Note: Current account is seasonally adjusted.

Figure 8.22 depicts the results for 1990–2003. The left axis shows the share of net flows used to finance current account deficits. Negative values correspond to years of positive current account balance (1992 and 2003), and values greater than 100 percent refer to periods of current account deficit and reduction in reserves (1991, 1997–99). The values in the right axis—shown in inverse scale—represent the share of net flows that translated

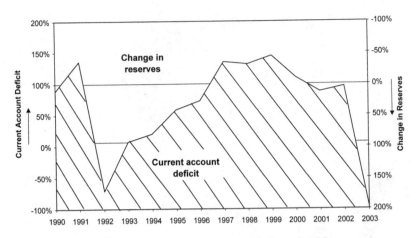

Fig. 8.22   Share of the capital and finance account balance used for current account and for change in reserves (1990–2003)

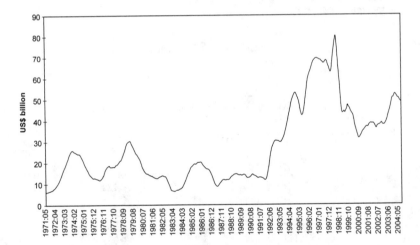

Fig. 8.23   International reserves: Liquidity concept (six-month moving average, May 1971:5–March 2004:9, at 2003 prices)

into reserve increases. Negative values refer to periods of a reduction in reserves. Note, however, that the figure shows only proportions and not the amount of the values involved.

Capital flows were used basically to finance current account deficits, especially during the cycle from 1995 through 2002. The exception to the rule was from 1992 through 1994, when most net flows were employed to finance reserve accumulation. Actually, as we can see in figure 8.23, there was an intense process of reserve accumulation from 1992 through 1996. Reserves rose from US$9.4 billion at end 1991 to US$60.1 billion at end

1996, and were fundamental for the implementation of Real Plan. The other exception took place in 2003, eased by positive current account results.[27]

8.5.2   What Have Capital Flows Financed? Consumption or Investment?

After averaging 0.6 percent over 1990–94, the ratio of current account deficit to GDP rose by 2.8 percentage points in the 1995–97 period, reaching 4.1 percent in the latter year. The high deficits continued in the following years, averaging 4.4 percent over 1998–2001. They reverted in 2002, with a deficit of 1.2 percent, and turned into surplus in the following years. This section uses the national accounts to have an indication of the main aggregate components that accounted for the deficits. National account statistics, however, have to be used with care because they do not necessarily reflect relationships of causality.

We use the well-known basic identities of the national accounts:[28]

$$CA = S - I$$

$$GNDY = GDP + NYCT$$

$$S = GNDY - C$$

$$C = C_h + C_g,$$

where CA = current account balance, S = gross domestic saving, I = investment, GNDY = gross national disposable income, GDP = gross domestic product, NYCT = net income from abroad and net current transfers, C = consumption, C_h = household consumption, and C_g = government consumption.

Tables 8.9 and 8.10 divide the current account deficit period into two phases: (a) 1995–97, characterized by a large increase in the deficit and in domestic expenditure rates; and (b) 1998–2001, characterized by some increase in the deficit and by a prominent role of the deficit in the net income from abroad. We estimate the contribution of the variables to the increase in the current account deficit comparing the first phase to 1990–94, and the second phase to the first one.

According to table 8.9, the increase in the current account deficit in the first period corresponded to both an increase in the investment ratio and a reduction in domestic saving. The rise in the investment ratio responded for 43.2 percent of the deficit increase in the period. In contrast, in the second period, the reduction in domestic saving was accompanied by a decrease, at a lower value, in the investment ratio. Table 8.10 allows us to discriminate the elements behind the reduction in domestic saving.

The current account deficit cycle was accompanied by an increase of 2.1

27. During the 1980s, the exception was 1984–85, with high trade balance surpluses.
28. See, for instance, IMF (1993).

Table 8.9   Domestic saving and investment as a share of GDP and their contribution to the increase in the current account (CA) deficit, 1990–2001

	Current account deficit (A) = (C) – (B)	Domestic saving (B)	Investment (C)
1. 1990–1994 (%)	0.6	19.8	20.4
2. 1995–1997 (%)	3.4	18.2	21.6
3. 1998–2001 (%)	4.4	16.6	21.0
Row 2 minus row 1	2.8	–1.6	1.2
Contribution to the increase in the CA deficit (%)	100.0	56.8	43.2
Row 3 minus row 2	1.1	–1.6	–0.6
Contribution to the increase in the CA deficit (%)	100.0	153.2	–53.2

Sources: IBGE and authors' calculations.

Table 8.10   Components of national accounts as a share of GDP and their contribution to the increase in the current account (CA) deficit, 1990–2001

	Current account deficit	Income deficit	Investment	Consumption	Household consumption	Government consumption
1. 1990–1994 (%)	0.6	1.8	20.4	78.4	60.4	18.0
2. 1995–1997 (%)	3.4	1.4	21.6	80.4	61.7	18.8
3. 1998–2001 (%)	4.4	2.9	21.0	80.6	61.4	19.1
Row 2 minus row 1	2.8	–0.5	1.2	2.1	1.3	0.8
Contribution to the increase in the CA deficit (%)	100.0	–17.8	43.2	74.6	45.5	29.1
Row 3 minus row 2	1.1	1.5	–0.6	0.1	–0.3	0.4
Contribution to the increase in the CA deficit (%)	100.0	143.3	–53.2	9.9	–17.3	139.9

Sources: IBGE and authors' calculations.

percentage points in the consumption share in the GDP, which took place basically in 1995 and 1996, as we can see in figure 8.24.[29] In fact, under the point of view of the national accounts, consumption—household and government—accounted for the larger part (74.6 percent) of the increase in the current account deficit. On the other hand, because the share of consumption is approximately four times higher than that of investment, the percentage increase in the consumption ratio was lower than that of investment (2.7 percent against 5.9 percent). The combination of an increase

29. Note that the values in the right axis refer to the consumption ratio.

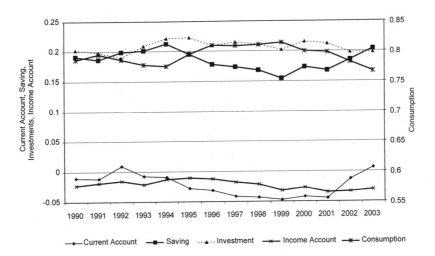

Fig. 8.24   Components of national accounts as a proportion of GDP (1990–2003)

in investment and consumption comprised 117.8 percent of the deficit increase (net income from abroad contributed with −17.8 percent).

In the 1998–2001 period, however, it was an increase in the net income deficit that accounted for most of the increase in the current account deficit. The ratio of net income deficit to GDP rose by 1.5 percentage points, reflecting basically the debt accumulation and foreign investments of the previous period, besides some movements related to the domestic crises.

In summary, the role of net financial flows in the 1990s was to finance (a) a strong accumulation of international reserves between 1992 and 1996; (b) a large expansion of the current account deficit over 1995–97, representing an expansion of both investment and consumption; and (c) an increase in the current account deficit over 1998–2001, resulting from a higher deficit in the net income from abroad.

8.5.3   GDP Growth

Since the 1980s, the Brazilian economy has experienced short-lived business cycles. Figure 8.25 shows the four-quarter moving average of GDP growth and the four-quarter cumulative balance of the private capital account since 1992. Economic expansions have lasted approximately two years. The figure also shows that there is an association between capital flows and output movements. The two expansions before the adoption of the floating exchange rate regime benefited from the large capital inflows. Figure 8.3 shows clearly the appreciation trend and the large trade deficit of the period.

In comparison to the 1990s growth episodes, economic growth in 2000–

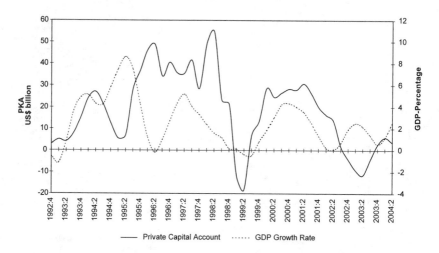

Fig. 8.25   Private capital account balance (four-quarter cumulative balance at 2003 prices) and GDP growth rate (four-quarter moving average, 1992:Q1–2004:Q2)

2001 and at the time of this writing (2004) took place in a different context. First, net capital flows have been of lower magnitude and have been dominated by FDI. Actually, since 1998, net direct investment has comprised more than 100 percent of the private capital account balance. There has been no significant surge of short-term flows or portfolio investment. Second, the expansions have been accompanied by a more favorable situation in the trade balance. Third, the policy regime has changed to improve fundamentals. Furthermore, the economic slowdown was less intense in the Brazilian confidence crisis than in other countries' sudden-stop crises. Figure 8.26 shows GDP growth in the year following the crises for a few comparable cases.

8.5.4   Consumption Smoothing

Based on the intertemporal approach to the current account, capital flows are deemed to bring about greater consumption smoothing.[30] When facing idiosyncratic shocks, a country's consumers can borrow (or lend) abroad and reduce consumption volatility. Table 8.11 shows consumption volatility for three periods. We compare volatility after capital account openness with the periods of absence of capital flows and of the 1970s debt accumulation. In fact, consumption—its growth rate or share in GDP—is more stable in the recent period than in the 1980s.[31] The standard deviation

30. See Obstfeld and Rogoff (1994, 1996).
31. In contrast, Prasad et al. (2003) have found that the median of the consumption volatility of twenty-two more financially integrated developing countries—which include Brazil—increased in the 1990s in comparison to the 1980s.

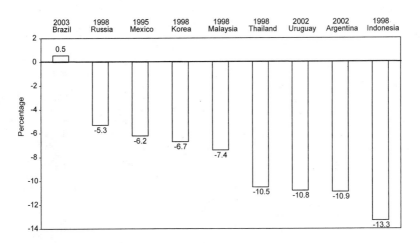

Fig. 8.26 GDP growth after crises

Table 8.11   **Growth rate and volatility of consumption and GDP in Brazil, 1974–2003**

	Consumption growth rate			Consumption share in GDP		GDP growth rate		
	Average	Standard deviation	Coefficient of variation	Average	Standard deviation	Average	Standard deviation	Coefficient of variation
1974–1982	4.95	5.30	1.07	78.5	1.4	5.03	4.49	0.89
1983–1991	2.18	4.30	1.97	75.3	3.7	2.27	4.31	1.90
1992–2003	2.20	2.54	1.15	79.3	1.6	2.43	2.08	0.86

Sources: IBGE and authors' calculations.

of consumption growth is also lower after the capital account liberalization in comparison to the 1970s, even though the variation coefficient is slightly higher because of the lower growth rate.[32]

8.5.5 What Determines Capital Flows and Their Components?

To assess the main determinants of capital flows, we have estimated regressions for selected items: private capital account, official agency–related loans, net foreign direct investment, and net foreign investment in debt securities, equities, and loans. In particular, we are interested in the role played by the external and domestic interest rates and the crises. The main

---

32. One should be cautious about these comparisons because the periods may involve different moments in the cycle, and of course GDP has additional determinants. In particular, the 1983–91 period was marked by external adjustment resulting from the debt crisis and by the recession brought about by the Collor Plan in 1990. On the other hand, the 1970s was a period of great economic expansion, and the last decade was featured by several financial crises.

Table 8.12   Determinants of capital flows (January 1995–August 2004)

Regressor	Private capital account	Debt securities	Equities	Loans	Direct investment	Official-agency loans
			Dependent variable			
Constant	1,938.9*	506.3*	488.2	122.2	1,237.0**	−882.4
	(1,164.9)	(262.3)	(701.8)	(450.8)	(537.9)	(865.9)
U.S. interest rate	238.7	−14.0	147.4*	86.1	332.3***	−81.9
	(175.7)	(38.8)	(78.0)	(77.3)	(64.8)	(126.5)
Domestic interest rate[a]	95.5**	20.7**	30.0*	33.7**	−70.2***	19.7
	(39.1)	(8.7)	(16.3)	(15.6)	(10.4)	(29.6)
EMBI+ Brazil	−426.6***	−0.7***	−1.7**	−1.6***	1.0*	114.2**
	(127.8)	(0.3)	(0.8)	(0.6)	(0.6)	(55.5)
R^2	0.3201	0.1857	0.1914	0.2302	0.1810	0.0518
Adjusted R^2	0.3015	0.1635	0.1693	0.2092	0.1587	0.0260
Unit root test for the dependent variable: p-value[b]	0.0071	0.0000	0.0984	0.0146	0.2343	0.0302

Notes: Standard errors (shown in parentheses) were corrected by Newey-West heteroskedasticity and autocorrelation consistent covariance matrix estimator. Estimation using two-stage least squares. Instrumental variables: constant U.S. interest rate and the variable domestic rate and EMBI lagged one and two periods. The variables Debt Securities, Equities, Loans, and Direct Investment refer to net foreign investment.

[a]Minus expected exchange rate depreciation.

[b]p-value found using the augmented Dickey-Fuller test. Number of lags selected according to modified AIC, which generated the same number of lags as modified SIC.

***Significant at the 1 percent level.

**Significant at the 5 percent level.

*Significant at the 10 percent level.

results are recorded in table 8.12. We have used as explanatory variables the Federal Reserve funds rate, domestic interest rate minus expected depreciation,[33] and EMBI+ Brazil (sovereign spread). Although the EMBI is also affected by the Federal Reserve funds rate, it tends to basically reflect the several crises. The correlation coefficient between the Federal Reserve funds rate and the EMBI is −0.208. Thus, we do not include dummies for the crises, whose specification implies some arbitrariness and may distort the estimations.[34]

33. Calculated using the Selic in the first working day of the month divided by the expected exchange rate change, measured as the ratio between the forward rate for contracts due at the beginning of the following month and the spot rate. All dependent variables are measured at constant U.S. prices.

34. Initially, we conducted unit root tests (augmented Dickey-Fuller formulation), basically to avoid incurring spurious regression. We reject the null for all dependent variables except for direct investment. In the case of the regressors, we accept the null of presence of a unit root in the U.S. and domestic interest rates, and reject it for the EMBI. In the estimations, we

The role played by the EMBI and the domestic interest rate is evident. In the regressions of the variables representing private capital flows, the EMBI enters significantly with a negative sign and the domestic interest rate with a positive sign, except in the case of direct investment. Greater yields in domestic bonds attract capital inflows, and financial crises stimulate net outflows. The Federal Reserve funds rate enters significantly only in the equity and direct investment equations, but with a positive sign. One possible explanation is that increases in the U.S. interest rate tend to generate economic slowdown, discouraging investment in that country and thus stimulating investment abroad.

In contrast to the other private flows, the coefficient on the domestic interest rate is negative in the direct investment equation. In this case, as an increase in the domestic interest rate generates an economic slowdown, inward direct investment is discouraged.[35] The equation for official agency loans appears with a positive coefficient on the EMBI, indicating the role played by these loans in working as compensatory flows during some crises.[36]

8.5.6   The Relationship between Capital Flows and Macroeconomic Performance: A VAR Approach

We have estimated a structural VAR to further examine the role played by capital flows. Our interest is to assess the importance and impact of capital flow movements on other macroeconomic variables as well as the factors behind those movements.

To estimate the VAR, we choose variables that are related to the behavior of the current account and capital flows: industrial production, current account balance, private capital account, terms of trade (measured as the ratio of export prices to import prices), EMBI+ Brazil, real effective exchange rate (measured as the value of foreign currency in terms of domestic currency), and domestic real interest rate (Selic rate). The exogenous variables are the Fed Funds interest rate and the U.S. industrial production.

The sample goes from January 1995 through August 2004. Unfortunately, although we are using monthly data, some of the results are sensi-

---

used two-stage least squares, employing standard errors corrected by Newey-West heteroskedasticity and autocorrelation consistent covariance matrix. The instrumental variables for the domestic interest rate and the EMBI Brazil were these variables lagged one and two periods. We consider that the Federal Reserve funds rate is not affected contemporaneously by shocks to capital flows to Brazil.

35. Since we could not reject the null of presence of a unit root in the direct investment, we have also estimated in first differences, after having rejected the presence of cointegration. None of the coefficients is significant.

36. We have also tested for the inclusion of other variables, such as output (level and growth) and exchange rate (measured as deviation of a trend estimated using the Hodrick-Prescott filter), but they did not enter significantly.

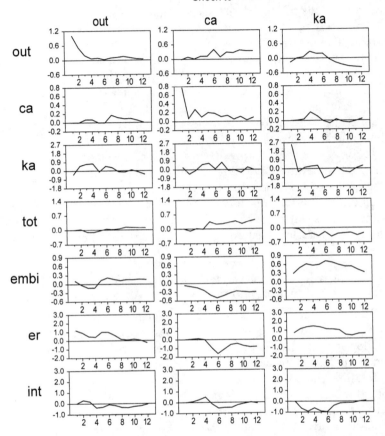

Fig. 8.27   Impulse-response functions: SVAR (January 1995–August 2004)

tive to the identification structure assumed concerning the contemporaneous effects of the shocks. Therefore, the results have to be viewed with caution. Appendix D provides a more detailed explanation of the variables and identification structure used.

For simplicity, we show only the resulting impulse response functions and the variance error decomposition (figure 8.27 and table 8.13). In general, the results using the point estimates of the impulse response functions are consistent with the theory and historical evidence. The most interesting result refers to the behavior of the variables when the economy is hit by a shock to the EMBI. An increase in the country risk premium clearly leads to a positive response of interest rate, exchange rate depreciation (depreciation of domestic currency), and a reduction in capital flows (measured by the private capital account balance). Although with some lag, output falls.

Shock to

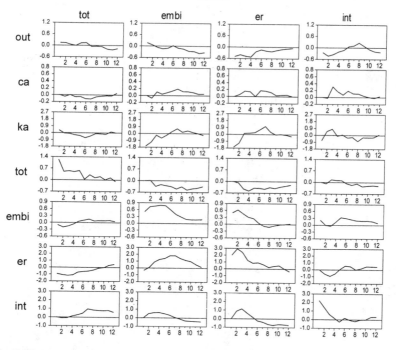

Fig. 8.27   (cont.)

As exchange rate depreciates, terms of trade deteriorate. These results are in line with the historical evidence concerning the effects of several crises on the economy.

As expected, in response to positive interest rate shocks, output falls. Positive shocks to the current account, in turn, lead to an exchange rate appreciation, reduction in the EMBI, and some improvement in terms of trade and output levels. Positive shocks to capital flows are not persistent but lead to a reduction in the interest rate, which seems to cause exchange rate depreciation. In response to a favorable shock to terms of trade, exchange rate tends to appreciate. Finally, positive shocks to the exchange rate are followed by an increase in the interest rate and EMBI. The increase in the country risk premium, in turn, tends to cause a reduction in the capital flows. Current account tends to respond somewhat positively. Output, however, declines, but it reverts as the exchange rate, EMBI, and interest rate return to their previous values.

The variance error decomposition allows us to have an idea of the importance of certain shocks for forecast errors. Shocks to the current account, private capital account, and exchange rate explain a large part of

Table 8.13   Variance error decomposition (%), SVAR (January 1995–August 2004)

Variables	Standard error	Output	Current account	Private capital account	Terms of trade	EMBI Brazil	Real effective exchange rate	Real interest rate
Output								
3 steps	1.6	54.0	0.3	1.1	1.8	1.5	26.0	15.3
12 steps	2.3	26.3	14.1	12.9	3.9	9.4	21.5	11.8
24 steps	2.7	19.5	19.0	20.1	5.6	9.7	16.4	9.9
Current account								
3 steps	0.9	0.5	82.0	0.1	0.3	2.0	3.3	11.8
12 steps	1.2	4.7	57.8	4.1	3.1	8.4	8.6	13.5
24 steps	1.2	4.3	54.1	6.9	3.3	9.0	8.6	13.7
Private capital account								
3 steps	4.1	5.1	1.5	37.6	0.8	23.1	23.7	8.2
12 steps	5.1	7.4	6.4	31.9	3.7	19.2	22.3	9.2
24 steps	5.3	7.2	6.7	31.2	3.9	18.6	22.1	10.2
Terms of trade								
3 steps	1.6	0.5	0.4	4.0	80.6	4.6	8.6	1.3
12 steps	2.9	1.1	10.9	11.2	33.8	19.7	19.7	3.6
24 steps	3.7	0.9	23.5	19.7	22.6	17.4	12.7	3.1
EMBI Brazil								
3 steps	1.8	0.9	1.3	22.5	2.4	44.3	27.2	1.5
12 steps	3.2	2.5	11.8	35.3	1.5	33.7	10.5	4.8
24 steps	3.4	2.7	15.6	34.1	1.6	30.8	9.9	5.4
Real effective exchange rate								
3 steps	5.5	8.1	0.1	12.2	11.2	3.0	61.2	4.2
12 steps	8.4	7.2	9.9	16.8	8.7	21.8	31.7	4.0
24 steps	8.9	6.8	14.3	16.5	9.0	19.8	29.1	4.4
Real interest rate								
3 steps	3.4	1.1	0.6	11.5	0.1	5.1	18.5	63.2
12 steps	4.9	3.2	4.6	15.1	17.2	7.8	21.1	31.0
24 steps	5.6	3.2	7.2	13.2	15.5	12.2	22.3	26.3

Note: Standard errors are underestimated because their estimation assumes that coefficients are known.

output forecast errors in a twelve- or twenty-four-month horizon. Interest rate shocks affect output forecast errors more strongly over a short horizon. Private capital account forecast errors, in turn, are largely explained by shocks to the EMBI, exchange rate, and interest rate. In the case of exchange rate, shocks to the country risk premium, private capital account, and current account are responsible for a large part of its forecast errors. Interest rate forecast errors, in turn, are explained by shocks to the private capital account, terms of trade, EMBI, and exchange rate, besides shocks to itself.

8.6   Conclusions

Notwithstanding the financial crises and macroeconomic volatility of the recent past, financial liberalization has led to reduced external vulnerability. Balance-of-payments patterns have changed. Recent growth has been accompanied by a more favorable trade balance position. The profile of external financing has improved after the floating of the currency. The private sector has decreased significantly its issuance of external debt, and FDI has replaced portfolio investment as the main financing source.

Liberalization of the capital account in the last fifteen years has provided more convertibility to the currency. The new rules, however, coexist with an old legislation that was established in a more control-prone environment. Therefore, the result is a complex web of regulations and rules that require consolidation and a mentality that still associates transfers abroad with illicit or antipatriotic practices (based on the capital flight legislation period).

We believe further progress in capital account convertibility is warranted. Liberalization should be accompanied by a broad range of reforms to improve and foster stronger institutions—such as approval of de jure central bank independence (not only de facto)—establish a longer track record of responsible fiscal policy (under the fiscal responsibility law), and reduce microeconomic inefficiencies and contractual uncertainties.

Appendix A

Main Exchange Restrictions in Brazil

Export Surrender

- Export proceeds are required to be converted into domestic currency ("export surrender"). Furthermore, the netting of payments is not allowed (e.g., exporters cannot use their proceeds to pay for an import or an external debt before converting them into domestic currency).

Controls on Capital Flows

- There are generally no current taxes on capital flows. Two exceptions. Short-term fixed income flows (up to ninety days) are taxed at a 5 percent rate. Payments of credit card transactions are taxed at 2 percent.
- All capital flows must be registered at the Central Bank of Brazil.

Transfers of Currency

- Transfers abroad by residents are allowed but have to be registered at the Central Bank.

- Travelers may take out or bring into the country domestic or foreign banknotes, checks, or traveler's checks without restriction but must declare to customs any amount over R$10,000 or its equivalent.

Limits on Transactions and Deposits in Foreign Currency

- Settlements of transactions among residents and pricing of contracts or goods in foreign currency are prohibited.
- Lending in foreign currency is prohibited, except for on-lending of external foreign currency loans by banks.
- Deposits in foreign currency are generally not allowed. There are several exceptions. For residents these are authorized foreign exchange dealers, tourist agencies, Brazilian citizens living abroad, the Brazilian Post Office Administration, credit card administration companies, companies responsible for the development and execution of projects in the energy sector, and insurance and reinsurance companies and reinsurance brokers. For nonresidents, the exceptions are embassies, foreign delegations, international organizations, foreign transportation companies, foreign citizens in transit in the country, and reinsurance companies.

Direct Investment

- Foreign direct investment in Brazil is generally free. However, there are legal restrictions on participation in certain economic activities.
- Brazilian direct investment abroad requires prior approval by the Central Bank. The exception is transfers of up to the equivalent of US$5 million, including all remittances in the previous twelve months.

Nonresident Participation in Local Markets

- There is no restriction on the purchase of debt instruments. The purchase by nonresident of shares is also generally free. There are restrictions in certain economic activities.
- Nonresidents may issue shares (or other securities that represent ownership) only through Brazilian depositary receipts (BDRs). The exception is for Mercosur countries, where direct sales are also allowed.

Resident Restrictions on Investment and Issues Abroad

- Residents may purchase bonds or other debt securities through dedicated offshore investment funds (FIEX).
- Residents may invest only in stock exchanges in Mercosur countries. Brazilians are allowed to purchase depositary receipts issued abroad by companies headquartered in Brazil.
- Corporations may issue depositary receipts abroad.

Appendix B

Table B.1   Chronology of Main Changes to Capital Account Regulation (1990–2004)

Normative measure	Date	Nature of measure	Direction of flows	Description
A. Resident and nonresident accounts: Regulations implemented prior to the 1990s				
Decree 23, 501, replaced by Decree-Law 857	11/27/33, 9/11/69			Establishment of the domestic currency as the only legal tender. In other words, payments in foreign currency are not allowed (exceptions included contracts related to imports and exports, exchange contracts, and debt involving nonresidents as creditor or debtor). Law 10,192 of 2/14/01 (previously Provisory Measure 1,053 of 6/30/95) reaffirmed those restrictions and also clarified that restriction includes indexation to a foreign currency.
Decree 42,820	12/16/57			Determination that "it is permissible to take out or bring in domestic and foreign paper currency, as well as stocks and any other financial assets that have monetary value" (article 17). The National Monetary Council (CMN), if necessary, can restrict the entry and exit of domestic paper money (article 20).
Decree 55,762	2/17/65			Permission for nonresidents to transfer abroad, without prior authorization, the balance resulting from foreign exchange sales or money orders in foreign currency (article 57).
Circular Letter 5	2/27/69			Classification of nonresidents' deposit accounts into two categories: (a) "free accounts—coming from exchange sales," and (b) "free accounts—from other origins." The balance of the former that is not withdrawn is freely convertible into foreign currency; however, if the balance is withdrawn and then subsequently returned to the account, it is classified in the second category.

(continued)

In panel A, we focus on the so-called CC5 accounts.

Table B.1 (continued)

Normative measure	Date	Nature of measure	Direction of flows	Description
Resolution 1,552	12/22/88			Creation of the "floating exchange rate market"—also called "dollar-tourism market"—alongside the "commercial or free exchange rate market." Permission for authorized institutions to transfer their long foreign currency position to nonresident institutions in exchange for domestic currency. Furthermore, permission for the Central Bank to change the conditions of the floating exchange rate market at any time.
Main changes Circular Letter 2,259	2/20/92	L	O	Creation of a third category in the free accounts established in Circular Letter 5, complementing Resolution 1,552: "free accounts—financial institutions—floating exchange rate market," which can be opened by nonresident financial institutions and whose withdrawals and deposits are freely available, including those coming from exchange sales or purchases.
Resolution 1,946, Circular 2,242	7/29/92, 10/7/92	R	O	Requirement that international transfers in domestic currency should be identified and registered in the central bank information system (Sisbacen) when equal to or greater than US$10,000.00.
Circular 2,677, Circular 2,242	4/10/96, 10/7/92	E	O	Consolidation and revision of the regulation on nonresidents' accounts and international transfers in reais. Requirement of Sisbacen identification when withdrawals or deposits are equal to or greater than R$10,000.00 (revoked Circular Letter 5).
B. Foreign direct investment: Regulation implemented prior to the 1990s				
Law 4,131, Law 4,390, and Decree 55,762	9/3/62, 8/29/64, 2/17/65			Regulation of foreign capital in Brazil, basically direct investment and loans, and the associated remittance of income abroad.
Resolution 1,460	2/1/88			Regulation of the conversion of external debt into investment in the country.
Constitution	10/5/88			Restriction on foreign investment in some economic sectors.
Main changes Resolution 1,810	3/27/91	L	I	Authorization of the conversion of external debt instruments of the federal public sector, bonds, and deposits denominated in foreign currency for use in the National Privatization Program.

Normative measure	Date	Nature of measure	Direction of flows	Description
Law 8,383	12/30/91	L	O	Elimination of the additional tax, ranging from 40% to 60%, on remittance of profits and dividends abroad that exceeded 12% of registered capital, effective 1/1/92. Reduction to 15% of the withholding tax on profits and dividends of nonresidents, effective 1/1/93.
Resolution 1,894	1/9/92	L	I	Reduction from twelve to six years of the period that investments resulting from the conversion of external debt instruments for use in the National Privatization Program are required to remain in Brazil.
Circular 2,487	10/5/94	R	I	Prohibition of inflows in the form of both advances for future capital increases and bridge investments in anticipation of future conversion of debts into investment.
Law 8,987	2/13/95	L	I	Opening of new possibilities for investment in public utilities with the concession law.
Constitutional Amendment 6	8/15/95	L	I	Removal of the constitutional distinction between Brazilian firms—licensed under Brazilian laws and with headquarters and administration in the country—and Brazilian firms of national capital—restricted to those under control of residents—and the related special treatment given to the latter. Regardless of owner nationality, firms licensed under Brazilian laws and with headquarters and administration in the country were guaranteed (a) special treatment in the case of small firms and (b) exclusivity rights in the mining sector.
Constitutional Amendment 7	8/15/95	L	I	Removal of the constitutional requirement that navigation along the coast and in the inland waterways be conducted by national vessels.
Statement of Reasons 311, Communications 5,796 and 10,844	8/23/95, 9/9/97, 3/19/03	L	I	Possibility for an increase in the ownership participation of nonresidents in financial institutions, after case-by-case analysis by the monetary authority, and republic president's final decision.
Law 9,249	12/26/95	L	O	Removal of income tax, previously of 15%, on remittance of profits and dividends abroad.

(continued)

Table B.1 (continued)

Normative measure	Date	Nature of measure	Direction of flows	Description
Directive MF 28	2/8/96	R	I	Imposition of a financial transaction tax (IOF) of 5% on privatization funds, when the resources enter the country.
Directive MF 85	4/24/97	L	I	Reduction in IOF from 5% to 0% on privatization funds.
Circular 2,997	8/15/00	E		Introduction of electronic registration (RDE) for foreign direct investment.
Resolution 2,815	1/24/01	L	I	Revocation of rule set in Resolution 2,099 o 8/17/94, which precluded the opening of new bank branches controlled by nonresidents.

C. Foreign portfolio investment and external loans: Regulation implemented prior to the 1990s

Law 4,131 and 4,390, Decree 55,762	9/3/62, 8/29/64, 2/17/65			Regulation of foreign capital in Brazil, basically direct investment and loans, and the associated remittance of income abroad.
Resolution 63	8/21/67			Regulation of external loans that are on-lent by resident financial institutions.
Resolution 64	8/23/67			Inclusion of BNDES among the institutions authorized to on-lend loans under Resolution 63.
Resolution 125	12/12/69			Requirement that external loans be previously approved by the Central Bank.
Resolution 498	11/22/78			Determination of a minimum maturity of ten years for external loans to be eligible for reimbursement, reduction, or exemption from income tax.
Resolution 644	10/22/80			Exemption from tax on the remittance abroad of interest, commission, and issuance expenditures of commercial paper.
Resolution 1, 289, with Annexes I to III	3/20/87			Regulation of the creation, operation, and management of foreign capital investment companies, foreign capital investment funds, and stock and bond portfolios.
Resolution 1,460	2/1/88			Regulation of the conversion of external debt into investment in the country.

Main changes

Resolution 1,734	7/31/90	L	I	Authorization for certain financial institutions to issue commercial paper abroad.

Table B.1 (continued)

Normative measure	Date	Nature of measure	Direction of flows	Description
Resolution 1,803	3/27/91	L	I	Reduction in the minimum maturity of external loans from ten to five years for those to be eligible for reimbursement, reduction, or exemption from income tax (revoked Resolution 498).
Debt agreement	4/1/91	E		Preliminary agreement with nonresident creditor banks for the elimination of arrears outstanding at the end of 1990.
Resolution 1,832	5/31/91	L	I	Liberalization of the securities market to foreign institutional investors, via Annex IV to Resolution 1,289. These investments were given exempted from income and capital gains tax, but were subject to a 15% tax on income remitted abroad.
Circular 1,969, replaced by Circular 2,199	6/6/91, 7/16/92	L	I	Authorization for the issuance of convertible debentures abroad.
Resolution 1,853	7/31/91	L	O	Tax exemption for the remittance abroad of interest, commission, and issuance expenditures, applied to commercial paper and extended to floating-rate notes, fixed-rate notes, floating-rate certificates of deposit, fixed-rate certificates of deposit, publicly issued bonds, and privately issued bonds.
Resolution 1,848, replaced by Resolution 1,927	8/1/91, 5/18/92	L	I	Authorization for the issuance abroad of depository receipts representing Brazilian securities (ADRs and International Depositary Receipts [IDRs])—Annex V.
Resolution 1,872	9/25/91	L	I	Permission for external borrowing for agricultural financing.
Circular 2,083	11/7/91	L	I	Reduction in the minimum term for onlending operations related to Resolution 63 from one year (investment banks and BNDES) or six months (commercial banks) to ninety days.
Resolution 1,901	1/29/92	L		Authorization for natural and juridical persons to invest in securities in Mercosur countries.
Communications 2,747 and 2,757	3/12/92, 3/13/92	R	I	Increase in the minimum average maturity of debt securities (commercial paper and those listed in Resolution 1,853 of 7/31/91) to thirty months to be eligible for tax exemptions.

(continued)

Table B.1 (continued)

Normative measure	Date	Nature of measure	Direction of flows	Description
Circular Letter 2,269	4/24/92	R	I	Requirement that the minimum average maturity for issuance of debt securities must be thirty months, and increase, from thirty to sixty months, in the minimum average maturity required for those to be eligible for tax exemptions (revoked Communications 2,747 and 2,757).
Resolution 1,921	4/30/92	L		Authorization for hedge operations against interest rate risk in the international market.
Resolution 1,935	6/30/92	L	I	Authorization for foreign investors represented by funds, investment companies, and institutional investors to operate in the options and futures markets for securities, exchange, and interest rates.
Resolution 1,968	8/30/92	L		Authorization for natural and juridical persons to invest in derivatives markets as hedge operations in Mercosur countries (replaced Resolution 1,901).
Circular Letter 2,333	10/29/92	R	I	Authorization for external loans only for those with a minimum average maturity of thirty months.
Circular Letter 2,372	6/16/93	R	I	Increase in the minimum average maturity required for the issuance of debt securities from thirty to thirty-six months, and in the minimum average maturity from sixty to ninety-six months for eligibility for reimbursement, reduction, or exemption from income tax (revoked Circular Letter 2,269).
Circular Letter 2,373	6/16/93	R	I	Increase in the minimum average maturity required for loans from thirty to thirty-six months (revoked Circular Letter 2,333).
Resolution 1,986	6/28/93	R	I	Increase in the minimum average maturity of loans from sixty to ninety-six months for those to be eligible for reimbursement, reduction, or exemption from income tax (revoked Resolution 1,803).
Resolution 2,012	7/30/93	L		Expansion of the hedge operations that firms are allowed to undertake, including, besides those related to interest rates previously allowed, those related to exchange rate and commodity prices (revoked Resolution 1,921).

Table B.1 (continued)

Normative measure	Date	Nature of measure	Direction of flows	Description
Resolution 2,013	8/19/93	R	I	Prohibition of foreign capital, registered under Annexes I to IV, to invest in fixed-income bonds.
Decree 995	11/25/93	R	I	Imposition of IOF of 5% on investments in fixed-income funds and 3% on external loans when entering the country.
Resolution 2,028	11/25/93	R	I	Prohibition of foreign capital, registered under Annexes I to IV, to invest in debentures, accompanied by the creation of foreign capital fixed-income funds (FRF-CE) to invest in private debt securities. Portfolio investment by foreign investors in fixed-income instruments was restricted to those new funds.
Circular 2,384	11/26/93	L	I	In the absence of objection by the Central Bank of Brazil, automatic authorization for the issuance of debt securities by the private sector after five working days of the request for authorization.
Resolution 2,034	12/17/93	R	I	Prohibition of foreign capital, registered under Annexes I to IV, to invest in derivatives markets—unless as a hedge—including operations that result in fixed income. FRF-CE funds were allowed to invest in federal bonds, derivatives, and financial investment funds (FAFs; revoked Resolution 2,028).
Resolution 2,042	1/13/94	L		Authorization for certain institutions to conduct swap operations involving gold, exchange rates, interest rates, and price indexes in the over-the-counter market.
Resolution 2,046	1/19/94	R	I	Change in the regulation of investments under Annexes I to IV, including prohibition of investment in debentures (revoked Resolution 2,013).
Circular 2,410	3/2/94	R	I	Termination of the automatic authorization for the issuance of debt securities abroad that had been set by Circular 2,384 of 11/26/93.
Circular Letter 2,444	3/14/94	R	I	Renewal or extension of contracts of debt securities subject to the same rules as new contracts established by Circular Letter 2,372 of 6/16/93.

(continued)

Table B.1 (continued)

Normative measure	Date	Nature of measure	Direction of flows	Description
Debt Agreement	4/15/94	E		Conclusion of the arrangements to reschedule Brazil's external debts to commercial bank creditors.
Resolution 2,079	6/15/94	R	I	Prohibition of foreign capital, registered under Annexes I to IV, to invest in certificates of privatization and related securities.
Resolution 2,105	8/31/94	L	O	Permission for prepayment of external loans and import financing.
Resolution 2,115	10/19/94	R	I	Prohibition of foreign capital, registered under Annexes I to IV, to invest in FAFs.
Directive MF 534	10/19/94	R	I	Increase in the IOF from 5% to 9% on foreign investment in fixed-income funds, and from 3% to 7% on external loans, and imposition of a tax of 1% on foreign investment in securities.
Circular 2,492	10/19/94	R	I	Increase in the minimum maturity for on-lending operations under Resolution 63 from 90 to 540 days (revoked Circular 2,083).
Circular 2,545	3/9/95	L	I	Reduction in the minimum term for on-lending operations related to Resolution 63 from 540 days to 90 days (revoked Circular 2,492).
Circular 2,546	3/9/95	L	I	Reduction in the minimum average maturity required for loans from thirty-six to twenty-four months, with maintenance of the minimum average maturity of ninety-six months for those to be eligible for reimbursement, reduction, or exemption from income tax (revoked Circular Letters 2,372 and 2,373).
Circular 2,547, replaced by Circular 2,559	3/9/95, 4/20/95	L	I	Reduction in the minimum average maturity required for the renewal and extension of debt securities contracts from thirty-six months to 180 days, with maintenance of the minimum average maturity of ninety-six months for eligibility for reimbursement, reduction, or exemption from income tax (revoked Circular Letter 2,444).
Directive MF 95	3/9/95	L	I	Reduction in the IOF from 9% to 5% on foreign investment in fixed-income funds, from 1% to 0% on foreign investment in securities, and from 7% to 0% on external loans.

Normative measure	Date	Nature of measure	Direction of flows	Description
Resolution 2,147	3/9/95	R	O	Revocation of the permission for prepayment of external loans and import financing (revoked Resolution 2,105).
Resolution 2,148	3/16/95	L	I	Permission for external borrowing for the financing of agricultural investment. Minimum maturity for these external loans of 180 days (revoked Resolution 1,872).
Resolution 2,170	6/30/95	L	I	Permission for financial institutions to contract resources abroad, with a minimum maturity of 720 days, for the financing of construction or acquisition of new real estate ventures.
Directive MF 202	8/10/95	R	I	Increase in the IOF from 5% to 7% on foreign investment in fixed-income funds, and from 0% to 5% on external loans, and imposition of a 7% rate on interbank foreign exchange operations between financial institutions abroad and institutions authorized to operate in the foreign exchange market, and on the formation of short-term cash holdings (*disponibilidades*) of nonresidents.
Directive MF 228	9/15/95	L	I	Imposition of a differentiated IOF on external loans according to average maturity: 5% for those with an average maturity of two years, 4% for three years, 2% for four years, 1% for five years, and 0% for six years.
Resolution 2,188	10/8/95	R	I	Prohibition of foreign capital, registered under Annexes I to IV, to invest in futures and options markets (revoked Resolution 2,115).
Circular 2,661	2/8/96	R	I	Increase in the minimum average maturity required for external credits to thirty-six months, with maintenance of the minimum average maturity of ninety-six months for debt securities to be eligible for reimbursement, reduction, or exemption from income tax (revoked Circulars 2,546 and 2,559).
Resolution 2,246	2/8/96	R	I	Prohibition of foreign capital, registered under Annexes I to IV, to invest in agrarian debt bonds (TDAs), national development fund bonds (OFNDs), and Siderbras debentures (revoked Resolution 2,188).
Resolution 2,247	2/8/96	L	I	Permission for nonresidents to invest in mutual investment funds in emerging firms.

(*continued*)

Table B.1 (continued)

Normative measure	Date	Nature of measure	Direction of flows	Description
Resolution 2,248	2/8/96	L	I	Permission for nonresidents to invest in real estate investment funds.
Resolution 2,266	3/29/96	L	I	Expansion of permission for external borrowing to finance agricultural activities to all financial institutions, not only those participating of the national system of rural credit.
Resolution 2,271	4/18/96	R	I	Restriction of external financing for states, federal district, and municipalities, and their dependencies, foundations, and firms, to the refinancing of their domestic debt.
Resolution 2,280	5/22/96	L	I	Establishment of some exceptions to the restrictions set in Resolution 2,271 (revoked Resolution 2,271).
Directive MF 241	10/31/96	L	I	Reduction in the differentiated IOF on external loans according to average maturity: 3% for those with an average maturity less than three years, 2% for four years, 1% for five years, and 0% for equal to or above five years.
Resolution 2,337 and Circular 2,728	11/28/96, 11/28/96	E		Introduction of electronic registration (RDE) for inward and outward flows, starting with foreign portfolio investment.
Resolution 2,345	12/19/96	L	I	Authorization for the issuance abroad of depository receipts representing nonvoting shares of resident financial institutions with shares traded in the stock market—Annex V.
Law 9,430	12/27/96	E		Revocation of the decrees that gave authority to the National Monetary Council to set some rules on nonresident income tax. As a consequence, termination of tax rules set in Resolution 1,853, and Circulars 2,546 and 2,661.
Provisory Measure 1,563, turned into Law 9,481	12/31/96, 8/13/97	R	I	Exemption from income tax on interest, commission, and issuance expenditures of debt securities with a minimum average maturity of ninety-six months. Exemption from income tax on interest of loans with a minimum maturity of fifteen years.

Normative measure	Date	Nature of measure	Direction of flows	Description
Directive MF 85	4/24/97	L	I	Reduction in the IOF from 7% to 2% on foreign investment in fixed-income funds, from the differentiated rates to a flat rate of 0% on loans, and from 7% to 2% on interbank exchange operations between financial institutions abroad and institutions authorized to operate in the exchange market, and on the formation of short-term cash holdings of nonresidents.
Resolution 2,384	5/22/97	L	I	Permission for foreign capital, registered under Annexes I to IV, to invest in convertible debentures and futures and options markets as hedge operations.
Resolution 2,406	6/26/97	L	I	Authorization for creation of investment funds in emerging firms—foreign capital.
Circular 2,783	11/13/97	L	I	Reduction in the minimum average maturity required for loans from thirty-six to twelve months for new loans, and to six months for renewed or extended loans.
Circular 2,807	2/26/98	R	I	Increase in the minimum average maturity required for loans from twelve to twenty-four months for new loans, and from six to twelve months for renewed or extended loans (revoked Circular 2,661 and replaced Circular 2,783).
Circular 2,834, replaced by Circular 2,850	8/24/98, 11/30/98	L	I	Reduction in the minimum average maturity required for loans from twenty-four to twelve months for new loans, and from twelve to six months for renewed or extended loans (revoked Circular 2,807).
Directive MF 348	12/30/98	R	I	Increase in the IOF from 2% to 2.38% on foreign investment in fixed-income funds, on interbank exchange operations between financial institutions abroad and institutions authorized to operate in the exchange market, and on the formation of short-term cash holdings of nonresidents, and from 0% to 0.38% on foreign investment in securities. Imposition of a 0.38% rate on financial transfers abroad and from abroad.
Circular 2,859	1/27/99	L	I	Reduction in the minimum average maturity required for loans from twelve to nine months for new loans, and from nine to six months for renewed or extended loans (revoked Circular 2,850).

(*continued*)

Table B.1 (continued)

Table B.1 (continued)

Normative measure	Date	Nature of measure	Direction of flows	Description
Resolution 2,590	1/28/99	L	I	Reduction in the minimum average maturity from 180 to 90 days for agricultural loans.
Resolution 2,591	1/28/99	L	I	Permission for foreign capital, registered under Annexes I to IV, to invest in public debt securities of the federal government.
Directives MF 56 and 157	3/12/99, 6/24/99	L	I	Reduction in the IOF from 2.38% to 0.5% on foreign investment in fixed-income funds, on interbank exchange operations between financial institutions abroad and institutions authorized to operate in the exchange market, and on the formation of short-term cash holdings of nonresidents.
Resolution 2,625	7/29/99	L	I	Permission for financial institutions to issue bonds abroad and use the proceeds freely in the domestic market as long as those resources stay a minimum of five years in the country.
Resolution 2,622	7/29/99	L	I	Permission for nonresidents to invest in futures contracts related to agricultural products.
Directive MF 306	8/18/99	L	I	Reduction in the IOF from 0.5 to 0% on foreign investment in fixed-income funds, on interbank exchange operations between financial institutions abroad and institutions authorized to operate in the exchange market, and on the formation of short-term cash holdings of nonresidents (revoked Directives MF 56 and 157).
Directive MF 306	8/18/99	L	I	Reduction in the IOF from 0.5 to 0% on foreign investment in fixed-income funds, on interbank exchange operations between financial institutions abroad and institutions authorized to operate in the exchange market, and on the formation of short-term cash holdings of nonresidents (revoked Directives MF 56 and 157).
Resolution 2,628	8/6/99	L	I	Permission for foreign capital, registered under Annexes I to IV, to invest in fixed-income instruments, although within some limits (replaced Resolutions 2,384 and 2,591).

Normative measure	Date	Nature of measure	Direction of flows	Description
Resolution 2,683	12/29/99	L	I	Elimination of the requirement of five years for the proceeds from the bonds issued abroad by financial institutions to stay in the country. Elimination of minimum average maturity required for external loans (revoked Resolution 2,625).
Directive MF 492	12/29/99	R	I	Determination of the IOF on external loans at a rate of 0% for those with average maturity above ninety days, and 5% for those with average maturity up to ninety days.
Provisory Measure 2,013-4, turned into Law 9,959	12/30/99, 1/27/00	R	O	Termination of the income tax exemption on interest, commission, and issuance expenses for debt securities with a minimum average maturity of ninety-six months, and of the income tax exemption for loans with maturity greater than fifteen years. Interest payments on all external loans and debt securities, regardless of the maturity, taxed at 15%.
Resolution 2,689	1/26/00	L	I	Regulation of investment in the financial and capital markets, allowing nonresidents to invest in the same instruments as residents. Inward investment must be registered at the Central Bank.
Circular 2,975	3/29/00	E		Update on conditions for the RDE of portfolio investment (replaced Circular 2,728).
Resolution 2,770	8/30/00	L	I	Consolidation of the regulation on external loans, including debt securities. Termination of the requirement of prior approval by the Central Bank for those operations, except for those involving the public sector as a debtor. Maintenance of the requirement of registration at the Central Bank for those operations (revoked sixty-seven resolutions, ninety-six circulars, and fifty-one circular letters, including Resolutions 63, 64, 125, and 1,986, and Circular 2,410).
Circular 3,027	2/22/01	E		Introduction of RDE for external loans, including debt securities.
Constitutional Amendment 37, and Decree 4,296	6/12/02, 7/10/02	L	I	Exemption from the Provisional Contribution on Financial Transactions (CPMF) for entries into foreign investor accounts involving inflows of financial resources to the country and remittances abroad when such resources are used exclusively in stock operations.

(continued)

Table B.1   (continued)

Normative measure	Date	Nature of measure	Direction of flows	Description
Resolution 3,217	6/30/04	L	O	Permission for the prepayment of external debt, including debt securities.
Resolution 3,221	7/29/04	L	I	Establishment of conditions for the issuance of real-denominated external debt.

D. Brazilian capital abroad: Regulation implemented prior to the 1990s

Circular 1,280	1/18/88			Requirement that Brazilian investments abroad be compensated by a sale to the Central Bank of gold bought in the domestic market for a value equivalent to the investment. Previously, authorization for Brazilian investment abroad was decided on a case-by-case basis by the monetary authority.
Resolution 1,534	11/30/88			As an alternative to the exchange compensation with gold mechanism, investment abroad by Brazilian enterprises may be authorized at the official exchange rate in an amount equal to foreign direct investment received by the firm.

Main changes

Resolution 1,925	5/5/92	L	O	Termination of the mechanism of exchange compensation with gold, transferring the operations of investment abroad to the floating exchange rate market.
Circular 2,243	10/14/92	L	O	Authorization for nonfinancial resident firms to invest abroad up to US$1 million without prior authorization, for each twelve months by economic group. When above this value, investors must provide information to the Central Bank thirty days ahead of the exchange transaction.
Circular 2,472	8/31/94	L	O	Increase in the limit of the value of Brazilian investments abroad that do not require previous authorization from US$1 to US$5 million.

Table B.1   (continued)

Normative measure	Date	Nature of measure	Direction of flows	Description
Resolution 2,111	9/22/94	L	O	Authorization of Foreign Investment Funds (FIEX) for investment in debt securities in international markets.
Resolution 2,318	9/26/96	L	O	Regulation of residents' investments in BDRs.
Resolution 2,356	2/27/97	L	O	Permission for residents to invest in depository receipts issued abroad representing resident firms' securities.
Circular 2,863	2/10/99	R	O	Increase in the minimum share of Brazilian sovereign bonds in FIEX funds from 60% to 80%.
Circular 2,877	3/17/99	R	O	Prohibition of financial institutions to invest directly or indirectly in FIEX funds.
Resolution 2,716	4/12/00	L	O	Permission for private pension funds to invest up to 10% of their resources in BDRs.
Resolution 2,717	4/12/00	L	O	Permission for insurance companies, capitalization companies, and open private pension funds to invest up to 10% of their resources in BDRs.
Resolution 2,763	8/9/00	E		New regulation on residents' investments in BDRs, which represent securities of nonresident companies (replaced Resolution 2,318).
Decree-Law 1,060, Circular 3,039 and Resolution 2,911	10/21/69, 6/8/01, 11/29/01	E		Implementation of the first survey of Brazilian capital abroad, which has subsequently been conducted on an annual basis. The provision of information from residents on their assets abroad is mandatory.

Notes: L = liberalizing; R = restrictive; E = regulatory; I = inflows; O = outflows. We focus on regulation of the capital account and convertibility of domestic currency into foreign currency. Thus, we do not deal, for example, with export and import payments. Resolutions are rules set by the National Monetary Council; circulars, circular letters, and communications by the Central Bank of Brazil; and directives by the Ministry of Finance. This chronology was written directly consulting the rules, but initially using the IMF's *Annual Report on Exchange Arrangements and Exchange Restrictions* and Soheit (2002).

Appendix C

Classification of Capital Flows

In the text, we classify the items of the capital and financial account into six groups: net direct investment, portfolio investment, loans and trade credits, other short-term assets, official agency–related loans, and other items.[37] We do not use the category "other investments" from the IMF's classification because it consists of disparate flows. In particular, it includes both compensatory flows and private bank loans; thus, using the balance of this category may be misleading. For example, in 2002, despite negative net loan flows and large currency transfers abroad, the "other investments" balance does not appear as significantly negative (only –$0.2 billion in U.S. dollars) because of IMF loans (a net inflow of US$11.5 billion). Descriptions of our six categories follow.

1. *Net direct investment.* This category follows the IMF's definition. It covers inflows (outflows) related to acquisition, subscription, and increase in the capital of resident (nonresident) enterprises, and similarly flows related to partial or total sale of the capital. It also includes intercompany loans.[38] Unlike the investor in equities, the "direct investor seeks a significant voice in the management" of the enterprise (IMF 1993, p. 80). In general, the criterion used is that the direct investor owns 10 percent or more of the ordinary shares or voting power (for an incorporated enterprise) or the equivalent (for an unincorporated enterprise; IMF 1993, p. 86).

2. *Portfolio investment.* This category follows the IMF's definition as well. It is represented by cross-border investment in equity securities that is not classified as direct investment, and debt securities.[39] We also consider these two items separately when relevant. This category includes securities negotiated in Brazil and abroad.

3. *Loans and trade credits.* This category comprises loans not related to official agencies—which we call loans—and suppliers' and buyers' credits.

---

37. The balance-of-payments statistics are produced by the Central Bank of Brazil and are available on its website (http://www.bcb.gov.br). The statistics follow the IMF's recommendations (IMF 1993; Central Bank of Brazil, 2001). Although those recommendations were implemented in 2001, the historical statistics were conformed to the new methodology. We do not use the statistics published in the International Financial Statistics (IFS) database of the IMF, because its high level of aggregation does not allow us to make the classification used in this paper.

38. It should include reinvested earnings as well, but because the data do not include this item since 1999, we exclude it to maintain the coherence throughout the series. The statistics do not include intercompany trade credits either.

39. Throughout the paper, we have excluded from the series of portfolio investment and loans the values related to the conversion of debt under the Brady Plan, which appear in the second quarter of 1994. Maintaining them in the series would distort the analysis.

4. *Other short-term assets.* This group aims to capture the movements of currency and deposits, which played an important role during the crises. For example, in 1998, the negative balance of this category reached –$17.6 billion in U.S. dollars. It consists of three items of the balance-of-payments statistics: "currency and deposits of nonresidents," which includes flows through the CC5 accounts classified as "disposable funds"; "currency and deposits of non-financial residents," which includes deposits available abroad; and "other short-term assets" within other domestic investments, which includes flows through the CC5 accounts below 10,000 reais.

5. *Official agency–related loans.* This category consists of loans to the monetary authority (such as those from the IMF, BIS, Bank of Japan, and U.S. Treasury) and long-term financing from bilateral or multilateral organizations (such as IBD and World Bank Group).[40] These loans have clearly worked as compensatory flows. For instance, in the crisis years of 1998 and 2002, the balance of this group was largely positive, US$10.9 billion and US$12.2 billion, respectively.

6. *Other items.* This category corresponds to the remaining items of the capital and financial account. It includes diverse items, but quantitatively the most important ones are "currency and deposits of financial residents" and "other liabilities" within other foreign investments (mainly external liabilities assumed by the Central Bank, but whose repayments and interests were not sent abroad duly).[41] The latter were the bulk of the group through the mid-1990s because of the arrears that occurred in some periods.

We also classify flows according to their maturity. Short-term debt flows correspond to equities and short-term debt securities, loans, and trade credits. When including other short-term assets, we call them "short-term flows expanded." Long-term debt flows in turn comprise long-term debt securities, loans, and trade credits, which, according to the balance-of-payments classification, correspond to contracts with maturity superior to 360 days. When including net direct investment, we call this group "long-term flows expanded."

40. Before 1979, some of the items that comprise official agency–related loans are available only on an annual basis. We distributed the annual values over the four quarters and added to the data available quarterly.

41. The other items are "capital account" (according to IMF's [1993] definition, which covers capital transfers and acquisition or disposal of nonproduced, nonfinancial assets), financial derivatives, and other long-term assets of residents (Brazil's participation in multilateral organizations, and greater-than-one-year escrow deposits). We do not classify "currency and deposits of financial residents" into the group "other short-term assets" because they are the main counterpart of the payments registered in the balance of payments. For example, when a resident repays a loan, it represents a reduction in external liabilities (increase in net assets of residents), but as counterpart there is a reduction in the foreign assets of the bank that sold the foreign currency (reduction in net assets of residents). In fact, the balance of this item was positive in 1998 and 2002.

Appendix D

Methodology Used in the VAR Estimation

To estimate the VAR, we have used the following endogenous variables:[42] (a) log-level of industrial production in Brazil (seasonally adjusted); (b) current account balance at constant prices (seasonally adjusted by the authors; ratio to the average GDP in the period);[43] (c) private capital account (ratio to the average GDP in the period); (d) log of terms of trade, measured as the ratio of export prices to import prices; (e) EMBI+ Brazil, sovereign spread;[44] (f) log of real effective exchange rate (measured as the value of foreign currency in terms of domestic currency);[45] and (g) real interest rate, measured as the Selic interest rate deflated by the IPCA.[46] The exogenous variables are the Federal Reserve funds rate and the U.S. industrial production (seasonally adjusted).

The sample goes from January 1995 through August 2004. It starts when the balance-of-payments statistics are available on a monthly basis according to the IMF's (1993) methodology. Furthermore, it does not include the high-inflation period.[47] We have estimated the VAR using the variables in levels,[48] employing six lags for the endogenous variables.[49] For the exogenous variables, we use their contemporaneous and one-period lagged values.[50]

42. The data sources are the following: (a) IBGE; (b) and (c) Central Bank of Brazil; (d) Funcex, available in Ipeadata; (e) JPMorgan; (f) and (g) Central Bank of Brazil. The estimations were conducted using basically the Rats software.

43. We do not use the ratio to current GDP because the large movements in the exchange ratio tend to distort the analysis: movements in the ratio can reflect changes in the exchange ratio rather than capital account changes. On the other hand, the absence of normalization generated problems for the convergence of the algorithm to estimate the structural parameters. The same reasoning is valid for the private capital account.

44. Average of daily data of the EMBI Brazil from January 1992 through December 1996, and the EMBI+ Brazil thereafter.

45. Estimated by the Central Bank of Brazil using the IPCA as internal deflator and U.S. CPI as external deflator. It corresponds to the average of the domestic currency value in relation to fifteen countries weighted by the participation of these countries in Brazil's exports.

46. We use the inflation accumulated in the last twelve months because of the difficulties in using a measure for expected inflation for the whole sample. We use twelve months because of the volatility of the inflation rate of one or even six months. From January 1995 through July 1995, however, we use the average inflation in the period starting in September 1994 instead of twelve months to avoid the distortions caused by the high-inflation period.

47. Thus, we do not face the problem of measuring the real interest rate in the high-inflation period and making it comparable to the low-inflation period.

48. The estimation is consistent even in the presence of variables integrated of order one (Sims, Stock, and Watson 1990; Hamilton 1994).

49. The Schwarz criterion has indicated two lags, but, using a Lagrange multiplier test, we reject the null hypothesis of absence of serial correlation in the residuals. We then add lags until accepting the null of no serial correlation.

50. Further lags were not significant. The presence of one lag also avoids the problem of spurious regression (Hamilton 1994).

To determine the identification structure concerning the contemporaneous effects of the shocks, we have considered the relationships between variables and possible lags in the effects of one variable on another as well as the correlation of the estimated reduced-form residuals. First, we have assumed that current account, terms of trade, and interest rate are not affected contemporaneously by shocks to other variables. Effective exports and imports are usually the result of contracts set in advance.[51] Terms of trade, besides depending on exogenous variables, are affected by pricing-to-market decisions, which tend to react with some lag. Although interest rate is a financial variable, we are using the rate whose target is set by the Central Bank. We are assuming that there is a one-month lag in the reaction of the Central Bank either because information is not available promptly or because there is some lag in the Central Bank's decisions. In particular, the target for the basic interest rate is usually set on a monthly basis rather than on a daily basis.[52] Second, since the EMBI and exchange rate are financial variables, they tend to react more quickly. We assume then that reduced-form shocks to the other variables affect those variables contemporaneously. Third, for output and capital flows, we have used the matrix of correlation coefficients of reduced-form residuals. We have considered only residuals that have a correlation coefficient greater than 0.1, which led to assume that output responds contemporaneously to terms of trade, EMBI, exchange rate,[53] and interest rate, and capital flows to EMBI, exchange rate, and interest rate.

The resulting structure was the following (time subscripts were omitted):

$$
\begin{bmatrix}
1 & 0 & 0 & a_{14} & a_{15} & a_{16} & a_{17} \\
0 & 1 & 0 & 0 & 0 & 0 & 0 \\
0 & 0 & 1 & 0 & a_{35} & a_{36} & a_{37} \\
0 & 0 & 0 & 1 & 0 & 0 & 0 \\
a_{51} & a_{52} & a_{53} & a_{54} & 1 & a_{56} & a_{57} \\
a_{61} & a_{62} & a_{63} & a_{64} & a_{65} & 1 & a_{67} \\
0 & 0 & 0 & 0 & 0 & 0 & 1
\end{bmatrix}
\begin{bmatrix}
\text{OUT} \\ \text{CA} \\ \text{KA} \\ \text{TOT} \\ \text{EMBI} \\ \text{ER} \\ \text{INT}
\end{bmatrix}
= C + A(L)
\begin{bmatrix}
\text{OUT} \\ \text{CA} \\ \text{KA} \\ \text{TOT} \\ \text{EMBI} \\ \text{ER} \\ \text{INT}
\end{bmatrix}
+ H(L)
\begin{bmatrix}
\text{OUT\_US} \\ \text{INT\_US}
\end{bmatrix}
+
\begin{bmatrix}
e_{\text{OUT}} \\ e_{\text{CA}} \\ e_{\text{KA}} \\ e_{\text{TOT}} \\ e_{\text{EMBI}} \\ e_{\text{ER}} \\ e_{\text{INT}}
\end{bmatrix},
$$

51. Even in the case of terms of trade, the correlation coefficient between the reduced-form shock to that variable and the shock to the current account balance was not positive (−0.02).

52. Even in the case of crises, the basic interest rate did not react in the same month.

53. The correlation with exchange rate is low, but the coefficient was included to ease the convergence of the algorithm.

where OUT, CA, KA, TOT, EMBI, ER, INT, OUT_US, and INT_US stand for output, current account, private capital account, terms of trade, EMBI+ Brazil, real effective exchange rate, real interest rate, U.S. output, and U.S. interest rate, respectively; C is a vector of constants; A and H are coefficient matrices; L is the lag operator; and e is the structural shock. Since there are twenty-six free parameters, the model is overidentified. Even though most of the structural coefficients are not significant, we can accept the identification restrictions (p-value of 0.293).

References

Arida, Persio. 2003a. Ainda sobre a conversibilidade. *Revista de Economia Política* 23 (3): 135–42.
———. 2003b. Por uma moeda plenamente conversível. *Revista de Economia Política* 23 (3): 151–54.
———. 2004. Aspectos macroeconômicos da conversibilidade: Uma discussão do caso Brasileiro. Casa das Garças, Rio de Janeiro: Instituto de Estudos de Política Econômica. Mimeograph.
Arida, Persio, Edmar L. Bacha, and André Lara-Resende. 2005. Credit, interest, and jurisdictional uncertainty: Conjectures on the case of Brazil. In *Inflation targeting, debt and the Brazilian experience, 1999 to 2003,* ed. Francesco Giavazzi, Ilan Goldfajn, and Santiago Herrera, 265–93. Cambridge, MA: MIT Press.
Ariyoshi, Akira, Karl Habermeier, Bernard Laurens, Inci Otker-Robe, Jorge I. Canales-Kriljenko, and Andrei Kirilenko. 2000. Capital controls: Country experiences with their use and liberalization. IMF Occasional Paper no. 190. Washington, DC: International Monetary Fund.
Bosworth, Barry P., and Susan M. Collins. 1999. Capital flows to developing economies: Implications for saving and investment. *Brookings Papers on Economic Activity,* Issue no. 1:143–80.
Cardoso, Eliana, and Ilan Goldfajn. 1998. Capital flows to Brazil: The endogeneity of capital controls. *IMF Staff Papers* 45 (1): 161–202.
Carvalho, Bernardo S. de M. 2005. A eficácia dos controles de entrada de capitais. Master's thesis, Pontifical Catholic University of Rio de Janeiro.
Central Bank of Brazil. 1993. O regime cambial brasileiro: Evolução recente e perspectivas. Série Banco Central do Brasil. Brasília: Central Bank of Brazil.
———. 2001. Methodological notes on the balance of payments. Central Bank of Brazil Technical Notes no. 1. Brasília: Central Bank of Brazil, June.
Cerqueira, Ceres A. 2003. *Dívida externa brasileira.* 2nd ed. Brasília: Central Bank of Brazil.
Edwards, Sebastian. 2005. Capital controls, sudden stops and current account reversals. NBER Working Paper no. 11170. Cambridge, MA: National Bureau of Economic Research, March.
Ferrari Filho, Fernando, Frederico G. Jayme, Jr., Gilberto T. Lima, José L. Oreiro, and Luiz F. Paula. 2005. Uma avaliação crítica da proposta de conversibilidade plena do real. *Revista de Economia Política* 25 (1): 133–51.
Franco, Gustavo H. B., and Demosthenes M. Pinho Neto. 2004. A desregulamentação da conta de capitais: Limitações macroeconômicas e regulatórias. Work-

ing Paper no. 479. Pontifical Catholic University of Rio de Janeiro, Department of Economics, January.

Garcia, Márcio G. P., and Alexandre Barcinski. 1998. Capital flows to Brazil in the nineties: Macroeconomic aspects and the effectiveness of capital controls. *Quarterly Review of Economics and Finance* 38 (3): 319–57.

Garcia, Márcio G. P., and Marcus V. F. Valpassos. 1998. Capital flows, capital controls and currency crisis: The case of Brazil in the nineties. Working Paper no. 389. Pontifical Catholic University of Rio de Janeiro, Department of Economics, November.

Giavazzi, Francesco, Ilan Goldfajn, and Santiago Herrera, eds. 2005. *Inflation targeting, debt and the Brazilian experience, 1999 to 2003.* Cambridge, MA: MIT Press.

Gleizer, Daniel, ed. 2005. *Aprimorando o mercado de câmbio brasileiro.* São Paulo, Brazil: Bolsa de Mercadorias & Futuros.

Hamilton, James D. 1994. *Time series analysis.* Princeton, NJ: Princeton University Press.

International Monetary Fund (IMF). Various issues. *Annual report on exchange arrangements and exchange restrictions.* Washington, DC: International Monetary Fund.

———. 1993. *Balance of payments manual.* Washington, DC: International Monetary Fund.

Obstfeld, Maurice, and Kenneth Rogoff. 1994. The intertemporal approach to the current account. NBER Working Paper no. 4893. Cambridge, MA: National Bureau of Economic Research, October.

———. 1996. *Foundations of international macroeconomics.* Cambridge, MA: MIT Press.

Prasad, Eswar, Kenneth Rogoff, Shang-Jin Wei, and M. Ayhan Kose. 2003. Effects of financial globalization on developing countries: Some empirical evidence. IMF Occasional Paper no. 220. Washington, DC: International Monetary Fund, March.

Schwartsman, Alexandre. 2004. Descontrole nas contas CC5. *Valor Econômico.* August 30.

Sims, Christopher A., James H. Stock, and Mark W. Watson. 1990. Inference in linear time series models with some unit roots. *Econometrica* 58 (1): 113–44.

Soihet, Elena. 2002. Índice de controle de capitais: Uma análise da legislação e dos determinantes do fluxo de capital no período 1990–2000. Master's thesis, Getulio Vargas Foundation.

Stiglitz, Joseph. 2002. *Globalization and its discontents.* New York: W. W. Norton.

The Chinese Approach to Capital Inflows
Patterns and Possible Explanations

Eswar Prasad and Shang-Jin Wei

9.1 Introduction

China has in many ways taken the world by storm. In addition to its swiftly rising prominence in the global trading system, where it now accounts for over 6 percent of total world trade, it has also become a magnet for foreign direct investment (FDI), overtaking the United States (in 2003) as the number one destination for FDI.

It was not always thus. China's integration with the global economy began in earnest only after the market-oriented reforms that were instituted in 1978. Capital inflows, in particular, were minimal in the 1970s and 1980s, impeded by capital controls and the reluctance of international investors to undertake investment in a socialist economy with weak institutions and limited exposure to international trade. All of this changed in the early 1990s, when FDI inflows surged dramatically because of the selective opening of China's capital account as well as the rapid trade expansion that, in conjunction with China's large labor pool, created opportunities for foreign investors. These inflows have remained strong ever since, even during the Asian crisis of the late 1990s.

Eswar Prasad is the Tolani Senior Professor of Trade Policy at Cornell University. He was chief of the China division at the International Monetary Fund (IMF) during 2002–4. Shang-Jin Wei is assistant director and chief of the Trade and Investment division in the research department of the IMF and a research associate and director of the Working Group on the Chinese Economy at the National Bureau of Economic Research (NBER).

We are grateful to Jahangir Aziz, Ray Brooks, Michael Dooley, Sebastian Edwards, Mark Wright, and participants at the NBER capital flows conference, the Stanford China Conference, and a seminar at the China Center for Economic Research for helpful comments and suggestions. We are indebted to members of the IMF's China team, from whose work we have drawn extensively. We owe a particular debt to Qing Wang, who provided many useful suggestions and comments. Ioana Hussiada provided excellent research assistance.

Given China's status as a global economic power, characterizing the nature and determinants of China's capital inflows is of considerable interest for analytical reasons as well as for understanding the implications for the regional and global allocation of capital. Our primary objective in this paper is to provide a detailed descriptive analysis of the main aspects of capital inflows into China. Given the degree of interest in China and the relative paucity of data, we aim to provide a benchmark reference tool for other researchers, in part by providing some critical perspectives on the numbers that we report.

Section 9.2 presents a detailed picture of the evolution of China's capital inflows. A feature of particular interest is that China's capital inflows have generally been dominated by FDI, which, for an emerging market, constitutes a preferred form of inflows, since FDI tends to be stable and associated with other benefits such as transfers of technological and managerial expertise. An interesting aspect of these inflows is that, contrary to some popular perceptions, they come mainly from other advanced Asian countries that have net trade surpluses with China, rather than from the United States and Europe, which constitute China's main export markets. As for other types of inflows, China has limited its external debt to low levels, and non-FDI private capital inflows have typically been quite limited, until recently.

In section 9.3, we examine the evolution of the balance of payments and dissect the recent surge in the pace of accumulation of international reserves. A key finding is that, although current account surpluses and FDI have remained important contributors to reserve accumulation, the dramatic surge in the pace of reserve accumulation since 2001 is largely attributable to non-FDI capital inflows. We provide some analytical perspectives on the costs and benefits of holding a stock of reserves that now amounts to nearly 40 percent of gross domestic product (GDP). There has also been considerable international attention focused recently on the issue of the currency composition of China's massive stock of international reserves (which is now second only to that of Japan). Despite data constraints, we attempt to shed what little light we can on this issue, both by carefully examining a popular source of data for China's holding of U.S. securities and by calculating the potential balance-of-payments implications of reserve valuation effects associated with the depreciation of the U.S. dollar in recent years.

Section 9.4 discusses the broader composition of China's capital inflows in the context of the burgeoning literature on financial globalization. Notwithstanding the recent surge of non-FDI inflows, FDI remains historically the dominant source of inflows into China. The literature on the benefits and risks of financial globalization suggests that China may have benefited greatly in terms of improving the risk-return trade-offs by having its inflows tilted so much toward FDI.

Whether this composition of inflows is a result of enlightened policies, the structure of institutions, or plain luck is an intriguing question. In section 9.5, we examine various hypotheses that have been put forward to explain why China has its inflows so heavily tilted toward FDI. In this context, we provide a detailed description of China's capital account restrictions and how these have evolved over time. While controls on non-FDI inflows as well as tax and other incentives appear to be proximate factors for explaining the FDI-heavy composition of inflows, other factors may also have contributed to this outcome. It is not straightforward to disentangle the quantitative relevance of alternative hypotheses. We argue, nonetheless, that at least a few of the hypotheses—including some mercantilist-type arguments that have been advanced recently—are not consistent with the facts.

9.2 The Chinese Pattern of Inflows and Some International Comparisons

9.2.1 The Evolution of Capital Inflows

Gross capital inflows into China were minuscule before the early 1980s. After 1984, the "other investment" category, which includes bank lending, increased significantly and accounted for the largest share of total inflows during the 1980s (figure 9.1). FDI rose gradually from the early 1980s to early 1991 and then rose dramatically through the mid-1990s. During the 1990s, FDI accounted for the lion's share of inflows. It is interesting to note that FDI inflows were only marginally affected during the Asian crisis. Figure 9.2 provides some more detail on the evolutions of the main compo-

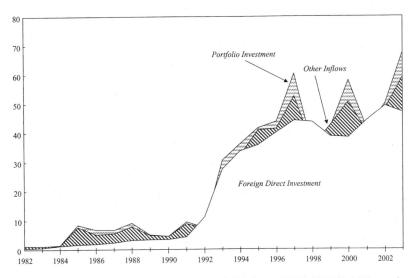

Fig. 9.1   Level and composition of gross capital inflows, 1982–2003 (in billions of U.S. dollars)

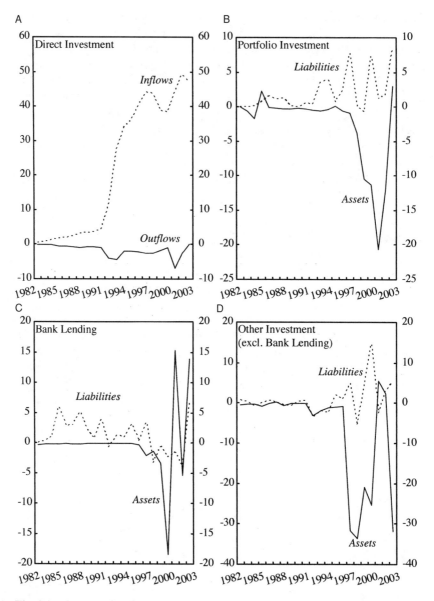

Fig. 9.2   Gross capital flows by component (in billions of U.S. dollars): *A*, **direct investment;** *B*, **portfolio investment;** *C*, **bank lending;** *D*, **other investment (excluding bank lending)**

Source: CEIC database.

Note: Scales differ across the four panels of this figure.

nents of the capital account, in terms of both gross outflows and inflows. Note that all components other than FDI show sharp increases in outflows in the period immediately after the Asian crisis, with the subsequent recovery in net inflows of these components taking two to three years to materialize. Recent data indicate that, after remaining in a range of around $50 billion during 2002–3, gross FDI inflows increased to almost $61 billion in 2004.

From a cross-country perspective, China's net capital inflows are of course large in absolute magnitude but hardly remarkable relative to the size of the economy. Before the Asian crisis, many of the other "Asian tigers" had significantly larger inflows relative to their GDP (figure 9.3, panel A). What is striking, however, is that, except for Singapore, the share of FDI in total inflows is clearly the highest for China. Its total net inflows as a share of GDP rank among the highest across all emerging markets after the Asian crisis, especially since many of the Asian tigers were no longer the darlings of international investors (figure 9.3, panel B). While the net inflows dropped sharply across all emerging markets after the late 1990s, the interesting thing to note is that most of the inflows that did come into the emerging markets after 1999 took the form of FDI.

China's average net inflows, and the share of FDI in those inflows, look quite similar during the periods 1990–96 and 1999–2003. Since FDI is clearly the main story in the context of China's capital inflows, we now turn to a more detailed examination of these flows.

9.2.2 Foreign Direct Investment

Over the past decade, China has accounted for about one-third of gross FDI flows to all emerging markets and about 60 percent of these flows to Asian emerging markets (figure 9.4, panel A). Even excluding flows from Hong Kong to China from these calculations (on the extreme assumption that all of these flows represent "round-tripping" of funds originating in China—this point is discussed further below), China's share in these flows to emerging markets is substantial (figure 9.4, panel B). The shares spike upward during the Asian crisis and, more recently, in 2002, when weaknesses in the global economy resulted in a slowdown in flows from industrial countries to most emerging markets other than China. With the pickup in flows to emerging markets in 2003, there was a corresponding decline in China's share, even though flows to China remained essentially unchanged.

Where are China's FDI inflows coming from? Table 9.1 shows the share of utilized FDI by source country. Some aspects of the results are worth noting. First of all, the share of Hong Kong has declined steadily over the past decade, from 58 percent in 1994 to 32 percent in 2004. One of the concerns in interpreting FDI data for China is that a significant portion of these flows could potentially represent round-tripping to take advantage of

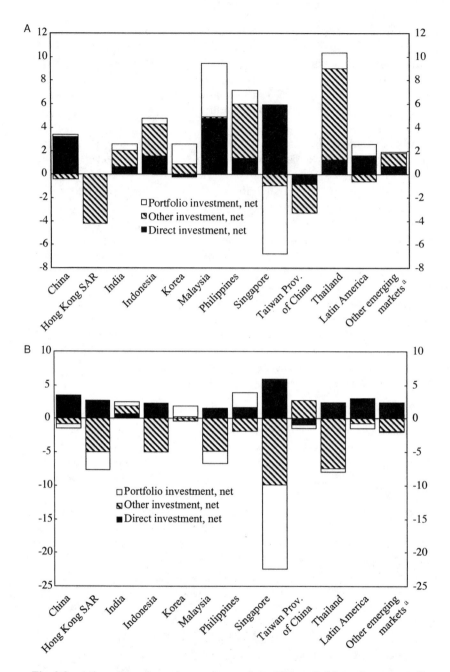

Fig. 9.3   Asian economies and emerging markets: Net capital flows (in percent of GDP): *A,* **before Asian crisis (average 1990–96);** *B,* **after Asian crisis (average 1999–2003)**

Source: World Economic Outlook database.

[a]Average for emerging markets in EMBI+ index, excluding Latin America and Asian countries.

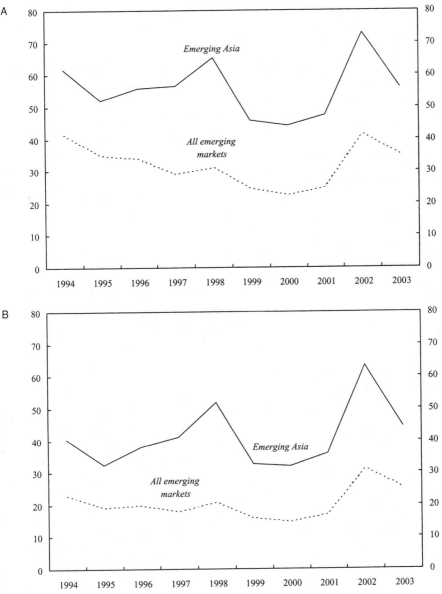

Fig. 9.4 China's share of foreign direct investment inflows to emerging markets: *A,* **FDI to China;** *B,* **FDI to China minus FDI from Hong Kong**

Sources: World Economic Outlook database, CEIC database, and authors' calculations.

Notes: This figure uses data on gross FDI flows in percent of FDI to emerging Asia and all emerging markets. Panel B excludes gross FDI flows to China originating from Hong Kong from both the numerator and the denominator of the two ratios shown.

Table 9.1   FDI inflows by source country (percent share)

	1994	1995	1996	1997	1998	1999	2000	2001	2002	2003	2004 (September)
Hong Kong	58.2	53.4	49.6	45.6	40.7	40.6	38.1	35.7	33.9	33.1	31.7
Virgin Islands			8.8	9.6	8.9	6.6	9.4	10.8	11.6	10.8	11.5
Japan	6.1	8.2	8.8	9.6	7.5	7.4	7.2	9.3	7.9	9.4	8.7
Korea	2.1	2.8	3.3	4.7	4.0	3.2	3.7	4.6	5.2	8.4	10.7
United States	7.4	8.2	8.2	7.2	8.6	10.5	10.8	9.5	10.3	7.8	6.9
European Union						11.1	11.0	8.9	7.0	7.3	7.3[a]
Taiwan	10.0	8.4	8.3	7.3	6.4	6.4	5.6	6.4	7.5	6.3	5.4
Singapore	3.5	4.9	5.4	5.8	7.5	6.6	5.3	4.6	4.4	3.8	3.5
Australia	0.6	0.6	0.5	0.7	0.6	0.0	0.8	0.7	0.7	1.1	1.0
Western Samoa					0.3	0.5	0.7	1.1	1.7	1.8	2.0
Macao					0.9	0.8	0.9	0.7	0.9	0.8	0.8[a]
Others	12.0	13.4	16.0	19.3	14.7	6.5	6.7	7.9	8.9	9.2	10.4
Total	100	100	100	100	100	100	100	100	100	100	100

Sources: CEIC database and CEIC China database.

Note: This table is based upon data for utilized (rather than contracted) FDI.

[a]Data for these two regions for 2004 were not available at the time of this writing, so the same share has been assumed as in 2003.

preferential tax treatment of foreign investment relative to domestic investment. Much of this round-tripping is believed to take place through Hong Kong. While it is difficult to estimate the extent of round-tripping, the declining share of Hong Kong in total inflows at least suggests that the magnitude of round-tripping as a share of total FDI inflows may have been declining over time. On the other hand, the shares of small economies like the Virgin Islands and Western Samoa, which have risen over the past few years, could now be accounting for some of these round-tripping flows.[1]

Asian economies account for a substantial fraction of China's FDI inflows. For instance, over the period 2001–4, five Asian economies—Hong Kong, Japan, Korea, Taiwan, and Singapore—together account for about 60 percent of FDI inflows. That a lot of China's FDI comes from these relatively advanced Asian economies suggests that these flows do bring the usual benefits associated with FDI, including transfers of technological and managerial expertise. The other interesting point to note is that—contrary to the widespread perception of large direct investment flows from western industrial economies to China—the United States and the European Union (EU) economies together accounted for only 15 percent of total inflows in 2003, and even that is down from a share of 22 percent in 1999–2000. Even if one were to assume that half of the reported FDI inflows from Hong Kong are accounted for by round-tripping and that all of the share of the Virgin Islands in fact represents flows originating in the United States, the share of the United States and the EU in China's total FDI inflows would be about 30 percent, a large but hardly dominant share. Preliminary data for 2004 indicate that the share of Hong Kong has declined by about 1.5 percentage points and that of the United States is down by 1 percentage point, while Korea's share has increased by over 2 percentage points.

To which parts and regions of China's economy are FDI inflows being directed? Table 9.2 shows that about two-thirds of these flows have been going into manufacturing, with real estate accounting for about another 10 percent. Within manufacturing, the largest identifiable share has consistently gone to electronics and communication equipment. The share of manufacturing has risen by almost 15 percentage points since 1998, largely at the expense of the shares of utilities, construction, transport and telecommunication services, and real estate. Since the industries with declining FDI shares are largely focused on nontraded goods, the evolution of this pattern of FDI seems to be consistent with the notion that these inflows have been stimulated by China's increasing access (both actual and anticipated) to world export markets following its accession to the World Trade Organization (WTO).

---

1. A more likely possibility is that those could be flows from sources such as Japan, Taiwan, and the United States that are channeled through such offshore financial centers in order to evade taxes in the source countries.

Table 9.2   Utilized FDI by sector (percent share)

	1998	1999	2000	2001	2002	2003	2004 (September)
Primary sector	1.4	1.8	1.7	1.9	1.9	1.9	1.8
Extraction industries	1.3	1.4	1.4	1.7	1.1	0.6	0.6
Manufacturing	56.3	56.1	63.5	65.9	69.8	69.0	70.9
Textiles	3.4	3.4	3.4	4.1	5.6	4.1	3.6
Chemicals and raw materials	4.3	4.8	4.4	4.7	6.0	4.9	4.4
Medicine	0.8	1.7	1.3	1.3	1.7	1.4	1.2
Ordinary machinery	2.1	2.4	2.6	2.8	3.2	2.9	3.4
Special use equipment		1.3	1.3	1.7	2.5	2.3	3.5
Electronics and communication equipment	5.3	7.8	11.3	15.1	20.0	11.9	13.0
Utilities	6.8	9.2	5.5	4.8	2.6	2.4	2.0
Construction	4.5	2.3	2.2	1.7	1.3	1.1	1.3
Transport and telecommunication services	3.6	3.8	2.5	1.9	1.7	1.6	2.2
Distribution industries	2.6	2.4	2.1	2.5	1.8	2.1	1.3
Banking and finance		0.2	0.2	0.1	0.2	0.4	0.4
Real estate	14.1	13.9	11.4	11.0	10.7	9.8	9.4
Development and operations	12.0	11.7	10.7	10.2	9.9	9.5	8.9
Social services	6.5	6.3	5.4	5.5	5.6	5.9	5.9
Hotels	1.1	1.8	1.1	1.0	0.9	0.9	0.6
Healthcare, sports, and social welfare	0.2	0.4	0.3	0.3	0.2	0.2	0.1
Media and broadcasting	0.2	0.2	0.1	0.1	0.1	0.1	1.8
Scientific research services	0.1	0.3	0.1	0.3	0.4	0.5	0.5
Other	2.4	1.9	3.6	2.3	2.5	4.2	1.7

Source: CEIC database.

The regional distribution within China of utilized FDI inflows has shown some changes over time (table 9.3). Guangdong Province has typically accounted for about one-quarter of FDI inflows, consistent with its proximity to Hong Kong and its reputation as an exporting powerhouse, but its share fell by about 7 percentage points from 1995–97 to 2003. The big winner over the past few years has been Jiangsu Province (next to Shanghai), which increased its share from 12 percent in 1995–97 to 25 percent in 2003, thereby displacing Guangdong from the lead position.[2] This has come at the expense of the relative shares of provinces such as Fujian,

2. In the early 1980s, Guangdong was heavily promoted as a leading experimental lab for market-oriented reforms, due in part to its proximity to Hong Kong. By contrast, the reform of the Yangtze River Delta region (especially Jiangsu, Shanghai, and Zhejiang) was held back in the 1980s. Shanghai was a key provider of revenue to the central government and, since the experiment with a market economy was considered risky, central planning features were largely retained there until the late 1980s. Once it was clear that the market economy experiment was working well, reforms in Shanghai went into full swing.

Table 9.3   Foreign direct investment inflows into China by region (in percent of total FDI inflows)

	Average 1995–2003	Average 1995–1997	Average 2000–2003	2003
Guandong	25.1	27.0	22.3	14.6
Jiangsu	15.3	12.8	17.4	19.7
Shanghai	8.5	8.8	8.8	10.2
Fujian	8.7	9.9	7.2	4.9
Shandong	7.1	6.2	8.8	11.2
Beijing	3.9	3.4	3.8	4.1
Zhejiang	4.5	3.4	6.0	9.3
Tianjin	4.1	4.8	3.3	2.9
Liaoning	4.7	4.3	5.5	5.3
Hebei	2.0	2.0	1.6	1.8
Guangxi	1.4	1.8	0.9	0.8
Hubei	2.2	1.7	2.6	2.9
Hainan	1.4	2.1	1.0	0.8
Hunan	1.7	1.7	1.8	1.9
Jiangxi	1.2	0.8	1.6	3.0
Henan	1.2	1.4	1.0	1.0
Anhui	0.8	1.2	0.7	0.7
Sichuan	1.0	1.0	1.0	0.8
Heilongjiang	1.0	1.4	0.7	0.6
Jilin	0.8	1.0	0.6	0.4
Shaanxi	0.8	1.0	0.7	0.6
Chongqing	0.6	0.9	0.5	0.5
Shanxi	0.5	0.4	0.5	0.4
Inner Mongolia	0.4	0.2	0.8	0.2
Yunnan	0.3	0.3	0.2	0.2
Quizhou	0.1	0.1	0.1	0.1
Gansu	0.1	0.2	0.1	
Qinghai			0.1	
Ningxia			0.1	
Xinjiang		0.1	0.1	

Source: CEIC database.

Tianjin, Hebei, and Hainan. Except for Fujian, however, the other provinces didn't have large shares to begin with.

Another phenomenon of some interest is the increase in FDI outflows from China. As China intensifies its trade linkages with other Asian economies, anecdotal evidence suggests that its FDI outflows have increased significantly in recent years. This phenomenon has been actively encouraged by the Chinese government as part of its policy of gradual capital account liberalization. Since 2001, some steps have been taken each year to ease restrictions on FDI outflows (see appendix B). However, while it is true that FDI outflows have risen almost tenfold from the mid-1990s to 2003, the total outflows are still small, amounting to only about $3 billion in 2003 (table 9.4). Much of these outflows has indeed gone to other Asian economies, es-

Table 9.4   Total outward foreign direct investment (%; for top ten countries with the highest average percent share between 2001 and 2003)

	1995	1996	1997	1998	1999	2000	2001	2002	2003	Average 1995–2000	Average 2001–2003
Hong Kong SAR	18.9	39.9	4.0	4.9	4.1	3.2	25.6	13.2	40.4	12.5	26.4
United States	22.0	2.0	0.0	9.9	13.7	4.2	6.8	5.6	2.3	8.6	4.9
Thailand	60.7	1.7	0.0	0.3	0.3	0.6	15.5	0.1	2.0	10.6	5.9
Republic of Korea	3.5	0.1	0.0	0.4	0.0	0.8	0.1	3.1	5.4	0.8	2.9
Vietnam	1.8	0.7	0.3	0.9	1.1	3.2	3.4	1.0		1.3	
Australia	0.9	0.3	0.0	-0.1	0.3	1.8	1.3	1.8		0.5	
Cambodia	0.0	7.9	6.1	2.3	5.6	3.1	4.4	0.2		4.2	
Brazil	0.5	0.6	13.7	0.6	0.1	3.8	4.0	0.3		3.2	
Russia	0.1	0.0	0.8	1.0	0.6	2.5	1.6	1.3	1.1	0.8	1.3
Yemen	0.0	0.0	0.0	0.0	0.0	2.0	2.7	0.0		0.3	1.3
Total amount (in US$ millions)	110.0	290.0	200.0	260.0	590.0	551.0	785.0	2,701.0	2,850.0		

Source: CEIC China database.

pecially Hong Kong. The United States has, over the past decade, accounted for about 8 percent of China's FDI outflows. More recently, the Chinese government has encouraged FDI outflows to countries in Asia and Latin America in order to ensure more reliable sources of raw materials (for instance, by purchasing mining operations) and upstream products for processing in China. Preliminary data for 2004 indicate that China's FDI outflows amounted to about $3.6 billion in 2004, with about half of this investment going to Latin America and 40 percent to other Asian countries.[3]

9.2.3   External Debt

Unlike some other emerging markets, China has been quite cautious about taking on external debt (figure 9.5). There has been little sovereign borrowing until very recently, and, as a matter of policy, enterprises have been discouraged from taking on external debt. As a consequence, notwithstanding the significant increase in the absolute amount of external debt since the mid-1980s, the ratio of external debt to GDP has remained relatively stable at around 15 percent since the early 1990s.

However, it is not just the level of external debt but also the maturity structure of this debt that has been shown to be associated with currency and financial crises. As discussed earlier, countries that have more short-term debt relative to long-term debt tend to be more susceptible to such crises. On this score, one noteworthy development is that the share of short-term debt in China's total external debt has risen significantly, from 9 percent in 2000 to over 45 percent in 2004 (figure 9.6 and table 9.5).[4] This level is close to the threshold that some studies have identified as posing a high risk of crises. However, this increase could appear more dramatic than warranted, since this ratio appears to have bottomed in 2000. Furthermore, a significant part of the increase in the relative importance of short-term debt since 2001 can be accounted for by the surge in trade credits. Trade credits constituted 19 percent of total external debt in 2003, up from 13 percent in 2001 (table 9.5). The increase in trade credits accounts for about two-fifths of the total increase in outstanding external credit from 2001 to 2004.[5] While trade credits often have short maturities, they do not pose the same type of risks as other short-term borrowing since they tend to be closely linked to subsequent export receipts.

3. Official reports note that the cumulative amount of outward FDI as of the end of 2004 was $37 billion, which does not seem to match the annual data shown in this table. Based on anecdotal and other evidence, however, the upward trend in FDI outflows is incontrovertible even if the magnitudes may be suspect.

4. The ratio of short-term external debt to GDP has risen from 1.2 percent to 5.5 percent over this period.

5. One cautionary note about the trade credit data in the external debt statistics is that they are estimated partly from data on imports. Consequently, they do not always match the balance-of-payments data on trade credits (discussed below), which are based on sample surveys. But the broad trends revealed by these two sources are similar.

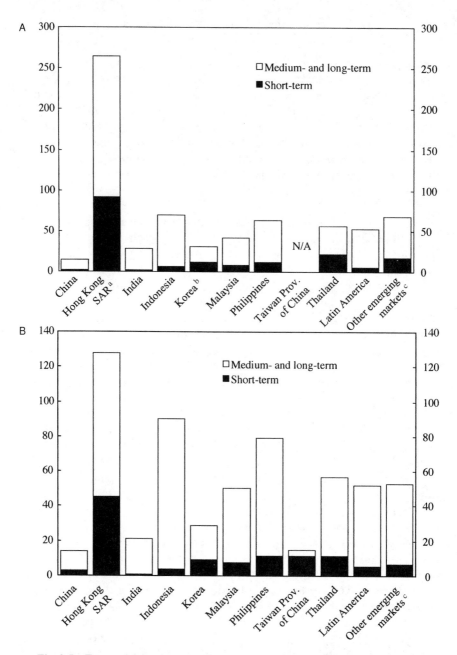

Fig. 9.5   External debt: Cross-country comparison (in percent of GDP): *A,* **average 1990–98;** *B,* **average 1999–2003**

Sources: World Economic Outlook database, CEIC database, and joint BIS-OECD-IMF-WB statistics on external debt. Includes private-sector debt.

[a]Average for Hong Kong consists of data between 1996 and 1998.

[b]Average for Korea consists of data between 1994 and 1998.

[c]Average for emerging markets in EMBI+ index, excluding Latin America and Asian countries.

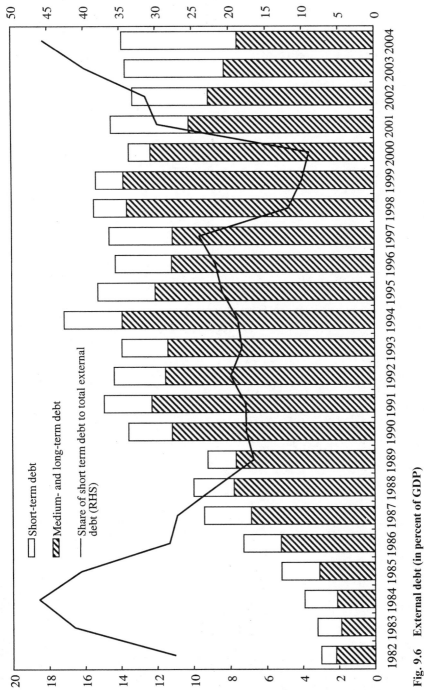

Fig. 9.6   External debt (in percent of GDP)

Source: China State Am for Foreign Exchange (SAFE) and World Bank Global Development Finance database.

Table 9.5   External debt

	1995	1996	1997	1998	1999	2000	2001	2002	2003	2004
Total										
In billions of U.S. dollars	106.6	116.3	131.0	146.0	151.8	145.7	170.1	171.4	193.6	228.6
In % of GDP	15.2	14.2	14.6	15.4	15.3	13.5	14.5	13.5	13.7	14.2
By maturity (in % of total debt)										
Short-term[a]	11.2	12.2	13.8	11.9	10.0	9.0	29.7	32.5	39.8	45.6
Medium and long-term debt	88.8	87.8	86.2	88.1	90.0	91.0	74.2	72.0	62.3	54.4
By type (in % of total debt)										
Registered external debt							87.3	84.6	81.1	80.8[b]
Trade credit							12.7	15.4	18.9	19.2[b]
Registered external debt by debtor (in % of registered external debt)[c]										
Public and publicly guaranteed	29.2	28.8	27.5	28.5	31.2	33.6	33.5	34.8	33.6	18.8[b]
Chinese-funded enterprises	11.0	10.6	10.2	10.6	9.7	9.3	7.6	6.9	4.9	3.4[b]
Chinese-funded financial institutions	33.5	29.6	25.3	23.3	22.7	20.5	20.2	22.0	21.2	35.8[b]
Chinese-funded nonfinancial institutions	10.8	9.7	8.5	6.6	5.3	3.9	2.9	3.0	2.7	
Foreign-funded enterprises	2.1	3.2	5.3	6.3			23.7	22.9	24.1	23.3[b]
Foreign-funded financial institutions							11.5	10.4	13.3	18.5[b]
Other	13.5	18.1	23.2	24.6	31.2	32.7	0.5	0.0	0.2	0.2[b]

Sources: CEIC database, Chinese authorities, and authors' calculations.

Note: Maturity structure is based on classification by residual maturity of outstanding debt.

[a] Assumes original maturity through 2000 and remaining maturity from 2001 onward.

[b] As of September 2004.

[c] Effective June 2004, loans from foreign governments that are assumed by policy banks were reclassified under debt of Chinese-funded financial institutions (rather than debt of government departments). Furthermore, in 2004, the outstanding external debt of government departments decreased, but that of Chinese-funded financial institutions increased by US$18.7 billion. This accounts for the sharp shift in the shares of these two categories in 2004.

In short, while the stock of debt is in itself not a source of concern, the maturity structure and composition of this debt bear careful observation.[6]

9.3   International Reserves

9.3.1   Recent Developments

A different perspective on China's capital inflows is provided by examining the evolution of the balance of payments and the stock of international reserves.[7] Table 9.6 shows that China's gross international reserves have risen sharply over the past decade, from well below $50 billion during 1990–93 to $457 billion at the end of 2003, with almost a third of this buildup occurring in 2003.[8] This has left China with the second largest stock of international reserves in the world, behind Japan alone, amounting to about 32 percent of its nominal GDP at the end of 2003.

In 2004, gross reserves rose at an even faster pace than in previous years, reaching $619 billion at the end of the year, according to official figures. However, it is necessary to add the $45 billion used for bank recapitalization at the end of 2003 to this stock in order to allow for comparability of the stock levels in 2003 and 2004 (these adjusted figures are reported in table 9.6). Thus, we arrive at an increase of $206 billion, or an average of about $17.2 billion a month, during 2004 (compared to $162 billion, or about $13.5 billion a month, during 2003). Since balance-of-payments data for 2004 were not available at the time of this writing, the remainder of this section focuses on data through 2003.

Of the total increase of about $430 billion in reserves over the past decade, cumulative flows on the current account balance amount to about $216 billion, while flows on the capital account sum up to $300 billion. The residual is given by cumulative errors and omissions, which amount to about –$85 billion over this period.

It is instructive to examine the factors underlying changes in the pace of reserve accumulation over time. After registering relatively small changes over the period 1985–93, reserve accumulation rose sharply and averaged $30 billion a year over the period 1994–97. This was largely due to a strong

---

6. The World Bank's 2003 *Global Development Finance Report* (pp. 136–39) indicates that, in recent years, about 70 percent of China's outstanding long-term external debt has been denominated in U.S. dollars, and about 15 percent has been denominated in Japanese yen. Data on the currency composition of short-term external debt are not available in this report.

7. Some of the analysis in section 9.3 draws upon work done by members of the IMF's China team.

8. The figure for 2003 includes the $45 billion used to recapitalize two state commercial banks at the end of that year. Hence, the numbers reported in this table for foreign exchange reserve accumulation during 2003 and the level of gross official reserves at the end of 2003 are higher by $45 billion than the corresponding official figures. To understand the evolution of the capital account, it is relevant to include that figure in the calculations.

Table 9.6   The balance of payments (in billions of U.S. dollars)

	1990	1991	1992	1993	1994	1995	1996	1997	1998	1999	2000	2001	2002	2003	2004
Gross international reserves	30.2	44.3	21.2	23.0	53.6	76.0	107.7	143.4	149.8	158.3	168.9	218.7	295.2	457.2[a]	663.6[a]
Foreign exchange reserves	28.6	42.7	19.4	21.2	51.6	73.6	105.0	139.9	145.0	154.7	165.6	212.2	286.4	448.3[a]	654.9[a]
Increase in international reserves	12.1	14.6	-2.1	1.8	30.5	22.5	31.6	35.7	6.4	8.5	10.5	47.3	75.5	162.0[a]	206.3
Current account balance	12.0	13.3	6.4	-11.9	7.7	1.6	7.2	29.7	29.3	21.1	20.5	17.4	35.4	45.9	70.0[b]
Merchandise trade balance	9.2	8.7	5.2	-10.7	7.3	18.1	19.5	46.2	46.6	36.0	34.5	34.0	44.2	44.7	
Services trade balance	1.5	2.9	-0.2	-1.1	0.1	-6.1	-2.0	-5.7	-4.9	-5.3	-5.6	-5.9	-6.8	-8.6	
Net investment balance	1.1	0.8	0.2	-1.3	-1.0	-11.8	-12.4	-15.9	-16.6	-14.5	-14.7	-19.2	-14.9	-7.8	
Net transfers	0.3	0.8	1.2	1.2	1.3	1.4	2.1	5.1	4.3	4.9	6.3	8.5	13.0	17.6	
Capital account balance	-2.8	4.6	-0.3	23.5	32.6	38.7	40.0	23.0	-6.3	5.2	2.0	34.8	32.3	97.8	112.0[b]
FDI, net	2.7	3.5	7.2	23.1	31.8	33.8	38.1	41.7	41.1	37.0	37.5	37.4	46.8	47.2	55.0[b]
Portfolio, net	-0.2	0.2	-0.1	3.1	3.5	0.8	1.7	6.8	-3.7	-11.2	-4.0	-19.4	-10.3	11.4	
Other investment, net	-5.2	0.9	-7.4	-2.7	-2.7	4.0	0.2	-25.5	-43.7	-20.5	-31.5	16.9	-4.1	39.1[b]	24.3[b]
Errors and omissions, net	-3.1	-6.7	-8.3	-9.8	-9.8	-17.8	-15.6	-17.0	-16.6	-17.8	-11.9	-4.9	7.8	18.4	
Non-FDI capital account balance (including errors and omissions)	-8.6	-5.6	-15.7	-9.4	-8.9	-13.0	-13.7	-35.6	-64.0	-49.6	-47.4	-7.4	-6.7	69.0	81.3[b]

Sources: CEIC database, PBC, the State Administration of Foreign Exchange (SAFE), and authors' calculations.

Notes: In 1992, foreign exchange reserves were reclassified to exclude foreign-exchange deposits of state-owned entities with the Bank of China. There are minor discrepancies in some years between row 3 (increase in international reserves) and changes in the numbers in row 1 (stock of gross international reserves). This is attributable to the fact that the numbers in row 3, which come from the balance of payments, do not include valuation changes in holdings of gold.

[a] Reserve data for 2003 and 2004 include the $45 billion used for bank recapitalization at the end of 2003. This affects the increase in international reserves shown for 2003 and the stocks of reserves shown for 2003 and 2004.

[b] These very preliminary data for 2004 are taken from the PBC's monetary policy report for 2004:Q4. The figure for FDI net is an assumption based on a reported gross inflow of about $60 billion and an assumed outflow of $5 billion (up from about $3 billion in 2003). Errors and omissions are calculated as a residual (and, hence, so is the non-FDI capital account balance).

Table 9.7   **Decomposition of the recent reserve buildup (in billions of U.S. dollars)**

	Average 1998–2000 (1)	Average 2001–2003 (2)	Change (2) – (1)	Average 2001–2004 (3)	Change (3) – (1)
Foreign reserve increase	8.5	95.0	86.5	122.8	114.3
Current account balance	23.7	32.9	9.2	42.2	18.5
Capital account balance	0.3	55.0	54.7	69.3	69.0
FDI, net	38.5	43.8	5.3	46.6	8.1
Errors and omissions, net	–15.4	7.1	22.5	11.4	26.8
Non-FDI capital account balance (including errors and omissions)	–53.6	18.3	72.0	34.1	87.7

Sources: CEIC database, PBC, and authors' calculations.

Notes: The numbers shown in this table are annual averages over the relevant periods (underlying annual data are in table 9.6). Balance-of-payments data for 2004 that are used in the calculations in the last two columns are very preliminary and are mostly taken from the PBC's monetary policy report for 2004:Q4. The numbers used for 2004 are as follows: increase in gross international reserves, $206.3 billion; current account balance, $70.0 billion; capital account balance, $112.0 billion; FDI, net, $55 billion; errors and omissions, net, $24.3 billion; non-FDI capital account balance, $81.3 billion. The 2004 figure for FDI net is based on a reported gross inflow of about $60 billion and an assumed outflow of $5 billion (up from about $3 billion in 2003). Net errors and omissions are calculated as a residual (and, hence, so is the non-FDI capital account balance).

capital account, which in turn reflected robust FDI inflows on the order of $30–40 billion a year. Interestingly, the errors and omissions category was significantly negative over this period (averaging about –$15 billion a year), suggesting that unofficial capital outflows were occurring at the same time that significant FDI inflows were coming in through official channels.

Reserve accumulation then tapered off during 1998–2000, the years right after the Asian crisis. A sharp rise in outflows on other investment and large negative errors and omissions together offset much of the effect of continued robust FDI inflows and a strong current account, the latter reflecting an increase in the trade surplus.

The subsequent sharp increase in reserves since 2001 is noteworthy, particularly because it was accompanied by a sustained export boom and the possibility—according to a number of observers and analysts—that the renminbi may have become significantly undervalued over this period.[9] It is instructive to compare the factors underlying the accumulation of reserves in 2001–3 relative to the previous three-year period.

Table 9.7 shows that the average annual increase in foreign exchange reserves during 2001–3 was an order of magnitude higher than during 1998–

9. There is a considerable range of opinions about the degree of undervaluation of the renminbi. IMF (2004) and Funke and Rahn (2005) conclude that there is no strong evidence that the renminbi is substantially undervalued. Goldstein (2004) and Frankel (2004), on the other hand, argue that the renminbi may be undervalued by at least 25–30 percent. Market analysts have a similarly broad range of views.

2000. The current account surplus was on average larger in the latter period, but it does not account for much of the increase in the pace of reserve accumulation since 2001. Similarly, while FDI inflows are an important contributor to reserve accumulation, there is little evidence of a major increase in the pace of these inflows in the latter period. The most significant increase is in non-FDI capital inflows (including errors and omissions), which swung from an average of –$53.6 billion in 1998–2000 to $18.3 billion in 2001–3, a turnaround of $72 billion on an annual basis. Errors and omissions, in particular, changed from an average of –$15.4 billion in the first period to $7.1 billion in the second.

This decomposition is significant as it shows that much of the recent increase in the pace of reserve accumulation is potentially related to "hot money" rather than a rising trade surplus or capital flows such as FDI that are viewed as being driven by fundamentals. In fact, the merchandise trade balance has been relatively stable in the range of $35–45 billion since 1997. The moderate increase in the average current account surplus is largely accounted for by the surge in net transfers.

To better understand recorded non-FDI capital inflows, we examine more detailed information from capital and financial account transactions. Table 9.8 shows how the main items changed from 2000 to 2003. Of the total increase of $96 billion in the capital and financial account over this period, the increases in net FDI inflows and net portfolio flows account for $10 billion and $15 billion, respectively. This leaves a substantial portion, about $71 billion, to be explained by other capital flows. The two biggest increases, adding up to about $60 billion, are in the categories of inward loans—representing offshore borrowing by Chinese households and firms—and other assets. This includes significant withdrawals of overseas lending by Chinese banks in order to meet rising domestic demand for foreign currency–denominated loans. The general direction of all of these flows is consistent with expectations during this period of an appreciation of the renminbi.

Similarly, the large switch in the errors and omissions category could potentially be indicative of unrecorded capital flows into China, stimulated by the prospect of an appreciation of the renminbi against the U.S. dollar. Such speculative pressures may have been exacerbated by the positive interest differential between China and the United States, which implies that investors may have seen a move into renminbi-denominated instruments as essentially a one-way bet, and one without even an associated carrying cost.

This raises the prospect that, as long as the perception of an undervalued renminbi persists—and unless the interest differential between China and the United States narrows further or shifts—these speculative inflows could continue. It should nevertheless be noted that, given the apparent one-way bet on the renminbi, the fact that these flows are not larger than they are suggests that capital controls may be at least partially effective.

In this context, it is worth trying to investigate in more detail where the un-

Table 9.8   Capital flows under the financial account (in billions of U.S. dollars)

	2000			2003			Change in balance (2003 less 2000)
	Balance	Credit	Debit	Balance	Credit	Debit	
Financial account	2	92	90	98	220	122	96
Direct investment	37	42	5	47	56	8	10
Inward	38	41	2	47	54	6	9
Outward	−1	1	2	0	2	2	1
Portfolio investment	−4	8	12	11	12	1	15
Assets	−11	0	11	3	3	0	14
Equity securities							
Debt securities							
Liabilities	7	8	0	8	9	1	1
Equity securities							
Debt securities							
Other investment	−32	42	74	39	152	113	71
Assets	−44	5	49	27	52	25	71
Trade credit	−13	0	13	−1	0	1	11
Loans	−18	0	19	14	22	8	32
Currency, deposits	−6	1	7	−7	1	7	−1
Other assets	−6	3	10	21	30	8	28
Liabilities	12	37	25	12	100	88	0
Trade credit	18	18	0	5	5	0	−14
Loans	−2	−12	15	7	79	72	9
Currency, deposits	0	0	0	1	9	8	1
Other liabilities	−3	7	10	0	7	7	3

Source: CEIC database.

recorded flows are coming from, how much larger could they be in the absence of capital controls, and how much money may try to find its way around the capital controls. Anecdotal evidence suggests that the money flowing in is primarily accounted for by a reversal of outflows from Chinese households and corporations that took place during the 1990s to evade taxes or to avoid losses associated with a possible depreciation of the renminbi. It is difficult to answer precisely the question of how much such money is outside of China and could potentially come back into the country.

We take the simple and admittedly naive approach of adding up errors and omissions and portfolio flows and labeling the total as hot money that could potentially switch directions within a short time horizon. Figure 9.7 shows the amount of such hot money flows over the past two decades.[10] The

10. Capital flight through underinvoicing of exports or overinvoicing of imports may not show up in the errors and omissions or any other part of the balance of payments statistics. Net errors and omissions may also understate unrecorded capital flows to the extent that there are offsetting unrecorded flows on current and capital account transactions, or even among transactions within each of these categories. Gunter (2004) estimates that capital flight during the 1990s may have been greater than suggested by such crude estimates.

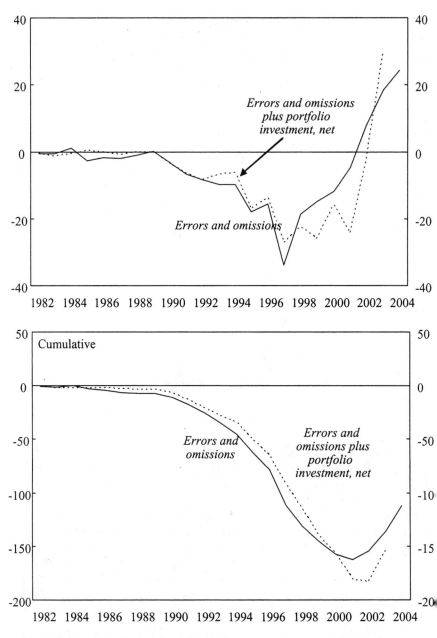

Fig. 9.7   Errors and omissions and portfolio investment, net (in billions of U.S. dollars)

Source: World Economic Outlook database.

Note: Data for 2004 are preliminary (see notes to table 9.6).

lower panel shows that the cumulative amount of errors and omissions since the early 1990s is quite large, peaking at about $150 billion, and the recent swing has reversed at best a small part of this flow. Under this interpretation, there could potentially be significant amounts of further inflows if there continues to be a strong expectation of an appreciation of the renminbi.

An alternative, and more benign, possibility is that the errors and omissions category may in part reflect an accounting issue.[11] China's officially reported holdings of foreign bonds are not marked to market in terms of exchange rate valuations, while the stock of international reserves on the People's Bank of China's (PBC's) balance sheet does reflect these currency valuation effects. This implies, for instance, that any changes in the dollar value of reserve holdings could end up in the balance of payments under the errors and omissions category.[12] In the absence of published data on the currency composition of foreign exchange reserves, it is widely believed that a substantial fraction of China's foreign exchange reserve holdings is in U.S. treasury bonds, with the remainder in government bonds denominated in euros and other currencies.[13] Given the recent large swings in the value of the U.S. dollar, however, even modest holdings of reserves in instruments denominated in other major currencies could have a significant quantitative impact on the dollar value of gross reserves.

Table 9.9 shows the effects of some simple simulations to illustrate how large these valuation effects could potentially be. For instance, in panel A, we assume that 80 percent of China's foreign reserve holdings are in U.S. dollar–denominated instruments, with the remainder in euro-denominated instruments. This calculation suggests that, in 2003, roughly $16 billion, representing about 85 percent of the errors and omissions amount for the year, could be accounted for by valuation changes on the stock of reserves. In 2004, valuation changes could account for about $11 billion of unrecorded capital inflows, although, in the absence of full balance-of-payments data at this stage, one cannot tell how this fits into the bigger picture. But, as a share of the total change in reserves, valuation effects are clearly going to be a lot less important in 2004 than in 2003, both because the underlying exchange rate changes were smaller and because the change in reserves was larger in 2004.

The remaining panels of this table show how the results change under

11. The calculations that follow are based upon unpublished work by Ray Brooks.
12. China does not report its international investment position, which would clarify this matter.
13. There has been a great deal of recent interest in the share of Chinese official reserve holdings accounted for by U.S. dollar–denominated instruments, particularly treasury bonds. The recent depreciation of the U.S. dollar has fueled speculation that China has been diversifying away from U.S. dollar bonds into other currencies. Appendix A provides a detailed analysis, including some cautionary notes, about one source of data that has been used by many analysts to examine this issue.

Table 9.9   Possible effects of valuation changes on reserves

Year	Foreign exchange reserves (in US$ billions)	Increase/decrease in reserves due to foreign exchange rate change			Errors and omissions (in US$ billions)	US$/euro exchange rate		US$/yen · 100 exchange rate	
		Euro	Yen	Total		Beginning of period	End of period	Beginning of period	End of period
A. Assumed composition of reserves: 80% U.S. dollars and 20% euros									
2000	165.6	−2.4		−2.4	−11.9	1.00	0.93		
2001	212.2	−2.2		−2.2	−4.9	0.93	0.88		
2002	286.4	10.4		10.4	7.8	0.88	1.04		
2003	403.3	16.1		16.1	18.4	1.04	1.25		
2004	609.9	10.8		10.8	24.3[a]	1.25	1.36		
B. Assumed composition of reserves: 90% U.S. dollars and 10% euros									
2000	165.6	−1.2		−1.2	−11.9	1.00	0.93		
2001	212.2	−1.1		−1.1	−4.9	0.93	0.88		
2002	286.4	5.2		5.2	7.8	0.88	1.04		
2003	403.3	8.1		8.1	18.4	1.04	1.25		
2004	609.9	5.4		5.4	24.3[a]	1.25	1.36		
C. Assumed composition of reserves: 70% U.S. dollars, 20% euros, and 10% Japanese yen									
2000	165.6	−2.4	−1.8	−4.2	−11.9	1.00	0.93	0.98	0.87
2001	212.2	−2.2	−2.7	−4.9	−4.9	0.93	0.88	0.87	0.76
2002	286.4	10.4	2.9	13.3	7.8	0.88	1.04	0.76	0.84
2003	403.3	16.1	4.3	20.5	18.4	1.04	1.25	0.84	0.93
2004	609.9	10.8	2.7	13.5	24.3[a]	1.25	1.36	0.93	0.97

Sources: *International Financial Statistics*, CEIC database, Datastream, and authors' calculations.

Notes: Foreign exchange reserves shown in the first column are end-of-year stocks. In this table, we do not include the US$45 billion used for bank recapitalization at end 2003 to the reserve stock numbers for 2003 and 2004. In principle, any currency valuation changes of that amount should affect the balance sheets of the banks to which those reserves were transferred. Thus, the currency valuation effects would matter for the net international investment position but not for official reserves.

[a]Errors and omissions data for 2004 are based on very preliminary estimates (see notes for table 9.6).

different assumptions about (a) the share of reserves held in U.S. dollar–denominated bonds and (b) the other Group of Three (G3) currencies in which the remainder of the reserves are held. The results generally seem to confirm the possibility that errors and omissions in recent years may, to a significant extent, reflect currency valuation effects rather than unrecorded capital inflows. This is clearly an issue that bears further investigation in the future.

9.3.2 Implications of the Recent Reserve Buildup

The fact that China's capital inflows over the past decade have been dominated by FDI is a positive outcome. As documented above, however, non-FDI capital inflows have accounted for much of the recent surge in the pace of reserve accumulation. This raises a question about whether, from China's domestic perspective, the continued rapid buildup of reserves is desirable.

The literature on the optimal level of reserves (see, e.g., Aizenman and Marion 2004 and references therein) does not provide a clear-cut way of answering this question. The usefulness of a large stock of reserves is essentially that, especially for a country with a fixed exchange rate system, it can be useful to stave off downward pressures on the exchange rate. The trade-off results from the fact that developing-country reserves are typically held in treasury bonds denominated in hard currencies. The rate of return on these instruments is presumably lower than that which could be earned by physical capital investment within the developing country, which would typically have a scarcity of capital. In addition, the capital inflows that are reflected in reserve accumulation could increase liquidity in the banking system, creating potential problems in a weakly supervised banking system because banks have an incentive to relax their prudential standards in order to increase lending. Sterilization of capital inflows to avoid this outcome could generate fiscal costs, because the rate of return on domestic sterilization instruments is typically higher than that earned on reserve holdings.

China, however, appears to be a special case in some respects. China's low (controlled) interest rates imply that, since its reserve holdings are believed to be held primarily in medium- and long-term industrial-country treasury instruments and government agency bonds, there are in fact net marginal *benefits* to sterilization. This is of course enabled by domestic financial repression—with no effective competition for the state-owned banking sector—and capital controls.[14] Furthermore, with domestic in-

---

14. This suggests that there are implicit costs to these sterilization efforts. However, determining the incidence of these costs is not straightforward; much of these costs is presumably borne by depositors in the state banks. Recent data suggest that longer-term central bank bills (original maturity of one year or longer) have replaced short-term bills as the primary sterilization instrument used by the Chinese authorities. This may have been driven by concerns about frequently rolling over the stock of short-term bills. In addition, purchases of shorter-term U.S. Treasury instruments appear to have increased (see appendix A). Thus, traditional sterilization costs may also soon start coming into play.

vestment rates of above 45 percent (supported mainly by domestic saving, which is an order of magnitude larger than FDI inflows), capital scarcity is apparently not a concern, and it is not obvious that the marginal return on investment is higher than the rate of return on reserve holdings, particularly in the likely scenario in which the allocation of capital remains the sole prerogative of an improving but still inefficient state banking system.[15]

Commonly used reserve adequacy indicators provide one way of assessing the insurance value provided by reserve holdings (figure 9.8).[16] China's reserve holdings provide comfortable coverage of its imports, more so than most other emerging markets. The stock of reserves at the end of 2004 accounted for about fifty-three weeks' worth of imports in that year (and for about forty-three weeks of the IMF's forecast of imports in 2005), significantly above the corresponding figures for most other emerging markets. In terms of reserve coverage of short-term external debt, China outperforms virtually every other emerging market, with its reserves amounting to more than ten times short-term external debt.[17] One area where China's position looks less favorable relative to other emerging markets is the reserve coverage of the monetary base, which is a useful indicator of reserve adequacy in the context of a currency peg. Reflecting the high degree of monetization of the Chinese economy (the ratio of M2 to GDP at end 2004 was about 1.9), reserves cover only about 20 percent of M2.

As a related matter, in addition to providing a buffer to stave off any future downward pressures on the fixed exchange rate, the high level of reserves has in fact been cited as necessary to cushion the financial sector from external shocks. Reported nonperforming loans (NPLs) in the banking system amounted to about 30 percent of GDP in 2003 (see Prasad 2004), similar in magnitude to the stock of reserves, suggesting that the present level of reserves could be used to finance a bailout of the banking system if the need should arise. Indeed, the recapitalization of two major state commercial banks at the end of 2003 using $45 billion of reserves is indicative of the intention of the Chinese authorities to use reserve holdings to help strengthen the books of state banks. However, there are concerns that deficiencies in accounting practices and the reporting of NPLs could mean that their true level is higher than the reported numbers. Furthermore, the rapid expansion of credit during 2003 and the first half of 2004 that contributed to an investment boom could result in a new wave of problem loans in the future if the surge in investment results in excess

15. See Boyreau-Debray and Wei (2004) for evidence of low returns to lending by state banks.

16. The cross-country comparison in figure 9.8 shows data only through 2003. The discussion in this paragraph uses updated data for China through end 2004.

17. Figure 9.8 uses Bank for International Settlements (BIS) data on external debt that are, in principle, comparable across countries. Based on official Chinese data, reserves amount to about six times the stock of short-term external debt, still above comparable ratios in almost all other emerging markets.

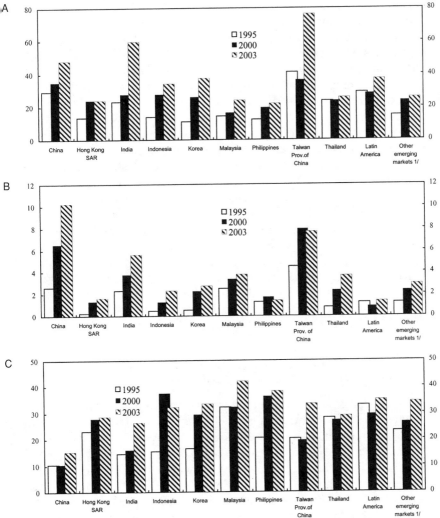

Fig. 9.8   Reserve adequacy indicators: *A,* **reserves/imports (weeks of imports);**
B, **reserves/short-term external debt;** *C,* **reserves/M2 (percentage)**

Sources: IFS, DOT, WEO and Joint BIS/IMF/OECD/World Bank Statistics of External
Debt.

Note: In panel A, end-of-year reserves are shown as a ratio to the number of weeks' worth of
imports in that year.

capacity being built up in some sectors (Goldstein and Lardy 2004). This could justify maintaining a high level of reserves.[18]

One risk associated with maintaining a high level of reserves, however, is the vulnerability of the balance sheet of the PBC to changes in the industrial country treasury yield curve. An upward shift in the yield curve could significantly reduce the mark-to-market value of Chinese holdings of industrial country treasury instruments.[19] Similarly, an appreciation of the currency relative to, for example, the U.S. dollar could lead to a fall in the renminbi value of dollar-denominated treasury bond holdings. Since the primary sterilization instrument in China—central bank bills—is denominated in renminbi, this would lead to a net capital loss in domestic currency terms. Interestingly, this suggests that, at least on this dimension, the costs of a move toward greater exchange rate flexibility (which, under present circumstances, is expected to lead to some appreciation of the renminbi in the short run) could increase as the stock of reserves rises.[20] It could also increase the incentive to diversify out of dollar assets and into other hard currencies.

To summarize, there is no clear evidence that the buildup of reserves in China has significant direct sterilization costs, although it could have some efficiency costs and also expose the balance sheet of the PBC to some exchange rate and capital risks, at least on a mark-to-market basis.

9.4   Viewing China's Capital Inflows through the Prism of the Literature on Financial Globalization

It has long been an article of faith among most economists that international capital flows allow for a more efficient global allocation of capital. For capital-poor developing countries in particular, financial integration (with world capital markets) was seen as key to moving onto a high-growth path. In addition, financial integration in theory provides enhanced possibilities for consumption smoothing through better sharing of income risk across countries. Those developing countries that subscribed to this logic by liberalizing their capital accounts starting in the mid-1980s—a group that has come to be known as the emerging markets—captured the lion's

---

18. Preliminary indications are that the reported ratio of NPLs to GDP declined in 2004, but this may be attributable partly to the transfer of some NPLs off the books of state commercial banks.

19. One could argue that these notional capital losses in mark-to-market terms should not be of concern if the Chinese authorities' intention is to hold the bonds to maturity. This argument has validity only so long as the reserves do not need to be liquidated before maturity.

20. A related point is that if the accumulation of reserves continues apace, the potential capital loss from any appreciation would grow over time, suggesting that an earlier move toward exchange rate flexibility would be preferable from this narrow perspective (if such a move was regarded as being inevitable). In any event, we doubt that this factor will play a significant role in influencing the timing of a move toward greater flexibility.

share of the net capital flows from industrial to developing economies that took place over the subsequent decade. Capital account liberalization proved, however, to be a mixed blessing, with many emerging markets suffering debilitating financial and balance-of-payments crises in the late 1990s. But do the crises by themselves imply that financial integration is not advisable for developing countries? A closer look at the evidence is in order.[21]

9.4.1   Financial Integration and Growth

In theory, there are a number of channels through which capital inflows can help to raise economic growth in developing countries. These include direct channels such as augmentation of domestic savings, lower cost of capital, transfer of technology, and development of the domestic financial sector. Indirect channels include the inducements for better domestic policies offered by capital account openness and the promotion of specialization of production. Theory drives one inexorably to the conclusion that financial integration *must* be good for growth.

The empirical evidence, however, paints a far more sobering picture. It is true that emerging markets as a group have posted much higher growth on average than other developing economies over the past two decades. Notwithstanding the painful crises that many of them experienced, these countries have done far better overall in terms of raising per capita incomes. However, this does not by itself imply a causal relationship. Indeed, while there is a considerable divergence of results among different studies, the weight of the evidence seems to tilt toward the conclusion that it is difficult to find a strong and robust causal link once one controls for other factors that could affect growth (Prasad et al. 2003 provide an extensive survey of this literature). There is of course an element of endogeneity here—financial integration could induce countries to have better macroeconomic policies and improve their institutions, but this effect would not be picked up in a regression framework. However, there is at best mixed evidence that financial integration induces a country to pursue better macroeconomic policies (Tytell and Wei 2004). More research is needed on this question, but the bottom line is that it is difficult to make a prima facie case that financial integration provides a strong boost to growth in emerging markets.

9.4.2   Financial Integration and Volatility

As for volatility, economic theory has the strong implication that access to financial markets—at either the household or the national level—must be welfare enhancing from a consumption-smoothing perspective. So long as aggregate shocks (at the relevant level of aggregation) are not dominant

21. The discussion in section 9.4 draws on Prasad et al. (2003).

in explaining variations in household or national income growth, financial markets should improve welfare by providing a mechanism that allows individual economic units to share their idiosyncratic income risk. The reason countries (and households) like to do this, of course, is to smooth their consumption growth and reduce the otherwise necessarily close linkage of national consumption growth to national income growth and its intrinsic volatility. Although some countries may not be able to take full advantage of such risk-sharing opportunities (e.g., due to problems of monitoring and moral hazard), access to international financial markets should improve their welfare—in terms of reducing consumption volatility—at least marginally.

The reality for emerging markets is starkly different. Recent research suggests that, for these countries, the ratio of consumption growth volatility to output growth volatility in fact increased on average in the 1990s, precisely during the key period of financial globalization (Kose, Prasad, and Terrones 2003). Note that this result cannot be ascribed simply to the fact that some of these countries experienced crises during this period. In principle, a country should be able to do no worse than having its consumption growth be as volatile as its income growth. Formal regression analysis controlling for a variety of other determinants of volatility and growth suggests the existence of a nonlinearity in the relationship between the degree of financial integration and the relative volatility of consumption growth.[22]

An increase in financial integration from a low to a medium level tends to be associated with a rise in the relative volatility of consumption growth. At one end of the spectrum, for countries with very limited access to international financial markets, consumption growth tends to be about as volatile as income growth.[23] At the other end, industrial countries, which tend to be highly integrated into global financial markets, appear to be able to take advantage of financial openness to effectively reduce their relative consumption growth volatility. For emerging markets, the problem of course is that although international investors are willing to provide capital when times are good, these countries often lose access to international capital markets when times are bad (see, e.g., Kaminsky, Reinhart, and Végh 2004). Thus, sadly, it is precisely those countries that dip their toes into the waters of financial globalization that appear to be penalized by the procyclical nature of their access to world capital markets.

The situation appears bleak. Developing countries need external capital to grow. But is financial integration just "snake oil"—delivering at best weak growth effects and exposing countries to higher volatility? The answer, it turns out, depends.

---

22. In this subsection, "relative" volatility of consumption growth should always be taken to mean its volatility relative to that of income growth.

23. Even in a closed economy, of course, the existence of investment opportunities should allow for some degree of intertemporal smoothing of national consumption.

9.4.3   The Composition of Capital Inflows Matters

A large literature shows that it is not just the degree of financial openness, but also the composition of capital inflows, that determines the quality of a developing country's experiences with globalization (see Prasad et al. 2003 for a survey and additional references for the points made below). For instance, FDI inflows tend to be far less volatile than other types of inflows. In particular, FDI appears to be less subject to sharp reversals than other types of inflows, particularly bank lending.[24] External debt, on the other hand, clearly increases vulnerability to the risks of financial globalization. In particular, debt crises are more likely to occur in countries where external debt is of relatively short maturity (see, e.g., Frankel and Rose 1996 and Detragiache and Spilimbergo 2001).

The problem, of course, is that the composition of inflows and related matters such as the maturity structure of external debt are not entirely under the control of developing-country governments. Countries with weak macroeconomic fundamentals are often forced to rely more on external debt and end up having little choice but to borrow at short maturities. Financial integration can in fact aggravate the risks associated with weak macroeconomic policies. Access to world capital markets could lead to excessive borrowing that is channeled into unproductive government spending, ultimately increasing vulnerability to external shocks or changes in investor sentiment. In addition, lack of transparency has been shown to be associated with increased herding behavior by international investors, which can destabilize financial markets in an emerging market economy. Furthermore, a high degree of corruption tends to adversely affect the composition of a country's inflows, making it more vulnerable to the risks of speculative attacks and contagion effects.

Thus, the apparently negative effects of globalization appear to be related to a particular kind of threshold effect. Only countries with good institutions and sound macroeconomic policies tend to have lower vulnerability to the risks associated with the initial phase of financial integration and are able to realize its full benefits.

9.4.4   The Right Composition of Inflows for China

From a number of different perspectives, China is a prototypical developing country that is best served by FDI rather than other types of inflows. In the context of the above discussion on the benefits and potential risks of financial globalization, the dominance of FDI in China's capital inflows implies that it has been able to control the risks and get more of the promised benefits of financial integration than many emerging mar-

---

24. See Wei (2001). The evidence that net FDI flows to emerging markets are less volatile than portfolio flows is weaker (see Dooley, Claessens, and Warner 1995; Wei 2001).

kets that have taken a less cautious approach to capital account liberalization.

FDI may have served China well in other ways also. Given the low level of human capital and technical expertise in China, FDI could serve as a useful conduit for importing technical and managerial know-how (Borensztein, De Gregorio, and Lee 1998). Furthermore, the state-owned banking system is inefficient at allocating credit. This system has improved over time, particularly with the much-heralded end of the directed policy lending that these banks were forced to undertake until the late 1990s. However, most bank credit still goes to the public sector, especially since, with the controls on lending rates that existed until end October 2004, banks were not able to price in the higher risk of lending to new and/or small firms in the private sector (see Dunaway and Prasad 2004). As the experiences of some of the Asian crisis countries have shown, a weakly supervised banking system that is allowed to raise funds abroad and channel them into the domestic economy can generate serious imbalances. Thus, restrictions on bank borrowing from abroad can serve a useful purpose.

With a fixed exchange rate, openness to other types of financial flows, which tend to be less stable and are subject to sudden stops or reversals, would be less advisable. For instance, external borrowing by banks could cause instability in exchange markets and would have at best dubious effects on growth. Substantial opening of the capital account would also be inadvisable in this context, which suggests that the sort of selective opening that China has pursued may have some advantages (see Prasad, Rumbaugh, and Wang 2005).

9.5   What Explains the Composition of China's Capital Inflows?

China appears to have benefited from a pattern of capital inflows heavily tilted toward FDI. A key question is how China has attained such a composition of its inflows, one that many emerging markets aspire to but that few achieve. Some context is important before addressing this question. Earlier work by Wei (2000c) suggests that the size of FDI inflows into China relative to its GDP and other "natural" determinants is not unusually high. If anything, China seems to be an underperformer as a host of FDI from the world's five major source countries. In more recent years, with the continued rise in FDI, China may have become a normal country in terms of its attractiveness as a destination for FDI.

One explanation for the composition of China's capital inflows is that it is the result of a pragmatic strategy that has been adjusted over time through trial and error. The pattern in the 1980s and early 1990s could well have reflected a combination of inertia and luck, with the post-1997 pattern reflecting the scare of the Asian financial crisis. Indeed, at the beginning of the reform period in the late 1970s and early 1980s, there were few capital inflows of any kind.

The early stage of reform sought to import only the type of foreign capital that was thought to help transmit technical and marketing know-how; thus, the policy enunciated was "welcome to FDI, but no thank you to foreign debt and portfolio flows." Export performance and foreign exchange balance requirements were initially imposed even on foreign-invested firms. The restrictions on FDI were relaxed step by step, together with certain "supernational treatment" (of incentives) for foreign-owned enterprises and joint ventures. Over time, the government also started to relax restrictions on foreign borrowing by corporations (and take steps to expand the set of Chinese stocks listed on Shanghai's B-share market and the Hong Kong and U.S. stock exchanges). The government declared in the mid-1990s that it intended to implement capital account convertibility by 2000.

The psychological impact of the subsequent Asian financial crisis may have been profound. Several countries that China had regarded as role models for its own development process (especially Korea) went into deep crises in a very short period of time. It was a common perception among policymakers in China that the swings in the non-FDI part of the international capital flows had played a crucial role in the process. In this sense, the Asian financial crisis caused a rethinking of the Chinese approach to capital inflows. The idea of capital account liberalization by 2000 disappeared, and in its place rose the notion that the higher the level of foreign exchange reserves, the better the chance of avoiding painful crises.

9.5.1   Incentives and Distortions Affecting FDI

A more traditional explanation for the composition of China's capital inflows is that the unusually high share of FDI could reflect a policy mix of simultaneously discouraging foreign debt and foreign portfolio inflows while providing incentives for FDI.[25] Indeed, the existence of tax benefits for FDI has meant that, until recently, the playing field was in fact tilted in favor of foreign-funded firms. This was conceivably a part of an enlightened policy choice, which included restricting other types of inflows using capital controls.

Since China promulgated laws governing foreign investment at the start of the reform, the government has offered generous tax treatment to foreign firms. In the first two years that a foreign-invested firm makes a profit, it is exempt from corporate income tax. In subsequent years, foreign com-

---

25. Tseng and Zebregs (2002) discuss other factors that may have helped to attract FDI, such as market size, infrastructure, and the establishment of open economic zones, which have more liberal investment and trade regimes than other areas.

panies are subject to an average corporate income tax of 15 percent, less than half the normal rate of 33 percent paid by Chinese companies.

Tax exemptions and reductions constitute only one aspect of government incentives favoring FDI. To capture these incentives more comprehensively and to place the Chinese FDI regime in a cross-country comparative context, we now make use of the description of the legal FDI regimes for forty-nine countries in 2000 constructed by Wei (2000b), who in turn relied on detailed textual descriptions prepared by PricewaterhouseCoopers (PwC) in a series of country reports entitled "Doing Business and Investing in [the country that is the subject of the report]." The "Doing Business and Investing in . . ." series is written for multinational firms that intend to do business in a particular country. They are collected in one CD-ROM titled "Doing Business and Investing Worldwide" (PwC 2000). For each country, the relevant PwC country report covers a variety of legal and regulatory issues of interest to foreign investors, including restrictions on foreign investment and investors (typically chapter 5), investment incentives (typically chapter 4), and taxation of foreign corporations (typically chapter 16).

To convert the textual information in these reports into numerical codes, we read through the relevant chapters for all countries that the PwC series covers. PwC (2000) contains information on incentives for FDI in the following four categories:

1. Existence of special incentives to invest in certain industries or certain geographic areas
2. Tax concessions specific to foreign firms (including tax holidays and tax rebates, but excluding tax concessions specifically designed for export promotion, which is in a separate category)
3. Cash grants, subsidized loans, reduced rent for land use, or other nontax concessions, specific to foreign firms
4. Special promotion for exports (including existence of export processing zones, special economic zones, etc.)

For each category of incentives, we then created a dummy variable, which takes the value 1 if a particular type of incentive is present. An overall "FDI incentives" variable can then be constructed as the sum of the above four dummies. This variable takes a value of zero if there is no incentive in any of the categories, and 4 if there are incentives in all of them.

Of the forty-nine countries for which one can obtain information, none has incentives in all four categories. The median number of incentives is 1 (mean = 1.65). China is one of only three countries that have incentives for FDI in three categories—the other two countries being Israel and Egypt. Therefore, based on this information, we might conclude that China offers more incentives to attract FDI than most countries in the world.

Of course, legal incentives are not the only things that matter for international investors. To obtain a more complete picture, one also has to look at legal restrictions. The same PwC source also offers information, in a standardized format, on the presence or absence of restrictions in four areas:

1. Existence of foreign exchange control (which may interfere with foreign firms' ability to import intermediate inputs or repatriate profits abroad)
2. Exclusion of foreign firms from certain strategic sectors (particularly national defense and mass media)
3. Exclusion of foreign firms from additional sectors that would otherwise be open in most developed countries
4. Restrictions on foreign ownership (e.g., they may not per permitted 100 percent ownership)

We generated dummy variables for each category of restrictions and created an overall "FDI restriction" variable that is equal to the sum of those four dummies. This variable takes the value of zero if there is no restriction in any category, and 4 if there are restrictions in all of them.

The median number of restrictions is 1 (mean = 1.69). Interesting, China is one of only five countries in the sample that place restrictions on FDI in all four categories. Different restrictions and incentives may have different effects on FDI, so they cannot be assigned equal weights. Notwithstanding this caveat, in terms of the overall legal regime, it is not obvious that China makes for a particularly attractive FDI destination (as of 2000).[26]

So far, we have been discussing explicit incentives and restrictions that are written into laws and regulations. Of course, there can be many other implicit incentives or restrictions that are nonetheless an important part of the overall investment climate in the mind of potential investors. For example, corruption and bureaucratic red tape raise business costs and are part of the implicit disincentives for investment. Statistical analyses by Wei (2000a, 2000b, 2000c) suggest that these costs are economically as well as statistically significant.

To sum up, while the Chinese laws and regulations offer many legal incentives to attract FDI, they should be placed in context along with many implicit disincentives as well as explicit legal restrictions in order to form a more complete assessment of the overall investment climate.

9.5.2 A Mercantilist Story

Another hypothesis for explaining China's pattern of capital inflows is that the encouragement of FDI inflows is part of a mercantilist strategy to

---

26. The regression analysis in Wei (2000b, 2001) suggests that these FDI incentive and restriction variables explain a part of the cross-country variation in inward FDI.

foster export-led growth, abetted by the maintenance of an undervalued exchange rate (see Dooley, Folkerts-Landau, and Garber 2004a, 2004b; henceforth DFG). The basic premise of DFG is that, with a large pool of surplus labor and a banking system that is assumed to be irremediably inefficient, a more appropriate growth strategy for China is to use FDI to spur "good" investment in the export sector and to maintain an undervalued exchange rate in order to maintain export competitiveness. To support this equilibrium, China allows manufacturers in its export markets (the U.S. market in particular) to bring in FDI and take advantage of the cheap labor to reap substantial profits, thereby building a constituency in the United States to inhibit any action to force China to change its exchange rate regime. In addition, China's purchase of U.S. government securities as a part of its reserve holdings acts as a collateral or insurance policy for foreign firms that invest in China.

While this is an intriguing story, the facts do not support it. For instance, most of the FDI inflows into China have come from countries that are exporting to China rather than importing from it (see section 9.2). Furthermore, it is worth noting that (a) China chose not to devalue in 1997–98, even though that would have increased its exports; (b) the massive buildup of foreign exchange reserves is a relatively recent phenomenon; and (c) for much of the two decades up to 2001, the Chinese currency was likely to be overvalued rather than undervalued according to the black market premium. Even if one were to accept the DFG approach as a sustainable one, there is a conceptual question of whether it is the right approach. To take just one aspect, the sheer size of domestic saving (more than $500 billion a year) eclipses FDI (at about $45–50 billion a year, an order of magnitude smaller). Hence, writing off the domestic banking sector and focusing solely on FDI-led growth can hardly be regarded as a reasonable strategy. In short, while the DFG story is a seductive one and has many plausible elements, it does not appear to be a viable overall approach to fostering sustainable growth in China.[27]

9.5.3   Institutions and Governance

A different possibility, suggested by the work of Yasheng Huang (2003), is that the dominant share of FDI in China's inflows over the past decade reflects deficiencies in domestic capital markets. In particular, private firms have faced discrimination relative to state-owned enterprises, from both the banking system (in terms of loan decisions by state-owned banks) and the equity market (in terms of approval of stock listings). As a result, private firms have taken advantage of pro-FDI policies in an unexpected way and used foreign joint ventures as a way to acquire needed capital in

27. Roubini (2004) and Goldstein and Lardy (2005) present broader arguments against the DFG story.

order to undertake investment. Foreign investors have presumably been willing to go along because they are appropriately compensated by their Chinese partners in the form of profit shares, even in cases where the foreign investors may have no particular technological, managerial, or marketing know-how to offer. If the Chinese financial system had no such discrimination in place, much of the foreign investment in the form of joint ventures might not have taken place. In this sense, the deficiency of the domestic financial system may have artificially raised the level of inward FDI.

This is an interesting hypothesis and may well explain part of the inward FDI in the 1980s. However, there is some mismatch between this hypothesis and the data, especially in terms of the time series patterns of FDI inflows. On the one hand, inward FDI has been increasing at a rapid rate—indeed, more than half of the cumulative stock of inward FDI can be accounted for by recent inflows over the period 1998–2003. This hypothesis would require a financial system ever more discriminatory of private firms. On the other hand, domestic banks have become increasingly willing to make loans to non-state-owned firms. Similarly, in the equity market, both the absolute number and the relative share of the non-state-owned firms in the two stock exchanges have been rising. Therefore, it seems to us that Huang's hypothesis is unlikely to be a major part of the explanation for the rapid rise in inward FDI in recent years.

Governance, which includes various aspects of public administration, is another potentially important determinant of the composition of inflows. Unlike other types of inflows, FDI that is used to build plants with joint ownership by Chinese entrepreneurs provides foreign investors with the best possibility of being able to successfully negotiate the bureaucratic maze in China. However, this is somewhat at odds with recent literature that has examined the role of weak institutions (e.g., those with a high level of corruption, lack of transparency, weak judicial system) in the volume and patterns of capital inflows. Low levels of transparency typically tend to discourage international portfolio investment (Gelos and Wei 2005). Weak public governance—especially rampant insider trading—tends to exacerbate stock market volatility, further discouraging foreign portfolio inflows (Du and Wei 2004). High corruption also tends to discourage FDI (Wei 2000a, 2000b). However, taken together, these factors are unlikely to explain the particular composition of the Chinese capital inflows, since weak public governance by itself should tend to tilt the composition away from FDI and toward foreign debt (Wei and Wu 2002).

It is not easy to empirically disentangle the various hypotheses that we have reviewed above to explain why China gets more FDI than other types of inflows. In our view, the nature of the capital controls regime and the incentives for FDI appear to have played a big part in encouraging FDI inflows. But the story is not quite that straightforward, since one would expect a counteracting effect from factors such as weak governance, legal restrictions on investment by foreigners, and poor legal infrastructure and property rights. Furthermore, it is useful to keep in mind that FDI inflow figures may have been artificially inflated by the incentives for disguising other forms of inflows as FDI in order to get around capital account restrictions and to take advantage of tax and other policies favoring FDI.

9.6   Concluding Remarks

In this paper, we have provided an overview of developments in China's capital inflows and analyzed the composition of these inflows in the context of a rapidly burgeoning literature on financial globalization. We have also examined a number of hypotheses for China's success in attracting FDI inflows. Further research will be needed to disentangle the competing explanations for this phenomenon, but there is little evidence that mercantilist stories are the right answer. Understanding the reasons for China's success in tilting inflows toward FDI is important, especially as China continues its integration into world financial market and becomes more exposed to the vagaries of these markets. China has done well so far in managing the risks associated with financial globalization, but major challenges remain to ensure that continued integration with financial markets does not worsen the risk-return trade-off.

Appendix A

Some Information on China's Foreign Holdings of U.S. Dollar Securities

China does not publicly report the currency composition of its foreign exchange reserves.[28] With its reserves at well over $600 billion and continuing to rise, there is growing interest in the question of what currencies and maturities these reserves are held in. The U.S. Treasury International Capital (TIC) System database is a popular source of data for attempting to shed some light on this issue. This appendix provides some information on China's holdings of U.S. dollar–denominated instruments that can be gleaned from this source—including a discussion of what can and cannot be learned from these data—and reviews the major caveats that should be kept in mind while analyzing these data.

One of the main TIC databases provides information on U.S. transac-

---

28. We are grateful to Eisuke Okada for his help in preparing this appendix and to Carol Bertaut for helping us to understand these data better. The descriptions and data reported here are taken from the U.S. Treasury web site: http://www.treas.gov/tic.

tions with foreigners in long-term domestic and foreign securities. The data are based on mandatory reports filed by banks, securities dealers, investors, and other entities resident in the United States that deal directly with foreign residents in purchases and sales of long-term securities—composed of equity and debt issues with an original maturity of more than one year—that are issued by the U.S. government and U.S. firms or by foreign governments and foreign-based firms.

These data reflect only transactions between U.S. residents and counterparties located outside the United States. Because they are designed to capture cross-border transactions on a U.S. balance-of-payments basis, these data do not necessarily indicate the country of beneficial owner or issuer, or the currency of denomination of securities.[29] This implies that purchases of U.S. securities by China could be significantly understated if any of these purchases are routed through financial intermediaries in other countries. Purchases of U.S. dollar–denominated instruments outside the United States would also not be captured here. Another key issue is that these numbers include not just purchases by central banks but also those by other financial institutions.

A different TIC data source, "U.S. Banking Liabilities to Foreigners," reports data on foreign holdings of short-term treasury bills and notes. The data from these two TIC sources are combined into a table showing major foreign holders of treasury securities that is available on the U.S. Treasury website. This table shows stock data including holdings of short-term treasury bills and certificates, estimated holdings of long-term treasury securities, and a small amount of nonmarketable treasury bonds and notes issued to foreigners.[30] The monthly figures for holdings of long-term treasury securities since end June 2003, for example, begin with accurate data for end June from the annual survey of foreign holdings of U.S. securities as of that date. Holdings are then estimated for the end of each successive month by adding to the previous month's figure the net foreign transactions in treasury bills, notes, and bonds during the month as reported in the securities transactions data. This process of estimation has created a data series with breaks at each new survey of foreign holdings of U.S. securities, which generally takes place every year or two.

There are country identification problems with these data as well. First, a custodial bias is introduced in the survey data when foreign owners of treasury securities entrust the safekeeping of their securities to financial institu-

29. For instance, if an intermediary in London were used by someone in India to buy a U.S. or Mexican security in the United States, that transaction would be recorded opposite the United Kingdom, not India.
30. Foreign holdings of short-term treasury bills are recorded at face value. Holdings of and transactions in long-term treasury securities are collected at market value (including commissions and taxes in the case of the transactions data), although no change is made to adjust these data to account for price changes occurring subsequent to the survey or transaction dates. Holdings of nonmarketable securities are included at current value.

tions in third countries. Second, since a large volume of cross-border transactions takes place in major international financial centers, the procedure of adding net transactions to the original survey positions for long-term marketable securities can generate large geographic distortions over time.

Data on net purchases of treasury bills (with original maturities of less than one year) can be derived from changes in the stock data for treasury bills as reported in "U.S. Banking Liabilities to Foreigners."

Panel A of table 9A.1 shows the net purchases of treasury bills and long-term domestic and foreign securities in the United States that are recorded against China. Over the period 2001–4, treasury instruments constitute about 43 percent of total net purchases over the period 2001–4, and government agency bonds account for 40 percent. One important point to note is that, during 2001–3, net purchases of government agency bonds exceeded purchases of treasury instruments by China. Another interesting point is that in 2004 net purchases of shorter-term treasury bills increased sharply, becoming as important as purchases of long-term treasury securities and government agency bonds.

How much of China's reserve accumulation could potentially be accounted for by these flows? Panel B of table 9A.1 shows the ratio of net purchases of treasury bills and long-term securities in the United States to China's foreign exchange reserve accumulation. This ratio has fluctuated considerably over the years.[31] It has fallen sharply in recent years, from over 1 in 2001 to 0.33 in 2004, suggesting a drop-off in the share of reserve accumulation that is flowing into U.S. instruments.

Panel C of table 9A.1 shows that China is now a large holder of U.S. Treasury securities (the second largest, in fact, behind only Japan). As of December 2004, China accounted for $194 billion of outstanding U.S. Treasury securities recorded against foreign holders (compared to $712 billion for Japan and $164 billion for the United Kingdom). Under some strong assumptions, these numbers could be read as suggesting that, as of December 2004, about 30 percent of China's foreign exchange reserves were held in U.S. Treasury instruments, down from 41 percent in January 2003. But the caveat about inadequate coverage of the TIC data may be especially relevant here.

Overall, one could infer suggestive evidence from the data presented in this appendix that China's purchases of U.S. Treasury securities and other U.S. dollar–denominated holdings may be accounting for a smaller proportion of its accumulation of foreign exchange reserves than in the past. These data should, however, be interpreted with extreme caution since they are subject to serious shortcomings (as clearly noted on the TIC web site itself, from which we have drawn many of the caveats discussed above).

---

31. A ratio above 1 suggests some reallocation of reserve holdings from outside to inside the United States.

Table 9A.1   China's purchases and holdings of U.S. financial instruments (in billions of U.S. dollars)

| | A: Net purchases of securities in the U.S. | | | | | | B: Annual flows | | | C: End-of-year stocks | | |
| | | Long-term securities | | | | | | | | | | |
	Total	Treasury bills	Treasury bonds	Government agency bonds	Corporate bonds and stocks	Foreign bonds and stocks	Net purchases of securities (1)	Foreign exchange reserves (2)	Ratio (1)/(2)	Holdings of U.S. Treasury securities (1)	Foreign exchange reserves (2)	Ratio (1)/(2)
1990	0.3	−0.2	0.3	0.0	0.0	0.2	0.3	5.5	0.06		11.1	
1991	0.6	0.0	0.1	0.0	0.0	0.4	0.6	10.6	0.06		21.7	
1992	5.3	0.3	3.4	0.5	0.7	0.4	5.3	−2.3	−2.32		19.4	
1993	0.7	−0.1	0.5	0.6	0.1	−0.3	0.7	1.8	0.39		21.2	
1994	16.1	3.7	12.2	0.5	0.1	−0.4	16.1	30.4	0.53		51.6	
1995	14.8	13.7	0.7	0.9	0.0	−0.4	14.8	22.0	0.67		73.6	
1996	14.6	−2.8	14.5	2.8	0.3	0.0	14.6	31.4	0.47		105.0	
1997	2.1	−7.4	8.2	1.7	0.1	−0.4	2.1	34.9	0.06		139.9	
1998	1.1	−4.1	2.6	0.9	0.0	1.7	1.1	5.1	0.21		145.0	
1999	14.7	−2.7	8.2	8.3	0.7	0.1	14.7	9.7	1.51		154.7	
2000	17.6	0.4	−4.0	18.8	0.7	1.6	17.6	10.9	1.61	60.3	165.6	0.36
2001	55.0	−0.9	19.1	26.0	6.7	4.1	55.0	46.6	1.18	78.6	212.2	0.37
2002	63.1	0.2	24.1	29.3	6.1	3.5	63.1	74.2	0.85	118.4	286.4	0.41
2003	68.4	0.3	30.1	29.4	4.5	4.0	68.4	161.8	0.42	157.7	448.3	0.35
2004	67.5	17.2	18.9	16.4	12.1	3.0	67.5	206.7	0.33	193.8	654.9	0.30

Sources: Treasury International Capital System, CEIC database, and authors' calculations.

Notes: The data in panel A are taken from the tables entitled "U.S. Banking Liabilities to Foreigners" and "U.S. Transactions with Foreigners in Long-Term Securities" on the U.S. Treasury web site (http://www.treas.gov/tic/). Treasury bills have an original maturity of less than one year. Treasury bonds include marketable treasury and federal bank bonds and notes with an original maturity of one year or longer. Government agency bonds include bonds of U.S. government corporations and federally sponsored agencies. The stock data on holdings of U.S. Treasury securities (panel C) are taken from "Major Foreign Holders of U.S. Treasury Securities" on the U.S. Treasury web site. Data on foreign exchange reserve increase in 2003 and corresponding stocks in 2003 and 2004 include the $45 billion used for bank recapitalization at the end of 2003. Note that the flow data on net purchases of treasury bills and treasury bonds in panel A cannot be fully reconciled with the estimated stock of treasury securities in panel C (e.g., for 2002 and 2003), because the stock data are rebenchmarked whenever a new survey is conducted.

Appendix B

Evolution of Capital Controls in China

This appendix provides an extensive chronology of controls on capital account transactions over the period 1980–January 2005.[32] It is drawn from the IMF's *Annual Reports on Exchange Arrangements and Exchange Restrictions* (various issues). Following a detailed description of controls existing in 1980, changes to those restrictions in each subsequent year are then listed. The reporting format for the capital account transactions changed in 1996, the year in which China accepted the obligations of Article VIII of the IMF's Articles of Agreement. Another detailed overview of the restrictions in place at the end of 1996 is therefore provided, followed by a listing of changes to those restrictions in subsequent years.

Existing Controls on Capital Transactions as of December 31, 1980

A policy of permitting foreign borrowing on a planned basis has been instituted. Loans for vital projects or projects that have a rapid rate of return are given priority approval. All sections and departments wishing to borrow abroad must prepare a plan showing the kinds of imports for which the loan is intended. Such plans must show the amount of foreign exchange needed and how much of this will be earned and how much borrowed from abroad. All such plans are submitted to the State Planning Commission, which reviews them in cooperation with the Foreign Investment Control Commission. If the imports are for new construction, the plans are also reviewed by the State Construction Commission (all three commissions are under the supervision of the State Council).

Approval of foreign loans is based on a consideration of the need for foreign capital, and the ability of the borrowing unit to repay, and the overall debt-service ratio of China. Most loans are made through the Bank of China or, in the case of some loans to provinces or enterprises that are able to repay the loan themselves, with Bank of China guarantees. External borrowing plans by entities other than the Bank of China must be submitted to the State General Administration of Exchange Control (SGAEC) and the Foreign Investment Control Commission for approval, before loans from abroad or from the Hong Kong and Macao regions can be incurred. Resident organizations may not issue securities for foreign exchange unless approved by the State Council.

All foreign investment projects are subject to the approval of the Foreign Investment Control Commission. The policy with respect to foreign capital is designed both to make up the insufficiency of domestic capital and to

---

32. We are indebted to Qing Wang for his help in preparing this appendix.

facilitate the introduction of modern technology and management. All foreign exchange earned by joint ventures should be kept in a Bank of China account. Transfers of capital require SGAEC approval. When a joint venture is wound up, the net claims belonging to the foreign investor may be remitted with SGAEC approval through the foreign exchange account of the joint venture. Alternatively, the foreign investor may apply for repayment of his paid-in capital.

Profits of joint ventures, besides firms in special export zones and those exploiting petroleum, natural gas, and other resources, are subject to tax at 33 percent (30 percent basis rate plus a 10 percent surcharge on the assessed tax). As mentioned above, remitted profits are subject to an additional tax of 10 percent. A joint venture scheduled to operate for ten years or more may be exempted from income tax in the first year of operation and be allowed a 50 percent reduction for the second and third years. Joint ventures in low-profit operations, or those located in remote, economically underdeveloped outlying areas, may be allowed a further 15–30 percent reduction in income tax for the following ten years. A participant in a joint venture that reinvests its share of profit in China for a period of not less than five years may obtain a refund of 40 percent of the tax paid on the reinvested amount. Some joint ventures concluded before the passing of tax regulations in August 1980 are subject to taxes at different rates.

Foreign investment by Chinese enterprises is subject to approval; profits thereby earned must be sold to the Bank of China, except for a working balance. Chinese diplomatic and commercial organizations abroad and undertakings abroad and in Hong Kong and Macao are required to draw up annual foreign exchange plans.

Changes during 1981

None.

Changes during 1982

January 1. The Law on Income Taxes for Foreign Enterprises, which was adopted by the National People's Congress on December 13, 1981, came into force.

January 30. The State Council promulgated regulations on the exploitation of offshore petroleum resources in cooperation with foreign enterprises.

March 6. The Bank of China decided (a) to grant foreign currency loans at preferential interest rates to support the development of export commodities, projects of energy saving most pressing to the state, technical transformation of enterprises of light industries (including the textile and engineering industries), purchases by domestic enterprises of raw and semifinished materials in short supply, and projects of the packing industry; and (b) to finance export services relating to projects contracted with foreign countries.

Changes during 1983

January 1. The tax rate on income earned by foreign firms from interest on loans in respect of contracts signed during the period of 1983–85 was reduced by 50 percent; a similar reduction was extended to income earned from agriculture, energy development, communications and transport, education, and scientific research.

August 1. New rules (approved by the State Council on July 19, 1983) were introduced for the implementation of exchange controls in respect of enterprises with foreign and overseas Chinese capital and joint ventures.

September 2. The Standing Committee of the National People's Congress approved certain changes in the income tax law for joint ventures.

September 20. The State Council issued a body of regulations for the implementation of the law on joint ventures involving China and foreign capitals.

Changes during 1984

January 23. The State Council announced that Shanghai region would be given the authority to approve FDI projects to a value of up to US$10 million.

April 27. The State Council announced that fourteen selected coastal cities would be allowed to open up further to the outside world, in order to help speed up the introduction of advanced foreign technologies, notably through FDI.

May 3. The harbor city of Beihai, one of the fourteen coastal cities selected by the State Council for wider opening up to the outside world, was officially designated as an economic and technological development zone opened to FDI by small and medium-sized electronics and light industry enterprises. Foreign nationals investing in Beihai would be given a preferential tax treatment similar to that prevailing in the four special economic zones.

June 6. The municipality of Shanghai announced that foreigners investing in the economic and technological development zone in Shanghai would be given preferential tax treatment in regard to local income tax, comparable to the tax treatment provided in the Shenzhen economic zones.

July 14. As part of various steps announced by the State Council with the objective of speeding up a wider opening up of the fourteen designated coastal cities to the outside world, it was decided that these cities would not have the status of the existing special economic zones but would be allowed, at their own initiative, to offer additional tax incentives to foreign investors providing advanced technology. In addition, such cities could set up special economic and technological development areas where the 10 percent tax on profits remitted abroad by foreign investors would be waived. As in the special economic zones, the profits of joint venture established in the designated areas would be subject to a 15 percent income tax, and machinery, equipment, and other inputs imported by or for joint ventures operating in the fourteen coastal cities would be exempt from customs duties as well as from the consolidated industrial and commercial tax. Exports would also be exempt from export duties, and a certain proportion of products requiring advanced manufacturing techniques would be permitted to be marketed domestically.

July 31. Joint ventures operating in the fourteen coastal cities were formally made subject to an income tax of only 15 percent (instead of the standard 33 percent), with the approval of the Ministry of Finance. In addition, the 10 percent tax on onward remittances of foreign investment income would be waived if the foreign investment was undertaken in designated economic and technological development areas in these cities.

August 20. Special foreign currency lending facilities were set up by the Bank of China and the Industrial and Commercial Bank of China for domestic borrowers to help finance imports of advanced foreign technology.

September 1. Authorization was granted for the State Administration of Exchange Control (SAEC) and the Bank of China to settle payments of outstanding foreign currency debts of foreign and overseas Chinese banks in China (including branches undergoing or already in liquidation) that were contracted through 1949.

November 7. The Industrial and Commercial Bank of China was authorized to carry out business transactions in foreign exchange in the special economic zones.

November 19. New provisional regulations concerning the application of income taxes and the consolidated industrial and commerce tax in the special economic zones and in the new technology development zone in fourteen newly opened-up coastal cities were issued by the State Council. The income taxes payable by joint ventures in the specified zones and areas would be reduced from the standard rate of 33 percent to 15 percent, with the approval of the Ministry of Finance. Income taxes for other long-term industrial, communication, transport, agricultural, and service trade undertakings in their first one or two profit-taking years would be waived with the approval of the taxation authority, and reductions of 50 percent would be allowed in the following two or three years, but profits made by the older sectors of the fourteen coastal cities would be subject to taxation by up to 80 percent of the standard tax rate of 33 percent. In addition, consolidated industrial and commercial tax exemptions would be granted on imports of machinery and equipment, raw materials, building supplies, spare parts, other specified inputs, and exports other than those controlled by the state. Foreign participants in the joint ventures in these zones and areas were also allowed to remit their share of the profits overseas tax free, but a 10 percent tax was levied on income from royalties, dividends, interest, and rentals, compared with the standard rate of 20 percent elsewhere in China. The exemption and reductions of income tax were made applicable to the whole of 1984, while the exemption and reductions of industrial and commercial consolidated tax were to take effect from December 1, 1984.

December 13. In a move aimed at attracting FDI, the municipal authorities of Shanghai announced new concessions on tax and other policies, including reduced customs duties and preferential access to specified domestic markets. In addition, the income tax could, with approval from the Ministry of Finance, be decreased to 15 percent on condition that the project be operated with advanced technology or that the investment be for over US$30 million, and customs duties on certain imported equipment and raw materials could be waived.

December 22. Foreign banks were allowed to accept deposits from foreign organizations, nonresidents, enterprises with foreign capital as well as capital belong to overseas Chinese, and Chinese and foreign joint ventures, and to make loans in foreign currency in Shanghai.

Changes during 1985

January 3. New plans to open four large industrial regions to foreign investment and trade were announced. The move represented the third stage in China's current open-door policy, following experiments in the four special economic zones and the fourteen coastal cities.

March 14. Regulations governing the establishment of foreign joint ventures in Shanghai were relaxed.

March 15. China and India signed a three-year agreement to develop economic and trade relations; the accord provided for encouraging joint ventures, the creating of consultancy services, the exchange of economic, trade, and technical delegations; and participation in international fairs in the two countries.

March 26. The Foreign Economic Contract Law was adopted.

April 1. The Chinese Patent Law, enacted in 1984, came into effect. In addition, China joined the Paris Convention for the Protection of Industrial Property.

April 1. The Ministry of Petroleum and Industry announced that foreign oil companies would be allowed to participate in exploration and development of oil and gas reserves in nine provinces and one autonomous region.

April 2. The State Council introduced a regulation on the control of foreign banks and joint venture banks in special economic zones.

August 22. China approved the establishment of the first foreign branch bank office in the country since 1949. In addition, the Hong Kong and Shanghai Banking Corporation (HSBC) announced a plan to begin branch operations in Shenzhen, a special economic zone, in October 1985.

November 6. China and Libya signed a protocol aimed at consolidating bilateral cooperation between the two countries.

December 3. A joint venture bank, the first with foreign capital participation, was opened in Xiamen, a special economic zone, with the Panin Group of Hong Kong.

Changes during 1986

None.

Changes during 1987

February 5. Provisional regulations were approved permitting financial institutions and enterprises with sources of foreign exchange income to guarantee foreign exchange obligations of other debtors.

August 27. Provisional regulations were issued on a new system requiring the timely registration of external borrowing with the State Administration of Foreign Exchange (SAFE).

Changes during 1988

April 13. The National People's Congress adopted a new Chinese-foreign cooperative joint ventures law.

Changes during 1989

February 14. The State Council issued regulations that all foreign commercial borrowing required the approval of the People's Bank of China (PBC). All commercial borrowing is to be channeled through one of ten domestic entities—the Bank of China, the Communications Bank of China, the China International Trust and Investment Corporation, the China Investment Bank, and six regional international trust and investment corporations. The short-term debt of each entity may not exceed 20 percent of the entity's total debt, and short-term borrowing is to be used only for working capital purposes.

March 6. The SAEC announced procedures governing Chinese direct investment abroad. Such investments would require government and

SAEC approval, a deposit of 5 percent of the investment to secure repatriation of dividends and other income from the investment, and repatriation of earnings within six months.

Changes during 1990

April 4. The National People's Congress adopted an amendment to the law on Chinese foreign equity joint ventures. The amendment stipulated that the state would not nationalize joint ventures, simplified the approval procedures for new foreign investment enterprises (requiring a decision by the competent government authority within three months), and extended the management rights of foreigners (including permitting foreigners to assume the chairmanship of the board of directors of joint ventures).

May 14. The Shanghai City Government announced plans for the development of the Pudong New Area (an area adjacent to Shanghai that covers 135 square miles). It was envisaged that the multibillion-dollar project would take thirty to forty years to complete. To attract foreign capital into the area, Chinese foreign joint ventures were to be offered tax incentives similar to those available in the special economic zones, and overseas businesses would be permitted to invest in the construction of airports, ports, railways, highways, and utilities, as well as to open foreign bank branches in Shanghai. Detailed regulations were announced in October 1990.

May 19. The State Council issued regulations for the sale and transfer of land use rights in cities and towns to encourage foreign investors to plan long-term investment. Under these regulations, companies, enterprises, other organizations, and individuals within and outside China would be permitted to obtain land use rights and undertake land development. The maximum period for land use rights ranged from forty years for commercial, tourism, or recreational users to fifty years for industrial use and seventy years for residential use. The State Council issued provisional regulations for investment in large tracts of land to attract foreign firms' investment in tract development. Under these regulations, tract development referred to the obtaining of land use rights for state land and the development of infrastructure and other investments.

Changes during 1991

April 9. The National People's Congress adopted the Law Concerning the Income Tax of Foreign-Funded Enterprises and Foreign Enterprises and eliminated a 10 percent tax imposed on distributed profits remitted abroad by the foreign investors in foreign-funded enterprises. This law unified the tax rates for Chinese foreign equity joint ventures and wholly owned foreign enterprise. It would also provide for more tax benefits in the priority industrial sectors, with effect from July 1, 1991.

September 26. "Regulations on Borrowing Overseas of Commercial Loans by Resident Institutions" and "Rules on Foreign Exchange Guarantee by Resident Institutions in China" were issued.

Changes during 1992

March 1. The policy on foreign trade and investment was further liberalized, opening a large number of inland and border areas to such activities.

Changes during 1993

None.

Changes during 1994

None.

Changes during 1995

None.

Changes during 1996

September 25. The Regulation on External Guarantees Provided by Domestic Entities was passed, allowing for the provision of guarantees by authorized financial institutions and nonfinancial legal entities that had foreign exchange receipt.

Existing Controls on Capital Transactions as of December 31, 1996

Controls on Capital and Money Market Instruments

On capital market securities

Purchase locally by nonresidents	Nonresidents may only purchase B shares. The face value of B shares is denominated in renminbi, which are listed on the Chinese Securities Exchange and can only be bought by foreign investors.

Sale or issue locally by nonresidents	These transactions are not permitted.
Purchase abroad by residents	Residents, except financial institutions permitted to engage in foreign borrowing and authorized industrial and trade enterprises or groups, are not permitted to purchase securities abroad. A qualifications review by the SAFE is required for financial institutions to purchase securities abroad.
Sale or issue abroad by residents	Prior approval by the PBC, the SAFE, or the Securities Supervisory Board is required. Issuing bonds abroad must be integrated within the state's plan for utilizing foreign capital. Bonds can only be issued by financial institutions approved by the PBC.

On money market instruments

Purchase locally by nonresidents	Nonresidents are not allowed to purchase money market instruments.
Sale or issue locally by nonresidents	Nonresidents are not allowed to sell or issue money market instruments.
Purchase abroad by residents	Residents, except financial institutions permitted to engage in foreign borrowing, and authorized industrial and trade enterprises or groups are not allowed to purchase money market instruments. Financial institutions must undergo a review of qualifications by the SAFE before purchasing foreign money market instruments.
Sale or issue abroad by residents	Sale or issue abroad of securities, other than stocks, requires PBC and SAFE approval.

On collective investment securities

Purchase locally by nonresidents	These transactions are not allowed.
Sale or issue locally by nonresidents	There are no regulations, and if these instruments are traded they must be approved by the Securities Policy Commission.
Purchase abroad by residents	Same regulations as for purchase of money market instruments apply.
Sale or issue abroad by residents	Same regulations as for sale or issue of money market instruments apply.

Controls on Derivatives and Other Instruments

Purchase locally by nonresidents	These transactions are not allowed.
Sale or issue locally by nonresidents	These transactions are not allowed.

Purchase abroad by residents	Operations in such instruments by financial institutions are subject to prior review of qualifications and to limits on open foreign exchange positions.
Sale or issue abroad by residents	Same regulations as for purchases apply.

Controls on Credit Operations

Commercial credits

By residents to nonresidents	Industrial and commercial enterprises may not provide lending to nonresidents. Provision of loans to nonresidents by financial institutions is subject to review of qualifications by the SAFE and to a foreign exchange asset-liability ratio requirement.
To residents from nonresidents	Only financial institutions permitted by the SAFE to engage in external borrowing and authorized industrial and commercial enterprises or groups can engage in external borrowing of commercial credit. For credit over one-year maturity, the loan must be part of the state plan for utilizing foreign capital and must be approved by the SAFE. Short-term commercial credit (with a maturity of one year or less) is subject to foreign exchange balance requirements. Financial institutions permitted to engage in foreign borrowing are free to conduct short-term foreign borrowing within the target balance without obtaining approval, but must register the borrowing with the SAFE.

Short-term foreign financing with maturity of three months or less provided to enterprises—excluding foreign funded enterprises (FFEs)—is not subject to limitations, but short-term financing of longer than three months is subject to short-term foreign exchange balance requirements, and the borrowing must be registered with the SAFE.

FFEs may borrow from nonresidents without obtaining approval, but must report the borrowing to SAFE.

Financial credits	Same regulations as for commercial credits apply.

Guarantees, sureties, and financial backup facilities

By residents to nonresidents	The regulation on External Guarantees Provided by Domestic Entities of September 1996 allows

the provision of guarantees by authorized financial institutions and nonfinancial legal entities
that have foreign exchange receipts. Government
agencies or institutions cannot provide guarantees.

Controls on Direct Investment

Outward direct investment	Foreign exchange is provided for the investment after a SAFE review of sources of foreign exchange assets and an assessment of the investment risk involved, approval by the Ministry of Foreign Trade and Economic Cooperation (MOFTEC), and registration with the SAFE.
Inward direct investment	As long as nonresidents meet requirements under Sino-foreign joint venture laws and other relevant regulations, and are approved by MOFTEC, non-residents are free to invest in China. There is no restriction on the inward remittance of funds as far as exchange control is concerned. For environmental and security reasons, inward direct investment in some industries is prohibited.

Controls on Liquidation of Direct Investment

None.

Controls on Real Estate Transactions

Purchase abroad by residents	Same regulations as for direct investment apply.
Purchase locally by nonresidents	Same regulations as for direct investment apply.
Sale locally by nonresidents	Not available.

Provisions Specific to Commercial Banks and Other Credit Institutions

Borrowing abroad	Same regulations as for commercial credits apply.
Maintenance of accounts abroad	Prior approval by the SAFE is required for domestic entities opening foreign exchange accounts abroad.
Lending to nonresidents (financial or commercial credits	Lending is allowed subject to review of qualifications by the SAFE and to asset-liability ratio requirements.
Lending locally in foreign exchange	Lending is mainly subject to qualifications review by the SAFE and to asset-liability ratio requirements.

Purchase of locally issued securities denominated in foreign exchange	China does not issue securities denominated in foreign currency.

Differential Treatment of Nonresident Deposit Accounts and/or Deposit Accounts in Foreign Exchange

Reserve requirements	There are different reserve requirements for deposits in renminbi and in foreign currency, and also between the latter in domestic banks and in FFEs (i.e., 13 percent for deposits in renminbi, 5 percent for any foreign currency deposit in domestic banks, and 3 percent for deposits in foreign currency for over three months and 5 percent for less than three months, in FFEs).
Liquid asset requirements	Bank foreign exchange liquid assets (one year or less) should not be less than 60 percent of liquid liabilities (one year or less) and 30 percent of total foreign exchange assets. Total deposits with three-month maturities, deposits in both domestic and foreign banks, funds used for purchasing transferable foreign currency–denominated securities, deposits with the central bank, and cash holdings should not be less than 15 percent of total foreign exchange assets. Nonbank foreign exchange liquid assets (one year or less) should not be less than 60 percent of liquid liabilities (one year or less) and 25 percent of total assets. Total deposits with three-month maturities, deposits in both domestic and foreign banks, funds used for purchasing transferable foreign currency–denominated securities, deposits with the central bank, and cash holdings should not be less than 10 percent of total assets.
Credit controls	Total loans, investment guarantees (calculated as 50 percent of the balance guaranteed), and other foreign exchange credits provided to a legal entity by banks or nonbank financial institutions should not exceed 30 percent of the foreign exchange capital owned by the banks or nonbank financial institutions.
Investment regulations	Bank equity investment should not exceed the difference between bank capital and mandatory paid-in capital. Nonbank financial institutions'

	total equity investment (excluding trust accounts) should not exceed the difference between their capital and mandatory paid-in capital.
Open foreign exchange position limits	For financial institutions trading foreign exchange on their own behalf, the daily total amount traded (total open foreign exchange position) should not exceed 20 percent of the foreign exchange working capital. As authorized by the highest level of management, financial institutions trading foreign exchange on their own behalf may retain a small amount of overnight open position, but this should not exceed 1 percent of the foreign exchange working capital.

Provisions Specific to Institutional Investors

None.

Changes during 1997

None.

Changes during 1998

Controls on capital and money market instruments	*January 1.* Regulations for issuing bonds denominated in foreign currency by domestic institutions were issued.
Controls on credit operations	*January 1.* The implementation bylaws of regulations for external guarantees by domestic institutions were issued. Forward letters of credit (LCs) with a maturity exceeding 90 days and less than 365 days were included in the category of short-term credit, while those exceeding one year were included in the category of medium- and long-term international commercial loans. External borrowing regulations were changed.
	August 20. Enterprises were barred from advance prepayment of debt.

Changes during 1999

Controls on credit operations	*July 15.* Some controls on renminbi loans to FFEs under foreign exchange liens or guarantees were eased.

Changes during 2000

None.

Changes during 2001

Controls on capital and money market instruments

February 22. Domestic investors were allowed to purchase B shares with existing foreign currency deposits.

June 1. Domestic investors were allowed to purchase B shares with new foreign currency deposits.

Controls on credit operations

September 19. Restrictions were liberalized on purchases of foreign exchange for advance repayments of domestic and foreign currency loans, loans converted from foreign debt, and foreign debts, as follows: if the loan contract contains an advance repayment clause, the party may use its own foreign exchange to make advance repayment, subject to SAFE approval; and, subject to SAFE approval, a party may purchase foreign exchange to make advance repayments of loans, including (a) loans made with approval of the State Council; (b) loans for enterprise debt restructuring, for permanent or temporary closure, or for merger or transfer of ownership due to a change in national policy; and (c) loans where advance repayments are deemed necessary by a court.

Controls on direct investment

September 19. The purchase of foreign exchange was authorized for investments abroad in strategic foreign projects that have been approved by the State Council, projects that entail importing of materials into China for processing, and foreign aid projects.

Changes during 2002

Controls on capital and money market instruments

September 1. Prior approval by the China Securities Regulatory Commission (CSRC) was required for overseas listed domestic companies (OLDCs) and China-held foreign listed companies (CHFLCs) to sell shares overseas. The foreign exchange proceeds must not be retained overseas without SAFE approval and must be repatriated within thirty days and kept in OLDCs' foreign exchange accounts or converted into renminbi (with SAFE approval).

December 1. Qualified foreign institutional investors (QFIIs) were allowed to invest domestically in A shares, subject to restrictions.

Controls on direct investment

April 1. A new four-tier classification was introduced, defining activities in which foreign investment is encouraged, permitted, restricted, or banned. As a result, many industries that were previously closed to foreign investment, particularly in the services sector, were opened.

Changes during 2003

Provisions specific to commercial banks and other credit institutions

January 1. Registration with and permission from the SAFE to repay the principal were no longer required for residents to borrow foreign exchange from domestic Chinese financial institutions.

Controls on direct investment

November 1. In some provinces and regions, the limit on outward investment was increased to the equivalent of US$3 million from US$1 million.

Provisions specific to commercial banks and other credit institutions

January 1. Registration with and permission from the SAFE to repay the principal were no longer required for residents to borrow foreign exchange from domestic Chinese financial institutions.

November 19. A memorandum of understanding between the Hong Kong Monetary Authority and the China Banking Regulatory Commission to share supervisory information on banks operating in mainland China and Hong Kong and to ensure that parent banks maintain effective control over their cross-border branches and subsidiaries came into effect.

Changes during 2004

Controls on capital market securities purchased locally by nonresidents

QFIIs may invest domestically in A shares, subject to the following restrictions: (a) a QFII must have minimum experience in the industry (five years for fund managers, thirty years for insurance companies) and the equivalent of at least US$10 billion in assets under management in the latest financial year and must be clear of any major irregularities in its home market over the past three years; (b) a QFII that is a bank must have assets that rank it among the top 100 internationally in the latest financial year; (c) a QFII that is an insurance or a securities company must have minimum paid-up capital of the equivalent of US$1 billion; and (d) ownership of any Chinese company listed on the Shanghai or Shenzhen stock exchange by a QFII may not exceed 10 percent, and the total shares owned by QFIIs in a single Chinese company may not exceed 20 percent. QFIIs must set up special renminbi accounts with domestic banks and use the services of domestic securities companies. Closed-end QFIIs may only remit capital after three years, in installments of no more than 20 percent of the total each time, at intervals of one month or more. Other QFIIs may only remit capital after one year, in installments of no more than 20 percent of the total, and at intervals of three months or longer.

Provisions specific to commercial banks and other credit institutions

January 1. Under the Closer Economic Partnership Arrangement, (a) the asset requirement for Hong Kong–incorporated banks to open branches in mainland China was reduced to US$6 billion from US$20 billion; (b) the requirement for setting up a representative office in mainland China before a Hong Kong bank establishes a joint-venture bank or joint-venture finance company in mainland China was lifted; and (c) for mainland China branches of Hong Kong banks to apply to conduct renminbi business, the minimum number of years of business operations on the mainland required of the banks was reduced to two years from three years.

The official ceiling on foreign bank ownership of a Chinese bank was raised to 25 percent (from 20 percent), and the ceiling for any one bank was increased to 20 percent (from 15 percent).

June 27. Domestic foreign-funded banks were not permitted to convert debt contracted abroad into renminbi and were not allowed to purchase foreign exchange for servicing such debts. Capital obtained through FDI could only be converted into renminbi upon proof of a domestic payment order.

| Inward direct investment | *June 27.* Capital remitted through FDI could only be converted to renminbi upon proof of domestic payment order. |
| Controls on personal capital movements | *December 1.* Foreign heirs, including those from Hong Kong and Macau, were permitted to take inheritances off of the mainland. Emigrants were allowed to take legally obtained personal assets with them; amounts up to US$200,000 could be moved without restriction, while amounts in excess of US$200,000 could be transferred in stages over a minimum of two years. |

Changes during January 2005

| Provisions specific to commercial banks and other credit institutions | *January 15.* The reserve requirements on deposits in renminbi and foreign currencies were unified at 3 percent. |

References

Aizenman, Joshua, and Nancy Marion. 2004. International reserve holdings with sovereign risk and costly tax collection. *Economic Journal* 114 (July): 569–91.

Borensztein, Eduardo, José De Gregorio, and Jong-Wha Lee. 1998. How does foreign direct investment affect growth? *Journal of International Economics* 45 (June): 115–35.

Boyreau-Debray, Genevieve, and Shang-Jin Wei. 2004. Pitfalls of a state-dominated financial system: Evidence from China. CEPR Discussion Paper no. 4471. London: Centre for Economic Policy Research.

Dooley, Michael P., Stijn Claessens, and Andrew Warner. 1995. Portfolio capital flows: Hot or cold? *World Bank Economic Review* 9 (1): 53–174.

Dooley, Michael P., David Folkerts-Landau, and Peter Garber. 2004a. Direct investment, rising real wages and the absorption of excess labor in the periphery. NBER Working Paper no. 10626. Cambridge, MA: National Bureau of Economic Research, July.

———. 2004b. The revived Bretton Woods system: The effects of periphery intervention and reserve management on interest rates and exchange rates in center countries. NBER Working Paper no. 10332. Cambridge, MA: National Bureau of Economic Research, March.

Du, Julan, and Shang-Jin Wei. 2004. Does insider trading raise market volatility? *Economic Journal* 114 (498): 916–42.

Dunaway, Steven, and Eswar Prasad. 2004. Interest rate liberalization in China. *International Herald-Tribune,* December 3.

Frankel, Jeffrey A. 2004. On the renminbi: The choice between adjustment under a fixed exchange rate and adjustment under a flexible rate. Harvard University, Kennedy School of Government. Unpublished manuscript.

Frankel, Jeffrey A., and Andrew Rose. 1996. Currency crashes in emerging markets: An empirical treatment. *Journal of International Economics* 41 (3–4): 351–66.

Funke, Michael, and Jorg Rahn. 2005. Just how undervalued is the Chinese renminbi? *World Economy* 28 (4): 465–89.

Gelos, Gastos R., and Shang-Jin Wei. 2005. Transparency and international portfolio holdings. *Journal of Finance* 60 (6): 2987–3020.

Goldstein, Morris. 2004. Adjusting China's exchange rate policies. Institute for International Economics Working Paper no. 04/126. Washington, DC: Institute for International Economics.

Goldstein, Morris, and Nicholas R. Lardy. 2004. What kind of landing for the Chinese economy? Policy Briefs in International Economics no. PB04-7. Washington, DC: Institute for International Economics.

———. 2005. China's role in the revived Bretton Woods system: A case of mistaken identity. IIE Working Paper no. 05-2. Washington, DC: Institute for International Economics.

Gunter, Frank R. 2004. Capital flight from China. *China Economic Review* 15:63–85.

Huang, Yasheng. 2003. *Selling China: Foreign direct investment during the reform era.* Cambridge: Cambridge University Press.

International Monetary Fund (IMF). 2004. People's Republic of China: Article IV consultation—staff report. Washington, DC: International Monetary Fund.

Kaminsky, Graciela, Carmen Reinhart, and Carlos Végh. 2004. When it rains, it pours: Procyclical capital flows and macroeconomic policies. In *NBER macroeconomics annual 2004,* ed. Mark Gertler and Ken Rogoff, 11–82. Cambridge, MA: National Bureau of Economic Research.

Kose, M. Ayhan, Eswar S. Prasad, and Marco E. Terrones. 2003. Financial integration and macroeconomic volatility. *IMF Staff Papers* 50:119–42.

Prasad, Eswar, ed. 2004. China's growth and integration into the world economy: Prospects and challenges. IMF Occasional Paper no. 232. Washington, DC: International Monetary Fund.

Prasad, Eswar, Kenneth Rogoff, Shang-Jin Wei, and M. Ayhan Kose. 2003. The effects of financial globalization on developing countries: Some empirical evidence. IMF Occasional Paper no. 220. Washington, DC: International Monetary Fund.

Prasad, Eswar, Thomas Rumbaugh, and Qing Wang. 2005. Putting the cart before the horse? Capital account liberalization and exchange rate flexibility in China. IMF Policy Discussion Paper no. 05/1. Washington, DC: International Monetary Fund.

PricewaterhouseCoopers (PwC). 2000. Doing business and investing worldwide. New York: PricewaterhouseCooopers. CD-ROM.

Roubini, Nouriel. 2004. BW2: Are we back to a new stable Bretton Woods regime of global fixed exchange rates? Nouriel Roubini's Global Economics Blog, October 8. http://www.roubiniglobal.com/archives/2004/10/are_we_back_to.html.

Tseng, Wanda, and Harm Zebregs. 2002. FDI in China: Lessons for other countries. IMF Policy Discussion Paper no. 02/3. Washington, DC: International Monetary Fund.

Tytell, Irina, and Shang-Jin Wei. 2004. Does financial globalization induce better macroeconomic policies? Washington, DC: International Monetary Fund. Unpublished manuscript.

Wei, Shang-Jin. 2000a. How taxing is corruption on international investors? *Review of Economics and Statistics* 82 (1): 1–11.

———. 2000b. Local corruption and global capital flows. *Brookings Papers on Economic Activity,* Issue no. 2:303–54.

———. 2000c. Why does China attract so little foreign direct investment? In *The role of foreign direct investment in East Asian economic development,* ed. Takatoshi Ito and Anne O. Krueger, 239–61. Chicago: University of Chicago Press.

———. 2001. Domestic crony capitalism and international fickle capital: Is there a connection? *International Finance* 4 (1): 15–45.

Wei, Shang-Jin, and Yi Wu. 2002. Negative alchemy? Corruption, composition of capital flows, and currency crises. In *Preventing currency crises in emerging markets,* ed. Sebastian Edwards and Jeffrey Frankel, 461–501. Chicago: University of Chicago Press.

10

South Korea's Experience with International Capital Flows

Marcus Noland

South Korean economic performance over the last four decades has been nothing short of spectacular. During this period the country experienced only two years of negative growth—1980, in the wake of the second oil shock and the assassination of President Park Chung-Hee, and 1998, in the midst of the Asian financial crisis (figure 10.1). Between the initiation of a wide-ranging economic reform program by Park in 1963 and the financial crisis in 1997, real per capita income growth measured in purchasing power adjusted terms averaged more than 6 percent annually, and per capita income stood at more than eight times its level when reforms began. According to the Penn World Tables, at the start of that period the country's income level was lower than that of Bolivia and Mozambique; by the end it was higher than that of Greece and Portugal.[1]

Most economists would probably subscribe to the rough notion that more complete markets are preferable to less complete markets. In the case of financial markets, there is a large theoretical and empirical literature supporting the notion that the development of local financial markets and their integration into international markets encourages a variety of desirable outcomes. Yet during its period of rapid growth, South Korea deliberately eschewed the purported gains of international financial integration and instead maintained extensive controls on international capital flows as

Marcus Noland is a senior fellow at the Institute for International Economics.

I would like to thank Paul Karner for research assistance and participants in the National Bureau of Economic Research preconference for comments on an earlier draft.

1. South Korea was "deceptively poor" in the 1950s, in that per capita income was unusually low relative to human capital (Noland and Pack 2002, table 2.1), a situation presumably explained in large part by the destruction of much of the physical capital stock during the Korean War (1950–53). That said, South Korea also accumulated human capital extremely rapidly relative to other large developing countries of that era (Noland and Pack 2002, figure 2.3).

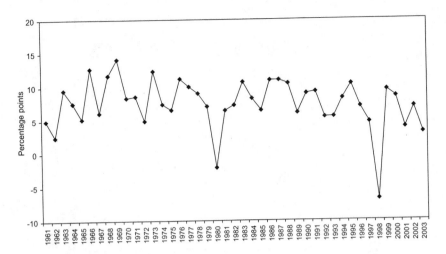

Fig. 10.1   South Korean real GDP growth, 1961–2003
Source: World Development Indicators 2004.

part of a more general policy of financial repression undertaken in the context of a state-led development strategy. In other words, rapid sustained growth occurred in the presence of capital controls for a period of several decades. This is not to argue that capital controls were causal: this paper will not speculate on the counterfactual of what South Korean economic performance might have been under a different policy package, but will simply acknowledge that this period of rapid growth coincided with the existence of capital controls, and that these controls and the delinking of domestic and international financial markets was an essential component of the country's state-led development strategy.

Problems arose as the country approached the international technological frontier and opportunities for easy technological catch-up began to erode. The disappearance of straightforward paths for industrial upgrading based on imitating the prior trajectories of more advanced economies put a heightened premium on the ability of corporate managements and their financiers to discern emerging profit opportunities. The old development strategy was no longer adequate, but decades of state-led growth had bureaucratized the financial system and created a formidable constellation of incumbent stakeholders opposed to liberalization and transition toward a more market-oriented development model. As rents dissipated, both financial and nonfinancial firms scrambled to claim the dwindling low-hanging fruit.

Under these conditions, the liberalization undertaken in the early 1990s was less a product of textbook economic analysis than of parochial politicking. A combination of South Korean policy, its accession to the Organization for Economic Cooperation and Development (OECD), and the Basel Accords on capital adequacy created unintended incentives for short-term bank borrowing. The highly leveraged nature of the South Korean economy, together with the currency and term mismatches embodied in the mid-1990s surge of foreign debt exposure, left the economy vulnerable to a variety of negative shocks, and in 1997, in the context of the broader Asian upheaval, South Korea experienced a financial crisis with net cleanup costs that eventually amounted to 16 percent of 2001 gross domestic product (GDP).[2] The South Korean case is interesting precisely because it combines in an unparalleled manner the characteristics of sustained success, capital controls, and financial crisis.

To preview the conclusions of this paper, capital controls were a necessary component of the state-led development process. The problem is that it is difficult to transition out of the state-led model—interventions create their own constituencies, and the 1990s liberalization was a function of political competition among domestic financial and corporate institutions over declining rents and foreign financial service providers seeking to enter the South Korean market.

Two concerns were expressed contemporaneously in South Korea about capital account liberalization—that it would adversely affect incumbent South Korean financial service firms and that it could be macroeconomically destabilizing. Systemic risk was sufficiently high that South Korea might well have experienced a financial crisis regardless of capital account liberalization; the liberalization program affected the timing, magnitude, and particulars of the crisis.

The degree of financial market integration between South Korea and the rest of the world is considerably higher as a result of the crisis-driven removal of capital controls. Yet the "dumbing down" of the financial system produced by decades of financial repression may have left lingering effects. South Korea seems to have emerged from the crisis relatively successfully, but concerns remain, largely centering on the apparent difficulty of changing the lending culture of until recently bureaucratized financial institutions and the counterpart challenge of improving the quality of market-oriented financial oversight by regulators more experienced in systems of greater direct command and control. In the specific historical and political circumstances of South Korea, whether the use of capital controls could have been separated from the more general policy of financial repression and more dynamic domestic financial markets fostered in their presence is an open question.

---

2. In these regards, the South Korean case is similar to those of Japan and Taiwan, which also combined state-led growth and capital controls, and in the 1990s experienced financial crises costing double-digit shares of GDP.

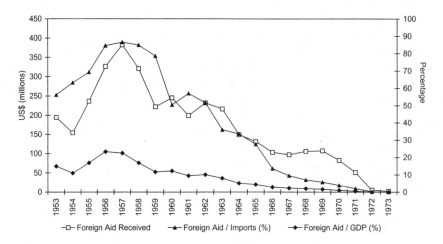

Fig. 10.2   Foreign aid to South Korea, 1953–73
Sources: Collins and Park (1989); World Bank's World Development Indicators; Bank of Korea.

10.1   Historical Context

South Korea inherited a legacy of financial repression from Japanese colonial occupation (1910–45) that carried into the period of independence (1948), reflecting the dirigiste character of Japanese colonial administration and the continuation of extensive controls by the U.S. military authorities in the immediate postwar period. A continuing theme throughout South Korean economic history has been the critical role of the state, its role in the generation of rents, and the politicization of their distribution, starting with the first postcolonial president of South Korea, Rhee Syng-Man, who exploited the policy-generated rents to build political power.[3] According to S. Cho (1994), South Korean economic policy was aimed at maximizing the value of American aid in the aftermath of the Korean War (1950–53), which had left the country devastated, and the ensuing Cold War standoff. Aid financed most capital accumulation and, at its peak in the late 1950s, more than half of imports (figure 10.2).

A military government led by General Park Chung-Hee took control in 1961. As shown in figure 10.3, when Park seized power, gross domestic saving net of aid was derisory. Gross investment, financed mostly by aid, stood at a bit more than 10 percent of GDP, and the current account was in rough balance. After two years of poor economic performance, the military government unified the existing multiple exchange rate system, devalued the

---

3. See Cargill (1999) for a comparison of the Japanese and South Korean financial systems. See Jones and SaKong (1980) and Woo (1991) for examples of the use of state-derived rents for political power building.

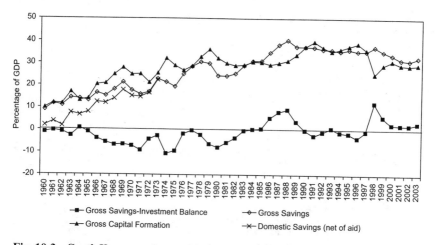

Fig. 10.3   South Korean savings and investment, 1960–2003
Source: Bank of Korea Economic Statistics System and *World Development Indicators* 2004.

currency, and initiated a series of wide-ranging reforms. After a brief experiment with floating, the currency was pegged to the U.S. dollar, and it would remain so until 1980 (Koo and Park 1990). Domestic saving net of aid began rising rapidly (looking at figure 10.3, one can understand why development economists adopted Rostow's take-off metaphor). Domestic investment began rising even faster.

While in some ways Park's reform package marked a fundamental departure from past practices (with respect to trade policy, for example), it retained an important role for the state in the development process. Pervasive regulatory entry barriers (and thus protection from competition for incumbents), and Park's penchant for sole-sourcing important infrastructural and other large-scale government-supported projects, in effect socialized risk and created opportunities for cross-subsidization across different business ventures, encouraging the *chaebol* (family-dominated conglomerates) to diversify into otherwise unrelated lines of business. By the 1980s, the top ten *chaebol* accounted for more than 20 percent of national income (SaKong 1993, table A.20). Bank of Korea independence was ended and the Bank made subservient to the Ministry of Finance and, ultimately, the Blue House.

The accumulation of capital contributed to rapid technological upgrading and a stunning transformation of the composition of output. In 1963 nonfuel primary products accounted for more than half of South Korea's exports, and human hair wigs were the third leading item. A decade later South Korea's exports were dominated by manufactures such as textiles, electrical products, and iron and steel; only one primary product category, fish, made the top ten. As seen in figure 10.3, capital accumulation was fi-

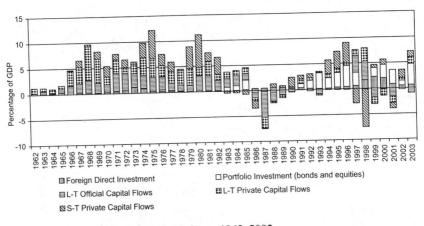

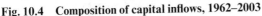

Fig. 10.4   Composition of capital inflows, 1962–2003

Sources: Park (1984); IMF Balance of Payments Statistics; Collins and Park (1989); Bank of Korea Economic Statistics System; *World Development Indicators* 2004; author's calculations.

Note: Portfolio investment is assumed to be zero from 1962 to 1973.

nanced primarily by growing domestic saving, augmented by a significant inflow of saving from abroad, reaching nearly 10 percent of GDP in 1971, and actually breaching this threshold in 1974 after the first oil shock.

These inflows predominately took the form of long-term loans and trade credits from private lenders and public institutions (including the multilateral development banks) all subject to Bank of Korea regulation (figure 10.4). Portfolio inflows and inward foreign direct investments were negligible during this period. A substantial academic literature exists (e.g., Westphal, Rhee, and Pursell 1981; Westphal, Kim, and Dahlman 1985) that attempts to understand the sources of South Korean industrial competence and that documents the varied forms of technological transfer and interaction between South Korean and foreign firms. Figure 10.4 indicates that whatever the origins of South Korean technical mastery, much of the foreign capital arrived in the form of technologically disembodied loans.

In 1972, Park, who had been reelected for a third term, pushed through the Yushin (Revitalization) Constitution, which in essence made him president for life. For a variety of reasons, he initiated the intensive promotion of heavy industry through what came to be known as the Heavy and Chemical Industry (HCI) policy. Modest financial-sector liberalizations that had been undertaken in the late 1960s were reversed in 1972, when interest rates were lowered and direct government control of the banking system was increased in order to channel capital to preferred sectors, projects, or firms (figure 10.5). In order to finance large-scale projects, special public financial institutions were established, and private commercial banks were instructed to make loans to strategic projects on a preferential basis. By the late 1970s, the share of these "policy loans" had risen to 60 percent (J.-H.

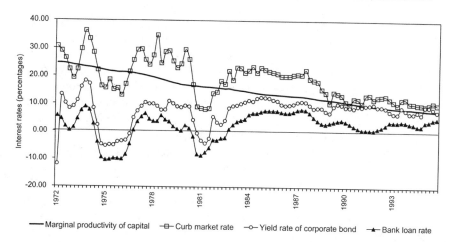

Fig. 10.5   Real interest rates
Source: D. Cho and Koh (1996).

Yoo 1994). These loans carried, on average, negative real interest rates, and the annual interest subsidy grew from about 3 percent of gross national product (GNP) in 1962–71 to approximately 10 percent of GNP on average between 1972 and 1979 (Pyo 1989).[4] With such a large share of national income at stake, the allocation of these highly subsidized loans became the focus of intense political activity.

Park was assassinated in 1979 during what amounted to a palace coup. General Chun Doo-Hwan and his fellow officers more or less stumbled into power, driven more by intramilitary rivalries and narrow career interests than by any real sense of where they wanted to take the country (Clifford 1997). Facing deteriorating economic performance, which was exacerbated by the second oil shock, Chun and his cronies turned to Western-trained economic technocrats, who were already attempting to introduce a stabilization policy and reverse the worst excesses of the HCI policy, to fix the economy and shore up the generals' political legitimacy.[5]

Despite at times carrying a large volume of fixed-interest loan debt, South Korea managed to avoided financial trouble until the early 1980s slowdown in global growth in the wake of the second oil shock. The external shocks that hit South Korea during the period 1979–1981 were actually larger than those experienced by a number of other countries discussed at

4. The definition of "policy loans" is imprecise, and various sources report significantly different figures. See S. Cho (1994) for discussion, and see SaKong (1993, tables A.18–A.19) and Krueger and Yoo (2002) for alternative calculations.

5. Chun literally scheduled early-morning tutoring sessions. Perhaps there is something peculiarly Korean about this: it is hard to imagine the typical military dictator staying up late to study for his daily economics lesson.

this conference, including Argentina, Brazil, Chile, and Mexico (Balassa 1985, table 1). Although external debt and debt service ratios had increased substantially in the late 1970s, South Korea was able to re-attain high sustained growth by 1983, more rapidly than its comparators, through a combination of a reduction in imports associated with a sharp, though brief, decline in income, together with real exchange rate depreciation achieved through a 20 percent nominal devaluation. (The currency had also been devalued by 20 percent in 1974 following the first oil shock.) This pattern of relatively a sharp income decline and real depreciation followed by rapid recovery was to be repeated in the 1997 crisis (J.-W. Lee and Rhee 2000). The technocrats around Chun implemented a policy of macroeconomic stabilization, through which they began to liberalize and deregulate the South Korean economy. A liberalization of the financial sector initiated under the Fifth Five-Year Plan (1982–86) and extended under the Sixth Five-Year Plan (1987–91) attenuated "policy lending."

10.1.1   Domestic Finance

The capital channeling development strategy pursued up through the 1980s rested on the twin pillars of financial repression and capital controls to delink the domestic and international financial markets. The government had to limit capital markets to institutions that could be dominated if not controlled, and it had to limit the firms' financing options to those institutions. At the core was a positive list system through which anything not explicitly permitted was prohibited. This hampered the introduction of new instruments throughout the financial sector. In practice this meant emphasizing indirect finance and maintaining limitations on foreign participation in financial markets and domestic firms' access to foreign capital. Presumptively less compliant foreign banks could not be allowed into the market in any significant way, for if they were allowed to establish a significant presence, they would undermine domestic banks operating under the burdens of "policy lending."[6] Thus, the financial system had to be built around a relatively small number of South Korean banks, and corporate finance had to be largely limited through regulatory fiat and tax provisions to borrowing from those intermediaries.

Alternative sources of corporate finance were suppressed: the development of money markets and bond markets was retarded and restricted to a limited range of maturities with no real secondary markets, and issuance was effectively dependent on bank guarantees. The government discouraged the development of an efficient auction and secondary market for

---

6. In the characterization of one South Korean economist, "Dominance of the Korean financial market by foreign institutions was abhorred, as it would deprive authority over various instruments of monetary control, weaken many customary, informal practices associated with industrial policy, and might also alter the public-good nature of the financial system" (C.-P. Lee 1993, p. 7).

government bonds, and no swap, bond, or interest futures markets existed. As for the stock market, in 1990 the government established a quarterly quota on new issues, and prior to the 1997 crisis a backlog of more than 360 companies was waiting to be listed (relative to the 776 that were already on the exchange). Criminal proceedings documented that firms were forced to resort to bribing officials to bring their initial public offerings to the market.[7] As a result of these policies, corporate capital sourced through bank loans exceeded equity, bonds, and commercial paper combined until the late 1980s, and indirect finance from all sources was the primary form of corporate finance until 1991 (Y. Cho 2002, table 4).

There were multiple implications of these policies. First, the firms emphasized growth, not profitability, since risk was socialized and increased borrowing made further borrowing advantageous under the "too big to fail" notion, promoted by the government's habitual interventions. From the standpoint of a lender, the bigger the firm, the more creditworthy the firm, since size increased the likelihood that the government would intervene in the event that the firm got into financial trouble, which it did on a fairly routine basis. The implication was that firms became extraordinarily leveraged as growth became the name of the game.[8] Loans were the mechanism for growth, and, paradoxically, debt signaled creditworthiness, a state of affairs that S.-M. Yoo (1999) described as the "survival of the fattest." Indeed, one study of corporate finance covering the decade 1977–86 found that "the largest firms have the weakest financial structure," as measured by the degree of equity in their capital structures (E. Kim 1990, p. 342), while another found that the major *chaebol* were systematically less profitable than other South Korean firms (Krueger and Yoo 2002). A corollary to this system of corporate financing was the encouragement of extensive cross-shareholding, cross-loan guarantees, and nontransparency, all of which served to facilitate borrowing and had the effect of disadvantaging outside shareholders.

10.1.2 Capital Controls

Comprehensive capital controls were used to insulate the domestic financial market from the global market.[9] Inward remittances were monitored to impede unauthorized foreign exchange transactions and inward investments. Inward foreign direct investment (FDI) was discouraged by

7. In June 1996, the governor of the Securities and Exchange Commission (SEC) and a director of the Ministry of Finance and Economy (MFE) were arrested for taking bribes to get firms listed. Six other SEC executives were forced to resign.

8. In July 1997, just prior to the crisis, the average debt-equity ratio of the thirty largest *chaebol* exceeded 400 percent (S.-M. Yoo 1999, table 9). By the end of 1997, it stood at 500 percent, and 600 percent of the debt of subsidiaries was included on a consolidated basis (Claessens, Ghosh, and Scott 1999). See also Krueger and Yoo (2002, table 6).

9. See Linder (1994) and S. Kim, Kim, and Wang (2001) for descriptions. The appendix contains a detailed chronology of the policies applied.

permitting entry only into a limited range of sectors, imposing minority ownership requirements, requiring technology transfer (in the absence of any intellectual property rights enforcement), and imposing strict export requirements. And while there were modest relaxations beginning in the late 1970s, actual FDI inflows remained minuscule until a wide-ranging liberalization was undertaken in response to the 1997 crisis (figure 10.4). On the eve of the crisis, South Korea and India were the only countries in Asia where the dominant modality of U.S. foreign investment was minority-stake joint ventures, as opposed to majority-stake joint ventures or wholly owned subsidiaries.

Stock market investment by nonresidents was prohibited until 1992, and then it was subject to stringent quantitative ceilings.[10] At the time of the 1997 crisis, foreign ownership of listed companies was limited to 20 percent of capital, with individual stakes limited to 5 percent. Investment by non-residents in domestic bonds was prohibited until 1996, and then it was subject to quantitative limitations. The local presence and activity of foreign financial institutions were highly circumscribed.

For much of this period outbound investment was similarly restricted. Domestic residents were not permitted to open foreign bank accounts or purchase foreign securities, nor were foreign entities permitted to issue won-denominated securities domestically. Export earning had to be repatriated within six months. Outward direct investment required official approval and was subject to regulations that had the effect of encouraging the intermediation of South Korean banks.[11]

The local currency, the won, was nonconvertible, and the South Korean government discouraged the development of any offshore market in won or won-denominated instruments. A rapid real appreciation of the Japanese yen beginning in 1985 encouraged a process of relocation of manufacturing activities from Japan to South Korea. The Bank of Korea accommodated the capital inflow, and between 1985 and 1989 the money supply increased by 105 percent, the price level rose by 3 percent, and the stock market increased by 458 percent, becoming the world's ninth largest in terms of capitalization.

In February 1980, following a 20 percent devaluation the previous month, South Korea moved off a strict dollar peg and began pegging the

---

10. Initially this was set at 10 percent in January 1992; it was raised to 12 percent in December 1994, 15 percent in July 1995, and 18 percent in April 1996. In June 1996, the government announced a further phased opening that would increase the ceiling to 20 percent in 1996, and 3 additional percentage points annually thereafter to 29 percent by 1999, and the government added that it might abolish the ceiling entirely in 2000 if "economic circumstances" were appropriate.

11. For example, there were restrictions on firms' ability to issue securities abroad and on contracting foreign loans at rates more than 100 basis points above the London interbank offered rate (LIBOR).

won to a basket of currencies that constituted the Special Drawing Right (whose respective weights in the basket were undisclosed) plus a "policy adjustment" factor. In the words of Jeffrey A. Frankel (1993), this was a basket peg "in name only." As observed by Balassa and Williamson (1990), the policy adjustment factor predominated: between 1984 and 1987 the won depreciated against all five currencies in the basket, generating an undervalued currency (I.-J. Kim 1993). The International Monetary Fund (IMF) was astute enough to classify South Korea's exchange rate regime as a managed float rather than a basket peg.

The undervalued won, the relocation of productive activities from Japan to South Korea, and expansionary macroeconomic policies in the United States, generated a growing bilateral surplus with the United States (Noland 1993). Through the experience of the yen-dollar talks, the U.S. political system had become enamored with negotiating with other countries over exchange rate and financial market policies. The United States initially sought to use the IMF's special consultative mechanism to pressure South Korea over its exchange rate policy despite the fact that as late as 1985 the IMF had been advising further depreciation of the won. Starting in 1986 the U.S. Treasury began publicly to pressure South Korea to revalue the won. Although Japan was the primary focus of the financial provisions of the Omnibus Trade and Competitiveness Act of 1988 (the "Trade Act"), South Korea emerged as a secondary target.

In its first three congressionally mandated reports under Section 3004 of the Trade Act, the Treasury identified South Korea as an "exchange rate manipulator," removing South Korea from the list in April 1990, after a new exchange rate management system called the market average exchange rate system was introduced. Under this arrangement, the mid-band won-dollar rate was calculated as an average of the previous day's transactions and then allowed to float within officially prescribed margins around this rate. In 1991 the government began a process of very gradually widening the bands, with the putative expectation that as the bands were widened a freely floating exchange rate would emerge (B. Kim 1993). Needless to say, things did not work out this way.

The pervasive pattern of government intervention created a symbiotic relationship between the government and the private sector, eroding private-sector autonomy and facilitating the corruption of the political system. The move toward more genuine political competition in the late 1980s arguably shifted the balance of power away from the government and toward the private sector, which became the source of badly needed campaign funds (Kang 2002a, 2002b). In the words of one contemporary observer, corruption "exploded" (Clifford 1997). With the exception of current president Roh Moo-Hyun, every South Korean president since Park Chung-Hee and/or at least one of his sons has been imprisoned on corruption offenses.

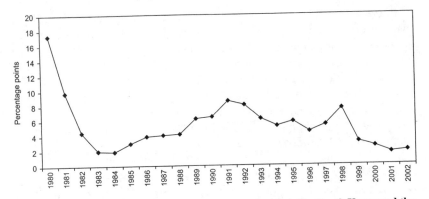

Fig. 10.6   Spread between long-term government bond yields, South Korea and the United States

Source: International Financial Statistics, IMF.

Notes: For Korea, the yield reported is on national housing bonds. For the United States, the yield reported is on the ten-year treasury note.

10.2   Financial Liberalization in the 1990s

Over time, pressure for liberalization developed both from domestic firms disadvantaged in international competition by relatively high domestic interest rates and limited options for corporate finance, and from the U.S. government, promoting the interests of American financial service providers (figure 10.6).[12] The outcome of this tension was a political compromise that resulted in a gradual, uneven, and ultimately problematic liberalization program that both contributed to and was overtaken by the 1997 financial crisis. (A chronology of policies actually applied is provided in the appendix.)

The United States had begun pressuring South Korea for improved market access for U.S. financial services providers in the late 1980s, initiating a more or less ongoing process of bilateral consultations on the issue of financial market liberalization. The conclusion of the Sixth Five-Year Plan (1986–91) provided treasury officials an opening to talk to their South Korean counterparts about "the vision thing."[13] Some commentators (Park,

---

12. In figure 10.6 the interest rate differential is calculated as the difference between yields on South Korean won-denominated ten-year government bonds and U.S. government bonds of the same maturity. If one expected the Balassa-Samuelson effect to hold and the won to appreciate in real terms over the long run, then, from the standpoint of a South Korean firm, the implicit differential was even larger.

13. Wang Yen-Kyun (1993, p. 186) quotes the November 1991 treasury report to Congress mandated under Section 3004 of the Trade Act as reading in part, "Most troubling at this stage is that the Korean government appears to lack a 'vision' and well-defined strategy for the liberalization of its financial markets. [Recent reforms] are steps in the right direction but do not appear to go fast enough."

Song, and Wang 2003) argue that these discussions formed the basis of the first of a series of multiyear financial sector policy plans, the most important of which was promulgated in 1995 and scheduled to run through 1999 (Kwon 1996).[14] Additional reforms were announced as part of South Korea's 1996 accession to the OECD, which itself was undertaken for largely politically symbolic reasons by President Kim Young-Sam. Nevertheless, there was considerable domestic opposition to these initiatives (from underwriters of domestic securities, for example), and the 1995 plan and South Korea's application to join the OECD became the focal points in the internal battle over reform (as well as an opportunity for further U.S. government pressure).

The aspects of the plan itself were arguably captured by special interests through corruption. Part of the process of unifying the financial markets had been the regularization of curb market lenders as investment and finance companies. The traditional commercial banks began to get squeezed: their share of deposits and lending fell steadily from roughly 80 percent in 1975 to less than 50 percent in 1990. This process accelerated in the mid-1990s when a new class of institutions was established: merchant banks, which had a broader remit than the existing nonbank financial intermediaries. Merchant bank licenses were issued in two tranches in 1994 and 1996. The issuance of licenses was dominated by bribery and kickbacks, and a later investigation by the Board of Audit and Inspection determined that three of the fifteen merchant banks approved in 1996 were insolvent when the licenses were issued (Haggard 2000). The merchant banks played a significant role in the subsequent crisis both at home and abroad through connected lending to their *chaebol* owners, particularly the financing of unviable investments in steel, automobiles, and chemicals during the mid-1990s investment boom, and reckless investments in Russia and Southeast Asia (Ishii and Habermeier 2002, p. 69). The commercial banks were experiencing erosion of both market share and margins: in 1996 their share of deposits and lending had fallen to 33 percent and 43 percent, respectively, and returns on assets and equity were declining as well.

Out of the OECD application process came a phased multiyear financial liberalization plan to break down some barriers within the domestic market and liberalize capital outflows before capital inflows. The plan amounted to a continuation of the ongoing liberalization process on a variety of fronts, though many of its provisions would leave the government with significant discretion. It was unclear what controls would remain in 1999, the terminal year of the plan. At the end of 1995, domestic market in-

---

14. American demands for financial market opening are a hardy perennial. Invariant to partisan control of the government, they continue to this day. See Frankel (1989, 1993), Wang Yen-Kyun (1993), Blustein (2003), Stiglitz (2003), and U.S. Trade Representative (USTR; 2004) for examples.

terest rates had largely been freed (indeed, a year ahead of schedule). However, the government still regulated the portfolios of commercial banks. It still owned a large number of financial institutions (of which the Korea Development Bank was the largest), and state-owned financial institutions dominated some markets (such as mortgage lending). It announced in August 1996 that foreign investors would be allowed to invest in convertible bonds issued by large corporations beginning in 1998, but that full opening of the bond market would be delayed until the differential between Korean and overseas interest rates (at the time 500–600 basis points) narrowed to 200 basis points.[15] Of course there was no guarantee that this condition would ever be met.

Government control over the introduction of new instruments had retarded the adoption of innovations in the securities market, and would be expected to continue to do so under this plan. Despite the decline of policy loans, the central bank would still act as a source of subsidized lending to preferred borrowers. Foreign participation in South Korean financial markets would continue to be circumscribed, and access by residents to international capital markets would still be restricted. Under this plan, the South Korean financial system would have remained among the most repressed in Asia. Reservations to OECD codes are permitted, and the average acceptance rate of financial liberalization codes in the financial services area is 89 percent; South Korea used its exceptions remit liberally, accepting only 65 percent of the OECD's financial system codes (although, in fairness, some of these exceptions were scheduled for phaseout by 2000; Dobson and Jacquet 1998). The Presidential Commission for Financial Reform was established in January 1997 to propose broad follow-on recommendations for the modernization of the financial system (Cargill 1999). Needless to say, its recommendations were overtaken by events.

The case for international financial market integration is well known: the benefits include enhanced opportunities for intertemporal consumption, greater opportunities for portfolio diversification and risk reduction for both borrowers and lenders, enhanced competition and technology transfer in both financial and nonfinancial sectors, and a reduction in systemic risk. Conversely, the symptoms of financial repression include low rates of return to savers, banking-sector inefficiency manifested by high spreads between lending and deposit rates, poor allocation of funds across alternative uses, politicization of lending decisions, and the existence of large informal and unregulated credit markets ("the curb market"). Financial repression tends to retard the development of the economy by dis-

---

15. The *chaebol* had been lobbying to be allowed to access foreign capital directly through the bond market. The government had been reluctant to do so, fearing that this would further advantage the *chaebol* relative to smaller firms that would be less able to take advantage of this opportunity. The banks presumably also preferred to their privileged position as financial intermediaries.

couraging the accumulation of capital. Savers are offered low rates of return, while firms face a high cost of capital for their investment needs. At the same time financial repression impedes the efficient allocation of what capital is accumulated. Projects are typically not funded according to their rates of return but rather on the basis of noneconomic considerations, which may include political connections or bribery of the relevant officials. The likely result of financial repression is that the total amount of savings is lower than it should be and the allocation of the total among its possible uses is inefficient. Disequilibrium in the financial markets generates rents that may be allocated through corruption. These distortions become severe when the real economy develops rapidly and profitable real investment opportunities abound yet the financial system lags behind. Capital controls act as an implicit tax on holders of government debt. By restricting international capital flows, the government can in effect force domestic residents to accept government debt at lower interest rates than would be the case if there were no controls on capital.

These arguments are easily applicable to the South Korean case, and indeed supporting evidence could be observed contemporaneously. Opportunities for intertemporal consumption smoothing could be particularly important for a country like South Korea, where the rate of return on capital during this period was quite high (figure 10.5) and the economy was subject to major financial shocks, such as the need to finance unification (Noland 1996b).[16] With respect to portfolio diversification, during the period under consideration, foreign investment in the South Korean stock market was legally restricted, and in statistical terms it was "mildly segmented" from the rest of the world (Claessens and Rhee 1994; Watanabe 1996). There was even some evidence that the correlation between movements in the South Korean and foreign markets was declining, which would have enhanced the attractiveness of cross-border diversification. Although it was sometimes argued that foreign investment in the stock market amounted to "hot money," the dominant behavior of foreign investors was to reinvest sales as part of the process of portfolio realignment (Jun 1995). Giovanni and deMelo (1993) estimate that in the case of South Korea for the period 1975–87, the "financial repression tax"—the reduction in borrowing costs to the central government generated by capital controls that effectively force domestic residents to invest in local instruments or the implicit tax rate—was more than 5 percent, amounting to 0.25 percent of national income, or 1–2 percent of actual tax revenues.

Not only were the prospective gains to relaxation capital controls discernable, but the implicit costs were also evident. There were enormous spreads across borrowers, reflecting the segmentation and repression of fi-

---

16. See Y. Cho (2002, fig. 1) and Krueger and Yoo (2002, tables 3–4, figs. 1–2) for alternative estimates of rates of return.

nancial markets (figure 10.5). The South Korean financial service sector was bureaucratized, bloated, and backward. This was reflected in the low average rate of return on bank assets, which was among the lowest of those observed in emerging markets (Goldstein and Turner 1996, table 5). The role of foreign firms was highly circumscribed. Given the highly concentrated South Korean industrial structure with respect to both firms (a relatively small number of firms accounted for a large share of national income) and the composition of output and exports (highly concentrated in a few products such as automobiles and computer chips), systemic risk was a real concern. The situation was exacerbated by a relaxation in 1995 of bank provisioning requirements and by fragmented regulatory authority, in which the Bank of Korea was responsible for oversight of the commercial banks while "poor supervision [of the merchant banks] by the MOFE [Ministry of Finance and Economy] created the possibility for regulatory arbitrage and high risk practices" (Ishii and Habermeier 2002, p. 69).[17] Macroeconomic volatility was higher than in other Asian economies, and data from the Bank of International Settlements (BIS) indicated that the risk-adjusted capital adequacy ratio of South Korean banks was among the lowest of all developing countries (Goldstein and Turner 1996).

South Korean reluctance to deregulate reflected a mixture of motivations. There were two sorts of counterarguments offered in opposition to liberalization. The first was that the South Korean financial service firms simply could not compete. Some South Koreans probably opposed liberalization out of self-interest, since liberalization would erode their privileged position within the South Korean financial system. (Likewise, some foreign calls for opening the Korean financial market were surely motivated by similar self-interest.) For example, Park Yung-Chul (1995, p. 7) argued that "domestic financial institutions have little competitive advan-

---

17. Writing prior to the crisis, the present author summarized the situation as follows:

The potential problem with the system is the implicit guarantee that banks not be allowed to fail; this, together with deposit insurance, simultaneously creates an incentive for banks to seek risk, while it relieves depositors of the incentive to monitor bank health. . . . Moreover, the Korean definition of bad loans is narrower than that commonly used abroad, and foreign bankers estimate the true bad loan problem may be three times as large as admitted. . . . Concerns about the banking system are further aggravated by the MFE's dual function as a promoter and supervisor of financial institutions, and legitimate questions can be raised about the degree of independence of the regulatory authorities. . . . The bottom line is that Korea should be concerned about the strength of its banking system, *and much of this concern is related to domestic financial repression and is unrelated to the issue of external financial liberalization.* Market discipline does not work when there is a lack of information, or when the notion that banks cannot fail is widely held. The appropriate responses are to deal with the structural problems of the banking system (which are likely to involve both domestic and international liberalization together with strengthened prudential supervision by public authorities), to strengthen public disclosure requirements, and to signal limits on public bailouts. (Noland 1996a, pp. 12–14; emphasis in the original)

tage over their foreign counterparts. At best Korea's financial sector remains an infant industry and may need market protection."[18] On some level this was undoubtedly true (although irrelevant): the South Korean banking sector was highly inefficient, as could easily be observed at the time. This was subsequently confirmed by the industry's postcrisis consolidation, which, despite a strong union presence in the industry, was accompanied by a roughly 40 percent decline in sectoral employment and no apparent diminution in service.

A more serious argument was that destabilizing capital flows would create macroeconomic instability. Park and Song (1996, p. 14) wrote, "Korean policymakers have been reluctant to liberalize the capital account rapidly. There is concern that devastating macroeconomic instability would result from a sudden opening of financial markets. In contrast efficiency gains to the economy from liberalization are considered to be small, possibly even insignificant, and at best realized in the long run." Johnston et al. (1999, p. 71) write that upon joining the OECD, South Korean government officials expressed their disinclination to ease capital controls further and explicitly stressed that they wished to maintain controls over short-term capital inflows that may "hamper macroeconomic and financial market stability." A major source of reluctance to remove barriers to capital inflows was the fear that inflows of reserves would increase the money supply excessively and lead to real exchange rate appreciation, either through inflation or through nominal appreciation of the currency.[19]

A striking aspect of the South Korean case is that while a variety of policy responses to this concern were suggested, it does not appear that any were seriously considered. One way of avoiding excessive appreciation would have been to continue to sterilize the capital inflows, as South Korean policymakers had done throughout the 1980s and 1990s by forcing domestic financial institutions to purchase monetary stabilization bonds (MSBs) to offset the expansionary impact on the money supply of foreign capital inflows. Indeed, research cited by Park Yung-Chul (1995) indicated that the optimal policy from a South Korean standpoint would have been a mixture of exchange rate adjustment and sterilization. Sterilization may

18. Another South Korean economist wrote, "Unless the weakness in domestic financial institutions is improved, financial markets in Korea could eventually be controlled by foreign firms. Fortunately, [under the agreement with the OECD] it is predicted that liberalization of capital movements will not result in foreign control of domestic financial industries. Such prediction is supported by the fact that foreign banks operating in Korea have experienced a decline in their asset size, and foreign insurance firms' market share is less than one percent" (Chae 1997, pp. 71–2).

19. For example, in an NBER paper, D. Cho and Koh (1996) write, "With the current level of interest rate differentials between Korea and developed economies, drastic full-scale liberalization would certainly induce a large amount of capital inflows and appreciate the Korean won. This would affect the price competitiveness of Korean products in international markets, which could bring about significant macro-instability in an economy like Korea which relies heavily upon external transactions" (p. 1).

have been advisable in the short run, but it is doubtful whether this is a good long-term policy: such a policy generates quasi-fiscal costs as long as the interest rate on the MSBs exceeds the return on holding foreign exchange. (In the case of comparable Latin American countries, Leiderman [1995] estimated their annual costs at 0.25 percent to 0.50 percent of national income.) In any event, since domestic rates were higher than foreign rates, it would be desirable to reduce domestic rates and obtain the benefits of higher investment and growth.[20] Moreover, as *domestic* financial markets became more complex, the ability of the Bank of Korea to exercise monetary control through administrative guidance and MSBs would be increasingly less possible, underscoring the advisability of developing the capacity for indirect control through open market operations. Another alternative, proposed by Dornbusch and Park (1995), was for the government to create a long-term (six years or more) won currency bond exclusively for foreigners for use when sterilizing capital inflows.

If it is not possible to adequately sterilize or otherwise offset inflows, and the capital inflows are financing consumption (instead of investment), another response would be to reintroduce some controls on capital inflows, presumably in the form of "Tobin taxes" that would throw some sand in the external financial market wheels.[21] Park Yung-Chul and colleagues (Dornbusch and Park 1995; Park 1995; Park and Song 1996) devoted considerable effort to thinking about this in the South Korean context. They raised two possibilities, which they appeared to regard as temporary measures for extreme situations. The first was a variable deposit requirement (VDR), in which reserve or deposit requirements are imposed on capital inflows, with the deposit varying according to type of inflow and investor. It is possible, in principle, that the reserve requirement could be set exactly so that the opportunity cost of the deposit sitting in a non-interest-bearing Bank of Korea account could exactly offset the international interest rate differential. Apparently the legal framework existed for the imposition of this deposit requirement, and the existing procedures would make it feasible to impose this on foreigners. The main problem (beyond damage to future credibility with foreign investors) would appear to be that this would also most certainly generate conflicts with foreign governments and investors and, depending on its implementation, possibly amount to a violation of South Korea's World Trade Organization commitments. These emergency

---

20. Park (1995) suggested central bank swaps as a possible alternative to sterilization. When central bank foreign exchange holdings got too high, the central bank would sell foreign exchange to domestic financial institutions to invest abroad. At the end of a specified time, the swap would be reversed, and the central bank would compensate financial institutions for losses due to interest rate differentials and exchange rate movements. The problem, as in the case of sterilization, is that the quasi-fiscal cost could be high.

21. If the foreign capital inflows were going into productivity-enhancing investment, the proper response would be to allow the exchange rate to appreciate with productivity gains and allow the capital inflows to continue.

safeguards were to be explicitly authorized postcrisis in the Foreign Exchange Transaction Act of 1999.

The alternative to controlling quantity (in terms of setting the size of the deposit) would be to control price, and Park and Song (1996) raised the issue of a transaction tax, for which, like the VDR, the necessary legal framework apparently already existed. The transaction tax could be confined to capital account transactions and, in principle, could be imposed solely on foreigners. Like the VDR, this would surely raise hackles with foreign firms and governments. Moreover, although the won could not legally trade outside of South Korea, it is hard to see why interested parties could not simply move their activities offshore and avoid the tax. More generally, the market for the won was already relatively thin, and it is not clear that reducing the volume of transactions would be desirable.

Finally, one might fight destabilizing inflows by encouraging outflows. At first blush, encouraging outflows to offset inflows would appear to be the natural response to concerns about excessive net inflows. There are two arguments as to why encouraging outflows may actually exacerbate the problem, however. First, barriers to outflows create an element of irreversibility to foreign investors, and if there is uncertainty about the future conduct of economic policy, then this irreversibility may deter investment. Elimination of irreversibility through the removal of capital controls could reduce foreign investor caution and paradoxically lead to higher net inflows. Second, since barriers to external flows are sometimes maintained to facilitate the collection of financial repression taxes, the removal of the impediments may be regarded as a signal of a lower permanent rate of taxation on capital, and thus it can induce capital inflow. It is unclear whether either of these arguments carried much force in the South Korean case.

In any event, South Korean authorities appeared to be proceeding more rapidly with liberalization on outbound flows than on inbound flows. To the extent that one believes that, for conventional portfolio diversification reasons, domestic residents wish to hold foreign currency assets and have been prevented from doing so, the elimination of these impediments would encourage capital outflow. If the fundamental concern about external financial liberalization is that it would lead to destabilizing net inflows, the South Korean policy amounted to firing the guns before the enemy was in sight.

Not only that, but the effect of government policy was to encourage those inflows to take the form of short-term lending to South Korean banks. The closure to foreign investors of the long-term corporate bond market created the perverse incentive to raise capital through short-term borrowing. This was significant because South Korean firms were highly concentrated in relatively footloose manufacturing industries and subject to contentious labor relations at home. As a consequence, South Korean firms began investing abroad at a scale that was unusually large for an economy at its level of income and industrial development.

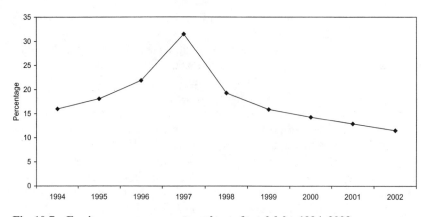

Fig. 10.7   Foreign currency percentage share of total debt, 1994–2002
Source: Goldstein and Turner (2004), table 4.4.

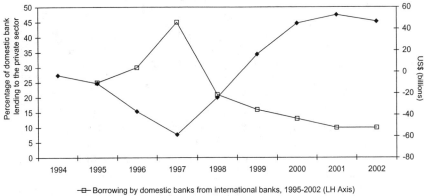

Fig. 10.8   Borrowing by domestic banks from international banks and net foreign currency assets
Source: Goldstein and Turner (2004), tables 2.2 and 4.3.

In 1993, the government expanded the scope for short-term foreign currency borrowing by allowing firms to borrow abroad directly or through South Korean banks to finance the importation of capital goods (figure 10.7). With interest rates relatively high in South Korea, and continued restrictions on firms' ability to issue long-term bonds or secure long-term loans in foreign markets still in effect, firms were encouraged to increase their reliance on short-term foreign borrowing, and South Korean banks were encouraged to step up their on-lending activities (figure 10.8).[22]

22. Further impetus was provided in October 1995 when the government announced that, in the case of direct investments abroad by South Korean corporations of $100 million or more, at least one-fifth of the funds would have to be raised at home.

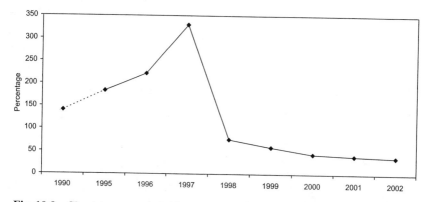

Fig. 10.9   Short-term external debt as a percentage of foreign exchange reserves
Source: Goldstein and Turner (2004), table 9.1.

The following year, the government removed restrictions on banks' foreign currency loans, resulting in a massive increase in net foreign currency liabilities (figure 10.8). Moreover, the Bank of Korea applied window guidance to limit medium- and long-term borrowing on international markets, apparently due to concerns about potential loss of control over domestic financial institutions through debt-equity swaps biasing borrowing toward the short end of the term spectrum (Johnston et al. 1999). Short-term external debt rose from $40 billion in U.S. dollars in 1993 to US$98 billion at the end of September 1997, representing more than half of external liabilities and more than three times the amount of foreign exchange reserves (figure 10.9). The growth of short-term debt outstripped the growth in usable reserves, raising the specter of a liquidity crunch. The ratio of usable international reserves—official reserves less the amount of illiquid funds that had been deposited at overseas bank branches to cover short-term debt repayments—to short-term debt declined from 42 percent in 1993 to 29 percent at year-end 1996 (Chopra et al. 2002).

These demand-side factors were reinforced by supply-side effects through the Basel Accords. Lending to other OECD banks, irrespective of the term of the loan, is assigned a risk weight of 20 percent in the capital adequacy requirements. However, in the case of non-OECD banks, the assessments vary with the term of the loan: loans of less than one year's duration receive the 20 percent risk weight while those with a duration of more than one year are assigned a 100 percent risk rate. Since all corporate lending receives the 100 percent risk weight, Basel Accord incentives arguably encouraged lending to South Korea to take the form of short-term bank lending, reinforcing South Korean government policy (Johnston et al. 1999). When South Korea joined the OECD, the effect was to reduce the risk premium on lending to South Korea.

The net result was currency and term mismatching on a massive scale. One way of getting a handle on the implications of this is suggested by

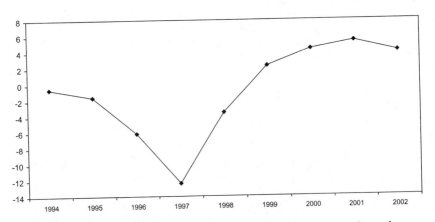

Fig. 10.10   Modified Goldstein-Turner aggregate effective currency mismatch (AECM) estimates, 1994–2002
Source: Goldstein and Turner (2004), table 4.6.

Goldstein and Turner (2004), who propose an aggregate effective currency mismatch measure—the net foreign currency asset position normalized by a country's export openness and the foreign currency share of total debt—as a shorthand stress indicator of the vulnerability of an economy to an exchange rate depreciation. As shown in figure 10.10, South Korea moved from a small net negative position in 1994 (i.e., an exchange rate depreciation would slightly reduce the net worth of the economy) to a sizable negative position in 1996, as the economy experienced a tenfold rise in net currency liabilities and a smaller increase in the foreign currency share of total debt, in the absence of a significant increase in export openness. The implication of this movement in the Goldstein-Turner measure was that, heading into 1997, a South Korean currency collapse was both more likely to occur and more likely to have a severe impact on the economy.[23] Although internal vulnerabilities could be easily observed contemporaneously, few if any analysts properly understood the external vulnerabilities created by the borrowing activities of overseas bank affiliates.

10.3   The 1997 Crisis and Its Aftermath

Between 1994 and 1996 South Korea experienced an investment boom that was increasingly financed by mismatched foreign borrowing. Unlike Southeast Asia, where the investment boom was concentrated in the real estate sector, much of the capital was flowing into manufacturing, pre-

23. To be clear the effective mismatch index is retrospective—the data requirements preclude contemporaneous calculation of the measure. However, the index is now reported on the Asian Development Bank's AsianBondsOnline Web site, http://asianbondsonline.adb .org/asianbondindicators/ave_effect_currmsmatch.php.

sumptively giving less cause for concern.[24] However, a substantial share was invested in industries that were already arguably characterized by excess capacity, and by the mid-1990s South Korea was experiencing slowing total factor productivity growth, deteriorating terms of trade, and declining profitability. South Korea's largest export market, Japan, went into recession in 1996, and the yen began to depreciate significantly against the dollar, generating an effective real appreciation of the won. Export growth slowed in 1996 and turned negative the following year. Stock market prices, which peaked in 1994, accelerated their decline.

As conditions worsened in 1996, the margin of error for the highly leveraged *chaebol* evaporated. In January 1997 Hanbo Steel, the seventeenth-largest *chaebol* ranked by sales, collapsed amid $6 billion of outstanding debts. The collapse of Hanbo, the first major *chaebol* to go bankrupt in more than a decade, was to have repercussions beyond its debts: a subsequent series of bribery arrests culminating in the arrest and conviction of President Kim Young-Sam's son and political confidante, Kim Hyun-Chol, shook the political establishment and greatly damaged the elder Kim. The Hanbo collapse was followed by the failures of two more *chaebol,* driving up interest rates in the large corporate bond market and imposing negative externalities on all corporate borrowers. During the second quarter of 1997, spreads on South Korean government bonds began to widen, while, as points of comparison, those on Indonesian and Malaysian government bonds remained unchanged. The market was signaling an increase in South Korean country risk. The turning point arguably came in June with the failed nationalization of Kia, the country's third-largest automaker.

Despite these worsening conditions, the vulnerability of the South Korean economy was not universally appreciated, by either forecasters, whose expectations for the South Korean economy were myopic in the extreme (figure 10.11), South Korean government officials, or the IMF.[25]

If domestic turmoil had been its only problem, South Korea might have been able to avoid the conflagration that was to engulf it. Instead, in the second half of 1997 South Korea was rocked by the shocks emanating from the financial crisis that had seized Southeast Asia and an emerging bank-

---

24. There is a gargantuan literature on the South Korean crisis of 1997–98. For entry points into this literature, see Wang Yunjong and Zang (1998), Noland (2000), Smith (2000), Coe and Kim (2002), and Web sites maintained by the NBER, http://www.nber.org/~confer/2000/korea00/korea00.html, and Nouriel Roubini, http://www.stern.nyu.edu/globalmacro/.

25. For example, the head of one government think tank, after accurately diagnosing the labor problems, loss of political confidence, and macroeconomic imbalances emerging in South Korea, in a public address in Washington, DC, in April 1997, dismissed concerns over the short-term debt and concluded: "There is, in fact, no economic crisis in Korea, if, by a crisis, we mean that there is imminent danger to the national economy—as was the case with Mexico in 1994" (Young 1997, p. 4). He was not alone—as late as September 1997, IMF missions to Seoul were giving the economy a clean bill of health.

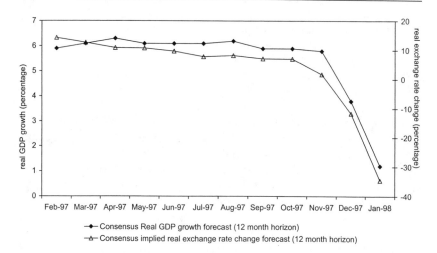

Fig. 10.11   Real GDP growth forecast and expected real exchange rate change
Source: Noland (2000), figure 6.5.

ing crisis in Japan, its principal source of foreign loans. The South Korean economy was adversely affected through three channels: spillovers in real terms as the depreciations of its competitors (especially Taiwan) effectively acted as competitive devaluations; contagion in financial terms; and a precipitous decline in rollover rates as Japanese banks hunkered down. The result was a collapse in private capital inflows (figure 10.4).

These forces put considerable downward pressure on the won in the latter part of 1997. South Korean authorities spent billions of dollars in an unsuccessful attempt to maintain their quasi-peg, but by December they were forced to abandon any pretense of controlling the exchange rate.[26] The currency went into a free fall. Developments in the currency market rebounded on the domestic financial system. As the exchange rate collapsed, financial and nonfinancial firms with unhedged foreign currency–denominated debt were crushed by a mounting debt burden in domestic resource cost terms. By the year's end the stock market had lost more than half its value in a period of eight months.

South Korea initially sought assistance from Japan and the United States bilaterally; after being rebuffed, it approached the IMF. The IMF,

---

26. On 27 August a high-ranking official of the MFE, in one of history's weirder abuses of metaphor, told a Seoul press conference that the Bank of Korea would defend its "Maginot Line" of 900 won to the dollar. Unfortunately, this new Maginot Line was as ineffective as the original, and the level was soon breached. The Bank of Korea continued to intervene in the foreign exchange market in a futile attempt to defend the won. On November 17, in a press conference that would have been farcical if not for the stakes, MFE officials again invoked the Maginot Line imagery, solemnly declaring that they would defend their newest line of 1,000 won to the dollar. They spent billions of dollars trying, but the following day the barrier was breached once again.

the multilateral development banks, and bilateral donors agreed to contribute to a rescue. Agreement was reached in November on a US$57 billion package—then the largest in history, and nearly twenty times South Korea's IMF quota—in return for broad, though vaguely worded, reforms. This agreement was promptly denounced by all three candidates in the ongoing presidential campaign. The National Assembly refused to consider a package of financial reform legislation proposed by MFE, and the bank regulators marched on the National Assembly to protest their possible reorganization. Moreover, given the vagueness of the reform commitments, outside observers expressed skepticism about their eventual implementation. South Korean asset prices continued to plummet. On December 18 a former political dissident, Kim Dae-Jung, was elected president. The following week, default was avoided when a second agreement involving expedited disbursements was concluded, and William McDonough, chairman of the New York Federal Reserve, persuaded the international banks to keep their credit lines open. Ultimately, South Korea's creditors were persuaded to exchange their existing short-term loans for government-guaranteed bonds of longer maturity.[27]

In negotiating the second package, the IMF extracted significant policy commitments, including both monetary and fiscal tightening (despite the fact that the 1996 general government budget surplus was 5 percent of GDP), as well as a variety of structural reforms, some unrelated to the financial crisis, such as the removal of the ban on the importation of Japanese automobiles. Although trade liberalization had been a staple of other IMF programs, the inclusion of these items contributed to the perception in South Korea that the IMF was simply being used as a tool of Japanese, and especially U.S. commercial policy.

Feldstein (1998) argues that the South Korean case could be thought of as a fundamentally well-functioning economy experiencing a temporary liquidity crisis. Had the IMF initially acted to coordinate a restructuring of private-sector lending while providing temporary credits (in essence a bridge loan), the huge official money package could have been avoided and along with it the intrusive conditionality that the IMF demanded as part of the second deal. Indeed, South Korea ultimately borrowed less than $29 billion and in fact did not draw down the entire IMF portion of the loan.

The South Korean crisis presented the IMF, the major finance ministries, and the multilateral development banks with a difficult situation. It occurred in the context of a cascading set of crises, which threatened to spread to Brazil and Russia. The South Korean government's willingness to guarantee the short-term foreign debt of private entities socialized risk, creating moral hazard and ultimately increasing the severity of the crisis. It waited too long to approach the IMF, and once it did, it engaged in un-

27. See IMF (2003) for a detailed description of the coordinated rollover.

helpful tactics such as leaking confidential documents. The IMF and its allies had little control over these events, and in November 1997 they confronted a situation that arguably posed a systemic risk to the international financial system.

When push came to shove, the IMF and its collaborators provided South Korea with an enormous package, far beyond its past lending practices in other cases, and a timely infusion of cash that undoubtedly prevented a chaotic default. That said, the macroeconomic conditionality imposed on South Korea was too severe.[28] It needlessly intensified the recession that was to come to be known colloquially as "the IMF recession" as the growth rate collapsed from 7 percent in 1996 to –7 percent in 1998 before rebounding to more than 10 percent in 1999 (figure 10.1). Yet the South Korean economy had been beset with some significant structural problems, and, given the vast scope of the December 1997 standby agreement, considerable demands for structural reform could be expected, at least with regard to financial market regulation and corporate governance. Other aspects of the program, requiring specific trade and labor market reforms, or demanding an independent central bank with price stability as its sole mandate, were intrusive and at best only tangentially connected to the crisis.[29] Yet one could argue that the existence of such a demanding international organization allowed Kim Dae-Jung to advance his own relatively liberal economic agenda more effectively than if the IMF or some similar organization had not existed.

In a sense South Korea benefited from the vagaries of the electoral calendar—President Kim entered the Blue House essentially owing nothing to the dominant interests in the society and could blame the mishap on his predecessor. Given this freedom to maneuver, he moved resolutely to extract concessions from both the labor unions and the *chaebol*. In the financial sector, the government immediately closed two brokerage houses and a number of merchant banks (including some affiliated with *chaebol*). The government began the process of auctioning off two nationalized commercial banks, while putting other financial institutions on short tethers. Despite the austerity and dislocation that would accompany the process of restructuring, the financial markets responded positively to these actions.

The crisis forced a restructuring of South Korea's systems of finance, regulation, and corporate governance, and a dismantling of the pervasive controls on international capital flows that characterized the precrisis

28. There is a substantial academic literature on the monetary policy aspects of the crisis response that reaches ambiguous conclusions about the interest rate increases embodied in the IMF program. There is less disagreement that the fiscal tightening was inappropriate. See IMF (2003) for a review.

29. The IMF appears to have belatedly acquiesced on this point, observing that "the IMF may have been better advised to confine its advice and conditionality to a narrower range of issues, and then let the Korean authorities define their own agenda for implementation on a more focused set of policy issues" (IMF 2003, p. 111).

regime. Since the crisis South Korea has arguably made better progress on economic reform than the other heavily affected Asian crisis countries, or Japan, for that matter.

One manifestation of this has been an increase in FDI. As noted earlier, before the crisis, South Korea was unusual in that the dominant modality of investment was minority stake joint ventures. FDI spiked in 1999 and 2000 and has fallen considerably since then (H.-K. Kim 2004, table 1). The temporary hike stemmed in large part from foreign minority partners buying out their South Korean counterparts—given the opacity of South Korean accounting practices at the time, incumbent investors were uniquely informed about the franchise value of these businesses.[30] Subsequent FDI has mostly taken the form of greenfield investments.

In the financial sector, prudential regulation has been consolidated and strengthened through the creation of the Financial Supervisory Commission and the introduction of new regulatory practices, approaches, and standards. Competition was injected into the financial sector by the increased role of foreigners through a variety of institutional arrangements. What appears to be more difficult to change has been the lending culture of South Korean financial institutions (Mann 2000). In the aftermath of the crisis, lenders went from bingeing on corporate lending to bingeing on household lending: South Korean household debt registered the fastest growth in the world, increasing 18 percentage points of GDP in two years, before ending in crisis with the insolvency of the country's largest credit card issuer.[31] A current challenge centers on the rapidly growing use of financial derivatives by South Korean financial institutions and the concern that the regulatory regime may not have kept pace with financial innovation.

Nevertheless, the improvement in the function of South Korea's financial system can be seen in firm-level balance sheet data: South Korean corporations on the whole have reduced their leverage, and access to capital is increasingly a function of profitability (Alexander 2003). This development is, in turn, facilitated by improved corporate governance through enhanced financial transparency, stricter enforcement of existing laws, and expanded scope for minority shareholders to seek legal redress.

What has not happened is the development of independent institutional investors capable of monitoring management. To the extent that such institutional investors exist in South Korea, they tend to be affiliated with the major *chaebol,* and although some foreign institutional investors and the nascent shareholder rights movement have exerted some salutary influence, it is fair to say that the country still lacks a real market for corporate

---

30. One issue is whether these acquisitions amounted to a "fire sale" of assets by financially distressed South Korean firms. Econometric results reported by Chari, Ouimet, and Tesar (2004) suggest not.

31. See IMF (2004) for a summary of the credit card debacle.

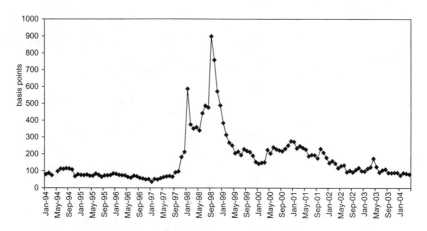

Fig. 10.12   JPMorgan Emerging Markets Bond Index global strip spread for South Korea, 1994–2004

Source: JPMorgan's MorganMarkets database.

control. South Korean equity markets have become more integrated with markets elsewhere. In part this increase reflects the natural integration of markets following the removal of restrictions on foreign ownerships of South Korean stocks (foreigners now own more than 40 percent of the shares on the Korean Stock Exchange) and the removal of restrictions on South Korean residents' ability to invest abroad. Yet despite these developments, the interest rate spread on South Korean debt remains higher than it was precrisis (figure 10.12).

In June 1998 the government announced a plan to liberalize all foreign exchange transactions in two stages. The first stage took effect on April 1, 1999, with the implementation of the Foreign Exchange Transaction Act, which liberalized most existing restrictions on current account transactions and established a negative list system for capital account transactions under which transactions are legal unless stipulated by law or decree. (See the appendix in K.-S. Kim 2001 for a complete description.) The second stage of the exchange control liberalization took effect January 1, 2002.

In April 2002 the government announced "The Plan for the Development of the Korean Foreign Exchange Market," which envisions full liberalization of foreign exchange regulations by 2011 as part of the government's attempt to establish South Korea as a regional business hub for Northeast Asia. At present the exchange rate system is classified as independently floating in an inflation-targeting framework by the IMF. In recent years, however, exchange rate interventions have been sizable: they appear to go beyond the smoothing operations as characterized by the IMF and instead involve an attempt to prevent appreciation of the won. As of August 2004, South Korea had accumulated US$171 billion in official reserves, and exchange rate policy and the magnitude of currency market interventions have emerged as a source of controversy within the South Korean government.

10.4 Conclusion

South Korea is a fascinating case in that it combines the characteristics of sustained prosperity, capital controls, and financial crisis in a striking manner. Pervasive capital controls, which delinked South Korea's internal financial markets from the rest of the world, were a necessary component of the country's capital-channeling development strategy. This strategy clearly was consistent with rapid and sustained economic development, although it may or may not have been causal.

These interventions create domestic political constituencies for both their perpetuation and dissolution, and the implementation of liberalization programs will reflect political competition among these groups. Transition is also affected by the demands of foreign financial services providers, which, having developed greater efficiency in a more competitive environment, regard the protected market as an opportunity. All of these phenomena are evident in the South Korean case.

Because of its somewhat amorphous nature, perhaps the most difficult challenge is the legacy of financial repression in "dumbing down" both private-sector actors and their public-sector regulatory counterparts. The main ongoing concern in South Korea is not the macroeconomic adjustment to the removal of capital controls per se, but rather the lingering concerns about both the lending culture of South Korean financial-sector firms and the capacity of South Korean authorities to successfully regulate the more complex financial system enabled by liberalization.

The obvious question is whether South Korea could have developed a more dynamic and market-oriented financial system in the presence of international capital controls. In theory there is no reason why this could not have happened if South Korea had chosen this path. Indeed, the strengthening of domestic financial institutions prior to opening the capital account is a staple of the sequencing literature, and South Korea in the late 1980s appeared to meet the basic preconditions for a successful transition, such as fiscal health (Edwards 1989). Similarly, one can imagine a greater (or lesser) role for foreign financial service providers under a variety of institutional and regulatory constructs. Yet it is doubtful whether this could have been obtained in practice. Neither South Korean government officials nor the intelligentsia evinced much ideological commitment to the notion of freer financial markets, and, perhaps more important, there were some very large and powerful interest groups that were opposed to liberalization. For better or worse, given the specifics of the South Korean situation, freer international capital flows, a less regulated domestic financial system, and an increased role for foreign financial service providers were probably not greatly separable components of financial-sector reform.

Appendix

Chronology of Capital Flow Liberalization in South Korea

This appendix provides a timeline of capital flow liberalization in South Korea. It is derived primarily, though not exclusively, from Johnston et al. (1999) and the Bank of Korea web site, http://www.bok.or.kr. The chronology is organized by topic: FDI, portfolio investment, other capital flows, capital market organization, and foreign exchange.

Foreign Direct Investment

1983
- Revision of the Foreign Capital Inducement Law establishes the principle that inward FDI, subject to approval, is permitted except in specific "negative list" sectors.

1985
- More than 100 sectors are eliminated from the negative list. The "liberalization ratio" (share of industries open to FDI) reaches 76 percent, 92 percent in manufacturing.

1986
- Initial liberalization of restrictions on direct investment abroad begins.

1987
- Twenty-six additional manufacturing sectors are eliminated from the negative list.
- Tax incentives for FDI in strategic sectors are reduced.

1988
- Restrictions on FDI in advertising, motion pictures, and insurance are relaxed.

1989
- Six manufacturing sectors are opened to FDI, raising the liberalization ratio to 79 percent, 98 percent in manufacturing.
- Limit on automatic approval is raised to US$5 million from US$3 million.

1990
- The limit on automatic approval is raised to US$100 million from US$3 million.
- Two more sectors are opened to FDI.

1991
- The approval requirement is replaced with notification system for projects with foreign participation of less than 50 percent.

- Exemptions are granted to foreign firms on corporate profit taxes for three years, while a 50 percent exemption is established for the two successive years.
- Restrictions on foreign ownership of retail businesses are relaxed.

1992
- The approval requirement is replaced by a notification system for investments in most business sectors.

1994
- The Foreign Capital Inducement Act is amended to streamline application procedures. Rules on land ownership are relaxed.

1995
- Investment in 101 sectors is permitted or greatly liberalized.

1997
- August: The debt limits on corporations making overseas direct investments, whereby 20 percent of investments exceeding US$100 million had to be financed by a firm's own capital, are abolished.

1998
- The Foreign Investment Promotion Act establishes the principle of national treatment; further narrows the negative list down to 5 percent of all sectors and 1 percent of manufacturing (twenty-two sectors, including real estate rentals and sales, land development, waterworks, and investment companies and trusts, fully open to foreign investment); broadens the scope of tax incentives available to foreign investors; simplifies approval procedures; and establishes foreign investment zones.

1999
- Five more categories—book publishing, alcoholic beverages, external maritime transport, blood-related products, and casinos—are fully opened.
- Investment in foreign real estate by domestic entities is permitted.

2000
- Regulations on FDI are brought into compliance with OECD standards.
- Cattle husbandry and news agencies are partly liberalized.

2001
- Meat wholesaling is partly liberalized.

Present situation: Out of 1,121 industries, 29 remain partially or completely closed to FDI. There is no limit on the amount that corporations can invest abroad, but all direct investments require notification of the corporations' banks, and for financial, banking, and insurance companies, acceptance is required by the Ministry of Finance and Economy (MOFE).

Notification of the Bank of Korea (BOK) and foreign exchange banks is also required for purchases of foreign real estate by domestic companies or purchases of domestic real estate by foreigners. Minimum standards of domestic companies' foreign exchange earnings must be met in order for them to establish branches overseas.

Portfolio Investment

1984
- The Korea Fund is listed on the New York Stock Exchange, providing international investors with an indirect means of investing in the Korean stock market.

1985
- South Korean firms are allowed to issue depository notes and warrants up to 15 percent of their outstanding share volume provided that no single foreign entity can acquire more than 3 percent of the capital by exercising conversion rights.

1987
- The Korea Europe Fund is established, further enabling foreigners to invest in the stock market.
- Inward remittances greater than US$20,000 are monitored to discourage investments in the stock exchange.

1989
- Foreigners are allowed to trade among themselves. South Korean shares are permitted to be acquired through the exercise of bond conversion rights.
- Foreign exchange banks are allowed to issue foreign currency bonds offshore and to underwrite and trade foreign currency bonds issued by nonresidents.

1990
- The government allows the three domestic investment trusts each to establish a US$100 million fund (of which US$60 million is to be raised abroad) to invest in South Korean companies (70 percent of the capital) and foreign securities.

1991
- The Korea Asian Fund is established
- Nonresidents are allowed to convert into won up to US$100,000 to invest in development trusts with a maturity of more than two years.
- Securities in foreign currencies are permitted to be issued by residents to finance import of inputs and machinery for which no domestic substitute is available.
- Nonresidents who had acquired South Korean shares through convertible bonds are allowed to trade them in the stock exchange.

1992
- Foreign investment directly in the South Korean stock market by non-residents subject to ceilings of 3 percent for a particular investor and 10 percent for foreign investors in the aggregate is permitted.
- Investments in stocks by resident foreign financial institutions are subject to the same limits as those of institutions owned by nationals.
- Authorization for the issuance abroad of bonds, callable bonds, warrants, and stock depository receipts by residents is simplified, and receipts can be maintained in accounts abroad.

1993
- Issues of securities denominated in foreign currency are not subject to permission but only to reporting requirements; the class of eligible issuers is widened to include those with positive cumulative profits over the past three years.

1994
- The ceiling on nonresidents holdings of individual South Korean firms' capital is raised from 10 percent to 12 percent. Nonresidents' holdings of individual South Korean public corporations are allowed up to an 8 percent ceiling.

1995
- The ceiling on nonresidents' holdings of private South Korean firms' capital is raised from 12 percent to 15 percent.
- Brokers are allowed to engage in foreign exchange transactions related to nonresidents' investments in the stock market.
- Issuance of exchangeable bonds overseas is permitted, provided that they do not exceed 15 percent of the firm's capital.
- Limits on offshore security issuance by small and medium-sized companies are relaxed.

1996
- Investment in domestic bonds by foreigners is allowed through the US$100 million Korea Bond Fund listed in London.
- Limits on foreign ownership of listed Korean firms are raised to 20 percent and 15 percent for private and public enterprises, respectively; the ceiling on individual ownership is increased to 5 percent.
- Up to 50 percent of won-denominated securities issued by nonresidents can be sold abroad.

1997
- Foreigners can collectively purchase up to 30 percent of convertible bonds issued by small and medium-sized companies and only 5 percent individually.
- June: Regulations are relaxed so that foreign investors are allowed access to nonguaranteed bonds of small and medium-sized companies

(maturities over three years and up to 50 percent of the amount listed) and of conglomerates (up to 30 percent limit of an issue together with a 6 percent individual limit).

- The issue abroad of won-denominated securities requires approval by the MOFE. The issue of foreign currency–denominated securities must be reported to the MOFE.
- December 11: Authorities raise the ceiling on aggregate foreign ownership of listed Korean shares from 26 percent to 50 percent and the individual ceiling from 7 percent to 50 percent; eliminate all limits on foreign investment in nonguaranteed bonds issued by small and medium-sized companies; and allow foreign investment in the guaranteed corporate bond market (for maturities greater than three years) with limits at 10 percent and 30 percent for individuals and in aggregate, respectively.
- December 12: Authorities raise aggregate limits for foreign investment in nonguaranteed corporate (convertible) bonds from 30 percent to 50 percent.
- December 23: Authorities allow foreigners to invest in government and special bonds, up to the aggregate ceiling of 30 percent, and eliminate all individual limits for foreign investment in corporate bonds.
- December 30: Authorities eliminate all foreign investment ceilings for the government, special, and corporate bond markets, including for maturities of less than three years; lift the restriction on foreign borrowing of over three years' maturity; and raise the aggregate ceiling on foreign investment in Korean equities to 55 percent.

1998
- Restrictions on the amount of foreign investment in Korean equities are lifted; domestic bond and money markets are opened to foreigners.

1999
- Offshore issuance of securities with a maturity of less than one year by domestic entities is permitted.
- Issuance of won-denominated and foreign currency–denominated securities by foreign entities is permitted.
- Investment in foreign financial and insurance markets by domestic entities is permitted.

Present situation: Ceilings on purchases of Korean stocks remain in place for twenty-three domestic firms.

Other Capital Flows

1981
- Issuance of foreign beneficiary certificates by Korean trust companies is allowed.

1985
• Some restrictions on foreign loans to domestic firms are relaxed.

1986
• Regulations on foreign currency loans are tightened.

1987
• The government directs financial institutions to repay foreign short-term borrowing and bank loans that bear "unfavorable conditions." Special deposits by the central bank are made at Korean foreign exchange banks for this purpose.

1988
• Nonresidents are prohibited from converting in won amounts withdrawn from their accounts. Sales of foreign currency by nonresidents to domestic banks are limited to US$10,000.
• Limits on banks' foreign exchange loans to small and medium-sized enterprises and export firms are strictly enforced.

1989
• A limit of US$200 million is set on special foreign currency loans granted to a firm during a year.
• Currency loans are now admissible for investment operations abroad, subject to a ten-year maturity limit and ceilings of 60 percent and 80 percent of the investment for large and small firms, respectively.
• The amount of foreign currency allowed in the country without notification to the tax authorities is raised in two steps to US$10,000.

1990
• Central bank loans for the redemption of the foreign currency loans by banks and firms are abolished.

1991
• Limits on foreign currency loans for investments abroad are reduced to 40 percent and 60 percent of the total for large and small enterprises, respectively.

1992
• The maximum amount of loans of overseas investments is increased to 60 percent and 70 percent for large and small enterprises, respectively.
• Residents can issue abroad negotiable certificates of deposit and commercial papers.

1993
• Nonresidents are allowed to hold won accounts.
• Manufacturing companies can obtain loans in foreign currencies for all imports of inputs and equipment; the BOK raises the amount of

foreign exchange reserves earmarked for supporting foreign currency loans by domestic banks from US$1 billion to US$4 billion.

1994

- Ceilings are abolished on borrowing by resident corporations and their foreign branches from nonresident financial institutions located abroad.
- Foreign-financed general manufacturing companies are eligible for short-term overseas borrowing, while the overseas borrowing by foreign-financed, high-tech firms is raised to 100 percent of the foreign capital share.

1995

- Eight leasing companies are allowed to undertake medium- and long-term borrowing offshore without intermediation from foreign exchange banks.
- Direct foreign borrowing by enterprises engaged in social projects and foreign-financed, high-tech firms is allowed up to 100 percent of capital (90 percent for large corporations) for redemption of import-related debts.
- The ratio of foreign currency loans taken by large companies for import of inputs and machinery is lowered to 70 percent of total cost.

1996

- Restrictions on foreign borrowing are eliminated for certain small and medium-sized firms.
- Nonresidents are allowed to open won accounts in overseas branches of domestic banks.

1997

- April: The period for importing on a deferred-payment basis is lengthened by 30 days for raw materials used in manufacturing export commodities for small and medium-sized enterprises. The period is extended for large enterprises as well in August.
- July: The MOFE abolishes regulations on the usage of long-term loans with maturities of over five years brought into the country by foreign manufacturers.
- Foreign investment funds approved by the MOFE can purchase domestic money market instruments. Other foreign institutions and domestic individuals require the prior approval of the MOFE. The issuance abroad of other securities, like certificates of deposit in foreign currency denominations, requires the MOFE's approval.
- Certain forms of trade credit are allowed without prior approval; however, deferred payments for the import of goods and export advances (except those by small and medium-sized firms) are subject to binding value limits. Export down payments up to 8 percent of the value are allowed for ships and plant building during production.

- Foreign exchange banks can borrow from abroad. They need to report foreign borrowing to the MOFE when the maturity exceeds one year and when the amount is over US$10 million.
- Credits from nonresidents to nonbank residents require prior approval by the MOFE.
- Foreign-financed, high-tech companies can borrow up to 100 percent of the foreign invested capital with maturity limited to three years.
- Foreign borrowing with a maturity of less than three years is governed by the Foreign Exchange Act.
- Residents cannot lend abroad without the approval of the MOFE.

1998
- February 16: Authorities removed restrictions on corporate borrowing from abroad up to US$2 million for venture companies.
- Authorities opened up money market instruments issued by nonfinancial institutions (commercial papers, commercial bills, and trade bills) to foreigners without limits.
- The requirement that foreign borrowing from abroad exceed US$1 million is eliminated.

1999
- The Foreign Exchange Management Act is abolished and replaced by the Foreign Exchange Transaction Act, which liberalizes most current account transactions. It also authorizes safeguard mechanisms, including freezing of transactions; a permission-based transaction system; the funneling of foreign currency to the BOK; activation of a VDR system; and requirement that a certain percentage of capital flows be deposited in a non-interest-bearing account.
- Overseas short-term borrowing by "financially sound" domestic firms is permitted.
- Nonresidents are permitted to make deposits and open won-denominated savings and trust accounts with maturities in excess of one year.
- The requirement that foreign-invested firms receive government approval for intrafirm transactions exceeding $1 million is abolished.

2001
- All restrictions are lifted on foreign currency loans to residents by domestic banks.
- The remaining ceilings on current account transactions by individuals are eliminated.

2002
- Regulations on individuals' external payments are eased.

Present situation: Requirements for the repatriation of overseas claims, limits on nonresident won funding aimed at hedge funds, and restrictions on short-term external borrowing by "financially unsound" corporations are still in place. The Foreign Exchange Transactions Act contained sunset provisions expiring December 31, 2005, relating to the permission system for certain capital account transactions. This expiring system was replaced by a streamlined reporting system on January 1, 2006. Sale by nonresidents of foreign exchange over US$20,000 without documentation is subject to notification requirements. Purchase by nonresidents of foreign exchange without documentation of previous sale in excess of US$10,000 is subject to notification requirements. Notification requirements remain on foreign currency loans for nonbank firms, in particular loans in excess of US$30 million. Firms whose debt ratio is greater than their industry average and/ or whose credit rating is below investment grade are considered financially unsound and are subject to special notification requirements for short-term foreign currency borrowing. Exceptions exist for certain general manufacturing or high-tech industries.

Capital Market Organization

1985
- The underwriting of foreign assets by domestic securities companies is permitted.

1987
- Foreign exchange banks begin offshore banking at the initiative of the government.
- Nine additional foreign banks are allowed to enter the trust investment business.

1993
- Overseas branches of domestic banks are allowed to supply loans to residents who trade commodities futures and financial futures.

1997
- Foreign exchange banks can conduct all form of transactions in the foreign currency market, including swaps, options, forwards, and futures, but the terms of the forward transaction between banks and nonbank customers must be based on bona fide transactions.
- December 29: Restrictions on commercial bank ownership are eased to encourage foreign investment in domestic financial institutions. The financial-sector legislation passed on December 29 abolishes the 4 percent ownership limit for commercial banks. Purchase of bank equity by foreign banks is now permitted without limit, but requires approval at three stages: 10 percent, 25 percent, and 31 percent. Domestic ownership above 4 percent is permitted provided that an equal or larger share is held by a foreign bank.
- Commercial bank open positions in foreign currencies are subject to

the following limits: (a) the overall overbought position must be lower than 15 percent of the equity capital and the oversold position lower than 10 percent of the equity capital or US$20 million, whichever is larger; and (b) the spot oversold positions cannot exceed 3 percent of the equity capital or US$5 million, whichever is larger.

1998
- March 31: Authorities allow foreign banks and brokerage houses to establish subsidiaries.

1999
- Domestic institutions are permitted to engage in derivative transactions.
- The principle is established under the Foreign Exchange Transaction Act that any financial institution meeting certain requirements need merely notify MOFE before engaging in foreign exchange–related business.

2002
- Securities and insurance companies are allowed entry into the interbank market.

Present situation: Sixty-one institutions are recognized as "foreign exchange banks" and authorized to engage in foreign exchange transactions for third parties. A larger number of businesses are authorized to engage in foreign exchange transactions on their own behalf. The overall open overbought (oversold) position in foreign currencies of foreign exchange banks must be lower than 20 percent of the equity capital. A foreign exchange bank must maintain reserves amounting to a prescribed proportion of its foreign currency deposit liabilities in the form of foreign currency deposits at the BOK. The current requirements are 5 percent for demand deposits, 2 percent for saving deposits, and 1 percent for foreign currency deposits by nonresidents and other banks. The banks are also subject to foreign currency mismatch regulations: 80 percent of short-term (less than three months) liabilities must be covered by deposits, and 50 percent of long-term loans must be financed by long-term borrowings.

Foreign Exchange

1963
- The multiple exchange rate system is unified; the won is pegged to the dollar.

1980
- A "multibasket" peg for the won is introduced, determined by the weighted average of the special drawing rights (SDR) basket and a

trade-weighted basket of major currencies, plus an additional "policy" adjustment factor.

1985
- Currency swaps are permitted.

1986
- Regulations on swaps are further liberalized.

1987
- Restrictions on futures and options are lifted. The limit on the forward contract period is eliminated.
- The ceiling on foreign banks' swap operations is relaxed by 10 percent.

1988
- The limit on swaps by foreign banks is relaxed again by 10 percent.

1989
- The ceilings on swap operations by foreign banks are relaxed by another 10 percent.

1990
- The Market Average Exchange Rate (MAR) System is adopted, in which the won is allowed to float within certain bands of daily fluctuation. The band is initially set at ±0.4 percent.

1991
- The band is widened to ±0.6 percent.

1992
- The range of admissible forward exchange contracts is extended.
- The band is widened to ±0.8 percent.

1993
- Regulations on forward foreign exchange transactions are relaxed; ceilings held on foreign exchange deposits payable in domestic currency are abrogated.
- The band is widened to ±1.0 percent.

1994
- The band is widened to ±1.5 percent.

1995
- The band is widened to ±2.25 percent.

1996
- The yen-won spot and forward market are established.
- Foreign currency–derivative transactions are opened to nonresidents. Documentation requirements for forward and futures transactions are eliminated, but transactions still need to be based on real demand.

- The ceiling on the swap facility provided to foreign banks is relaxed by 10 percent.
- Swaps are allowed for portfolio investments abroad by financial and insurance companies.

1997
- All settlements with other countries can be made in any convertible currency except the won. Export earnings exceeding US$50,000 must be repatriated within six months.
- Residents can purchase derivatives through a foreign exchange bank, but issuance abroad requires MOFE's approval.
- November 11: The band is widened to ±10 percent.
- December 16: South Korea floats the won.

1999
- The real demand principle for forward and derivative transactions is abolished, permitting further development of these markets. The Korea Futures Exchange (KOFEX) is established.

2002
- The Plan for the Development of the Korean Foreign Exchange Market, which envisions full liberalization of foreign exchange regulations by 2011, is announced.

Present situation: The exchange rate system is classified as independently floating in an inflation-targeting framework by the IMF. Interventions are sizable and would appear to go beyond the smoothing function as characterized by the IMF.

References

Alexander, Arthur. 2003. Korea's capital investment: Returns at the level of the economy, industry, and firm. Special Studies Series no. 2. Washington, DC: Korea Economic Institute.

Balassa, Bela. 1985. Adjusting to external shocks: The newly-industrializing developing economies in 1974–76 and 1979–81. *Weltwirtschaftliches Archiv* 121 (1): 116–41.

Balassa, Bela, and John Williamson. 1990. Adjusting to success: Balance of payments policy in the East Asian NICS. Policy Analyses in International Economics no. 17 (revised). Washington, DC: Institute for International Economics, April.

Blustein, Paul. 2003. *The chastening.* Rev. ed. New York: Public Affairs.

Cargill, Thomas F. 1999. Economic and financial crisis in Korea, the Japanese financial regime, and the need for a new financial paradigm. *Joint U.S.-Korea Academic Studies* 9:111–30.

Chae, Wook. 1997. Korea's admission to the OECD: Implications and economic effects. *Korea's Economy* 1997 (13): 68–72.

Chari, Anusha, Paige P. Ouimet, and Linda L. Tesar. 2004. Acquiring control in emerging markets: Evidence from the stock market. NBER Working Paper no. 10872. Cambridge, MA: National Bureau of Economic Research.

Cho, Dongchul, and Youngsun Koh. 1996. Liberalization of capital inflows in Korea: Big bang or gradualism? NBER Working Paper no. 5824. Cambridge, MA: National Bureau of Economic Research.

Cho, Soon. 1994. *The dynamics of Korean development.* Washington, DC: Institute for International Economics.

Cho, Yoon Je. 2002. What have we learned from the Korean economic adjustment program? In *Korean crisis and recovery,* ed. David Coe and Se-Jik Kim, 105–27. Washington, DC: International Monetary Fund and Korea Institute for International Economic Policy.

Chopra, Ajai, Kenneth Kang, Meral Karasulu, Hong Liang, Henry Ma, and Anthony Richards. 2002. From crisis to recovery in Korea: Strategies, achievements, and lessons. In *Korean crisis and recovery,* ed. David T. Coe and Se-Jik Kim, 13–104. Washington, DC: International Monetary Fund and Korea Institute for International Economic Policy.

Claessens, Stijn, Swati Ghosh, and David Scott. 1999. Korea's financial sector reforms. *Joint U.S.-Korea Academic Studies* 9:83–110.

Claessens, Stijn, and Moon-Whoan Rhee. 1994. The effect of barriers to equity investment in developing countries. In *The internationalization of equity markets,* ed. Jeffrey A. Frankel, 231–75. Chicago: University of Chicago Press.

Clifford, Mark. 1997. *Troubled tiger.* Rev. ed. Singapore: Butterworth-Heinemann Asia.

Coe, David T., and Se-Jik Kim. 2002. *Korean crisis and recovery.* Washington, DC: International Monetary Fund and Korea Institute for International Economic Policy.

Collins, Susan, and Won-Am Park. 1989. External debt and macroeconomic performance in South Korea. In *Developing country debt and economic performance,* vol. 3, ed. Jeffrey Sachs and Susan Collins, 153–369. Chicago: University of Chicago Press.

Dobson, Wendy, and Pierre Jacquet. 1998. *Financial services liberalization in the WTO.* Washington, DC: Institute for International Economics.

Dornbusch, Rudiger, and Yung Chul Park. 1995. *Financial opening: Policy lessons for Korea.* Seoul: Korea Institute of Finance.

Edwards, Sebastian. 1989. The sequencing of economic reform: Analytical issues and Latin American experiences. In *Korea's macroeconomic and financial policies,* 177–98. Seoul: Korea Development Institute.

Feldstein, Martin. 1998. Refocusing the IMF. *Foreign Affairs,* March/April.

Frankel, Jeffrey A. 1989. And now won/dollar negotiations? Lessons from the yen/dollar agreement of 1984. In *Korea's macroeconomic and financial policies,* 109–29. Seoul: Korea Development Institute.

———. 1993. Liberalization of Korea's foreign exchange markets and the role of trade relations with the United States. In *Shaping a new economic relationship: The Republic of Korea and the United States,* ed. Jongryn Mo and Ramon Myers, 119–42. Stanford, CA: Hoover Institution Press.

Giovanni, Alberto, and Martha deMelo. 1993. Government revenue from financial repression. *American Economic Review* 83 (4): 953–63.

Goldstein, Morris, and Philip Turner. 1996. Banking crises in emerging economies: Origins and policy options. BIS Economic Papers no. 46. Basel, Switzerland: Bank of International Settlements, October.

————. 2004. *Controlling currency mismatches in emerging markets.* Washington, DC: Institute for International Economics.

Haggard, Stephan. 2000. *The political economy of the Asian financial crisis.* Washington, DC: Institute for International Economics.

International Monetary Fund (IMF). 2003. The IMF and recent capital account crises. Evaluation Report. Washington, DC: International Monetary Fund.

————. 2004. Republic of Korea: Article IV consultation—Staff report; staff statement; public information notice on the executive board discussion; and statement by the executive director for the Republic of Korea. Washington, DC: International Monetary Fund, February.

Ishii, Shogo, and Karl Habermeier. 2002. Capital account liberalization and financial sector stability. Occasional Paper no. 211. Washington, DC: International Monetary Fund.

Johnston, R. Barry, Mark Swinburne, Alexander Kyei, Bernard Laurens, David Mitchem, Inci Otker, Susana Sosa, and Natalia Tamirisa. 1999. Exchange rate arrangements and currency convertibility. World Economic and Financial Surveys. Washington, DC: International Monetary Fund.

Jones, Leroy P., and Il SaKong. 1980. *Government, business, and entrepreneurship in economic development: The Korean case.* Cambridge, MA: Harvard University Press.

Jun, Kwang W. 1995. Effects of capital market liberalization in Korea. In *The U.S.-Korea economic partnership,* ed. Youn-Suk Kim and Kap-Soo Oh. Aldershot, UK: Avebury Press.

Kang, David C. 2002a. Bad loans to good friends: Money, politics, and the developmental state in South Korea. *International Organization* 56 (1): 177–207.

————. 2002b. *Crony capitalism: Corruption and development in South Korea and the Philippines.* Cambridge: Cambridge University Press.

Kim, Benjamin Jin-Chun. 1993. An empirical assessment of the multiple currency basket peg system and the market average system in Korea. *Joint U.S.-Korea Academic Studies* 3:113–27.

Kim, E. Han. 1990. Financing Korean corporations: Evidence and theory. In *Korean economic development,* ed. Jene K. Kwon, 341–57. New York: Greenwood.

Kim, Hee-Kyung. 2004. FDI in Korea: Recent trends and policy issues. *Korea Focus* 12 (6): 133–52.

Kim, In-June. 1993. Fluctuating foreign-exchange rates and price competitiveness. In *Shaping a new economic relationship: The Republic of Korea and the United States,* ed. Jongryn Mo and Ramon Myers, 143–52. Stanford, CA: Hoover Institution Press.

Kim, Kyung-Soo. 2001. Managing international capital flows: The case of Korea. In *New international financial architecture and Korean perspectives,* ed. Tae-Jun Kim and Doo Yong Yang, 35–58. Seoul: Korea Institute for International Economic Policy.

Kim, Soyoung, Sunghyun H. Kim, and Yunjong Wang. 2001. *Capital account liberalization and macroeconomic performance: The case of Korea.* Seoul: Korea Institute for International Economic Policy.

Koo, Bon Ho, and Won Am Park. 1990. Exchange rate policy in Korea. In *Korean economic development,* ed. Jene K. Kwon, 79–98. Westport, CT: Greenwood.

Krueger, Anne O., and Jungho Yoo. 2002. Falling profitability, higher borrowing costs, and *chaebol* finances during the Korean crisis. In *Korean crisis and recovery,* ed. David T. Coe and Se-Jik Kim, 157–96. Washington, DC: International Monetary Fund and Korea Institute for International Economic Policy.

Kwon, Jae-Jung. 1996. Financial liberalization: 1995 accomplishments and future plans. *Korea's Economy* 1996 (12): 31–39.

Lee, Chon-Pyo. 1993. Preconditions for a successful liberalization and a feedback process of managing progressive liberalization. *Joint U.S.-Korea Academic Studies* 3:1–23.

Lee, Jong-Wha, and Changyong Rhee. 2000. Macroeconomic impacts of the Korean financial crisis: Comparison with the cross-country patterns. *World Economy* 25 (4): 539–62.

Leiderman, Leonardo. 1995. Policy lessons from Latin America's experience with capital inflows. In *Financial opening,* ed. Rudiger Dornbusch and Yung Chul Park, 80–105. Seoul: Korea Institute for Finance.

Linder, Deborah J. 1994. Foreign exchange policy, monetary policy, and capital market liberalization in Korea. In *The Korean economy at a crossroad,* ed. Sung Yeung Kwack, 123–39. Westport, CT: Praeger.

Mann, Catherine L. 2000. Korea and the brave new world of finance. *Joint U.S.-Korea Academic Studies* 10:55–68.

Noland, Marcus. 1993. The origins of U.S.-Korea trade frictions. In *Shaping a new economic relationship: The Republic of Korea and the United States,* ed. Jongryn Mo and Ramon Myers, 13–39. Stanford, CA: Hoover Institution Press.

———. 1996a. Restructuring the Korean financial system for greater competitiveness. Working Papers in Asia-Pacific Economic Cooperation no. 96-14. Washington, DC: Institute for International Economics.

———. 1996b. Some unpleasant arithmetic concerning unification. Working Papers in Asia-Pacific Economic Cooperation no. 96-13. Washington, DC: Institute for International Economics.

———. 2000. *Avoiding the apocalypse: The future of the two Koreas.* Washington, DC: Institute for International Economics.

Noland, Marcus, and Howard Pack. 2002. *Industrial policy in an era of globalization.* Washington, DC: Institute for International Economics.

Park, Yung Chul. 1984. Korea's experience with external debt management. Korea University, Department of Economics. Manuscript, April.

———. 1995. Korea's experience with managing foreign capital flows. Seoul, Korea: Korea University and Korea Institute of Finance. Manuscript, September.

Park, Yung Chul, and Chi-Young Song. 1996. Managing foreign capital flows: The experiences of Korea, Thailand, Malaysia and Indonesia. Jerome Levy Economics Institute Working Paper no. 163. Annandale-on-Hudson, NY: Bard College, May.

Park, Yung Chul, Wonho Song, and Yunjong Wang. 2003. Finance and economic development in Korea. In *Financial development and integration in East Asia,* ed. Choong Yong Ahn, Takatoshi Ito, Masahiro Kawai, and Yung Chul Park, 317–45. Seoul: Korea Institute for International Economic Policy.

Pyo, Hak K. 1989. Export-led growth, domestic distortions, and trade liberalization. Paper presented at the United States–Korea Financial Policy Discussions. 12 December, Washington, DC.

SaKong, Il. 1993. *Korea in the world economy.* Washington, DC: Institute for International Economics.

Smith, Heather. 2000. *Looking forward: Korea after the economic crisis.* Canberra, Australia: Asia Pacific Press.

Stiglitz, Joseph E. 2003. *Globalization and its discontents.* New York: Norton.

U.S. Trade Representative (USTR). 2004. *2004 national trade estimate report on foreign trade barriers.* Washington, DC: Government Printing Office.

Wang, Yen-Kyun. 1993. Exchange rates, current accounts balance of Korea, and U.S.-Korea negotiations on exchange rate matters. In *Shaping a new economic relationship: The Republic of Korea and the United States,* ed. Jongryn Mo and Ramon Myers, 153–70. Stanford, CA: Hoover Institution Press.

Wang, Yunjong, and Hyoungsoo Zang. 1998. *Adjustment reforms in Korea since the financial crisis.* Seoul: Korea Institute for International Economic Policy.
Watanabe, Toshiaki. 1996. Pacific Basin stock market returns and volatility: Statistical properties and correlations. Paper presented at the International Symposium on Macroeconomic Interdependence in the Asia-Pacific Region, Economic Planning Agency. 22–23 October, Tokyo, Japan.
Westphal, Larry E., Yung W. Rhee, and Garry Pursell. 1981. Korean industrial competence: Where it came from. World Bank Staff Working Paper no. 469. Washington, DC: World Bank.
Westphal, Larry E., Linsu Kim, and Carl Dahlman. 1985. Reflections on Korea's acquisition of technological capability. In *International technology transfer,* ed. Nathan Rosenberg and Claudio Frischtak, 167–221. New York: Praeger.
Woo, Jung-En. 1991. *Race to the swift.* New York: Columbia University Press.
Yoo, Jung-Ho. 1994. South Korea's manufactured exports and industrial targeting policy. In *Manufactured exports of East Asian industrializing economies,* ed. Shu-Chin Yang, 149–73. Armonk, NY: M. E. Sharpe.
Yoo, Seong-Min. 1999. Corporate restructuring in Korea. *Joint U.S.-Korea Academic Studies* 9:131–99.
Young, Soo-Gil. 1997. The end of Korea's economic miracle? Paper presented at congressional roundtable discussion. Washington, DC.

Comment   Gita Gopinath

This paper provides a detailed characterization of economic policy events, particularly those related to international capital flows, in South Korea from the early 1960s to the present. It describes the policy stance on internal and external financial liberalization in South Korea over this period. It notes that several years of high growth in South Korea prior to the 1980s took place in a climate of financial repression: only starting in the 1980s and later were there signs of financial liberalization. The paper also discusses the origins of the financial crisis of 1997–98 and the subsequent reforms.

This paper contributes to the literature that identifies turning points in financial liberalization policies in developing countries. A related paper that performs an analysis of policy changes with respect to financial-sector liberalization and generates an index of financial liberalization for several developing and developed economies is Abiad and Mody (2003). Their index of financial liberalization can potentially take values from 0 to 18, with higher numbers implying greater levels of financial liberalization. Consistent with this paper, they also find that until 1980 Korea had extensive controls on domestic financial institutions and international capital flows. Figure 10C.1 indicates this. Further, there is no evidence of substantial

Gita Gopinath is an assistant professor of economics at Harvard University and a faculty research fellow of the National Bureau of Economic Research.

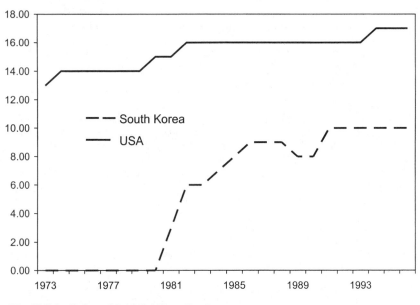

Fig. 10C.1   Index of financial liberalization
Note: For details regarding construction of this index see Abiad and Mody (2003).

reversals in the steps toward financial liberalization, as seen in figure 10C.2. This is contrary to the experience of certain other emerging markets, especially Argentina, when liberalization measures were adopted in the 1970s and almost completely reversed following the debt crisis of the 1980s. Also, comparing the level of financial development in Korea to a developed economy indicates that Korea is still below the frontier.

Country studies of this nature help answer questions about what drives changes in policy. Is it political events, crisis events, or IMF interventions? In the case of Korea it appears that at different points in time different factors were at work. Phase I, prior to 1980, was a period of extensive capital controls. This appears to be a result of the political/economic ideology at the time, which led to a state-led development strategy. A question that can be raised about this period is why savings rates were so high in Korea. Savings rates were as high as 40 percent of GDP in the initial decades, which allowed high levels of investment even when the economy was closed to foreign capital flows. To ensure policy-directed lending only, there was a need to keep domestic and international markets segmented. This involved limiting firms' financing options to regulated banks and limiting lending institutions to those that could be controlled. Until 1991, capital was mainly sourced through banks, and alternative sources of corporate finance were suppressed. This period saw the growth of the *chaebol,* and studies find that indeed the largest firms had the weakest financial structure.

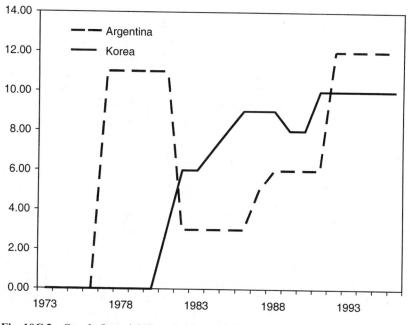

Fig. 10C.2   Steady financial liberalization

Phase II, which started around the 1980s, involved stop-and-go liberalization. The move to more liberalization was spurred partly by domestic institutions' desire to borrow at lower rates. Foreign financial service providers, especially from the United States, also desired to enter the South Korean market, and accordingly there was external pressure to open up. Also, South Korea was attempting to join the OECD. Phase III was the 1997–98 crisis phase, in which IMF-imposed policies were adopted by Korea. So the reform during this period had a substantial IMF component.

The financial crisis in South Korea in 1997–98 has often been blamed on the short-term nature of capital flows into the country. An important question, then, is why capital flows took this form. A country study, like that in this paper, is a very useful tool to decipher different stories. This paper suggests that short-term flows were very much an outcome of government policy. According to policy, foreign investors were prevented from investing in the long-term corporate bond market. There were concerns with longer-term lending because of ownership issues: The government wished to retain control over domestic financial institutions, and most of the lending went through banks. Policy therefore created an incentive to borrow short term. Further, Basel Accord incentives encouraged lending to South Korea to take the form of short-term bank lending.

This explanation for short-term flows contrasts with the explanation put forth by Diamond and Rajan (2001a, 2001b). According to this view, poor information in emerging markets and relationship banking results in foreign investors' primarily lending to banks. This is also the reason why foreign investors keep their lending short term: to safeguard themselves against the risk of bad investments by banks. It was a combination of the nature of investments being financed and lack of foreign investor confidence that resulted in a short-term debt buildup. This hypothesis is presumably testable given the policy details in this paper.

In the 1990s there was a rise in foreign currency liabilities held by Korean banks, with currency and maturity mismatches. This meant that an exchange rate adjustment would have strong negative effects on bank balance sheets. The source of the crisis in South Korea has been much debated. This paper finds a combination of explanations, including domestic shocks associated with failures of the *chaebol* and domestic political turmoil. The financial crisis in other parts of Southeast Asia and the emerging banking crisis in Japan, which was the principal source of foreign loans to South Korea, were added problems.

The question of what fundamentally changed during the crisis period in Korea is an open one. Alternative hypotheses include the view that the crisis was a liquidity crisis. An interesting feature of the crisis episode was the entry of foreign direct investment into South Korea even during crisis years. Aguiar and Gopinath (2005) find evidence that a significant portion of acquisitions took the form of fire sale of assets. That is, domestic firms that were liquidity constrained were, all else being equal, more likely to be acquired during the crisis.

Following the financial crisis, Korea took several steps to improve financial institutions by introducing new regulatory practices and standards. The paper notes that while attempts have been made to improve corporate governance, the years of financial repression have left a legacy that makes it difficult to efficiently regulate bank lending to large corporations and to enforce the new regulations. This provides an interesting perspective into the role of institutions and the persistent effect they have on future developments in an economy.

References

Abiad, Abdul, and Ashoka Mody. 2003. Financial reform: What shakes it? What shapes it? IMF Working Paper no. 07/03. Washington, DC: International Monetary Fund.

Aguiar, Mark, and Gita Gopinath. 2005. Fire-sale FDI and liquidity crises. *Review of Economics and Statistics* 87 (3): 439–52.

Diamond, Doug, and Raghuram Rajan. 2001a. Banks, short-term debt and financial crises: Theory, policy implications and applications. *Proceedings of Carnegie-Rochester Series on Public Policy* 54:37–71.

———. 2001b. Liquidity risk, liquidity creation and financial fragility: A theory of banking. *Journal of Political Economy* 109 (2): 287–327.

Malaysian Capital Controls
Macroeconomics and Institutions

Simon Johnson, Kalpana Kochhar, Todd Mitton, and
Natalia Tamirisa

11.1 Introduction

Until the late 1970s, capital controls were widely used to prevent the free
flow of funds between countries. A cautious relaxation of such controls
during the 1980s proved consistent with greater economic integration
among advanced countries and strengthened the case for capital market
opening more generally. By the early 1990s, capital controls appeared to be
finished as a serious policy tool for relatively open economies (Bhagwati
1998a). Today, however, in the aftermath of the Asian crisis, the role of capital controls is being reconsidered.

In this reassessment of capital controls, recent experience in Malaysia—
which reimposed capital controls in September 1998—has been central to
the two main views on capital controls. The more established view emphasizes macroeconomics. If a country faces a severe external crisis, particularly one caused by pure panic, and if orthodox macroeconomic policies
have failed to restore confidence, Krugman (1998) argues that imposing
capital controls may be an effective way to stabilize the economy.[1] More

Simon Johnson is the Ronald A. Kurtz Professor at the Sloan School of Management, Massachusetts Institute of Technology, and a research associate of the National Bureau of Economic Research (NBER). Kalpana Kochhar is a senior advisor in the research department of
the International Monetary Fund. Todd Mitton is an assistant professor of business management at Brigham Young University. Natalia Tamirisa is a senior economist at the International Monetary Fund (IMF).

For helpful comments we thank Sebastian Edwards, Peter Henry, participants at the NBER
preconference and conference on international capital flows, and colleagues at the IMF. Ioan-
nis Tokatlidis provided outstanding assistance. All the information used in this paper is from
publicly available sources.

1. Krugman was making policy recommendations for some Asian countries, including
Malaysia.

generally, Bhagwati (1998a, 1998b) and Rodrik (2000) oppose the conventional wisdom that free capital flows help countries benefit from trade liberalization, and argue instead that capital market liberalization invites speculative attacks. In this context, Malaysia's experience has been interpreted as demonstrating that capital controls can have positive macroeconomic effects (Kaplan and Rodrik 2001), but this claim is controversial and has been forcefully opposed by Dornbusch (2001).[2]

The second view of capital controls puts greater emphasis on institutions (i.e., the rules, practices, and organizations that govern an economy). Specifically, Rajan and Zingales (1998) argue that capital controls are an essential part of the package of policies that allows "relationship-based" capitalism to function. In this system, informal relationships between politicians and banks channel lending toward approved firms, and this is easier to sustain when a country is relatively isolated from international capital flows. If capital controls are relaxed, as in some parts of Asia in the early 1990s, the result may be overborrowing and financial collapse (Rajan and Zingales 1998).[3] In this context, Rajan and Zingales (2003) suggest that reimposing capital controls may be attractive if it enables politicians to support the financing of particular firms. If this view is correct, we should expect capital controls to be associated with more resources for favored firms. In the context of economic crises, there are two testable implications at the firm level. Firms with stronger political connections should (a) suffer more when a macroeconomic shock reduces the government's ability to provide advantages and (b) benefit more when the imposition of capital controls allows a higher level of support for particular firms.

For the macroeconomic debate, the Malaysian experience is inconclusive. The capital controls worked in the sense that they were not circumvented on a large scale. However, they also never came under serious pressure. Controls might have played a preventive role—that is, to guard against risks to financial stability—but they were never tested in this role. At the same time, there is no convincing evidence of adverse macroeconomic consequences from the controls.

In contrast, the firm-level evidence lends support to the Rajan and Zingales view of capital controls. Our estimates indicate that in the initial phase of the crisis, from July 1997 to August 1998, roughly 9 percent of the estimated US$60 billion loss in market value for politically connected firms may be attributed to the fall in the expected value of their connections.

---

2. See also Perkins and Woo (2000) and Hutchison (2003).

3. Theoretically, relaxing capital controls can lead to financial distress in at least three ways. First, local financial institutions respond by taking on more risk. Second, local firms borrow directly from international lenders, who are either unable to assess risks appropriately or believe that there is an implicit sovereign guarantee. Third, after they lose their monopolies, local banks are less willing to bail out firms that encounter problems, as in Petersen and Rajan (1995).

With the imposition of capital controls in September 1998, up to 32 percent of the estimated $5 billion gain in market value for firms connected to the prime minister may be attributed to the increase in the value of their connections. For connected firms, the value of political connections was in the range of 12–23 percent of their total market value at the end of September 1998.

The paper closest to our firm-level analysis is Fisman (2001), who estimates the value of political connections in Indonesia by looking at how stock prices moved when former president Suharto's health was reported to change. Fisman measures the direct effect of health shocks to a dictator, which is presumably quite specific to authoritarian systems, during a period of relative economic stability. The Malaysian experience lets us examine the interaction of connections and capital controls in a democracy. In addition, we are able to use variation between firms connected to politicians who continue in power and those who lose out. This helps ensure that political connections rather than some other unobservable characteristics of firms drive our results.

Our paper is part of a growing literature that examines the performance of relatively privileged firms. La Porta, Lopez de Silanes, and Zamarippa (2003) show that well-connected Mexican banks engaged in a considerable amount of irresponsible lending before the 1995 crisis, and this presumably contributed to the severity of the crisis when it came. To our knowledge, no previous papers have tried to measure the combined effects of connections and capital controls.

Our work is also related to the recent literature that shows important links between institutions, firm-level governance, and macroeconomic outcomes. Johnson et al. (2000) present evidence that the Asian financial crisis had more severe effects in countries with weaker institutions in general and weaker investor protection in particular (as measured by La Porta et al. 1997, 1998). Mitton (2002) finds firm-level evidence that weaker corporate governance was associated with worse stock price performance in the Asian crisis, and Lemmon and Lins (2003) confirm these results using different definitions of governance and outcomes. More broadly, Morck, Yeung, and Yu (2000) argue that in countries with weak property rights protection, stock price movements are predominantly driven by political shocks.

The paper is organized as follows. Section 11.2 summarizes the history of Malaysian capital controls.[4] Section 11.3 reviews the macroeconomic

---

4. Sections 11.2 and 11.3 draw on publicly available data and documents, in particular, press releases, exchange notices, and annual reports of Bank Negara Malaysia (available at http://www.bnm.gov.my) as well as the IMF's *Annual Report on Exchange Arrangements and Exchange Restrictions.* For more details on the chronology of crisis in Malaysia and the authorities' response, see Meesook et al. (2001) and Tamirisa (2006). Section 11.4 draws on Johnson and Mitton (2003).

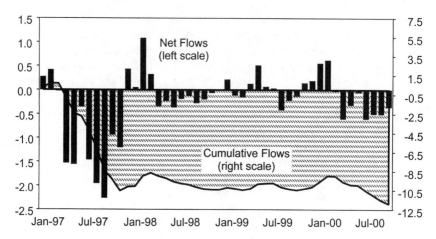

Fig. 11.1   Malaysia: Cumulative and net portfolio flows, 1997–2000 (in billions of U.S. dollars)

Source: Meesook et al. (2001).

evidence. Section 11.4 assesses the firm-level evidence. Section 11.5 concludes.

11.2   Brief Chronology of Capital Controls and Macroeconomic Policies

In 1968 Malaysia removed restrictions on payments and transfers for current international transactions, accepting the obligations of the IMF's Article VIII. Exchange and capital account regulations were relaxed further in 1973, and Malaysia moved from a fixed to a floating exchange rate. Subsequently the authorities gradually liberalized capital controls, particularly in 1986–87.[5]

Appendix A reports the details of Malaysian capital controls since 1992. At the time of the Asian crisis, portfolio flows were generally free of restrictions. Domestic and international credit transactions in foreign currency were carefully controlled, but international trade and financial transactions denominated in ringgit were allowed and perhaps even promoted. As a result, an active and largely unregulated offshore market in ringgit developed.

After Thailand devalued in July 1997, the Malaysian ringgit came under severe pressure. Portfolio outflows intensified (figure 11.1), and foreign exchange reserves plummeted (figure 11.2). As currency traders took speculative positions against the ringgit in the offshore market, offshore ringgit

5. In 1994, Malaysia temporarily reintroduced some controls to stem inflows of short-term capital.

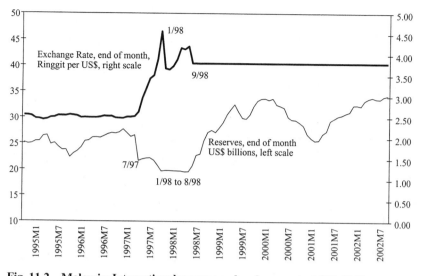

Fig. 11.2   Malaysia: International reserves and exchange rate, 1995–2000
Source: IMF, *International Financial Statistics.*

interest rates rose markedly relative to onshore rates (figure 11.3). This further intensified the movement of ringgit funds offshore.

The initial response of the authorities was to tighten macroeconomic policies.[6] Spending cuts were introduced in 1997, and the 1998 budget was drafted to target a surplus of 2.5 percent of gross domestic product (GDP). Base lending rates were allowed to rise somewhat in response to higher interbank interest rates (figure 11.4), and lending targets were adjusted to reduce growth of credit for financing purchases of real estate and securities. These measures had little stabilizing impact on financial markets as crisis continued to spread in the region. When the extent of the output collapse became clearer, by early 1998, fiscal policy became more expansionary. The target for the 1998 budget was relaxed to a surplus of 0.5 percent of GDP in March 1998. A package of measures to strengthen the financial sector was also introduced at the same time.

In early September 1998, arguing that the measures and reforms that had been put in place by all countries affected by the Asian crisis did not appear to be returning stability to financial markets, the Malaysian authorities imposed capital controls and pegged the ringgit to the U.S. dollar.[7]

---

6. The Malaysian authorities intervened heavily in the foreign exchange market and sharply raised interest rates in July 1997. These measures were abandoned after a few days. In August 1997, the authorities introduced limits on ringgit swap transactions with nonresidents to stabilize the offshore market. They also restricted trading in blue chip stocks on the Kuala Lumpur Stock Exchange. For more details, see Meesook et al. (2001).

7. See appendix A and Bank Negara Malaysia (1998).

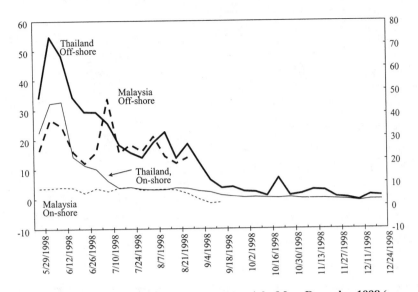

Fig. 11.3   Malaysia and Thailand: Swap differentials, May–December 1998 (swap premia, one month forward)
Sources: Data provided by Malaysian authorities; Consensus Economics, Inc.; Asia Pacific Consensus Forecasts; and IMF staff estimates.

To close the offshore market in ringgit and ringgit assets, investors were re-quired to repatriate all ringgit held offshore back to Malaysia, licensed offshore banks were prohibited from trading in ringgit assets, and residents were prohibited from granting or receiving ringgit credit vis-à-vis nonresi-dents. Among supporting measures, the authorities prohibited offshore trading of ringgit assets and brought to a halt long-standing trading in Malaysian shares in Singapore.[8] In addition to controls on international transactions in the ringgit, the authorities imposed controls on portfolio outflows, particularly a one-year holding period on nonresidents' repatri-ating proceeds from the sale of Malaysian securities and a prior approval requirement—above a certain limit—for residents to transfer capital abroad.

The controls were carefully designed to withstand pressure—that is, to close all known channels and loopholes for the supply of the ringgit to the offshore market and major portfolio outflows—while attempting not to affect foreign direct investment and current account convertibility (see ap-pendix A). The authorities also stressed the temporary nature of the con-trols. Furthermore, a number of preconditions facilitated the implementa-tion of capital controls—a history of using some controls, effective state

---

8. The controls were gradually relaxed, beginning in December 1998. See appendix A for more details.

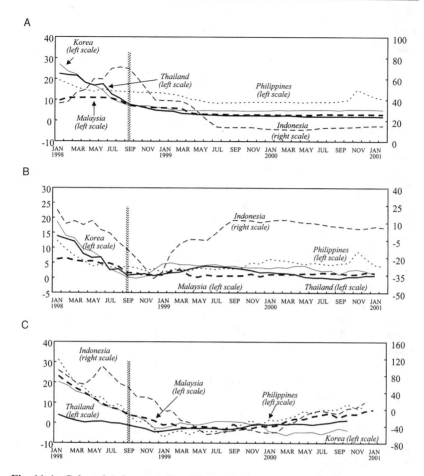

Fig. 11.4   Selected Asian countries: Monetary indicators, 1998–2001: *A,* **nominal interest rates (percent per annum, end of period);** *B,* **real interest rate (percent per annum, end of period);** *C,* **private-sector credit growth (twelve-month percent change)**
Sources: IMF's *International Financial Statistics* and Asia Pacific department databases.

capacity, and generally strong bank supervision and regulation (Meesook et al. 2001; Latifah 2002).

11.3   Macroeconomic Issues

11.3.1   Understanding the Motivation for the Controls

The authorities emphasized financial stability as the primary motivation for these controls. The official press releases that accompanied the introduction of capital controls underscored the following objectives: "(i) to limit the contagion effects of external developments on the Malaysian economy; (ii) to preserve the recent gains made in terms of the policy measures to stabilize the domestic economy; and (iii) to ensure stability in domestic prices and the ringgit exchange rate and create an environment that is conducive for a revival in investor and consumer confidence and facilitate economic recovery."[9]

Although interpreting data in real time is more difficult than it is ex post, it is now clear that the risks to financial stability in Asia had diminished by the summer of 1998. A significant portion of capital had already flowed out by the time the controls were imposed (figure 11.1). The ringgit had already depreciated by 70 percent, and pressure on the currency was letting up by the summer of 1998 (figure 11.2). Offshore swap differentials for Malaysia (as for Thailand) were trending down (figure 11.3). And quarterly GDP growth data showed that the crisis had bottomed out in the first quarter of 1998 (figure 11.5).

The Malaysian authorities acknowledged that the political and social fallout from the crisis in other countries did weigh in their decision to impose controls (Latifah 2002). The authorities were concerned about political and social stability, "which defined the country even more than the deterioration in the level of wealth" (Meesook et al. 2001). These concerns were consistent with a worsening of political risk indicators during the summer of 1998 (figure 11.6, where a lower score indicates higher perceived risk), particularly following the political turmoil in Indonesia. Theoretically, in September 1998 there was a worst-case scenario of domestic capital flight and increased offshore speculation against the ringgit that would have entailed significant economic and political costs for the country. Seen in this light, the controls played a role in guarding against the eventuality of this scenario.

The worst-case scenario did not come to pass in September 1998.[10] To a large extent, this reflected increased incentives for holding the ringgit, given the improvement in market sentiment about the region as signs of an economic turnaround became clearer, and also the increase in global liquidity following cuts in U.S. interest rates. Several observers have also noted that the ex post undervaluation of the ringgit made avoiding the capital controls unappealing (see, for example, IMF 1999; Meesook et al. 2001; World Bank 2000; and Jeong and Mazier 2003).[11]

---

9. See Bank Negara Malaysia (1998). The authorities considered the capital controls as complementing the introduction of the peg, which in turn was seen as an appropriate "strategic response to the unique circumstances at the time" and a way "to introduce a large degree of stability and predictability to mitigate the impact of market volatility on the real economy" (Latifah 2002).

10. Malaysia has turned out to be the only Asian-crisis country that did not have a government change during 1997–98.

11. Capital controls and other measures aimed at closing the offshore market prompted an influx of ringgit funds into the stock market, causing it to rally.

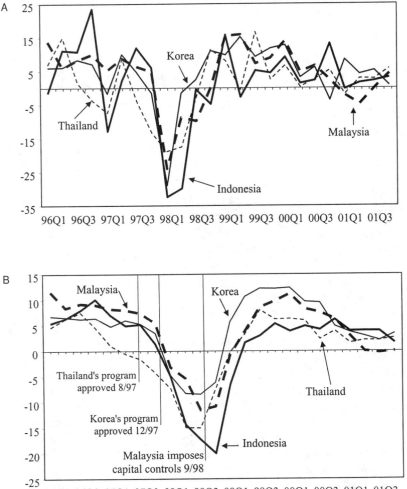

Fig. 11.5   Selected Asian countries: Real GDP growth, 1996–2001: *A,* **quarter-on-quarter (annualized and seasonally adjusted);** *B,* **year-on-year**
Sources: IMF's Asia Pacific department databases for Indonesia, Korea, and Thailand; Haver Analytics for Malaysia; and IMF's *International Financial Statistics.*

11.3.2   Macroeconomic Impact

Kaplan and Rodrik (2001) argue that the capital controls enabled a faster and less painful recovery in Malaysia compared with the experience in Korea and Thailand. But their argument is based on the assumption that Malaysia in September 1998 should be compared with other countries

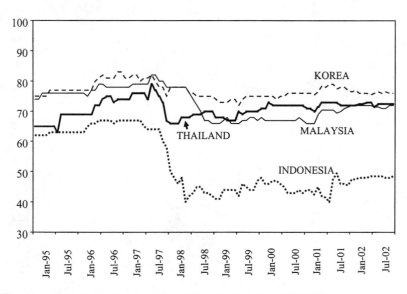

Fig. 11.6   Selected Asian countries: Political risk index, 1995–2002
Source: International Country Risk Guide (http://www.icrgonline.com).

when they adopted IMF programs (six to twelve months earlier). It is hard to make this position persuasive.

Independent of capital controls, Malaysia was well placed to experience a shallower downturn and a faster recovery than other countries. As emphasized by Dornbusch (2001), initial conditions, particularly the "burden" of short-term corporate debt, were more favorable in Malaysia than in other Asian crisis countries.[12] In terms of institutional indicators, Malaysia also stands out among its regional peers, with higher rankings of government effectiveness, regulatory quality, rule of law, and control of corruption (figure 11.7).

In the event, the timing and magnitude of the output decline were similar in the four countries most seriously affected by the Asia-wide crisis (Indonesia, Korea, Malaysia, and Thailand, hereinafter referred to as crisis countries). Hutchison's (2003) empirical assessment leads to a similar conclusion. Hutchison also points out that Kaplan and Rodrik's analysis does not take into account the fact that the Malaysian currency crisis might not

12. Malaysia has had a long-standing policy of controlling external borrowing by the domestic private sector. Besides prudential controls on external borrowing by banks and their domestic lending in foreign currency, external borrowing by domestic corporations above a certain limit required approval, which reportedly was given for projects that generated or saved foreign currency. The authorities see this measure as helping promote "natural hedging" of private debt service payments, whereby residents borrowing externally could meet their external (non-ringgit) obligations through their own foreign currency earnings (Latifah 2002).

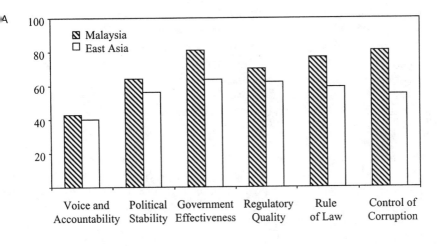

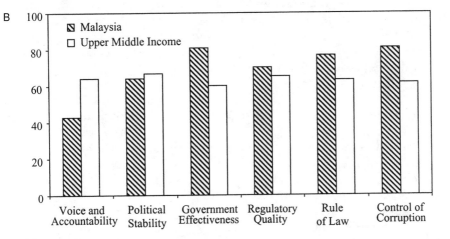

Fig. 11.7   Governance indicators in percentile rankings, 1998: *A,* **Malaysia and East Asia;** *B,* **Malaysia and upper middle-income countries**

Source: Kaufmann, Kraay, and Mastruzzi (2005).

Note: The upper middle-income countries, according to World Bank's classification, is represented by the average value of the following group: Argentina, Belize, Botswana, Chile, Costa Rica, Croatia, Czech Republic, Dominica, Estonia, Gabon, Grenada, Hungary, Latvia, Lebanon, Lithuania, Mauritius, Mexico, Oman, Panama, Poland, Saudi Arabia, Seychelles, Slovak Republic, Saint Kitts–Nevis, Saint Lucia, Trinidad and Tobago, Uruguay, and Venezuela.

have lasted until September 1998 if an IMF program had been in place from 1997.

Likewise, the timing and strength of the recovery of the Malaysian economy were similar to those of the other Asian crisis countries. By the summer of 1998, all the crisis-affected countries had begun to show recovery (figure 11.5), and Malaysia recovered at about the same rate as Korea and Thailand (the momentum of recovery in Indonesia was weaker than in the other countries). There is thus no evidence to suggest that the Malaysian economy performed better than the others following the imposition of the controls. This is not surprising, given that Malaysia's macroeconomic policies were broadly similar to those in other crisis countries.

Some commentators argued that the controls could be used to allow the government to undertake expansionary fiscal and monetary policy without fear of worsening external imbalances (e.g., Perkins and Woo 2000). However, the evidence shows that the Malaysian authorities did not use controls to pursue heterodox policies such as a substantial lowering of interest rates or providing a particularly aggressive fiscal stimulus. In the event, the timing and pace of interest rate reductions in Malaysia were not out of line with those in the other crisis countries, where there were no capital controls (figure 11.4). A comparison with Korea is particularly instructive in this context. In nominal terms, interest rates in Korea and Malaysia were similar during the period in question. But in real terms, interest rates were brought down earlier and more aggressively in Korea: by the summer of 1998, they were already below those in Malaysia, and remained below after the controls were imposed. Moreover, the fiscal impulse provided in Malaysia was smaller than in other crisis countries in 1998 and broadly similar in 1999 (figure 11.8 and Meesook et al. 2001).[13] The current account surplus and increases in reserves during the recovery stage were larger in Malaysia than in other countries, in part reflecting the undervaluation of the ringgit. Throughout the crisis and into the capital control period the authorities pursued what are generally considered to be orthodox macroeconomic and structural policies.

All in all, there is no evidence in the data to suggest that capital controls made a visible difference in Malaysia's recovery process. Responsible macroeconomic policies and commitment to financial- and corporate-sector reforms, together with strong initial conditions and institutional capacity, should receive the main credit for the recovery in Malaysia.[14] As the experience of other crisis countries shows, these policies were possible without capital controls.

13. The fiscal impulse was larger in 2000, but by this time controls had been significantly relaxed.
14. See Lindgren et al. (1999), Meesook et al. (2001), and Latifah (2002) for a detailed discussion of structural reforms in Malaysia during and after the crisis.

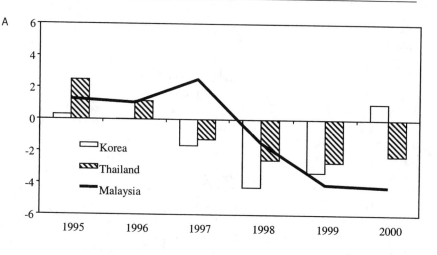

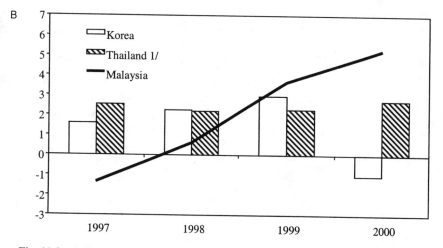

Fig. 11.8   Asian countries: Fiscal indicators, 1995–2000 (percent of GDP):
A, **overall fiscal balance;** *B,* **cumulative fiscal impulse**
Source: Meesook et al. (2001).
Note: In panel B, Thailand is on a fiscal-year basis, where the fiscal year ends in September.

At the same time, there is no evidence that controls had lasting costs by
affecting Malaysia's access to international portfolio capital. While Thailand, Korea, and Indonesia also suffered lower investor ratings after the
crisis hit, Malaysia suffered a particularly steep fall from 1998 to 1999. But
by 2003, all four countries had regained their previous relative rankings.
Three of the countries had slightly lower absolute rankings than before—
only Indonesia was much lower. Malaysia's spreads widened by more than

those of other countries after capital controls were introduced, but these effects unwound relatively rapidly.

One open question is whether there is any evidence that, after the capital controls, investors perceived Malaysia as a less desirable destination for foreign direct investment (FDI). According to the 2004 United Nations Conference on Trade and Development (UNCTAD) annual report on FDI, Malaysia has maintained a steady ranking (around 33rd–34th in the world) in terms of FDI "potential" (measured on the basis of "structural factors" such as physical infrastructure, GDP per capita, total exports and imports of natural resources, education, energy use, and the stock of FDI), but in terms of capital attracted it has slipped from around 5th–10th in the world before the crisis to 70th–75th after the crisis. Other Asian countries affected by the crisis—with the exception of Indonesia—did not experience similarly sharp falls in actual inward FDI performance, as assessed by UNCTAD.

In addition, the recovery in Malaysia's private fixed investment has been slower than in other crisis countries (figure 11.9). The decline from high precrisis levels is consistent with the view that these countries were investing too much in the early and mid-1990s. While we do not yet have enough data to draw definite conclusions, it is striking that Korea, Thailand, and Indonesia have all shown a stronger recovery in private investment than

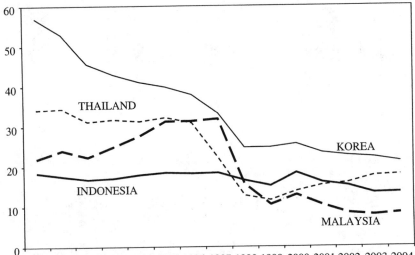

Fig. 11.9   Selected Asian countries: Private fixed investment, 1990–2004 (private gross fixed capital formation as percent of GDP)

Sources: IMF World Economic Outlook Database; for Korea, OECD database.

Note: Observations for Indonesia before 1999 are estimated on the assumption that the ratio of private to public fixed investment is constant and equal to its average for the period 1999–2004.

has Malaysia. Private investment, as a percent of GDP, has recently been remarkably low—under 10 percent—in Malaysia, and only about half the regional average.

11.4   Firm-Level Evidence

11.4.1   Political Connections in Malaysia

Gomez and Jomo (1997) suggest there were two forms of political connections in Malaysia prior to 1997. The first is the official status awarded to firms that are run by ethnic Malays. The second consists of much more informal ties that exist between leading politicians and firms that are run by both Malay and Chinese businesspeople.

Although ethnic Malays (known as Bumiputras, literally "sons of the soil") account for some 60 percent of the population, business in Malaysia has historically been dominated by ethnic Chinese. With an eye toward correcting this imbalance, and partly in response to ethnic rioting in 1969, the government instituted the New Economic Policy (NEP) in 1970. Since that time, Bumiputras have been given, among other privileges, priority for government contracts, increased access to capital, opportunities to buy assets that are privatized, and other subsidies. The ruling coalition in Malaysia for over three decades has been the Barisan Nasional, which is dominated by the United Malays' National Organisation (UMNO). Dr. Mahathir bin Mohamad, president of UMNO and prime minister of Malaysia from 1981 to 2003, consistently promoted Bumiputra capitalism (Gomez and Jomo 1997).

The increased state intervention required for implementation of the NEP opened the door to greater political involvement in the financing of firms in Malaysia. During the 1990s, two government officials were most influential in promoting firms in Malaysia. The first was the prime minister. The second was Anwar Ibrahim, finance minister during the Asian crisis.[15] Below we denote the first type of firm as PMC (prime minister connected) and the second type as FMC (finance minister connected).

11.4.2   Identifying Firm-Level Political Connections

To identify which firms have political connections with government officials, we rely on the analysis of Gomez and Jomo (1997). This analysis has

15. Before moving on to the coding of political connections, it is important to note that there is no evidence suggesting that any unobserved characteristics of these firms determined their political affiliations. Before the Asian financial crisis, the evidence suggests that affiliations to either the finance minister or the prime minister were close substitutes. Indeed, there is no evidence that the alliances between firms and specific politicians were the result of anything other than chance personal relationships (Gomez and Jomo 1997, pp. 126, 148–49). Any systematic differences in the performance of these firms should therefore be due to the changing relative value of their political connections.

been used extensively to identify political connections in Malaysia in previous work, including Johnson and Mitton (2003), Faccio (2006), Faccio, Masulis, and McConnell (2006), and Chong, Liu, and Tan (2005).

Using the analysis of Gomez and Jomo (1997) to identify connections creates some limitations. First, these authors do not claim to have exhaustively identified every firm with political connections in Malaysia. Second, although all connections identified by Gomez and Jomo (1997) are from before the Asian crisis, some are identified from earlier in the 1990s, creating the possibility that a connection could have disappeared prior to the beginning of the crisis.[16] However, given the relative stability of the government over this period, it seems unlikely that changes in political connections would be prevalent during this period. Many political connections identified by Gomez and Jomo are unofficial and have not been verified by other sources. Finally, the coding of political connections does not measure the strength of these connections. Nevertheless, Gomez and Jomo offer an extensive analysis, and we take a systematic approach to identifying connections based on their work. Consequently, our coding of connections likely presents a fairly clear picture of investors' perceptions of political connections during this time period. See appendix B for more details and examples of our coding.

11.4.3 Sample and Descriptive Statistics

Our sample is taken from the set of Malaysian firms in the Worldscope database. Worldscope maintains data on active and inactive firms, so there is no sample selection bias due to firms dropping out of the data set. The firms in our sample are representative of the firms listed on the main board of the Kuala Lumpur Stock Exchange. Firms not included in our sample include smaller unlisted Malaysian firms and multinationals with no local listing.

Table 11.1 reports the basic descriptive data for these firms. In this table we compare the performance of politically connected firms to that of unconnected firms prior to the crisis. We define political connections for each firm in our sample as outlined in the previous section. Table 11.1 also compares the performance of PMC firms to FMC firms, and shows the performance of nonfinancial firms separately. Row 1 reports the number of firms in each category of our sample; the total number of firms with available precrisis data is 424, of which 67 had identifiable political connections.

Row 2 of table 11.1 shows that politically connected firms had significantly worse returns (compared with unconnected firms) during the crisis

---

16. In the second edition of their book, which was prepared in late 1997 and appeared in 1998, Gomez and Jomo (1998) updated their list of political connections. We have used this revised list as a robustness check and find that it does not affect any of our main results. However, we prefer to use their precrisis list, as this was complete before there was any sign of economic trouble.

Table 11.1 Summary statistics of firm-level sample

	All Worldscope firms							Nonfinancial firms only			
	All	Politically connected	Unconnected	p-value	PM connected	FM connected	p-value	All	Politically connected	Unconnected	p-value
1. Number of firms	424	67	357		53	14		312	50	262	
Stock returns											
2. July 1997 to August 1998	−78.5%	−83.0%	−77.7%	0.010	−83.4%	−81.3%	0.529	−78.1%	−82.1%	−77.3%	0.065
3. September 1998	39.7%	53.2%	37.1%	0.000	61.7%	31.3%	0.021	38.7%	50.5%	36.1%	0.007
4. October 1998 to September 2000	81.9%	83.5%	81.7%	0.897	69.8%	132.2%	0.036	81.6%	94.8%	79.1%	0.348
Precrisis performance measures											
5. Size (total assets in $000)	986,606	1,845,217	820,423	0.012	1,799,914	2,013,485	0.816	599,554	1,299,733	465,535	0.000
6. Growth (in assets, one year)	50.3%	67.3%	46.8%	0.301	81.7%	20.3%	0.376	42.3%	39.3%	42.9%	0.834
7. Profitability (return on assets)	4.0%	−1.2%	4.9%	0.041	−3.0%	5.2%	0.604	3.7%	−2.7%	4.9%	0.062
8. Liquidity (current ratio)	1.77	1.53	1.82	0.432	1.52	1.61	0.846	1.69	1.54	1.72	0.516
9. Efficiency (asset turnover)	0.55	0.47	0.56	0.147	0.44	0.55	0.421	0.65	0.56	0.66	0.170
10. Valuation (book-market ratio)	0.45	0.47	0.45	0.568	0.50	0.36	0.105	0.42	0.45	0.42	0.450
Precrisis leverage											
11. Leverage (total debt/total assets)	23.7%	33.7%	21.9%	0.000	36.0%	24.6%	0.298	26.1%	36.9%	24.0%	0.000
12. Precrisis increase in leverage (one year)	2.7%	6.3%	2.0%	0.062	8.4%	−70.0%	0.334	3.2%	7.7%	2.3%	0.046
13. Maturity (short-term debt/total debt)	61.8%	57.1%	62.8%	0.216	56.8%	58.5%	0.869	61.7%	59.3%	62.2%	0.573
14. Precrisis increase (one year)	−2.2%	−7.7%	−1.1%	0.088	−7.6%	−7.9%	0.975	−1.9%	−8.9%	−0.5%	0.062

Notes: The table presents summary statistics of Malaysian firms in the Worldscope database. The numbers reported are simple averages except as noted. Listed p-values are from t-tests of differences of means. "Politically connected" refers to a firm with identifiable political connections from Gomez and Jomo (1997). A financial firm is defined as one with primary SIC in the range 6000–6999. Financial figures are based on the last reported financial statements prior to July 1997. Data points are missing for some items; thus, the number of observations included for each average may vary. PM = prime minister; FM = financial minister.

period of July 1997 to August 1998, although there was no significant difference between PMC and FMC firms. Row 3 shows that politically connected firms had significantly better returns (compared with unconnected firms) after the imposition of capital controls in September 1998, and that PMC firms performed much better than FMC firms during this period. Row 4 shows no significant differences between politically connected and unconnected firms in returns after September 1998.

Row 5 of table 11.1 shows that, in terms of total assets, politically connected firms were significantly larger than unconnected firms (about twice the size on average), although asset growth immediately before the crisis was not significantly greater in connected firms (row 6). There is no evidence that PMC firms had larger size on average than FMC firms.

Row 7 of table 11.1 suggests that politically connected firms were less profitable than unconnected firms (in terms of return on assets) before the crisis.[17] However, in regression analysis (not reported here but available on request) we control for other firm characteristics, such as firm size and industry, and find no evidence that politically connected firms had lower profitability before the crisis (Johnson and Mitton 2003).[18] Rows 8 and 9 show no differences in the liquidity (current ratio) and efficiency (asset turnover ratio), respectively, across the dimensions of political connections (in terms of t-tests of the means). The book-market ratio is one way to examine whether investors perceive that there is expropriation of assets by managers or controlling shareholders. Row 10 shows that these ratios are not significantly different for any group of firms before the crisis.

In the next section of table 11.1 we examine the financial leverage of firms prior to the crisis period. If politically connected firms had greater leverage prior to the crisis, then this could explain some or all of the performance differences in stock price performance. A firm with higher debt would naturally be expected to perform worse in a crisis (compared to a firm with less debt) both because of the effect of leverage on a firm's covariation with the market and also because the depreciation of the local currency hurts a firm if any of its debt is denominated in foreign currency. In addition, if the government responds to the crisis by raising interest rates—as in Malaysia early in the crisis—this raises the cost of servicing corporate debt. The data on leverage in table 11.1 show that firms with political connections had debt-asset ratios more than 11 percentage points higher, on average, than unconnected firms prior to the crisis (row 11). In addition, leverage was rising significantly faster for connected firms prior

---

17. This is consistent with the notion that politically connected firms were not well run, at least with respect to performance reported in audited statements (as opposed to private benefits).

18. Using data through 1995, fewer firms, and a different specification, Samad (n.d.) finds that politically connected firms have higher profitability but no difference in investment behavior.

to the crisis (row 12). However, politically connected firms had less short-term debt (maturity less than one year) as a percentage of total debt (row 13), and connected firms had a lower percentage increase in short-term debt prior to the crisis (row 14). These apparent differences in leverage between connected and unconnected firms are only rough measures, of course, in that they do not account for differences in industry or other firm characteristics.

In further regression analysis (not reported here but available on request) we control for other factors, and we still find that politically connected firms had more debt before the crisis (see Johnson and Mitton 2003). Controlling for standard determinants of leverage—size, profitability, growth, and industry—accounts for some, but not all, of the difference in leverage between favored and other firms.[19] After controlling for all these factors, among nonfinancial firms politically connected firms still had debt ratios 5 percentage points higher (with the coefficient significant at the 10 percent level).

Overall, the evidence in table 11.1 does not suggest that favored firms performed differently during the crisis primarily because they were operated any better or worse (than unconnected firms) before the crisis. However, size and leverage stand out as the primary characteristics that differ between connected and unconnected firms, and we will control for these characteristics in subsequent regression analysis.

11.4.4 Hypotheses and Regression Specification

We now turn to analysis of firm-level performance of connected firms relative to unconnected firms during the crisis period and imposition of capital controls. Note that the nature of the data does not let us distinguish the market perception of the capital controls separately from other events that took place at the same time and were associated with the imposition of these controls.

If political connections mattered in Malaysia, then the Rajan and Zingales view suggests three specific hypotheses:

- The stock price of politically connected firms should have fallen more in the early crisis period.
- When capital controls were imposed, the stock price of politically connected firms should have risen (relative to unconnected firms). Within the set of politically connected firms, the benefits of capital controls should be concentrated in PMC firms rather than FMC firms in September 1998.

---

19. Specifically, larger firms had higher debt ratios, as predicted by Titman and Wessels (1988); more-profitable firms had lower debt ratios, as suggested by Myers (1977); and firms with higher growth had higher debt ratios.

- After the imposition of capital controls, PMC firms should have shown some evidence of having received advantages.

We examine the evidence for each of these hypotheses in turn. We begin by assessing the impact of political connections on stock price performance during the crisis period and after the imposition of capital controls. Because we use monthly stock return data, we define the "crisis period" as July 1997 through August 1998.[20] Other studies have focused on September 1998 as a key date in the Malaysian crisis.[21] The most detailed account of Malaysia's economic crisis, by Jomo (2001, chap. 7), also identifies the beginning of September 1998 as the critical turning point. Returns for the month of September 1998 are used to assess the stock price impact of capital controls.

To study stock price performance, we estimate the following cross-sectional return model:

$$(1) \quad \text{Stock return}_i = \alpha + \text{Political connection}_i + \text{Size}_i + \text{Leverage}_i + \text{Industry}_i + \varepsilon_i,$$

where the stock return for firm i is measured over a specified period. Stock returns are dividend inclusive and expressed in ringgit.[22] The political connection variables change according to the specification. Equation (1) also shows that we control for other factors that may influence returns; in particular, we control for those factors for which differences were demonstrated between connected and unconnected firms in table 11.1 Size$_i$ and Leverage$_i$ for each firm i are as defined in table 11.1, and Industry$_i$ corresponds to a set of dummy variables corresponding to the primary industry of firm i, where industries are defined broadly, as in Campbell (1996).

11.4.5 The Crisis Period: July 1997–August 1998

Table 11.2 presents the results from these regressions for the period from July 1997 to August 1998. In the first three columns, the politically connected dummy variable is included. For nonfinancial firms, the coefficient on the politically connected dummy is –0.075, indicating that a political connection is associated with a greater stock price decline of 7.5 percent-

20. The beginning of the crisis period corresponds to the devaluation of the Thai baht on July 2, 1997, a date generally considered to be the starting point of the Asian financial crisis. The end of the crisis period and start of the "rebound period" corresponds to the imposition of capital controls on September 2, 1998, when the stock index began a sustained upward trend.

21. Capital controls were announced on September 1, and the ringgit-dollar rate was fixed in the early afternoon of September 2, 1998.

22. We do not calculate abnormal returns using historical betas because data limitations prevent calculation of precrisis betas for many of the firms in the sample. Even requiring a price history of just twenty-four months, we can calculate betas for only 65 percent of the firms in our sample. In this subsample, all of our key results are robust to including beta in the regressions.

Table 11.2   Political connections and crisis-period stock returns (dependent variables: stock return from July 1997 to August 1998)

	Political connections			PM and FM connections		
	Nonfinancial firms	Financial firms	All firms	Nonfinancial firms	Financial firms	All firms
Politically connected	−0.075***	−0.077***	−0.077***			
	(−2.97)	(−3.42)	(−3.88)			
PM connected				−0.079***	−0.091***	−0.083***
				(−2.78)	(−3.58)	(−3.64)
FM connected				−0.059	−0.046	−0.056**
				(−1.61)	(−1.34)	(−2.06)
Firm size	0.074***	0.041*	0.070***	0.074***	0.042*	0.070***
	(5.19)	(1.71)	(5.56)	(5.19)	(1.75)	(5.56)
Debt ratio	−0.0014*	−0.0011	−0.0014**	−0.0014*	−0.0010	−0.0014**
	(−1.87)	(−1.65)	(−2.10)	(−1.85)	(−1.53)	(−2.07)
No. of observations	312	112	424	312	112	424
R-squared	0.269	0.095	0.236	0.269	0.099	0.237

Notes: The table reports coefficient estimates from regressions of stock returns on political connection variables and control variables over the Asian crisis period of July 1997 to August 1998. All Malaysian firms with available data in the Worldscope database are included. Also estimated but not reported are a constant term and industry dummy variables. "Politically connected" means the firm has an identifiable connection with key government officials from Gomez and Jomo (1997). "PM connected" and "FM connected" indicate the source of the political connection to prime minister and finance minister, respectively, as in Gomez and Jomo (1997). Firm size is measured as the log of total assets; the debt ratio is measured as total debt over total assets. Numbers in parentheses are heteroskedasticity-robust *t*-statistics.

***Significant at the 1 percent level.
**Significant at the 5 percent level.
*Significant at the 10 percent level.

age points, on average, during the crisis period of July 1997 through August 1998.[23] For financial firms, the coefficient is similar, at −0.077. These coefficients are significant at the 1 percent level of confidence. The control variables for size and leverage are also significant in these regressions, with larger size being associated with higher returns during the crisis, and higher leverage with lower returns.

In the last three columns, we include separate dummies for PMC and FMC. Both types of politically connected firms had worse stock price performance than did unconnected firms, but the difference in performance between PMC and FMC firms is small in this time period. Among nonfinancial firms, PMC firms had a greater decline of 7.9 percentage points, and FMC firms had a greater decline of 5.9 percentage points.

Note that, depending on the precise specification, as many as six of the

---

23. See table 11.1 for average declines in stock price: 83 percent for connected firms and 77.7 percent for unconnected firms in this first phase of the crisis.

twelve industry dummies are significant in our crisis-period regressions.[24] However, including industry dummies does not weaken the coefficients on the political connection variables.

In the first phase of the financial crisis, therefore, political connections were associated with a significant negative effect on the stock price performance of Malaysian firms (although the total decline in all stock prices was larger than the connection-specific effect). This is broadly consistent with the Rajan and Zingales (1998) view that firms with strong political connections suffer more in a financial crisis, presumably because the expected value of government support declines. It is hard to know exactly what the Malaysian government was doing with regard to such support in 1997–98, but the finance minister's stated policy was to follow tight budget discipline along the lines of a de facto IMF program (although Malaysia did not sign up for official IMF conditionality). There was also a certain amount of political rhetoric regarding the need to reduce cronyism (and various statements from both the finance minister and the prime minister about who was or was not a "crony"). Our results indicate that the market interpreted the policies of July 1997 to August 1998 as squeezing politically connected firms.[25]

11.4.6   The Effects of Capital Controls: September 1998

If politically connected firms performed poorly during the first phase of the crisis because the connections themselves decreased in value, then connected firms should rebound more than unconnected firms when capital controls were imposed. (Again, we are measuring not the effects of the controls alone, but rather the market's view—which may have been incorrect—of all the events associated with the controls.)

In general, it could be difficult to differentiate a rebound based on political connections from a rebound based on operating characteristics of firms. But Malaysian political events allow for a cleaner test. September 1998 marked both the imposition of capital controls and also the downfall of the finance minister. Once considered the prime minister's certain successor, the finance minister was fired on September 2, 1998, and then jailed on charges of corruption on September 20, 1998. Over the course of September 1998, investors' perceptions were that these events reduced the value of political connections for firms with strong ties to the finance minister. To the extent that politically connected firms enjoyed a rebound in September due to the increased value of their connections, investors would not expect the same increase in value to be enjoyed by FMC firms.

Table 11.3 presents the results of regressions of stock returns for Sep-

---

24. Following Campbell (1996, table 1) the industries are petroleum, finance/real estate, consumer durables, basic industry, food/tobacco, construction, capital goods, transportation, utilities, textiles/trade, services, and leisure.

25. We have performed a number of robustness tests on these results that are not reported here but are discussed in Johnson and Mitton (2003). In particular, the regression results are robust to controlling for political favoritism of Bumiputra firms.

Table 11.3   **Political connections and stock returns following the imposition of capital controls (dependent variable: stock return for September 1998)**

	Political connections			PM and FM connections		
	Nonfinancial firms	Financial firms	All firms	Nonfinancial firms	Financial firms	All firms
Politically connected	0.081	0.285***	0.138**			
	(1.23)	(2.69)	(2.42)			
PM connected				0.130*	0.403***	0.199***
				(1.76)	(3.02)	(2.98)
FM connected				−0.116	0.027	−0.063
				(−1.11)	(0.24)	(−0.81)
Firm size	0.014	−0.038	0.001	0.015	−0.043	0.000
	(0.42)	(−0.50)	(0.04)	(0.43)	(−0.58)	(0.01)
Debt ratio	0.0036***	0.0018	0.0032***	0.0035***	0.0012	0.0031***
	(3.48)	(0.89)	(3.53)	(3.40)	(0.58)	(3.35)
No. of observations	302	111	413	302	111	413
R-squared	0.142	0.115	0.128	0.154	0.153	0.143

Notes: The table reports coefficient estimates from regressions of stock returns on political connection variables and control variables for September 1998. All Malaysian firms with available data in the Worldscope database are included. Also estimated but not reported are a constant term and industry dummy variables. "Politically connected" means the firm has an identifiable connection with key officials from Gomez and Jomo (1997). "PM connected" and "FM connected" indicate the source of the political connection to prime minister and finance minister, respectively, as in Gomez and Jomo (1997). Firm size is measured as the log of total assets; the debt ratio is measured as total debt over total assets. Numbers in parentheses are heteroskedasticity-robust *t*-statistics.
***Significant at the 1 percent level.
**Significant at the 5 percent level.
*Significant at the 10 percent level.

tember 1998 on the same variables as in table 11.2. The first three columns present results for the political connections indicator. Politically connected firms as a whole enjoyed a rebound in September 1998 (their total increase in average stock price was 53.2 percent, compared with 37.1 percent for unconnected firms; see table 11.1). Among nonfinancial firms, a higher return of 8.1 percentage points, not significant at standard levels, may be attributed to political connections. The effect appears to be stronger among financial firms, where connected firms on average had a higher return of 28.5 percentage points, which is significant at the 1 percent level. For all firms combined, the political connections coefficient shows a higher return of 13.8 percentage points, and is significant at the 5 percent level.

The final three columns of table 11.3 present results for the differences in PMC and FMC firms. Among nonfinancial firms, PMC firms on average experienced higher returns of 13 percentage points, significant at the 10 percent level, while the dummy on FMC firms is −11.6 percentage points (but is not statistically significant), for a total net difference of 24.6 percentage points (13 plus 11.6) between PMC and FMC firms. The effect seems even stronger among financial firms, where PMC firms had higher returns of 40.3 percentage points, significant at the 1 percent level. Among all firms combined, PMC firms on average had higher returns of 19.9 percentage points, significant at the 1 percent level, while FMC firms on average had lower returns of 6.3 percentage points (not statistically significant). This result suggests that the value of political connections themselves was an important determinant of the fortunes of Malaysian firms when capital controls were imposed.

As a further test of whether the observed differences are due to the effects of capital controls, we examine cross-sectional differences in stock price gains following the imposition of capital controls. If capital controls constrain financial flows across borders, we would expect to see smaller gains for connected firms having access to international capital markets compared to connected firms without such access. In additional regressions (not reported here, but see Johnson and Mitton 2003) we compare gains for connected firms that had foreign capital access (defined as having international stock listings or bond placements) with connected firms that did not have foreign capital access. While the evidence is mixed at times, on balance the results show that politically connected firms without foreign capital access performed better than connected firms with foreign capital access when capital controls were imposed (Johnson and Mitton 2003).[26] The results are consistent with the idea that capital controls affected Malaysian firms' access to foreign finance.

11.4.7   Economic Significance of Political Connections

For a measure of economic significance, we use our regression coefficients to estimate the impact of connections on the total market value of firms. We find that during the crisis period, roughly $5.7 billion of the total market value lost by connected firms is attributable to their political connections. When capital controls were imposed in September 1998, although market valuations were then on a smaller scale, political connections are estimated to have accounted for an incremental gain of roughly $1.3 billion in market value for connected firms.[27]

By looking at the outcomes for connected firms in September 1998, we can obtain an estimate of the perceived value of political connections as a percentage of total firm value after capital controls were imposed. If we as-

---

26. Our results are weakest when we limit the sample to just firms that were included in the International Finance Corporation's investable index (i.e., those regarded as being more liquid). In this case, the coefficient on prime minister connections falls to 0.129, with a t-statistic of 1.1. However, this sample is only 109 firms, which is about one-quarter of our main sample, so the loss of significance is not surprising.

27. The estimates of the effects of political connections on market value are based on our estimated regression coefficients, monthly stock prices, and available data on the number of shares outstanding for each firm. Because the number of shares outstanding is not known for every month and is missing for three of the connected firms, the estimated figures are not exact calculations but reasonable estimates.

sume that the events of September 1998 restored the full value of connections to the prime minister, then the estimated gain attributable to prime minister connections in September 1998 should give an indication of the percentage of firm value attributable to political connections. Our regression coefficients show that prime minister connections account for about a 20 percent increase in firm value in September 1998. In terms of (higher) valuations at the end of September 1998, this increase would be 12 percent of firm value. This would suggest that 12 percent is a low estimate of investors' perceptions of the percentage of firm value attributable to connections, with the actual percentage being higher to the extent that connections still accounted for some value prior to September 1998. While this is clearly only a rough estimate, the estimated proportion of value attributable to connections seems to be within the 12–23 percent range estimated by Fisman (2001) for connected firms in Indonesia.

Regarding the effect of political connections in relation to the total variation in returns, we note that in regressions with September 1998 returns, the R-squared of the regression rises incrementally from 0.109 to 0.143 when the political connection variables are added. This suggests that roughly 3.4 percent of the total variation in returns is explained by differences in political connections (alternatively, about one-quarter of the systematic, explainable variation in stock prices is due to political connections). For regressions of returns for the initial crisis period, adding political connection variables increases the R-squared from 0.210 to 0.237, suggesting that 2.7 percent of the total variation in returns is explained by differences in political connections.

11.4.8   After the Imposition of Capital Controls: 1999–2003

What did the Malaysian government do once capital controls were imposed? Some general reflationary measures were taken, including cutting interest rates and making credit more readily available to consumers and firms (Kaplan and Rodrik 2001; Mahathir 2000, chap. 8). A new expansionary budget was introduced in October 1998 (Perkins and Woo 2000). Overall, however, as discussed above, macroeconomic policy remained cautious and responsible after the controls were imposed.

At the firm level, evidence from the public record suggests that the government may have used the economy's isolation from short-term capital flows to restore advantages for some favored firms. The precise distribution of these advantages is hard to measure, as they are usually not reported publicly. However, high-profile incidents that have been reported in the international media suggest three types of benefits for favored firms.[28]

---

28. These three forms of advantages for favored firms could benefit minority shareholders, in part because they put the supported firms on a stronger financial basis and reduce the incentives to transfer resources out of the firms (Johnson et al. 2000). In other cases, however, the government has permitted companies to carry out actions that might be detrimental to minority shareholders (see, e.g., Restall 2000b; Perkins and Woo 2000; Jayasankaran 2000).

First, the state-owned oil company was called upon to provide bailouts to particular distressed firms (see, e.g., Jayasankaran 1999b; Restall 2000a; Lopez 2001).[29] Second, some companies with perceived political connections appeared to receive advantageous deals directly from the government (see, e.g., Prystay 2000).[30] Third, in the banking sector, the government introduced a consolidation plan that appeared beneficial to connected firms, and some large companies were allowed to repeatedly roll over their debts (see, e.g., Jayasankaran 1999a; Dhume et al. 2001).[31]

While these extracts from the public record provide anecdotal evidence that certain firms were favored after the imposition of capital controls, it is impossible to directly measure the extent to which connected firms received benefits. In order to address the issue more systematically, we turn again to the firm-level data. Specifically, we examine the operating performance of all Malaysian firms in Worldscope over the period 1990–2003. We study four firm-level measures of operating performance: investment, growth, profitability, and leverage. Here we define investment as the ratio of capital expenditures to gross fixed assets, growth as the log annual growth rate in sales, profitability as the return on assets, and leverage as the ratio of total debt to total assets.

In table 11.4, we show the median firm-level operating performance for each of these measures for each year from 1990 to 2003. To assess the effect of having political connections in each year, we also show the results of regressing these performance measures on a full set of two-digit standard industrial classification (SIC) sector dummy variables, a control for firm size, and a dummy for whether a firm was, according to Gomez and Jomo (1997), connected to the prime minister. Each year is covered in a separate regression.

The results in table 11.4 indicate that PMC firms showed higher investment, higher growth, higher leverage, and lower profitability in most precrisis years (compared with non-PMC firms). However, in the years following the crisis, the differences in investment and growth were largely

---

29. "Since the Asian financial crisis hit, Petronas has helped buy debt-burdened shipping assets controlled by Mahathir's eldest son; now it's preparing to buy control of the national car maker, Proton. Looking ahead, Mahathir told the *Review* in June that he didn't see why Petronas should not take over the ailing national carrier, Malaysian Airlines, although Petronas itself says it has no such plan" (Jayasankaran 1999b).

30. "On Friday, the government announced it will raise six billion ringgit [$1.58 billion] in a bond issue to buy back the assets of two unprofitable privatized light-rail projects in Kuala Lumpur. Two key beneficiaries of the bailout: debt-laden conglomerate Renong Bhd., which owns one of the rail projects, and Renong's controlling shareholder, Halim Saad. The move comes days after the Finance Ministry agreed to repurchase a 29 percent interest in ailing Malaysian Airlines System from businessman Tajudin Ramli for 1.79 billion ringgit—the same price he paid the government for the MAS stake in 1994" (Prystay 2000).

31. "A major worry is that the government seems to have weighed political ties in choosing some of the leader banks. . . . Just as there are losers in the merger stakes, so are there winners. One of them is Multipurpose Bank, a small institution controlled by businessmen widely viewed by analysts as being close to Finance Minister Daim" (Jayasankaran 1999a).

Table 11.4   **Political connections and median operating performance**

	Investment				Growth		Leverage		Profitability	
Year	Median, all firms	Compare: Thailand	Compare: Korea	PM effect	Median, all firms	PM effect	Median, all firms	PM effect	Median, all firms	PM effect
1990	0.079	0.288	0.156	-0.014	0.206	0.259	0.126	0.102	0.049	-0.006
1991	0.126	0.267	0.133	0.005	0.135	0.498***	0.105	0.101	0.046	-0.011
1992	0.124	0.170	0.120	0.025	0.081	0.381	0.088	0.062	0.053	-0.088
1993	0.118	0.155	0.102	0.130**	0.058	0.277**	0.101	0.039	0.048	0.001
1994	0.121	0.147	0.102	0.094*	0.101	0.170	0.153	0.077	0.046	-0.011
1995	0.127	0.137	0.144	0.042	0.145	0.170	0.187	0.099**	0.051	-0.018
1996	0.126	0.116	0.142	0.073*	0.139	0.301*	0.228	0.113**	0.044	-0.012
1997	0.114	0.076	0.124	0.060*	0.090	0.015	0.259	0.188***	0.033	-0.082*
1998	0.079	0.029	0.060	0.052	-0.082	0.067	0.290	0.395**	0.005	-0.223
1999	0.044	0.030	0.061	0.017	-0.088	-0.188	0.253	0.321*	0.019	-0.026
2000	0.042	0.030	0.071	-0.003	0.010	-0.098	0.232	0.347*	0.021	-0.096
2001	0.041	0.037	0.069	0.023	-0.018	-0.171	0.223	0.297	0.016	-0.014
2002	0.038	0.045	0.056	-0.011	0.005	-0.019	0.223	0.261	0.018	0.003
2003	0.041	0.057	0.058	-0.015	0.059	-0.020	0.210	0.248*	0.025	-0.010

Notes: The table reports median operating performance for Malaysian firms for the years 1990 to 2003. For investment, comparative figures are given for Thailand and Korea. "PM effect" refers to coefficient estimates for a "PM connected" indicator from regressions of performance measures on a PM indicator for each year 1990 to 2003. Included, but not reported, in each regression is a full set of two-digit SIC dummy variables and a control for firm size. All Malaysian firms with available data in the Worldscope database are included. "PM connected" means the firm has an identifiable connection with key government officials from Gomez and Jomo (1997). Investment is capital expenditure/gross fixed assets, growth is the log annual real growth rate in sales, leverage is total debt/total assets, and profitability is return on assets.

***Significant at the 1 percent level.

**Significant at the 5 percent level.

*Significant at the 10 percent level.

reversed: the PMC firms had lower investment and growth. In addition, in the years following the crisis, PMC firms appear to have had even higher leverage than other firms compared with the years before the crisis. On balance, the results show that the effects of being connected to the prime minister, in terms of firm operating performance, were very different after the imposition of capital controls from what they were prior to the crisis.

To further assess the operating performance of connected firms, in panel A of table 11.5, we estimate the following panel regression:

$$(2) \quad Performance_{it} = \alpha + Firm_i + PMC_i \times Crisis_t + PMC_i \times Postcrisis_t$$
$$+ Year_t + \varepsilon_{it},$$

where $Performance_{it}$ is one of the four measures of operating performance for firm i in year t. $Firm_i$ represents firm fixed effects. PMC_i is a dummy variable indicating whether firm i is connected to the prime minister. As we have a full set of firm fixed effects, we cannot estimate the direct PMC effect, but this framework allows us to look at how the effects of connections varied over time. $Crisis_t$ is a dummy variable set to 1 for years 1997–98, and $Postcrisis_t$ is a dummy variable set to 1 for years 1999–2003. $Year_t$ represents a full set of year-specific dummy variables.

These results show that, compared with unconnected firms, PMC firms suffered a large drop in relative investment and growth from the precrisis to postcrisis period. They also had less growth and higher leverage, relative to unconnected firms, in the crisis period compared with the precrisis period. The effects in question are large and consistent with the data shown in table 11.4.[32]

However, it is possible that the standard errors in panel A of table 11.5 are too low—for example, if there is serial correlation in the error term. As a more conservative approach, in panels B, C, and D we estimate the following cross-sectional regression:

$$(3) \qquad AvgPerformance_i = \alpha + PMC_i + Industry_i + \varepsilon_i,$$

where $AvgPerformance_i$ is the average of one of the four performance measures over all years in the precrisis period (panel B), the crisis period (panel C), or the postcrisis period (panel D). PMC_i is a dummy variable indicating whether firm i is connected to the prime minister. $Industry_i$ represents a full set of industry dummy variables.[33]

In addition, panel A of table 11.5 shows the value of prime minister connections after the crisis relative to before (or during) the crisis. Panels B, C,

32. We obtain similar results for investment, leverage, and profitability using Arellano-Bond generalized method of moments (GMM). A balanced panel also gives similar results, although the standard errors are higher because the sample is much smaller (about 20 percent of the full sample).

33. The only difference between the regression in table 11.4 and the one in panels B, C, and D of table 11.5 is that table 11.4 also includes a control for firm size.

Table 11.5   **Political connections and operating performance: Regression analysis**

	Investment	Growth	Leverage	Profitability
A. 1990–2003 (dependent variable: the performance measure indicated)				
PM connected × crisis	0.001	–0.128*	0.232*	–0.075
	(0.02)	(–1.67)	(1.92)	(–1.04)
PM connected × postcrisis	–0.050*	–0.213***	0.210	–0.003
	(–1.93)	(–2.91)	(1.46)	(–0.11)
No. of observations	3,035	3,557	3,786	3,792
R-squared	0.312	0.196	0.538	0.176
B. Precrisis period (dependent variable: the average performance measure over period)				
PM connected	0.048	0.264**	0.049	–0.009
	(1.27)	(2.50)	(1.62)	(–0.74)
No. of observations	279	263	324	324
R-squared	0.174	0.680	0.244	0.195
C. Crisis period (dependent variable: the average performance measure over period)				
PM connected	0.053	0.022	0.287**	–0.131*
	(1.49)	(0.38)	(2.27)	(–1.70)
No. of observations	283	347	355	355
R-squared	0.173	0.258	0.195	0.123
D. Postcrisis period (dependent variable: the average performance measure over period)				
PM connected	0.008	–0.013	0.241	0.012
	(0.74)	(–0.16)	(1.38)	(0.33)
No. of observations	287	354	355	355
R-squared	0.162	0.149	0.166	0.155

Notes: Panel A reports coefficient estimates from panel regressions of performance measures on a political connection indicator over the period 1990 to 2003. Panel A includes firm fixed effects and a full set of year-specific dummies are included. Panels B, C, and D regress average performance measures over the given time period on the political connections indicator. Panels B, C, and D include a full set of industry dummies. "PM connected" means the firm has an identifiable connection with key government officials from Gomez and Jomo (1997). The precrisis period refers to 1990–96, the crisis period refers to 1997–98, and postcrisis to the period 1999–2003. Investment is capital expenditures/gross fixed assets, growth is the log annual real growth rate in sales, leverage is total debt/total assets, and profitability is return on assets. Numbers in parentheses are heteroskedasticity-robust *t*-statistics (adjusted for firm-level clustering in panel A).

***Significant at the 1 percent level.
**Significant at the 5 percent level.
*Significant at the 10 percent level.

and D show the PMC versus unconnected (non-PMC) comparison within each time period, which enables us also to check the absolute value of these connections. PMC firms had a growth advantage in the precrisis period, and this disappeared after the crisis.[34] These connected firms also had more leverage and less profitability during the crisis. Taken with the rest of table

34. In panels B, C, and D, the results are very similar if we use the same set of firms in each.

11.5 and table 11.4, these results suggest that PMC firms' advantages were not manifested in better performance after the resolution of the crisis.[35]

11.5 Conclusion

We do not find evidence that Malaysia's September 1998 controls were essential for recovery or structural reforms. Our analysis of the key macroeconomic and financial indicators confirms the empirical findings of Hutchison (2003) that Malaysia's macroeconomic performance after the imposition of capital controls was comparable to that of other countries recovering from the Asian financial crisis. The controls were imposed late, after a big depreciation and after a large amount of capital had already left the country, and this limited the potential macroeconomic benefits. At best, the controls played a preventive role in guarding against perceived risks to financial stability, but in this role they were not tested by any observable pressure. As far as we can determine, Malaysia's successful recovery resulted from the country's strong fundamentals, sound policies, and effective institutions, rather than from the capital controls. It would thus be misleading to draw any general lessons applicable to other countries based on Malaysia's experience with capital controls during the Asian crisis.

However, the firm-level evidence from Malaysia supports the idea that the stock market interpreted the events of September 1998 as helping politically connected firms (relative to unconnected firms). Firms with political connections were expected by the stock market to lose benefits in the first phase of the Asian crisis. Conversely, firms connected to the prime minister were expected to gain benefits when capital controls were imposed in September 1998.

The presence of political connections in East Asian economies does not mean that these connections caused the crisis or even that relationship-based capitalism was necessarily a suboptimal system for these countries. While politically connected firms were hit harder during the crisis, the data do not indicate that this was a punishment for past misdeeds and deficiencies. The evidence suggests rather that investors interpreted the crisis as indicating that previously favored firms would lose valuable advantages, while the imposition of capital controls indicated—at least initially—that these advantages would be restored for some firms.

Based on the actual financial performance of firms after the crisis, it is hard to discern the extent to which firms actually received special advantages. This could be because financial- and corporate-sector reforms resulted in fewer advantages for connected firms or because connected firms did not end up making good use of their privileges.

---

35. Tables 11.4 and 11.5 include both financial and nonfinancial firms. We ran the same regressions separately for nonfinancial firms only, without finding any significant differences.

Appendix A

Table A.1   Malaysian Capital Controls (1992–2004)

Date	Measure	Category
1991	No changes	
4/20/1992	Total borrowing by residents in foreign currency from domestic commercial and merchant banks to finance imports of goods and services is restricted to the equivalent of 1 million ringgit (RM; previously there were no limits).	Borrowing in foreign currency domestically and abroad
7/9/1992	Borrowing under the Export Credit Refinance Facilities (both pre- and postshipment financing) by nonresident-controlled companies will be considered domestic borrowing.	Borrowing in foreign currency domestically and abroad
10/24/1992	Offshore guarantees obtained by residents to secure domestic borrowing, except offshore guarantees (whether denominated in ringgit or foreign currency) without resource to Malaysian residents and obtained from the licensed offshore banks in Labuan to secure domestic borrowing, are deemed foreign borrowing. In cases where an offshore guarantee is denominated in ringgit, it is subject to the condition that, in the event the guarantee is called on, the licensed offshore banks in Labuan must make payments in foreign currency (with some exceptions), not in ringgit.	Borrowing in foreign currency domestically and abroad
11/1/1992	The guidelines on foreign equity capital ownership are liberalized. Companies exporting at least 80 percent of their production are no longer subject to any equity requirements, whereas companies exporting between 50 percent and 79 percent of their production were permitted to hold 100 percent equity, provided that they have invested $50 million or more in fixed assets or completed projects with at least 50 percent local value added and that the company's products do not compete with those produced by domestic firms. These guidelines are not to apply to sectors in which limits on foreign equity participation have been established.	Foreign direct investment
12/14/1992	Residents and the offshore companies in Labuan are prohibited from transacting with the residents of dealing in the currency of Yugoslavia (Serbia and Montenegro) without specific prior approval from the Controller of Foreign Exchange (COFE).	Currency requirements
12/22/1993	Nonresident-controlled companies involved in manufacturing and tourism-related activities are freely allowed to obtain domestic credit facilities to finance the acquisition and/or the development of immovable property required for their own business activities.	International transactions in ringgit
1/17/1994	A ceiling is placed on the net external liability position of domestic banks (excluding trade-related and direct investment inflows); removed on January 20, 1995.	Bank and foreign exchange transactions
1/24/1994	Residents are prohibited from selling the following Malaysian securities to nonresidents: banker's acceptances; negotiable instruments of deposit; Bank Negara bills; treasury bills; government securities (including Islamic securities) with a remaining maturity of one year or less.	Inflows of portfolio and other capital

(*continued*)

Table A.1   (continued)

Date	Measure	Category
2/7/1994	Residents are prohibited from selling to nonresidents all forms of private debt securities (including commercial papers, but excluding securities convertible into ordinary shares) with a remaining maturity of one year or less.	Inflows of portfolio and other capital
2/7/1994	The restriction on the sale of Malaysian securities to nonresidents is extended to both the initial issue of the relevant security and the subsequent secondary market trade.	Inflows of portfolio and other capital
2/23/1994	Prohibition of forward transactions (on bid side) and nontrade-related swaps by commercial banks with foreign customers to curtail the speculative activities of offshore agents seeking long positions in ringgit (lifted on August 16, 1994).	Bank and foreign exchange transactions
8/12/1994	Residents are permitted to sell to nonresidents any Malaysian securities.	Inflows of portfolio and other capital
12/1/1994	Residents may borrow in foreign currency up to a total of the equivalent of RM5 million from nonresidents and from commercial and merchant banks in Malaysia.	Borrowing in foreign currency domestically and abroad
12/1/1994	Nonresident-controlled companies are allowed to obtain credit facilities, including immovable property loans, up to RM10 million without specific approval, provided that at least 60 percent of their total credit facilities from banking institutions are obtained from Malaysian-owned financial institutions.	International transactions in ringgit
12/1/1994	Nonresidents with valid work permits may obtain domestic borrowing to finance up to 60 percent of the purchase price of residential property for their own accommodation.	International transactions in ringgit
6/27/1995	Corporate residents with a domestic credit facility are allowed to remit funds up to the equivalent of RM10 million for overseas investment purposes each calendar year.	Outflows of portfolio and other capital
2/1/1996	The threshold for the completion of the statistical forms for each remittance to, or receipt of funds from, nonresidents is raised from RM50,000 to RM100,000 or its equivalent in foreign currency.	Payments for invisible transactions
8/4/1997	Controls are imposed on banks to limit outstanding noncommercial-related ringgit offer-side swap transactions (i.e., forward order/spot purchases of ringgit by foreign customers) to $2 million per foreign customer or its equivalent. Hedging requirements of foreigners for trade-related and genuine portfolio and foreign direct investment investments are excluded.	Bank and foreign exchange transactions
8/4/1997	Residents are allowed to enter into non-commercial-related swap transactions up to a limit (no limits existed previously).	Bank and foreign exchange transactions
8/28/1997	A ban on short-selling of the listed securities on the Kuala Lumpur Stock Exchange (KLSE) is introduced to limit speculative pressures on stock prices and exchange rates.	Stock market transactions

Table A.1   (continued)

Date	Measure	Category
9/1/1998	A requirement is introduced to repatriate all ringgit held offshore (including ringgit deposits in overseas banks) by October 1, 1998 (Bank Negara approval thereafter).	International transactions in ringgit
9/1/1998	Approval requirement is imposed to transfer funds between external accounts (freely allowed previously) and for the use of funds other than permitted purposes (i.e., purchase of RM assets).	International transactions in ringgit
9/1/1998	Licensed offshore banks are prohibited from trading in ringgit assets (allowed up to permitted limits previously).	International transactions in ringgit
9/1/1998	A limit is introduced on exports and imports of ringgit by residents and nonresident travelers, effective September 1, 1998 (no limits existed previously).	International transactions in ringgit
9/1/1998	Residents are prohibited from granting ringgit credit facilities to nonresident corresponding banks and stockbroking companies (subject to a limit previously).	International transactions in ringgit
9/1/1998	Residents are prohibited from obtaining ringgit credit facilities from nonresidents (subject to a limit previously).	International transactions in ringgit
9/1/1998	All imports and exports are required to be settled in foreign currency.	International transactions in ringgit
9/1/1998	All purchases and sales of ringgit facilities can only be transacted through authorized depository institutions.	International transactions in ringgit
9/1/1998	Approval requirement for nonresidents to convert ringgit in external accounts into foreign currency, except for purchases of ringgit assets, conversion of profits, dividends, interest, and other permitted purposes (no such restrictions previously).	Outflows of portfolio and other capital
9/1/1998	No restriction on conversion of ringgit funds in external accounts of nonresidents with work permits, embassies, high commissions, central banks, international organizations, and missions of foreign countries in Malaysia.	Outflows of portfolio and other capital
9/1/1998	A twelve-month waiting period for nonresidents to convert ringgit proceeds from the sale of Malaysian securities held in external accounts (excluding FDI, repatriation of interest, dividends, fees, commissions, and rental income from portfolio investment). No such restrictions previously.	Outflows of portfolio and other capital
9/1/1998	A prior approval requirement beyond a certain limit for all residents to invest abroad in any form (previously applied only to corporate residents with domestic borrowing).	Outflows of portfolio and other capital
9/1/1998	Trading in Malaysian shares on Singapore's Central Limit Order Bank (CLOB) over-the-counter market becomes de facto prohibited as a result of strict enforcement of the existing law requiring Malaysian shares to be registered in KLSE prior to trade.	Stock market transactions

(*continued*)

Table A.1   (continued)

Date	Measure	Category
9/1/1998	A specific limit on exports of foreign currency by residents and up to the amount brought into Malaysia for nonresidents (previously, no restriction on export of foreign currency on person or in baggage of a traveler; export by other means required approval, regardless of amount).	Export and import of currency
9/1/1998	No restriction on conversion of ringgit funds in external accounts of nonresidents with work permits, embassies, high commissions, central banks, international organizations, and missions of foreign countries in Malaysia.	Controls on portfolio outflows
9/1/1998	A specific limit on exports of foreign currency by residents and the amount brought into Malaysia for nonresidents (previously, no restriction on export of foreign currency on person or in baggage of a traveler; export by other means required approval, regardless of amount).	Export of foreign currency
12/12/1998	Residents are allowed to grant loans to nonresidents for purchases of immovable properties from December 12, 1998, to January 12, 1999.	International transactions in ringgit
1/13/1999	Designated nonresident accounts for futures trading are allowed and exempt from the twelve-month holding period.	Derivatives
1/13/1999	Capital flows for the purpose of trading derivatives on the commodity and monetary exchange of Malaysia and the Kuala Lumpur options and financial futures exchange are permitted for nonresidents, without being subject to the rules governing external accounts, when transactions are conducted through "designated external accounts" that can be created with tier 1 commercial banks in Malaysia. (From September 1999, the classification of tier 1 and tier 2 banks became no longer applicable: all commercial banks were allowed to open designated accounts for nonresidents.)	Derivatives
2/15/1999	The twelve-month waiting period is replaced with a graduated system of exit levies on the repatriation of the principal of capital investments (in shares, bonds, and other financial instruments, except for property investments) made prior to February 15, 1999. The levy decreases over the duration of the investment, and thus penalizes earlier repatriations; the levy is 30 percent if repatriated less than seven months after entry, 20 percent if repatriated in seven to nine months; and 10 percent if nine to twelve months. No levy on principal if repatriated after twelve months.	Outflows of portfolio and other capital
2/18/1999	Repatriation of funds relating to investments in immovable property is exempted from the exit levy regulations.	Outflows of portfolio and other capital
3/1/1999	The ceiling on the import and export of ringgit for border trade with Thailand is raised.	International transactions in ringgit
4/5/1999	Investors in the Malaysian Exchange of Securities Dealing and Automated Quotation (MESDAQ) are exempted from the exit levy introduced on February 15, 1999.	Outflows of portfolio and other capital

Table A.1   (continued)

Date	Measure	Category
7/8/1999	Residents are allowed to grant overdraft facility in aggregate not exceeding RM200 million for intraday and not exceeding RM5 million for overnight to a foreign stockbroking company, subject to certain conditions.	International transactions in ringgit
9/21/1999	Commercial banks are allowed to enter into short-term currency swap arrangement with nonresident stockbrokers to cover for payment for purchases of shares on the KLSE and in outright ringgit forward sale contract with nonresidents who have firm commitment to purchase shares on the KLSE, for maturity period not exceeding five working days and with no rollover option.	Bank and foreign exchange transactions
10/4/1999	Residents are allowed to grant ringgit loans to nonresidents for purchases of immovable properties from October 29, 1999, to December 7, 1999.	International transactions in ringgit
3/14/2000	Funds arising from sale of securities purchased by nonresidents on the CLOB can be repatriated without payment of exit levy.	Outflows of portfolio and other capital
4/24/2000	Nonresident-controlled companies raising domestic credit through private debt securities are exempted from RM19 million limit and the 50:50 requirement for issuance of private debt securities on tender basis through the fully automated system for tendering, to develop domestic bond market.	International transactions in ringgit
6/29/2000	Administrative procedures issued to facilitate classification of proceeds from the sale of CLOB securities as being free from levy.	Outflows of portfolio and other capital
7/27/2000	Residents and nonresidents are no longer required to make a declaration in the traveler's declaration form as long as they carry currency notes and/or traveler's checks within the permissible limits. For nonresidents, the declaration is incorporated into the embarkation card issued by the immigration department.	Export and import of currency
9/30/2000	Licensed offshore banks in the Labuan international offshore finance center are allowed to invest in ringgit assets and instruments in Malaysia for their own accounts only and not on behalf of clients. The investments cannot be financed by ringgit borrowing.	International transactions in ringgit
12/1/2000	Foreign-owned banks in Malaysia are allowed to extend up to 50 percent (previously 40 percent) of the total domestic credit facilities to nonresident-controlled companies, in case of credit facilities extended by resident banks. This is to fulfill Malaysia's commitment under the General Agreement on Trade in Services.	Domestic lending by foreign-owned banks
12/10/2000	Licensed commercial banks are allowed to extend intraday overdraft facilities not exceeding RM200 million in aggregate and overnight facilities not exceeding RM10 million (previously 5 million) to foreign stockbroking companies and foreign global custodian banks.	International transactions in ringgit
2/1/2001	The exit levy on profits repatriated after one year from the month the profits are realized is abolished. Portfolio profits repatriated within one year remain subject to the 10 percent levy.	Outflows of portfolio and other capital

(continued)

Table A.1 (continued)

Date	Measure	Category
5/1/2001	The 10 percent exit levy imposed on profits arising from portfolio investments repatriated within one year of realization is abolished.	Outflows of portfolio and other capital
6/1/2001	All controls on the trading of futures and options by nonresidents on the Malaysian Derivatives Exchange (MDEX) are eliminated. The Commodity and Monetary Exchange of Malaysia and the KLSE merge to form the MDEX.	Derivatives
6/13/2001	Resident insurance companies are allowed to extend ringgit policy loans to nonresident policy holders with the terms and conditions of the policies. The amount of ringgit loans extended may not exceed the policy's attained cash surrender value and may be for the duration of the policies.	International transactions in ringgit
7/10/2001	Resident financial institutions are allowed to extent ringgit loans to nonresidents to finance the purchase or construction of any immovable property in Malaysia (excluding financing for purchases of land only) up to a maximum of three property loans in aggregate.	International transactions in ringgit
11/21/2002	Banks are allowed to extend additional ringgit credit facilities to nonresidents up to an aggregate of RM5 million per nonresident to finance projects undertaken in Malaysia. Prior to this, credit facilities in ringgit to nonresidents for purposes other than purchases of three immovable properties or a vehicle were limited to RM2000,000.	International transactions in ringgit
12/3/2002	In addition to obtaining property loans to finance new purchases or construction of any property in Malaysia, nonresidents may also refinance their ringgit domestic property loans. The above is subject to a maximum of three property loans.	International transactions in ringgit
12/3/2002	The limit of RM10,000 equivalent in foreign currency for investment abroad by residents under the Employee Share Option/ Purchase Scheme is removed. Effective this date, general permission is granted for overseas investment for this purpose.	Outflows of portfolio and other capital
12/3/2002	Payments between residents and nonresidents as well as between nonresidents for ringgit assets are liberalized to allow payments to be made in either ringgit or foreign currency (previously, only in ringgit).	Settlement
3/7/2003	Banking institutions as a group are permitted to extend ringgit overdraft facilities, not exceeding RM500,000 in aggregate, to a nonresident customer, if the credit facilities are fully covered at all times by fixed deposits placed by the nonresident customer with the banking institutions extending the credit facilities.	International transactions in ringgit
4/1/2003	Exporters are allowed to retain a portion of their export proceeds in foreign currency accounts with onshore licensed banks in Malaysia with overnight limits ranging between the equivalent of US$1 million and US$70 million, or any other amount that has been approved (previously, the limit was between US$1 million and US$10 million).	Export proceeds

Table A.1   (continued)

Date	Measure	Category
4/1/2003	Residents are allowed to sell up to twelve months forward foreign currency receivables for ringgit to an authorized dealer for any purpose, if the transaction is supported by a firm underlying commitment to receive such currency.	Bank and foreign exchange transactions
4/1/2003	The overnight limit on foreign currency export proceeds that may be retained by resident exporters in foreign currency accounts with designated banks in Malaysia is raised to a range between the equivalent of US$1 million and US$70 million, from overnight limits of between US$1 and US$10 million.	Export proceeds
4/1/2003	The maximum amount of payment of profits, dividends, rental income, and interest to a nonresident on all bona fide investments that may be remitted without prior approval, but upon completion of statistical forms, is increased from RM10,000 to RM50,000, or its equivalent in foreign currency, per transaction.	Outflows of portfolio and other capital
5/21/2003	The threshold level for acquisition by foreign and Malaysian interests exempted from Foreign Investment Committee (FIC) approval is raised from RM5 million to RM10 million. Acquisition proposals by licensed manufacturing companies are centralized at the Ministry of International Trade and Industry (MITI), while corporate proposals are centralized at the Securities Commission. These proposals no longer require FIC consideration.	Foreign direct investment
6/17/2003	Foreign equity holding in manufacturing projects is allowed up to 100 percent for all types of investment.	Foreign direct investment
4/1/2004	Residents are allowed to sell forward nonexport foreign currency receivables for ringgit or another foreign currency to an authorized dealer or an approved merchant bank for any purpose, provided the transaction is supported by an underlying commitment to receive currency.	Bank and foreign exchange transactions
4/1/2004	Residents with permitted foreign currency borrowing are allowed to enter into interest rate swaps with onshore licensed banks, approved merchant banks, or licensed offshore banks in Labuan, provided that the transaction is supported by a firm underlying commitment.	Bank and foreign exchange transactions
4/1/2004	Resident individuals with funds abroad (not converted from ringgit) are allowed to maintain nonexport foreign currency accounts offshore without any limit imposed on overnight balances.	Outflows of portfolio and other capital
4/1/2004	Resident companies with domestic borrowing are allowed to open nonexport foreign currency accounts with licensed onshore banks in Malaysia to retain foreign currency receivables other than export proceeds with no limit on the overnight balances. Resident companies without domestic borrowing are allowed to open nonexport foreign currency accounts in licensed offshore banks in Labuan up to an overnight limit of $500,000 or its equivalent.	Bank and foreign exchange transactions

(continued)

Table A.1   (continued)

Date	Measure	Category
4/1/2004	Resident individuals are permitted to open foreign currency accounts to facilitate payments for education and employment overseas, with an aggregate overnight limit equivalent to $150,000 with Labuan offshore banks. Previously, the limit was $100,000 ($50,000 for overseas banks).	Bank and foreign exchange transactions
4/1/2004	Resident individuals who have foreign currency funds are allowed to invest freely in any foreign currency products offered by onshore licensed banks.	Bank and foreign exchange transactions
4/1/2004	The amount of export proceeds that residents may retain in foreign currency accounts with licensed onshore banks is increased from the range of $1 million to $70 million to the range of $30 million to $70 million.	Export proceeds
4/1/2004	COFE approval is required for the issuance of ringgit bonds in Malaysia by multinational development institutions and foreign multinational corporations.	International transactions in ringgit
4/1/2004	Resident banks and nonbanks are permitted to extend ringgit loans to finance or refinance the purchase or construction of any immovable property in Malaysia (excluding financing for purchases of land only) up to a maximum of three property loans in aggregate.	International transactions in ringgit
4/1/2004	The limit for banking institutions on loans to nonresidents (excluding stockbroking companies, custodian banks and correspondent banks) is raised from RM200,000 to RM10,000,000.	International transactions in ringgit
4/1/2004	Licensed insurers and takaful operators (Islamic insurance) are allowed to invest abroad up to 5 percent of their margins of solvency and total assets. These entities are also allowed to invest up to 10 percent of net asset value in their own investment-linked funds.	Outflows of portfolio and other capital
4/1/2004	Unit trust management companies are allowed to invest abroad the full amount of net asset value attributed to nonresidents, and up to 10 percent of net asset value attributed to residents, without prior COFE approval. In addition, fund/asset managers are allowed to invest abroad up to the full amount of investments of nonresident clients and up to 10 percent of investments of their resident clients.	Outflows of portfolio and other capital
4/1/2004	Bank Negara Malaysia liberalizes its foreign exchange administration rules to facilitate multilateral development banks (MDBs) or multilateral financial institutions (MFIs) to raise ringgit-denominated bonds in the Malaysian capital market. The size of the bond to be issued by MDBs or MFIs should be large enough to contribute to the development of the domestic bond market, and the minimum tenure of the bonds should be three years. Ringgit funds raised from the issuance of ringgit-denominated bonds can be used either in Malaysia or overseas. There will be no restriction for MDB or MFI issuers and nonresident investors of ringgit-denominated bonds to maintain foreign currency accounts, or ringgit accounts as external accounts with onshore licensed banks in Malaysia. MDBs, MFIs, or nonresident investors can enter into forward foreign exchange contracts or swap arrangements to hedge ringgit exposure, and MDB or MFI issuers can enter into interest rate swap arrangements with onshore banks.	International transactions in ringgit

Table A.1   (continued)

Date	Measure	Category
4/1/2004	Bank Negara Malaysia liberalizes rules to facilitate foreign multinational corporations (MNCs) to raise ringgit-denominated bonds in the Malaysian capital market. The ringgit funds raised from such issues can be used in Malaysia or overseas.	International transactions in ringgit
	MNC issuers and nonresident investors of ringgit-denominated bonds can maintain, without restrictions, foreign currency accounts or ringgit accounts as external accounts with any onshore licensed bank. MNC issuers or nonresident investors will be allowed forward exchange contracts of swap arrangements to hedge ringgit exposures, and MNC issuers will be allowed interest rate swap arrangements with onshore banks.	Bank and foreign exchange transactions

Sources: IMF, *Annual Report on Exchange Arrangements and Exchange Restrictions,* and Bank Negara Malaysia, *Annual Report* and *Exchange Notices,* various years.

Appendix B

Coding of Firms

We code as "politically connected" any firm that Gomez and Jomo (1997) identify as having officers or major shareholders with close relationships with key government officials—primarily the prime minister and the finance minister (and their allies). For example, Gomez and Jomo (1997) state that a firm we will call Firm A is "controlled by [Person X], who is closely linked to [an ally of the Prime Minister]" (p. 103), so Firm A is coded as politically connected, with the prime minister as the primary connection (Gomez and Jomo reveal actual names; we have dropped these here). As another example, Gomez and Jomo (1997) state, "The chairman of [Firm B] was [Person Y] of the [Group J], a close friend of [the] Prime Minister" (p. 59). Thus, Firm B is coded as politically connected, with its primary connection listed as the prime minister. As a final example, Gomez and Jomo (1997) state that "[Person Z], probably [the Finance Minister's] closest confidant, has an interest" in Firm C (p. 57). This results in Firm C being coded as politically connected, with the finance minister as the primary connection. We search the entire text of Gomez and Jomo (1997) for all such indications of connections and code them accordingly.[36]

36. The detailed coding is available from the authors upon request.

References

Bank Negara Malaysia. 1998. Measures to regain monetary independence. Press release, 1 September.

Bhagwati, J. 1998a. The capital myth. *Foreign Affairs* 77 (May/June): 7–12.

————. 1998b. Why free capital mobility may be hazardous to your health: Lessons from the latest financial crisis. Paper presented at NBER Conference on Capital Controls. 7 November, Cambridge, Massachusetts.

Campbell, J. 1996. Understanding risk and return. *Journal of Political Economy* 104:298–345.

Chong, B., M.-H. Liu, and K. Tan. 2005. The wealth effect of forced bank mergers and cronyism. Nanyang Technological University Working Paper.

Dhume, S., S. Crispin, S. Jayasankaran, and J. Larkin. 2001. Economic reform: Running out of steam. *Far Eastern Economic Review* 164 (2): 44–47.

Dornbusch, R. 2001. Malaysia: Was it different? NBER Working Paper no. 8325. Cambridge, MA: National Bureau of Economic Research.

Faccio, M. 2006. Politically connected firms. *American Economic Review* 96 (1): 369–86.

Faccio, M., R. Masulis, and J. McConnell. 2006. Political connections and corporate bailouts. *Journal of Finance,* forthcoming.

Fisman, R. 2001. It's not what you know: Estimating the value of political connections. *American Economic Review* 91:1095–1102.

Gomez, E. T., and K. S. Jomo. 1997. *Malaysia's political economy: Politics, patronage and profits.* Cambridge: Cambridge University Press.

————. 1998. *Malaysia's political economy: Politics, patronage and profits.* 2nd ed. Cambridge: Cambridge University Press.

Hutchison, M. M. 2003. A cure worse than the disease? Currency crises and the output costs of IMF-supported programs. Chap. 10 in *Managing currency crises in emerging markets,* ed. M. Dooley and J. A. Frankel. Chicago: University of Chicago Press.

International Monetary Fund (IMF). 1999. IMF concludes Article IV consultation with Malaysia. Public Information Notice no. 99/88. Washington, DC: International Monetary Fund, September 8.

Jayasankaran, S. 1999a. Merger by decree. *Far Eastern Economic Review* 162 (36): 10–14.

————. 1999b. Saviour complex. *Far Eastern Economic Review* 162 (32): 10–13.

————. 2000. Entrepreneurs—a question of honour: Renong Group Chairman Halim Saad wins a postponement of a purchase of shares he is committed to buy; the markets are appalled. *Far Eastern Economic Review* 163 (51): 60–62.

Jeong, S., and J. Mazier. 2003. Equilibrium exchange rates of eight East Asian currencies: A fundamental equilibrium exchange rate (FEER) approach. CEPN Working Paper no. 09. Paris: Centre d'Economie de l'Université Paris Nord.

Johnson, S., P. Boone, A. Breach, and E. Friedman. 2000. Corporate governance in the Asian financial crisis, 1997–98. *Journal of Financial Economics* 58:141–86.

Johnson, S., and T. Mitton. 2003. Cronyism and capital controls: Evidence from Malaysia. *Journal of Financial Economics* 67 (2): 351–82.

Jomo, K. S. 2001. *Malaysian eclipse: Economic crisis and recovery.* London: Zed Books.

Kaplan, E., and D. Rodrik. 2001. Did the Malaysian capital controls work? NBER Working Paper no. 8142. Cambridge, MA: National Bureau of Economic Research.

Kaufmann, D., A. Kraay, and M. Mastruzzi. 2005. Governance matters IV: Governance indicators for 1996–2004. World Bank Policy Research Working Paper no. 3630. Washington, DC: World Bank, May.

Krugman, P. 1998. Saving Asia: It's time to get radical. *Fortune*. September 7.

La Porta, R., F. Lopez de Silanes, A. Shleifer, and R. Vishny. 1997. Legal determinants of external finance. *Journal of Finance* 52:1131–50.

———. 1998. Law and finance. *Journal of Political Economy* 106:1115–55.

La Porta, R., F. Lopez de Silanes, and G. Zamarippa. 2003. Related lending. *Quarterly Journal of Economics* 118:231–68.

Latifah, M. C. 2002. Capital flows and capital controls: The Malaysian experience. Chap. 7 in *Globalization and the Asian Pacific economy,* ed. Kyung Tae Lee. London: Routledge.

Lemmon, M., and K. Lins. 2003. Ownership structure, corporate governance, and firm value: Evidence from the East Asian financial crisis. *Journal of Finance* 58:1445–68.

Lindgren, C., T. Balino, C. Enoch, A.-M. Gulde, M. Quintyn, and L. Teo. 1999. Financial sector crisis and restructuring: Lessons from Asia. IMF Occasional Paper no. 188. Washington, DC: International Monetary Fund.

Lopez, L. 2001. Mokhzani Mahathir exits two firms: Prime minister's son says he wants to put to rest accusations of nepotism. *Asian Wall Street Journal.* April 30.

Meesook, K., I. H. Lee, O. Liu, Y. Khatri, and N. Tamirisa. 2001. Malaysia: From crisis to recovery. IMF Occasional Paper no. 207. Washington, DC: International Monetary Fund.

Mitton, T. 2002. Across-firm analysis of the impact of corporate governance on the East Asian financial crisis. *Journal of Financial Economics* 64:215–41.

Mohamad, M. bin. 2000. *The Malaysian currency crisis: How and why it happened.* Kuala Lumpur, Malaysia: Pelanduk Publications.

Morck, R., B. Yeung, and W. Yu. 2000. The information content of stock markets: Why do emerging markets have synchronous stock price movements? *Journal of Financial Economics* 58:215–60.

Myers, S. 1977. The determinants of corporate borrowing. *Journal of Financial Economics* 5:147–75.

Perkins, D. H., and W. T. Woo. 2000. Malaysia: Adjusting to deep integration with the world economy. In *The Asian financial crisis: Lessons for a resilient Asia,* ed. W. T. Woo, J. Sachs, and K. Schwab, 227–55. Cambridge, MA: MIT Press.

Petersen, M., and R. Rajan. 1995. The effect of credit market competition on lending relationships. *Quarterly Journal of Economics* 110:407–43.

Prystay, C. 2000. Malaysia reverses course in privatization program: Government nationalizes two light-rail projects. *Asian Wall Street Journal.* December 27.

Rajan, R., and L. Zingales. 1998. Which capitalism? Lessons from the East Asian crisis. *Journal of Applied Corporate Finance* 11:40–48.

———. 2003. The great reversals: The politics of financial development in the 20th century. *Journal of Financial Economics* 69:5–50.

Restall, H. 2000a. Malaysia's national car hurts Malaysians. *Asian Wall Street Journal* (weekly edition). August 28–September 3.

———. 2000b. Reading Malaysia's Rorschach test. *Asian Wall Street Journal* (weekly edition). December 11–17.

Rodrik, D. 2000. Exchange rate regimes and institutional arrangements in the shadow of capital flows. Harvard University, John F. Kennedy School of Government. Working paper.

Samad, M. F. B. A. n.d. Performance of politically-affiliated businesses in Malaysia: A summary of principal findings. University of Malaya. Working Paper.

Tamirisa, N. 2006. Do macroeconomic effects of capital controls vary by their type? Evidence from Malaysia. *ASEAN Economic Bulletin,* forthcoming.

Titman, S., and R. Wessels. 1988. The determinants of capital structure choice. *Journal of Finance* 43:1–19.
World Bank. 2000. Malaysia: Social and structural review update. http://site resources.worldbank.org/INTMALAYSIA/Resources/malaysia_STR_update .pdf.

Comment   Peter Blair Henry

I like this paper a lot. Discussions of capital controls can be highly ideo-logical and strangely unencumbered by the facts. In contrast, this paper takes a sensible look at the data and does not force them to tell a story that is not really there.

The paper focuses on two central questions, one macroeconomic in nature and the other microeconomic. The macro question is the obvious one: did the Malaysian capital controls ease the impact of the Asian crisis on the Malaysian economy? Since GDP plummeted in 1998 and bounced back in 1999, it is tempting to conclude that the controls had a positive effect. However, the paper argues that the data are actually inconclusive. The problem is that we observe a similar V-shaped pattern in the GDP of two East Asian economies that did not impose capital controls: Korea and Thailand.

Furthermore, capital controls in Malaysia were imposed at the depth of the crisis—too late for any reasonable analysis to conclude that the controls had an effect, for good or ill. In the ideal real-world experiment, Malaysia would have imposed capital controls at the same time that Korea and Thailand signed agreements with the International Monetary Fund (IMF). But Malaysia did not impose capital controls until several months after the Korea and Thailand IMF agreements. Therefore, a comparison of Malaysia versus Korea and Thailand is legitimate only if you assume that in September of 1998 Malaysia was in the same place that Korea and Thailand were when they signed their agreements. The authors do not think that this is a legitimate assumption. I agree.

Overall, the paper argues that Malaysia weathered the crisis by following sound macroeconomic policy. The authors declare: "We should emphasize that throughout the crisis and the capital control period the authorities pursued good macroeconomic and structural policies." This observation notwithstanding, the paper also notes a slightly worrisome macro fact: private investment in Malaysia has fallen from an average of 25 percent of GDP before the crisis to less than 15 percent of GDP

Peter Blair Henry is an associate professor of economics and the John and Cynthia Fry Gunn Faculty Scholar in the Graduate School of Business at Stanford University, and a faculty research fellow of the National Bureau of Economic Research.

after the crisis. The paper argues that a deterioration of institutions stemming from the imposition of capital controls may explain the fall in private investment. Toward the end of my comments I will suggest a more pedestrian explanation that also questions the assertion that Malaysia pursued "good" macro policy.

The paper also asks a microeconomic question: did firms with political connections benefit from the imposition of capital controls? In the aftermath of the Asian crisis, Malaysia was one of a number of countries accused of crony capitalism: firms with connections to the government enjoyed subsidies and benefits that unconnected firms did not. The onset of the crisis provides an opportunity to use the stock market to examine the validity of such assertions. If politically connected firms benefited from crony capitalism and the onset of a financial crisis signaled the end of that arrangement, then we would expect the stock prices of connected firms to be affected more adversely by the onset of a financial crisis than the prices of unconnected firms.

This is exactly what the paper shows. While the aggregate value of the Malaysian stock market declined from July 1997 through August 1998 (the period of the crisis), the stock price decline of firms with political connections to Prime Minister Mahathir was 8 percentage points larger than that of unconnected firms. Similarly, when capital controls were imposed on September 1, 1998, stock prices rose, but the average stock price increase of firms with connections to Mahathir was 19.9 percentage points greater than that of the typical unconnected firm. Furthermore, firms with connections to Anwar, the former minister of finance (he was fired on September 2, 1998) experienced a stock price increase that was 6.3 percentage points less than that of the unconnected firms. In other words, from July 1997 to August 1998, the market considered political connections a liability. Once controls were imposed, connections with Mahathir became an asset, while connections with Anwar were a liability (more on this later).

While the firm-level results support the paper's central thesis that political connections affect corporate valuation, they also raise two important issues of interpretation. First, why did the market interpret the onset of the crisis in July 1997 as the imminent end of crony capitalism, and why was the imposition of capital controls in September 1998 viewed in exactly the opposite fashion? The paper argues that relationships between politicians, banks, and firms are easier to maintain when the economy is isolated from international capital flows (Rajan and Zingales 2003). The problem with this argument is that it does not explain how government-firm relationships persisted in the face of free capital flows before the crisis. Moreover, I think there is a simpler story that relates to the second point of interpretation I want to raise.

The paper shows that the overall value of the stock market (both connected and unconnected firms) rose by 40 percent in September of 1998. If the capital controls had no macroeconomic impact, then why did the stock prices of unconnected firms rebound at all? It is true that the stock price increase may have been driven by news that the economy was recovering. But if the economy seemed to be recovering, then why did the government impose capital controls? One answer to this question is that Mahathir wanted to undermine his political opponent, Anwar, the minister of finance (and deputy prime minister). The chronology of events in Malaysia justifies this assertion and provides a more direct explanation for why the stock market reacted so differently to the onset of the crisis in 1997 and the imposition of capital controls in 1998.

Remember, while Prime Minister Mahathir was famously blaming George Soros and hedge fund managers for Malaysia's economic and financial woes, Anwar was trying to reassure investors that Malaysia would not adopt economic policies to match Mahathir's populist, anti-western-capitalist rhetoric. So there was a battle of ideas, as it were. The following exchange between Mahathir and Anwar at a press conference in October 1997 best illustrates the mounting tension between the two men (Freedman 2004):

Mahathir: "The press is asking questions. I'm answering and tomorrow the currency traders will push the Ringgit down because I opened my mouth."
Anwar (laughing): "Then I will clarify and the press will say we are quarreling." (Jayasankaran 1997)

Two months after that exchange, in December 1997, Anwar announced a series of austerity measures that were seen as an attempt to reverse Mahathir's long-standing policy of subsidizing favored corporations. In the months following the exchange, Mahathir became even more aggressive about bailing out high-profile companies (Freedman 2004).

The political events in Indonesia during early 1998 provide important additional context for understanding the link between Mahathir and Anwar's political struggle, capital controls, and the stock market. In April of 1998, President Suharto of Indonesia agreed to adopt a number of economic reform measures in return for financial assistance from the IMF. One month later, amid protests sparked (in part) by the hardships caused by the reforms, Suharto was forced to resign after thirty-two years as Indonesian head of state.

I am not suggesting that Indonesia's signing of an IMF agreement was responsible for Suharto's downfall, but Mahathir clearly seemed to link the two events in his mind. Following Suharto's resignation, Mahathir began moving more aggressively to bring down Anwar. On June 24, 1998, Mahathir placed Daim Zainuddin in charge of economic policy. On September 1, 1998, Mahathir imposed capital controls. The next day he fired Anwar.

The implementation of capital controls and the sacking of his finance minister gave the clearest possible indication that Mahathir had no intention of taking the economy in the direction of economic reforms and fiscal austerity. In other words, what this sequence of events reveals is not that capital controls per se make it easier to maintain subsidies, but rather that the imposition of capital controls was an unambiguous signal that Mahathir had no intention of signing an IMF agreement that would bring an end to subsidies.

Now we see why prices fell more for connected firms during the period prior to the imposition of capital controls. In addition to the macroeconomic shock of the Asian financial crisis, there was concern that the end of politically driven subsidies was nigh. Reserves were falling because the central bank was defending the currency, the fall in reserves might force the government to borrow money from the IMF, and IMF conditionality would likely put a stop to the gravy train for politically connected firms.

The sacking of Anwar paved the way for expansionary fiscal policy that allowed the government to maintain corporate subsidies even in the face of a contracting economy—this is where the macro and micro stories converge. To illustrate the point more clearly, I present table 11C.1. It shows that Malaysia's overall fiscal balance went from five straight years of surplus, including a surplus of 2.4 percent of GDP in 1997, to five straight years of deficits. The interesting point is that in the aftermath of capital controls, Malaysia followed a policy in diametric opposition to the one that would have been required under an IMF agreement.

Does this table reveal a pattern of reckless spending, or Keynesian fiscal stimulus of a distinctly East Asian variety? Apparently, the definition of "good" macroeconomic policy depends on whether you are sitting in Kuala Lumpur or at the corner of 19th and H! Irrespective of the stance you take on the soundness of Malaysia's fiscal response to the crisis, one has to wonder whether an old-fashioned crowding-out story lies behind the

Table 11C.1   Malaysia's deteriorating fiscal balance following the imposition of capital controls

1993	0.2
1994	2.3
1995	0.8
1996	0.7
1997	2.4
1998	−1.8
1999	−3.2
2000	−5.8
2001	−5.5
2002	−5.6
2003	−5.4

subsequent fall in private investment to which the authors allude. This seems like an issue worthy of further investigation.

References

Freedman, Amy L. 2004. Economic crises and political change: Indonesia, South Korea, and Malaysia. *World Affairs* 166 (4): 185–96.
Jayasankaran, S. 1997. High wire act. *Far Eastern Economic Review,* October 9, 1997, 12.
Rajan, Raghuram, and Luigi Zingales. 2003. The great reversals: The politics of financial development in the 20th century. *Journal of Financial Economics* 69 (1): 5–50.

Capital Flows and Exchange Rate Volatility
Singapore's Experience

Basant K. Kapur

12.1 Introduction

Singapore's experience with international capital flows over the past two decades or so has been a rather—although not completely—benign one, owing to strong fundamentals and generally well-conceived macroeconomic policies. At the same time, useful lessons can be learned regarding issues such as exchange rate policy, the policy of noninternationalization of the Singapore dollar, and unavoidable fallout effects of capital flow volatility even in generally sound environments and how these may best be dealt with.

A feature of Singapore's economy that sets it apart from various other countries discussed in this volume is its well-developed banking system and equities market, and the fact that it is on a (modified) currency board (CB) system. Its bond market is, however, less developed, although in recent years measures have been taken to foster its growth, as discussed below. It may be useful, therefore, to begin by comparing Singapore's experience with that of another state with a well-developed financial system, namely Hong Kong: the latter, in addition, operates what may be termed a "pure" CB system. Notwithstanding their economic similarities, Singapore and Hong Kong have had rather different experiences with capital flows, and an examination of why this has been so turns out to be rather instructive. In section 12.2, therefore, we briefly examine Hong Kong's experience during the Asian crisis of 1997–98 and identify its areas of vulnerability. In section 12.3, we discuss Singapore's policy background and how it responded

Basant K. Kapur is a professor of economics at the National University of Singapore.

I wish to thank Sebastian Edwards, Martin Feldstein, Anusha Chari (the discussant), and other participants for their most helpful comments. The usual disclaimer applies.

to a significant speculative attack in 1985, and draw lessons from this. Further lessons are drawn in section 12.4, in which we consider Singapore's experience during the Asian crisis. Section 12.5 discusses Singapore's debt markets, an interesting feature being that both Singapore and Hong Kong have in recent years encouraged foreign enterprises to *float* bond issues in Singapore dollars (S$) and Hong Kong dollars (HK$), respectively. Section 12.6 concludes. An appendix provides a chronology of the evolution of capital controls (specifically, the evolution of the noninternationalization policy) in Singapore.

12.2   Hong Kong: The 1997–98 Experience

As indicated above, our discussion here will be fairly brief, given that our main focus is on Singapore, and is designed primarily to provide a comparative perspective on Singapore's experience.[1] A minimalist definition of a pure CB system is that it is one in which domestic currency is issued or redeemed (a) only in exchange for foreign currency and (b) at a fixed exchange rate, usually vis-à-vis a single foreign currency, termed the reserve currency. A modified CB system, discussed further below, is then one in which criterion (a) holds, but not (b). A pure system aptly describes the Hong Kong situation, with the exchange rate fixed at HK$7.8 to the U.S. dollar (US$) since October 1983. Moreover, the monetary base in Hong Kong was rather small, given that it does not impose reserve requirements on banks and has an efficient, real-time interbank payment system so that "the aggregate balance that banks maintain in their clearing accounts held with the currency board" (Yam 1998a) is low. This rendered Hong Kong vulnerable to speculative capital outflows, of which there were a number in mid-1997 through mid-1998: these did not succeed, in part because the resulting high interest rates adversely affected the speculators too, who had borrowed Hong Kong dollars in the interbank market to launch their attacks. The high interest rates (the overnight interest rate actually rose to 280 percent on October 23, 1997) and their adverse effects on the stock market and economic activity in general were, however, a source of concern.[2]

The really major attack, however, occurred in August 1998, and Yam (1998a) describes the so-called double play thus:

1. Here we draw mainly on Rzepkowski (2000), Yam (1998a, 1998b), and Corsetti, Pesenti, and Roubini (2001).
2. The attacks reflected contagion from crises elsewhere in the region (Rzepkowski 2000; Hashimoto and Ito 2004) and uncertainties associated with Hong Kong's accession to China. While Yam (1998a) refers to the interest rate increases as an "autopilot mechanism"—an inevitable concomitant of the CB system—Rzepkowski contends (2000, p. 15) that they were partly induced, on occasion, by discretionary increases in the Hong Kong Monetary Authority's (HKMA's) discount rate.

In August [after an announcement that first-quarter gross domestic product growth had been negative] the speculators adopted a more sophisticated ploy. They introduced a form of double play aimed at playing off the currency board system against the stock and futures markets. First, to avoid being squeezed by high interest rates, they prefunded themselves in Hong Kong dollars in the debt market, swapping US dollars for Hong Kong dollars with multilateral institutions that have raised Hong Kong dollars through the issue of debt. At the same time, they accumulated large short positions in the stock index futures market. They then sought to engineer extreme conditions in the money market by dumping huge amounts of Hong Kong dollars. This sell-off was intended to cause [either a devaluation or] a sharp interest rate hike, which in turn would have sent the stock market plummeting. The collapse of the stock market would have enabled them to reap a handsome profit from the futures contracts they had taken out.

Presumably, a double play facilitates a stronger currency attack, since the higher interest cost resulting from an attack of a given size is at least partly offset by the possible gains from short selling in the stock index futures market. Rzepkowski (2000) points out that speculators also engaged in short selling of stocks, and that "the hedge funds involved in the speculation were identified as being the Quantum Fund of George Soros, the Tiger Fund, the Moore Global Investment, and the Long Term Capital Management" (p. 17). Their prefunding activities had driven the Hong Kong interest rate premium over the U.S. dollar to about 5 percentage points (Yam 1998b). It was estimated (Yam 1998a) that "the hedge funds involved had amassed in excess of HK$30 billion in currency borrowings, at an interest cost of around HK$4 million a day. They also held an estimated 80,000 short contracts, which translated into the following calculation: for every fall of 1,000 points in the Hang Seng index they stood to make a profit of HK$4 billion." Owing to the marking-to-market of their margin accounts with the Futures Exchange, they stood to gain daily from incremental falls in the Hang Seng Index (Rzepkowski 2000, pp. 17–18).

In the event, the attack proved unsuccessful. Like Singapore, Hong Kong has very substantial nonmonetary foreign reserves—reserves in excess of what is required to back the monetary base. At the time, it was unexpectedly confronted with a fiscal deficit, and had to convert part of these reserves into Hong Kong dollars to meet its fiscal obligations. "The immediate impact of this sale [of foreign currency], of an amount exceeding the HK$30 billion accumulated by the hedge funds, was the non-trigger of high interest rate" (Rzepkowski 2000, p. 19). In addition, and quite unconventionally,

between the 14th and 28th August 1998, the HKMA intervened via the Exchange Fund on the stock and futures markets. It acquired a portfolio of equities and HSI [Hang Seng Index] futures for an amount of about

US$15 billion, that is 7% of the capitalization and around 30% of the current [1998] Hang Seng Index value. . . . About 13% of its nonmonetary reserves . . . were allocated to these interventions, inducing an important injection of liquidity into the money market. (Rzepkowski 2000, p. 19)

By November, the portfolio had risen to US$19 billion in value, and during the interim speculators "were forced to close out their short positions, in many cases with heavy losses" (Yam 1998a). The portfolio was subsequently placed under the management of a separate company at arm's length from the HKMA, with the aim of divesting it gradually.

After August 1998, systemic improvements were introduced, with the intention of minimizing the occurrence of future attacks. The Exchange Fund, which manages Hong Kong's monetary and nonmonetary reserves, had since 1990 issued bills to promote the development of the local bond market, and in September 1998 virtually unrestricted discounting of Exchange Fund bills by commercial banks at the discount window of the HKMA, at nonpenal rates, was introduced. Effectively, this almost doubled the size of the monetary base, and it served to significantly reduce the interest rate response to a capital outflow of a given magnitude (Rzepkowski 2000, pp. 18–20). In addition, the government

brought in a 30-Point package tightening the regulation of the securities and future markets. Measures in the package include the strict enforcement of the T+2 settlement process, imposing a super margin on brokers with highly concentrated positions, introducing the client identity rule, increasing the penalty for naked short selling, creating a new offence for unreported short sales, and introducing new requirements for stock lenders to keep proper records of their lending activities. In parallel, SEHK [the Stock Exchange of Hong Kong] re-introduced the up-tick rule (no short selling below the current best ask price) for covered short selling and HKFE [the Hong Kong Futures Exchange] tightened the large open position reporting requirements and imposed position limits for HSI 33 Futures and Option Contracts. (Dickens 2002, p. 3).[3]

Subsequently, "relaxation measures applicable to certain market neutral transactions [were] introduced" (Dickens 2002, p. 3).

While the Hong Kong authorities have taken the view that the hedge funds were engaged in predatory market manipulation, Corsetti, Pesenti,

---

3. Prior to launching their attack in August, the hedge funds had borrowed Hong Kong stocks, to a large extent in the more efficient offshore market, from international fund managers and custodians (Rzepkowski 2000, n. 20). In addition, owing to "lax settlement requirements" (Yam 1998b, quoted in Rzepkowski 2000, n. 22), naked short selling was also practiced, even though it was against the law. Corsetti, Pesenti, and Roubini (2001, p. 43) also quote a study by the Financial Stability Forum (2000): "Aggressive trading practices by HLIs [highly leveraged institutions] reportedly included concentrated selling intended to move market prices, large sales in illiquid offshore trading hours, and spoofing of the electronic brokering services to give the impression that the exchange rate had moved beyond the HKMA's intervention level. There were frequent market rumours, often in offshore Friday trading, that a devaluation of the Hong Kong dollar or Chinese renminbi would occur over the weekend."

and Roubini (2001) adopt a more agnostic position, stating that "the hypothesis of rational investors taking short positions in two markets (based on an assessment of economic fundamentals) and the hypothesis of a double play (suggesting market manipulation) are observationally equivalent" (p. 44). One could hypothesize, alternatively, that the weakening fundamentals, due to both domestic and regional developments, had pushed the economy into a zone in which multiple equilibria (discussed further below) existed. Speculators then endeavored to drive the economy to the unfavorable equilibrium (possibly hoping that their actions would serve as a signal to others), seeking to reap large profits in the process, and were not averse to resorting to questionable means (such as naked short selling) to do so. One would then interpret the HKMA's actions as seeking to maintain the economy at the favorable equilibrium—successfully, as it turned out. In this framework, the equilibria themselves—in particular the equilibrium level of stock prices—depend inter alia on the extent of policy intervention by the authorities.[4]

The foregoing account permits (preliminary) identification of areas of vulnerability to speculative attack, or fault lines, in the Hong Kong environment of 1997–98. The first is the commitment to a fixed exchange rate. The Hong Kong authorities probably felt that they had no alternative in the matter, since any devaluation so soon after the accession to China could, it was felt, trigger a massive loss of confidence—a multiple-equilibria scenario analogous to Diamond-Dybvig-style bank panics, but affecting asset (including stock) prices in Hong Kong's case.[5] (Instead, real

---

4. In their theoretical discussion, Corsetti, Pesenti, and Roubini (2001) recognize that large players can influence market outcomes, but the authors appear reluctant to hypothesize that this occurred in Hong Kong's case. Their formal analyses deal with speculative attacks in a single market, and they then informally extrapolate their results to the Hong Kong case. However, in a double-play situation, if a devaluation does not occur, speculators can either lose or gain (Corsetti and his coauthors simply assume that they will lose), depending on the actions of other speculators and of the authorities, which affect interest rates and present and future stock prices. It is also entirely conceivable that in the Hong Kong case speculators failed to fully anticipate the extent and nature of the authorities' reaction. Rzepkowski (2000, p. 28) adopts a view of the underlying process somewhat similar to ours, arguing that "the logic underlying the several attacks against the HK dollar rests essentially on self-fulfilling expectations and on a pure contagion." Next, Chakravorti and Lall (2000) formally model a speculative double play and conclude that "government intervention in the equity market may either reduce interest rate or reduce the downward price pressure in equity markets but not both" (p. 23), owing to countervailing actions by speculators. They very peculiarly assume, however, that such intervention has no monetary effects, contrary to Rzepkowski's observation earlier, and they also overlook the fact that in Hong Kong, as indicated above, a fairly large sum of nonmonetary reserves was converted into Hong Kong dollars to meet fiscal obligations. A useful policy lesson here is that, if intervention is to be undertaken in response to a double play, it should be targeted at both equities and money markets.

5. This is a possibility that Devereux (2003) does not address in his comparison of the implications of the differing exchange rate regimes of Hong Kong and Singapore for longer-run trends in inflation and real exchange rates, and for short-run macroeconomic and real exchange rate volatility. It is also not clear whether his short-run simulation analysis imposes expectational rationality with regard to changes in the exchange rate (equal, in his model, to the expected rate of inflation of traded-goods prices) and the price of land.

gross domestic product [GDP] grew by 3 percent in 1999 and 10.2 percent in 2000.) In more normal situations, however, an adjustable peg (a) provides, as is well known, speculators with a one-way bet (especially if the band around the peg is fairly narrow), and (b) does not permit gradual exchange rate adjustments in the light of slowly changing fundamentals. The second vulnerable area is the ease with which speculators could borrow Hong Kong dollars, either in the interbank market or from multilateral institutions. The third is the unrestricted ease of short selling, in stock spot and index futures markets, and the laxity in enforcement of settlement requirements. Last is the initial small size of the monetary base, coupled with reliance on the autopilot mechanism of the CB system.[6] We turn now to a discussion of some of Singapore's experiences with capital flow volatility, and we should also recognize that not infrequently a tension exists between the desire for short-run stability and the desire to foster deeper and more open financial and capital markets for purposes of long-run growth and development of the economy.

12.3   Singapore: Policy Background and Early Experience

Any discussion of Singapore's experience must assign a prominent place to a major, long-standing (but recently relaxed, as discussed below) cornerstone of its monetary policy: the policy of noninternationalization of the Singapore dollar.[7] In Notice 621 of November 1, 1983, the Monetary Authority of Singapore (MAS) stated:

> Banks should observe the Authority's policy of discouraging the internationalization of the Singapore dollar. Specifically, banks should consult with the Authority before considering Singapore dollar credit facilities exceeding S$5 million (per entity) to nonresidents, or to residents where the Singapore dollars are to be used outside Singapore. Banks managing syndicated loans, bond issues, or other financial papers exceeding S$5 million should do likewise. The terms "residents" or "non-

6. In his empirical work, Rzepkowski utilizes the information in currency option prices to infer the expected intensity of a Hong Kong dollar devaluation, and then, in a vector autoregression framework, demonstrates the existence of a speculative double play: "A circular scheme characterized the formation of self-fulfilling expectations. The [expected] intensity of a HK dollar devaluation induced a sharp decrease in the index futures prices, which contributed to make the volatility of the HSI soar, in turn exacerbating the speculative pressures against the HK dollar" (p. 27). However, he then argues that the HKMA's stock market interventions in August 1998 were ineffective, since they "achieved to push up temporarily the index futures price, but induced a significant rise in the market volatility." Instead, it was the technical measures introduced in September 1998 to strengthen the CB system (see p. 578, this volume) that, he claims, dampened the pressures against the currency. Rzepkowski acknowledges that his options analysis abstracts from the possibility of a time-varying risk premium and imposes "strong assumptions on the underlying dynamics" (p. 29), and so the robustness of his findings remains an open issue.
7. We draw here mainly on Chan and Ngiam (1996, 1998), but we critique their formal analysis below; we draw as well on Lee (2001).

residents" include bank and nonbank customers (quoted in Chan and Ngiam 1996, p. 5).[8]

Chan and Ngiam (1996, p. 6) point out that "To ensure that its regulations are not being circumvented through financial derivatives, the MAS has defined Singapore dollar credit facilities to cover a wide range of financial instruments, including loans, foreign exchange swaps, currency swaps, interest rate swaps, facilities incorporating options, and forward rate agreements in Singapore dollars."[9] Subsequently, on July 18, 1992, the MAS issued a circular amending the policy. Consultation with the MAS was not required for credit facilities extended in Singapore dollars, in any amount, to residents or nonresidents to facilitate direct exports from and imports to Singapore, and for payment bonds in favor of Singapore parties, or payment guarantees, in respect of "economic activities" in Singapore, where the latter specifically excluded financial and portfolio investments. Forward sales of Singapore dollars earned from exports to Singapore were also permitted.

At the same time, banks were told that they should not finance in Singapore dollars "activities which have no bearing on Singapore" (Chan and Ngiam 1996, p. 5), including direct or portfolio investments outside Singapore by nonresidents, third-country trade by nonresident-controlled companies, and nonresident subscription to equity in a Singapore company where the proceeds are used for takeovers or financial investments. Moreover, note Chan and Ngiam (1996), banks were "advised against granting Singapore-dollar credit facilities to nonresidents for speculating in the local financial and property markets." For all other activities—which are quite wide ranging, and include third-country trade as well as direct and portfolio investments overseas by residents, and direct investment and housing development in Singapore by nonresidents—the 1983 ruling calling for consultation with the MAS continued to apply.

It perhaps bears noting that there are no restrictions against nonresidents' building up Singapore dollar holdings by converting their own foreign currency resources (or resources borrowed abroad) into Singapore dollars and placing them with the domestic banking units (DBUs). Moreover, by 1994 "the ACUs and the banks outside Singapore [had] amassed some S$51.6 billion worth of Singapore-dollar deposits (or 25 percent of

---

8. Singapore also has a very active offshore Asian currency market (in non-Singapore currencies), and banks are required to maintain separate accounts for Asian currency units (ACUs; Chan and Ngiam 1996, p. 4). "Nonresidents include Singapore-incorporated companies, which are majority-owned or otherwise controlled by nonresidents" (Lee 2001, p. 34).

9. Chan and Ngiam (1996) state, "Without any restrictions, a firm or individual can borrow Singapore dollars indirectly by first borrowing U.S. dollars and then doing a foreign exchange swap (which involves the buying of the Singapore dollar spot with the simultaneous selling of the Singapore dollar forward). This effectively replicates, or synthesizes, a Singapore dollar money market loan with a 'lock-in' Singapore dollar interest rate" (p. 6).

total liabilities) in the DBUs" (Chan and Ngiam 1996, p. 7). Such holdings could be converted into foreign currencies if sentiment regarding the Singapore dollar turned adverse; however, any *further* pressure through nonresidents' borrowing domestic currency and converting it, as occurred in Hong Kong, was obviated.[10] "Further pressure" here refers not to any increased likelihood of the country's reserves being unable to support capital outflows—which obviously cannot occur under a CB system—but to heightened short-term interest rates and their effects on the economy, as well as the enhanced complexity of monetary management.

Commencing in August 1998, a series of steps was undertaken to gradually liberalize the noninternationalization policy, in conjunction with moves to promote the development of the Singapore dollar bond market. These are discussed in greater detail in section 12.5. Throughout, however, the MAS made it clear that "banks shall not extend S$ credit facilities [exceeding S$5 million] to non-resident financial institutions if there is reason to believe that the S$ proceeds may be used for S$ currency speculation" (MAS Notice 757 of May 28, 2004). In the "frequently asked questions" document accompanying this notice, it was stated that banks were "expected to institute appropriate internal controls and processes to comply with this restriction"; these could include "written confirmation from the non-resident financial institution specifying the purpose of funding" and a "formal evaluation process of the client profile, which provides a clear basis for assessing that the client is unlikely to use the S$ proceeds for currency speculation." Banks were also required to report to MAS monthly their aggregate outstanding Singapore dollar lending to nonresident financial institutions. Clearly, there is an element of judgment involved in assessing that a client is unlikely to engage in speculation, but to date this does not appear to have created difficulties for banks.

The noninternationalization policy thus rather effectively blocked one of the channels of vulnerability that existed in Hong Kong. What about another channel, that of short selling of shares?[11] This, too, was circumscribed in Singapore: Poitras (2002, p. 147) points out that "sales for same day delivery" are permitted, and in its *Report on Transparency of Short Selling* the Technical Committee of the International Organization of Securities Commissions (IOSCO; 2003, p. 10) states that the Stock Exchange

10. Chan and Ngiam (1996, p. 8) also suggest that "as the forward market involving the Singapore dollar is rather thin, it cannot provide an effective vehicle for speculation"; moreover, the MAS monitors forward transactions with a view to ensuring that these are used for hedging and not for speculation. Chan and Ngiam further suggest that borrowing by residents for speculative purposes does "not seem to be a major concern as the Government can bring them to task if they bring down the Singapore dollar" (n. 27); the point being made here probably relates to the greater ease of monitoring, and if necessary regulating, the activities of residents, and perhaps also the greater sophistication and speed of action of foreign hedge funds and the like.

11. As discussed below, stock index futures were only introduced in 1998.

of Singapore (SES) "may suspend individual securities if speculative activity is excessive or abuse is suspected."[12] We thus observe a role being assigned to discretion in decision making, and both this and the same-day covering rule are in all likelihood reflective of the literature's ambiguity regarding the net benefit of short selling, especially in the presence of large players.

Discussion of the other two channels of vulnerability—the fixity of the exchange rate and the narrowness of the monetary base—is best carried out in the context of Singapore's exchange rate experience in the 1980s. As Teh (1988) points out,

> The Singapore dollar exchange rate is managed and set against a trade-weighted basket of currencies of its major trading partners. The trade-weighted Singapore dollar is allowed to float within a target band. The MAS keeps the trade-weighted dollar within the band through foreign exchange interventions [in U.S. dollars]. . . . The level at which the trade-weighted dollar is set is determined by what world inflation and domestic inflation are expected to be. Generally, the aim is to reduce imported inflation in domestic prices by appreciating the trade-weighted dollar.[13]

Departures from the foregoing general objective have occurred under recessionary conditions, during which the Singapore dollar has been permitted to depreciate to a certain extent. The first post-1965 recession in Singapore occurred in 1985, when real GDP fell by 1.6 percent, followed by slow growth of 2.3 percent in 1986 (Peebles and Wilson 2002). In response, as figure 12.1 shows, the dollar depreciated gradually from 1985 to the beginning of 1987. The depreciation was not an entirely smooth affair, however, as we now discuss.

It appears that speculators overestimated the extent to which the authorities were prepared to permit the exchange rate to depreciate. By August 1985, the currency had depreciated to about S$2.20:US$1 (from about S$2.10:US$1 earlier), and it then came under speculative pressure, primarily through spot conversions of Singapore dollars into foreign currencies (Chan and Ngiam 1996, pp. 7–8). By Thursday, September 12, it had fallen

---

12. There appears to be some confusion of interpretation about the issue. Bris, Goetzmann, and Zhu (2003, p. 33) say that in Singapore short selling is "not allowed" but is "practiced," while Morgan Stanley (2003) says, "There are no by-laws under the SGX [Singapore Exchange Ltd.] that forbid short-selling[;] however the present CDP [Central Depository] system actively works against it. This is because short sellers must cover their positions within the same day or face a buy-in by the SGX" (p. 4). Poitras (2002) says that "Except in very restrictive circumstances, short selling of stock on the SES is prohibited," while the technical committee of IOSCO (2003) states that short selling is "unrestricted," except for the caveat mentioned above. Market practitioners confirm, however, that short sellers are expected to cover their positions by the end of the same day, after which a buy-in by the SGX can occur; as mentioned, suspension of individual securities can also be instituted.

13. As the MAS (2000b) points out, under a pure CB system the rate used by the CB determines the market exchange rate, whereas in Singapore the exchange rates used by the CB "depend on the current rates in the foreign exchange market" (p. 24).

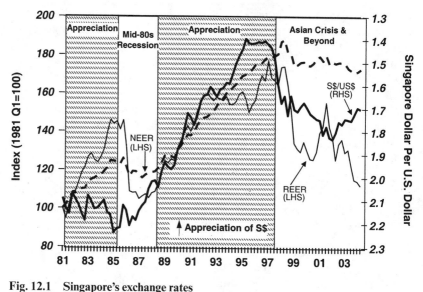

Fig. 12.1   Singapore's exchange rates

Source: MAS (2001), kindly updated by the MAS.

Note: REER uses export competitiveness weights and is deflated by relative unit labor costs.

to almost S$2.31:US$1 (Starr 1985). The following Monday, the MAS intervened, by spending US$100 million (amounting to less than 0.1 percent of its foreign reserves, according to Chan and Ngiam) to purchase Singapore dollars. The consequence was an immediate rise in the overnight interbank rate, which reached 120 percent on September 18, and the currency strengthened to S$2.20:US$1—an appreciation of about 5 percent in just four days. A news source noted that "substantial losses have almost certainly been incurred by foreign banks as a result of speculating against the Singapore dollar" (Textline 1985). Thereafter, liquidity was gradually restored to the money market, but it was also made clear that the MAS would not hesitate to act again if necessary.

Clearly, in addition to the noninternationalization policy and the discouragement of speculative short selling of shares, the exchange rate policy played a significant role in defusing the speculative attack. Initially permitting the exchange rate to depreciate to S$2.20:US$1, in line with weakening fundamentals, took some of the edge off speculative pressure. It would appear that the authorities then permitted, for some time, a further depreciation owing to uncertainty regarding the path of fundamentals. When it was determined that this depreciation was excessive, they were in a position to inflict substantial losses on speculators. As in the case of Hong Kong, Singapore's very healthy reserve position was a valuable asset in this regard. Unlike the case of Hong Kong, however, nonadherence to a fixed peg implied that speculators faced a "two-way bet": this may have constrained the intensity of the attack then, and, by strengthening the MAS's reputation for toughness, reduced speculators' willingness to attack in the future as well. Finally, the flexibility with which the MAS generally permits short-term uncollateralized borrowing by banks, in support of its exchange rate policy (MAS, n.d., p. 6), meant that the speculative pressure prior to the MAS intervention did not appreciably raise short-term interest rates (Textline 1985). We proceed next to examine lessons learned during the Asian crisis of 1997–98.[14]

12.4 Singapore: The 1997 Experience

We begin with a succinct statement by Chan and Ngiam (1998, p. 259):

> During the recent Asian currency crisis, which began when Thailand allowed its baht to float on July 2, 1997, the Singapore dollar, along with all the regional currencies, showed a significant fall against the US dollar for six months. From a high of $1.43 per US dollar on the day before the float of the baht, the Singapore dollar went all the way down to S$1.75 per US dollar on January 7, 1998, a decline of 18.3 percent over the period. . . . Although the Singapore dollar depreciated against the US dollar, it appreciated sharply against the regional currencies. Hence, on a trade-weighted basis, the Singapore dollar actually showed a slight appreciation since July 1, 1997. The Singapore dollar has withstood the currency storm lashing the region because of its extremely strong economic fundamentals . . . [including] low foreign debt, huge foreign exchange reserves, large current account surpluses, substantial budget surpluses, high savings rates, strong inflow of foreign direct investment, a sound financial system and prudent government policies.

We thus observe a significant difference between Singapore's exchange rate experience in 1997 and its experience in 1985. The greater depreciation in 1997, compared to the initial depreciation of only about 5 percent from S$2.10 to S$2.20 per U.S. dollar in 1985, might have reflected a judgment that the economic situation was more serious in 1997; at the same time, a larger depreciation might have been more in line with speculators' priors,

14. Chan and Ngiam's (1998) formal analysis of the 1985 episode appears, however, to be flawed. They erroneously assume that the exchange rate appreciated from a preexisting disequilibrium level but that interest rates nonetheless fell because, by underscoring the authorities' determination not to allow the currency to weaken, the appreciation reduced the perceived probability of a devaluation. In fact, however, interest rates did (as indicated above) rise after the appreciation, owing to the liquidity squeeze, and only fell subsequently. The key element of losses imposed on speculators by the appreciation is not included in the Chan and Ngiam analysis; nor do they recognize that the appreciation was intended to bring the exchange rate to an (equilibrium?) level that was lower than the original S$2.10 level. Indeed, it is difficult to imagine the perceived devaluation probability, and the interest rate, falling for good if the exchange rate did indeed remain overvalued.

and the latter might also still have had memories of the 1985 experience.[15] In both years, the noninternationalization policy and the short-sale restrictions would also have helped. Singapore's experience also exemplifies the point made in section 12.2 regarding the merits of gradual rather than discrete adjustments in situations that are not too extreme.

Notwithstanding the fairly smooth exchange rate adjustment, Singapore was not spared from volatility in other asset markets, particularly equities and property. From a high of 2055.44 in January 1997, the Straits Times index of stock prices dropped by 60 percent to 856.43 in September 1998 before recovering (Ngiam 2000, p. 6 and fig. 2). The private property price index dropped monotonically by about 40 percent from 270.0 in the first quarter of 1997 to 163.7 in the fourth quarter of 1998 (Ngiam 2000, p. 6 and fig. 3). Real GDP in fact declined by 0.9 percent in 1998 (table 12.1). It would not be correct to ascribe these developments solely to contagion effects, and trade and banking exposure to the region. Other factors, such as the global electronics slowdown, the downturn in the domestic real estate cycle, and (over time) the gradually increasing competition from China and India, also played a significant part. However, Singapore's experience in 1997–98 underscores the fact that countries that plug into the global economic grid will tend to experience not only higher mean growth rates but also greater variability of those growth rates. As has often been noted, capital can flow out of a country as well as into it. Selective measures aimed at particular sectors can mitigate the degree of volatility, but are unlikely to be capable of effectively eliminating it. Of course, economic agents will in due course learn to make improved risk-return calculations, and at the same time governments would be well advised to develop various coping mechanisms, such as a reasonable degree of social insurance and provision of skill upgrading and retraining facilities to help those who are severely affected by shorter-term cyclical changes as well as longer-term structural ones.

12.5   Debt Markets in Singapore

We begin with some figures for the 1990s. Table 12.2, from Ong (1998), provides information on the debt-asset ratio (DAR) of nonfinancial corporations in Singapore, Canada, and the United States. The ratio in Singapore declined somewhat in the 1990s, being fairly modest at 0.31, of which 0.21

15. Hashimoto (2003, p. 256) obtains "puzzling" results in seeking to identify speculative pressure against the Singapore dollar in 1997, including the fact that a large depreciation occurred when her estimated depreciation likelihood was lowest. Methodologically, her assumption that speculators condition only on the M2–foreign exchange reserves ratio in deciding when to launch an attack appears rather restrictive, and it is also not clear what her estimated critical level of 0.25 for this ratio for Singapore signifies, since the actual ratio was above this throughout her sample period (1986–97).

Table 12.1   Key national income statistics, Singapore

Year	GNI (in S$ millions)	Per capita GNI (in S$)	Gross national saving (in S$ millions)	Gross capital formation (in S$ millions)	Gross domestic product (in S$ millions)	Gross fixed capital formation (in S$ millions)
1993	94,604.0	28,535	42,062.4	35,258.2	98,838.2	32,439.3
1998	141,068.3	35,968	75,416.8	44,316.0	138,345.0	51,253.3
1999	142,617.3	36,097	70,644.6	44,739.5	147,834.4	48,717.8
2000	159,097.0	39,599	73,984.6	51,150.6	162,162.3	52,933.8
2001	155,472.3	37,634	67,150.2	38,296.3	159,073.0	50,549.3
2002	157,818.5	37,834	67,238.5	33,444.1	162,493.2	45,530.6
2003	157,173.9	37,555	70,351.3	21,245.0	164,265.9	43,779.4
				Percentage change over previous year		
1993	13.0	10.1	8.7	21.3	12.3	10.3
1998	-4.3	-7.4	-3.0	-20.3	-0.9	-6.0
1999	1.1	0.4	-6.3	1.0	6.9	-4.9
2000	11.6	9.7	4.7	14.3	9.7	8.7
2001	-2.3	-5.0	-9.2	-25.1	-1.9	-4.5
2002	1.5	0.5	0.1	-12.7	2.2	-9.9
2003	-0.4	-0.7	4.6	-36.5	1.1	-3.8

Source: Singapore Department of Statistics 2004 *Yearbook of Statistics.*

Notes: GNI = gross national income. All dollar amounts in Singapore dollars, and all are shown at current market prices except for the final two, "Gross domestic product" and "Gross fixed capital formation," which are at 1995 market prices.

Table 12.2   Average leverage ratio during the 1970s, 1980s, and 1990s

	1970s	1980s	1990s
Singapore			
DAR	0.33	0.36	0.31
Short-term DAR	0.24	0.24	0.21
Long-term DAR	0.09	0.12	0.10
Short- to long-term debt ratio	2.55	1.97	1.98
Canada			
DAR	0.24	0.28	0.30
Short-term DAR	0.11	0.17	0.15
Long-term DAR	0.13	0.11	0.15
Short- to long-term debt ratio	0.86	1.53	1.04
United States			
DAR	0.30	0.33	0.37
Short-term DAR	0.11	0.15	0.17
Long-term DAR	0.19	0.18	0.21
Short- to long-term debt ratio	0.59	0.85	0.80

Source: Ong (1998).
Notes: DAR = debt-asset ratio. For Singapore, data refer to period 1990–97. For Canada, data refer to period 1990–96. For the United States, data refer to period 1990–94.

was due to short-term debt (defined by Ong 1998, p. 9, as "the sum of bank loans and overdrafts, short-term commercial papers and other short-term loans"), and 0.10 to long-term debt ("the sum of preference shares, bonds and debentures, and other long-term loans," as defined by Ong).

With regard to external debt, the Singapore Department of Statistics (SDOS) distinguished between external debt per se—defined as "all overseas loans drawn by our corporate, government and household sectors, but exclud[ing] our banks' overseas inter-bank loans" (SDOS 2000, p. 1; we discuss bank borrowing below)—and "secondary forms of external debt," comprising negotiable debt securities (SDOS 1998, p. 2) such as bonds, debentures, treasury bills, and trade credits (defined by SDOS 1998 as "direct extension of credit by suppliers and buyers for goods and services transactions and advance payments for work that is in progress"). Tables 12.3–12.8 provide information on these forms of debt during the 1990s. According to the SDOS (1998, p. 2), "Singapore has had no public external debt since 1995," owing to its regular budget surpluses. Its debt sustainability ratios were much more favorable than those of other countries in the region. About three-quarters of the external corporate debt was contracted by foreign-owned companies.[16]

---

16. The figure for nonbank loans at end 97, $4.518 billion, is the same in tables 12.3 and 12.6, but the figure for bank loans is larger in the former, since it includes loans to households as well; nonbank lending to households is not significant.

Table 12.3   Singapore's external debt, end 1995 to end 1998 (in S$ millions)

	End 1995	End 1996	End 1997	End 1998
Private sector	9,801	12,341	16,490	14,734
Loans				
BIS banks	6,921	7,390	11,161	9,274
Non-BIS banks	434	1,053	811	808
Other nonresidents	2,446	3,898	4,518	4,652
Public sector	0	0	0	0
Total	9,801	12,341	16,490	14,734
Previous estimates	9,801	10,927	15,631	

Source: SDOS (2000).
Notes: Data for 1998 are preliminary. BIS = Bank for International Settlements.

Table 12.4   Singapore debt sustainability ratios, end 1995 to end 1998 (%)

	End 1995	End 1996	End 1997	End 1998
Debt to GNP	8.1	9.3	11.2	10.0
Debt to (domestic) exports	10.0	11.9	15.3	13.9

Source: SDOS (2000).
Note: Data for 1998 are preliminary.

Table 12.5   External debt sustainability ratios of selected countries (%)

	End 1993	End 1994	End 1995	End 1996
External debt to GNP				
Indonesia	58.9	57.4	56.9	59.9
Malaysia	38.7	36.9	42.6	42.1
The Philippines	64.1	59.3	51.5	47.3
Thailand	37.1	43.1	34.9	50.3
External debt to exports				
Indonesia	211.9	195.8	202.9	222.2
Malaysia	43.5	37.7	40.8	42.4
The Philippines	187.0	160.6	121.8	97.6
Thailand	93.0	103.1	76.6	120.5

Source: World Bank, *World Debt Tables,* reproduced from SDOS (1998).

Turning to secondary forms of external debt, the SDOS (2000) observes, in regard to table 12.7, that "Singapore's external liability in debt securities nearly doubled from $2.0 billion at end-95 to $3.7 billion at end-98. . . . It was dominated by 4 foreign (3 Japanese and 1 U.S.) companies. The debt securities are mostly short and medium term notes issued to provide additional funds for the companies' operation." Regarding foreign direct investment (FDI) nonequity liabilities, and excluding debt securities, a

Table 12.6　　　　Overseas loans of local and foreign-owned companies, end 1997

	Identified bank loans		Nonbank loans		Total	
	Value (US$ millions)	Share (%)	Value (US$ millions)	Share (%)	Value (US$ millions)	Share (%)
Local-owned	1,258	21	1,445	32	2,703	26
Foreign-owned	4,754	79	3,073	68	7,827	74
Total	6,01		4,518		10,530	

Source: SDOS (2000).
Note: "Identified bank loans" refers to bank loans that are identified in SDOS surveys.

Table 12.7　　　　Secondary forms of external debt, end 1995 to end 1998 (in US$ millions)

	End 1995	End 1996	End 1997	End 1998
Debt securities	1,952	2,419	3,585	3,662
FDI nonequity capital: Net liability	5,194	5,687	7,808	7,792
Loans		4,074	5,437	5,752
Trade credits: Liabilities	9,852	6,830	7,431	6,825
Trade credits: Assets	4,658	5,217	5,050	4,785
Non-FDI trade credits: Net asset	3,267	6,238	8,092	7,072
Assets	16,662	17,632	21,148	19,639
Liabilities	13,395	11,394	13,056	12,567

Source: SDOS (2000).
Note: Data for 1995 have been revised. Data for 1998 are preliminary.

Table 12.8　　　　Net external position: Loans and debt securities, end 1996 to end 1997 (in US$ millions)

	End 1996	End 1997
Debt securities	6,303	7,454
Assets	8,722	11,039
Liabilities	2,419	3,585
Loans: Other nonresidents	4,804	6,846
Assets	8,702	11,364
Liabilities	3,898	4,518
Loans: FDI	3,518	3,944
Assets (outward FDI)	7,592	9,381
Liabilities (inward FDI)	4,074	5,437

Source: SDOS (2000).

significant portion comprised loans from parent companies. After 1995, Singapore was a net creditor in all trade credit transactions (FDI and non-FDI). As table 12.8 shows, it was also a net creditor in all the other categories covered in the preceding tables, namely debt securities, FDI-related loans, and loans to other nonresidents, with the exception of borrowing from external banks (table 12.3): the figure of almost S$12 billion here is modest relative to other figures below, and it has not been netted against lending by Singapore banks to external nonbank entities, on which data are not provided.

The overall picture that emerges is that of a comfortable external debt position, as far as nonbank entities are concerned. Turning to banks, as of December 1997 the DBUs owed S$94.7 billion to banks outside Singapore (including to the head offices of foreign-owned banks); however, they had also lent S$69.7 billion to banks outside Singapore (both figures are inclusive of DBU transactions with ACUs, and all figures are from the *Monthly Digest of Statistics, Singapore,* July 1998).[17] The total asset base of DBUs at that time (after deducting interbank lending between DBUs, but inclusive of dealings with ACUs and other foreign banks) was S$163.7 billion, and their total deposits from nonbank customers amounted to S$124.1 billion, with a further S$25.8 billion of deposits with the Post Office Savings Bank. Also by way of comparison, Singapore's stock market capitalization was about S$180 billion in 1997 (Thiam 2002, table 1), notwithstanding the depressed state of security prices at the time. Finally, with regard to bond issuance specifically, total outstanding corporate bonds at that time, sold to both domestic and foreign asset holders, amounted to S$8.4 billion (S$6.7 billion being Singapore dollar issuance, and S$1.7 billion being non–Singapore dollar issuance), and total outstanding governmental debt (secondary debt according to the SDOS classification) comprised S$15.0 billion worth of bonds and S$6.9 billion worth of treasury bills (all figures from the MAS web site's sections on Singapore's bond markets).

Given Singapore's modest overall external debt position, its large foreign exchange reserves (amounting to about six times the size of the monetary base[18]), and its small exchange rate depreciation relative to that of

17. We focus here on DBUs, since the offshore market or the ACUs transact virtually entirely in foreign currencies.

18. These very large reserves are to a not insignificant degree a reflection of Singapore's fairly low domestic absorption capacity (given its small size), juxtaposed against its large savings rate over many years. Nor does it appear that such large reserve holdings impose a significant opportunity cost on the economy: a *Straits Times* (Singapore) report of July 22, 2004, by Audrey Tan quotes the assistant managing director of the MAS, Ong Chong Tee, as saying, "we are invested across a diversified range of markets and currencies" and that owing to "the better performance of global equity markets," the MAS's profits in the year ending March 31, 2004, jumped to S$4.99 billion (from just S$623 million the previous year). The bulk of these profits arose from investing its foreign reserves, which totaled US$96.3 billion at the beginning of the year. The report adds that the MAS "does not disclose the rate of return on its investments" but that, according to Ong, "on average, MAS' performance would

other countries in the region, it is not surprising that its external indebtedness was not a noticeable aggravating factor in the 1997–98 downturn. It is, however, of interest to examine the reasons for the historical underdevelopment of Singapore's bond markets (as seen above, its banking system and equities market are much more developed) and to review the measures taken since 1998 to foster their growth, with particular reference to their implications for the noninternationalization policy.[19]

We may divide the reasons for the historical underdevelopment into supply and demand factors, while recognizing that there is some interaction between the two. Perhaps the most important supply factor has been the healthy fiscal position of the government, which has resulted in a limited need for it to issue bonds. Moreover, the bonds that were issued were of low maturity (not more than seven years, prior to 1998), and the bulk of them, and of treasury bills, were held by banks and finance companies (to a significant extent to meet minimum liquidity requirements), as well as insurance companies, resulting in a very limited secondary bond market. It should, however, be noted that we exclude here "specially-issued, non-tradable, long-term government bonds which are held by the CPF [Central Provident Fund] until maturity" (Ngiam and Loh 2002, p. 6). The CPF is Singapore's compulsory saving scheme, and its holdings of these special bonds substantially exceed the outstanding amount of other, tradable government securities. Ngiam and Loh add, "Most of the proceeds from such [CPF-purchased] bonds are probably channeled to the Government of Singapore Investment Corporation (GSIC) for investment in foreign assets" (p. 6).

An important consequence of the underdevelopment of the governmental bond market, particularly the secondary market, was the absence of a benchmark yield curve to facilitate corporate issuance, and active trading, of bonds. At the same time, it may be hypothesized that Singaporeans' appetite for a secure, long-term asset has to a large extent been met, albeit compulsorily, by their CPF savings, notwithstanding the somewhat low return on such savings (Asher 2004). They may thus wish to channel most if not all of their remaining discretionary savings (beyond that used to finance home ownership) to more liquid bank deposits and to higher-yielding but risky equity investments, an explanation that would help account for the more advanced state of development of Singapore's banking system and equities market—which in turn makes it easier for Singapore corporations to raise funds from these sources.

---

place it in the top 25th percentile of its peer group of fund managers." Substantial sums are also invested by the Government of Singapore Investment Corporation (in financial and real assets abroad) and Temasek Holdings (until recently, mostly in government-linked-companies domestically), but the precise amounts are not known, and neither is the former's rate of return on its investments.

19. Valuable references here are Ngiam and Loh (2002), Lee (2001), and U.S. Embassy (2001).

With a largely captive market for government securities, the government could afford to pay low yields on these. Moreover, until recently, "Singapore investors [had] to pay tax on interest income whereas they [did] not have to pay tax on capital gains obtained from investing in equities and properties" (Ngiam and Loh 2002, p. 11). Lastly, much of Singapore's economic growth has historically been driven by large inflows of FDI, with foreign-owned companies receiving major infusions of equity and loans from their parent companies.

The Asian crisis of 1997–98 provided a major impetus to a shift in policy thinking regarding bond market development in Singapore. The crisis highlighted the dangers of currency and maturity mismatches in corporate borrowing, and Singapore banks also suffered losses due to exposure to the region, although none was in danger of collapsing. It therefore appeared prudent to diversify the sources of borrowing on the part of Singapore corporations, particularly long-term borrowing, and encourage them to borrow in Singapore dollars. Also, with economic growth the pool of discretionary saving was growing substantially, notwithstanding the high CPF contribution rate, and fund management companies had become increasingly active in the economy. One may surmise that concomitantly the demand for market determination of bond yields, and of greater market liquidity, was also growing. This was underscored by the severe fall in equity and property prices during the crisis. From a longer-term, developmental perspective, fostering of a further pillar of Singapore's dynamic financial sector was also deemed desirable. The intention was to encourage not only Singaporean but also foreign corporations, and multilateral institutions, to float bond issues in Singapore.

Accordingly, since 1999 the MAS has issued, on a regular basis, more Singapore government securities (SGSs), with larger issuances and longer maturities (up to fifteen years). The healthy fiscal position of the government has enabled it to offer lower yields on such securities and yet ensure their acceptance by investors.[20] Statutory boards and government-linked corporations (GLCs) have also become active in bond issuance, relying less on bank borrowing: for example, the Jurong Town Corporation launched a S$200 million twelve-year issue in 2000, and Singapore

---

20. See figures 12.2 and 12.3 (from Wong 2004) in respect of Singapore and U.S. government ten-year bond yields in the recent past. The former yield has almost invariably been below the latter, while tracking its movement fairly closely, except in recent months, which Wong attributes to expectations of continued weakening of the U.S. dollar. The IMF Country Report of October 2001 on Singapore (Kochhar et al. 2001) also points out that SGSs offer lower yields than U.S. Treasury bonds but have nonetheless been included in JPMorgan's Government Bond Index (GBI) Broad since April 2001 (with a weight of one-third percent) because of their low cross-correlations with returns from most other government bonds and their very low volatility of returns, "which help to expand the efficient portfolio frontier for bonds" (p. 24). McCauley and Jiang (2004) provide a detailed analysis of the diversification benefits from holding a range of Asian currency bonds in addition to those from other areas.

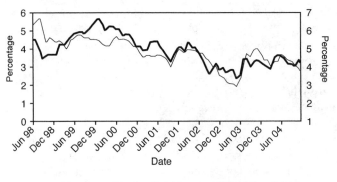

Fig. 12.2   Singapore dollar and U.S. dollar bond yields
Source: Wong (2004).
Note: The left column measures the Singapore bond yield.

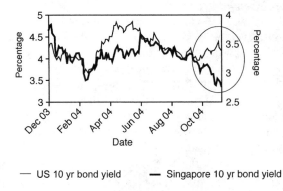

Fig. 12.3   U.S. dollar and Singapore dollar bond yields
Source: Wong (2004).
Note: The left column measures the U.S. bond yield.

Telecommunications launched a S$1 billion five-year issue in February 2001. The intention has been "to stimulate the emergence of a debt market, and to establish benchmark rates" (U.S. Embassy 2001, p. 2). Secondary markets are still fairly small (Ngiam and Loh 2002), although growing. Tax exemption for fee income earned by financial institutions arranging debt securities in Singapore (in Singapore dollars as well as foreign currencies) was also granted, interest income earned by nonresidents was exempted from withholding tax, and a concessionary tax rate of 10 percent was introduced on interest income earned by financial institutions and corporations from holding debt securities. Interest rate futures contracts were introduced, and restrictions on Singapore dollar over-the-counter (OTC) interest rate derivatives such as interest rate swaps, forward rate agreements, and interest rate and swap options were lifted (Ngiam and Loh 2002, p. 13).[21] The authorities have also attempted to foster primary and secondary market liquidity through measures such as the introduction of an SGS repurchase facility for primary dealers and a five-year SGS bond futures contract.

Of particular interest for our purpose is "the opening up of the S$ bond market to foreign issuers . . . accomplished through MAS Notice 757, introduced in August 1998 and amended in November 1999" (Ngiam and Loh 2002, p. 8).[22] The proceeds from such issues could be retained in the form of domestic currency deposits with banks in Singapore pending use; however, if and when the proceeds were to be used outside Singapore, they had to be converted or swapped into foreign currency before remitting abroad (Ngiam and Loh 2002). Funds raised for use in Singapore by nonbank nonresidents for designated economic activities—excluding, for example, "speculating in the S$ currency and interest rate markets" (Lee 2001, p. 36)—did not require prior MAS approval. Prior approval was also not required for transacting in several derivative products (fuller details are provided in the appendix). Lee (2001) also points out that Notice 757 (of August 1998) "fully liberalized the extension of S$ credit facilities to residents" (p. 35). Interestingly, in the revised Notice 757 of May 28, 2004, the MAS has stated that, effective from that date, nonresident nonfinancial issuers of Singapore dollar bonds and equities were no longer required to swap or convert their proceeds into foreign currencies before remitting abroad, adding that this revision "would allow the issuers greater flexibility in managing their S$ funds." For nonresident financial institutions, however, the requirement was retained.

A short time after the policy of August 1998 was announced, according to the U.S. Embassy (2001),

> the International Finance Corporation became the first foreign entity to issue S$ bonds, with a S$300 million three-year issue. GE Capital followed in Q1 1999 as the first foreign private issuer, with a S$300 million issue, followed by the Nordic Investment Bank and the European Bank for Reconstruction and Development. A wide range of foreign financial institutions and other corporates have launched issues since early 1999

---

21. "However," Ngiam and Loh add, "banks are required to submit monthly reports on details of interest rate derivative transactions exceeding S$5 million with counter-parties outside Singapore" (p. 13).

22. Foreign entities have also been permitted to list Singapore dollar–denominated shares since late 1998, but similar restrictions to those discussed immediately below on the use of the proceeds outside Singapore have applied (Shook Lin and Bok 2001).

(including US issuers such as Ford Motor Credit, JPMorgan, UPS, Morgan Stanley, John Hancock, General Motors Acceptance, and Goldman Sachs, as well as a wide range of European entities and some Asian entities).

By the first quarter of 2002, total Singapore dollar bond issue by foreign entities amounted to S$7.2 billion (Ngiam and Loh 2002, p. 8), and the market continues to grow, thereby helping to meet the demand of both domestic and foreign investors (including fund managers) for such instruments.

Ngiam and Loh (2002, p. 20) further mention that "from December 2000 onward, non-residents have been allowed to borrow Singapore dollars [from banks] to buy SGS and SDCB [Singapore dollar corporate bonds]," as well as Singapore dollar equities and real estate (U.S. Embassy 2001). Banks were also permitted to "extend S$ credit facilities exceeding S$5 million to nonresidents to fund offshore activities, as long as the S$ proceeds are swapped into foreign currency" (Lee 2001, p. 37), to transact in Singapore dollars currency options with other banks and financial institutions in Singapore, and to transact with nonresidents in a broad range of derivative products (Lee 2001, p. 37; the appendix provides further details). Foreign securities intermediaries were permitted to freely obtain Singapore dollar financing domestically, and, effective March 1, 2001, offshore banks were permitted to freely engage in Singapore dollar swap activity with nonbanks (U.S. Embassy 2001). In March 2002, Singapore dollar credit facilities to nonresident nonfinancial entities (such as corporate treasury centers) were liberalized, so that only credit in excess of S$5 million to nonresident financial entities for speculating against the Singapore dollar was prohibited, and even these entities were permitted to engage in a wider range of derivative transactions (such as Singapore dollar currency options) with financial institutions. The intention was to promote the deepening of such markets. We discuss the overall implications of measures to promote financial market development in the conclusion.

12.6   Conclusion

Singapore clearly has strong defenses against what it deems excessive exchange rate volatility triggered by destabilizing capital flows. These include its strong fundamentals (discussed in the Chan and Ngiam quotation at the beginning of section 12.4), the adoption of a CB system, and the nonadherence to a fixed currency peg when the economic situation changes. (Indeed, an important lesson is that it is the *package* of policies in totality that can meaningfully be evaluated, rather than individual policies in isolation from the overall policy context.) Under the imperative of promoting the continued growth and diversification of its financial sector—an important pillar of the economy, accounting for about 12 percent of its GDP—quite a number of administrative restrictions have been relaxed since 1997. This was heralded in a key address on November 4, 1997, by then Deputy Prime Minister Lee Hsien Loong:

> In order to meet the upcoming challenges, DPM Lee proposed a fundamental change in Singapore's attitude towards risk management. . . . In contrast to Hong Kong, "where anything not expressly forbidden is permitted," Lee noted that in Singapore "anything not expressly permitted is forbidden." At this stage, however, the government needed to regulate the financial sector "with a lighter touch, accept more calculated risks, and give the industry more room to innovate and stretch the envelope" in order to promote a more competitive, dynamic and innovative environment. Lee argued for a disclosure-based regulatory system to protect investors, rather than . . . extensive regulations. (U.S. Embassy 1999)

The progressive relaxations of the Singapore dollar noninternationalization policy, which in any event was a rather limited form of capital control, may be viewed in this light.[23] Such relaxations, including those on a wide variety of derivative transactions, were necessary to foster bond market development in Singapore, and the evidence provided in this chapter indicates that this objective (including the attraction of foreign bond-issuers) is well on the way to being achieved. Since May 2004, the only remaining restriction of any significance is the onus placed on banks to determine, as far as possible, that the Singapore dollar credit facilities they extend to nonresident financial institutions will not be used for currency speculation. This would appear to be a reasonable restriction, especially in light of the very high interest rate volatility experienced by Hong Kong (which did not impose such a restriction) during speculative periods (see the beginning of section 12.2). Given the MAS's reputation for toughness, one would expect that banks will err on the side of caution in implementing this policy. Financial market development is thereby facilitated, and at the same time the risk of heightened currency speculation during turbulent periods is reduced, along with the associated macroeconomic instability. It is also quite conceivable that restrictions—for example, on swap transactions—would be reintroduced if it was felt that the situation so warranted.

A similar policy orientation may be seen in the securities market. In 1998, Morgan Stanley launched the Morgan Stanley Capital International (MSCI) Singapore stock index futures contract, and in 2000 the *Straits Times* Singapore stock index futures contract was launched, both on Singapore International Monetary Exchange (SIMEX). However, SIMEX is

---

23. A study by the MAS (2000a) found that during the 1990s, and prior to the Asian crisis, covered and uncovered interest parity tended to hold between Singapore and U.S. one- and three-month interbank rates respectively, indicating, as one might expect, a high degree of financial integration.

authorized by the MAS to "establish position and trading limits to diminish or prevent excessive speculation" (Lawton 1999, section 3) and also maintains a large trader reporting system. Somewhat ironically, in the light of (now) Prime Minister Lee's observations, while Singapore has moved to a more relaxed regulatory regime, Hong Kong has tightened up somewhat, and the two systems are closer than they previously were. This perhaps is where the golden mean lies—a fairly, although not completely, unrestrictive, rule-based system in general, but with provision for discretionary intervention when the situation warrants. Do such discretionary provisions create uncertainty for business, and can they be abused? If they are intelligently employed, they can be very valuable in times of stress, and perhaps the best safeguard against abuse is public analysis and discussion whenever they are employed.

Appendix

Chronology of Capital Controls in Singapore

June 1, 1978

Exchange controls are completely liberalized, in line with efforts to develop Singapore as a banking and financial center (including offshore banking). From then on, "residents are allowed to borrow, lend and invest freely in foreign currencies. Banks in Singapore that are licensed to deal in Asian Currency Units can freely accept deposits in foreign currencies. Residents may deal freely in spot and forward foreign exchange transactions. Nonresidents are freely allowed to make direct and portfolio investments in the country" (MAS 1999, p. 2).

November 1, 1983

MAS Notice 621, setting out the policy of noninternationalization of the Singapore dollar, is issued (see section 12.3).

July 18, 1992

The MAS amends the policy by distinguishing three categories of activities:

1. *The approved category:* Consultation with the MAS is not required for credit facilities extended in Singapore dollars, in any amount, to residents or nonresidents to facilitate direct exports from and imports to Singapore, and for payment bonds in favor of Singapore parties, or payment guarantees (including guarantees for tax payments), in respect of "economic activities" in Singapore, where the latter specifically excludes finan-

cial and portfolio investments. Forward sales of Singapore dollars earned from exports to Singapore are also permitted.

2. *The banned category:* Banks are not to finance in Singapore dollars "activities which have no bearing on Singapore," including direct or portfolio investments outside Singapore by nonresidents, third-country trade by nonresident-controlled companies, and nonresident subscription to equity in a Singapore company where the proceeds are used for takeovers or financial investments. Banks are also not to extend Singapore dollar credit facilities, in any amount, to nonresidents for speculating in the local financial and property markets.

3. *The unlisted category:* The 1983 ruling calling for consultation with the MAS continues to apply for all other activities, which are quite wide ranging; these include third-country trade as well as direct and portfolio investments overseas by residents, and direct investment and housing development in Singapore by nonresidents.

August 1998

In conjunction with an "extensive program of financial sector liberalization" (Lee 2001, p. 35), the MAS issues the first version of Notice 757, which replaces Notice 621; this and subsequent versions seek to successively relax restrictions against various financial transactions. While concluding that "the basic policy remains sound," the MAS states that "some judicious relaxation of specific restrictions would foster the development of capital markets with minimal incremental risks" (quoted in Lee 2001, p. 35).

The notice fully liberalizes the extension of Singapore dollar credit facilities to residents. In addition, banks can now engage in the following activities without prior consultation with the MAS (Lee 2001):

1. Extension of Singapore dollar credit facilities to, and arranging Singapore dollar equity listings or bond issues for, nonbank nonresidents if the Singapore dollar proceeds are used for designated economic activities in Singapore.

2. Extension of Singapore dollar credit facilities to nonbank nonresidents for financial investments—shares, bonds, deposits, and commercial properties in Singapore—up to S$5 million.

3. Extension of Singapore dollar credit facilities up to S$20 million to nonresidents, via repurchase agreements of SGSs.

4. A limited list of derivative transactions, including hedging of currency or interest rates from the activities listed in item 1 above, and transacting in Singapore dollar interest rate futures with nonresidents.

For other activities, consultation with the MAS continues to be required, and in addition the Singapore dollar proceeds from credit facilities and bond and equity listings arranged for nonbank nonresidents have to be converted or swapped into foreign currency if they are to be used outside

Singapore. Also, the extension of Singapore dollar credit facilities to non-residents for certain purposes—including speculating in the Singapore dollar currency and interest rate markets, financing third-country trades, and financing acquisition of shares of companies not listed on the stock exchange or Central Limit Order Book—is explicitly prohibited.

November 1999

Banks are permitted to engage in an expanded range of activities without prior consultation with the MAS, including extension of Singapore dollar credit facilities to, and transacting in Singapore dollar interest rate products with, other banks, merchant banks, finance companies, and insurance companies in Singapore; extension of Singapore dollar credit facilities of any amount to nonresidents via repurchases of SGSs or other Singapore dollar bonds; arranging Singapore dollar equity listings for nonresident companies as long as the Singapore dollar proceeds are converted into foreign currency before being used outside Singapore; and all Singapore dollar derivative transactions with residents, as well as an expanded range of derivative transactions with nonresidents, including option-related products with nonfinancial counterparts. However, banks are still required to consult with the MAS before transacting in Singapore dollars currency options or option-related products with nonbank financial institutions, and before extending Singapore dollar credit facilities exceeding S$5 million to banks and other financial institutions outside Singapore, and they are not permitted to transact in Singapore dollars currency options or option-related products with other banks.

December 2000

Nonresidents are permitted to borrow Singapore dollars (from banks) to buy SGSs and SDCBs, as well as Singapore dollar equities and real estate. Banks are also permitted to extend Singapore dollar credit facilities exceeding S$5 million to nonresidents to fund offshore activities, as long as the proceeds are swapped into foreign currency; to transact in Singapore dollars currency options with other banks and financial institutions in Singapore; and to transact with nonresidents in a broad range of derivative products, including cross-currency swaps and currency options for hedging purposes, Singapore dollar interest rate derivatives, and equity derivatives. Foreign securities intermediaries are permitted to freely obtain Singapore dollar financing domestically, and, effective March 1, 2001, offshore banks are permitted to engage freely in Singapore dollar swap activity with nonbanks.

March 2002

Singapore dollar credit facilities to nonresident nonfinancial entities (such as corporate treasury centers) are liberalized, so that only credit in excess of S\$5 million to nonresident financial entities—including banks, finance companies, insurance companies, hedge funds, and securities dealers and brokers—for speculating against the Singapore dollar is prohibited. Even the latter entities are permitted to engage in a wider range of derivative transactions (such as Singapore dollar currency options) with financial institutions, except that foreign exchange swaps involving a spot sale of Singapore dollars to the nonresident in the first leg remain under the rubric of Singapore dollar credit facilities. Apart from this, transactions involving asset swaps, cross-currency swaps, and cross-currency repurchases are fully liberalized. The intention is to promote the deepening of such markets and make it easier for Singapore dollar equities and debts to be swapped into foreign currencies for overseas use. Financial institutions are also no longer required to ensure that Singapore dollar credit facilities extended to finance investments be withdrawn when the investments are liquidated, thereby lessening the burden of tracking fund use.

May 28, 2004

Nonresident nonfinancial issuers of Singapore dollar bonds and equities are no longer required to swap or convert their Singapore dollar proceeds into foreign currencies before remitting abroad, so as to "allow the issuers greater flexibility in managing their S\$ funds" (MAS Notice 757). For nonresident financial institutions, however, the requirement is retained for Singapore dollar proceeds from equity and bond listings and from borrowing from banks. Banks are also required to report to the MAS monthly their aggregate outstanding Singapore dollar lending to nonresident financial institutions. It is reiterated in Notice 757 that "banks shall not extend S\$ credit facilities [exceeding S\$5 million] to non-resident financial institutions if there is reason to believe that the S\$ proceeds may be used for S\$ currency speculation."

References

Asher, M. 2004. Retirement financing in Singapore. National University of Singapore, School of Public Policy. Manuscript, June.

Bris, A., W. N. Goetzmann, and N. Zhu. 2003. Efficiency and the bear: Short sales and markets around the world. NBER Working Paper no. W9466. Cambridge, MA: National Bureau of Economic Research, January.

Chakravorti, S., and S. Lall. 2000. The double play: Simultaneous speculative attacks on currency and equity markets. FRBC Working Paper no. 2000-17. Chicago: Federal Reserve Bank of Chicago, December.

Chan, K. S., and K. J. Ngiam. 1996. Currency speculation and the optimum control of bank lending in Singapore dollars: a case for partial liberalization. IMF Working Paper WP/96/95. Washington, DC: International Monetary Fund, August.

———. 1998. Currency crises and the modified currency board system in Singapore. *Pacific Economic Review* 3 (3): 243–63.

Corsetti, G., P. A. Pesenti, and N. Roubini. 2001. The role of large players in currency crises. NBER Working Paper no. W8303. Cambridge, MA: National Bureau of Economic Research, May.

Devereux, M. B. 2003. A tale of two currencies: The Asian crisis and the exchange rate regimes of Hong Kong and Singapore. *Review of International Economics* 11 (1): 38–54.

Dickens, M. 2002. Development of the Hong Kong Securities and Futures Market. Paper presented at fourth Round Table on Capital Market Reform in Asia. 9–10 April, Tokyo, Japan.

Financial Stability Forum. 2000. Report of the Working Group on Highly Leveraged Institutions. April.

Hashimoto, Y. 2003. An empirical test of likelihood and timing of speculative attacks: The case of Malaysia and Singapore. *Japan and the World Economy* 15 (2): 245–59.

Hashimoto, Y., and T. Ito. 2004. High-frequency contagion between the exchange rates and stock prices. NBER Working Paper no. 10448. Cambridge, MA: National Bureau of Economic Research, April.

Kochhar, K., A. Senhadji, J. Lee, and Y. Nishigaki. 2001. *Singapore: Selected issues.* IMF Country Report no. 01/177. Washington, DC: International Monetary Fund, October.

Lawton, J. C. (acting director, Commodity Futures Trading Commission). 1999. Letter to J. K. Thorpe, Singapore international monetary exchange limited; Request for no-action relief from the contract market designation requirement. Letter to J. K. Thorpe. December 17.

Lee, J. 2001. Evolution of the policy on noninternationalization of the Singapore dollar. In *Singapore: Selected issues,* ed. K. Kochhar, A. Senhadji, J. Lee, and Y. Nishigaki, 33–41. Washington, DC: International Monetary Fund.

McCauley, R., and G. Jiang. 2004. Diversifying with Asian local currency bonds. *BIS Quarterly Review* 2004 (September): 51–66.

Monetary Authority of Singapore (MAS). n.d. Monetary policy operating procedures in Singapore. BIS Policy Paper. Basel, Switzerland: Bank for International Settlements.

———. 1999. Capital account and exchange rate management in a surplus economy: The case of Singapore. Occasional Paper no. 11. Monetary Authority of Singapore, March.

———. 2000a. Financial market integration in Singapore: The narrow and the broad views. Occasional Paper no. 20. Monetary Authority of Singapore, May.

———. 2000b. A survey of Singapore's monetary history. Occasional Paper no. 18. Monetary Authority of Singapore, January.

———. 2001. Singapore's exchange rate policy. Monetary Authority of Singapore, February.

Morgan Stanley. 2003. Short-selling details: Equities. March 27. https://www.oecd.org/dataoecd/5/43/18465550.pdf.

Ngiam, K. J. 2000. Coping with the Asian financial crisis: The Singapore experience. Visiting Researchers Series no. 8. Singapore: Institute of Southeast Asian Studies, March.

Ngiam, K. J., and L. Loh. 2002. Developing a viable corporate bond market: The Singapore experience. Economics and Finance Series no. 2(2002). Singapore: Institute of Southeast Asian Studies, June.

Ong, L. H. 1998. Financial leverage of Singapore corporations, 1971–1997. *Statistics Singapore Newsletter.* April, pp. 9–14.

Peebles, G., and P. Wilson. 2002. Economic growth and development in Singapore. London: Edward Elgar.

Poitras, G. 2002. Short sales restrictions, dilution, and the pricing of rights issues on the Singapore Stock Exchange. *Pacific-Basin Finance Journal* 10 (2): 141–62.

Rzepkowski, B. 2000. The expectations of Hong Kong dollar devaluation and their determinants. CEPII Working Paper no. 2000-04. Paris: Centre d'études prospectives ed d'informations internationales, February.

Shook Lin and Bok. 2001. MAS liberalizes Singapore dollar policy. *Legal Newsletter.* January 4.

Singapore Department of Statistics (SDOS). 1998. *Monthly digest of statistics.* Singapore Department of Statistics, July.

————. 1998b. Singapore's external debt. Occasional Paper on Economic Statistics. Singapore Department of Statistics, December.

————. 2000. Singapore's external debt: Definition and 1998 assessment. Information Paper on Economic Statistics. Singapore Department of Statistics, January.

Starr, P. 1985. Singapore props up currency. *Australian Financial Review.* September 18.

Tan, A. 2004. MAS chalks up handsome $5b gain. *Straits Times* (Singapore). July 22.

Technical Committee, International Organization of Securities Commissions. 2003. Report on transparency of short selling. June.

Teh, K. P. 1988. Monetary policy in an open economy: Singapore. Lecture delivered at seventeenth SEANZA (South-East Asia, New Zealand, Australia) Central Banking Course. Sydney, Australia.

Textline Multiple Source Collection. 1985. Singapore's foreign exchange market is virtually back to normal. 20 September.

Thiam, H. N. 2002. Stock market linkages in South-East Asia. *Asian Economic Journal* 16 (4): 353–77.

U.S. Embassy, Singapore. 1999. Reforming Singapore's financial services sector: A background and progress report. May.

————. 2001. Singapore: The Singapore dollar bond market develops. March.

Wong, S. J. 2004. Rising bond prices. December 10. http://www.fundsupermart.com.

Yam, J. 1998a. Defending Hong Kong's monetary stability. Speech at Trade Development Council networking luncheon. 14 October, Singapore.

Yam, J. 1998b. Coping with financial turmoil. Inside Asia lecture. 23 November, Sydney, Australia.

Comment   Anusha Chari

Introduction

Singapore's macroeconomic history sets it apart from the other countries discussed in this volume. A number of developing countries have lurched from crisis to crisis, plagued by a variety of economic ills such as unsustainable fiscal positions, current account deficits, lax monetary poli-

Anusha Chari is an assistant professor of finance in the Stephen M. Ross School of Business, University of Michigan.

cies, rampant inflation, high unemployment rates, and weak corporate governance mechanisms. In contrast, Singapore's economic good fortune is one of budget and current account surpluses, a high savings rate, low inflation, good institutions, a sound financial system, and—last but not least—a stable currency.

Closer examination reveals that a cornerstone of Singapore's policy on capital account openness is the noninternationalization of the Singapore dollar. Banks are required to follow a policy of noninternationalization in large part because the government is concerned about the buildup of offshore deposits of the Singapore dollar that could be used by speculators to destabilize the currency. The policy is applied to a broad range of financial instruments including bond issues and derivative products.

The policy is in part also designed to help Singapore maintain the "soft peg" that has been crucial for its export-led strategy of development. Singapore's successful maintenance of its soft peg defies the conventional wisdom that soft pegs are not viable (Eichengreen 1999).

It is worth noting that, following revisions in March 2002, only two core requirements of the policy on capital controls remain. First, financial institutions are not allowed to extend Singapore dollar credit facilities in excess of S\$5 million to nonresident financial entities, if they have reason to believe that the proceeds may be used for speculation against the Singapore dollar. Second, for a Singapore dollar loan to a nonresident financial entity exceeding S\$5 million, or for a Singapore dollar equity or bond issue by a nonresident entity that is used to fund overseas activities, the Singapore dollar proceeds must be swapped or converted into foreign currency before use outside Singapore. According to the Monetary Authority of Singapore (2002), the policy continues to be necessary to prevent offshore speculators from accessing the liquidity in Singapore's onshore foreign exchange swaps and money markets.

In these comments I will argue that the policy of noninternationalization has perhaps outlived its use and may in fact be a factor that hinders the development of an active bond market in Singapore.

Destabilizing Speculation versus Deteriorating Fundamentals

Basant Kapur argues that Singapore has adopted a policy of noninternationalization to ward off financial instability of the sort experienced by Hong Kong in 1998. Hong Kong and Singapore are often thought of as being very similar. Indeed, both are city-states with a British colonial heritage, and both have been in the set of "Asian tigers" that achieved extremely rapid economic growth from the 1960s until very recently. Kapur contends that the "double play" by foreign speculators—simultaneously shorting the Hong Kong stock index futures and selling the Hong Kong dollar forward—was the root cause of the crisis in 1998.

There has been a long-standing academic and policy debate about the factors that drive currency crises. In this context, the role of large players has been particularly important. On the one hand, large traders and arbitrageurs may improve the efficiency of the price mechanism because they are well suited to collecting and processing information. Alternatively, following crisis episodes, the machinations of large players have been blamed as catalysts of market panic and short-termism (Corsetti, Pesenti, and Roubini 2002). The literature provides many an example in which market efficiency is jeopardized by the behavior of large traders as destabilizing speculators (Krugman 2000).

According to Kapur, Hong Kong in 1998 provides an important example of an economy that came close to the collapse of its currency board regime as a result of aggressive speculation against its foreign exchange and stock markets. In this example, only direct intervention by the authorities in the stock market prevented the collapse of the currency peg and a further meltdown of its stock market. However, the effects of defending the peg, which probably exacerbated the recessionary effects of the Asian crisis on the domestic economy, were quite costly (Corsetti, Pesenti, and Roubini 2002).

In fact, it is rather hard to prove that speculation by large traders alone caused a currency or stock market crisis episode. Crisis episodes generally take place against a backdrop of deteriorating macro fundamentals, policy uncertainties, and structural weaknesses (Corsetti, Pesenti, and Roubini 2002). In other words, was the double play in Hong Kong a rational response to deteriorating fundamentals?

Kapur concedes that the empirical findings do not provide evidence of market manipulation per se. Indeed, Hong Kong experienced a sharp recession in 1998, and GDP growth in the first quarter was negative. Coupled with worsening macroeconomic conditions in East Asia, a falling yen, and the threat of Chinese devaluation, this may have led to a loss of confidence in the Hong Kong stock market and the survival of the currency peg.

Shorting both the Hong Kong stock market and its currency at that time could therefore be interpreted as a rational strategy for all investors, domestic and foreign, highly leveraged or not (Corsetti, Pesenti, and Roubini 2002). In other words, the hypothesis of rational investors taking short positions in two markets (based on an assessment of economic fundamentals) and the hypothesis of a double play (suggesting market manipulation) are observationally equivalent. Kapur acknowledges this point. The rationale for the continued maintenance of the policy of noninternationalization in Singapore is therefore not apparent.

Developing a Viable Bond Market

The second issue that Kapur focuses on is the concerted effort being made by Singapore to develop its bond market. It is interesting to note the unique factors separate from the policy of noninternationalization that hinder the development of the bond market in Singapore. In many countries, the need to develop active bond markets stems from a public finance motive—namely, to finance government deficits. In contrast, Singapore has consistently run budget surpluses since the 1980s. Therefore, the government's borrowing needs have not spawned a domestic bond market. Many large companies in Singapore also do not require bond financing, as they tend to be cash rich.

Moreover, Singapore has a sophisticated bank lending network and equity capital market, which provide viable financing alternatives in the absence of bond markets. Hence, the need to develop the debt markets in Singapore must be governed by other imperatives.

One imperative may be the desire on the part of the government to develop the island state as a financial services hub for the region. In the longer term, Singapore may aspire to become a center for the issuing and trading of regional currency bonds. Like Switzerland, Singapore has all the necessary ingredients of an active corporate bond market—low borrowing costs, political stability, sound fundamentals, a stable currency, and a AAA sovereign rating.

Despite these attractive features, Singapore has been characterized by a historic underdevelopment of its bond market or suffers from original sin on the supply side. It is important to note that the greater part of international bond issuance takes place in relatively few currencies. For example, international bonds and notes denominated in the U.S. dollar, the euro, and the British pound account for approximately 88 percent of the total amounts outstanding for these instruments (*BIS Quarterly Review* 2005). This may prove to be an obstacle for a small country like Singapore as it tries to develop as a regional hub for international bond issuance in its own currency.

Interestingly, despite the fact that the government has run budget surpluses since the 1980s and maintains huge reserves, the government has actively promoted the development of a government bond market. In fact, the government securities market remains the biggest segment of the debt markets in Singapore. In part, developing the government bond market may fulfill the important purpose of providing a benchmark yield curve as a reference for the term structure of corporate issues.

The second measure that Singapore has undertaken to develop its bond market has been the opening up of the Singapore dollar bond market to foreign issuers. Foreign issuers may be attracted to the Singapore market because of low borrowing costs and a large pool of Singapore dollar funds. However, the policy of noninternationalization continues to apply to Singapore dollar bond issuance by foreigners. If Singapore dollar proceeds from the bond issuance are not used for economic activity in Singapore, they must be swapped into a foreign currency before being remitted abroad.

Note that a Singapore dollar loan combined with a currency swap results in a "synthetic" foreign currency loan. Also note that the swap market involving the Singapore dollar is illiquid and has wide bid-ask spreads. It is therefore not evident why foreign issuers would prefer to issue Singapore dollar bonds and incur the heavy costs of swapping rather than directly issuing foreign currency bonds in the Eurodollar bond market. By imposing swapping costs on foreign issuers, Singapore may in fact deter potential foreign issuers from the Singapore dollar bond market.

However, there is another point worth noting in the context of the currency denomination of international bond issuance: This context further highlights the idea that the policy of noninternationalization may have outlived its purpose. Corporate risk management strategies require companies to swap foreign currency–denominated loans (here, the Singapore dollar) into their domestic currency (say, the U.S. dollar) so as to avoid a currency mismatch between domestic assets and liabilities. The rationale for the government maintaining the noninternationalization "requirement" is therefore unclear.

References

BIS Quarterly Review. 2005. International banking and financial market developments. March.

Corsetti, Giancarlo, Paolo Pesenti, and Nouriel Roubini. 2002. The role of large players in currency crises. In *Preventing currency crises in emerging markets: Crisis prevention,* ed. S. Edwards and J. Frankel, 197–268. Chicago: University of Chicago Press.

Eichengreen, Barry. 1999. *Toward a new international financial architecture: A practical post-Asia agenda.* Washington, DC: Institute for International Economics.

Krugman, Paul, ed. 2000. *Currency crises.* Chicago: University of Chicago Press.

Monetary Authority of Singapore (MAS). 2002. Singapore: Policy of noninternationalization of the S$ and the Asian dollar market. Paper presented at the BIS/SAFE Seminar on Capital Account Liberalization. 12–13 September, Beijing, China.

India's Experience with Capital Flows
The Elusive Quest for a Sustainable Current Account Deficit

Ajay Shah and Ila Patnaik

13.1 Introduction

Indian economic policy witnessed a marked shift following a balance-of-payments crisis in 1991. Prior to this, India had a "less developed country (LDC) style" composition of capital flows, where current account deficits were financed using official flows and debt flows. As in other countries that were liberalizing capital flows in this period, the conceptual framework underlying the reforms of the 1990s was based on experiences with volatile debt flows, views about the sustainability of debt flows, and views about a desirable composition of flows.

The new approach, which has been broadly stable from 1992 till 2006, consisted of liberalizing the current account, opening up to foreign direct investment (FDI) for domestic and foreign firms, opening up to portfolio flows for foreigners, and restricting debt flows. The currency regime was shifted away from a fixed-but-adjustable exchange rate to a "market-determined exchange rate," which was pegged to the U.S. dollar through extensive trading on the currency market by the central bank.

Indian capital controls consist of an intricate web of a very large number

Ajay Shah is an independent scholar. Ila Patnaik is the economics editor at *Indian Express* in New Delhi and a senior fellow of the Indian Council for Research in International Economic Relations.

The views expressed in this paper are those of the authors and not of their employers. We are grateful to the Centre for Monitoring Indian Economy for help on data. We are grateful to Takatoshi Ito, Vijay Kelkar, Joydeep Mukherji, Brian Pinto, and participants of the 2004 National Bureau of Economic Research (NBER) International Capital Flows conference and the 2005 National Centre for Applied Economics Research–NBER conference for many ideas and improvements; to Shashank Saksena, H. A. C. Prasad, and P. R. Suresh for myriad clarifications about capital controls; to Vikram Nirula of G. W. Capital for facts about call centers; and to Sumanta Basak for outstanding research assistance.

of quantitative restrictions, operated by a substantial bureaucratic apparatus. Liberalization of FDI and portfolio flows was done in a gradual manner, with a large number of incremental and partial changes to the large number of rules. While some major decisions were taken in 1992, there has been a continual process, which continues even in 2006, of changing restrictions in small steps.

Liberalization of the current account has been highly successful. Positive technological shocks and dropping prices of international telecommunications helped India obtain high growth rates of services exports. The removal of quantitative restrictions, and the sharp drop in tariffs, served to spur both imports and exports. Through these, gross flows on the current account rose from 25 percent of gross domestic product (GDP) in 1992–93 to 35 percent in 2003–4.

Major changes took place on the capital account also. The policy bias against debt flows led to an outcome where net debt inflows stagnated at roughly 1 percent of GDP between 1992–93 and 2003–4. Owing to the debt aversion of the policy framework, gross debt flows dropped from 13.5 percent of GDP in 1992–93 to 10.6 percent in 2003–4. Official flows faded into insignificance.

Restrictions on both equity portfolio investors and on FDI were eased in this period. However, net FDI flows into India have remained small, either when compared to Indian GDP or when compared to global FDI flows. In contrast with the Chinese experience, relatively little FDI has come into India in setting up factories that are parts of global production chains. This may be associated with infirmities of Indian indirect taxes and transportation infrastructure. India is more important as a platform for service production as a part of global production chains, where difficulties of indirect taxes and transportation infrastructure are less important. However, service production is less capital intensive and is associated with smaller net FDI flows.

Given the size of the Indian economy, and the relative lack of correlation with the global business cycle, Indian equities have had low correlations with global risk factors. In addition, India has fared well in creating the institutional mechanisms of a modern, liquid equity market. Through these factors, portfolio flows have predominated. India's share in global portfolio flows is higher than India's share in global FDI flows, and net portfolio flows are substantial when compared to Indian GDP.

In many countries, there has been a close interplay between foreign investment and growth in trade. India has increased its share in world trade without having substantial FDI. A partial explanation lies in the low capital intensity of export-oriented production. Another aspect is the initial conditions, which consisted of a strong set of domestic firms. Portfolio flows have delivered capital to these domestic firms, which have gone on to obtain growth in exports. The growth of domestic firms has been assisted by relaxations of capital controls, which enabled them to engage in outbound FDI. Consequently, FDI inflows are somewhat larger than the data for net inflows make them appear.

While portfolio flows are sometimes considered volatile, in India's experience, there has been no episode of a significant retreat by foreign investors. Net FDI and net portfolio flows have been fairly stable. Debt flows have been relatively volatile, reflecting frequent changes in capital controls applicable to debt flows, and changing currency expectations.

Through these policy initiatives, gross flows on the capital account grew from 15 percent of GDP in 1992–93 to 20 percent of GDP in 2003–4, along with sharp changes in the composition of flows. In 2003–4, gross portfolio flows amounted to as much as 7 percent of GDP.

The growth of the capital account, and the shift toward less government control of the flows, has generated increasing difficulties in terms of reconciling currency policy and monetary policy autonomy with the increasingly open capital account. Speculative views of the currency have been expressed by economic agents in many ways. For example, in this paper, we find that currency expectations are important in explaining the time series dynamics of portfolio flows.

The ability of economic agents to express speculative views on the currency in an increasingly open economy has generated difficulties in implementing the currency regime that had not been experienced in preceding decades. As an example, from late 2001 to early 2004, the demands of the pegged exchange rate regime involved trading by the Reserve Bank of India (RBI) to prevent rupee appreciation. The private sector had expectations of a gradual INR appreciation, and thus had incentives to bring capital into India. This led to a large increase in inflows on both the current account and the capital account. In order to uphold the pegged exchange rate, the RBI traded extensively on the currency market, with a sharp rise in reserves from $40 billion to $115 billion from 2001 to 2004. In 2003–4, net capital inflows of $21 billion were accompanied by addition to reserves of $31 billion. This constituted a net outward flow of capital of $10.6 billion.

In retrospect, India's approach of gradual liberalization of the capital account has worked well in many ways. India has reaped microeconomic benefits of an open current account, and from FDI and portfolio flows. India has encountered no balance-of-payments crisis in the post-1992 period. From the macroeconomic standpoint, there have been episodes where monetary policy autonomy was significantly attenuated in the implementation of the currency regime. One key element of India's original policy quest—the search for a sustainable framework for augmenting investment through current account deficits—has as yet not been achieved.

In this paper, we explore the causes and consequences of the major empirical features of India's experience with capital flows. The paper begins with a review of India's quest for a current account deficit (section 13.2) and broad empirical features (section 13.3). We review the evolution of the currency regime (section 13.4) and capital controls (section 13.5). We examine FDI and portfolio flows in section 13.6, where we also explore the interplay between currency expectations and portfolio flows. Section 13.7 examines India's experience from the viewpoint of the impossible trinity of open economy macroeconomics, with an accent on the events of 2003–4. Finally, section 13.8 concludes.

13.2 The Quest for a Sustainable Current Account Deficit

India had low savings rates in the early period, with values of 9.8 percent in the 1950s, 12.5 percent in the 1960s, and 17.2 percent in the 1970s. Economic policy thinking was very aware of the opportunity to use current account deficits, and net capital inflows, in order to supplement domestic savings, augment investment, and thus enjoy a faster growth trajectory.

However, India persistently encountered difficulties in obtaining a sustained and economically significant current account deficit. In the late 1970s, a combination of high domestic inflation, a world oil price hike, and a pegged exchange rate generated low exports, a large current account deficit, and near exhaustion of reserves. In response to this, India undertook an International Monetary Fund (IMF) program in 1981. Conditionalities associated with this program included a revision of the exchange rate (Joshi and Little 1994).

By the late 1980s, India had built up a significant stock of external debt. In a period of political instability in 1990, there was a crisis of confidence, which gave a flight of debt and conditions of a speculative attack on the pegged exchange rate. In response to this, India undertook an IMF program in 1991. Conditionalities associated with this program included revision of the exchange rate and a shift to a market-determined exchange rate.

In recent years, several prominent documents in policy analysis have advocated larger but sustainable current account deficits. The expert group on commercialisation of infrastructure projects, chaired by Rakesh Mohan (1996, p. 49) states that

> The sustainability of such economic growth would require continuing high growth in exports, perhaps declining from the current 20 per cent annual growth to about 10 per cent by the end of the next decade, giving an average of about 15 per cent annual growth over the period. If this takes place, total exports should reach about $66 billion in 2000–01 and $115 billion by 2005–06. At these levels, exports would comprise about 15 per cent of GDP in 2000–01 and 17 per cent of GDP by 2005–06, up from the current levels of about 10 per cent. If exports manage to increase to these levels, it would become feasible for India to sustain a wider current account deficit which is required for the non-inflationary

absorption of external capital inflows. It is suggested that a sustainable level of current account deficit would increase from the current level of 1.5 per cent of GDP to 2.5 per cent in 2000–01 and 3 per cent in 2005–06. It would then be possible for the net capital inflow to rise from the current level of about $7 billion to $8 billion to about $17 billion to $20 billion by 2000–01 and about $25 billion to $30 billion by 2005–06. As table 13.1 shows, India did better than anticipated. Total exports reached $118 billion, or 18.4 percent of GDP in 2003–4, and net capital inflows reached $20.5 billion. However, far from obtaining a larger current

Table 13.1   **Indian capital flows: 1992–93 versus 2003–4**

	1992–93 (in US$ billions)	2003–4 (in US$ billions)	Growth percent	Percent to GDP 1992–93	2003–4
GDP at market prices	239.09	639.90	9.36		
Current account (net)	–3.53	10.56		–1.47	1.65
Merchandise					
Outflows	24.32	80.18	11.46	10.17	12.53
Inflows	18.87	64.72	11.86	7.89	10.11
Invisibles					
Outflows	7.41	26.97	12.46	3.10	4.21
Inflows	9.33	52.98	17.10	3.90	8.28
Capital account (net)	3.88	20.54	16.37	1.62	3.21
Official flows					
Outflows	2.66	6.46	8.40	1.11	1.01
Inflows	4.92	3.34	–3.47	2.06	0.52
FDI					
Outflows	0.03	1.47	42.42	0.01	0.23
Inflows	0.34	4.89	27.25	0.14	0.76
Portfolio equity					
Outflows	0.00	16.86	127.46	0.00	2.64
Inflows	0.24	28.22	54.01	0.10	4.41
Debt					
Outflows	14.99	31.01	6.83	6.27	4.85
Inflows	17.37	37.14	7.15	7.26	5.80
Miscellaneous					
Outflows	2.34	2.27	–0.27	0.98	0.35
Inflows	1.36	5.35	13.26	0.57	0.84
Reserves at year end	6.43	107.45	29.17	2.69	16.79
Addition to reserves	0.70	31.42	41.35	0.29	4.91
Metric of integration	96.60	352.05	12.47	40.40	55.02
Trade integration	59.93	224.85	12.77	25.07	35.14
Financial integration	36.67	127.20	11.97	15.34	19.88

Notes: "Official flows" comprise external assistance, rupee debt service with respect to Russia, and IMF-related monetary movements. "Debt" comprises commercial borrowing, short-term loans, and banking capital. "Miscellaneous" is the sum of "Other capital flows" and errors and omissions. The Indian fiscal year runs from April to March, so 2003–4 runs from April 1, 2003, to March 31, 2004.

account deficit, as had been envisaged in this prominent and influential report, India ended up with a current account surplus of 1.7 percent of GDP in 2003–4.

The 10th plan document, which is a medium-term economic policy analysis effort, expresses regrets at the inadequate levels of the current account deficit in recent years (volume 1, paragraph 4.18): "The current account deficit narrowed down and on the average was 0.8 per cent of GDP, less than one half of the 2.1 per cent envisaged in the plan."

There has been considerable discussion about a development strategy where countries might desire current account surpluses (Dooley, Folkerts-Landau, and Garber 2003). In India's case, public statements on development policy were in favor of current account deficits. Many economists argued that the current account surplus in 2003–4, of 1.7 percent of GDP, implied a significant opportunity cost in terms of investment forgone and thus lower GDP growth (Lal, Bery, and Pant 2003).

13.3   Broad Empirical Features

Broad facts about Indian capital flows are presented in table 13.1, which shows two years: 1992–93 and 2003–4. The year 1992–93 was chosen since it reflects the last year of "the previous regime" of highly restricted capital flows.[1] The year 2003–4 is the most recent year observed.

GDP: Over this eleven-year period, GDP measured in current dollars grew by an average of 9.4 percent per annum.

Current account: India undertook major initiatives in trade liberalization in this period (Panagariya 2005). This led to growth rates of roughly 12 percent per annum in imports and exports of merchandise, and imports of invisibles. The dropping prices of global telecommunications led to an increase in service exports from India, giving a higher invisibles export growth rate of 17 percent per annum. Putting these together, trade integration (measured as gross current account flows as percent to GDP) rose sharply from 25.1 percent of GDP in 1992–93 to 35.1 percent of GDP in 2003–4: an increase of 10 percentage points in eleven years. In addition, over this period, the current account switched from a deficit of 1.5 percent of GDP to a surplus of 1.7 percent of GDP.

Net capital flows: On the surface, net capital flows appear to have changed little, from 1.6 percent of GDP in 1992–93 to 3.2 percent of GDP

---

1. Significant capital flows through FDI and portfolio investment commenced in 1993–94, which justifies the choice of 1992–93 as the last year of the previous policy regime.

The year-end exchange rate used for 1992–93 incorporates the sharp devaluation that took place when the rupee became a market-determined exchange rate in 1992. Hence, 1992–93 is also the first year for which it is meaningful to convert between rupees and dollars (e.g., for the purposes of reexpressing British pounds in U.S. dollars). All values are shown in U.S. dollars to ease interpretation and international comparison, and to avoid noise induced by domestic inflation volatility in this period.

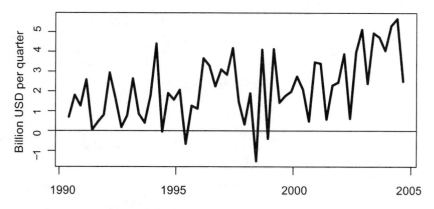

Fig. 13.1   Net capital flows (US$ billions per quarter)

in 2003–4 (see figure 13.1). Yet major changes took place in the structure of capital flows.

Debt flows: In 1992–93, which reflects the previous policy regime, the capital account was dominated by official flows and debt flows. Over this eleven-year period, net official flows switched from +0.9 percent of GDP to –0.5 percent, and net debt flows stagnated at 1 percent of GDP. Given the limited accretion of debt, and high export growth, the debt service ratio dropped from 27.5 percent in 1992–93 to 18.1 percent in 2003–4.

FDI and portfolio investment: Major growth was seen in FDI and portfolio investment. Gross flows in these two channels grew sharply from 0.3 percent of GDP to 8 percent of GDP. The average annual growth rate of net FDI flows was 24.2 percent, and that for net portfolio flows was 41.9 percent. Through these high growth rates, over this period, India switched from LDC-style capital flows, emphasizing official flows and debt, to an "emerging market style" structure of capital flows, emphasizing FDI and portfolio investment. Gross flows on the capital account reached 19.9 percent of GDP in 2003–4, an increase of 4.5 percentage points as compared with 1992–93.

Portfolio flows are more prominent when measuring *gross* flows on the capital account, since they involve larger two-way flows of capital. In 2003–4, FDI inflows were 3.33 times bigger than FDI outflows, but portfolio inflows were only 1.67 times bigger than portfolio outflows. Hence, even though net flows through portfolio investment were 3.3 times larger than net FDI flows in 2003–4, gross portfolio flows in 2003–4 amounted to 7 percent of GDP, while gross FDI flows amounted to only 1 percent of GDP.

Outward flows: These changes were accompanied by a substantial outward flow of capital through purchases of foreign exchange reserves. The year-end reserves rose sharply from 2.7 percent of GDP in 1992–93 to 16.8

percent of GDP in 2003–4. In 2003–4 alone, the addition to reserves was 4.9 percent of GDP. In this year, net capital inflows of $20.5 billion and a current account surplus of $10.6 billion were associated with an addition to reserves of $31.4 billion.

Global integration: The sum of gross flows on the current and capital account serves as an overall metric of integration into the world economy. This rose by 14.6 percentage points over this eleven-year period, from 40.4 percent in 1992–93 to 55 percent in 2003–4.

These data and this description suggest that the two major features of India's experience with capital flows have been

- Rapid growth of foreign investment—particularly portfolio investment—accompanied by slow growth of debt flows.
- A substantial extent of outward flows through reserve accumulation.

This paper seeks to shed some light on the causes and consequences of these major features.

13.4   Currency Regime

In India, there has been a rich interplay between policies and outcomes on capital flows and the currency regime. According to the RBI, the Indian rupee is a market-determined exchange rate, in the sense that there is a currency market and the exchange rate is not administratively determined. India has clearly moved away from fixed exchange rates. However, the RBI actively trades on the market, with the goal of containing volatility and influencing the market price.

In India, as in most developing countries, there has been a distinction between the de facto and the de jure currency regime. Patnaik (2003) argues that there is a de facto pegged exchange rate, for the following reasons:

- There is extremely low volatility of the rupee-dollar exchange rate alongside high volatilities of other exchange rates such as the rupee-euro and rupee-yen. Table 13.2 shows that the volatility of daily returns on the rupee-dollar has been 0.277 percent, while the volatility of (say) the rupee-yen has been 0.848 percent per day. The latter value is remarkably close to the dollar-yen volatility of 0.836 percent per day. In the polar case where the rupee-dollar were a fixed exchange, the rupee-yen volatility would be exactly equal to the dollar-yen volatility. Volatilities of the rupee against the British pound, euro, and yen take on large values, similar to those of floating exchange rates such as the dollar-euro or the euro-pound.
- Tests based on Frankel and Wei (1994) show that the U.S. dollar is overwhelmingly the dominant currency in explaining fluctuations of

Table 13.2 Cross-currency volatility (daily returns, August 1992 to November 2004)

	U.S. dollar	British pound	Euro	Yen
Rupee	0.277	0.634	0.778	0.848
U.S. dollar		0.588	0.738	0.836
British pound			0.601	0.896
Euro				0.932

the Indian currency (table 13.3).[2] The coefficient of the dollar–Swiss franc returns is 0.9345, which is near 1, while other coefficients are near 0. The R^2 of this regression is 87.45 percent.

- India's enormous reserve buildup after mid-2002 cannot be explained by a quest for reserves as insurance.
- Extending the Calvo and Reinhart (2002) λ metric of currency flexibility beyond 1999 shows that there has been no change in this metric over 1979–2003.

The *extent* of pegging has varied through this period. There have been multimonth periods where the rupee-dollar exchange rate was fixed, but there have also been periods where the volatility of the rupee-dollar exchange rate was closer to that of the rupee-euro or the rupee-yen. The facts shown above represent the average behavior over the period from August 1992 to November 2004.

As is typical with pegged exchange rates, the nominal rupee-dollar exchange rate has had low volatility, while all other measures of the exchange rate have been more volatile. As an example, there has been significant volatility of the real effective exchange rate (REER; figure 13.2). A substantial appreciation of the REER took place through a pegged rupee-dollar exchange rate coupled with higher domestic inflation.

13.5 Capital Controls

13.5.1 Evolution of Capital Controls

Foreign institutional investors (FIIs) were given permission to participate on the Indian market on September 14, 1992. Limits were put in place

2. Frankel and Wei (1994) developed a regression-based approach for testing for pegging. In this approach, an independent currency, such as the Swiss franc, is chosen as a numeraire. The model estimated is

$$d\log\left(\frac{\text{rupee}}{\text{franc}}\right) = \beta_1 + \beta_2 d\log\left(\frac{\text{dollar}}{\text{franc}}\right) + \beta_3 d\log\left(\frac{\text{yen}}{\text{franc}}\right) + \beta_4 d\log\left(\frac{\text{deutsche mark}}{\text{franc}}\right) + \varepsilon.$$

This regression picks up the extent to which the rupee-franc rate fluctuates in response to fluctuations in the dollar-franc rate. If there is pegging to the dollar, then fluctuations in the yen and deutsche mark will be irrelevant, and we will observe $\beta_3 = \beta_4 = 0$ while $\beta_2 = 1$. If there is no pegging, then all the three coefficients will be different from 0. The R^2 of this regression is also of interest; values near 1 would suggest reduced exchange rate flexibility.

Table 13.3   Frankel-Wei regression (daily returns, August 1992 to November 2004)

Parameter	Coefficient
$d\log\left(\dfrac{\text{USD}}{\text{CHF}}\right)$	0.9345
	(72.73)
$d\log\left(\dfrac{\text{JPY}}{\text{CHF}}\right)$	0.0519
	(6.47)
$d\log\left(\dfrac{\text{EUR}}{\text{CHF}}\right)$	−0.0134
	(−0.7)
$d\log\left(\dfrac{\text{GBP}}{\text{CHF}}\right)$	0.0186
	(1.27)
Intercept	0.0151
	(2.46)
T	2,854
R^2	0.8745
σ_ε^2	0.08

Notes: USD = U.S. dollar; CHF = Swiss franc; JPY = Japanese yen; EUR = euro; GBP = British pound. *t*-statistics in parentheses.

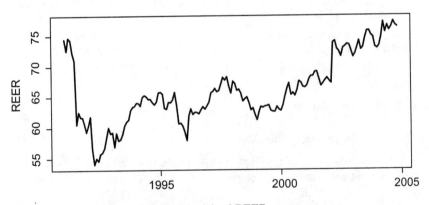

Fig. 13.2   Thirty-six-country trade weighted REER

to ensure that no one FII could own more than 5 percent of a company and all FIIs (put together) could not own more than 24 percent of a company.

From 1992 onward, restrictions on portfolio equity investment have been steadily eased, while sharp constraints on bond investment have been preserved. Table 13.4 shows the major events of the 1992–2004 period in

Table 13.4	Chronology of easing controls on portfolio flows
September 14, 1992	Foreign institutional investors (FIIs) permitted into the country: these included pension funds, mutual funds, endowments, etc., proposing to invest in India as broad-based funds with at least 50 investors and no investor with more than 5 percent. Permitted access to primary and secondary market for securities, and products sold by mutual funds, with a minimum 70 percent investment in equities. Ceiling upon one FII of 5 percent ownership of any firm, and ceiling upon total of all FIIs at 24 percent.
November 1996	New concept of "100 percent debt FIIs" permitted, which could invest in corporate bonds but not government bonds.
April 4, 1997	Ceiling upon total ownership by all FIIs of local firms raised from 24 percent to 30 percent (required shareholder resolution).
April 1998	FIIs permitted to invest in government bonds, subject to a ceiling upon all FIIs put together of $1 billion.
June 11, 1998	Ceiling upon ownership by one FII in one firm raised from 5 percent to 10 percent. FIIs permitted to partially hedge currency exposure using the currency forward market. FIIs permitted to trade on the equity derivatives market in a limited way.
August 1999	Requirement that FII must have at least 50 investors eased to 20 investors.
February 2000	Foreign firms and individuals permitted access to the Indian market through FIIs as "subaccounts." Local fund managers also permitted to do fund management for foreign firms and individuals through subaccounts. Requirement that no investor can have over 5 percent of the FII fund eased to 10 percent.
March 1, 2000	Ceiling upon total ownership by all FIIs of local firms raised from 30 percent to 40 percent (required shareholder resolution).
March 8, 2001	Ceiling upon total ownership by all FIIs of local firms raised from 40 percent to 49 percent (required shareholder resolution).
September 20, 2001	Ceiling upon total ownership by all FIIs of local firms raised from 49 percent to "the sectoral cap for the industry" (required shareholder resolution).
January 8, 2003	Limitations upon FIIs hedging using the currency forward market removed.
December 2003	Twin approvals for FIIs at both SEBI and RBI replaced by single approval at SEBI.
November 2004	New ceiling placed upon ownership of all FIIs of all corporate bonds of $0.5 billion.
February 2006	The ceiling upon ownership of all FIIs of government bonds raised to $2 billion and ceiling upon ownership of all FIIs of corporate bonds raised to $1.5 billion.

the easing of capital controls on portfolio flows. It also gives a sense of the detailed system of quantitative restrictions operated by the RBI and the intricate steps through which reform has come about. Through this reform process, portfolio investors are now able to trade in the spot and derivative markets for both equities and currency. However, the changes in rules have not always been only in the direction of liberalization—sometimes reforms have been reversed.

Under the Indian policy framework, entities eligible to become FIIs have an essentially open capital account, while being required to suffer overhead costs of registration and reporting in India. There are two kinds of entities that do not trade in the Indian market through the FII framework: those that are ineligible and those that find the overhead costs unacceptable. In order to overcome these constraints, an over-the-counter (OTC) derivatives market has sprung up for access products called participatory notes. In this market, eligible FIIs sell call options or linear exposures to others. In early 2006, roughly half of the outstanding FII investments into India had come through access products sold by 17 out of the 733 registered FIIs. The rise of access products underlines the extent to which India's FII framework implies that there is de facto capital account convertibility when it comes to equity investment.

While considerable openness on FDI exists, there are restrictions on foreign ownership in certain industries. For example, the foreign company engaging in FDI in insurance is limited to 26 percent ownership. Another major constraint influencing FDI is "Press Note 18," whereby a foreign firm that wishes to start a second project in India is required to take approval of its first domestic partner.

In recent years, some databases have sought to distill the system of capital controls prevalent in a country at a point in time into a simple score (Johnston and Tamirisa 1998). It is instructive to examine their values for India. The IMF single-dummy indexes have India as 1 from 1983 to 1995, a period over which major changes took place. Miniane (2004) reports a composite measure based on fourteen disaggregated indexes and finds that India moved from 0.917 in 1983 to 0.923 in 2000 (an increase in capital controls). The level and the change in both these indexes appear inconsistent with India's experience, where substantial openness has come about through a large number of small steps.

13.5.2   Restrictions on CIP Arbitrage

One element of the capital controls consists of barriers to arbitrage on the currency forward market. In an ordinary forward market, arbitrage and only arbitrage defines the forward rate. Even if there are strong speculative views and positions on the market, there is relatively little that can be inferred from forward premium, since this is primarily determined by covered interest parity (CIP).[3] When violations of market efficiency arise, near-infinite capital should come into play in arbitrage. Through this process, arbitrageurs restore market efficiency and push the forward price back to fair value.

In India, banking regulations place sharp restrictions upon the ability of banks to engage in CIP arbitrage. Importers and exporters are permitted access to the forward market, where they are free to either hedge or not hedge. The supply and demand for forward dollars by these "permitted hedgers" determines the forward price, and banks are prevented from engaging in CIP arbitrage. This serves to break the link between the spot and the derivative.[4] In addition, the empirical experience with the RBI's trading shows that while the RBI trades extensively on the spot market, the observed forward price tends to be a market-determined rate that is not distorted through trading by the central bank.

As shown in figure 13.3, in the rupee-dollar forward market, deviations from the covered parity condition have tended to persist over multimonth periods. In an unrestricted market, arbitrage would have wiped out such deviations almost instantly. However, the restrictions against CIP arbitrage that are in force have prevented arbitrage from restoring market efficiency.

This situation—where restrictions on CIP arbitrage are coupled with a largely undistorted forward market—has generated *a remarkable information source* as a side effect. If economic agents expect the rupee to depreciate, there would be a greater interest in selling rupees forward—exporters would stay unhedged, and importers would be likely to hedge. Conversely, if economic agents expect the rupee to appreciate, there would be greater interest in buying rupees forward while those expecting to import would stay unhedged. Lacking adequate arbitrage capital, the forward price does not get restored to the fair value. The deviation between the fair value of

3. The arithmetic of forward pricing in an efficient market is based on "covered interest parity." Covered interest parity involves comparing two routes for riskless dollar investment. An investor could convert \$1 into $(1 + r_u)^T$ through r_u, which is obtained from the U.S. zero coupon yield curve for T years. Alternatively, the investor could convert into rupees at the spot price S, invest in the government of India zero coupon yield curve, and obtain a locked-in cash flow of $S(1 + r_i)^T/F$ by converting back into dollars at the rate F at date T. Under no-arbitrage, these two investment strategies have to yield an identical return, through which the fair value for F can be computed.

4. Currency derivatives can trade either OTC or on exchanges. In India, trading of currency derivatives on exchange is infeasible owing to legal difficulties. Hence, our treatment is limited to currency forwards and does not utilize data from a currency futures market.

Offshore cash-settled forward markets, named "nondeliverable forward (NDF) markets," exist on the Indian rupee. However, the mere existence of a currency forward market outside the reach of domestic currency controls is not enough to generate informative prices in the sense of a forward market that is immune to CIP. The essential and unique feature of India's forward market is the restrictions upon CIP arbitrage. If (for example) a forward market existed outside the country, but if arbitrage were feasible, then it would also obey CIP and the prices observed there would be noninformative.

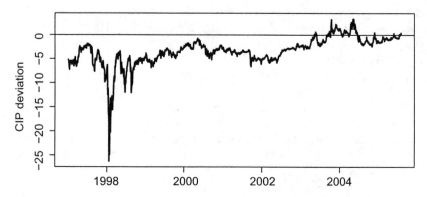

Fig. 13.3   Deviation between actual and fair trade value of rupee-dollar forward premium

the forward premium and the observed value on the market then serves as a measure of the *speculative* views in the market about the future course of the currency.[5] As figure 13.3 shows, in the period from 1997 to 2000, the CIP deviation was generally negative, which suggests that rupee depreciation was expected. In 2003, the CIP deviation changed sign, which suggested expectations of rupee appreciation.

If arbitrage was unrestricted, the forward premium would not have such an interpretation and would be relatively noninformative. Under the existing policy framework, the CIP deviation is a uniquely useful high-frequency market-based measure of future expectations, one that is not available in most countries where regulators do not inhibit arbitrage.[6]

Given the nature of rules governing importers and exporters, there is little doubt that CIP deviations in India reflect the views of economic agents who are given the choice between hedging and not hedging. However, the extent of correctness of these views is a distinct question. An important question concerns the extent to which the speculative views of the market predict future exchange rate movements.

Two specific episodes can be isolated in which the views of the market proved to be wrong. In 1993 and 1994, with strong portfolio inflows, the CIP deviation was strong and positive, suggesting that private agents expected a currency appreciation. However, the RBI chose to effectively have a fixed exchange rate of 31.37 rupees (Rs), and the expectations of agents

5. Apart from conveying expectations of the market, the deviation between the observed forward premium and its fair value also shows the arbitrage opportunity available to the few economic agents who are permitted to engage in the trading required for doing CIP arbitrage. Their mass has thus far not been large enough to remove CIP deviations.
6. Internationally, empirical research related to currency expectations uses data based on surveys (Frankel and Okongwu 1996). Market participants, central bankers, multinational companies, and economics departments of banks are interviewed on a weekly or monthly basis. Survey data such as the *Currency Forecasters' Digest,* now known as the *Financial Times Currency Forecast,* forms the basis for a number of papers in the field (Chinn and Frankel 1994).

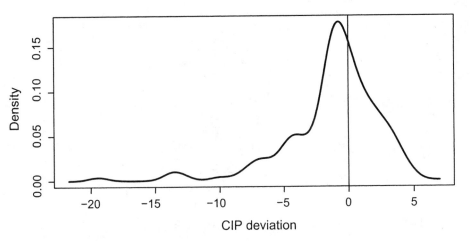

Fig. 13.4   Kernel density plot of CIP deviation

proved to be wrong. In late 1997 and early 1998, in the aftermath of the East Asian crisis, there were strong expectations that the rupee would devalue sharply, giving very large negative values of the CIP deviation (see figure 13.3). In the event, domestic interest rates were raised sharply in an "interest rate defense," and the rupee did *not* devalue, so the expectations of agents proved to be wrong (Patnaik 2005).

We can test the extent to which lagged CIP deviations explain current changes of the exchange rate. If market expectations are (on average) correct, when past values of the CIP deviation are positive, this should be associated with currency appreciation (negative slopes).

A difficulty faced in this regression is the distribution of the CIP deviation (figure 13.4), where there are some extreme values (from late 1997 and early 1998). These extreme values for the CIP deviation prove to be influential observations in a regression. Hence, in addition to showing ordinary least squares (OLS) results, we investigate this question using a robust regression using an M-estimator (Venables and Ripley 2002).

The results for weekly data (table 13.5) and monthly data (table 13.6) suggest that the CIP deviation at a given point in time is a statistically significant predictor of future currency returns over a considerable future time period.[7]

The picture that the rupee spot and forward markets represent may hence be summarized as the following elements:

7. These regressions are based on a daily time series from January 1, 1997, to February 4, 2005. The last observed value for the week or the month is used in converting to weekly or monthly frequencies. The simplest model (currency returns on lagged CIP deviation) juxtaposes the currency returns of this month with the CIP deviation prevalent at the end of the last month.

Table 13.5   CIP deviation as predictor of future currency returns (weekly data)

	OLS (1)	OLS (2)	Robust LS (3)	Robust LS (4)
CIP deviation lag 1	−0.025	0.009	−0.023	−0.010
	(−2.83)	(0.36)	(−5.21)	(−0.78)
Lag 2		−0.028		−0.014
		(−0.84)		(−0.82)
Lag 3		−0.009		0.001
		(−0.36)		(0.05)
R^2	0.019	0.024		

Notes: CIP = covered interest parity; OLS = ordinary least squares; LS = least squares.

Table 13.6   CIP deviation as predictor of future currency returns (monthly data)

	OLS (1)	OLS (2)	Robust LS (3)	Robust LS (4)
CIP deviation lag 1	−0.121	−0.130	−0.097	−0.111
	(−2.42)	(−1.77)	(−3.43)	(−2.67)
Lag 2		0.171		0.080
		(1.91)		(1.58)
Lag 3		−0.205		−0.099
		(−2.78)		(−2.36)
R^2	0.058	0.134		

1. The rupee-dollar spot market is a pegged exchange rate. It is not a floating rate. It is not a random walk. Violations of market efficiency are detected. It may hence be possible for economic agents to form useful predictions of future currency movements.

2. There are strong restrictions that inhibit CIP arbitrage.

3. Hence, sustained CIP deviations are found.

4. In the absence of adequate arbitrage capital, the CIP deviation reflects the speculative views of economic agents who choose to hedge or not hedge depending on expectations about future exchange rate fluctuations.

5. CIP deviations do have some forecasting power in predicting future exchange rate fluctuations.

13.5.3   Capital Controls Prevalent in 2005

The state of capital controls in 2005 may be summarized as follows:[8]

Current account: There are no current account restrictions, other than the limit upon individuals of purchasing no more than $10,000 per year for the purpose of foreign travel.

---

8. The discussant of the paper, Takatoshi Ito, remarked that these capital controls were reminiscent of Japan in the mid-1960s to the mid-1970s (Ito 1983).

Restrictions upon the currency market: Market access to the currency market is severely restricted, primarily to banks. Only economic agents with a direct current account or capital account exposure are permitted to trade in the market. Exchange traded currency derivatives are absent. Importers and exporters face binding restrictions on the size of their currency forward positions.

Outward flows by individuals: Individuals are limited to taking $25,000 per year out of the country.

Outward flows by firms: Firms are limited to taking capital out of the country that is equal to their net worth.

Borrowing by firms: External borrowing by firms must be of at least three years' maturity below $20 million and of at least five years' maturity beyond. Borrowing up to $500 million by a firm "for certain specified end-users" (e.g., expanding a factory, importing capital goods) is allowed without requiring permissions. There is a ceiling whereby approvals for borrowing by all firms (put together), in a year, should not exceed $9 billion per year. This limit, of $9 billion, is revised upward roughly every one to two years.

Firms are "required to hedge their currency exposure," but there is no mechanism for verifying this, and substantial restrictions on their activities on the currency forward market are in place.

Borrowing by banks: The central bank controls the interest rate at which banks borrow from foreigners through "nonresident deposits."[9]

Generic restrictions upon portfolio flows: Only FIIs are permitted to invest in the country.

Debt investment by foreign portfolio investors: The aggregate investment in government bonds by all foreign investors cannot exceed $2 billion. The aggregate bond investments by any one fund cannot exceed 30 percent. The total corporate bond ownership by all foreign investors cannot exceed $1.5 billion.

Equity investments by foreign portfolio investors: The aggregate foreign holding in a company is subject to a limit that can be set by the shareholders of the company. This limit is, in turn, subject to "sectoral limits" that apply in certain sectors. No one foreign portfolio investor can own more than 10 percent of a company. Foreign ownership in certain sectors (telecommunications, insurance, banking) is capped at various levels. Firms are free to issue global depository receipts (GDRs) or American depository receipts (ADRs) outside the country, which can be sold to a broad swathe of global investors. Within these restrictions, foreign investors are fully able to convert currency, hedge currency risk, and trade in the equity spot or derivatives markets.

FDI: Foreign ownership in certain sectors (e.g., telecommunications, insurance, banking) is capped at various levels (table 13.7). Foreign compa-

---

9. Gordon and Gupta (2004) analyze the determinants of nonresident deposits.

Table 13.7   Ownership restrictions on FDI

Sector	Limit on foreign ownership (%)
FDI prohibited	
Retail, plantations, real estate	0
FDI with limits on foreign ownership	
Broadcasting	20/49
Defense	26
Insurance	26
Petroleum refining	26
Airlines	49
Oil and gas pipelines	51
Trading	51
Petroleum exploration	51 to 100
Petroleum distribution	74
Mining for diamonds, precious stones	74
Coal mining	74
Telecommunications	74
Banking	74
Advertising	74
Airports	74/100
All other areas	100

nies require approval of the first firm they choose to do a joint venture with in the country, if they wish to start a related business.

13.6   Investment Flows

13.6.1   FDI

Figure 13.5 shows the time series of quarterly flows of FDI. In order to aid comparability, it has the same scale as figures 13.1 and (in section 13.6.2) 13.6.

In many countries, high exports growth has been strongly associated with FDI. As shown in table 13.1, India has experienced annual dollar growth rates of merchandise exports of 12 percent and services exports of 17 percent. Thus, India's share in world trade of both goods and services has been increasing, without high FDI. Two elements of an explanation might be labor-intensive exports and the strength of India's domestic firms.

Labor-Intensive Exports

This may partly reflect the higher extent to which FDI into India has emphasized labor-intensive economic activities, such as service exports. As an example, call centers have a capital output ratio of just 0.75; hence, an annual flow of exports worth $10 billion requires a stock of capital of only

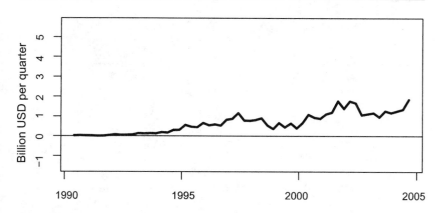

Fig. 13.5   Net FDI flows (US$ billions per quarter)

Table 13.8   Sectoral composition of FDI: August 1991 to November 2004

Sector	FDI flows (in US$ billions)	Percent of total
Oil and electricity	2.5	9.8
Telecommunications	2.7	10.5
Transportation	2.9	11.4
Electrical, electronics, software	3.8	15.1
Metals	0.5	1.9
Chemicals	1.7	6.0
Food processing	1.1	4.2
Services	2.2	8.2
Others	15.0	32.9
Total	32.3	100.0

$7.5 billion.[10] Table 13.8 shows the sectoral composition of FDI, which shows that, like the Indian exports basket, FDI has been diversified across a broad range of sectors. The service sector—which includes export-oriented services and domestic services—accounted for only 8.2 percent of total FDI.

Strength of Domestic Firms

Unlike many emerging markets or transition economies, India had a strong set of domestic firms in place by the 1990s. A steady flow of startups and initial public offerings (IPOs) has fueled a large domestic corporate sector. These domestic firms were able to engage in export-oriented activities, as opposed to the higher reliance seen in other countries upon foreign

10. The rough financial structure of a 1,000-seat call center, as of 2004, is as follows. The project cost is roughly $15 million, of which $10 million is fixed capital (excluding real estate). The annual revenue works out to roughly $25 million, of which the value added is roughly $20 million.

Table 13.9   Country composition of Indian trade and FDI

Country	Share in FDI	Share in trade
United States	18.8	9.6
Japan	8.1	3.0
The Netherlands	7.7	1.0
United Kingdom	7.3	3.8
Germany	5.6	3.2

Note: FDI share computed over 1991–2004, trade shares over 1998–2004.

firms who would first bring in FDI and then export. In India's case, the role of foreign capital flows has worked, to a greater extent, through portfolio flows into the domestic equity market, through domestic firms to exports.

Domestic firms have been given an increasingly liberal framework for outward FDI flows so that they can become multinational corporations. In 2003–4, gross FDI inflows of $4.89 billion were accompanied by gross outflows of $1.47 billion. Offshore investments by Indian firms made up part of the latter. To this extent, Indian data show lower net FDI flows.

Table 13.9 shows the country composition of FDI into India.[11] In the case of each of the top five countries by FDI share, the FDI share of the country considerably exceeds the trade share of the country. China and United Arab Emirates (UAE) are examples of countries where India has substantial trade but that are not sources of FDI to India.

13.6.2 Portfolio Flows

Indian Securities in a Global Portfolio

In the portfolio optimization of a globally diversified investor, the appeal of Indian securities is related to their lack of correlation with global risk factors. Some correlations of weekly returns, in the period from October 1995 to February 2004, are in table 10.[12]

In many small countries, liberalization efforts in terms of a more open current account, FDI, and portfolio flows have led to increased correlations, which has served to diminish the benefits from diversification. In or-

11. These fractions have been computed using the following adjustment. The largest country that sends FDI to India, in the data, is the island of Mauritius (34.5 percent). India has an advantageous tax treaty with Mauritius, and many investors choose to incorporate in Mauritius in order to benefit from this tax treatment. The values given here show the fraction of countries in the non-Mauritius FDI into India, and are only accurate insofar as the country composition of FDI into India that is routed through Mauritius is the same as the country composition of FDI that comes directly to India.

12. October 1995 is used as the starting point for this data set, since it reflects the point by which the early sharp increase in foreign portfolio flows had been completed, and some major changes in the domestic equity market design had been completed. Hence, the period from October 1995 onward represents a comparable period.

Table 13.10   Correlation matrix of some stock market indexes

	Nifty Jr.	Kospi	Nifty	S&P 500
A. Full period				
Cospi	0.862	0.254	0.911	0.159
Nifty Jr.		0.233	0.776	0.099
Kospi			0.280	0.312
Nifty				0.221
B. First half of period: October 1995–December 1999				
Cospi	0.868	0.105	0.935	0.101
Nifty Jr.		0.101	0.803	0.023
Kospi			0.155	0.237
Nifty				0.169
C. Second half of period: December 1999–February 2004				
Cospi	0.863	0.424	0.892	0.209
Nifty Jr.		0.377	0.760	0.142
Kospi			0.441	0.396
Nifty				0.272

Notes: This table uses weekly returns data from October 1995 to February 2004. Nifty is the Indian stock market index of the top fifty stocks. Nifty Jr. is the second rung of fifty stocks. Cospi is the Indian index encompassing all active stocks, which number around 2,000. Kospi is the Korean stock market index.

der to explore this issue, table 13.10 also breaks the overall period into two halves. The correlation of the overall index (Cospi) against the Standard and Poor's (S&P) 500 doubled from 0.1 in the first half to 0.21 in the second half. However, 0.21 remains a small number by world standards. For example, it is lower than the correlation of Korea's Kospi against the S&P 500 in the first half. It is also significantly lower than the Korean correlation of 0.396 in the second half.

These low correlations suggest that Indian equities can play a useful role in improving the Sharpe's ratio of globally diversified portfolios. As an illustrative example, applying a portfolio optimizer to the historical covariance matrix over this period yields weights of 61.6 percent for the S&P 500, 11.5 percent for the Korean Kospi, and the remainder in India (19.1 percent in Nifty and 7.8 percent in Cospi). This aspect constitutes one feature of understanding India's large equity portfolio inflows.

Factors Influencing Home Bias

In a rational world, decisions about including securities from a given country in global portfolios should be based on the improvements in diversification obtained therein. At the same time, a strong problem that is well known in the literature is that of the home bias, whereby individual and institutional portfolios tend to hold higher weights of local-country securities. In the literature, home bias is believed to be related to informational asymmetries and transaction costs. For example, Portes and Rey

(2001) find that the geography of information—rather than the quest for efficient portfolios through diversification—dominates patterns of cross-border equity flows. Other constraints include size, liquidity, and corporate governance.

India's success at attracting substantial portfolio flows relates to strengths on these issues of information, size, and liquidity.

Size: India is a large economy, with a strong set of domestic firms in place by the 1990s when portfolio flows commenced. A steady flow of start-ups and IPOs has fueled a large domestic corporate sector. As of February 2006, the market capitalization of the equity market was $600 billion.

Information: On the issues of informational asymmetries and transaction costs, India had strengths in terms of a century-old tradition of law, accounting, and stock market trading with extensive participation by domestic households. This implied that many issues about law, information disclosure, and corporate governance, which were important to foreign investors, were broadly in place in India before portfolio flows commenced. India's extensive use of English, and the extensive presence of individuals of Indian origin in global finance companies, has helped reduce the informational asymmetry faced by foreign investors. Familiarity with India among global finance companies was further heightened from the late 1990s onward, when most major global finance companies started moving parts of their production process to India, including areas such as call centers, accounting, back office processing, research, and software development.

Liquidity: While the extensive participation by domestic households offered the possibility of a liquid and active stock market, in the early 1990s there were many weaknesses in the market design, which led to high transaction costs. As a response to these weaknesses, many domestic firms chose to disintermediate the domestic securities markets and engage in offshore issuance through ADR or GDR markets. This allowed these firms to exploit the superior market design that was available outside in London or New York. However, securities issued outside the country did suffer from poor liquidity owing to the incompatible time zone and lack of widespread trading interest.

Partly as a response to the difficulties faced by foreign investors on domestic stock markets, India embarked on a major program of modifying incentives and institutions on the securities markets (Shah and Thomas 2000; Thomas 2006). This involved a new securities regulator (SEBI) and a new set of securities trading institutions (NSE, NSCC, and NSDL). These institutions innovated on the market design, introducing all the elements of world-class securities infrastructure: demutualization of the exchange (1993), electronic limit order book market (1994), elimination of entry barriers into intermediation (1994), nationwide access (1994), novation at the clearing corporation (1996), dematerialized settlement (1996), equity de-

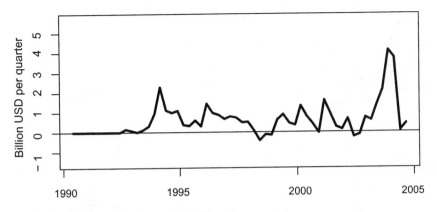

Fig. 13.6   Net portfolio flows (US$ billions per quarter)

rivatives trading (2000–2001), and T + 3 and then T + 2 rolling settlement (2001, 2002).

This reform program had a profound impact upon transaction costs (Shah and Thomas 1997). It helped foster IPOs, the growth of market capitalization, and foreign investment. It also eliminated the rationale for offshore issuance as a mechanism to disintermediate an inefficient domestic market.

In the process of institution building on the securities markets, India harnessed the scale economies associated with a large number of listed companies and a large number of active speculators. The two stock markets in India—NSE and BSE—are ranked third and fifth in the world by number of transactions. These economies of scale in India were a sharp contrast with the difficulties faced by many small countries in building liquid securities markets (Shah and Thomas 2003).[13]

Growth of Net Portfolio Flows

Figure 13.6 shows the time series of quarterly portfolio flows. In order to aid comparability, it has the same scale as figures 13.1 and 13.5. India's share of world portfolio flows considerably exceeds India's share in world FDI flows.

FIIs and the Domestic Equity Market

India is a retail-dominated equity market, where institutional investors account for roughly 10.8 percent of spot market turnover and just 3.3 percent of derivatives turnover. The easing of capital controls for foreign port-

13. The bond market experienced a very different trajectory in the domestic reform process, and largely failed to achieve comparable results in terms of liquidity and transparency. However, the prevailing policy environment aimed to discourage debt-related flows. Hence, the weakness of the bond market was not a binding constraint in shaping portfolio flows.

Table 13.11   Foreign institutional investors (FIIs) on the equity market (in billions of rupees)

	2001	2002	2003	2004
End-year number of FIIs	490	502	540	637
End-year number of subaccounts	1,372	1,361	1,542	1,785
Spot market activity				
Gross buy	518	288	944	1,857
Gross sell	386	253	640	1,467
Net	131	35	305	390
Derivatives activity				
Gross buy	n.a.	n.a.	n.a.	842
Gross sell	n.a.	n.a.	n.a.	861
Net	n.a.	n.a.	n.a.	–19

Source: Ministry of Finance (2006).
Note: n.a. = not available.

folio investors has led to extensive trading by foreign portfolio investors. Putting the spot and derivatives markets together, in 2004, FIIs purchased Rs2,699 billion and sold Rs2,328 billion (table 13.11). From 2001 to 2004, the number of registered FIIs rose from 490 to 637, and the number of subaccounts rose from 1,372 to 1,785, showing a greater diversity of the foreign investors present.

Derivatives transactions by FIIs were not separately tracked prior to 2004. The inclusion of derivatives data from 2004 onward overstates the increase in FII turnover for 2004, which hence shows a sharp jump from Rs1,583 billion in 2003 to Rs5,027 billion in 2004. While Rs5,027 billion of gross FII turnover—summing across spot and derivatives markets—appears to be a large number, it now makes up only 5.83 percent of the overall Indian equity market (table 13.12).[14]

13.6.3   Determinants of Portfolio Flows

Given the prominence of portfolio flows into India, it is important to understand the factors that shape portfolio flows.[15] In the literature on portfolio flows into emerging markets, evidence has been found about the importance of the U.S. interest rate and flows into equity-oriented fund managers in the United States. If foreign fund managers react to information in India with a lag, then lagged output and lagged stock returns should help predict portfolio inflows. If decisions of foreign fund managers are

14. A key feature of measurement in table 13.12 is the use of "gross turnover." Trading volume data, as normally reported by exchanges, shows volume of Rs100 when one security worth Rs100 goes from a seller to a buyer. However, when data are captured about the gross trading of market participants, this transaction shows up twice, as Rs200 of trades. To ensure comparability, the table reexpresses all data as gross turnover, by doubling the trading volume as reported by exchanges.
15. This question has been recently addressed by Gordon and Gupta (2003).

Table 13.12   **Gross turnover (in billions of rupees)**

	2001	2002	2003	2004
Spot market				
NSE + BSE gross turnover	23,416	19,142	26,340	34,168
FIIs	904	540	1,583	3,323
Derivatives				
NSE + BSE gross turnover	838	6,927	28,804	51,118
FIIs				1,703
Equity spot + derivatives				
NSE + BSE gross turnover	24,254	26,070	55,145	86,286
FIIs	904	540	1,583	5,027

Source: Ministry of Finance (2006).

Table 13.13   **Explaining portfolio flows into the equity market: Monthly data, March 1998 to October 2004**

	Parsimonious	Kitchen sink
Intercept	238.245	207.209
CIP deviation	106.937	74.679
	(5.26)	(2.09)
Squared CIP deviation	8.985	4.121
	(2.10)	(0.76)
U.S. 90-day rate		−15.686
		(−0.51)

	Lag 1	Lag 2	Lag 3
Lagged Nifty returns	−0.350	6.960	8.550
	(−0.06)	(1.18)	(1.47)
Lagged industrial growth	−8.061	27.042	−4.12
	(−0.24)	(0.88)	(−0.14)
Lagged S&P 500 returns	5.052	9.196	4.961
	(0.58)	(1.05)	(0.53)

	Parsimonious	Kitchen sink
R^2	0.2668	0.3396
Adjusted R^2	0.2477	0.2213

shaped by expectations about the currency, then the CIP deviation should help predict portfolio inflows.[16]

Portfolio flows into government bonds are highly restricted by India's capital controls. Hence, we focus on portfolio flows into the equity market. Table 13.13 shows two OLS regressions that explain portfolio flows into the equity market. The time span available is short, from March 1998 until

16. As of late 2004, the Indian r_f was 4.5 percent, the historical equity premium was roughly 8 percent, and the annualized volatility of the equity index was roughly 20 percent. The Sharpe's ratio of the equity index—as viewed by a foreign investor—would hence be significantly affected by currency views of (say) ±5 percent on an annualized basis.

Table 13.14   Volatility of capital flows: Summary statistics of quarterly data from 1995:Q1 to 2004:Q2 (in US$ millions)

	Minimum	25th percentile	Median	75th percentile	Maximum	Interquartile range
Raw data						
Portfolio	−423	260	594	899	4,111	624
FDI	365	595	886	1,175	1,768	564
Debt	−1,257	270	826	2,330	3,895	1,825
Official	−2,657	−738	−24	210	857	921
Total	−1,514	1,436	2,426	3,969	5,315	2,496
Residuals about time trend						
Portfolio	−1,278	−531	−19	311	2,903	815
FDI	−534	−137	−26	115	666	246
Debt	−2,448	−826	−230	1,083	2,833	1,806
Official	−2,249	−555	261	511	1,214	1,017
Total	−3,648	−771	224	1,317	2,340	2,018

October 2004. None of the explanatory variables are significant in the "kitchen sink" model, other than the CIP deviation. The parsimonious model is a quadratic in the CIP deviation, where bigger flows come into the equity market when the currency is expected to appreciate, with a nonlinearity in response where bigger deviations induce bigger inflows.

These results suggest that in India's short experience, traditional explanatory variables appear to be relatively less important, and currency expectations do play a role in shaping portfolio flows into the equity market.

13.6.4   Volatility of Capital Flows

India's stance on liberalization of the capital account was strongly motivated by certain priors about the volatility of capital flows, and about the extent to which different kinds of capital flows would impinge upon implementation of the prevailing currency regime. In the literature, there has been disagreement about the volatility of the various kinds of capital flows, and the interplay between the currency regime adopted and the volatility of certain kinds of capital flows.[17]

We can use quarterly balance-of-payments data in order to review India's experience with volatility of the four components of capital flows. In order to avoid the formative period where large changes were taking place in response to the first easing of capital controls, we focus on the period after 1995. This helps us obtain information about the behavior in the postreform period.

Table 13.14 shows summary statistics about the four components of net

17. Alfaro, Kalemli-Ozcan, and Volosovych (2004) find that in Asia, in the decade of the 1990s, the volatility of capital flows was 1.2 for FDI, 15.4 for portfolio equity flows, and 1.6 for debt. They define volatility of capital flows as the standard deviation of per capita net capital flow divided by the average of gross inflow and gross outflow.

capital flows, using data for thirty-seven quarters from 1995:Q1 to 2004:Q2. Since the data often have unusual distributional characteristics, the interquartile range is used as a relatively nonparametric measure of dispersion.[18]

The raw data show that a net outflow was never observed in the case of FDI. FDI and portfolio flows have similar values for the interquartile range. Debt and official flows seem to be much more volatile than FDI and portfolio flows.

When expressed as residuals about a time trend, all four components have experienced significant negative outflows in the worst quarter. Viewed in this fashion, FDI flows seem to be highly stable, and more stable than other components. The ranking of volatility of components, when viewed in this fashion, appears to be debt > official > portfolio > FDI.

Over this period, fluctuations in debt and official flows frequently reflected changes in the policy framework. Capital controls and other policy levers were frequently used to encourage or discourage debt and official flows, depending on the tactical exigencies of implementing the currency peg. On some occasions, offshore borrowing was effectively initiated by the government, and banks were encouraged to borrow abroad at high rates (set by the RBI). At other times, strict controls have been placed on off-shore borrowing, and the interest rate at which banks borrow has been cut (Gordon and Gupta 2004). Hence, there is need for caution in interpreting the characteristics seen therein, which may reflect factors such as policy volatility and currency expectations. The volatility of debt flows and of official flows might have been very different if India's policies on capital controls had been stable, or if the currency regime had been different.

The results for the volatility of India's portfolio and FDI flows reflect the characteristics of these flows and of the Indian economy, since they reflect the outcomes obtained under a broadly stable policy framework, subject to a steady process of liberalization whereby controls have been slowly relaxed over the years, with an essentially one-way direction of reforms.

13.6.5   Evaluating India's Experience with the Composition of Capital Flows

India represents an unusual situation of a developing country where portfolio flows have been particularly important. Net portfolio flows are presently roughly three times the size of net FDI flows. India's experience is hence an opportunity to illuminate our understanding of the composition of capital flows.

Where many economists have argued in favor of FDI given that FDI is

---

18. The prob values obtained using the Shapiro-Wilk test of normality for the five time series are as follows: portfolio (4.672×10^{-6}), FDI (0.081), debt (0.035), official (0.0018), and total (0.57). Hence, we avoid the use of the standard deviations as a measure of dispersion.

"bolted down" and cannot flee in the event of a crisis, recent research has brought new perspectives to bear on this question. Hausmann and Fernandez-Arias (2000) find that when countries develop, while total capital flows go up, the share of FDI in capital flows goes down. They argue that portfolio flows require more sophisticated institutions and a greater degree of trust on the part of the investor. Their analysis suggests that a domination of FDI is found in countries with the weakest institutions. In addition, Fernandez-Arias and Hausmann (2000) argue that FDI is not necessarily "bolted down": a firm faced with a currency crisis can find many instrumentalities to take capital out, such as borrowing in the country against physical assets as collateral, and taking financial capital out of the country.

In this context, Bird and Rajan (2002) offer striking evidence from Malaysia. In the period from 1990 to 1997, Malaysia had no portfolio inflows, and FDI dominated their capital inflows. Yet Malaysia went on to experience a currency crisis.

The Indian experience is interesting from the viewpoint of this debate. India represents a large country where sophisticated institutions have helped obtain high success in attracting portfolio flows.

13.7   Impossible Trinity

As highlighted in table 13.1 early in this paper, the size of the current account and the capital account rose sharply from 1992–93 to 2003–4. Gross flows on the current account, expressed in U.S. dollars, grew at a compound rate of 12.77 percent per annum, and gross flows on the capital account grew at a similar rate of 11.97 percent per annum. Both these growth rates were faster than the growth of GDP expressed in nominal U.S. dollars of 9.36 percent per annum. Hence, the overall measure of integration (gross flows on capital account and current account, expressed as percent of GDP) rose sharply from 40.4 percent of GDP in 1992–93 to 55 percent in 2003–4.

Under these conditions, considerable movements of capital can take place in response to speculative views about the currency. As an example, the regression results of table 13.13 show that speculative views reflected in covered interest parity (CIP) deviations are an important explanatory variable in the model seeking to explain portfolio flows.

The period 2003–4 serves as a valuable illustration of how capital flows would behave under conditions where the currency regime induced a currency spot price process that gave private agents significant opportunities for speculative trading on the currency. When economic agents have views about future currency movements, all avenues are utilized for currency speculation. It is well known in the literature on capital controls that the current account can be used for implementing capital movements and currency speculation, through overinvoicing, underinvoicing, prepayment, and delayed payments (Patnaik and Vasudevan 2000). These issues have become more pertinent, given the sharp rise in the size of the current account, from 25 percent of GDP in 1992–93 to 35 percent in 2003–4. FDI and portfolio flows are fairly open. Even with the constraints that are in place in India on debt flows, it is striking to notice that in 2003–4, debt flows worked out to roughly $6 billion out of total net capital flows of $20 billion.

These arguments suggest that the impossible trinity is an increasingly important constraint faced by Indian macro policy (Joshi 2003). Patnaik (2005) examines how monetary policy was attenuated through implementation of the currency regime in two prominent episodes in the recent eleven-year period. The pressures in implementing the pegged exchange rate were heightened in 2003 and 2004, and while no public announcement has been made about a change in the currency regime, nominal rupee-dollar volatility rose significantly from 0.129 percent per day in some months to 0.355 percent per day in other months.

India continues to grapple with the trade-offs associated with the impossible trinity. On January 12, 2005, the head of the central bank proposed that India should reexamine the existing framework of capital controls and possibly introduce a fresh set of restrictions including quotas or ceilings on portfolio flows, enhancing "quality of flows" by restrictions upon eligible foreign investors, price-based measures such as taxes, and monitoring and restrictions upon voting rights of nonresidents. While no decisions were taken to introduce such capital controls, the speech highlights the tensions faced in Indian macro policy and the difficulties faced in the existing combination of a pegged exchange rate and a fairly open capital account.

As argued in section 13.3, a major feature of India's recent experience with capital flows has been the outward flows of capital taking place since the RBI's purchase of reserves exceeded net capital inflows. The recent experience with the stock of reserves and the flow of net purchases by the RBI on the currency market is shown in figures 13.7 and 13.8.

This shows a striking buildup of reserves, from roughly $40 billion to $115 billion, over the period from late 2001 to early 2004. Through this period, RBI purchases on the currency market went up to $7 billion in April 2004. Patnaik (2003) argues that this reserve buildup was related to implementing the currency regime. Through this period, India experienced current account surpluses. This was a paradoxical turnaround compared with the starting point of the reforms. A goal of the early reforms was to find a sustainable mechanism to sustain the import of capital (i.e., a current account deficit). In 2002, India found itself in a situation with persistent export of capital.

The currency regime has continued to evolve in response to the tensions between capital flows and the pegged exchange rate. In 2003, reserves grew

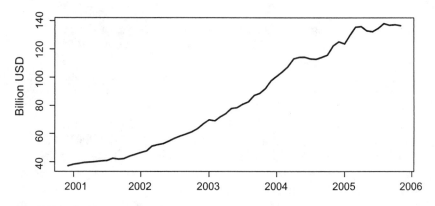

Fig. 13.7   Foreign currency reserves

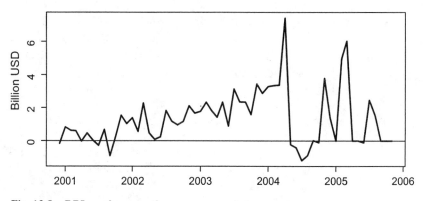

Fig. 13.8   RBI purchases on the currency market

dramatically while the steady currency appreciation, under the pegged rate, gave a one-way bet to private agents. This led to a change in the currency regime in March 2004. Table 13.15 shows the small daily fluctuations of the rupee-dollar rate going up to March 19, 2004, and the larger volatility from that date on. The first nine days shown in this table had a zero change in the exchange rate; the second nine days shown had an appreciation of 3.4 percent. In the period from January 1, 2000, to March 19, 2004, daily rupee-dollar returns had a volatility of 0.129 percent. For some of the following months (March 22, 2004, to February 11, 2005), the volatility had nearly tripled, to 0.355.

Such sharp changes in the time series process of the rupee-dollar spot price reflect the pressures of implementation of the pegged exchange rate in an increasingly open economy. Across these events, however, no changes in the currency regime were officially announced. The private sector suddenly saw an unexpected and sharp change in currency volatility.

Even in months when little trading was done by the RBI, reserves con-

Table 13.15   **The rupee-dollar exchange rate, March 9 to April 5, 2004**

Date	Rate	Returns (%)
March 9	45.21	–0.09
March 10	45.23	0.04
March 11	45.25	0.04
March 12	45.27	0.04
March 15	45.25	–0.04
March 16	45.24	–0.02
March 17	45.25	0.02
March 18	45.22	–0.07
March 19	45.22	0.00
March 22	45.15	–0.15
March 23	44.93	–0.49
March 24	44.76	–0.38
March 25	44.75	–0.02
March 26	44.73	–0.04
March 29	44.12	–1.37
March 31	43.39	–1.67
April 2	43.77	0.87
April 5	43.67	–0.23

tinued to fluctuate owing to the currency composition of the portfolio, and returns are earned on the fixed income instruments in which reserves are invested.[19] In addition, the period after May 2004 was one in which the U.S. dollar depreciated significantly against the euro. Since India held significant euro-denominated assets but reported foreign currency reserves in dollars, this showed up as higher reserves.

13.7.1   Lack of Sustained Current Account Deficit

As emphasized in section 13.2, India has long sought to augment domestic savings using capital flows so as to achieve a higher investment rate. As argued above, the currency regime chosen by India led to a failure to achieve this goal, despite considerable success in attracting sustained capital flows.

Table 13.16 shows how from 1995–96 to 2003–4 India lost 3.4 percent of GDP of an investment rate owing to the change in the current account balance. In the table, the savings rate rose strongly by 3.0 percentage points of GDP over an eight-year period, but the investment rate actually dropped by 0.6 percentage points of GDP.

19. India does not disclose the currency composition of the reserve portfolio. On April 30, 2004, disclosures under the IMF *Template on International Reserves* showed that of the reserve portfolio of $113 billion, $40 billion were held as securities, and $72.9 billion were held as "currency and deposits." Of the securities portfolio, the U.S. Treasury disclosure system (Sobol 1998) (http://www.ustreas.gov/tic/mfh.txt) showed that in December 2004, India had $12.9 billion of U.S. government bonds.

Table 13.16   Saving, investment, and current account balance

Year	Savings	Investment	Current account balance
1995–1996	25.1	26.9	–1.7
1996–1997	23.2	24.5	–1.2
1997–1998	23.1	24.6	–1.4
1998–1999	21.5	22.6	–1.0
1999–2000	24.2	25.3	–1.0
2000–2001	23.7	24.4	–0.6
2001–2002	23.4	22.6	0.7
2002–2003	26.1	24.8	1.2
2003–2004	28.1	26.3	1.7

13.8   Conclusion

India serves as an interesting case study in integration into the world economy. The initial conditions involved a small trade-GDP ratio and a highly repressed capital account. At the same time, India had many potential strengths for participating in financial globalization. These included strong traditions of law and accounting, a long tradition of equity ownership and price discovery on speculative markets, and an absence of a history of default.[20]

The goals of the reforms of the early 1990s were articulated by the policy makers of the time as comprising three elements:

1. Avoiding debt flows, particularly short-term debt flows, which were viewed as being potentially destabilizing.

2. Increasing India's trade integration into the world.

3. Spurring Indian growth by harnessing the growing global FDI and portfolio flows.

In the postwar period, two successful "Asian development models" are known. The first is the approach of a completely closed capital account, with no FDI and no portfolio flows, which was followed by Japan (1950s–1960s) and Korea and Taiwan (1970s–1980s). There is the alternative approach of encouraging FDI and having restricted portfolio flows, followed by Singapore (1970s–1980s), Malaysia and Thailand (1980s–1990s), and China (1980s). Both these models used substantial rigidity in the currency regime. India appears to have embarked on a different path, with considerable freedom for both FDI and portfolio flows, modern institutional development of securities markets, considerable success in attracting port-

---

20. As emphasized in Reinhart and Rogoff (2004), some countries are "serial defaulters" and pose high risks to foreign sources of capital. India has been through two IMF programs in situations where a fixed exchange rate regime was challenged owing to near exhaustion of reserves (in 1981 and 1991). However, India has never defaulted.

folio flows, and a pegged exchange rate regime with greater currency flexibility as compared with some Asian peers.

India did not engage in "big bang" liberalization. The full policy implications of this broad position were worked out through a steady pace of numerous reforms initiatives in the 1992–2004 period. The 2004 framework of tariffs, restrictions against FDI, and restrictions against portfolio flows implies that the reform agenda on the current account, on FDI, and on portfolio flows remained incomplete as of 2004.

Looking back, some of the goals have been achieved to a significant extent:

1. Net debt flows were at roughly 1 percent of GDP in both 1992–93 and 2003–4. Gross debt flows actually dropped sharply, from 13.5 percent of GDP in 1992–93 to 10.6 percent in 2003–4.

2. Trade integration has gone up sharply, with gross current account flows rising from 25 percent of GDP in 1992–93 to 35 percent in 2003–4.

3. FDI and portfolio flows have gone up sharply. India has fared particularly well in the institutional transformation of the equity market, which helped Indian equities obtain acceptance in global portfolios. The experience with FDI flows, while showing strong growth rates when compared with the initial conditions, lags behind that of other Asian countries, both in absolute terms and when expressed as percentage of GDP.

In an open economy, these three aspects of policy are closely intertwined with the currency regime. India has been in a quest for openness in trade, FDI, and portfolio flows, while continuing to have capital controls in most other respects, and trying to have both an independent monetary policy and a pegged exchange rate. A strong consensus exists in India about the usefulness of extensive trading by the central bank on the currency market in implementing currency policy. Indeed, issues about the currency regime were not debated in the 1992–2002 period.

As a consequence, India's experience with capital flows is deeply intertwined with India's experience with the currency regime. Capital flows have shaped the currency regime, and the currency regime has shaped capital flows.

Openness on the trade account, FDI, and portfolio flows has given economic agents opportunities to express speculative views about currency movements, and thus has thrown up new problems in the implementation of pegging. India differs from China in the importance of portfolio flows. Portfolio flows involve robust inflows *and* outflows. For example, in 2003–4, portfolio inflows were only 1.67 times bigger than portfolio outflows, and gross portfolio flows amounted to 7 percent of GDP.

Difficulties faced by the central bank in implementing the currency regime have continually influenced the pace of removal of controls on capital flows. In particular, there has been significant policy volatility with respect to debt flows, ranging from periods with government-sponsored offshore borrowing to periods with sharp restrictions upon offshore borrowing. Similarly, policies on outward capital flows have been ambivalent and have lacked the consistent direction of reform that was found on the current account, on FDI, and on portfolio flows.

The implementation of the currency regime has led to large capital outflows. One of the key goals of the reforms of the 1990s was to augment domestic GDP growth by attracting FDI and portfolio flows. In 2003–4, the total net capital inflows of $20.5 billion were accompanied by an outward official capital flow of over $31.4 billion. This leads to concerns about whether this policy framework has succeeded in serving the interests of accelerating GDP growth. India has undoubtedly reaped *microeconomic* benefits from the new presence of FDI and foreign investors on the equity market. However, the pegged exchange rate regime has not allowed capital inflows to augment domestic investment on a sustained basis.

References

Alfaro, L., S. Kalemli-Ozcan, and V. Volosovych. 2004. Volatility of capital flows: Bad policies or bad institutions? Harvard Business School and University of Houston. Working paper.

Bird, G., and R. S. Rajan. 2002. Does FDI guarantee the stability of international capital flows? Evidence from Malaysia. *Development Policy Review* 20 (2): 191–202.

Calvo, G. A., and C. M. Reinhart. 2002. Fear of floating. *Quarterly Journal of Economics* 117 (2): 379–408.

Chinn, M. D., and J. A. Frankel. 1994. More survey data on exchange rate expectations: More currencies, more horizons, more tests. Working Paper no. 312. University of California, Santa Cruz.

Dooley, M. P., D. Folkerts-Landau, and P. Garber. 2003. An essay on the revived Bretton Woods system. NBER Working Paper no. 9971. Cambridge, MA: National Bureau of Economic Research.

Fernandez-Arias, E., and R. Hausmann. 2000. Is FDI a safer form of financing? Working Paper no. 416. Washington, DC: Inter-American Development Bank.

Frankel, J., and C. Okongwu. 1996. Liberalised portfolio capital inflows in emerging markets: Sterilisation, expectations, and the incompleteness of interest rate convergence. *International Journal of Finance and Economics* 1 (1): 1–23.

Frankel, J., and S. J. Wei. 1994. Yen bloc or dollar bloc? Exchange rate policies of the East Asian countries. In *Macroeconomic linkage: Savings, exchange rates and capital flows,* ed. T. Ito and A. Krueger, 295–334. Chicago: University of Chicago Press.

Gordon, J., and P. Gupta. 2003. Portfolio flows in India: Do domestic fundamentals matter? IMF Working Paper no. 03/20. Washington, DC: International Monetary Fund.

———. 2004. Nonresident deposits in India: In search of return? IMF Working Paper no. 04/48. Washington, DC: International Monetary Fund.

Hausmann, R., and E. Fernandez-Arias. 2000. Foreign direct investment: Good cholesterol? Working Paper no. 417. Washington, DC: Inter-American Development Bank.

Ito, T. 1983. Capital controls and covered interest parity. NBER Working Paper no. 1187. Cambridge, MA: National Bureau of Economic Research.

Johnston, B. R., and N. T. Tamirisa. 1998. Why do countries use capital controls? IMF Working Paper no. 98/181. Washington, DC: International Monetary Fund.

Joshi, V. 2003. India and the impossible trinity. *World Economy* 26 (4): 555–83.

Joshi, V., and I. Little. 1994. *India: Macroeconomics and political economy, 1964–1991.* New York: Oxford University Press.

Lal, D., S. Bery, and D. Pant. 2003. The real exchange rate, fiscal deficits and capital flows India: 1981–2000. *Economic and Political Weekly* 38 (47): 4965–76.

Miniane, J. 2004. A new set of measures on capital account restrictions. *IMF Staff Papers* 51 (2): 276–308.

Ministry of Finance. 2006. *Economic survey.* New Delhi, India: Ministry of Finance, February.

Mohan, R. 1996. The India infrastructure report (Expert Group on the Commercialisation of Infrastructure Projects)." Committee report. New Delhi, India: Ministry of Finance.

Panagariya, A. 2005. India's trade reform. *India Policy Forum* 1:1–57.

Patnaik, I. 2003. India's policy stance on reserves and the currency. ICRIER Working Paper no. 108. New Delhi: Indian Council for International Economic Relations. http://www.icrier.org/pdf/wp108.pdf.

———. 2005. India's experience with a pegged exchange rate. *India Policy Forum* 1:189–216.

Patnaik, I., and D. Vasudevan. 2000. Trade misinvoicing and capital flight from India. *Journal of International Economic Studies* 14:99–108.

Portes, R., and H. Rey. 2001. The determinants of cross-border equity flows. London Business School and Princeton University. Working paper.

Reinhart, C., and K. Rogoff. 2004. Serial default and the "paradox" of rich to poor capital flows. NBER Working Paper no. 10296. Cambridge, MA: National Bureau of Economic Research.

Shah, A., and S. Thomas. 1997. Securities markets. In *India development report 1997,* ed. K. S. Parikh, 167–92. Delhi: Oxford University Press.

———. 2000. David and Goliath: Displacing a primary market. *Journal of Global Financial Markets* 1 (1): 14–21.

———. 2003. Securities market efficiency. In *Globalization and national financial systems,* ed. J. A. Hanson, P. Honohan, and G. Majnoni, 145–75. New York: Oxford University Press.

Sobol, D. M. 1998. Foreign ownership of U.S. Treasury securities: What the data show and do not show. *FRBNY Current Issues in Economics and Finance* 4 (5): 1–6.

Thomas, S. 2006. How the financial sector was reformed. In *Documenting reforms: Case studies from India,* ed. S. Narayan, 171–210. New Delhi, India: Macmillan.

Venables, W. N., and B. D. Ripley. 2002. *Modern applied statistics with S.* 4th ed. New York: Springer.

Capital Controls
An Evaluation

Nicolas Magud and Carmen M. Reinhart

14.1 Introduction

The literature on capital controls has (at least) four very serious issues that make it difficult, if not impossible, to compare across theoretical and empirical studies. We dub these apples-to-oranges problems, and they are as follows. First, there is no unified theoretical framework (say, as in the currency crisis literature) to analyze the macroeconomic consequences of controls. Second, there is significant heterogeneity across countries and time in the capital control measures implemented. Third, there are multiple definitions of what constitutes success (capital controls are a single policy instrument—but there are many policy objectives). Fourth, the empirical studies lack a common methodology and are furthermore significantly overweighted by the two poster children—Chile and Malaysia.

Our goal in this paper is to find a common ground among the noncomparabilities in the existing literature. Of course, there is usually a level of generality that is sufficiently encompassing. After all, an apples-to-oranges problem can be solved by calling everything fruit. Our goal is, as far as possible, to classify different measures of capital controls on a uniform basis. Once done, it should be easier to understand the cross-country and time series experience.

We attempt to address some of these apples-to-oranges shortcomings by being very explicit about what measures are construed as capital controls. We document not only the more drastic differences across countries or

Nicolas Magud is an assistant professor of economics at the University of Oregon. Carmen M. Reinhart is a professor in the School of Public Affairs and the Department of Economics of the University of Maryland, and a research associate of the National Bureau of Economic Research.

The authors thank conference participants and Vincent R. Reinhart and Miguel A. Savastano for useful comments and suggestions.

episodes and between controls on inflows and outflows, but also the more subtle differences in types of inflow or outflow controls. Also, given that success is measured so differently across studies, we standardize (wherever possible) the results of over thirty empirical studies summarized in this paper. As far as possible, we bring to bear the experiences of episodes less well known than those of Chile and Malaysia.

The standardization was done by constructing two indexes of capital controls: indexes of capital controls effectiveness and weighted capital control effectiveness. The difference between them lies only in the fact that the WCCE controls for the differentiated degree of methodological rigor applied to draw conclusions in each of the papers considered.

Our results from these indexes can be summarized briefly. Capital controls on inflows seem to make monetary policy more independent, alter the composition of capital flows, and reduce real exchange rate pressures (although the evidence there is more controversial). Capital controls on inflows seem not to reduce the volume of net flows (and hence the current account balance). As to controls on outflows, there is Malaysia and there is everybody else. In Malaysia, controls reduced outflows and may have given room for more independent monetary policy (the other poster child does not fare as well, in that our results are not as conclusive as for the Chilean controls on inflows). Absent the Malaysian experience, there is little systematic evidence of success in imposing controls, however defined.

The paper proceeds as follows. The next section summarizes some of the key reasons why capital controls—particularly capital controls on inflows—are either considered or implemented. Controls, as we note, help deal with what we dub the "four fears." Section 14.3 focuses on the distinctions among types of capital controls—highlighting the fact that not all capital control measures are created equal and therefore they cannot be simply lumped together in a rough capital controls index. Section 14.4 examines the existing empirical evidence by standardizing and sorting studies along a variety of criteria. Specifically, we focus on the following sorting strategy. First, we analyze separately cases where the study was multicountry or focused on a single case study; second, we distinguish the cases where the controls were primarily designed to deal with inflows or outflows; third, we provide an ad hoc (but uniform) criteria to rank the approach or econometric rigor applied in the study to test hypotheses about the effects of the controls; and, last, we evaluate the outcomes reported in the studies according to the definition of what constitutes a success. The last section discusses some of the policy implications of our findings.

14.2   The Rationale for Capital Controls and the "Four Fears"

Anyone examining the literature on capital controls, which spans many decades and all the regions around the globe, would be well advised to retain a sense of irony. Repeatedly, policymakers have sought refuge in tax laws, supervisory restraint, and regulation of financial transactions to cope with external forces that they deem to be unacceptable. Often they rationalize their actions on loftier grounds, sometimes so effectively as to make it difficult to clearly identify episodes of controls on capital. But in all these episodes, four fears lurk beneath the surface.

14.2.1 Fear of Appreciation

Being the darling of investors in global financial centers has the decided, albeit often temporary, advantage of having ample access to funds at favorable cost. With the capital inflow comes upward pressure on the exchange value of the currency, rendering domestic manufacturers less competitive in global markets, and especially so relative to their close competitors who are not so favored as an investment vehicle. A desire to stem such an appreciation (which Calvo and Reinhart 2002 refer to as "fear of floating") is typically manifested in the accumulation of foreign exchange reserves. Over time, though, sterilizing such reserve accumulation (the topic of Reinhart and Reinhart 1998) becomes more difficult, and more direct intervention more appealing.

14.2.2 Fear of "Hot Money"

For policymakers in developing countries, becoming the object of foreign investors' attention is particularly troubling if such affection is viewed as fleeting. The sudden injection of funds into a small market can cause an initial dislocation that is mirrored by the strains associated with their sudden withdrawal. Such a distrust of "hot money" was behind James Tobin's initial proposal to throw sand in the wheels of international finance, an idea that has been well received in at least some quarters. Simply put, a high enough tax (if effectively enforced) would dissuade the initial inflow and preempt the pain associated with the inevitable outflow.

14.2.3 Fear of Large Inflows

Policymakers in emerging market economies do not universally distrust the providers of foreign capital. Not all money is hot, but sometimes the sheer volume of flows matters. A large volume of capital inflows, particularly when it is sometimes indiscriminate in the search for higher yields (in the manner documented by Calvo, Leiderman, and Reinhart 1994), causes dislocations in the financial system. Foreign funds can fuel asset price bubbles and encourage excessive risk taking by cash-rich domestic intermediaries. Again, recourse to taxation may seem to yield a large benefit.

14.2.4 Fear of Loss of Monetary Autonomy

The interests of global investors and domestic policymakers need not always—or even often—align. But a trinity is always at work: it is not possible to have a fixed (or highly managed) exchange rate, monetary policy autonomy, and open capital markets (as discussed in Frankel 2001). If there is some attraction to retaining some element of monetary policy flexibility, something has to give. However, in the presence of the aforementioned fear of floating, giving up capital mobility may seem more attractive than surrendering monetary policy autonomy.

Whatever the reason for action, some forms of capital control were intended to control exchange rate pressures, stem large inflows, and regain an element of monetary autonomy. And this is more relevant for those policymakers who impose controls to reduce capital flight, because investors seeking safety—including, most important, domestic residents as well as foreigners—are seldom dissuaded by regulatory restraint.

14.3   What Do We Mean by Capital Controls?

In most of the empirical literature there are no distinctions between controls on outflows and controls on inflows; these exercises suffer from the same problems as the de jure International Monetary Fund (IMF) classification of exchange rate arrangements. Even when a distinction is made between inflows and outflows (as here), controls can and do range from the explicit to the subtle, from the market friendly to the coercive.[1]

Furthermore, when considering the impacts and effectiveness of capital controls one cannot lump together the experiences of countries that have not substantially liberalized (e.g., India and China) with countries that actually went down the path of financial and capital account liberalization and decided at some point to reintroduce controls, as the latter have developed institutions and practices that are integrated in varying degrees to international capital markets.

Appendices D and E, which squarely focus on measures targeted to affect inflows and outflows in countries that had already gone the route of capital account liberalization,[2] indeed highlight the heterogeneity in both subtlety and market friendliness of capital control measures that have been tried in Asia, Europe, and Latin America during booms (these involve controls on capital inflows) as well as crashes (and attempts to curb capital outflows). These measures differ not only in subtlety and other features but also in intensity.[3]

---

1. There is, of course, the important issue of temporary versus permanent policies, a distinction not addressed here because most empirical studies do not focus on this issue. For a model and a discussion of the temporary-versus-permanent issue, see Reinhart and Smith (2002).
2. Hence, these cases involve the reintroduction of controls.
3. For a measure that quantifies the intensity of these measures see Montiel and Reinhart (1999).

14.4   The Empirical Literature: Finding a Common Ground

This section aims to overcome (or at least take a step in that direction) two of the apples-to-oranges problems we have identified in the capital controls literature. Namely, we attempt to (a) ascertain when and in what capacity capital controls were successful in achieving the stated objectives of the authorities (this is not trivial, as what constitutes as a success is defined very differently across studies), and (b) standardize (to some extent) the very eclectic array of descriptive and empirical methodologies and approaches that have characterized the empirical literature on capital controls. Lastly, we bring to bear evidence on episodes less familiar than the "classics" (Chile's controls on inflows starting in 1990 and Malaysia's 1998 controls on outflows).

In what follows, we review more than thirty papers that study capital controls on either inflows or outflows around the world. Some are country case studies, some describe several individual country experiences, and some are multicountry studies that bunch several cases together. As noted earlier, the papers measure "success" differently; thus, our aim is to standardize methodology and results where possible so as to facilitate comparisons. Not only will this enable us to assess the effectiveness of alternative capital controls events, but it will also permit us to evaluate some of the policy implications of imposing controls on capital inflows and/or outflows under alternative scenarios.

14.4.1   Types of Studies

We proceed as follows. First, we cluster the papers into three broad groups: capital inflows (CI), capital outflows (CO), and multicountry (MC)—the latter including the analysis of capital inflows, capital outflows, or both. We collected studies of capital controls for the following countries (the number of papers is shown in parentheses). For CI, there are studies on Brazil (6), Chile (11), Colombia (3), the Czech Republic (1), Malaysia (2), and Thailand (1). For CO, we obtained information for Malaysia (5), Spain (3), and Thailand (2). For the MC group, we collected five papers, covering a wide array of countries.[4]

14.4.2   Objective(s) of Capital Controls

Given the multiple objectives that capital controls are expected to achieve, we approached each paper with a series of questions. We asked whether, according to each paper, capital controls were able to

- Reduce the volume of capital flows
- Alter the composition of capital flows (toward longer-maturity flows)

4. For example, one of the more comprehensive multicountry papers uses monthly data for the period 1971–98 for a panel of twenty-six countries.

- Reduce real exchange rate pressures
- Allow for a more independent monetary policy

As a first step in sorting this information, we constructed tables 14.1–14.3. Table 14.1 includes CI episodes, table 14.2 displays CO episodes, and table 14.3 focuses on MC studies. As can be seen in the tables, possible answers are "yes," "no," and blank space. If the table reads "yes" in any cell, it means that the paper finds that the corresponding objective of capital controls was achieved. "No" stands for the paper finding that there was not such effect as a result of the capital controls. A blank space means that the paper does not address whether there was an effect. Sometimes the answer is followed by (ST). This indicates that the effects were only temporary— that is, that an objective was achieved only in the short term. To give an example, in table 14.1, the paper by Laurens and Cardoso (1998) studying the case of the Chilean experience during the 1990s finds evidence that capital controls were able to reduce the volume of capital flows only in the short term, that they were able to alter the composition of these flows toward longer-maturity flows, and that they were not successful in reducing pressures on the real exchange rate. They do not report results regarding the effectiveness of capital controls in making monetary policy more independent.

In a first pass through this information, by inspection, we can summarize it as follows (see table 14.4). We observe that in general the results obtained in these papers suggest that capital controls were successful in altering the composition of capital flows toward longer maturities and in making monetary policy more independent. However, the papers are not very informative regarding the effectiveness of capital controls in reducing the volume of capital flows and reducing real exchange rate pressures.

14.4.3   Indexes of Capital Control Effectiveness

But this is not informative enough, since it still lacks some rigor to evaluate the effectiveness of capital controls episodes. In order to better understand this, we construct two indexes of capital controls effectiveness. We call them the capital controls effectiveness index (CCE index) and the weighted capital controls effectiveness index (WCCE index). The only difference in computing them is that the WCCE index weighs the results obtained in each paper by the degree of methodological rigor applied to drawing conclusions; we discuss this further below.

In both cases, following the information summarized in tables 14.1–14.3, we arbitrarily assigned the following values:

- If the answer is yes, the corresponding value is 1.
- If the answer is no, the value assigned is –1.
- If the question is not addressed at all, it corresponds to a value of 0.

Table 14.1   **The famous Chilean case and lesser deities: Summary of key findings on effectiveness**

		Did controls on outflows:			
Study	Sample	Reduce the volume of net capital outflows?	Alter the composition of flows?	Reduce real exchange rate pressures?	Make monetary policy more independent?
A. Brazil					
Cardoso and Goldfajn (1998)		Yes (ST)	Yes (ST)		
Edison and Reinhart (2001)	1994			No	No
Reinhart and Smith (1998)		Yes (ST)	Yes (ST)		
Ariyoshi et al. (2000)	1993–97	No	No	No	Yes (ST)
B. Chile					
De Gregorio, Edwards, and Valdés (2000)	1988:Q1– 1998:Q2	Yes	Yes (ST)	Yes (ST)	Yes (ST)
Edwards (1999b)			Yes	No	Yes (ST)
Edwards (1999a)	June 1991– September 1998	No	Yes	No	Yes
Edwards and Rigobon (2004)	January 1991– September 1999		Yes		
Gallego, Hernández, and Schmidt-Hebbel (1999)		Yes (ST)	Yes (ST)	No	Yes
Labán and Larraín (1998)					
Larraín, Labán, and Chumacero (2000)	1985–94	No	Yes		
Laurens and Cardoso (1998)		Yes (ST)	Yes	No	
Le Fort and Budnevich (1997)	1990–94	No	Yes	Yes	Yes
Reinhart and Smith (1998)		Yes (ST)	Yes (ST)		
Valdés-Prieto and Soto (2000)	1987–95	No	Yes	No	No
Ariyoshi et al. (2000)	1991–98	No	No	No	Yes
C. Colombia					
Le Fort and Budnevich (1997)	1990–95	Yes (ST)	Yes	Yes	Yes
Reinhart and Smith (1998)		No	No		
Ariyoshi et al. (2000)	1993–98	No	No	No	Yes

(continued)

Table 14.1   (continued)

		Did controls on outflows:			
Study	Sample	Reduce the volume of net capital outflows?	Alter the composition of flows?	Reduce real exchange rate pressures?	Make monetary policy more independent?
D. Czech Republic Reinhart and Smith (1998)		No	Yes (ST)		
E. Malaysia (1989)[a] Reinhart and Smith (1998)		Yes	Yes		
F. Malaysia (1994) Ariyoshi et al. (2000)	1994	Yes	Yes	Yes (ST)	Yes
G. Thailand Ariyoshi et al. (2000)	1995–97	Yes	Yes	Yes	Yes

Notes: A blank entry refers to the cases where the study in question did not analyze that particular relationship. (ST) refers to cases where only short-term effects were detected.
[a]Note that there are several studies on Malaysia's 1998 capital controls targeting *outflows*. Here, we are referring to the controls on capital *inflows* introduced in January 1994.

These values are designed to equally weigh the existence or nonexistence of effects as a result of the imposition of capital controls and to give no weight to questions not addressed, so as not to distort the results in case any objective of capital controls is not addressed by the paper. With these values at hand, for each country we computed simple averages of these numbers for each of the four questions we brought to the papers. This gives, for example, a CCE index for volume reduction for each country, a CCE index for real exchange rate pressure reduction for each country, and so on. With this information we are able to compare, for each objective, which country was most effective. We also used this information to compute an aggregate index of capital controls effectiveness, by averaging out the four CCE indexes for each country, and then compiled a global CCE index across countries.

However, as has already been mentioned, the methodology used in these papers to evaluate success is highly heterogeneous. Some papers are mainly descriptive, generating conclusions from the movements (or lack thereof) in the time series of the main variables, and lack any rigorous statistical or econometric analysis. Other papers use some statistical or econometric methodology to evaluate capital control events, but among them there is still wide variation in the degree of rigor used to extract conclusions from the data.

In order to control for these differences, we made another pass through

Table 14.2   **The famous Malaysian case and lesser deities: Summary of key findings on effectiveness**

		Did controls on outflows:			
Study	Episode	Reduce the volume of net capital outflows?	Alter the composition of flows?	Reduce real exchange rate pressures?	Make monetary policy more independent?
A. Malaysia					
Tamirisia (2004)	January 1991– December 2002	Malaysia		No	Yes
Dornbusch (2001)				No	
Edison and Reinhart (2001)				Yes	Yes
Kaplan and Rodrik (2002)	1992–96				Yes
Ariyoshi et al. (2000)	1998–2000	Yes		Yes	Yes
B. Spain					
Viñals (1992)	1992	No			
Edison and Reinhart (2001)	1995–99			No	No
Ariyoshi et al. (2000)	1992	Yes		Yes (ST)	Yes
C. Thailand					
Edison and Reinhart (2001)				No	No
Ariyoshi et al. (2000)	1997–98	Yes		Yes	Yes (ST)

Notes: See table 14.1 notes.

the information in the papers. We classify each study according to the degree of methodological rigor—low, intermediate, or high—according to the following criteria. "Low" includes studies that consist mainly of descriptive analysis of events and/or time series. "Intermediate" includes papers that draw conclusions from a more formal evaluation of events but still lack any formal hypothesis testing. An example would be papers that perform time rescaling to compare the effects of capital controls in a before-and-after analysis. "High" includes only those studies that have highly developed econometric techniques, with well-defined hypothesis testing. Appendices A–C summarize the methodology used in each paper, as well as the corresponding classification as low, intermediate, or high, following these definitions.

In order to compute the WCCE index, we assigned the following values: low, 0.1; intermediate, 0.5; and high, 1. With these values at hand, we compute the WCCE index similarly to the CCE index, in order to determine

Table 14.3   The others—Multicountry studies: Summary of key findings on effectiveness

Study	Sample	Did controls on inflows:			
		Reduce the volume of net capital inflows?	Alter the composition of flows?	Reduce real exchange rate pressures?	Make monetary policy more independent?
Montiel and Reinhart (1999)	Indonesia, Malaysia, Philippines, Sri Lanka, Thailand, Argentina, Brazil, Chile, Colombia, Costa Rica, Mexico, Czech Republic, Egypt, Kenya, and Uganda (1990–96)	No	Yes (ST)		No
Reinhart and Smith (1998)	Brazil, Chile, Colombia, Czech Republic, Malaysia, Mexico, Thailand, Indonesia, and the Philippines	Yes (ST)	Yes (ST)		
Kaplan and Rodrik (2002)	Korea, Thailand, Indonesia, Malaysia (monthly and quarterly data for 1992–96—before crisis—and from crisis time and one year ahead)				Yes
Edison and Reinhart (2001)	Spain (1991–93); Brazil, Malaysia, and Thailand (1995–99) Control group: the Philippines and South Korea (daily data)			No	No
Miniane and Rogers (2004)	Australia, Austria, Belgium, Canada, Chile, Colombia, Denmark, Finland, France, Germany, Greece, India, Italy, Japan, Korea, Malaysia, Mexico, the Netherlands, Norway, the Philippines, Portugal, South Africa, Spain, Sweden, Turkey, United Kingdom (monthly data for January 1971–December 1998)			Yes (ST)	No

Notes: See table 14.1 notes.

Table 14.4   **Summary of results by country and multicountry studies**

| | Did controls on outflows: | | | |
Study	Reduce the volume of net capital outflows?	Alter the composition of flows?	Reduce real exchange rate pressures?	Make monetary policy more independent?
Controls on inflows				
Brazil	Unclear	Unclear	No	Unclear
Chile	Unclear	Yes	Unclear	Yes
Colombia	Unclear	Unclear	Unclear	Yes
Czech Republic	No	Yes		
Malaysia (1989)	Yes	Yes		
Malaysia (1994)	Yes	Yes	Yes	Yes
Thailand	Yes	Yes	Yes	Yes
Controls on outflows				
Malaysia (1998)			Unclear	Yes
Spain	Unclear		Unclear	Unclear
Thailand	Yes		Yes	Yes
Multicountry studies	Yes	Yes	Yes	No
Complete sample	Unclear	Yes	Unclear	Yes

Note: Yes stands for yes, it worked; No for no, it did not work; Unclear for mixed results; and blanks for results not reported.

which country has been most effective in achieving each of the four objectives. We also compute an aggregate (per-country) WCCE index, which enables us to understand which countries capital controls were more useful in. Furthermore, given this information, we can, at least as a first approximation, find conditions under which capital controls tend to be effective. Once more, it is worth mentioning that these exercises were done separately for the three clusters into which we separated the papers: CI, CO, and MC.

14.4.4   Summary of Results

Summary results of the CCE and WCCE indexes are presented in tables 14.5–14.7. From these indexes, we can extract the following policy conclusions. Looking at the data on controls on inflows (table 14.5) along with the preliminary results in table 14.4, we see that capital controls were able to make monetary policy more independent, alter the composition of capital flows toward longer maturities, and reduce real exchange rate pressures (although the evidence on the latter is more controversial). Interestingly, the usual model economy for this type of controls, Chile, stands out as achieving these goals quite comfortably, as the WCCE index shows. In this regard, initial conditions or characteristics such as those in Chile in the early 1990s, along with the continuing reforms during the 1990s, appear to be

Table 14.5   **Capital inflows: The indexes**

Country	Index	Reduce the volume of net capital inflows	Alter the composition of flows	Reduce real exchange rate pressures	Make monetary policy independent	Country average
Brazil	CCE	0.00	0.00	−0.67	0.00	0
	WCCE	0.35	0.35	−0.275	−0.225	0.05
Chile	CCE	−0.09	0.64	−0.27	0.45	0.18
	WCCE	0.03	0.67	−0.27	0.29	0.18
Colombia	CCE	−0.33	−0.33	0.00	0.67	0.00
	WCCE	−0.17	−0.17	0.00	0.07	−0.07
Czech	CCE	−1.00	1.00	0.00	0.00	0.00
Republic	WCCE	−0.50	0.10	0.00	0.00	−0.10
Malaysia	CCE	1.00	1.00	0.50	0.50	0.75
	WCCE	0.30	0.30	0.05	0.05	0.18
Thailand	CCE	1.00	1.00	1.00	1.00	1.00
	WCCE	0.10	0.10	0.10	0.10	0.10

Source: Table 14.1 and sources cited therein.

Table 14.6   **Capital outflows: The indexes**

Country	Index	Reduce the volume of net capital inflows	Alter the composition of flows	Reduce real exchange rate pressures	Make monetary policy independent	Country average
Malaysia	CCE	0.20	0.00	0.00	0.80	0.25
	WCCE	0.02	0.00	0.00	0.62	0.16
Spain	CCE	0.50	0.00	0.50	0.50	0.38
	WCCE	0.05	0.00	0.20	0.20	0.11
Thailand	CCE	0.50	0.00	0.00	0.00	0.13
	WCCE	0.05	0.00	−0.50	−0.50	−0.24

Source: Table 14.2 and sources cited therein.

Table 14.7   **Multicountry studies: The indexes**

Index	Reduce the volume of net capital inflows	Alter the composition of flows	Reduce real exchange rate pressures	Make monetary policy more independent
CCE	0.00	0.40	0.00	−0.40
WCCE	−0.10	0.30	0.00	−0.40

Source: Table 14.1 and sources cited therein.

necessary in order for capital controls on inflows to be effective. On the other hand, capital controls on inflows were not very effective in reducing the volume of net flows (hence the impact of these flows on the current account balance).

Looking in more detail, we see that Malaysia (1994) stands out as the best performer in terms of reducing the volume of capital flows, Chile dominates regarding the change in capital flow maturity, Thailand is superior in reducing real exchange rate pressures, and Chile again dominates in regard to monetary policy independence. Overall, as the average of the WCCE index reflects, Chile emerges as the most successful example of capital controls on inflows.

Let us now focus on capital controls on outflows (table 4.6). The received wisdom is that Malaysia (1997) is the example to follow. From our results, we can see that these capital controls were effective in reducing capital outflows and in making monetary policy more independent. Yet the results from WCCE index are not as conclusive as those on the Chilean controls on inflows.

If we focus on reduction in capital flows, Thailand and Spain dominate Malaysia. Regarding a switch in capital flows toward longer maturity, no conclusion can be extracted. Spain emerges as the best in real exchange rate pressure reduction; on the other hand, Malaysia clearly dominates at making monetary policy more independent. On the aggregate, Malaysia appears to be the most successful in its experience of capital controls on outflows.

Some further comments are in order. First, it could be argued that these indexes are not taking into account many other variables that might be affecting the effectiveness of capital controls, especially the set of other reforms being put in place in each country during each capital controls episode. That is true. However, this paper is reviewing and assessing only the conclusions contained in previous papers, not the papers themselves. All the reviewed papers draw conclusions from their information sets, and we just put them together and try to extract the main message that these papers give as a group. Furthermore, it is precisely because of this omitted-variables bias problem that our WCCE index becomes more relevant. For example, any structural reform carried on in parallel with capital controls is not usually specifically reflected in the papers we review; in a sense, for us this is similar to running a regression with missing data that we have to control for. This is where the degree of methodological rigor becomes important. The more formal the analysis is, especially if it includes hypothesis testing, the more accurate the information contained in it.

Second, a similar reasoning applies to the endogeneity of capital controls. Some could argue that we should control for it. Again, we rely on the conclusions obtained in previous papers, thus giving more value to the results we obtain from WCCE index. Also, this is relevant for how controls on capital inflows affect capital outflows. Moreover, that is why we cluster CI and CO separately in our analysis.

Third, it is worth mentioning that the papers we review are clearly not the only ones dealing with capital controls. There are many papers that analyze the long-run effects of capital controls, whereas we focus on the short run only, as can be seen from the questions with which we approach the papers. Other chapters in this book study the effects of capital controls on growth; we don't go into further details since these papers are out of our scope.

Fourth, another interesting point is whether capital control regimes are transitory or permanent. Here, as the questions we focus on clearly reveal, we are interested only in transitory events. This is why episodes such as the Chinese or Indian approach to capital controls are not covered here; see the papers on these countries contained in this volume for that purpose.

Fifth, an interesting point to raise is related to the timing (and related endogeneity) of capital controls: whether they are imposed in response to events—crises—or if they are designed in advance. Here, once more, we lack information because we rely only on what the papers conclude. It is worth mentioning, though, that by inspection it appears that the Malaysian (1997) episode could have been designed in advance, unlike most of the other episodes, and contrary to common wisdom. This theory emerges from the chronologies given in appendices D and E. In the case of Malaysia, a great quantity of controls was imposed on September 1, 1997. Furthermore, their level of detail seems to suggest that they were not decided upon and designed just in response to the crises.

Sixth, sometimes temporary capital control events become permanent. This could be because of time consistency problems or just because of the current response to future changes: rational expectations call for incorporating into your current decision the fact that in a prespecified time period capital controls will be levied. Furthermore, even if a country imposed capital controls and did levy them at the preestablished date, this might work as a signal that capital controls could be imposed in the future if needed. However, this signal says nothing about the controls being either good or bad—many things will influence the latter, especially the controls' effectiveness, as well as their effects on property rights. At any rate, imposing capital controls once establishes a precedent regarding a country's position toward capital mobility, despite the costs and benefits of such controls. This is another dimension in which temporary capital controls might become permanent.

14.5 Conclusions

In sum, capital controls on inflows seem to make monetary policy more independent, alter the composition of capital flows, and reduce real exchange rate pressures (although the evidence here is more controversial).[5] Capital controls on inflows, however, seem not to reduce the volume of net flows (and, hence, the current account balance).

As for controls on capital outflows, there is Malaysia . . . and there is everybody else. In Malaysia, controls reduce outflows and may make room for more independent monetary policy.[6] There is little evidence of success in other countries that attempt to control outflows, either by altering volume or by regaining monetary policy independence. These findings are in line with those of the earlier literature focused on capital flight (as in Mathieson and Rojas-Suarez 1996) and dual or parallel exchange markets (as in Kiguel, Lizondo, and O'Connell 1997).

While the effectiveness of controls varies across time, country, and type of measures used, limiting private external borrowing in the good times plays an important prudential role, because more often than not countries are debt intolerant. Indeed, often the critical problem in good times is that countries borrow too much![7]

While our study has made the case for the need to distinguish measures primarily designed to discourage inflows from those that primarily aim at curbing outflows, it would be worthwhile for future research to attempt to ascertain whether there are also important differences in achieving success between measures that are more market friendly (as in the Chilean reserve requirements) versus those that are based on more blunt quantitative restrictions. Furthermore, in this study, owing to the nature of most of the empirical work reviewed here (which treats the control measures as single episodes), it would be interesting for policy purposes to examine differences between short-run and long-run impacts of the measures, to ascertain how quickly control measures lose their effectiveness.

As long as capital flows to emerging markets remain volatile and potentially disruptive, the discussion of capital controls in academic and policy circles will remain alive, and hence there is a real need to evaluate their effectiveness, however defined. As noted earlier, it is an old discussion. Tobin's seminal paper (Tobin 1978) dates back to the 1970s. Furthermore, capital controls have historically been used to deal with the fickle capital flow cycle for at least two hundred years. Indeed, as in past inflow episodes, at the time of this writing countries like Colombia and Argentina either have implemented controls on capital inflows or are contemplating doing so.

5. According to the WCCI, Chile stands out in achieving these goals.
6. Yet the results for Malaysia based on the WCCI are not as conclusive as those for the Chilean controls on inflows.
7. See Reinhart, Rogoff, and Savastano (2003) for details.

Appendix A

Table A.1   Capital Inflows: Methodology and Degree of Methodological Rigor

Study	Sample	Methodology	Econometric rigor
		A. Brazil	
Cardoso and Goldfajn (1998)	January 1988– December 1995	OLS controlling for heteroscedasticity and serial correlation, IV, and VAR. The authors control for endogeneity of capital controls (government's reaction function).	High
Edison and Reinhart (2001)	1995–2001	Test for equality of moments and changes in persistence between capital controls and no controls, principal-components analysis; block exogeneity tests (VAR) for causality; GARCH for the effects of controls on volatility; and Wald tests for structural brakes over a rolling window.	High
Reinhart and Smith (1998)	1994–1996	Event comparison through time rescaling (labeling the implementation of controls as period t, and analyzing the evolution of the series in $t − 1$ through $t + 2$). Detailed chronological description of the various measures applied in each economy.	Medium
Ariyoshi et al. (2000)	1993–1997	Extensive descriptive and comparative country-studies analysis of time series in each episode, dividing facts according to controls on capital inflows (limiting short-term flows), controls on capital outflows (financial crises), extensive exchange controls (financial crises), long-standing controls and their liberalization, and rapid liberalization.	Low
		B. Chile	
De Gregorio, Edwards, and Valdés (2000)	1988:Q1– 1998:Q2	IV and VAR. With these, the authors address simultaneity problems, exogenous upward trend in capital flow, bias due to measurement error because of loopholes in controls. They consider two alternative measures of expected devaluations: (a) effective rate of depreciation, and (b) one-step-ahead forecast from a rolling ARMA. They consider two alternative measures of flows: (a) short-term flows to GDP, and (b) total flows to GDP.	High
Edwards (1999a)	June 1991– September 1998	Descriptive analysis of the composition of capital flows during capital control times. VAR on the effects of capital controls on the real exchange rate. GARCH for changes in the short-term central bank nominal interest rate and changes in the log of the stock market index.	High

Table A.1   (continued)

Study	Sample	Methodology	Econometric rigor
Edwards (1999b)	October 1994–January 1999	GARCH for changes in the short-term central bank nominal interest rate, and changes in the log of the stock market index, using daily data. Descriptive analysis of the effects of capital controls on the composition of capital inflows, on domestic interest rates, and on monetary policy independence.	High
Edwards and Rigobon (2004)	January 1991–September 1999	Using stochastic calculus, the authors compute the shadow exchange rate and its bands. GARCH (effect of capital controls on propagation of external shocks). Estimate a mean and a variance equation.	High
Gallego, Hernández, and Schmidt-Hebbel (1999)	1989–1998:Q2 and July 1998–June 1999	Least squares estimation, controlling for spurious correlation, endogeneity of the RHS regressors, heteroskedasticity, and autocorrelation. Cointegration analysis and error correction model. 2SLS estimation also included.	High
Labán and Larraín (1998)	1985–1996	Descriptive analysis of events, describing the context for implementing capital controls and the main macroeconomic effects.	Low
Larraín, Labán, and Chumacero (2000)	1985–1994	Estimation of a special case of nonlinear models in which a particular variable may adopt a certain law of motion conditional on an observation past a threshold (special case of Markov switching regime models, with the threshold replacing the transition matrix). The authors run a full-sample parsimonious regression for each series, to determine variables to include in the threshold process; for given choice of threshold variable, they estimate the model and get the p-value associated with a null of a unique stable representation; if the latter is rejected in favor of threshold process, the authors choose the threshold variable that minimizes the sum of squares of residuals, and reduce the threshold model to a parsimonious representation.	High
Laurens and Cardoso (1998)	1985:Q1–1994:Q4	Linear and cubic approximations of net inflows as primary explanatory variables of interest rate differentials.	High
Le Fort and Budnevich (1997)	1990–1994	Descriptive analysis of events, describing the context for implementing capital controls and the main macroeconomic effects.	Low

(*continued*)

Table A.1   (continued)

Study	Sample	Methodology	Econometric rigor
Reinhart and Smith (1998)	1990–1994	Event comparison through time rescaling (labeling the implementation of controls as period t, and analyzing the evolution of the series in $t-1$ through $t+2$. Detailed chronological description of the various measures applied in each economy.	Medium
Valdés-Prieto and Soto (2000)	1987–1995	Error correction representation (that is efficient) with a two-step procedure: (a) OLS estimation of the real exchange rate on a set of explanatory variables to contrast the estimated residuals, and (b) using these residuals to estimate by OLS an error correction equation measuring the deviation of the dependent variable from its long-term equilibrium level (given by step [a]). The authors check for several endogeneity and simultaneity biases. They also look at the effect of controls on short-term credit.	High
		C. Colombia	
Le Fort and Budnevich (1997)	1990–1995	Descriptive analysis of events, describing the context for implementing capital controls and the main macroeconomic effects.	Low
Reinhart and Smith (1998)	1990–1995	Event comparison through time rescaling (labeling the implementation of controls as period t, and analyzing the evolution of the series in $t-1$ through $t+2$. Detailed chronological description of the various measures applied in each economy.	Medium
Ariyoshi et al. (2000)	1993–1998	Extensive descriptive and comparative country-studies analysis of time series in each episode, dividing facts according to controls on capital inflows (limiting short-term flows), controls on capital outflows (financial crises), extensive exchange controls (financial crises), long-standing controls and their liberalization, and rapid liberalization.	Low
		D. Czech Republic	
Reinhart and Smith (1998)	1994–1997	Event comparison through time rescaling (labeling the implementation of controls as period t, and analyzing the evolution of the series in $t-1$ through $t+2$. Detailed chronological description of the various measures applied in each economy.	Medium

Table A.1   (continued)

Study	Sample	Methodology	Econometric rigor
		E. Malaysia (1989)	
Reinhart and Smith (1998)	1993–1996	Event comparison through time rescaling (labeling the implementation of controls as period *t*, and analyzing the evolution of the series in *t* – 1 through *t* + 2. Detailed chronological description of the various measures applied in each economy.	Medium
		F. Malaysia (1994)	
Ariyoshi et al. (2000)	1994	Extensive descriptive and comparative country-studies analysis of time series in each episode, dividing facts according to controls on capital inflows (limiting short-term flows), controls on capital outflows (financial crises), extensive exchange controls (financial crises), long-standing controls and their liberalization, and rapid liberalization.	Low
		G. Thailand	
Ariyoshi et al. (2000)	1995–1997	Extensive descriptive and comparative country-studies analysis of time series in each episode, dividing facts according to controls on capital inflows (limiting short-term flows), controls on capital outflows (financial crises), extensive exchange controls (financial crises), long-standing controls and their liberalization, and rapid liberalization.	Low

Notes: OLS = ordinary least squares; IV = instrumental variables; VAR = vector autoregression; GARCH = generalized autoregressive conditional heteroskedastic; ARMA = autoregressive moving average; 2SLS = two-stage least squares.

Appendix B

Table B.1   Capital Outflows: Methodology and Degree of Methodological Rigor

Study	Sample	Methodology	Econometric rigor
		A. Malaysia	
Tamirisia (2004)	January 1991– December 2002	Error correction model. Series on net foreign portfolio assets are by foreign portfolio assets to isolate country-specific effects.	High
Dornbusch (2001)		Descriptive analysis of different variables.	Low
Edison and Reinhart (2001)		Test for equality of moments and changes in persistence between capital controls and no controls, principal-components analysis; block exogeneity tests (VAR) for causality; GARCH for the effects of controls on volatility; and Wald tests for structural brakes over a rolling window.	High
Kaplan and Rodrik (2002)	1992–1996	Shifted difference-in-differences to separate the counterfactual of capital controls versus IMF program–based recovery. This methodology enables the authors to reschedule the episodes by the timing of the crises (shifted). The difference-in-differences allows them to capture the comparison effect of the recovery with capital controls vis-à-vis with a successful IMF program, controlling for exogenous and country-specific effects (static and dynamic).	High
Ariyoshi et al. (2000)	1998–2000	Extensive descriptive and comparative country-studies analysis of time series in each episode, dividing facts according to controls on capital inflows (limiting short-term flows), controls on capital outflows (financial crises), extensive exchange controls (financial crises), long-standing controls and their liberalization, and rapid liberalization.	Low
		B. Spain	
Viñals (1992)	1992	Descriptive analysis of economic policy measures and their effect on various macroeconomic variables.	Low
Edison and Reinhart (2001)	1991–1993	Test for equality of moments and changes in persistence between capital controls and no controls, principal-components analysis; block exogeneity tests (VAR) for causality; GARCH for the effects of controls on volatility; and Wald tests for structural brakes over a rolling window.	High

Table B.1   (continued)

Study	Sample	Methodology	Econometric rigor
Ariyoshi et al. (2000)	1992	Extensive descriptive and comparative country-studies analysis of time series in each episode, dividing facts according to controls on capital inflows (limiting short-term flows), controls on capital outflows (financial crises), extensive exchange controls (financial crises), long-standing controls and their liberalization, and rapid liberalization.	Low
		C. Thailand	
Edison and Reinhart (2001)	1995–1999	Test for equality of moments and changes in persistence between capital controls and no controls, principal-components analysis; block exogeneity tests (VAR) for causality; GARCH for the effects of controls on volatility; and Wald tests for structural brakes over a rolling window.	High
Ariyoshi et al. (2000)	1997–1998	Extensive descriptive and comparative country-studies analysis of time series in each episode, dividing facts according to controls on capital inflows (limiting short-term flows), controls on capital outflows (financial crises), extensive exchange controls (financial crises), long-standing controls and their liberalization, and rapid liberalization.	Low

Appendix C

Table C.1   Multi-country Studies: Methodology and Degree of Methodological Rigor

Study	Sample	Methodology	Econometric rigor
Montiel and Reinhart (1999)	1990–1996	The authors construct indexes to measure incidence and intensity of capital account restrictions. Estimation of fixed-effect panel regressions to explain volume and composition of capital flows. Results are checked for robustness by IV estimations. Covers Indonesia, Malaysia, the Philippines, Sri Lanka, Thailand, Argentina, Brazil, Chile, Colombia, Costa Rica, Mexico, the Czech Republic, Egypt, Kenya, and Uganda.	High
Reinhart and Smith (1998)	1990–1997	Event comparison through time rescaling (labeling the implementation of controls as period t, and analyzing the evolution of the series in $t-1$ through $t+2$. Detailed chronological description of the various measures applied in each economy. Covers Brazil, Chile, Colombia, the Czech Republic, Malaysia, Mexico, Thailand, Indonesia, and the Philippines.	Intermediate
Kaplan and Rodrik (2002)	1992–1996	Shifted difference-in-differences to separate the counterfactual of capital controls versus IMF program–based recovery. This methodology enables the authors to reschedule the episodes by the timing of the crises (shifted). The difference-in-differences allows them to capture the comparison effect of the recovery with capital controls vis-à-vis with a successful IMF program, controlling for exogenous and country-specific effects (static and dynamic). Covers Korea, Thailand, Indonesia, Malaysia (monthly and quarterly data for 1992–96—before crisis—and from crisis time and one year after).	
Edison and Reinhart (2001)	1991–1999	Test for equality of moments and changes in persistence between capital controls and no controls, principal-components analysis; block exogeneity tests (VAR) for causality; GARCH for the effects of controls on volatility; and Wald tests for structural brakes over a rolling window. Covers 1991–93 for Spain and 1995–99 for Brazil, Malaysia, and Thailand. Control group: the Philippines and South Korea.	High

Table C.1   (continued)

Study	Sample	Methodology	Econometric rigor
Miniane and Rogers (2004)	January 1971– December 1998	Panel VAR and individual-country VAR of commodity prices, U.S. industrial production, U.S. consumer prices, foreign industrial production, foreign interest rates, U.S. Fed Funds rate, ratio of nonborrowed reserves to reserves, and nominal exchange rate in response to a 25 basis point increase in the Fed Funds rate. For the country-level VAR the authors regress each country separately, compute the cumulative exchange rate and interest rate responses, and finally regress country-specific responses on the values of capital control index, exchange rate regime, degree of dollarization, and trade integration. Covers Australia, Austria, Belgium, Canada, Chile, Colombia, Denmark, Finland, France, Germany, Greece, India, Italy, Japan, Korea, Malaysia, Mexico, the Netherlands, Norway, the Philippines, Portugal, South Africa, Spain, Sweden, Turkey, and the United Kingdom.	High

Appendix D

Restrictions on Inflows and Prudential Requirements

For each country, the date in parentheses denotes the first year of the surge in inflows. Sources for Asian countries are Alfiler (1994); Bank Indonesia annual report, various issues; Bank Negara annual report, various issues; and various Bank of Thailand reports. Sources for Eastern European and Latin American countries are Central Bank of Chile (1991, 1992), Banco de la Republica Colombia (1993, 1994); Banco de Mexico (1992); and Conselho Monetario Nacional Brasil (1994, 1995).

Asia

Indonesia (1990)

March 1991: The central bank adopts measures to discourage offshore borrowing. Bank Indonesia begins to scale down its swap operations by reducing individual banks' limits from 25 to 20 percent of capital. The three-month swap premium is raised by 5 percentage points.

October 1991: All state-related offshore commercial borrowing is made subject to prior approval by the Government and annual ceilings are set for new commitments over the next five years.

November 1991: Further measures are taken to discourage offshore borrowing. The limits on banks' net open market foreign exchange positions are tightened by placing a separate limit on off-balance sheet positions. Bank Indonesia also announces that future swap operations (except for "investment swaps" with maturities of more than two years) will be undertaken only at the initiative of Bank Indonesia.

Malaysia (1989)

June 1, 1992: Limits on non-trade-related swap transactions are imposed on commercial banks.

January 17, 1994–August 1994: Banks are subject to a ceiling on their non-trade- or non-investment-related external liabilities.

January 24, 1994–August 1994: Residents are prohibited from selling short-term monetary instruments to nonresidents.

February 2, 1994–August 1994: Commercial banks are required to place with Bank Negara the ringgit funds of foreign banking institutions (Vostro accounts) held in non-interest-bearing accounts. However, in the January-May period these accounts were considered part of the eligible liabilities base for the calculation of required reserves, resulting in a negative effective interest rate in Vostro balances.

February 23, 1994–August 1994: Commercial banks are not allowed to undertake non-trade-related swap and outright forward transactions on the bid side with foreign customers.

The Philippines (1992)

July 1994: The central bank begins to discourage forward cover arrangements with nonresident financial institutions.

Thailand (1988)

Banks' and finance companies' net foreign exchange positions may not exceed 20 percent of capital. Banks' and finance companies' net foreign liabilities may not exceed 20 percent of capital. Residents are not allowed to hold foreign currency deposits except for trade-related purposes.

April 1990: Banks' and finance companies' net foreign exchange position limit is raised to 25 percent of capital.

August 8, 1995: Reserve requirements, to be held in the form of non-interest-bearing deposits at the Bank of Thailand, on short-term nonresident baht accounts are raised from 2 percent to 7 percent. While reserve requirements on domestic deposits are also 7 percent, up to 5 percent can be held in the form of interest-bearing public bonds.

December 1995: The 7 percent reserve requirement is extended to finance companies' short-term (less than one year) promissory notes held by non-residents. A variety of measures aimed at reducing foreign-financed lending are introduced.

April 19, 1996: Offshore borrowing with maturities of less than one year by commercial banks, Bangkok International Banking Facility (BIBF) offices, finance companies, and finance and security companies will be subject to a 7 percent minimum reserve requirement in the form of a non-remunerated deposit with the Bank of Thailand. Loans for trade purposes will be exempt.

Eastern Europe and Latin America

Brazil (1992)

October 1994: A 1 percent tax on foreign investment in the stock market is imposed. The tax on Brazilian companies issuing bonds overseas is raised from 3 percent to 7 percent of the total. (These taxes are both eliminated on March 10, 1995.) The tax paid by foreigners on fixed-interest investments in Brazil is raised from 5 percent to 9 percent. (This is reduced to 5 percent on March 10, 1995.) The central bank raises limits on the amount of dollars that can be bought on foreign exchange markets.

Chile (1990)

June 1991: A nonrenumerated 20 percent reserve requirement is to be deposited at the central bank for a period of one year on liabilities in foreign currency for direct borrowing by firms. The stamp tax of 1.2 percent a year (previously paid by domestic currency credits only) is applied to foreign loans as well. This requirement applies to all credits during the first year, with the exception of trade loans.

May 1992: The reserve requirement on liabilities in foreign currency for direct borrowing by firms is raised to 30 percent. Hence, all foreign currency liabilities have a common reserve requirement.

Colombia (1991)

June 1991: A 3 percent withholding tax is imposed on foreign exchange receipts from personal services rendered abroad and other transfers that could be claimed as credit against income tax liability.

February 1992: Banco de la Republica increases its commission on its cash purchases of foreign exchange from 1.5 percent to 5 percent.

June 1992: Regulation of the entry of foreign currency as payment for services is introduced.

September 1993: A nonrenumerated 47 percent reserve requirement is to be deposited at the central bank on liabilities in foreign currency for direct borrowing by firms. The reserve requirement is to be maintained for the duration of the loan and applies to all loans with a maturity of eighteen months or less, except for trade credit.

August 1994: A nonrenumerated reserve requirement is to be deposited at the central bank on liabilities in foreign currency for direct borrowing by firms. The reserve requirement is to be maintained for the duration of the loan and applies to all loans with a maturity of five years or less, except for trade credit with a maturity of four months or less. The percentage of the requirement declines as the maturity lengthens, from 140 percent for funds that are thirty days or less to 42.8 percent for five-year funds.

Colombia (2002)

December 2004: Foreigners investing in domestic markets must now keep their money in the country for at least one year.

Czech Republic (1992)

April 1995: The central bank introduces a fee of 0.25 percent on its foreign exchange transactions with banks, with the aim of discouraging short-term speculative flows.

August 1, 1995: A limit on net short-term (less than one year) foreign borrowing by banks is introduced. Each bank is to ensure that its net short-term liabilities to nonresidents, in all currencies, do not exceed the smaller of 30 percent of claims on nonresidents or 500 million Czech koruna. Administrative approval procedures seek to slow down short-term borrowing by nonbanks.

Mexico (1990)

April 1992: A regulation is passed that limits foreign currency liabilities of commercial banks to 10 percent of their total loan portfolio. Banks must place 15 percent of these liabilities in highly liquid instruments.

Appendix E

Restrictions on Outflows: Asia, Europe, and Latin America

For each country, the date in parentheses denotes the first year of the surge in outflows (or crisis). Sources are Banco de España; Bank Negara annual report, various issues; various Bank of Thailand reports; Conselho Monetario Nacional Brasil; and Dominquez and Tesar (chap. 7 in this volume).

Argentina (crisis ending the Convertibility Plan, 2001)

December 2001: The *Corralito* is established, limiting bank withdrawal limits and restrictions on dollar transfers and loans. However, purchases through checks or credit cards are available, and purchases of government bonds. December 30: suspension of external payments (debt default). In January 2002 there is a 40 percent devaluation, and a dual exchange rate regime is introduced (1.4 pesos per dollar for trade operations, with a floating regime for all other transactions). Later in the month, there is an easing of bank withdrawal restrictions, followed by an asymmetric pesofication: pesofication of dollar deposits at 1.4 pesos per dollar, with dollar debts pesofied at market exchange rate. There is unification of exchange rate regimes in a floating scheme; right to withdraw wages and pension incomes in full is granted; *Corralon* is imposed; there is a freeze of bank term deposits. In September of that year it is required that stocks should be traded in domestic currency regulation. Since the latter is widely resisted, it is eased, but the new restriction significantly increases transaction costs. In December 2002 the *Corralito* is rescinded.

Brazil (crisis ending the Real Plan, 1999)

March 1999: The government orders local investment funds to increase their holdings of government bonds. The central bank raises the minimum amount of sovereign debt that must be held in the country's foreign investment fund to 80 percent from 60 percent. This lowers the share that can be held in other countries' debt.

Malaysia (Asian crisis, 1997)

September 1998: Bank and foreign exchange controls limit offshore swap operations and ban short-selling. There is repatriation of ringgits held offshore, and strict regulation of offshore operations and most international operations in ringgits; export and import operations are allowed in foreign currency only; there is a twelve-month waiting period for nonresidents to sell profits from Malaysian securities; approval is required to invest abroad (above certain limits). In December residents are allowed to grant loans to nonresidents to purchase immovable property. In January 1999 some derivative transactions for nonresidents are permitted. In February there is a gradual ease on the twelve-month waiting period, and some repatriation funds are exempted from exit regulations. In March export and import trade ceilings are raised for operations with Thailand. In September commercial banks are allowed to enter into some short-term currency swaps with nonresident stockbrokers. In March 2000 funds from the sale of securities purchased by nonresidents can be repatriated without paying an exit levy; in June administrative procedures ease classification of securities as being free from exit levy. September 30: Some offshore banks are allowed to invest in ringgit assets. December 1: Foreign-owned banks are allowed to increase domestic credit. In February 2001 the exit levy is abolished for some operations. In May of that year the remaining exit levy is abolished. In June all controls on nonresidents' futures and options are abolished. In July, resident financial institutions are allowed to extend ringgit loans to nonresidents investing in immovable property in Malaysia. In November 2002, resident banks' credit levels to finance nonresidents' projects in Malaysia are raised. December 3: The foreign currency limit for investment abroad by residents is abolished, and payments are liberalized to allow them to be in either ringgits or foreign currency.

Spain (ERM crisis, 1992)

September 1992: The Bank of Spain suspends regular money market operations and introduces foreign exchange controls. In October of that year the peseta is devalued, and some of the controls are lifted. In November the remaining foreign exchange controls are rescinded.

Thailand (Asian crisis, 1997)

May 1997: The Bank of Thailand (BOT) introduces restrictions on capital account transactions. In June the BOT introduces additional measures to limit capital flows. Baht proceeds from sales of stocks are required to be converted at the onshore exchange rate. Additional controls are introduced, and later in the month a two-tier exchange rate is introduced. In September of that year, additional controls on invisible and current account transactions are introduced. In January 1998 it is required that proceeds on exports and invisible transactions and current account transfers be surrendered after seven days (instead of fifteen days). At the end of January, the BOT ends the two-tier exchange rate regime.

References

Alfiler, F. Enrico. 1994. Monetary and exchange rate policy responses to surges in capital flows: The case of the Philippines. Paper presented at the eleventh Pacific Basin Central Bank Conference. 31 October–2 November, Hong Kong.

Ariyoshi, Akira, Karl Habermeier, Bernard Laurens, Inci Okter-Robe, Jorge Canales-Kriljenko, and Anderi Kirilenko. 2000. Capital controls: Country experiences with their use and liberalization. IMF Occasional Paper no. 190. Washington, DC: International Monetary Fund.

Calvo, Guillermo A., Leonardo Leiderman, and Carmen M. Reinhart. 1994. The capital inflows problem: Concepts and issues. *Contemporary Economic Policy* 11 (3): 54–66.

Calvo, Guillermo A., and Carmen M. Reinhart. 2002. Fear of floating. *Quarterly Journal of Economics* 117 (2): 379–408.

Cardoso, Eliana, and Ilan Goldfajn. 1998. Capital flows to Brazil: The endogeneity of capital controls. *IMF Staff Papers* 45 (March): 161–202.

De Gregorio, José, Sebastian Edwards, and Rodrigo Valdés. 2000. Controls on capital inflows: Do they work? *Journal of Development Economics* 3 (1): 59–83.

Dornbusch, Rudi. 2001. Malaysia: Was it different? NBER Working Paper no. 8325. Cambridge, MA: National Bureau of Economic Research, June.

Edwards, Sebastian. 1999a. How effective are capital controls? *Journal of Economic Perspectives* 13 (4): 65–84.

———. 1999b. How effective are controls on capital inflows? An evaluation of Chile's experience. University of California, Los Angeles, Anderson Graduate School of Management. Working Paper, June.

Edwards, Sebastian, and Roberto Rigobon. 2004. Capital controls, managed exchange rates, and external vulnerability. University of California, Los Angeles, Anderson Graduate School of Management, and Massachusetts Institute of Technology, Sloan School of Management. Working Paper, February.

Edison, Hali, and Carmen Reinhart. 2001. Stopping hot money: On the use of capital controls during financial crises. *Journal of Development Economics* 66 (2): 533–53.

Gallego, Francisco, Leonardo Hernandez, and Klaus Schmidt-Hebbel. 1999. Capital controls in Chile: Effective? Efficient? Central Bank of Chile Working Paper no. 59. Santiago: Central Bank of Chile.

Kaplan, Ethan, and Dani Rodrik. 2002. Did the Malaysian capital controls work? In *Preventing currency crises in emerging markets,* ed. S. Edwards and J. Frankel, 393–440. Chicago: University of Chicago Press.

Kiguel, M., J. Saul Lizondo, and Stephen O'Connell, eds. 1997. *Parallel exchange rates in developing countries.* London: Macmillan.

Labán, Raúl M., and Felipe Larraín. 1998. The return of private capital to Chile in the 1990s: Causes, effects, and policy reactions. Faculty Research Working Paper no. R98-02. Harvard University, John F. Kennedy School of Government, January.

Larraín, Felipe, Raúl Labán, and Rómulo Chumacero. 2000. What determines capital inflows? An empirical analysis for Chile. Chap. 4 in *Capital controls, capital flows, and currency crises,* ed. F. Larraín. Ann Arbor: University of Michigan Press.

Laurens, Bernard, and Jaime Cardoso. 1998. Managing capital flows: Lessons from the experience of Chile. IMF Working Paper no. 98. Washington, DC: International Monetary Fund.

Le Fort, Guillermo, and Carlos Budnevich. 1997. Capital account regulations and macroeconomic policy: Two Latin experiences. Santiago: Central Bank of Chile. Mimeograph, March.

Mathieson, Donald J., and Liliana Rojas-Suarez. 1996. Liberalization of the capital account: Experiences and issues. IMF Occasional Paper no. 103. Washington, DC: International Monetary Fund.

Miniane, Jacques, and John Rogers. 2004. Capital controls and the international transmission of U.S. money shocks. Washington, DC: Board of Governors of the Federal Reserve. Mimeograph, June.

Montiel, Peter, and Carmen M. Reinhart. 1999. Do capital controls and macroeconomic policies influence the volume and composition of capital flows? Evidence from the 1990s. *Journal of International Money and Finance* 18 (4): 619–35.

Reinhart, Carmen, and Vincent R. Reinhart. 1998. Some lessons for policy makers who deal with the mixed blessing of capital inflows. In *Capital flows and financial crises,* ed. Miles Kahler, 93–127. Ithaca, NY: Cornell University Press.

Reinhart, Carmen, Kenneth Rogoff, and Miguel Savastano. 2003. Debt intolerance. *Brookings Papers on Economic Activity,* Issue no. 1:1–74.

Reinhart, Carmen, and Todd Smith. 1998. Too much of a good thing: The macroeconomic effects of taxing capital inflows. In *Managing capital flows and exchange rates: Perspectives from the Pacific Basin,* ed. Reuven Glick, 436–64. Cambridge: Cambridge University Press.

———. 2002. Temporary controls on capital inflows. *Journal of International Economics* 57 (2): 327–51.

Tamirisia, Natalia. 2004. Do macroeconomic effects of capital controls vary by their type? Evidence from Malaysia. IMF Working Paper no. 04/3. Washington, DC: International Monetary Fund, January.

Tobin, James. 1978. A proposal for international monetary reform. *Eastern Economic Journal* 4:153–59.

Valdés-Prieto, Salvador, and Marcelo Soto. 2000. New selective capital controls in Chile: Are they effective? Chap. 3 in *Capital controls, capital flows, and currency crises,* ed. F. Larraín. Ann Arbor: University of Michigan Press.

Viñals, José. 1992. Spain's capital account shock. Center for Economic Policy Research.

Contributors

Joshua Aizenman
Department of Economics
1156 High Street
University of California
Santa Cruz, CA 95064

Laura Alfaro
Harvard Business School
Morgan Hall 263
Soldiers Field
Boston, MA 02163

Matías Braun
UCLA Anderson School of
  Management and Universidad
  Adolfo Ibáñez
110 Westwood Plaza
Los Angeles, CA 90095-1481

Charles W. Calomiris
Graduate School of Business
Columbia University
3022 Broadway Street, Uris Hall
New York, NY 10027

Anusha Chari
Stephen M. Ross School of Business
University of Michigan
701 Tappan Street
Ann Arbor, MI 48109-1234

Kevin Cowan
Central Bank of Chile
Agustinas 1180
Santiago, Chile

José De Gregorio
Central Bank of Chile
Agustinas 1180
Santiago, Chile

Kathryn M. E. Dominguez
University of Michigan Department
  of Economics and Ford School of
  Public Policy
735 S. State Street
Ann Arbor, MI 48109-1220

Sebastian Edwards
UCLA Anderson Graduate School of
  Management
110 Westwood Plaza
Box 951481
Los Angeles, CA 90095-1481

Barry Eichengreen
Department of Economics
University of California
549 Evans Hall 3880
Berkeley, CA 94720-3880

Kristin J. Forbes
Sloan School of Management
Massachusetts Institute of Technology
50 Memorial Drive
Cambridge, MA 02142

Linda S. Goldberg
Research Department
Federal Reserve Bank of New York
33 Liberty Street
New York, NY 10045

Ilan Goldfajn
Department of Economics
Pontifícia Universidade Católica
Rua Marquês de São Vicente 225,
    Gávea
22453-900 Rio de Janeiro, RJ
Brazil

Gita Gopinath
Department of Economics
Harvard University
1875 Cambridge Street
Cambridge, MA 02138

Gerd Häusler
International Capital Markets
    Department
International Monetary Fund
700 19th Street, NW
Washington, DC 20431

Ricardo Hausmann
John F. Kennedy School of
    Government
Harvard University
79 John F. Kennedy Street
Cambridge, MA 02138

Peter Blair Henry
Graduate School of Business
Stanford University
Stanford, CA 94305-5015

Simon Johnson
Sloan School of Management
Massachusetts Institute of Technology
50 Memorial Drive
Cambridge, MA 02142-1347

Sebnem Kalemli-Ozcan
Department of Economics
University of Houston
Houston, TX 77204

Basant K. Kapur
Department of Economics
Faculty of Arts and Social Sciences
National University of Singapore
Kent Ridge
Singapore 117570

Kalpana Kochhar
Research Department
International Monetary Fund
700 19th Street, NW
Washington, DC 20431

Nicolas Magud
Department of Economics
1285 University of Oregon
Eugene, OR 97403-1285

André Minella
Central Bank of Brazil
SBS Quadra 3 Bloco B, Edifício-Sede
70074-900 Brasilia DF
Brazil

Todd Mitton
Marriott School of Management
Brigham Young University
660 TNRB
Provo, UT 84602

Marcus Noland
Institute for International Economics
1750 Massachusetts Avenue, NW
Washington, DC 20036

Ugo Panizza
Research Department
Inter-American Development Bank
1300 New York Avenue, NW
Washington, DC 20577

Ila Patnaik
Indian Express
C-6, Qutub Institutional Area
New Delhi 110016
India

Eswar Prasad
Research Department
International Monetary Fund
700 19th Street, NW
Washington, DC 20431

Carmen M. Reinhart
School of Public Policy and
    Department of Economics
4105 Van Munching Hall
University of Maryland
College Park, MD 20742

Ajay Shah
Flat E7, IGIDR
Goregaon (E)
Bombay India 400065

Natalia Tamirisa
International Monetary Fund
700 19th Street, NW
Washington, DC 20431

Alan M. Taylor
Department of Economics
University of California
One Shields Avenue
Davis, CA 95616

Linda L. Tesar
Department of Economics
University of Michigan
Ann Arbor, MI 48109-1220

Vadym Volosovych
Department of Economics
Florida Atlantic University
777 Glades Road
Boca Raton, FL 33431

Shang-Jin Wei
International Monetary Fund
700 19th Street, NW
Washington, DC 20433

Author Index

Subject Index